0 km 250
0 miles 250

Belém

São Luís

arabá

Teresina

Fortaleza

Araguaína

NORTHEAST
BRAZIL

Natal

Palmas

Recife

Maceió

Feira de
Santana

Salvador

Brasília

Goiânia

Uberlândia

Belo Horizonte

Ribeirão
Preto

SOUTHEAST
BRAZIL

Vitória

Campinas

São Paulo

Rio de
Janeiro

Curitiba

Florianópolis

P9-DFE-089

Piauí & Maranhão

Paraíba, Rio Grande do Norte & Ceará

Sergipe, Alagoas & Pernambuco

Bahia

Rio de Janeiro City

Rio de Janeiro & Espírito Santo

São Paulo State

São Paulo City

Minas Gerais

EYEWITNESS TRAVEL

BRAZIL

EYEWITNESS TRAVEL

BRAZIL

DK

LONDON, NEW YORK,
MELBOURNE, MUNICH AND DELHI
www.dk.com

Managing Editor Aruna Ghose
Editorial Manager Ankita Awasthi
Design Manager Priyanka Thakur
Project Editor Alka Thakur
Project Designer Mathew Kurien
Editors Arundhti Bhanot, Nandita Jaishankar, Vandana Mohindra
Designers Rajnish Kashyap, Baishakhee Sengupta
Cartography Manager Uma Bhattacharya
Senior Cartographer Suresh Kumar
Senior Picture Researcher Taiyaba Khatoon
Picture Researcher Sumita Khatwani
Senior DTP Designer Vinod Harish

Contributors
Alex Bellos, Shawn Blore, Dilwyn Jenkins, Oliver Marshall,
Christopher Pickard, Alex Robinson, Neiva Augusta Silva

Consultant
Alex Robinson

Photographers
Demetrio Carrasco, Nigel Hicks, Alex Robinson, Linda Whitwam

Illustrators
Surat Kumar Mantoo, Arun Pottirayil, Gautam Trivedi, Mark Warner

Printed and bound in China

First American Edition, 2007
16 17 18 19 10 9 8 7 6 5 4 3 2 1

Published in the United States by DK Publishing,
345 Hudson Street, New York, New York 10014

Reprinted with revisions 2010, 2012, 2016

Copyright © 2007, 2016 Dorling Kindersley Limited, London
A Penguin Random House Company

ISSN:1552-1554
ISBN 978-1-4654-3959-8

**The information in this
DK Eyewitness Travel Guide is checked regularly.**
Every effort has been made to ensure that this book is as up to date as possible
at the time of going to press. Some details, however, such as telephone numbers,
opening hours, prices, gallery hanging arrangements, and travel information are
liable to change. The publishers cannot accept responsibility for any consequences
arising from the use of this book, nor for any material on third-party websites, and
cannot guarantee that any website address in this book will be a suitable source of
travel information. We value the views and suggestions of our readers very highly.
Please write to: Publisher, DK Eyewitness Travel Guides, Dorling Kindersley,
80 Strand, London WC2R 0RL, UK, or email: travelguides@dk.com.

Contents

Costumed performers in the Sambódromo,
or *samba* parade

Introducing Brazil

Statue of Dom Pedro II, Museu Imperial,
Petrópolis

Front cover main image: Christ the Redeemer and the Sugar Loaf Mountain, Rio de Janeiro

◀ Rio de Janeiro's beautiful coastline with Vermelha and Copacabana beaches

Aerial view of Rio de Janeiro City

Majestic waterfall in the Parque do Caracol, near Canela

The bustling Terra Brasilis restaurant, on Praia Vermelha, Urca, Rio de Janeiro

Igreja e Convento de São Francisco, Salvador

HOW TO USE THIS GUIDE

This guide helps you get the most from your visit to Brazil, providing expert recommendations and detailed practical information. *Introducing Brazil* maps the country and sets it in its historical and cultural context. The following sections are devoted to the country's capital and various regions, and include the major towns, sights and attractions. Information on accommodation, restaurants, shopping, entertainment, and activities can be found in the *Travelers' Needs* section, while the *Survival Guide* contains practical tips on everything you need to know, from money and language to getting around the country and seeking medical care.

Major Cities

In this guide, Brazil is described in 15 sections, two of which concentrate on the country's major cities – Rio de Janeiro and São Paulo. A section is devoted to each city. All the sights are numbered and plotted on an *Exploring Map*. Information on each sight is easy to locate within the chapter as it follows the numerical order on the map.

1 Introduction
An overview of the history and characteristics of each city.

Each city can be quickly identified by its color-coding.

Country maps show the location of each of the cities.

2 City Map For easy reference, the sights are numbered and located on a map. The main streets, bus stations and railway stations, parking areas and tourist offices are also shown. Sights in the city centre are also shown on the Street Finders for Rio de Janerio City *(see pp100–105)* and for São Paulo City *(see pp158–63)*.

Sights at a Glance lists the chapter's sights by category: churches, cathedrals, monasteries, historic buildings, museums, parks, gardens, streets, and neighborhoods.

3 Detailed Information All the sights in each city are described individually. Addresses, telephone numbers, opening hours, admission charges, and information on how to get there are given for each sight. The key to symbols is shown on the back flap.

Each area of Brazil is identified by color-coded thumb tabs.

Country maps show the location and area of each region of Brazil.

1 Introduction An overview of the history and characteristics of each region.

Brazil Area by Area

In this book, the country is described in 15 chapters, two of which concentrate on Brazil's major cities and 13 on the country's main regions. The map on the inside front cover shows this regional division. The most interesting places to visit are given on the *Regional Map* at the beginning of each chapter.

2 Regional Map This shows the main road network and gives an illustrated overview of the whole region. All interesting places to visit are numbered and there are useful tips on getting around.

Story boxes explore some of the region's historical and cultural subjects in detail.

3 Detailed Information All the important towns and other places to visit are dealt with individually. They are listed in order, following the numbering given on the *Regional Map*. Each entry also contains practical information such as map references, addresses, telephone numbers, and opening times.

Practical information at the beginning of each entry gives helpful information about visiting the sight or attraction.

The Visitors' Checklist provides a summary of the practical information you need to plan your visit.

Stars indicate the best sights and important features.

4 Brazil's Top Sights These are given two or more full pages. Buildings are dissected to show their interiors.

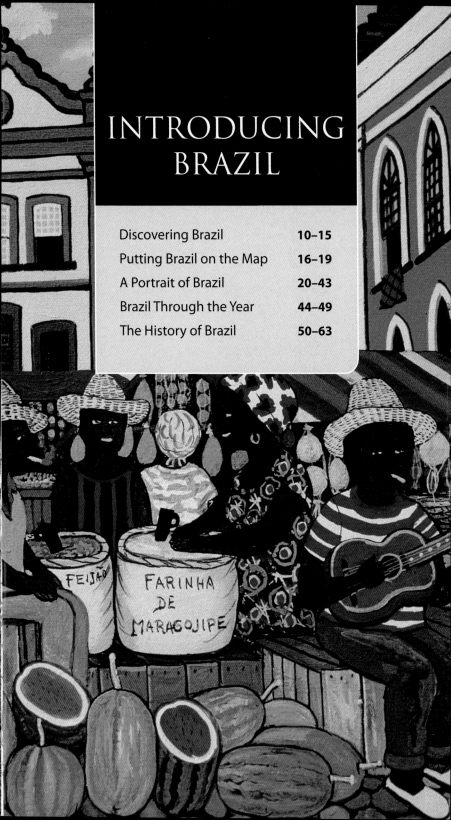

INTRODUCING BRAZIL

DISCOVERING BRAZIL

No visitor to Brazil should ever underestimate the size of the country or its largest cities. Brazil is a place of continental dimensions that can comfortably house all of Europe – with room to spare. Therefore, when we suggest a two-week itinerary of popular Brazilian highlights, keep in mind that this is the same as trying to visit all of Europe over a two-week period, and that it will require air travel. Brazilian highlights include the falls at Foz de Iguaçu; the Modernist Brazilian capital, Brasília; the world's largest wetland, the Pantanal; the Amazon rainforest; Salvador, one of the jewels of the country's northeast coast; and Rio de Janeiro itself. There is also the suggestion for a one-week coastal drive traveling from São Paulo, the country's business capital, to Rio de Janeiro, its leisure and culture hub. Finally, there are two-day itineraries for Rio de Janeiro and São Paulo, as well as Salvador. Time is tight on most of these itineraries, all of which are easy to extend and expand to the time available so that you can learn more about this gigantic and diverse country.

The large auditorium at the Teatro Amazonas in Manaus, in the northwest of the country, still features its original and impressive *belle époque* decor.

Two Weeks around Brazil

- Explore the Brazilian and Argentinian sides of **Foz do Iguaçu**, where a river is divided by 275 spectacular waterfalls.

- Marvel at the Modernist architecture and innovative urban planning in the Brazilian capital, **Brasília**.

- Get up close and personal with the flora and fauna that make up the **Pantanal**, the planet's largest wetlands.

- Travel along the **Amazon river** and experience a night in the **Amazon rainforest**.

- Visit the famous opera house in **Manaus**, in the heart of the Amazon.

- Discover the African influences behind **Bahia**'s cuisine, religion, music, dance, dress, and arts and crafts.

- Admire one of greatest collections of colonial architecture and treasures in the world in **Pelourinho, Salvador**'s historic center.

- Stand at the feet of **Rio de Janeiro**'s iconic statue of **Christ the Redeemer**, on the summit of **Corcovado**.

- Walk on the sands of some of the world's most famous beaches, including **Copacabana** and **Ipanema**.

- Tour the legendary **Maracanã** stadium in Rio de Janeiro, host to two soccer **World Cup** finals, as well as the **Olympics**.

- Appreciate the diversity of this great country in terms of landscapes, cuisine, culture, and its people.

◀ A painting in naive style by Calixto Sales, depicting a market scene in Maragojipe, Bahia

The Museu de Arte de São Paulo (MASP) is one of the most distinctive architectural landmarks in Brazil. Built in the 1960s, it contains a prestigious collection of art from Europe and Brazil.

A Week on the Costa Verde (Green Coast)

- Experience one of the world's great coastal drives.

- Discover **Rio de Janeiro**'s most westerly suburb, **Barra da Tijuca**, home to the **Olympic Village**.

- Enjoy the contrast between the greenery of the **Atlantic rainforest** and pristine **sandy beaches**.

- Stop off and enjoy a wide variety of **beaches** along the way.

- Explore the enchanting islands of **Ilha Grande** and **Ilhabela**.

- Wander the colonial-era streets of **Paraty** and soak up the atmosphere of times gone by.

- Enjoy the hospitality of some of Brazil's most charming and atmospheric small hotels, bars, and restaurants.

Key

— Two-week tour
— Costa Verde (Green Coast) tour

This aerial view of Rio de Janeiro highlights some of the city's most appealing aspects: its verdant mountains and its sandy coastline, gently caressed by the ocean.

Two Days in Rio de Janeiro

Rio de Janeiro is one of the world's most beautiful and exciting cities, blessed by a backdrop of mountains, rainforest, beaches, and the sea.

- **Arriving** Tom Jobim International Airport is located 12 miles (20 km) from the city. If traveling from São Paulo, you may land at the Santos Dumont airfield. Both have bus and taxi links.

- **Moving on** Take a flight or a long-distance bus to explore Brazil. Alternatively, rent a car and follow the coast to São Paulo *(see p14)*.

Day 1
Morning Start at the summit of **Morro do Corcovado** *(pp86–7)*, atop which stands the statue of **Cristo Redentor** (Christ the Redeemer; *p86*). From here, much of Rio is laid out before you. Take the **cog train** *(p87)* from the station in Rua Cosme Velho to the top. On the 17-minute journey you will pass through parts of the **Tijuca Forest** *(p87)*. Spend at least an hour at the summit. Back at the Rua Cosme Velho station, drop in on the neighboring **Museu Internacional de Arte Naïf** (International Naive Art Museum; *p87*) before taking a taxi across town for a tour of the **Estádio do Maracanã** *(p88)*, the stadium that hosted the 1950 and 2014 World Cup finals and will host the opening and closing ceremonies of the 2016 Olympics. Close by

is the Engenhão stadium, which has had its capacity increased to host the 2016 Olympic and Paralympic athletics program.

Afternoon A short metro or taxi ride takes you from the Maracanã stadium to the city's **historic center** *(pp74–9)*, an area that is packed with museums, galleries, cultural centers, and historic churches. The city center is fairly compact and easy to walk around, with plenty of options for a lunchtime break, such as the **Confeitaria Colombo** *(p76)*. In the evening, see a show at the **Theatro Municipal** *(p77)* or **Circo Voador** *(p78)*, or enjoy the nightlife and bohemian feel of **Lapa** *(p97)*.

Day 2
Morning Take a leisurely walk along the beachfront of **Copacabana** *(p82)*, **Ipanema** *(p83)*, or **Leblon** *(p83)*, soaking up the scenery and vibe. Swap the sand for greenery, and head across to the **Botanical Garden** *(p84)*. Nearby is the **Lagoa Rodrigo de Freitas** *(p84)*, where for lunch you can choose a lakeside kiosk or the more sophisticated Lagoon center, with views across the Lagoa to Corcovado.

Afternoon Pass through Botafogo, home to a number of museums, most notably the **Museu do Índio** *(p85)*, or stop off at the **Rio Sul** mall *(pp94–5)* for some retail therapy. Mid-afternoon, explore **Sugar Loaf Mountain** *(pp80–81)*, one of the city's iconic sights. Leave plenty of time to enjoy both **Morro da Urca** *(p80)* and the

summit. If your timing is right, you will be able to enjoy the change in light as darkness envelops the city below. After dinner, enjoy some *bossa nova* or *samba (p97)*, or return to Lapa.

> **To extend your trip…**
> Visit the historic mountain town of **Petrópolis** *(pp116–19)*, or head to the Costa do Sul and its highlight, the town of **Búzios** *(pp120–21)*. Also within a comfortable drive are the historic towns of **Minas Gerais** *(pp125–37)*.

Two Days in São Paulo

São Paulo is the business capital of Brazil and South America. The city spreads over a vast area, but many of its attractions sit close together or in clusters.

- **Arriving** Guarulhos International Airport is located 17 miles (28 km) northeast of the city. If coming from Rio de Janeiro, you may land at the smaller, more central Congonhas in the southwest.

- **Moving on** To explore Brazil, take a flight or a long-distance bus. Alternatively, rent a car and follow the coast to Rio *(see p14)*.

Day 1
Morning São Paulo's historic center *(pp142–6)* is well worth a visit. After rush hour, head for Praça de Sé, a good location from which to visit many of the area's attractions, including the **Catedral Metropolitana** *(p142)* and the **Pátio do Colégio** *(p142)*, where São Paulo was founded. Arrive at the **Edifício Itália** *(p143)* for lunch. The view may be better than the food, but you won't regret it. **Edifício Banespa** *(p143)*, a miniature version of the Empire State Building, also offers spectacular views across the city.

Afternoon Slightly north is another cluster of historic attractions, many located close to Praça da Luz. These include

Cog train traveling through the Tijuca Forest on its way to Morro do Corcovado, Rio de Janeiro

For practical information on traveling around Brazil's cities, see pp426–7

View across the Parque do Ibirapuera, which features many museums and is an important green lung in the city of São Paulo

one of South America's main museums, the **Pinacoteca do Estado** *(pp144–5)*, as well as the **Museu de Arte Sacra** *(p146)* and the Victorian-styled **Estação da Luz** *(p146)*. São Paulo's nightlife is highly rated, so in the evening catch a show or visit a club *(p156)*.

Day 2

Morning Head to the huge **Parque do Ibirapuera** *(pp150–51)*, which is home to a number of important museums and galleries, including the **Museu de Arte Moderna** *(p151)*, the Museu Afro Brasil, and the Bienal Building. Drive along **Avenida Paulista** *(p148)* to understand why São Paulo is the financial capital of South America, then go into the internationally acclaimed **Museu de Arte de São Paulo (MASP)** *(p147)*. Next, head to Rua Oscar Freire and Rua Bela Cintra, an area that offers plenty of charming options for lunch. Browse the distinctive, top-end boutiques around here.

Afternoon After lunch, go north to Praça Charles Miller, named for the Englishman who brought soccer to Brazil. Here is the Estádio do Pacaembu, built in 1940 and used for the 1950 World Cup, and also the highly celebrated **Museu do Futebol** *(pp148–9)*. Options for the rest of the afternoon include a visit to the **Instituto Butantã** *(p152)*, one of the world's most important research centers for venomous animals, or to **Liberdade** *(p149)*, the hub for the city's massive Japanese community. In the evening, experience the city's restaurants and nightlife.

Two Days in Salvador

Salvador, the first capital of Brazil, was also at the center of the slave trade, which makes it the most "African" of all Brazilian cities. The continent's influences can be found in everything from cuisine and arts to religion.

- **Arriving** The Deputado Luíz E. Magalhães International Airport is located 17 miles (28 km) to the north of the city. There are bus and taxi links.

- **Moving on** To explore Brazil, take a flight from the airport.

Day 1

Morning The crown jewel of Salvador is the restored historic center, **Pelourinho** *(pp190–93)*, a UNESCO World Heritage Site with colonial houses, Baroque churches, and museums. Don't miss the church and convent of **São Francisco** *(pp194–5)*. Spend the entire morning walking in and around Pelourinho, which offers many charming and atmospheric places for lunch.

Afternoon Take the **Elevador Lacerda** *(p193)*, built in 1873, down to the lower city to visit the **Mercado Modelo** *(p196)*, which houses a wide selection of northeastern arts and crafts. Since the market is popular with visitors, you can expect to see a demonstration of *capoeira* *(p203)*. Bahia is famous for its cuisine, so find a restaurant for dinner and experience the local dishes and delicacies.

Day 2

Morning Start the day in Nazaré, at the Arena Fonte Nova, one of the most admired stadiums of the 2014 World Cup. The tours start at 9am and take 1 hour and 15 minutes. Close by are the **Museu de Arte Sacra** *(p196)*, the **Museu de Arte Moderna** *(p196)*, and the **Solar do Unhão** *(p196)*, a 17th-century colonial sugar mill. The complex's atmospheric restaurant, with its wonderful views, is a great choice for lunch.

Afternoon Visit and enjoy the beaches of Salvador, which stretch west along the **Atlantic coast** *(pp198–9)*. Start at the most famous, Praia do Farol da Barra, which features a lighthouse and the **Forte de Santo Antônio** *(p197)*, a city landmark in its own right. Nearby, Porto da Barra is a popular beach from which to watch the sunset. Try Praia de Amaralina if you are interested in surfing or sailboarding.

To extend your trip...

Spend time exploring the coast of Bahia. To the south are **Ilha de Itaparica** *(p200)* and **Morro de São Paulo** *(p202)*. The coast to the north is known as the **Linha Verde**, or Green Line *(p211)*, and includes Praia do Forte and Costa do Sauípe. Or head inland to visit **Lençóis** *(p208)* and the spectacular **Parque Nacional de Chapada Diamantina** *(pp208–9)*.

Christian cross in front of the church and convent of São Francisco in Salvador

A Week on the Costa Verde (Green Coast)

Travel along a spectacular coastline and explore historic towns, beautiful beaches, and pretty islands.

- **Airports** Arrive and depart from São Paulo and Rio de Janeiro's international (Guarulhos/Tom Jobim) or domestic (Congonhas/ Santos Dumont) airports.

- **Transport** This itinerary is best done by rental car. It is also possible to do most of the route by using the bus services that link the towns.

- **Booking ahead** It is best to have all accommodation booked in advance, particularly on weekends. If you are sure of your timings, you can also pre-book the ferries to Ilhabela and Ilha Grande.

- **Tips** You can start this itinerary in Rio de Janeiro and work back to São Paulo.

Day 1: São Paulo
Pick a day from the city itinerary on pp12–13.

Day 2: São Paulo to Ilhabela
Plan to leave mid-morning, after the worst of the city's rush hour is over. Head for the 050 (SP-150), which will take you south, to the coast, via São Bernardo do Campo. As you leave the city, the scenery changes to a series of lakes surrounded by hills. You will wind your way through them before dropping down to **Guarujá** *(p169)* – this descent to the coast is spectacular. Guarujá offers excellent options for lunch on the beachfront. Continue east along the coastal road toward **São Sebastião** *(p168)*. You will pass many beautiful beaches, such as Camburi, Camburizinho, and **Maresias** *(p169)*. From São Sebastião, take the 15-minute ferry to **Ilhabela** *(p169)*, an island and yachting center offering mountain scenery, beaches, and waterfalls. Enjoy

the landscape and nightlife, and spend the night at one of the numerous *pousadas*. The island is especially lively at the weekend.

Day 3: Ilhabela to Paraty
Spend the morning exploring Ilhabela, before taking the ferry back to the mainland and following the coast east to **Ubatuba** *(p168)*, a small beach resort with a colonial center. This part of the coast offers nearly 60 miles (100 km) of beaches for you to discover, all wrapped up in Atlantic rainforest. Praia Grande, close to Ubatuba, is a popular location for lunch. Continue to the historic colonial town of **Paraty** *(pp110–11)*, much of which dates from the 18th century. En route, you will cross the state border between São Paulo and Rio de Janeiro, shortly after which the road will no longer hug the coast. Paraty's picturesque historic center is where the majority of the charming *pousadas*, bars, and restaurants are located.

Day 4: Paraty
Wander around Paraty's cobbled, pedestrian, sea-washed streets, popping into the beautifully restored colonial houses, museums, churches, and art galleries, or take a relaxing schooner ride around the many **islands** *(p112)* close by.

> **To extend your trip...**
> Consider staying two nights in Paraty to fully soak up the colonial atmosphere.

Days 5 and 6: Ilha Grande
It is quite possible to drive straight from Paraty to Rio de Janeiro. However, if you have time, stop at **Angra dos Reis** *(p114)*, leave the car, and take the ferry over to **Ilha Grande** *(p114)*, one of the largest of the 365 islands to be found in the bay. Spend at least two nights on this beautiful, underdeveloped island, and explore it on foot or by boat. You will need to take cash, since there are no banks or ATMs there, and no cars. Most of the main *pousadas* are a short distance from the ferry dock, at Vila do Abraão. There are nearly 100 miles (160 km) of trails that cover the entire island, so enjoy a hike and visit ruins, waterfalls, mountains, and beaches, including Lopes Mendes, one of the island's – and Brazil's – most beautiful. (You will need to take a boat taxi.)

Day 7: Rio de Janeiro
From the ferry terminal in Angra dos Reis, take the coastal road, following the signs to **Rio de Janeiro** *(pp70–105)* via **Barra da Tijuca** *(pp90–91)*. This is one of Rio's most affluent suburbs. If you have time, it is worth visiting a number of attractions as you pass through Barra, such as **Sitio Roberto Burle Marx** *(p91)* and **Casa do Pontal** *(p91)*. Alternatively, head to **Barra Shopping Center** *(p90)* for some retail therapy.

> **To extend your trip...**
> Spend a couple of days exploring Rio de Janeiro. See the city itinerary on p12.

A beach in the small town of Trindade, near Paraty, on the Costa Verde

For practical information on traveling around Brazil's cities, see pp426–7

Two Weeks around Brazil

This itinerary offers a tour of many iconic Brazilian sights, experiences, and highlights.

- **Airports** Because of the distances involved, you will need to fly between the main cities and gateways to be visited. Consider purchasing a Brazil Air Pass before arriving in Brazil. For more information about domestic air travel, see pp420–21.

- **Transport** Taxis and public transport are available. In most of the cities and locations, you will have the option to join an organized tour.

- **Booking ahead** It is best to book all city accommodations, Amazon lodges, and the trips to the Pantanal in advance.

Day 1: Iguaçu Falls (Brazilian side)

Start the tour in **Foz do Iguaçu** *(pp344–6)*. Visit the Brazilian side of the falls first – there are more than 275 spreading over 2 miles (3 km). If you have time, take an exhilarating inflatable-boat trip to the mouth of the falls (be prepared to get wet). There are many places to stay in Foz. If your budget allows, stay at the **Hotel das Cataratas Belmond** *(p381)*, the only hotel that lies in the national park next to the falls. It allows you to visit and view the falls when the park is closed to everyone else.

Day 2: Iguaçu Falls (Argentinian side)

Take an organized tour to the Argentinian **Parque Nacional Iguazú** *(p347)*; check in advance if you need a visa. The park offers many more walkways through and along the falls than are to be found on the Brazilian side. The popular Devil's Throat is the most impressive fall, so avoid the crowds by walking there first, then working your way back to the park entrance. In the evening, visit the falls on the Brazilian side again. Have dinner

at the Hotel das Cataratas, so you have access to the park. If you can time your visit with a full moon, you may get the chance to see a moonbow, or lunar rainbow – truly a memorable experience. If you have spare time on the second day, visit nearby **Itaipu Binacional** *(p346)*, one of the world's largest hydroelectric dams. Other options include **Parque das Aves** *(p346)*, an impressive aviary full of exotic birds, or a helicopter flight over the falls.

Day 3: Brasília

Take an early flight from Foz to the Brazilian capital, **Brasília** *(pp306–9)*. This relatively small and compact city has an array of attractions and can easily be explored on foot or as part of an organized tour. Visit the **TV Tower** *(p306)* for a bird's-eye view of the city and to appreciate its Modernist architecture and innovative urban planning. Brasília was one of the host cities of the 2014 World Cup, and the National Stadium (Estádio Nacional de Brasília Mané Garrincha) was built for the tournament.

Days 4 & 5: Pantanal

Head to the **Pantanal** *(pp324–5)*, the planet's largest wetland, which covers an area of 89,000 sq miles (230,000 sq km). To reach the Pantanal, take a short flight from Brasília to **Cuiabá** *(p322)*, credited with being the warmest city in Brazil. There is not a lot to see in Cuiabá, so you will be met at the airport and taken straight out to a lodge or farm. All accommodations in the Pantanal offer guided excursions to see the area's unique and rich ecosystem, with special tours for birders, visitors keen on tracking the Brazilian jaguar, horse riders, and those interested in the region's abundant fish life. It is much easier to spot Brazil's fauna and prolific birdlife in the Pantanal than in the more dense vegetation of the Amazon.

Day 6: Manaus

Return to Cuiabá for the flight to Manaus, in the heart of

Visitors at Foz do Iguaçu, the largest waterfalls in the world

the Amazon. On arrival in **Manaus** *(pp284–5)*, use the rest of the day to explore the city, the **Teatro Amazonas** *(pp286–7)*, the **Museu do Índio** *(p285)*, the waterfront, and the **market** *(p284)*.

Days 7 & 8: The Amazon

Spend two days out in a remote Amazon lodge. Take a cruise on a traditional Amazon riverboat to explore parts of the world's biggest rainforest *(pp288–9)*.

Days 9 & 10: Salvador

Return to Manaus for the flight to **Salvador** *(pp188–99)*. Follow the city itinerary on p13.

Days 11–14: Rio de Janeiro

Fly to **Rio de Janeiro** *(pp70–105)*. You will need at least two or three full days to do any justice to Brazil's most famous city. See the city itinerary on p12.

To extend your trip…

This itinerary could comfortably be extended to three weeks or more if you have the time, since virtually all the cities included offer the option to explore other areas of Brazil in more detail, be it the **south** *(pp328–63)* from Foz do Iguaçu; the **central west** *(pp294–327)* from Brasília; the **northeast** coast *(pp176–259)* from Salvador; or the historic towns of **Minas Gerais** *(pp124–137)* from Rio de Janeiro.

Putting Brazil on the Map

The largest country in South America, Brazil borders most other South American countries and covers over 3.3 million sq miles (8.5 million sq km), from the vast tropical Amazon region in the north to the cooler, more European-style South. It is divided into 26 states and one federal district – its political and administrative capital, Brasília. Brazil's population, now reaching almost 200 million, is mostly concentrated in the Southeast *(see pp18–19).*

VENEZUELA GUYAN

RORAIMA

Boa Vista

Caracaraí

Nora Paraís

Uaupés   Catrimani

Equator   *Negro*

COLOMBIA   Maraá

Itacoatiara

ECUADOR   Manaus

Guayaquil   Tefé *Amazon*

Iquitos   Novo
                              Aripuana

Loja   Tabatinga

AMAZONAS   *Purus*

Piura   Barra do
                    Lábrea   São Manuel
Tarapoto
                    Boco do   Humaitá   Conceição
                    Acre
            Feijó   Porto   B R A
Trujillo   Cruzeiro   Velho
        Pucallpa   do Sul   Ariquemes
                    Rio Branco   Ji-Paraná
            ACRE   RONDÔNIA

PERU   Costa   Vilhena
                            Marques
PACIFIC
OCEAN   Lima
                                                70

                    Puno   BOLIVIA

                    Nuestra Señora
                    de La Paz
                        Cochabamba
                                    Santa Cruzde
                                    de La Sierra

                                PARAGUAY

                    Tropic of Capricorn

                Antofagasta

            CHILE   Asuncic

                        San Miguel de
                        Tucuman
                    Cordoba

        Mendoza   Rosario

    Santiago   Buenos Aires

Greater Brasília

*Parque Nacional
de Brasília*   Sobradinho
                            20
*Represa
Santa Maria*

                    Paranoá

                BRASÍLIA
    Taguatinga   Cruzeiro   *Lago
                            Paranoa*
                Guará
        Núcleo
        Bandeirante
                Aeroporto Int. Pres
    Recanto   Juscelino Kubitschek
    das Emas   40   São
                            Sebastião
0 km   10
0 miles   10

Central & South America

Atlantic Ocean

NICARAGUA
COSTA RICA
PANAMA VENEZUELA GUYANA
COLOMBIA SURINAME FRENCH GUIANA
ECUADOR
PERU
BRAZIL
BOLIVIA
PARAGUAY
CHILE
ARGENTINA
URUGUAY
See pp18–19

Pacific Ocean

SURINAME

FRENCH GUIANA

Asoenangka AMAPÁ

ATLANTIC OCEAN

Serra do Navio
Macapá
Porteira
Óbidos
Parintins
Monte Alegre
Belém
Santarém
Itaituba
Equator
Amazon
Rio do Pará
Tapajós

PARÁ

Araras

São Luís

Fortaleza

Caxias
Marabá
Imperatriz
Timon
Teresina
CEARÁ
Mossoró
Ilha Fernando de Noronha
Natal

Araguaína

MARANHÃO

Juàzeiro do Norte

PARAÍBA
João Pessoa

Cachimbo

PIAUÍ

PERNAMBUCO
Recife

BRAZIL

Alta Floresta
Peixoto de Azevedo

Palmas

Petrolina
Juàzeiro
Paulo Afonso

Maceió

Sinop
Jacaré

TOCANTINS

Barreiras

Feira de Santana
Aracaju
Alagoinhas

MATO GROSSO

GOIÁS

BAHIA

Salvador

Cuiabá
Ceilândia
Brasília
Gama
Vitória da Conquista
Ilhéus

Várzea Grande
Rondonópolis
Anápolis
Goiânia

Jequié

MINAS GERAIS
Montes Claros

MATO GROSSO DO SUL
Rio Verde
Uberlândia

Teófilo Otôni

Campo Grande
São José do Rio Preto
Uberaba
Belo Horizonte
Ipatinga
ESPÍRITO SANTO

ATLANTIC OCEAN

Dourados
Ribeirão Preto
Juiz de Fora
Vitória
Vila Velha

Ponta Porã
Araçatuba
SÃO PAULO
Campinas
Campos dos Goitacazes

Maringá
Londrina
São Gonçalo

Cascavel
PARANÁ
São Paulo
Santos
Rio de Janeiro
Tropic of Capricorn

Foz do Iguaçu
Guarapuava
Curitiba
Joinville

SANTA CATARINA

Passo Fundo
Lajes
Florianópolis

RIO GRANDE DO SUL
Criciúma
Caxias do Sul

Uruguaiana
Porto Alegre

Bagé
Pelotas
Rio Grande

URUGUAY

| 0 km | 400 |
| 0 miles | 400 |

Key

═══ Highway

─── Major road

···· Minor road

─── Railroad

▓▓▓▓ International border

···· State border

Southeastern Brazil

The densely populated southeastern part of Brazil contains the country's two biggest cities. A dynamic, sprawling business center, São Paulo has more than 10 million inhabitants in the city proper. Beautiful Rio de Janeiro, with its legendary beaches, is home to around 7 million people. With a well-developed infrastructure and economy, this region has a stunning Atlantic coastline and a wealth of historic towns.

Itumbiara
Araguari
Patrocínio
Barragem de Emborcação
Uberlândia
Ituiutaba
Represa Nova Ponte
Araxá
Uberaba
Parque Nacional da Serra da Canastra
Planura
Franca
São José do Rio Preto
Barretos
São Sebastião do Paraíso
Bebedouro
Jaboticabal
Ribeirão Preto
Andradina
Araçatuba
Catanduva
Valparaíso
Birigüi
Taquaritinga
MATO GROSSO DO SUL
Panorama
SÃO PAULO
Lins
Araraquara
Piraçununga
Porto Alegre
Bataguaçu
Presidente Epitácio
Aroeira
Bauru
Rio Claro
Limeira
Piracicaba
Rio Brilhante
Presidente Prudente
Jaú
São Manuel
Campinas
Jundiá
Ivinheima
Teodoro Sampaio
Paranapanema
Porecatu
Assis
Ourinhos
Avaré
Botucatu
Nova Londrina
Loanda
Paranavaí
Londrina
Cornélio Procópio
BRAZIL
Buri
Sorocaba
Porto Camargo
Maringá
Arapongas
Umuarama
Apucarana
Itapeva
Capão Bonito
Juquiá
Goio-Erê
Cianorte
PARANÁ
Telêmaco Borba
Itararé
Eldorado
Peruíbe
Guaíra
Iguape
Toledo
Pitanga
Castro
Piraí do Sul
Cananéia
Cascavel
Prudentópolis
Ponta Grossa
Campo Largo
Ilha de Superagüí
Ilha do Mel
Paranaguá
Foz do Iguaçu
Guarapuava
Irati
Iguaçu
Curitiba
São José dos Pinhais
Baía de Guaratuba
Chopimzinho
Represa Salto Osório
Guaratuba
São Francisco do Sul
União da Vitória
Pato Branco
Jaraguá do Sul
Joinville
ARGENTINA
Campo Erê
Xanxerê
Caçador
Itajaí
Chapecó
Concórdia
SANTA CATARINA
Rio do Sul
Blumenau
Brusque
Porto Belo
Baía de Tijucas
Uruguai
Campo Novo
Erechim
Rio das Canas
Lages
São José
Florianópolis
Ilha de Santa Catarina
Palhoça
Santa Rosa
Palmeira das Missões
Passo Fundo
Antonio Prado
Santa Barbara do Sul
Imbituba
Santo Ângelo
Vacaria
Tubarão
Laguna
Cruz Alta
RIO GRANDE DO SUL
Criciúma
Tupancirentã
Barragem Passo Real
Bento Gonçalves
Flores da Cunha
Caxias do Sul
Torres
Jaguari
Santa Maria
Garibaldi
Gramado
Lajeado
Santa Cruz do Sul
Novo Hamburgo
Jacuí
Canoas
Cachoeira do Sul
Porto Alegre
Viamão

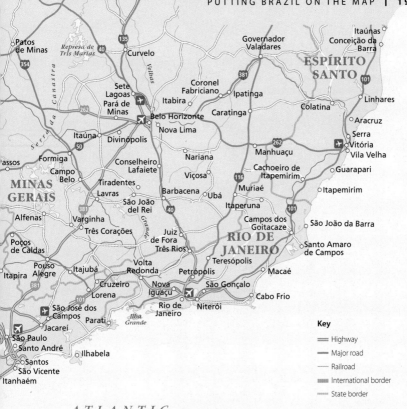

ESPÍRITO SANTO

MINAS GERAIS

RIO DE JANEIRO

ATLANTIC OCEAN

Key

▬▬ Highway
▬▬ Major road
---- Railroad
▬▬ International border
▬▬ State border

Mileage chart

Rio de Janeiro														
326 / 525	**Vitória**													
276 / 444	**327** / 526	**Belo Horizonte**												
720 / 1160	**776** / 1250	**460** / 741	**Brasília**											
1307 / 1669	**750** / 1207	**864** / 1391	**476** / 1542	**Salvador**										
1464 / 2357	**1174** / 1890	**1289** / 2075	**1381** / 2223	**523** / 842	**Recife**									
1537 / 2474	**1247** / 2007	**1363** / 2195	**1452** / 2338	**586** / 944	**78** / 125	**João Pessoa**								
1763 / 2838	**1491** / 2400	**1590** / 2559	**1422** / 2290	**872** / 1403	**496** / 799	**427** / 688	**Fortaleza**							
1898 / 3055	**1626** / 2618	**1724** / 2776	**1342** / 2161	**1006** / 1620	**995** / 1601	**1015** / 1635	**665** / 1070	**São Luís**						
2016 / 3246	**1904** / 3065	**1748** / 2814	**1326** / 2134	**1284** / 2068	**1270** / 2044	**1298** / 2090	**949** / 1527	**499** / 803	**Belém**					
2164 / 3483	**2229** / 3588	**1906** / 3068	**1610** / 2592	**2568** / 4133	**2995** / 4821	**3068** / 4938	**3108** / 5002	**2692** / 4333	**2756** / 4436	**Porto Velho**				
716 / 1153	**1042** / 1678	**811** / 1306	**1048** / 1687	**1670** / 2689	**2098** / 3377	**2171** / 3494	**2422** / 3858	**2248** / 3618	**2274** / 3661	**2153** / 3466	**Florianópolis**			
533 / 858	**859** / 1383	**628** / 1011	**865** / 1392	**1487** / 2394	**1915** / 3082	**1987** / 3199	**2213** / 3563	**2051** / 3302	**2039** / 3282	**1964** / 3161	**192** / 310	**Curitiba**		
266 / 429	**595** / 958	**364** / 586	**630** / 1015	**1232** / 1983	**1642** / 2643	**1732** / 2788	**1953** / 3144	**1861** / 2996	**1843** / 2967	**1949** / 3137	**432** / 695	**253** / 408	**São Paulo**	

10 = Distance in miles
10 = Distance in kilometers

0 km   100
0 miles   100

A PORTRAIT OF BRAZIL

Brazil evokes iconic images of lively Carnaval celebrations, brilliant soccer teams, *bossa nova* and *samba* performances, sensual Brazilians swaying across the sands of Ipanema and Copacabana, and the beautiful city of Rio de Janeiro. Beyond these popular images, however, there remains a lot to discover about Brazil, which is fast emerging as a global economic giant.

Covering over half of South America, Brazil is the world's fifth-largest nation. The sheer size of the country helps to explain the extraordinary diversity of environments and cultures. The larger cities are known for cosmopolitan sophistication and extensive technological development, while in the Amazon region there are indigenous peoples who still use ancient agricultural techniques.

The Portuguese colonization that began in the 1500s, combined with the influx of immigrants from a wide geographical and ethnic spectrum, has lent an eclectic character to the social fabric of the country. Portuguese is spoken by the vast majority of the 190 million Brazilians, although there are many commonly used words derived from indigenous and African languages.

The country's striking diversity is reflected in the major cities, each of which has its own distinctive character. The impressive Modernist architecture of the nation's capital Brasília, the ravishing cityscape of Rio de Janeiro, embraced by the gigantic statue of Cristo Redentor (Christ the Redeemer), the colonial buildings and Baroque gems of Minas Gerais, the historic cities of the Northeast, and the picturesque European-influenced, wine-producing towns in Southern Brazil, are just a few examples of this remarkable heterogeneity.

An aerial view of high-rise concrete towers in the ultra-modern city of São Paulo

◀ Carnival parade of *samba* dancers at the Sambódromo, held in Rio de Janeiro

Caiman and butterflies in the splendid Amazonian greenery

The diverse character of Brazil is reflected in its five distinct ecosystems – the Amazon rainforest, the semi-arid *sertão*, the central *cerrado* (savanna), the wildlife-rich Pantanal wetlands, and the lush Mata Atlântica. The varied natural attractions of the country include the spectacular falls at Foz do Iguaçu, captivating Amazônia, the splendid beaches of Rio de Janeiro and the Northeast, the luxuriant grasslands of Rio Grande do Sul, the pristine-white sand dunes of Lençóis Maranhenses, and the abundant, breathtaking flora and fauna of the Pantanal.

The Economy

The Brazilian economy is counted among the world's 10 largest, though it is riddled with contradictions – *favelas* (shantytowns) coexist with skyscrapers in the cities. The foundations for modern economic prosperity were laid, ironically, during the years of the military dictatorship from 1964 to 1984, when Brazil's rulers borrowed heavily from international banks to fund various large projects. However, it was only during the administration of Fernando Henrique Cardoso (1995–2002) that Brazil's economy became more market-orientated, a trend that was carried forward by his successor, Luiz Inácio Lula da Silva – "Lula."

Today, Brazil's major exports feature both manufactured goods, including machinery and automobiles, and agricultural products, such as soya beans and coffee. In recent years, Brazil has emerged as an economic powerhouse and a strong advocate of opening up global trade to developing nations. Its vision of exploring new energy production methods is manifested by Petrobras, Brazil's largest oil-producing company. Run by the state, Petrobras is a pioneer in the development of advanced technology from deep-water oil production.

Alongside Brazil's growing global significance, there still remain deep economic

The verdant countryside near Bento Gonçalves, a wine-producing town in the Serra Gaúcha, Rio Grande do Sul

Petrobras (Petróleo Brasileiro), Brazil's state-run gas and oil refinery, near Rio de Janeiro

disparities and regional differences. It is common to see the super-rich and the urban poor in Brazil's major cities, mainly Rio de Janeiro and São Paulo, two of the largest metropolises in the world. Inequitous growth is also visible not only in the undeveloped interiors, but also in the agriculture-dominated southern region where there is a rising number of landless peasants.

Political Life

Politicians have tremendous power in Brazil, and many start and make their way up through municipal and state politics. Some political positions outside of the capital are extremely powerful in their own right, especially that of mayor of one of the big cities, or governor of a state.

Since 1985, when the military dictatorship came to an end, Brazil has been one of the world's largest democracies. However, the country's current political elite have immersed Brazil in a series of scandals, involving corruption, misuse of public funds, and abuse of power.

When the leftist, ex-trade union leader Lula was elected president in 2002, Brazilians hoped for a democracy that favored the "majority of society," as promised in his Workers' Party (Partido dos Trabalhadores – PT) manifesto, but Brazil's underprivileged majority continued to be ruled by a wealthy minority. In 2011, Dilma Rousseff, also of the PT, was inaugurated as the country's first female president.

Brazilians, for the most part, are united in their distrust and lack of respect for their politicians and political parties.

Supporters waving flags of Lula during his 2002 electoral campaign

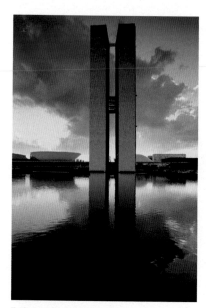

The Congresso Nacional at dusk, Brasília

The average educated Brazilian resents the perceived close alliance between the politicians and their ambitious business allies.

The People

Home to over half the population of South America, Brazil is the fifth most populous country in the world. The vast majority of people live in the coastal parts and major cities, and the population density grows progressively scantier toward the interior. Brazil has such a varied mix of races, nationalities, and ethnic groups that it is difficult to define a typical Brazilian. It is often argued that being Brazilian is more a state of mind than anything else.

The Portuguese, the first Europeans to explore Brazil, were followed by other colonial powers laying claim to areas along the Brazilian coast. However brief the influence of the French and the Dutch, and later the British, they all made their mark on Brazil, along with the dominant Portuguese. Their influence is still visible in its culture and its people. The millions of slaves brought to Brazil from West Africa, between the 16th and 19th centuries, have also played an important role in the development of Brazil as a country and as a vibrant culture. Between the 18th and 19th centuries, the influx of immigrants from Europe, especially Italy and Germany, and also from Japan and Korea, have played their part in forming the multicultural and ethnically diverse population of Brazil.

Although Brazil has reputedly the world's largest Catholic population, its unique mix of people has given rise to many different religions and sects. The animistic beliefs of the indigenous Brazilians, ritualistic Afro-Brazilian cults, and spiritualist Kardecism, coexist with other faiths including Judaism, Islam, and Buddhism. Candomblé, a syncretic cult practiced in Bahia, is a unique amalgamation of Catholicism and African beliefs.

Brazil upholds the ideal of racial harmony. However, though not blatant, racial discrimination does still exist. As well as having limited access to education and work opportunities, black people remain inadequately represented in the higher echelons of politics, academia, and business.

Baianas in front of the Convento de São Francisco, Salvador

Residents of Rio de Janeiro (Cariocas) playing soccer on Enseada de Botafogo

Sport & Culture

Brazil's sporting and cultural influence has made the "Brasil" brand known throughout the world. Brazil is the world's greatest soccer (*futebol*) nation, having won the

Ayrton Senna, winner of the Monaco Grand Prix in 1992

World Cup on five occasions and having been the only nation to play at every World Cup. Pelé *(see p172)*, hailed as a great national hero, is the most famous soccer player of all time.

Brazil's sporting prowess has not been restricted to soccer. In Ayrton Senna, Nelson Piquet, and Emerson Fittipaldi, it has had three Formula 1 World Champions, and in tennis it saw success in the 1950s and 1960s with Maria Esther Bueno and, more recently, with Gustavo Kuerten.

Culture has also played its part in establishing how the world views Brazil. The first musicians to make a mark internationally were composer Heitor Villa-Lobos and legendary performer Carmen Miranda. In literature too, writers as different in their subject matter as Jorge

Amado and Paulo Coelho, have helped spread the word about their homeland. The music of Brazil, be it *samba*, *bossa nova*, or one of the many other musical styles to be found across the country, has been a powerful calling card since the 1960s. In more recent times, talented filmmakers have gone on to produce critically acclaimed works, including Walter Salles with *Central do Brasil* (*Central Station*, 1998) and Fernando Meirelles with *Cidade de Deus* (*City of God*, 2002).

Brazilians celebrate life with their colorful festivals. Carnaval, the cultural event that helped put Brazil on the map, is perceived as the biggest and best in the world, and its revelry embraces the whole country.

A group of musicians rehearsing Brazil's country music *sertanejo*, in Cidade de Goiás

The Landscapes of Brazil

Larger than the US (excluding Alaska) and bordering 10 of the 12 other South American countries, Brazil is home to a wide variety of breathtaking landscapes, from vast swamps to desert, and thick rainforest to metropolitan cityscapes. Covering over 2 million sq miles (3.5 million sq km) and embracing over 40 percent of Brazilian territory, the Amazon rainforest is the most dominant landscape in Brazil and the best known. Although massive and spectacular, the Amazon Basin is only one biome out of several in Brazil, each with its own distinct scenery, fascinating wildlife, and climate.

Key

- The Amazon rainforest
- The Pantanal
- The *sertão*
- The *cerrado*
- Mata Atlântica
- •—• International border
- △ Peak

The Northern Highlands in Amazônia are impressive mountains, strung along the frontier with Venezuela and Guyana.

Branco

Pico da Neblina
9,888 ft (3,013 m)

Tiquié

Negro

Japurá

Amazonas

Içá

Juruá

Jutaí

Purus

Madeira

Tapajós

The Amazon rainforest *(see pp264–5)*, one of the most complex ecosystems in the world, is characterized by vast expanses of dense forest, with a wide range of vegetation. Large areas, such as the buriti palm-dominated *igapós*, are annually flooded by the waters of the Rio Negro.

The Pantanal *(see pp324–5)*, an immense wetland, is the largest seasonally flooded area on the planet, inundating as much as two-thirds of its total area for half the year, during the rainy season. Dotted with small, forested elevations, the southern Pantanal is used for cattle grazing during the dry season.

The Wet and the Dry Season

During the wet season, which lasts from December to March, the rising rivers inundate the flat land. This process creates *cordilhieras* (isolated islands) amid vast lakes and flowering shrubs. However, it is during the dry season (May to September), that wildlife is at its most spectacular in the Pantanal. During this time, the ponds teem with fish, and thousands of birds flock around the water holes.

The Pantanal in the wet season, near Porto Jofre

The Pantanal with tiny forests in the dry season

The ***sertão*** *(see p237)* is a semi-arid region in the interior of Brazil's northeast and parts of northern Minas Gerais. The essentially barren landscape, dominated by *caatinga*, is a uniquely Brazilian habitat. The *sertão* receives very little rainfall during the dry months, and is largely strewn with cacti and thorny shrubs. There are periods of intense drought, which makes it a harsh environment for wildlife and people alike. As a result, much of the flora and fauna have specially adapted themselves to the lack of water.

The cerrado *(see pp300–1)* features wide expanses of open, tropical grassland scattered with small, closed canopy forests. Brazil's central plateau is the world's most biologically rich savanna with over 10,000 plant species.

Mata Atlântica *(see p113)*, or the Atlantic rainforest, is a 4,600-mile (7,400-km) coastal band endowed with a stunning diversity of landscapes, from the granite peaks and sheer cliffs of the Great Escarpment to the beautiful white sands and surf of the Costa do Sol.

Brazil's Flora & Fauna

Home to over 55,000 plant species and three of the most diverse ecosystems on the planet, the wealth of flora and fauna in Brazil is unmatched. Some of the most valuable resources of the modern world, such as rubber, originate from the rainforests of the Amazon. As a result of the relative stability of the rainforest compared to temperate areas, the fauna here has had the freedom to evolve and to adapt to very specialized local conditions. With a few of the tributaries of the Amazon river still unexplored, there are numerous species yet to be discovered. Brazil has five principal ecosystems, each with its own distinct array of plant life. From forest and swamp to desert and savanna, these stark contrasts in climate and landscape have resulted in an immensely vibrant and diverse flora, much of which is unique to the country.

Aquatic plants, including the versatile water hyacinth, are commonly found in the Pantanal, which has the richest collection of these plants.

Amazônia

The Amazon rainforest *(see p264–5)* possesses a wealth of flora and fauna. It is characterized by vast expanses of dense forest, extensive savannas, and other ecosystems. Vegetation and wildlife vary because of the annual flooding of large areas.

Blue and gold macaws are brilliantly colored large birds that live on cliffs and high in trees in rainforests and swamps. They are considered an endangered species.

Aguapé is an invasive floating plant with medicinal properties. Found in the wetlands of the Pantanal and Amazônia, it acts as a natural water filter.

The Sertão

The arid *sertão (see p237)*, which comprises 75 percent of the land area in the northeast, has its own unique wildlife including lizards, snakes, and foxes. Birdlife manages to flourish in this minimalist, unfriendly landscape, and sheep and goats are also reared.

Juazeiro, a shrub-like tree indigenous to the *sertão*, is used in wine-making and medicine, as a hair tonic, and for timber.

Mandacaru cactus is a symbol of rebirth and resilience in the arid *sertão*. According to local legend, this tree-like cactus with fragrant blossoms originates on the site of a massacre.

The Cerrado

The *cerrado (see p300–1)* is a vast open savanna dotted with clusters of scattered woodlands. This is the world's most biologically rich grassland. There are over 4,000 endemic plant species. The *cerrado* is also home to maned wolves and giant anteaters.

The mutum, or crested currasow, is a large bird which is often seen in the forested areas of the *cerrado*.

Pequi, also known as souari nut, provides sweet berries with small thorns inside. It is eaten fresh, used in food, and made into a liqueur.

Giant anteaters are commonly spotted in the *cerrado*. These solitary animals have a long tail and tongue, a bristly brown coat, and five short, sharp claws on both their paws. They are sometimes hunted for their meat.

The Mata Atlântica

The Mata Atlântica *(see p113)*, or Atlantic rainforest, is formed by remnants of Brazil's coastal rainforest. The development of cities and intensive agriculture has severely reduced this habitat, but it remains home to monkeys and exotic birds.

The *piaçava* is a fibrous palm tree. Its fibers are extensively used to make brooms, thatch, mats, and cord.

Woolly spider monkeys are the largest primates in the Americas. This endangered species eats mainly fruits, leaves, and seeds.

The Pantanal

The largest inland wetland *(see pp324–5)* on the planet is constantly abuzz with bird- and wildlife. Hundreds of birds can be heard screeching overhead or fishing in the waters while caimans bask along the river banks. The best time to visit is the dry season.

The anaconda is a large water boa, which can grow to 32 ft (10 m) in length. It kills its prey, sometimes many times its size, by constriction as well as drowning.

The *gravatá* is a member of the *Bromeliaceae* family. *Gravatá* (also known as *karatas*) is a kind of fruit, similar to a pineapple, that grows on the ground.

Peoples of Brazil

When the Portuguese arrived in 1500, the Brazilian population consisted of over 5 million indigenous people divided into at least 1,000 communities. When their numbers began depleting due to the severity of slavery, the Portuguese started shipping slaves from Africa in the mid-16th century. Many of these slaves assimilated with the white and local population. Over the centuries, Brazil's peoples were diversified further by several waves of immigration from the Middle East, Asia, and Europe. After over 500 years of immigration and integration, modern Brazil is a true ethnic mosaic, where diverse elements combine to create a vibrant nation renowned for its spirit.

Indigenous Brazilians also include the Ticuna community, who are a large group with their own language and written literature.

Some indigenous groups *(see pp266–7)* continue to live as they had done before the arrival of the Portuguese, particularly in the forested interior.

Multiracial Brazil

Brazil is unique in its assimilation of various races and ethnic groups. A white-and-indigenous Brazilian is called a mestiço, *an Afro-Brazilian is called a cafuzo, while a mulatto is born of white and African parentage.*

European immigrants *(see pp332–3)* started moving to Brazil after slavery ended in 1888. They tended to concentrate in various parts of Southern Brazil, where people of Azorean, German, Italian, Slav, Dutch, Austrian, and other descents still thrive.

The Portuguese, the dominant ethnic group in Brazil today, introduced Catholicism *(see p38)*, and have given the country its official language.

Mulattoes, born of black and white parentage, make up at least half the population. Prominent in music, sports, and the arts, famous Brazilian mulattoes include pop music icon Gilberto Gil *(see p36)* and professional soccer player Ronaldo.

Baianas are recognizable in their lace dresses with colorful beads that represent the various *orixás*, or Afro-Brazilian deities *(see p181)*. Baianas play an integral role in keeping alive the Afro-Brazilian traditions that came to Brazil, especially in the slave ships from Angola and Nigeria.

Japanese Brazilians *(see p173)* are mainly descended from immigrants who came to Brazil around 1908 as laborers. There are numerous Buddhist and Shinto shrines around Brazil, and the Japanese influence can be seen in the art scene and in the popularity of its cuisine. São Paulo City's Liberdade district is home to the largest Japanese community outside of Japan.

Cariocas & Paulistanos

Cariocas frolicking on Copacabana beach, Rio City

Residents of Brazil's two largest cities, Rio de Janeiro and São Paulo, have successfully stereotyped themselves and each other. The fun-loving Cariocas of Rio are seen as too easygoing by the Paulistanos of São Paulo, whom the Cariocas regard as workaholics with no zest for life. Paulistanos see their city as the economic force driving Brazil, while Rio is considered to be a playground for Carnaval *(see pp68–9)*. The self-image of Cariocas is that they have better music and more beautiful people. The Paulistanos, on the other hand, take pride in their diligent nature and the distinct cadence of their spoken Portuguese. The key difference really revolves around beach life. Rio's long stretch of trendy beaches forms a vital part of the city's daily life *(see pp42–3)*. The beaches around São Paulo, on the other hand, demand the weekend to enjoy, being at least 40 miles (65 km) away from the city.

Architecture

The first buildings in Brazil were made by the indigenous peoples. As these structures were made from perishable materials, little is known of them beyond early European descriptions. Colonial churches and other buildings were in spectacular form in the 18th century during the Baroque era. After independence, Brazil followed European trends until Lúcio Costa and Oscar Niemeyer developed Brazilian Modernism, most strikingly expressed in the new capital Brasília. Today, Brazil is dominated by high-rises punctuated by the occasional striking building by a contemporary architect such as Ruy Ohtake.

Avenida Atlântica at Copacabana beach, Rio de Janeiro

Indigenous

Francisco de Orellana (1511–46), the first European to navigate the Amazon, described large cities created by Curucirari people extending for as much as 6 miles (10 km) and cut by large roads. These large cities no longer exist. Today, traditional indigenous villages are smaller and focus on a large communal maloca. Less traditional ones are made up of wattle-and-daub houses.

Dyed tree bark
Open entrance
Sloping thatched roof

Kayapó malocas, or *ocas*, are communal longhouses, usually measuring 92 ft (28 m) in length and 59 ft (18 m) in width. Their shape and design influenced many of Oscar Niemeyer's buildings.

Baroque

Baroque architecture began in 17th-century Europe but reached its most exuberant in Latin America. Brazilian Baroque is characterized by elaborately carved, painted interiors and ornate, florid forms set in modest, whitewash-and-raw-stone façades. The style found its zenith in Salvador and Recife, and in the sculptures of Aleijadinho *(see p135)* in Minas Gerais.

Elaborately carved stone tablet

The monumental door, offset by the modest façade

São Francisco de Assis, in Salvador, is a display of wealth and splendor. The interior of the church is covered with almost 900 lb (450 kg) of gold. Silver, gold leaf, and solid gold are coupled with stunning *azulejos*, that is blue Portuguese tile work.

São Pedro dos Clérigos, in Recife, is rich in ornamental flourishes typical of the Baroque. Its second tower was left incomplete in order to avoid a tax on churches.

Neo-Classical

Neo-Classicism is associated with Imperial Brazil and came to the country with the Portuguese monarchy who fled Napoleon in 1807, bringing the most fashionable European architectural ideas with them. The first Neo-Classical buildings were civic edifices in Rio de Janeiro and palaces in Petrópolis. These quickly became the norm for buildings of state in the rest of the Empire.

Typical Palladian portico
Frieze in bas-relief style
Ionic column

The Museu Imperial, in Petrópolis, marked the advent of the most popular form of Neo-Classicism. Its architect, Julius Köhler, was influenced by the English Palladian style.

Eclectic

Eclecticism is an architectural style associated with 19th-century Republican Brazil. Like the styles that preceded it, it was strongly influenced by European trends, particularly French and English. Eclecticism is characterized by a combination of forms, motifs, and styles from Neo-Classical and Baroque through to Manueline, a style that fuses together in one building Portuguese Late Gothic with ornamentation in portals, windows, and arcades, along with Oriental elements.

Teatro Amazonas's façade is rich with forms, motifs, and details selected from different historical periods and architectural styles.

Mock-Byzantine decorative cupola

Neo-Classical frieze

Windows fusing the Palladian style with Brazilian Baroque

Modernist

Modernism was shaped by architects such as Le Corbusier and Max Bill. Brazilian architects at first adhered to the strict precepts these Europeans laid down, but from the 1940s, architects such as Oscar Niemeyer developed a unique form of Brazilian Modernism, influenced by indigenous design and employing curved forms.

Le Corbusier canopy style

Brise-soleil façade

The Ministry of Education, built in Rio in 1943 with a striking glass *brise-soleil* façade, was the first Modernist building in the Americas to combine civic architecture with a contemporary medium.

Parliament buildings, in Brasília, are a harmony of simple lines and curves incorporating water and the landscape into the design.

Contemporary Brazil

Beyond Brasília and Oscar Niemeyer's continued output in Rio and Curitiba, contemporary Brazilian architecture is largely functional and not particularly inspiring. Cities are seas of identical tower-block flats broken by snaking highways. The most daring designs tend to be private homes hidden away behind high walls or corporate buildings such as Ruy Ohtake's stunning Hotel Unique *(see p373)* and Hotel Unique Garden in São Paulo.

Open-air Skye Bar

Glass set windows

Concrete Pillars supporting the hotel

Landscaped Garden

Hotel Unique is a combination of bravado and functionalism. Built by Ruy Ohtake, a leading figure in contemporary Brazilian architecture, the inverted arc has 3-ft- (1-m-) wide windows overlooking a stunning garden. The open-air rooftop bar has a spectacular view over the city.

Brazilian Artists & Writers

Brazil's first artists and writers were religious, and a tradition of uniquely Brazilian ecclesiastical art continued into the 20th century. Secular art in Brazil ceased to derive from Europe only in the 1920s after the emergence of the *antropofagismo* movement, which appropriated western themes into specifically Brazilian contexts. Brazil's writers found a voice in the work of 19th-century writers such as Joaquim Maria Machado de Assis and Euclides da Cunha. The explosion of Modernism in the early 20th century has left Brazil with a diverse literary output which remains largely unexplored by English-language publishers.

Ceiling painted by Dom Adelbert Gresnicht, Mosteiro São Bento, São Paulo

Church Art

Brazil's first great artists were European priests. Frei Domingos da Conceição (1643–1718) was responsible for the interiors of the São Bento monasteries in Rio and Olinda. Father Agostinho de Piedade (1580–1661) and 18th-century Francisco Xavier Brito, whose works can be found in Rio de Janeiro and Minas Gerais, introduced the Baroque style, developing it as uniquely Brazilian.

Brito almost certainly taught the great artist, Aleijadinho *(see p135)*, whose statuary mocks the racist Portuguese colonists, most notably at the basilica in Congonhas and the Igreja São Francisco in Ouro Preto. The latter also preserves the finest paintings by another subtle satiricist, Mestre (Manuel da Costa) Athayde (1762–1830). Illusionism in religious art was developed by José Joaquim da Rocha (1737–1807) in Salvador, Mestre Valentim (1750–1813)

in Rio, and José Joaquim da Veiga Valle (1806–74) in Goiás. In the 19th and 20th centuries, illusionism was largely lost but for the work of Benedito Calixto (1853–1927) in Santos and São Paulo, and the Dutch artist Adelbert Gresnicht, who painted the Beuronese interior of São Paulo's Mosteiro São Bento.

Secular Art

Brazil's first secular art was European in theme and technique, best seen in the

Alfredo Volpi, painter known for his signature Brazilian palette

pastoral idylls of the Dutch artist Frans Post (1612–80) and the formal portraits of the Frenchman Jean-Baptiste Debret (1768–1848).

The first painting to make use of Brazil's rich tropical light was *Caipira Picando Fumo* by José Ferraz de Almeida Júnior (1850–99). However, a truly Brazilian style emerged only in the 1920s with *antropofagismo*, a movement propagating "cultural cannibalism," which adapts ideas from European art and literature and reworks them in Brazilian terms. Tarsila do Amaral (1886–1973) produced the movement's most representative paintings, and was followed by Lasar Segall (1891–1957) and Anita Malfatti (1896–1964).

Other artists pursued Modernism according to their own ideas. Emiliano Di Cavalcanti (1897–1976) turned to the masses for inspiration, producing impressionistic, erotic icons of black Brazilian women. Candido Portinari (1903–62), with a far more obvious social conscience, produced *O Mestiço* that showed the dignity of Brazilian workers, while his *Os Retirantes* portrayed their misery. The sculptor Victor Brecheret (1894–1955) offered a Brazilian take on Art Deco, while Alfredo Volpi (1896–1988) brought Brazilian colors to abstract impressionism. São Paulo's large ethnic Japanese community continues to produce artists, such as Tomie Ohtake (b.1913), who pay Brazilian homage to the styles and techniques of Japan.

Brazil's contemporary art scene is lively and diverse. Most prominently, the works of photographer Sebastião Salgado (b.1944) are rooted in the ideas of Liberation Theology *(see p38)*. Artist Siron Franco (b.1947) uses naive, surreal forms to highlight social and environmental issues.

Colonial Literature

European Jesuits are credited with the earliest writing to come out of Brazil. José Anchieta (1534–97) chronicled his work and described the evangelization of the indigenous people. The sermons of Antônio Vieira (1608–97) are fine examples of Portuguese prose.

Gregório de Matos (1623–96), who was born in Bahia, is sometimes cited as Brazil's first celebrated homegrown literary figure. During the 18th century, poetry academies in Minas Gerais were producing writers such as Cláudio Manuel da Costa (1729–89), José Basílio da Gama (1740–95), and Tomás Antônio Gonzaga (1744–1810). They introduced revolutionary French ideas to Brazil and wrote lyric and epic poems on Brazilian themes, but in a lofty European classical style.

Legendary mulatto writer, Joaquim Maria Machado de Assis

The Empire & the Republic

Brazil began to find its own voice in the last days of the Empire with the great 19th-century mulatto novelist, Joaquim Maria Machado de Assis (1839–1908). Starting out with traditional sentimental romances, he later became celebrated for his darkly humorous novels with their subversive social criticism. *Dom Casmurro* is considered by some to be the greatest Latin American novel of the 19th

century. After independence in 1889, Machado de Assis's social criticisms were taken a step further by a generation of Republican novelists, influenced by scientific and nascent socialist ideas from Europe. In *Triste fim de Policarpo Quaresma*, the black novelist, Afonso Lima Barreto (1881–1922), was openly critical of the corruption that characterized the Republic. Euclides da Cunha's *Os Sertões* chronicled a gory and disastrous military campaign against a messianic rebel, Antônio Conselheiro *(see p210)*, and his bandit followers in the harsh landscape of the Bahian *sertão*.

Grande Sertão exhibition, Museum of Portuguese Language, São Paulo

Modernism in Literature

Modernism proper began in Brazil with Mário and Oswald de Andrade, who sought to articulate contemporary and uniquely Brazilian styles and themes. Mário (1893–1945) traveled throughout the country, searching for a unifying traditional culture which he enunciated in his comic rhapsody *Macunaíma*. Oswald (1890–1953), together with his wife Tarsila do Amaral, formulated the ideas behind the *antropofagismo cultural* movement. The de Andrades cleared the way for the Modernist poets Carlos Drummond (1902–87) and Manuel Bandeira (1886–1968), and the greatest of all Brazilian writers, João Guimarães Rosa (1908–67), whose grand metaphysical novel, *Grande Sertão: Veredas*, invented a new syntax based on the isolated idioms of the interior of Minas Gerais.

A string of writers, including Gilberto Freyre (1900–87), Sérgio Buarque de Holanda (1902–82), and Darcy Ribeiro (1922–97), emerged from the social sciences. The 20th century also produced major popular novelists, including Jorge Amado (1902–2001) and Clarice Lispector (1920–77). Vinícius de Moraes (1913–80),

a seminal figure in the contemporary Brazilian music scene, was the first to plough the furrow between music and literature by writing the lyrics of many famous songs. He has since been followed by song-writer Chico Buarque (b.1944), who wrote the novel *Budapest*.

Since 2000, writers from Brazil's manifold ethnic communities have risen to prominence. In *Relato de um Certo Oriente*, Milton Hatoum (b.1952) probes the psyche of an Arab immigrant, while Moacyr Scliar (b.1937) explores the Jewish-Brazilian experience in his writings.

Today, Brazilian fiction accounts for about half the literary output of Latin America. Writers include Paulo Coelho (b.1947), feminist novelist and short-story writer Lygia Fagundes Telles (b.1923), and Amazonian poet Aníbal Beça (b.1946).

Leading 20th-century novelist, Clarice Lispector

The Music of Brazil

The vibrant music of Brazil reflects the diversity of the cultural and ethnic backgrounds that make up the country's resident population. The music mirrors the influences of both the native and immigrant population. The rhythms of Africa are as important to the overall sound as the harmonies and melodies that were introduced from Europe. Brazil is not about one musical style, but a varied selection. Internationally, *samba* and *bossa nova* are the best known of the country's musical styles, but regional forms, such as *frevo (see p221)*, *axé*, *forró (see p240)*, and *sertanejo (see p237)*, are just as popular within Brazil.

Heitor Villa-Lobos, one of Brazil's greatest classical composers

Samba

Derived from Angolan religious rhythms, samba has permeated virtually every other Brazilian musical form that followed it. Historically strong in Rio, São Paulo, and Bahia, samba made a remarkable impact throughout the country in the 1930s. Samba comes in many forms, and most of these have a link to dance.

Zeca Pagodinho, who emerged in the late 1980s, is one of the most popular and best-selling artists of a new wave of *samba* stars.

Clara Nunes was one of the most prolific and popular *samba* singers of all time. Her career was tragically cut short when she died at the age of 39 in 1983.

Gilberto Gil went from political exile to Brazilian superstar before becoming Minister of Culture in 2003. He remains an active musical force.

Bossa nova

Bossa nova, *a marriage of Brazilian rhythms and American jazz, has been the most exportable form of Brazilian music since international audiences first discovered it through an album, Getz/Gilberto, recorded by Stan Getz and João Gilberto in 1964. The album included a number of compositions from a young and unknown composer from Rio, Antônio Carlos ("Tom") Jobim. Gilberto, Jobim, and Jobim's lyricist, Vinícius de Moraes, were to become the "Holy Trinity" of bossa nova.*

Antônio Carlos Jobim was responsible for many of the *bossa nova* classics including "The Girl From Ipanema," one of the most played and recorded songs in popular music history.

Sergio Mendes and his group, Brasil '66, helped launch *bossa nova* globally in the 1960s. They have recorded with acts such as Black Eyed Peas, Erykah Badu, and Justin Timberlake.

Bebel Gilberto has been the most internationally successful Brazilian artist in recent years. Her 2009 album *All in One* was her third to be nominated for a Grammy.

Caetano Veloso helped launch the *tropicalismo* movement in 1967, and is considered a Brazilian musical treasure.

Chico Buarque is a composer, lyricist, performer, and author. He is as popular today as when he first performed in 1964.

Tropicalismo & Música Popular Brasileira

Tropicalismo *was a form of Brazilian music that arose in the late 1960s from a mix of* bossa nova, *rock and roll,* Bahia folk, *and African music. Many* tropicalismo *artists, led by Caetano Veloso and Gilberto Gil, were driven by political activism following the coup of 1964. Inspired in part by* tropicalismo, música popular Brasileira (MPB), *or popular Brazilian music, includes many Brazilian musical styles and is the most popular music played on the radio and in the clubs and bars of Brazil.*

Daniela Mercury burst on to Bahia's *axé* and reggae music scene in the 1990s. Her explosive live performances have won her a growing international following.

Regional Music

Although MPB covers a multitude of Brazilian musical genres, there are a number of distinctive regional styles that include axé, choro, forró, frevo, *and* pagode. *Bahia, one of the powerhouses of regional Brazilian music, has its own versions of jazz, reggae, hip-hop, soul, funk, rock and roll, heavy metal, electronica, and the popular homegrown country and western style known as* sertanejo.

Carlinhos Brown, a prolific performer, composer, drummer, and dancer, is equally popular as a solo artist or when collaborating with others.

The São Paulo Scene

The residents of São Paulo work hard, but they have also learnt to play hard so that the city's club scene is now considered one of the world's most exciting and innovative, with top international DJs flying in to exchange ideas and sounds with their Brazilian counterparts. Break beat, drum and bass, electronica, house, lounge, speed, garage, techno, trance, and trip-hop all have a place in the Paulista scene. With a huge range of nightclubs and bars to choose from, Paulistanos can enjoy all genres of music through the week and all year round.

DJ playing in a São Paulo club

Religions of Brazil

Few countries in the world can match Brazil for religious diversity. A typical São Paulo or Rio neighborhood will be home to Catholic and Evangelical Protestant churches, Buddhist temples, synagogues, mosques, Spiritist churches, Afro-Brazilian ceremonial centers, as well as a range of smaller religious institutions. The practice of black magic is not uncommon, even in business and politics, and soothsayers and witches hand out leaflets on the streets. Only atheists are largely absent in Brazil; those who believe in nothing are looked upon with a mixture of incredulity and pity.

Igreja Nossa Senhora do Rosário dos Pretos in São Paulo

Catholicism

Catholicism arrived with the Portuguese, and Catholics remain Brazil's dominant religious group. Brazil has the largest number of Catholics of any country in the world.

From its earliest days, the Church in Brazil, as in most colonies, was divided into an establishment linked to the Crown (and later to the Emperor and the Republican State) and factions who campaigned on behalf of the oppressed. One of these factions was the Jesuits who, while treating the indigenous people as objects of pro-selytization, nonetheless fought doggedly against their enslavement and murder by the *bandeirantes* and the settlers on the Amazon. The Jesuits began to be seen as a threat to the Portuguese Crown and were expelled from the colonies in 1757.

The Church establishment in Brazil did little to criticize the treatment of the indigenous people, or the slaves from Africa who replaced them. Churches were divided along strict social and racial lines. The poorest churches were reserved for Afro-Brazilian slaves and were often dedicated to the black Madonna, Nossa Senhora do Rosário dos Pretos.

Latin American churches were instrumental in influencing Pope John XXIII and Pope Paul VI's groundbreaking Church reforms of the mid-1960s, known as Vatican II, and promoting a more egalitarian Catholic Church throughout the world. Vatican II led to the most important movement in the Catholic Church in the 20th century, Liberation Theology.

Churches in Brazil today are largely apolitical and gregarious, and are increasingly influenced by Evangelical preaching and musical styles.

Evangelical Protestants at Igreja Universal do Reino, São Paulo

Evangelical Protestantism

The Evangelical movement emphasizes the Protestant beliefs in the authority of the Bible and of every person's right to interpret the Scriptures for themselves. Services are emotive, with pastors making use of fiery language, and often strongly encouraging their congregation to donate a *dízima* (usually 10 percent of any monthly salary) to the Church. The movement has been widely criticized.

Liberation Theology

Leonardo Boff presiding over a service

In the 1970s, groups of Latin American Catholic thinkers preached what they called "a preferential option for the poor." In Brazil they were led by Leonardo Boff, Hélder Câmara, and Pedro Casaldáliga. They campaigned against the rich establishment and the dictatorships. Many of the priests involved were murdered or tortured and the movement was suppressed by the established Church.

Nonetheless, Evangelicalism is very popular in Brazil, so much so that populist politicians often campaign as Evangelicals in elections.

Spiritism

Developed by the Frenchman Allan Kardec, Spiritism is a systematization of divergent 19th-century occult practices dealing with communication with the spirits of the dead. Kardec called Spiritism "a science which deals with the nature, origin, and destiny of Spirits, as well as their relationship with the corporeal world." Brazil has the largest number of Kardecian Spiritists of any country in the world.

Chagdud Khadro Ling temple in Tres Coroàs, Rio Grande do Sul

Buddhism & Other Asian Religions

The largest population of ethnic Japanese in Latin America and immigrants from many other East Asian countries live in Brazil. Consequently, there are large communities of Nichiren Daishonin Mahayana Buddhists in the country. Their beliefs are based on the teachings of a 13th-century Japanese monk who stressed the need to elevate one's state of life from being trapped within the limits of desires and instincts. The method for achieving this is through strong ethical practice and the chanting of the Nam-Myoho-Renge-Kyo mantra. The movement has proved especially successful at bridging Brazil's trenchant class divide. Yoga and Krishna

Consciousness are also popular in Brazil, though often as alternative lifestyle options.

Afro-Brazilian Religions

West African religions came to Brazil with slaves and developed into cults, such as Candomblé (see p181), Batuque, and Umbanda. Worship involves the invocation of orixás – spirits who intervene between humans and Olorun, the supreme creator. The Brazilian government legalized their practice in the mid-19th century, but followers of these religions have been persecuted by the Church.

Indigenous Religions

Brazil is home to hundreds of different indigenous belief systems. These can all be loosely banded together as shamanism, which is not so much a religion as a distinct way of understanding reality. Rather than believing that we are made of material, indigenous peoples believe that material, time, and space itself are mere manifestations of a far deeper reality. Spiritual life is organized in harmony with this inner state by a shaman. A number of popular religious movements have grown up in Brazil from indigenous roots. The most widely practiced is Santo Daime, which makes use of Amazonian psychotropic plants to achieve a state of super-consciousness.

Al Iman Ali Ibn Abi Taleb mosque in Curitiba

Islam

Brazil has the largest Islamic community in Latin America, but Islamic fundamentalism is almost unknown. The community is private, conservative, and is generally more concerned with preserving links to Lebanese and Syrian culture and the Arabic language than it is with proselytizing. The community has produced numerous prolific writers and politicians.

Judaism

Brazil's Jewish community has about 150,000 members, most of whom are concentrated in São Paulo (which has the largest Ashkenazi synagogue on the continent), Recife, and Rio de Janeiro. Many are descended from the Jews who fled Europe in the 1930s. The community is active in political and cultural life. The writer Moacyr Scliar is one of the country's successful literary exports.

Santo Daime followers in Visconde de Mauá, Rio de Janeiro

Soccer in Brazil

In the first half of the 20th century, soccer went from being the private sport of Brazil's white European elite to becoming the greatest symbol of nationhood. The game united all sections of the population and, after the national team's first World Cup victory in 1958, brought about unprecedented national pride. The Brazilian way of playing *futebol* – with more emphasis on attacking, dribbling, and acrobatic ball skills – has become a benchmark for excellence, and is also known as *jogo bonito*, or "the beautiful game."

In a favela, the main leisure activity for children is always soccer. Rough terrain helps them develop trademark ball skills such as the dribble.

Charles Miller is the father of Brazilian soccer. In 1894, returning to the country after attending boarding school in Southampton, UK, he brought two footballs, a pump, and a rule book. The first reported game took place a few months later.

The 1938 national soccer team received a joyous welcome on their return home from France. Brazil, which came third after defeating Czechoslovakia, had also won the hearts of the Europeans.

The 1950 World Cup was hosted in Brazil. In the final game, favorites Brazil only needed a draw against Uruguay to win the tournament. However, they lost 2–1 in front of a record 200,000 crowd, causing the greatest moment of collective sporting tragedy in the country's history. The 7–1 defeat to Germany in the 2014 semifinals comes a close second.

The National Side

With their iconic yellow shirts, the Brazilian national team, known as the Seleção, or Selection, is the most glamorous soccer team in the world. It is the only team to have taken part in every World Cup and have won it more times than anyone – in 1958, 1962, 1970, 1994, and 2002.

Brazilian Greats

Brazil has produced more soccer legends than any other country and also the greatest player of all time: Pelé (see p172). The first great player was Artur Friedenreich in the 1910s. Each generation reveals new stars and the soccer factory shows no signs of stopping. Since the inauguration of FIFA's (Fédération Internationale de Football Association) World Player of the Year award in 1991, only Brazil has won it with more than one player: Romário (1994), Ronaldo (1996, 1997, 2002), Rivaldo (1999), and Ronaldinho (2004, 2005).

Leônidas da Silva, also called "Rubber Man" for his elasticity, was the highest scorer in the 1938 World Cup.

Garrincha, the "Little Bird," was born with bent legs and is considered to be the finest dribbler of all time.

The Dream Team of 1970 is considered the best soccer team of all time. Their 4–1 victory against Italy won them the World Cup for the third time.

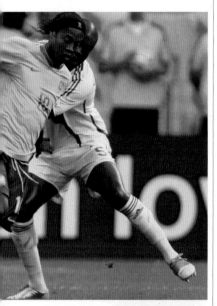

The torcidas, or soccer fans, have adapted aspects of Carnaval to *futebol*, playing lively music at stadia, dressing up in team colors, and bringing noisemakers, colorful banners, and flags.

Major Teams & Stadia

There are several hundred professional clubs in Brazil. The number is impossible to calculate, since local leagues are constantly changing and teams shutting down and starting up. Brazil's best-known stadia are the Maracanã *(see p88)* in Rio, which was built for the 1950 World Cup, and the Morumbi in São Paulo.

Estádio do Maracanã in Rio de Janeiro, one of the largest soccer stadia in the world

Brazil's Biggest Clubs & Stadia

 Sociedade Esportiva Palmeiras (1914)
Stadium: Allianz Parque, São Paulo
Capacity: 43,600

 Cruzeiro Esporte Clube (1921)
Stadium: Mineirão, Belo Horizonte, Minas Gerais
Capacity: 58,170

 Clube de Regatas do Flamengo (1895)
Stadium: Gávea/Maracanã, Rio de Janeiro
Capacity: 4,000 (Gávea)/78,838 (Maracanã)

 Fluminense Football Club (1902)
Stadium: Maracanã, Rio de Janeiro
Capacity: 78,838

 Grêmio Foot-Ball Porto Alegrense (1903)
Stadium: Arena do Grêmio
Capacity: 55,538

 São Paulo Futebol Clube (1930)
Stadium: Morumbi, São Paulo
Capacity: 72,000

 Sport Club Corinthians Paulista (1910)
Stadium: Parque São Jorge/Pacaembu, São Paulo
Capacity: 18,386 (P. São Jorge)/40,199 (Pacaembu)

Club de Regatas Vasco da Gama (1898)
Stadium: São Januário, Rio de Janeiro.
Capacity: 25,000

Pelé was a World Cup champion at 17, and scored a record-breaking 1,283 goals in 1,367 games.

Sócrates, the 1982 and 1986 World Cup captain, was famous for his back heels and his political beliefs.

Romário, the "Baixinho" (Shorty), was the star player in the 1994 World Cup, won by Brazil.

Ronaldo, with two World Cup winner's medals, broke the competition's goal-scoring record in 2006.

Brazilian Beach Culture

The beach represents a big playground for Brazilians. People living near Brazil's extensive coastline go to the beach daily to socialize and to eat and drink, while vacationers can spend all day near the sand and warm water. Brazilian music plays nonstop at the local beach stalls and, as dusk falls, beachgoers party long into the night. It is a Brazilian tradition to play soccer, beach volleyball, and footvolley, or go for a walk or bike ride along the beach or promenades. At some resorts, visitors can rent a horse or a beach buggy, or practice surfing, kayaking, paragliding, and *skibunda* (sandboarding).

Surfer at Praia Joaquina, Ilha de Santa Catarina

Urban Beaches are popular for their promenades and cycle lanes, where people go to exercise before or after work. Some beaches offer good facilities with bathrooms, showers, and gym equipment, and are illuminated at night for playing sports such as soccer and footvolley.

Colorful Food Stalls selling *coalho* cheese, corn-on-the-cob, peanuts, and shrimp sticks line the beaches. Popular local drinks include fresh coconut water, cold beer, and *caipirinha*.

Brazil's Beaches can vary from calm bays to unspoiled, wild beaches accessed only by tracks through the forest. There are also exclusive resort beaches with aquatic parks and modern facilities.

Beach sports are very popular. Besides soccer and volleyball, people play *frescobol* (a kind of tennis). Some beaches also offer paragliding and delta-wings during holidays.

Umbrellas in bright colors are rented for a small amount or lent by the food stalls to their patrons.

The *canga*, a Brazilian sarong, is worn to and from the beach, and also used as a towel to lie on.

Watersports, such as surfing, windsurfing, kayaking, scuba diving, and snorkeling, are popular throughout the year. All equipment can be easily rented at the beach.

Beach safety is monitored by lifeguards on buggies during holidays and at weekends. Flags offer advice on currents and deep water. Asking locals may be useful if there is no patrol.

Locals on the Beach

Relaxed and spontaneous by nature, Brazilians carry only the bare essentials with them to be free to walk, swim, play, or just lie on a canga to tan and watch the world go by.

Beach fashion for women popularly features tiny bikinis that ensure the smallest tan line. The men, on the other hand, can be seen wearing swimming trunks under informal shorts.

Beach parties, or *luaus* (moon parties), are kept alive all night by typical Brazilian dance music such as *forró (see p240)* or *axé*. Electronic music and live concerts are also played at these parties.

BRAZIL THROUGH THE YEAR

Brazilians are a fun-loving people. In this unique land of diverse ethnic groups and races, there is a colorful and vibrant culture, which is celebrated in the numerous parties, carnivals, festivals, rallies, and parades held through the year, but particularly in summer. The most significant events include the spectacular Carnaval and a series of popular religious festivals related to Catholicism and a combination of syncretic traditions. The climate varies, but on average it stays warm, making it favorable to outdoor celebrations. The seasons are not so perceptible, except in Southern and Southeastern Brazil where temperatures are moderate in autumn and spring and dip sharply in winter.

Spring

As flowers begin to decorate the landscape, Brazil prepares to display its wealth of spring flowers and gears up for festivities that last through the season. The most remarkable spring celebrations are related to the Catholic religion, but the highly charged Brazilian Grand Prix also generates great excitement.

September

Expoflora (*Sep weekends*), Holambra (São Paulo state). More than 1,000 species of flora are for sale. Dutch folk dances, music, and Dutch and Brazilian food are also featured, emphasizing the town's Dutch character.
International Fishing Festival (*2nd fortnight, but sometimes held in June*), Cáceres (Mato Grosso). Listed by the *Guinness World Records* as the biggest fishing tournament in the world, the angling event attracts more than 1,500 competitors.

October

São Paulo International Film Festival (*2nd fortnight*), São Paulo. Lasting two weeks, the festival screens around 350 critically acclaimed films from more than 50 countries.
São Paulo Art Biennial (*Oct–Dec, even years*), São Paulo. The Parque do Ibirapuera is the site of an amazing display of modern visual art.
Círio de Nazaré (*2nd Sun*), Belém. Our Lady of Nazareth procession follows the Romaria fluvial pilgrimage a day earlier.
Oktoberfest (*mid-Oct*), Blumenau (Santa Catarina). A lively street party, second only to Munich's, celebrates German music, beer, and way of life.
Brazilian Formula 1 Grand Prix (*late Oct*), São Paulo. Organized at Interlagos Circuit, the race is usually the final round of the Formula 1 season.
Recifolia (*last week*), Recife. A lively carnival with crowds dancing the whole week to Bahian bands.

Paying homage at Padre Cícero's towering statue, Juazeiro do Norte

November

Padre Cícero Pilgrimage (*Nov 2*), Juazeiro do Norte (Paraíba). On Dia de Finados (All Souls' Day), thousands of pilgrims visit patron saint Padre Cícero's statue and the church where he is buried.
National Handicraft Fair (*late Nov/early Dec*), Belo Horizonte. A major exhibition and sale of handicrafts from all over Brazil. There are interactive work-shops where many of the crafts can be learnt.

Smoke rising from the wheels of a Ferrari competing in the Brazilian Grand Prix, São Paulo

A spectacular display of Reveillon fireworks on Copacabana beach

Summer

Summer is the most important time of the year for Brazilians. It marks the beginning of the year and vacation time. It rains heavily in most parts, but the sun continues to shine through. Besides a number of outdoor events to mark the advent of summer, there are trade fairs and important religious festivals. The culmination of the summer is Carnaval.

December

Festa Santa Bárbara (*Dec 4*), Salvador. A popular three-day Candomblé ceremony at Fonte de Santa Bárbara. The image of Santa Bárbara, called Yansã in Candomblé, is carried through the streets of the historic center.

Carnatal (*early Dec*), Natal. Out-of-season Carnaval, where famous bands test their repertoire for the next Carnaval, with throngs of people singing and dancing through the streets.

São Silvestre Race (*Dec 31*), São Paulo. Amateur and recreational runners join professional athletes for a 9-mile (15-km) race through the streets of São Paulo.

Reveillon at Copacabana (*Dec 31*), Rio de Janeiro. A New Year's Eve party along Copacabana beach with performances by leading pop stars and a lavish midnight fireworks display at Forte de Copacabana and Windsor Atlântica Hotel.

January

Procissão dos Navegantes (*Jan 1*), Angra dos Reis. A *samba* school percussion group parade across the Baia de Ilha Grande in boats of different shapes and sizes.

Procissão do Bom Jesus dos Navegantes (*Jan 1*), Salvador. Hundreds of fishing boats follow a galliot, a long ship, that carries the image of Our Lord of Navigators.

Lavagem do Bonfim (*2nd Thu*), Salvador. A colorful parade and ceremonial washing (*lavagem*) of the steps of the Igreja de Nossa Senhora do Bonfim.

Fest Verão Paraíba (*early–mid-Jan*), João Pessoa. Taking place over three weeks, this is one of the country's largest music festivals, with big Brazilian acts.

Festas dos Ticumbi & Alardo (*Jan 19 & 20*), Itaúnas. People in colorful clothes pay homage to São Bento and São Sebastião to the strains of traditional music.

Pré Cajú (*end Jan*), Aracaju. One of the dozens of *micaretas* (out-of-season Carnaval) before the real Carnaval in February/March.

Festa de São Lázaro (*last Sun*), Salvador. A festival in honor of Candomblé deity Omolu, the God of Plague.

February

Pescadores do Rio Vermelho (*Feb 2*), Salvador. A procession of boats carrying offerings to Yemanjá, the Goddess of the Sea, accompanied by Afro-Brazilian music.

Nossa Senhora dos Navegantes (*Feb 2*), Porto Alegre. A boat procession on the Rio Guaíba carrying the image of Yemanjá.

Carnaval (*Feb/Mar, about 40 days before Easter*). The most famous Carnaval takes place in the city of Rio de Janeiro. Salvador and Olinda also have fantastic celebrations.

Festa Nacional da Uva (*Feb/Mar, biennial, even years*), Caxias do Sul. Wine production is the highlight of this festival that keeps alive the customs and traditions of the early Italian immigrants.

Carnaval performers in striking costumes, Rio de Janeiro City

Hooded torchbearers at the Procissão do Fogaréu, Cidade de Goiás

Autumn

In Southern Brazil and the Southeast, the autumn season is marked by steady breezes and comfortable temperatures. Religious festivals, such as the Semana Santa and Festa do Divino Espírito Santo, are celebrated with great involvement. The Hot-Air Balloon Festival is an additional attraction.

March
International Book Biennial (*Mar/Apr*), São Paulo (even years) and Rio de Janeiro (odd years). A 10-day fair marked by book launches, interactive author sessions, lectures, and cultural performances.
Semana Santa (*Mar/Apr*), across Pernambuco & Minas Gerais. In Nova Jerusalém, the play

Paixão de Cristo (Passion of Christ) is staged with over 500 professional actors; the audience also participates. In the historic towns of Minas Gerais, crowds accompany the religious processions.
São Paulo Fashion Week (*late Mar/early Apr*), São Paulo. Fashion shows featuring top Brazilian models and fashion designers are held (*see p149*). It also takes place in January.

April
Procissão do Fogaréu (*Wed before Good Friday*), Cidade de Goiás. The city glows with lights and the streets blaze with torches during the solemn procession of the Semana Santa, when the burial of Christ and the Resurrection are re-enacted to the sound of tambours.

Festa Nacional da Maçã (*Apr/May*), São Joaquim (Santa Catarina). Exhibitions, musical shows, and German folk performances, as well as bestowing of the "best apple producer" title.
Hot-Air Balloon Festival (*Easter week*), Torres. A spectacular annual hot-air balloon event that ahs been held since 1989. Other attractions include a parachute display and rodeo competition.

May
Festa do Bembé do Mercado (*approx May 13*), Santo Amaro. The festival marks the abolition of slavery in 1889. Traditional Bahian music and dance performances also take place.
Festa do Divino Espírito Santo (*May/Jun, 45 days after Easter*), Pirenópolis & Alcântara. Mock battles between Moors and Christians are enacted. Forró and *sertanejo* parties are held.

Winter

With cooler climatic conditions, the southern and southeastern regions are attractive to visitors. Across Brazil, the festivities begin in June, paving the way for international music and art festivals that are a huge draw. The GLBT (Gay, Lesbian, Bisexual, and Transgender) Parade is also significant.

Women in traditional dresses performing *samba-da-roda* at the Festa do Bembé do Mercado, Santo Amaro

Elaborate headgears for the Festa do Bumba-meu-boi, São Luís

June

Festas Juninas (*weekends through June*), across Southeast Brazil. Homage is offered to St. Antony (Jun 13), St. John (Jun 24), and St. Peter (Jun 29). The festivities that take place in the *arraiá* (imitations of old country villas) are marked by traditional feasting.

Festa do Pinhão (*early Jun*), Lages (Santa Catarina). Celebrating the edible *pinhão* (seed of the Paraná pine), the festival includes lively music performances.

GLBT Parade (*early Jun*), São Paulo. Organized since 1997, the parade is one of the biggest events of its kind in the world.

Festa do Bumba-meu-boi (*whole month*), São Luís. Improvised songs and dances by skilled performers tell the story of the death and resurrection of a bull.

Festa do Boi Bumbá (*Jun 28–30*), Parintins. In Amazonas, Bumba-meu-boi is known as Boi Bumbá. Two groups, Caprichoso (in blue) and Garantido (in red), compete inside a *bumbódromo* built to hold 35,000 spectators.

São João (*Jun/Jul*), Caruaru & Campina Grande. Forró is the predominant rhythm at the dance festival, which draws many leading performers.

International Puppet Theater Festival (*Jun/Oct*), Canela. Puppeteers perform in theaters, schools, and streets over four days.

Rally dos Sertões (*late Jun*), across Brazil. A 10-day event, when cars, truck pilots, and motorcycles drive 2,796 miles (4,500 km) through Brazil's rough interior.

July

Festival de Inverno (*Jul 1–30*), Campos do Jordão (São Paulo). Begun in 1990, this is the greatest festival of classical music in Latin America.

Festival Internacional da Dança (*2nd fortnight*), Joinville (Santa Catarina). Dance performances, workshops, and competitions take place at one of the world's largest dance festivals, featuring dance forms ranging from jazz and folk to classical ballet.

Ilhabela Sailing Week (*date varies*), Ilhabela. Known as the sailing capital, the island is famed for competitive races and regattas, organized by the Yacht Club de Ilhabela.

Fortal (*last week*), Fortaleza. The country's biggest *micareta*, held at Cidade Fortal, draws crowds with *axé* music and small schools of *samba*.

August

Festa da Nossa Senhora das Neves (*Aug 5*), João Pessoa. Street celebrations for 10 days to mark the day of the city's patroness, Our Lady of the Snow. The rhythm of *frevo* defines the mood.

Festival de Gramado (*2nd week*), Gramado. The most important film awards event in Brazil offers viewers the best in Brazilian and Latin American cinema.

Festa Literária Internacional de Paraty (FLIP) (*early Aug*), Paraty. An acclaimed literary gathering of Brazilian and international writers. Literary reunions, plays, lectures, and concerts feature on the versatile program list.

Festa do Peão de Boiadeiro (*beginning on the 3rd Thu*), Barretos (São Paulo state). The world's largest 10-day rodeo event receiving almost one million visitors every year. Concerts and food fairs.

Pinga Festival (*3rd weekend*), Paraty. Local *cachaça* samplings (*see p383*), also known as *pinga*, musical shows, and food stalls offering regional delicacies.

International Festival of Culture and Gastronomy (*date varies*), Tiradentes. A 10-day international gastronomic event with workshops and exhibitions in restaurants or at public squares all over the town.

Taking the bull by the horns, Festa do Peão de Boiadeiro, Barretos

The Climate of Brazil

Brazil's climate, divided into four broad zones, varies greatly from region to region. Amazônia is hot and humid all year round, though parts experience a distinct dry season from July to October. The central band of the country is also humid, with a marked dry season, while the coastal areas enjoy pleasant tropical breezes and short seasonal downpours. High temperatures and infrequent rainfall characterize the semi-arid desert in the Northeast. In Southern Brazil, cool, wet winters contrast with humid summers. Most of Brazil can be visited at any time of the year, with the exception of the wetlands of the Pantanal during the rainy season, and the extreme south of the country during winter, when it can get very cold.

Manaus and central Amazônia are constantly humid, but experience a distinct dry season from July to October.

Boa Vista

Novo Airão

Mac

Parintins
Manaus
Santa

Tefé

Porto Velho

Rio Branco

Alta Floresta

Cuiabá

Campo Grande

Foz D Iguaçu

Po Ale

Southwest Amazônia, lying near the Andes, sees even more rain than the northern parts.

The wetlands of the Pantanal are deluged by rain for most of the year, and seasonal flooding is common from October to April.

The central highlands of Santa Catarina occasionally receive snow in winter.

The lowest temperatures are in the far south of the country, where winters are cold, windy, and rainy.

MANAUS

month	Apr	Jul	Oct	Jan
°C/F max	30/85	32/89	33/91	31/88
min	23/73	23/73	24/75	24/75
hrs	4	8	7	4
in/mm	8/203	2/51	4/102	10/254

RIO BRANCO

month	Apr	Jul	Oct	Jan
°C/F max	33/91	33/91	34/93	33/91
min	20/68	17/62	21/70	21/70
hrs	7	8	7	3
in/mm	9/229	1/25	4/102	11/279

Average monthly maximum temperature

Average monthly minimum temperature

Average daily hours of sunshine

Average monthly rainfall

PORTO ALEGRE

month	Apr	Jul	Oct	Jan
°C/F max	25/77	20/68	24/75	31/88
min	16/61	10/50	15/59	21/70
hrs	6	5	7	8
in/mm	4/102	4/102	3/76	11/279

Climate Zones

- Humid: Heavy rainfall, high humidity.
- Tropical: Distinct hot humid and cold dry seasons.
- Semi-arid: Hot weather conditions, scanty rainfall.
- Humid subtropical: Cold winter, year-round rainfall.

0 kilometers 500

0 miles 500

Trade winds from the Atlantic bring moist air to Amazônia, where there is heavy precipitation all year round.

The semi-arid interior is so hot and dry that there is often no winter here.

The coastal region in the northeast of the country receives almost year-round sunshine and seasonal downpours.

The high-altitude plateau on which Brasília sits can become quite cool, with temperatures as low as 50° F (10° C) in winter.

BELÉM

°C/F	Apr	Jul	Oct	Jan
	31/88	**32**/90	**32**/90	**31**/88
	23/73	**22**/71	**22**/71	**23**/73
hrs	4	9	8	5
in/mm	**12**/304	**6**/152	**3**/76	**12**/304

RECIFE

°C/F	Apr	Jul	Oct	Jan
	31/88	**27**/81	**29**/84	**30**/86
	23/73	**21**/70	**23**/73	**25**/77
hrs	8	6	9	7
in/mm	**8**/203	**10**/254	**1**/25	**2**/51

SALVADOR

°C/F	Apr	Jul	Oct	Jan
	31/88	**26**/79	**28**/82	**29**/84
	23/73	**21**/70	**22**/72	**23**/73
hrs	6	5	6	7
in/mm	**7**/178	**5**/127	**3**/76	**2**/51

BRASÍLIA

°C/F	Apr	Jul	Oct	Jan
	28/82	**26**/79	**29**/84	**27**/81
	17/63	**13**/55	**18**/64	**18**/64
hrs	9	10	5	6
in/mm	**3**/76	**0.4**/10	**3**/76	**5**/127

SÃO PAULO

°C/F	Apr	Jul	Oct	Jan
	25/77	**21**/70	**25**/77	**28**/82
	15/59	**10**/50	**14**/57	**18**/64
hrs	5	6	7	6
in/mm	**2**/51	**1**/25	**6**/152	**9**/229

RIO DE JANEIRO

°C/F	Apr	Jul	Oct	Jan
	27/81	**24**/75	**25**/77	**29**/84
	21/70	**17**/63	**19**/66	**23**/73
hrs	6	7	5	7
in/mm	**4**/102	**1**/25	**3**/76	**5**/127

BELO HORIZONTE

°C/F	Apr	Jul	Oct	Jan
	27/81	**24**/75	**27**/81	**27**/81
	16/61	**10**/50	**16**/60	**18**/64
hrs	6	9	5	6
in/mm	**2**/51	**0.2**/6	**3**/76	**8**/203

Belém
São Luís
Fortaleza
Teresina
Natal
João Pessoa
Recife
Palmas
Maceió
Salvador
Brasília
Goiânia
Porto Seguro
Diamantina
Belo Horizonte
Vitória
Campinas
Rio de Janeiro
São Paulo
Curítiba
Florianópolis

THE HISTORY OF BRAZIL

Very little is known about the history of Brazil before 1500, when Europeans first traveled there. Archaeological remains, which consist mainly of pottery, suggest a complex society that was in existence long before the colonialists arrived. After more than 300 years of Portuguese colonization, Brazil became a republic in 1889. Long periods of totalitarian rule finally led to the return of democracy in 1989.

For over a millennium, before the Europeans arrived in Brazil, Amazônia had a vast network of sophisticated societies with populations of up to 100,000. The abundance of fish in the Amazon river and its tributaries was almost certainly one of the main reasons for the wealth and rapid growth of cultures in Amazônia.

Up until the beginning of the 16th century, the middle Amazon region around Santarém was an important center for ceramic art and trading. It was home to thousands of semi-settled indigenous people who grew maize and had access to plentiful fish. Living on higher land, up above the flood plain, as well as in longhouses along riverbanks, they left important ceramic remains. Archaeological evidence from the earth mounds near Santarém and also on the Ilha de Marajó (*see p274*) suggests that some of the shell mounds were part of these complex fishing societies. The most widespread of the 1,000 semi-nomadic indigenous peoples that inhabited the territory at the time of the European conquest were the Tupi-Guaraní Indians. While they lived off slash-and-burn farming, the Tupinambá, another large group, cultivated crops, primarily maize.

European Discovery

The coastline was widely inhabited when Spanish explorer Vicente Yáñez Pinzón disembarked on the northeastern shore in Pernambuco, on January 26, 1500. He could not claim the newfound land for Spain, as he was officially limited by the Tordesillas meridian. The Treaty of Tordesillas, signed in 1494 between Spain and Portugal, determined that all lands discovered west of a meridian located 3 miles (5 km) west of the Cape Verde Islands would belong to Spain, and those to the east of this line could be claimed by Portugal. On April 23, 1500, Pedro Álvares Cabral landed in southern Bahia, marking the Portuguese arrival in Brazil. Portugal, which already controlled the Indian Ocean and the spice trade, bolstered its position as a mercantile power rivaled only by Spain.

13,000 BC One of the early hunting communities flourishes near Pedra Furada, in Piauí state	*Detail of rock painting, dating from 2800 BC*	**1000 BC–AD 1000** Amazonian civilization, currently referred to as Patiti or Enin by archaeologists, develops a crop irrigation system		**AD 1000** Hierarchical societies settled along the Amazon

20,000 BC	**2000 BC**	**1000 BC**	**AD 1**	**AD 1000**
9500 BC Migration across the Pacific Ocean to mid-Amazon region	**2000 BC** Shell-mound sediment in Rio de Janeiro dated to this time is evidence of human activity			**AD 1500** Pedro Álvares Cabral of Portugal lands in Bahia
	3000 BC Prehistoric cultural developments in Marajoara and Santarém have been dated to this time			**AD 500–1300** Period of major growth and expansion of Marajoara culture

◀ Detail of a meeting of Portuguese sailors and natives of Brazil, a 1592 line engraving by Theodor de Bry

The Portuguese Conquest

When the Portuguese reached Brazil in 1500, their period of maritime expansion was at its peak. In 1501, Emperor Manuel I ordered Amerigo Vespucci to explore the new territory further, leading to the settlement of Guanabara Bay (Rio de Janeiro). In 1530, an expedition led by Martim Alfonso de Sousa resulted in the first colonial towns – São Vicente and São Paulo. Preoccupied with Africa and the Far East, Portugal neglected Brazil until 1532, when João III divided the land into 15 captaincies. The early settlers mainly comprised impoverished Portuguese peasants and nobles, who were expected to explore and govern these captaincies.

Armillary sphere, a globe used by early navigators

Manuel I (1469–1521)
An illuminated Portuguese manuscript features the royal coat of arms, as well as armillary spheres symbolizing Emperor Manuel's reign as a golden age of exploration.

Priests also joined the expedition, hoping to spread Christianity in the New World.

Cabral erected a cross and held a Catholic service to signify the ownership of Brazil.

Pedro Álvares Cabral

The commander of the fleet sent to India by Emperor Manuel I, Cabral landed at Porto Seguro in southern Bahia on April 23, 1500. The Portuguese navigator baptized the bay, where they anchored for 10 days, Terra de Vera Cruz, or "Land of the True Cross." His onward voyage to India was beset with calamities, and Cabral finally drowned in a shipwreck a few months later.

Indigenous People meeting the Portuguese
Initial Portuguese fleets were received by friendly indigenous people. Gradually, these confrontations and meetings became more hostile in nature.

The Naming of Brazil

Officially, the land was named for *pau-brasil*, or brazil wood, a tree yielding a valuable red dye. However, the name "Brazil" appeared in the Irish legend of St. Brendan as Hy Brazil ("Blessed Land" in Gaelic). It became part of European maritime folklore, designating a hypothetical land located somewhere in the Atlantic. When Cabral found a new land in that general area, he may have identified it with Brendan's Brazil. The tree might have been named after the land, rather than the other way around.

Early Brazil map, showing a couple under brazil wood

Botocudos Man
Still surviving in some parts of Brazil, the Botocudos were hunter-gatherers.

Woodcut Showing Tupinambá People
Ritually practicing cannibalism, the Tupinambá were some of the first Brazilians to make contact with the Portuguese. They soon died from diseases carried by the Europeans, and from the conditions of their capture and enslavement.

João III (1502–57)
King João III ascended to the throne while the Portuguese Empire was at the height of its mercantile and colonial power. Unable to directly govern Brazil, King João III divided the land into 15 *capitanias*, or captaincies. Settlement was focused mainly on the long coastline. Only São Vicente and Pernambuco immediately prospered. In 1548, the king repossessed the captaincies and brought Brazil under his direct control.

Skilled captains accompanied Cabral in his explorations to discover new territories.

A Jesuit Admonishing Indigenous People
The influence of the Jesuits accompanied this early period of colonization. The first missionaries had arrived in 1549 and acquired great power in Brazil through their influence on the Portuguese court. A zealous missionary movement began, aimed at converting the local people.

Painting showing a group of indigenous Brazilian slaves at work in a sugar plantation

Colonization & Expansion

King João III conferred special colonial privileges to the *donatários*, the aristocrats and minor gentry, who were expected to develop and govern the *capitanias* on behalf of the Crown. The *donatários*, however, met with adverse climatic conditions and hostile indigenous people. Some of the *capitanias* were attacked by the indigenous Brazilians. In 1549, the Crown was forced to send Tomé de Sousa as the first governor, who was assigned the task of protecting the few remaining captaincies.

Sugar & the Slave Trade

Introduced to Brazil in 1532, sugar replaced the country's first major export, brazil wood, which was nearly wiped out as a result of over-exploitation. Setting up his capital in Salvador, Tomé de Sousa enlisted the support of the Jesuits. The indigenous people who did not convert to Christianity were enslaved and sent to work in sugar plantations. As a result of the high demand for sugar in Europe, sugar cane grown in

engenhos (plantations) along the northeastern coast soon became the base of the Brazilian economy. Salvador and Olinda emerged as key centers for the sugar trade.

The hunting-gathering indigenous people, however, were found to be unsuitable slaves for the plantations. They were better suited for the brazil wood trade, and were made to log and transport timber instead. From the 1550s, the landowners turned to Africa, importing millions of slaves.

Colonial Wars

While the Portuguese Crown was still struggling to consolidate its hold on Brazil, the Dutch and French forces continued to encroach on its territories. In 1555, the French had made inroads into the bay of Guanabara, establishing their own colony, French Antarctic. Portuguese forces seized the colony in 1565, and founded a new city, Rio de Janeiro.

Throughout the first half of the 17th century, French and Dutch privateers continued to plunder the coastal cities. With a powerful fleet, the Dutch offered

African slaves in a sugar mill, using an early form of grinder for refining sugar

1532 King João III divides the land into 15 *capitanias*

1550 African slaves shipped to Brazil to work sugar plantations

1572 Construction of Salvador's Catholic cathedral completed

Slave ship

1630 The Dutch occupy Olinda

1500   **1550**   **1600**   16

1532 Sugar cane is introduced to Brazil

1549 Salvador founded by Tomé de Sousa

1554 Jesuits found São Paulo

1565 French Antarctic destroyed and Rio de Janeiro founded

1624 The Dutch capture Salvador, laying the city to siege for the next nine months

An engraving depicting naval combat between French and Portuguese ships off the coast of Brazil

a greater challenge. In 1624, the Dutch captured Salvador and laid siege to the city, until the combined fleet of the Portuguese and Spanish expelled them. The Dutch occupied Olinda in 1630 and, by 1641, controlled a vast stretch of coastline, ending Portugal's monopoly of the sugar trade. During 1648 and 1649, two battles were fought at Guararapes, in Pernambuco, where the Dutch were routed and their territory reduced to an enclave around Recife. Following several years of open warfare, the Dutch formally withdrew in 1661.

The Discovery of Gold

The decline of the sugar industry coincided with the discovery of gold. In 1695, gold was first discovered in Sabara, Minas Gerais, by the *bandeirantes* (paramilitary adventurers), who faced grueling conditions as they pressed inland toward the Andean foothills. Gold was also found in Cuiabá, Mato Grosso, in 1719. Both events led to

further development and expansion of the country's interior. Traffic to São Paulo and Rio de Janeiro rapidly increased and new communities drew people away from the Northeast coast. The focus of power in Brazil moved from the Northeast to the Southeast, and Rio de Janeiro was made the new capital in 1763.

Struggle for Independence

The gold rush lasted not more than 70 years. The decline of gold in the 18th century led to high taxes, as Brazil was forced to meet the quota set by the Crown for the minimum annual gold production. This, coupled with the Brazilian resentment at their exclusion from administration and the Portuguese dominance of foreign trade, culminated in the 1789 Inconfidência Mineira rebellion. Led by Tiradentes *(see pp130–31)*, who was eventually executed, the uprising was aimed at Brazilian independence from Portuguese rule.

1661 The Dutch formally withdraw from Portuguese territories

1719 Gold discovered in Cuiabá, Mato Grosso

1763 Rio de Janeiro made the new capital city of Brazil

1789 Inconfidência Mineira uprising is quelled, and the leader, Tiradentes, is hanged

1700

1750

1800

1695 Gold discovered in Sabará, Minas Gerais

Portrait of Tiradentes

Dom Pedro proclaiming "Independéncia ou Morte!" at the Rio Ipiranga, on September 7, 1822

The First Emperor of Brazil

The advance of French Emperor Napoleon, in 1808, forced King Dom João VI, who was ruling from Lisbon, to relocate his government to Brazil. In 1821, the royal family were forced to return to deal with rebels back home. Dom João's son, the Prince Regent, who had stayed back in Brazil, proclaimed independence from Portugal on September 7, 1822. In a famous scene at the Rio Ipiranga, he tore the Portuguese insignia from his uniform, drew his sword, and declared, "Independência ou Morte!" (Independence or Death). Three months later, he crowned himself Emperor Dom Pedro I.

Although the assumption of independence had been easy, Dom Pedro soon realized that organizing the new government was riddled with challenges. His own autocratic nature proved to be the biggest hurdle in winning the confidence of his subjects. The new consitution he proposed, based on his own unlimited power, was strongly opposed by the assembly. When Dom Pedro dismissed his assembly in 1831, demonstrators demanded its reinstatement.

Provincial Unrest

Dom Pedro I was forced to abdicate in favor of his five-year-old son, Dom Pedro II. From 1831 to 1840, three appointed regents ruled the country in the young Emperor's name, during a period of turmoil in which local factions struggled to gain control of their provinces and to keep the masses in line. The regency in Rio de Janeiro gave considerable power to the provinces in 1834, when Brazil became a federation of locally autonomous regional powers, with loose allegiance to the center. The rebellions, riots, and popular movements that marked these years did not spring from economic misery, but from attempts to share in the prosperity stemming from the North Atlantic demand for Brazil's exports.

The Coffee Industry

Coffee, which was introduced to Brazil in the early 1800s, filled the void left by the collapse of the sugar industry and the waning gold rush. An army officer,

A formal portrait of Brazil's Emperor Dom Pedro II (1825–91), depicting him in full regalia

Dom Pedro I

1808 Napoleon's advance forces Dom João to flee Portugal, and relocate to Brazil

1825 Britain and Portugal sign a treaty recognizing Brazilian independence

1837–38 The Sabinada Rebellion in Salvador

1842 Rebellions in Minas Gerais and São Paulo

1810   **1820**   **1830**   **1840**

1822 The Prince Regent proclaims independence from Portugal, crowning himself Emperor Dom Pedro I

1831 Pedro dismisses the Constituent Assembly after a draft constitution is proposed

1834 Brazil becomes a federation of autonomous regional powers

1838–41 The Balaiada Rebellion in Maranhão

Francisco de Mello, was believed to have brought the first coffee beans into Brazil, from his journey to French Guiana. The coffee industry began to flourish, mainly in Minas Gerais and São Paulo. Expanding coffee production in the 1850s and 1860s attracted British investment in railroads to speed transport of the beans to the coast. The coastal Santos–São Paulo railroad (1868) was followed by a series of railroads that linked the northeastern coast to the interior.

The Surrender of Uruguaiana, painted during the war

The War of the Triple Alliance

From 1864 to 1870, Paraguay and the allied countries of Argentina, Brazil, and Uruguay fought one of the bloodiest conflicts on the American continent. Also known as the Paraguayan War, it has been widely attributed to the expansionist ambitions of Paraguayan dictator Francisco Solano Lopez, and the Brazilian and Argentinian meddling in internal Uruguayan politics. The outcome of the war was the devastating defeat of Paraguay by the Triple Alliance, but at the cost of over 100,000 casualties.

Slavery Abolished

As coffee exports rose steadily, so did the numbers of imported slaves. In Rio de Janeiro alone, they soared from around 26,000 in 1825 to 44,000 in 1828. While slave owners argued that slavery was not demoralizing, others were in favor of replacing slavery with free European immigrant labor. Eventually, a contract system that was little better than slavery was established by the parliament. New laws and decrees, unacceptable to slave owners, were simply not enforced, such as the 1829 order forbidding slave ships to sail for Africa. The failure to enforce these orders caused regional slave rebellions throughout the 19th century. In 1850, British and domestic pressure finally forced the Brazilian

An 1857 portrayal of black slaves on a plantation

government to outlaw the African slave trade. Over the next five years, even clandestine landings stopped, ending the transatlantic trade. In 1871, the cabinet in Rio Branco approved a law freeing newborn slaves and requiring masters to care for them until they were eight years old. Between 1875 and 1887, 156,000 immigrants arrived in São Paulo to work as free laborers and fill the void created by the gradual decline in the slave population. By the 1880s, the slave population was reduced to half its size. In 1888, the Golden Law was passed, finally abolishing slavery.

Lady being served and fanned by a black slave

1850 British and domestic pressure force the Brazilian government to outlaw slave trade

1875–87 Approximately 156,000 immigrants arrive in São Paulo

1888 The Golden Law passed, ending slavery in Brazil

1850 — **1860** — **1870** — **1880**

1864–70 The War of the Triple Alliance

1868 Completion of the Santos–São Paulo railroad

1871 The Rio Branco cabinet enacts a law, ensuring the well-being of children born to slaves

1884 Slaves over 60 years old emancipated

The First Republic

In 1889, the monarchy was overthrown by a military coup, which was led by Marechal Deodoro da Fonseca and supported by Brazil's coffee barons. Dom Pedro II was exiled in Paris, where he died two years later. A republic was born, with Deodoro as the first president. The Constituent Assembly that drew up the 1891 constitution was a confrontation between the São Paulo coffee oligarchy that sought to limit executive power and the radical authoritarians who wanted to expand presidential authority. The growing opposition culminated in a navy revolt, forcing Deodoro to step down only a few months later. It was recognized that the central government could exercise control

The funeral of King Dom Pedro II in Paris, reported in a French journal

only through the local oligarchies, or *patrias*. The constitutional system was offset by the *coronelismo*, or the real system of unwritten agreements among these local bosses, by which local oligarchies chose the state governors, who in turn selected the president.

The informal distribution of power emerged as the result of armed struggles and bargaining. In order to check the nationalizing tendencies of the army, the oligarchic republic strengthened the navy and police, turning them into small armies in the larger states.

Scooping coffee beans for shipment after drying, on a São Paulo plantation

"Café Com Leite" Republic

The early years of the republic were called *café com leite* (coffee and milk) by its opponents. Brazilian politics was dominated by an oligarchy that comprised São Paulo coffee barons and Minas Gerais cattle ranchers. These groups controlled electoral politics, and the presidency alternated between the two wealthy states of coffee and milk.

The Struggle For Modernization

At the turn of the 19th century, Brazil lacked an integrated economy. Domestic consumption was largely neglected, and the middle class was not yet active in political life. The economy was organized around large agricultural estates, or *latifundia*. Brazil had lost its sugar market to Caribbean producers, while the rubber boom in Amazônia was beginning to lose its primacy to more efficient Southeast Asian plantations. The outbreak of World War I was the turning point for the dynamic urban sectors. Industrial production doubled, and agricultural diversity received an impetus, as the growing demand by the Allies for staple products sparked a new boom for goods other than sugar and coffee. The old order

1889 Military officers rebel against Dom Pedro II, establishing a republic

1897 Belo Horizonte founded in Minas Gerais, as Brazil's first modern planned city

Train station, Belo Horizonte

1916 A civil statute formally enshrines hierarchical and patriarchal view of family and sexual relations

1890   **1900**   **1910**   **1920**

1891 The first president of Brazil, Deodoro Fonseca, ousted by a navy revolt

1896 Teatro Amazonas (*see pp286–7*) opens in Manaus

1902 Euclides da Cunha writes *Os Sertões* (see p210)

1908 The first Japanese immigrants arrive in Santarém

1915 Southeast Asian rubber elbows out Brazil from the market gave way to the political aspirations of the new urban groups – government, white-collar workers, professionals, bankers, merchants, and industrialists. Increasing support for industrial protectionism marked Brazilian politics in the 1920s. Disparate social reform movements cropped up during this period. Between 1922 and 1926, junior military officers staged a revolt against the landed elite, demanding socio-economic modernization.

Brazilian army confronts rebels during the 1930 coup

The New State

A bloodless coup by the military installed Getúlio Vargas as provisional president in 1930. Between the World Wars, he built a corporatist, centralized state along fascist lines, although he did advocate some liberal reforms. The collapse of the old order had created a vacuum, which was filled by the fascist Integralistas and communists. The former had once enjoyed Vargas's support, but later turned against him when they realized that creating a strictly fascist state was not on his agenda. They were bidding to seize power in the 1938 election, which the Constitution barred Vargas from contesting. Months before the election, Vargas declared a state of emergency to avert an alleged communist plot. He dissolved the Constitution and established the Estado Novo (New State), which used repressive political tactics and rejected free-market liberal capitalism. Vargas's promise of a "postwar era of liberty" could not save the fall of the Estado Novo in 1945, when he was ousted by General Eurico Dutra. His return to the presidency in 1951 was marred by inflation, corruption, and a political scandal involving an attack on a journalist by the president's bodyguard. Faced with the ultimatum to resign, Vargas ended his life in 1954 by shooting himself.

Citizens of Rio de Janeiro welcoming rebel troops upon the success of the 1930 coup

Poster, World Cup, 1950

1930	1940	1950
1932 Young army officers lead their units against the old order in Minas Gerais and Rio	**1938** Vargas establishes the Estado Novo, or the "New State"	**1950** World Cup soccer held in Brazil **1954** Vargas commits suicide with a bullet to the heart
1930 A military coup installs Getúlio Vargas as provisional president	**1937** Vargas assumes dictatorial powers under a new constitution	**1945** The Estado Novo collapses, Eurico Dutra comes to power **1950** Vargas re-elected president

The Vargas Era (1930–54)

Spanning the creation of Brazil as a modern nation-state, the long political career of Getúlio Vargas exemplifies the various contradictions at the heart of the Brazilian national character. His rise to power in 1930 marked the resurgence of a generation of young, dynamic administrators, but also marked the beginning of an authoritarian rule. During his first term, he assumed absolute power to overthrow the old order, and established the Estado Novo. Forced to step down after World War II, he remained popular and was re-elected in 1950.

Getúlio Dornelles Vargas
A pro-industry nationalist and virulent anti-communist, Vargas possessed an authoritarian streak. The hero of the newly emerged urban working class, he favored capitalism and liberal reforms to some extent.

Crowd Cheering Vargas's Victory
A bloodless coup in 1930 ended the reign of President Washington Luis, and brought Vargas into power.

Nationalized Fascism

Exploiting communist paranoia, Vargas assumed dictatorship in 1937, abolishing opposition parties and imposing censorship. He tolerated anti-Semitism, initially encouraging the fascist Integralistas (see p59) until they decided to contest the elections against him in 1938.

Vargas, diminutive in stature, emulated Hitler and Mussolini in some ways.

Ties with Mussolini
In January 1931, 11 Italian aircraft, one of them piloted by Mussolini's son, were received in Brazil with great applause.

Integralistas in Rio de Janeiro, 1938
A group of Integralistas led a short-lived revolt against the corrupt Vargas regime. They attacked the Palácio Guanabara, and made a bid for Vargas's life, but government forces promptly suppressed the uprising.

**Carmen Miranda
(1909–55)**
During the Vargas era, the
Portuguese-Brazilian singer-
actress charmed post-World
War USA and the world.

1950 World Cup
Brazil was confident of winning the World Cup in the first tournament
to be held after World War II. The final was played on home ground
at Rio's Estádio Maracanã. However, in a surprise victory, Uruguay
defeated Brazil 2–1. With slighted pride, the humiliated nation
plunged into mourning.

New Ministry of Education
Vargas was responsible for the erection of a
sky-scraping new Ministry of Education, whose
cutting-edge design was emphasized by its
incongruous location behind a colonial church
in Rio de Janeiro.

Toward the Future
Vargas recognized that Brazil's strength lay in its
vast natural resources. He created Petrobras,
the state oil company, and invested in road and
air transport.

Daily Life
Under Vargas's rule, modern tramways were
constructed to carry white-collar employees
to their various offices in the capital city of
Rio de Janeiro.

President Juscelino Kubitschek on the cover of *Time* magazine dated January 13, 1970

Into Modernity

The reign of Juscelino Kubitschek, Vargas's successor, lasted from 1956 to 1961, ushering Brazil into modernity. Campaigning on a platform of "Fifty years of progress in five," Kubitschek tried to achieve this progress with generous incentives for foreign investors, such as low taxes, privileges for the importation of machinery, and donations of land. All this gave impetus to the economic growth rate, which paved the way for the economic boom in the next decade. The most notable

Trans-Amazon Highway construction near Altamira Brazil, July 1971

manifestation of Kubitschek's nationalistic aspirations was the creation of Brasília (*see pp298–9*) as the new capital of Brazil.

Despite instilling national confidence, Kubitschek's era was also beset with massive inflation. Also, the influx of foreign capital rapidly captured domestic industry, and the urban bourgeoisie found state control threatening rather than protective. Mild structural reforms took place under President João Goulart (1961–64), but the increasing political infighting between left and right culminated in the 1964 military junta.

The Era of Military Rule

A period of right-wing military dictatorship followed. In a bid to appease the hard-liners, the new president, Marshal Humberto Castelo Branco, recessed and purged Congress, and decreed the expansion of the president's powers at the expense of the legislature and the judiciary. His gamble curbed the populist left, but gave his successor, Artur da Costa e Silva (1967–69), a basis for authoritarian rule. Despite their victory, the hard-liners were still unable to institutionalize their agenda politically. They did not give up their liberal constitutionalism as they feared damage to their alliance with the US, the citadel of anti-communism. In 1969, the democratic mask fell off when General Médici came to power and

1960 Brasília inaugurated as the new capital of Brazil

1970 Brazil wins the soccer World Cup in Mexico

1977 *Dona Flor and Her Two Husbands* brings international fame to Brazilian cinema

1979 General Figueiredo is sworn in as president

1985 Civilian Tancredo Neves is elected to presidency

| 1960 | 1965 | 1970 | 1975 | 1980 | 1985 |

1961 Janio Quadros elected president, replaced by João Goulart in the same year

Jules Rimet trophy

1974 Ernesto Geisel's rule begins, marking a slow return to democracy

1980 Film *Bye Bye Brasil* brings more recognition to Brazilian cinema

1984 Benedita da Silva becomes the first black woman in Congress continued to rule an authoritarian regime without popular support. An extremely oppressive government apparatus hounded political opponents. Yet the Médici administration cloaked itself in the green and gold flag when Brazil won the Jules Rimet trophy for its third consecutive victory in the soccer World

Former President Luiz Inácio Lula da Silva, victorious after his re-election

Cup in 1970. From 1968 to 1974, during the darkest days of dictatorship, the military-civil alliance took shape as the economy boomed, reaching annual GDP growth rates of 12 percent. During this period, the Trans-Amazon Highway was built, and the Rio Paraná was dammed.

Geisel's accession in 1974 signaled a move toward democratic rule. He attempted to restrain the growing strength of the opposition parties by creating an electoral college that would approve his selected replacement. He allowed the return of exiles, restored *habeas corpus*, and installed General João Figueiredo as his successor in 1979. A 1981 bombing incident at Rio City's RioCentro confirmed direct military involvement in terrorism. The Figueiredo regime's inaction in punishing the guilty strengthened the public's resolve to end military rule, as Brazil faced inflation and mounting foreign debt.

The Return to Democracy

In 1985, civilian Tancredo Neves was voted into office as president. However, he died before taking office. Brazil completed its transition to a popularly elected govern-ment in 1989, when Fernando Collor de Mello won 53 percent of the vote. The democratization of the government was visible in the impeachment of the corrupt de Mello regime, forcing him to resign in 1992. The 1994 elections brought to power Fernando Henrique Cardoso, who served two terms but failed to match the growth of the country's wealth and power with better living conditions. Socio-economic contradictions helped usher in Lula da Silva in 2002 as Brazil's first elected left-wing president. His Workers' Party (Partido dos Trabalhadores – PT) government declined to nationalize private companies or collectivize land. This restored investor confidence in the country that underwrote strong economic growth and employment expansion. Despite an unfulfilled promise of economic and social revolution, Lula was re-elected to power in October 2006. Dilma Rousseff, also of the PT, was elected president in 2011 at the end of Lula's two terms in office, and re-elected in 2015.

A 1997 demonstration by landless farm workers, demanding jobs, justice, and land reform

Brazilian President Fernando Collor de Mello

1990	1995	2000	2005	2010	2015	2020
1994 Brazil defeats Italy to win the World Cup title	**1995** Fernando Cardoso takes office as president **2000** UNESCO declares the Atlantic rainforest a World Heritage Site	**2001** Congress approves a civil code, giving equal rights to men and women **2002** Brazil wins its fifth World Cup title defeating Germany	**2006** Lula da Silva is re-elected in a landslide victory, returning as Brazil's president	**2008** Brazil appointed as host country for the 2014 World Cup **2009** Rio announced as host city for the 2016 Olympics **2011** Dilma Rousseff elected first female president	**2016** Rio de Janeiro due to host the 2016 Olympics **2015** Dilma Rousseff begins second term as president **2014** Brazil hosted the 2014 FIFA World Cup	

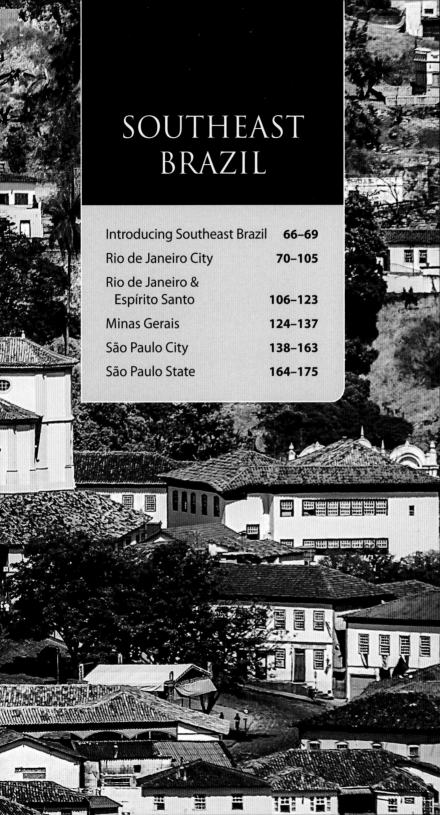

SOUTHEAST
BRAZIL

Introducing Southeast Brazil

The four states of Rio de Janeiro, Espírito Santo, Minas Gerais, and São Paulo constitute Brazil's economic heartland. The giant metropolises – Rio de Janeiro, Belo Horizonte, and São Paulo – burst with energetic cultural life. Rio de Janeiro holds the greatest attractions, with its Carnaval and breathtaking mountains and beaches. Beyond the urban hubs, nature and rural life exist undisturbed. Wild islands lie a short boat ride away. Inland, in the folds of the rugged Minas hills, are colonial towns whose cobbled streets, colorful Portuguese town houses, and ornate Baroque churches remain little changed since colonial times.

BRAZIL

SOUTHEAST
BRAZIL

Parque Nacional Serra da Canastra *(see p137)*, one of the protected areas dotting the region, preserves pristine rainforest and *cerrado*, as well as rich fauna.

São Paulo City *(see pp138–63)*, the capital of São Paulo state, is relentlessly urban and frenetic, but has Brazil's best restaurants, shops, and nightlife.

Uberlândia

Uberaba

São José
de Rio Preto

Ribeirão
Preto

SÃO PAULO STATE
(See pp164–75)

Presidente
Prudente

Campinas

Jacareí

SÃO PAULO CITY
(See pp138–63)

São Paulo's coast *(see pp168–75)*, stretching across 250 miles (400 km), features beaches and islands that serve as the weekend playground for the city.

◄ The pretty colonial city of Diamantina, Minas Gerais

0 km 100
0 miles 100

Montes Claros

Teófilo Otoni

MINAS GERAIS
(See pp124–37)

Ipatinga

Belo Horizonte

Congonhas

Juiz de Fora

Petrópolis

RIO DE JANEIRO CITY
(See pp70–105)

São Sebastião

RIO DE JANEIRO & ESPÍRITO SANTO
(See pp106–23)

Linhares

Vitória

Campos dos Goitacazes

Macaé

Diamantina *(see p128)*, once a diamond-mining town, set in a scenic landscape, is reputedly the finest of colonial towns in Minas Gerais. It was designated a UNESCO World Heritage Site in 1999.

Petrópolis *(see pp116–19)*, once the summer retreat of the Brazilian royal family, is still the home of Dom Pedro II's heir. The lovely mountain setting gives it a distinct character.

Rio de Janeiro
(see pp70–105) is a city of neighborhoods, each with its own unique character and most endowed with a great view. The panorama of Sugar Loaf and Botafogo from Mirante Dona Marta is simply unparalleled.

Carnaval in Rio

One of the world's most spectacular festivals, Carnaval is celebrated all over Brazil, but the celebrations in Rio are justly famous. They remain unmatched for their sheer scale and splendor. Falling in February or early March, Carnaval is linked to the calendar of the Catholic Church. Traditionally, Carnaval is the last celebration of excess and joy before the austerity and fasting of the Lenten period. Its key elements include street celebrations, carnival balls, and the world-famous parade of top *samba* schools, which traditionally takes place at the Sambódromo in downtown Rio.

Carnaval Dates

2016 Feb 5–10
2017 Feb 24–Mar 1
2018 Feb 9–14
2019 Mar 1–6
2020 Feb 21–26
2021 Feb 12–17
2022 Feb 25–Mar 2
2023 Feb 17–22

Samba Schools are large social clubs found in Rio's poorer communities and neighborhoods, often linked to the local *favelas*. Mangueira, one of the most prominent schools, was founded in 1928, and Portela, which began in 1923, has won the most Carnaval titles. Many top schools date from the 1940s and 1950s, while Grande Rio formed as late as 1988.

Giant Puppets are put together to decorate the floats and fascinating costumes are created for the participants. Craftspeople work throughout the year, as Carnaval is a year-round industry. Much of the work can now be seen at close quarters in the Cidade de Samba in downtown Rio.

Porta bandeira is the school's standard bearer, dressed in lavish 18th-century formal wear, regardless of the school's theme.

Street Carnivals take place wherever there is a band that can strike up a *samba* and move around the streets. Bands attract a large following who dance and sing through the neighborhoods.

Party-loving **Cariocas** consider Carnaval more important than any other event in the calendar, and that includes both Christmas and New Year. It is a week-long holiday for partying around the clock and a sign that summer is finally coming to a close.

Tips for Visitors

Transport: Take the metro. Use Central Station if your ticket is for an uneven-numbered sector and Praça Onze for an even one.

Winner's Parade: Those who missed the event can see part of the parade by winning schools on the Saturday after Carnaval.

Tickets: Book your tickets in advance (Maracanã stadium box office, (21) 2568 9962).

A different theme is chosen by every school, and conceptualized by the *carnavalesco* (director). The history of Espírito Santo, represented by the state colors, pink, blue, and white, was the theme of the Caprichosos de Pilares school in 2006. This float shows *antropofagismo*, the concept of "cultural cannibalism," putting foreign art, music, and literature in a Brazilian context.

The central display is the focal point of the float, and is often the most elaborately designed aspect, with the most creative costumes on display.

Passistas, or participants, numbering a minimum of 2,500, join each float with at least 200 in the *bateria* (percussion section).

The Parade

Each of the 12 main samba schools will have around 4,000 participants who must cover the Passarela do Samba in not less than 65 minutes and not more than 80 minutes. In that time, they will put on a performance every bit as complex and visually exciting as any musical showing on Broadway or in London's West End. Six schools parade each night.

Mestre sala is the school's dance master who, along with the *porta bandeira*, performs a complex series of dance steps as they move along the route.

Sambódromo, or Passarela do Samba, was inaugurated in 1984. Designed by Oscar Niemeyer, it can accommodate over 60,000 spectators at any one time. The end square is used for Carnaval, outdoor concerts, and festivals.

RIO DE JANEIRO CITY

Rio de Janeiro is quite simply one of the world's most beautiful and vibrant cities, and is the number-one destination for visitors coming to Brazil. Its unique setting, with dramatic mountains and beaches at its very center, sets it apart from the other great cities of the world. In addition, Rio's flamboyant Carnaval, *samba*, and *bossa nova* make for a heady mix that is impossible to ignore.

Rio de Janeiro was first discovered by European explorers on January 1, 1502. They mistook the huge Guanabara Bay for the mouth of a river (*rio*) and called the site "River of January," thus giving the city its name. Evidence of the city's colonial past can still be seen in downtown Rio, with buildings and artifacts dating from the 16th to the 19th centuries, including the imposing Paço Imperial and Palácio Tiradentes. In 1763, the city became the capital of Brazil's Vice-Royalty and in 1808, the Portuguese royal family and court abandoned Lisbon for Rio, making it the capital of both Brazil and the Portuguese Empire. It remained home to the Brazilian monarchy until 1889 and the capital of the Brazilian Republic until 1960, when the title was awarded to the newly built Bauhaus-style Brasília.

Today, Rio is an international metropolis and a spectacular tropical resort. It has several iconic sights, including the enormous statue of Christ that looms protectively over the city from Corcovado mountain, the easily recognizable Sugar Loaf Mountain at one end of Urca Bay, and the famous stadium, Estádio Maracanã, which opened for the 1950 World Cup and has hosted crowds of up to 200,000 people.

Rio's residents, affectionately called "Cariocas," are a laid-back, friendly people who love to go out. Visitors will be spoiled for choice in this hedonistic city, and can visit Lapa for its extravagant clubs, Gávea for its bars, and Ipanema and Leblon for their boutiques and restaurants. Rio's beaches provide ample opportunity for all manner of water sports and are a great meeting place for the city's residents, both rich and poor.

The colorful Copacabana beach, lined with palm trees

◄ Sunset over Botofogo Bay and the Sugar Loaf Mountain, Rio de Janeiro

Exploring Rio de Janeiro City

Rio de Janeiro covers a vast area of 473 sq miles (1,225 sq km) and is home to 6 million people, making it Brazil's second-largest and second most populous city after São Paulo. It has two main zones – Zona Norte (North Zone), encompassing miles of poor housing, known as *favelas*; and Zona Sul (South Zone), with plush neighborhoods and famous beaches such as Ipanema and Copacabana. Centro is Rio's main business district, and has a concentration of historic buildings, museums, and churches.

Sights at a Glance

Historic Buildings, Streets, Neighborhoods & Townships

1. *Praça XV & Centro pp74–5*
3. Docks & Avenida Rio Branco
5. Confeitaria Colombo
6. Theatro Municipal & Cinelândia
8. Santa Teresa
9. Lapa
27. *Morro do Corcovado & Cristo Redentor pp86–7*
29. Quinta da Boa Vista
30. Sambódromo & Cidade do Samba
31. Centro Cultural do Banco do Brasil
32. *Barra pp90–91*
35. *Niterói*

14. Museu da República
15. Museu Carmen Miranda
16. Oi Futuro Ipanema
24. Museu do Índio
25. Museu Villa-Lobos
26. Museu Casa de Rui Barbosa

National Parks

33. Parque Nacional da Tijuca

Soccer Clubs & Stadiums

22. Jóquei Clube Brasileiro
28. Estádio do Maracanã

Areas of Natural Beauty

17. *Sugar Loaf Mountain pp80–81*

Churches & Monasteries

2. Mosteiro de São Bento
4. Igreja de São Francisco da Penitência
7. Catedral Metropolitana
13. Igreja Nossa Senhora da Glória do Outeiro

Parks & Gardens

23. Jardim Botânico

Beaches & Lagoons

18. *Copacabana p82*
19. *Ipanema p83*
20. *Leblon p83*
21. Lagoa Rodrigo de Freitas
34. Baía de Guanabara

Museums

10. Museu Nacional de Belas Artes
11. Museu Histórico Nacional
12. Museu de Arte Moderna

0 meters 1000
0 yards 1000

For hotels and restaurants in this region see pp370–71 and pp386–8

DRIGUES ALVES
MORRO DA SAÚDE
AV VENEZUELA
Ilha das Cobras
Ilha Fiscal
Niterói
Uruguaiana
MO. DA CONCEIÇÃO
Central
Presidente Vargas
CENTRO
PRAÇA XV DE NOVEMBRE
AV RIO BRANCO
Carioca
AV GENERAL JUSTO
AVENIDA MEM DE SÁ
Cinelândia
Aeroporto Santos Dumont
LAPA
REI CANECA
RUA RIACHUELO
RIO MPRIDO
SANTA TERESA
RUA DO CATETE
Glória
CATETE
Catete
PARQUE GUINLE
PARQUE DO FLAMENGO
Largo do Machado
FLAMENGO
Flamengo
URCA
Praia de Urca
Praia de Fora
Enseada de Botafogo
RUA SÃO CLEMENTE
Botafogo
BOTAFOGO
MORRO DA URCA
PÃO DE AÇÚCAR
Praia Vermelha
MORRO DA BABILÔNIA
LEME
Ponta do Leme
Siqueira Campos
Copacabana
MORRO DO LEME
Praia do Leme
OPACABANA
Cantagalo
Praia do Copacabana
AVENIDA ATLÂNTICA
General Osório
PARQUE GAROTA DE IPANEMA
Praia do Diablo

VISITORS' CHECKLIST

Practical Information
6,000,000. Riotur Centro, Praça Pio X 119, Centro, (21) 2271 7000. Carnaval (Feb/Mar), Reveillon at Copacabana (Dec 31). **rio.rj.gov.br**

Transport
9 miles (15 km) N of center, then taxi. a short distance (1 km) E of Cinelândia metro station.

Greater Rio de Janeiro City

Aeroporto Internacional do Rio de Janeiro
São Gonçalo
RIO DE JANEIRO
ATLANTIC OCEAN

0 km 5
0 miles 3

Key
- Area of the main map
- Highway
- Main road
- Other road
- Railroad

Getting to & Around Rio

Rio is well connected and its international airport has daily flights to most major South and North American and European cities, as well as to several cities in Brazil. The city is also linked by Brazil's long-distance bus network, while a growing number of people also arrive here by cruise ship. Getting around Rio is fairly simple. Taxis are plentiful and cheap, and are the best option for visitors. The city's extensive bus network can sometimes be daunting, as it isn't always easy to decide which bus to take. Although limited, the metro is efficient and is the most convenient mode of traveling from Copacabana to the city center. From 2016, there will be a small light-rail network linking the port area to Centro. It is possible to rent a car, but first-time visitors may find driving here a little difficult.

For keys to symbols see back flap

❶ Street-by-Street: Praça XV de Novembro & Centro

Originally called the Largo do Paço, Praça XV de Novembro is the historic heart of Rio, even if it was only so named after the declaration of the republic on November 15, 1889. The Praça witnessed the arrival of Dom João VI of Portugal in 1808 as he fled with his court from Napoleon. The House of the Viceroy became the Paço Imperial, and for a time the square was the center of Brazil's political and commercial power. Today, Praça XV and the surrounding area is packed with historic buildings and streets. The square was given a new lease of life in the late 1980s with the restoration of the palace, which has acted as a catalyst in bringing culture and life back to the city center.

Statue of General Osório
General Manuel Luís Osório defended the Empire in the War of the Triple Alliance between 1864 and 1870 *(see p57)*.

Nossa Senhora do Monte do Carmo once served as the royal chapel.

★ Arco do Telles
Today a pedestrian exit, Arco de Telles dates from 1757 and is all that remains of the old Senate House that was destroyed by a fire in 1790. It is Rio's only surviving colonial arch.

AVENIDA RIO BRANCO

PRAÇA XV DE NOVEMBRO

Statue of General Osório

★ Paço Imperial
The Paço Imperial has been the backdrop for many key events in Brazilian history, including the signing of the Lei Aurea in 1888, abolishing slavery in Brazil.

0 meters	25
0 yards	25

Chafariz da Piramide was built in 1789 to distribute fresh water to the city and to visiting ships.

Barcas Metro Station

Key

— Suggested route

Locator Map
See Street Finder, map 5

AV PRES VARGAS

RUA DO ROSARIO

RUA I DE MARÇO

DO OUVIDOR

DO MERCADO

AV PRES KUBITSCHEK

★ **Nossa Senhora da
Candelária**
One of Rio's earliest
churches was built on this
site in 1630. The current
impressive structure dates
from 1775.

Espaço Cultural da Marinha,
the Navy's cultural center, was
inaugurated in 1996. Located in
the old docks, the center is the
starting point for tours of Baía
de Guanabara.

Casa França-Brasil (Franco-
Brazil Center) was opened in
1990. It is located in an 1820
customs house.

Travessa do Comércio
This photogenic pedestrian
street beyond Arco do Telles is
lined with bars and restaurants.
Carmen Miranda lived at No. 13 as a
small girl. The street is lively at lunch
and in the evening when the bars fill up.

Detail of the gilded Baroque interior of Mosteiro de São Bento

Two museums at the top of Avenida Rio Branco are worth visiting. The **Museu de Arte do Rio** has exhibitions that change regularly to show both classic and contemporary art. The **Museu do Amanhã** (Museum of Tomorrow) is a science museum that also encourages visitors to consider the Earth of the future.

❷ Mosteiro de São Bento

Rua Dom Gerardo 68 (entrance by elevator at No. 40), Centro. **Map** 5 D2. **Tel** (21) 2206 8100. Ⓜ Uruguaiana. **Open** 7am–6pm daily. 🅿️ ♿ 🕆 7:30am Mon–Sat, 10am & 6pm Sun. 🅦 osb.org.br

Benedictine monks from Bahia founded the São Bento Monastery in 1590 and much of the historic building, located on the hills of São Bento, has been structurally untouched since it was built between 1617 and 1641. The exterior of the main building reflects the simplicity of the time of its construction and gives no hint of the opulence of the gilded Baroque interior.

A number of the works on display were carved by one of the monks, Frei Domingos da Conceição (1643–1718). They include the main altar of the monastery's church. The painting displayed on it, which was created around 1676, is dedicated to Nossa Senhora de Montserrat (Black Virgin).

São Bento is still very much a working monastery. The Benedictine monks are protective of the monastery and their work and have tried hard to keep the church from becoming simply a tourist attraction. Many areas, such as the beautiful cloisters, remain out-of-bounds except on special occasions. Mass for the public is said daily, with a full Gregorian chant at 10am on Sundays. Visitors should remember to dress appropriately if they wish to view the interior of the monastery.

❸ Docks & Avenida Rio Branco

Praça Mauá, Centro. **Map** 5 D2. Ⓜ Carioca, Uruguaiana. ♿ Museu de Arte do Rio: **Tel** (21) 3031 2741. **Open** Tue–Sun. 🅿️ ♿ 🅦 museudeartedorio.org.br Museu do Amanhã: **Open** Tue–Sun. 🅿️ ♿ 🅦 museudoamanha.org.br

Though not as thriving as they once were, Rio's docks remain one of the most important in South America. The terminal in the old Touring Club do Brasil in Praça Mauá is the first port of call for visitors who arrive in Rio by ship. The docks are situated at the top end of Avenida Rio Branco, one of Brazil's important business streets. The street dates from 1904, when 590 buildings were demolished to make way for a modern central avenue, the spine of Rio's financial district. A handful of early 20th-century buildings survive, among them the glorious Theatro Municipal.

Lavish interior of the historic Confeitaria Colombo

❹ Igreja de São Francisco da Penitência

Largo de Carioca 5, Centro. **Map** 5 D4. Ⓜ Carioca. **Tel** (21) 2262 0197. **Open** 9am–noon, 1–4pm Tue–Fri. 🅿️ 🍴

Restored to its former glory, the church of São Francisco da Penitência is considered one of the richest and most beautiful examples of Baroque art in Brazil. Built between 1657 and 1772, the church exhibits various works of the Portuguese artist Francisco Xavier de Brito. His art heavily influenced the Brazilian artist Aleijadinho (see p135), whose own work spectacularly adorns many of the Baroque churches of Minas Gerais. One of the church's highlights is the 1738 painting of the glorification of St. Francis by Caetano da Costa Coelho, the first Brazilian painting to be done in perspective.

The neighboring Convento de Santo Antônio, dating back to 1615, is one of Rio's oldest structures. Its Baroque interiors contain priceless colonial art and *azulejos* (Portuguese tiles).

❺ Confeitaria Colombo

Rua Goçalves Dias 32, Centro. **Map** 5 D3. **Tel** (21) 2505 1500. Ⓜ Carioca. **Open** 9am–8pm Mon–Fri, 9am–5pm Sat. ♿ limited. 🅦 confeitariacolombo.com.br

The Colombo Tearoom dates from 1894 and remains a wonderful mix of Art Nouveau and *belle époque*. Located in what was then the very heart of Rio, it was a meeting point for intellectuals, artists, and politicians. Regulars included politician Ruy Barbosa, President

Getúlio Vargas, and composer Heitor Villa-Lobos.

The mirrors were shipped in from Belgium and the marble from Italy, while much of the original furniture is made of Brazilian jacaranda wood. Visitors can savor the atmosphere of Rio's past by eating a snack in the Bar Jardim, or a meal at the restaurant.

❻ Theatro Municipal & Cinelândia

Av Rio Branco, Centro. **Map** 5 D4.
Tel (21) 2332 9191.
Ⓜ Cinelândia. 🎫 ♿
Ⓦ theatromunicipal.rj.gov.br

Rio's Municipal Theater, built between 1905 and 1909, is the main venue for the city's ballet, opera, and orchestra (including the Brazilian Symphony Orchestra), and continues to attract the very best talent from both Brazil and abroad. Illustrious names include Nijinsky, Sarah Bernhard, Anna Pavlova, and Luciano Pavarotti, to name just a few.

Farther south along Avenida Rio Branco is the heart of Cinelândia or "cinema land," the area around which the city's movie houses sprang up in the 1920s. Many are still in operation, most notably the Cine Odeon BR which opened in 1926 and closed in 1999 to be renovated. It

Stained-glass window at the Catedral Metropolitana

reopened a year later as the headquarters of the Rio Film Festival. Other buildings in the area include the Museu Nacional de Belas Artes *(see p78)*, Biblioteca Nacional, and Palácio Pedro Ernesto.

❼ Catedral Metropolitana

Av República do Chile 245, Centro.
Map 5 D4. **Tel** (21) 2240 2669.
Ⓜ Cinelândia. **Open** 7:30am–6pm daily. ♿ ✝ 11am Mon–Fri, 10am Sat & Sun. Museu Arquidiocesano de Arte Sacra: **Open** 10am–4pm Wed, 9am–noon, 1–4pm Sat, 9am–noon Sun. ♿
Ⓦ catedral.com.br

Rio's striking Metropolitan Cathedral, with its truncated conical shape, was concept-

ualized by Ivo Calliari (1918–2005), a Catholic priest.

The cathedral's first stone was laid on January 20, 1964, and the inauguration of the still unfinished building was held 12 years later, in 1976, marking the 300th anniversary of the Diocese of Rio. Standing 248 ft (75 m) high with no interior columns, this huge cathedral has a seating capacity of 5,000 and can accommodate up to 20,000 people standing. The interior is dominated by four magnificent stained-glass windows that stretch 197 ft (60 m) to the ceiling. They represent the apostolic (yellow), Catholic (blue), ecclesiastical (green), and saintly (red) traditions.

The **Museu Arquidiocesano de Arte Sacra** (Sacred Art Museum) in the basement includes historical items in its collection, such as the baptismal fonts used for christening the Brazilian royal family, the golden rose gifted to Princess Isabel by Pope Leo XIII to celebrate her signing the abolition of slavery, and the throne of Dom Pedro II.

❽ Santa Teresa

Santa Teresa, Centro.
Ⓜ Cruz Vermelha.

At the top of the Santa Teresa hill, the neigborhood of Santa Teresa offers a magnificent view of the city, particularly from Parque das Ruínas. Its colonial charm has been retained through a resistance to development, and it is famed for its winding cobbled streets, old mansions, and for being an artistic hot spot. The construction of the Santa Teresa convent in the 18th century marked the beginning of the development of this area, and it is a popular tourist site, with restaurants, live music, cultural centers, and other attractions. A ride on the distinctive yellow streetcar, the Bondinho de Santa Teresa, is an experience not to be missed. This is the last of the many streetcars that used to crisscross the city, and it connects the neighborhood with downtown Rio.

Opulent façade of the Theatro Municipal

A Batalha do Avaí (1877) by Pedro Américo, Museu Nacional de Belas Artes

❾ Lapa

Lapa, Centro. Ⓜ Carioca.

The most famous image of the area known as Lapa is the **Arcos da Lapa**, an aqueduct built in 1724 to bring water down from the Santa Teresa forest to the public fountain in Largo da Carioca. In 1896, it became the base for the viaduct that carries streetcars to and from the city center.

Lapa has always had a slightly bohemian feel and during the first half of the 1900s was the center of Rio's alternative nightlife. The area still boasts a vibrant nightlife, attracting people from all over the city who come looking for the best of Brazilian music. Key hot spots include Rio Scenarium, Carioca de Gema, and Dama da Noite. In 2004, the area saw the return of the **Circo Voador** (Flying Circus), now held in a purpose-built music venue that replaced the earlier tent of the 1980s and early 1990s. Many of the leading names in contemporary Brazilian music – including Seu Jorge – got their first break at the Circo Voador.

🎪 **Circo Voador**
Rua dos Arcos, Lapa. **Tel** (21) 2533 0354. **Open** for shows only. 🅰 ♿

❿ Museu Nacional de Belas Artes

Av Rio Branco 199, Centro. **Map** 5 E4. **Tel** (21) 2240 0068. Ⓜ Cinelândia. **Open** 10am–6pm Tue–Fri, noon–5pm Sat, Sun & public hols. 🎟 free on Sun. 📷 by appt. ♿ 🌐 **mnba.gov.br**

The National Museum of Fine Arts is one of the most important permanent art collections in Latin America. The building in which it is housed dates from 1908.

The collection, which has over 16,000 pieces in its archive, features Brazilian artists from the colonial period as well as from the 19th and 20th centuries. Artists include Frans Post, who painted Brazilian landscapes in classical Dutch style, the Frenchman Jean Baptiste Debret, who painted the immortal *Battle of Guararapes* (1879), Vitor Meireles, and Pedro Américo, whose *A Batalha do Avaí* (1877) is one of the largest paintings in the world painted on an easel. There is also a gallery for contemporary exhibits.

The gallery has an extensive collection of non-Brazilian works and a particularly fine selection of Baroque Italian art dating from the 17th and 18th centuries. The museum was created on the basis of a prized art collection, brought to Brazil from Europe by Portugal's King Dom João VI and his court when they fled Napoleon in 1808 *(see p56)*.

⓫ Museu Histórico Nacional

Praça Marechal Âncora. **Map** 5 F4. **Tel** (21) 2550 9224. Ⓜ Cinelândia. **Open** 10am–6pm Tue–Fri, 2–6pm Sat, Sun & public hols. 🎟 ♿ restricted. 🌐 **museuhistoriconacional.com.br**

Founded in 1922, the country's leading history museum recounts the history of Brazil up to 1889. Its collection of 287,000 pieces includes everything from paintings and coins to carriages and rarities such as the pen used by Princess Isabel to sign the decree abolishing slavery. Apart from displaying period furniture, 19th-century firearms, and locomotives, the museum also traces Brazil's colonial past in its charts and written declarations. The building is one of the oldest in Rio, with a portion belonging to Santiago Fort, dating from 1603.

⓬ Museu de Arte Moderna

Av Infante Dom Henrique 85, Centro. **Map** 5 F5. **Tel** (21) 2240 4944. Ⓜ Cinelândia. **Open** noon–6pm Tue–Fri, noon–7pm Sat, Sun & public hols (last adm half hour before closing). 🅰 📷 ♿ 🌐 **mamrio.com.br**

Rio's Modern Art Museum (MAM) has one of the best collections of 20th-century art in Brazil, surpassed only by MASP in São Paulo *(see p147)*. The museum also houses one of the largest archives of Brazilian films.

The strikingly modern building that houses the MAM was far ahead of its time in its design and architecture when it was built in 1958. In 1978, a major fire destroyed many of its irreplaceable exhibits, including the works of Miró, Picasso, Salvador Dalí, Max Ernst, and René Magritte. It has taken time and the generosity of collectors in Brazil and abroad to rebuild the collection. Today, the MAM is once more a highly regarded institution, not only for its own archive but also for the visiting exhibitions from around the world that it stages through the year.

Entrance to the Museu de Arte Moderna (MAM)

Located close to its gardens is a monument to the victims of World War II. Inaugurated in 1960, it represents two arms raised with hands outstretched in prayer. In 1980, Pope John Paul II said mass from the steps of the monument to a crowd of more than 2 million people. Below the monument is a museum describing Brazil's participation in the Allied operations, known as the Italian Campaign, in and around Italy between 1944 and 1945.

Igreja Nossa Senhora da Glória do Outeiro rising above tree tops

⑬ Igreja Nossa Senhora da Glória do Outeiro

Praça Nossa Senhora da Glória 135, Glória. **Tel** (21) 2557 4600. Ⓜ Glória. **Open** 8am–5pm Tue–Fri, 8am–noon Sat & Sun. 🕒 9am–noon, 1–5pm Mon–Fri, 9–11am Sun.
Ⓦ **outeirodagloria.org.br**

Most visitors to downtown Rio cannot help but notice the beautiful octagonal church of Our Lady of Gloria, as it sits majestically on top of a hill beside the freeways cutting through Flamengo Park.

The spot where the church was built, in 1714, was first used as a place of worship in 1608, when the image of Our Lady of Gloria was placed in a grotto. The land was donated to the church in 1699 by the nobleman Cláudio Gurgel do Amaral.

The church, which was completed in 1739, came to national attention when it became the favorite place of worship for Dom Pedro VI and his family after their arrival from

Portugal in 1808. Known for its hand-painted tiles dating from the 1730s, it was declared a national monument by President Vargas in 1937.

The church can be reached by car, or by foot up the steps known as Ladeira de Nossa Senhora. It is also possible to take a small cable car from Rua do Russel 312. There are views across the bay and there is also a small sacred art museum.

⑭ Museu da República

Rua do Catete 153, Catete. **Tel** (21) 3235 3693. Ⓜ Catete. **Open** 8am–6pm daily (to 7pm in summer). 🎦 📷
Ⓦ **museudarepublica.org.br**

The story of Brazil's history, as told by the Museum of the Republic, picks up where the Museu Histórico Nacional left off. It begins with the Proclamation of the Republic in 1889, and covers events until 1960, when the capital and the then president, Kubitschek, moved from Rio de Janeiro to Brasília. What makes the museum particularly special is that its building, constructed between 1858 and 1866, was the presidential residence from 1897 until 1954. In that year, President Getúlio Vargas (see pp60–61), Brazil's most influential statesman who was president for 24 years, committed suicide in his bedroom. The third floor is dedicated to an exhibition about the life and work of Vargas. His bedroom has been preserved exactly as it used to be when he lived here. In total, the palace was home to 18 Brazilian presidents,

Attractive garden outside the Museu da República

all of whom feature in the museum's various exhibits.

Apart from the museum and palace, there is also an attractive garden on the grounds.

⑮ Museu Carmen Miranda

Av Rui Barbosa, Flamengo.
Tel (21) 2334 4293. Ⓜ Flamengo. **Open** 11am–5pm Tue–Fri, 2–5pm Sat, Sun & public hols.

Fans of Carmen Miranda will not want to miss this small museum in Flamengo Park. One of the most famous Brazilians of all time, Maria do Carmo Miranda da Cunha was born in Portugal in 1909, but moved to Rio with her family as a baby. Carmen cut her first record in 1929, but it was the big screen that would make her a global star. Her first film in 1932 shot her to international stardom, and in 1941, she became the first South American with a star on the Hollywood Walk of Fame. After her death on August 5, 1955, her body was returned to Rio where a crowd of almost 500,000 watched her burial.

The museum exhibits iconographic costumes, including her tall fruit hats and platform-heeled shoes, and artifacts belonging to Carmen, as well as many of her records and films.

This collection will be moved to the Museu da Imagem e do Som (see p82) in Copacabana in late 2015/early 2016.

⑯ Oi Futuro Ipanema

Rua Visconde de Piraja 53 (Third Floor). **Tel** (21) 3201 3010. **Open** 1–9pm Tue–Sun. Ⓦ **oifuturo.org.br**

A renovated 1918 building near Ipanema beach houses Oi Futuro, a hypermodern cultural center for art and technology. It hosts innovative exhibitions of avant-garde visual arts with multimedia installations that blend art forms such as painting, photography, film, music, and poetry. There are also film screenings, dance performances, and concerts of experimental musical styles from all over the world.

⑰ Sugar Loaf Mountain

Guarding the entrance to Guanabara Bay, the monolithic granite and quartz Sugar Loaf rises 1,300 ft (396 m) above the waters of the southern Atlantic Ocean. From the summit, it is easy to understand why the early explorers believed that they had sailed into the mouth of a great river they christened Rio de Janeiro. The Sugar Loaf experience takes in two mountains, Morro do Urca and Pão de Açúcar (Sugar Loaf). It is possible to scale both these mountains via organized climbs on most weekends. Demanding less effort, the cable car, originally opened in 1912, stops at the 705-ft- (224-m-) high Morro da Urca before ascending to the summit.

The original 1912 cable car, a remarkable feat of its times

Pão de Açúcar
The name of Sugar Loaf, adopted in the 19th century, is assumed to have been derived from the mountain's shape, which resembles conical clay molds used earlier to refine sugar. The Tupi Indians, however, called it "Pau-nh-Açuquá" (high, pointed, or isolated hill).

KEY

① **The summit** provides unforgettable views out over Copacabana, Ipanema, and the scenic Corcovado and Tijuca.

② **Helisight**, with a heliport base at Morro da Urca, offers flights around Sugar Loaf and Corcovado (see pp86–7).

③ **Morro da Urca** The flat summit of Morro da Urca has restaurants, bars, and a theater that hosts popular shows, concerts, and even Carnaval balls.

④ **Wooded Trails** A series of trails that lead to a number of good climbing locations wind their way up to the summit. The trails are also an ideal place to spot marmosets.

⑤ **Cable car station at Praia Vermelha**

⑥ **Boats** can be hired at many key locations for an enjoyable ride in the calm waters to the base of Sugar Loaf.

Rock Climbing
Since British nanny Henrietta Carstairs made the first recorded solo ascent in 1817, climbing the smooth Sugar Loaf has become a popular sport, with over 60 known routes to the towering summit.

Cable Car Ride
The current Italian cable system carries as many as 1,360 passengers every hour. The glass walls of the cable car allow sweeping views of the city.

VISITORS' CHECKLIST

Practical Information
Av Pasteur 520, Praia Vermelha, Urca. **Tel** (21) 2546 8400.
w bondinho.com.br
Helisight: **Tel** (21) 2511 2141.
Cable Car: Praia Vermelha.
Open 8am–9pm (ticket booth closes at 7:50pm).

Transport
107, 511, 512 & 2011.

Rio City at Night
The city of Rio de Janeiro boasts a stunning nightscape. The magnificent Sugar Loaf remains illuminated, even in the dead of the night, by powerful 1,000-watt projectors.

James Bond's Moonraker

In 1979, Sugar Loaf and the cable car formed the backdrop for a main action sequence in *Moonraker*, with Roger Moore playing James Bond. In real life, the Great Train Robber, Ronald Biggs, was kidnapped in 1981 by a group of British mercenaries from a restaurant, which was then located next to the cable car station. Ironically, during a first kidnap bid in 1979, the kidnappers had claimed to be part of the *Moonraker* crew.

A scene from the film *Moonraker*

Bustling Copacabana beach, popular with locals and vacationers

⑱ Copacabana

Ⓜ Siqueira Campos. 🛈 Av Princesa Isabel 183, (21) 2541 7522, 2542 8084.

One of the world's most celebrated beaches, Copacabana is the center of Rio's tourist trade. On New Year's eve, the neighborhood becomes Rio's spiritual and festive heart, as millions of Cariocas and visitors take to the beach to party, and honor Yemanjá, Goddess of the Sea.

The name Copacabana, or "Copa Caguana" (Luminous Place) in Quechua, an ancient language still spoken in Peru, was given by the Incas to a lovely site by the Lagoa Titicaca, where they built a temple. In the 17th century, the captain of a Spanish galleon erected a chapel in honor of Our Lady of Copacabana, who came to his aid during a shipwreck.

Built in 1914, on the promontory of the chapel as Rio's defense against attack, the **Forte de Copacabana** offers scenic views of the entire sweep of Copacabana.

The main attraction of Copacabana is the beach which, along with Leme, constitutes a magnificent 3-mile (5-km) stretch from Le Meridien hotel in the north on the corner of Avenida Princesa Isabel, to the Forte de Copacabana and Sofitel Rio in the south. Until 1892, it had been a leading trek for those from the city to reach Copacabana. In that year, a tunnel was cut through from Botafogo to Copacabana, followed by a second tunnel in 1904 that allowed the trams to reach the beach. The real turning point, however, was the creation of the Neo-Classical **Copacabana**

Palace hotel (see p370), a part of the fabric of Rio life since its opening in 1923. It has hosted both authentic royalty and the royalty of the entertainment world, including Queen Elizabeth II and Marlene Dietrich. The hotel continues to draw celebrities, as well as gays and transvestites.

The **Museu da Imagem e do Som** (Museum of Image and Sound) places an emphasis on the history of Brazilian music. It will soon also house the Carmen Miranda collection that is currently on display in Flamengo (see p79).

The beachfront kiosk bars lining Avenue Atlântica – the road that runs the length of the beach – are popular. The entire length of Copacabana is divided into stations (postos). Postos 5 and 6 attract older residents and favela youngsters. The fresh catch of the day can be bought at Posto 7 – at the southern end – known as the posto de pescadores (fisherman's post).

🔳 **Forte de Copacabana**
Av Atlântica Posto 6. **Tel** (21) 2521 1032. **Open** 10am–8pm Tue–Sun.
📷 🔲 ♿

🏛 **Museu da Imagem e do Som**
Av Atlântica 3432. **Tel** (21) 2146 1579.
Open see website for times.
🌐 mis.rj.gov.br 📷 🔲 ♿

Map of Copacabana, Ipanema & Leblon

Exterior of an upmarket jewelry store in Ipanema

The Girl from Ipanema

One of the most played and recorded songs in popular music history, "The Girl from Ipanema," or "A Garota de Ipanema," was written in 1962 by Antônio Carlos Jobim and Vinícius de Moraes. The duo are said to have been inspired by a sensual girl from Ipanema, Helô Pinheiro. A year later, the recording of the song's most famous version took place in New York's A&R Studio, featuring João and Astrud Gilberto, in the Portuguese and English versions, respectively. In 1964, Stan Getz, Jobim, and the Gilbertos took *bossa nova* to a global audience with the release of *Getz/Gilberto*. With "The Girl from Ipanema" as the opening track, the album stayed in the US charts for 96 weeks and won four Grammys.

Astrud Gilberto

⑲ Ipanema

Ⓜ General Osório. Feira Hippie de Ipanema: Praça General de Osório. **Open** 7am–7pm daily.

Almost as famous as Copacabana, Ipanema shot into the limelight in the 1960s with the globally famous song written by Antônio Jobim and Vinícius de Moraes, "The Girl from Ipanema" *(see p36)*.

The actual name of this fashionable area is credited to the native Tupi-Guaraní who called the area Y-panema, or "rough water." The first non-native residents moved into the area around 1884, and today Ipanema and neighboring

Leblon are considered the most desirable places to live in Rio. More residential than Copacabana, Ipanema is also more stylish, with its back streets dotted with chic boutiques, bars, restaurants, and nightclubs.

The most prestigious address in Rio is Avenida Vieira Souto, while running parallel, two streets back, is Rua Visconde de Pirajá, the backbone to the Ipanema shopping experience. At the Copacabana end is Praça General Osório, the public square that plays host to Rio's popular **Feira Hippie de Ipanema** (Hippie Fair), every Sunday. The fair has been a part of life in Ipanema and Rio since opening in 1968.

The mile-long stretch of Ipanema beach runs from Leblon in the west, up to Arpoador in the east. Arpoador extends the beach by another half-mile, and is popular with the surf set.

⑳ Leblon

🚎 Copacabana.

For many years, Leblon sat in the shadow of Ipanema. But today it is considered as fashionable and desirable as its neighbor, with perhaps an even greater density and mix of bars, clubs, and restaurants. Rua Dias

Ferreira, at the most westerly point, boasts a particularly eclectic mix. Like Ipanema, there are only a few hotels along the beachfront Avenida Delfim Moreira.

While the beaches of Copacabana and Leme flow seamlessly into each other, Leblon and Ipanema are separated by Jardim de Alá and the canal that links the Lagoa Rodrigo de Freitas with the sea. The 1-mile- (2-km-) long Leblon is said to have been given its name in honor of a blond foreigner, one of the first residents in the area. The nationality of "Le Blond" is debatable. Some scholars say that he was French, while others surmise he was Dutch.

Leblon is the headquarters of Clube de Regatas Flamengo, of which the most famous is the Flamengo Football Club, the World Club Champions in 1981.

The exclusive Leblon neighborhood and its fashionable beach

MORRO DE SÃO JOÃO

Siqueira Campos
Ⓜ Arcoverde

AV. PRINCESA ISABEL

COPACABANA

Copacabana
Palace Hotel ★

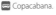

Praia de Copacabana

AVENIDA ATLÂNTICA

RUA FIGUEIREDO DE MAGALHÃES

SANTA CLARA

View of Lagoa Rodrigo de Freitas and Jóquei Clube Brasileiro from Corcovado

㉑ Lagoa Rodrigo de Freitas

Lagoa. **Map** 2 A3. 🚌 ♿
🌐 lagoarodrigodefreitas.com.br

The picturesque Lagoa Rodrigo de Freitas, or Lagoa (lagoon) as it is often called, sits at the foot of Corcovado peak and separates the Serra da Carioca from Ipanema and Leblon. A full circuit of the lagoon is about 5 miles (8 km) and is popular with joggers, cyclists, and parents with children in prams. There are plenty of halts en route, with kiosks selling everything from coconut water to full meals. Some kiosks even offer live music in the evenings.

The Lagoa is also bordered by more conventional restaurants and bars, especially along the Ipanema stretch. One of Rio's most traditional places, **Bar Lagoa** (see p387) opened here in 1934. Along the northern shore, highlights include Claude Troisgros' **Olympe** (see p388), which, despite a change in name since it opened in 1983, is still one of Rio's best restaurants.

Several sports clubs are also located here. Among the most famous are the Jockey Club Brasileiro, the **Sociedade Hípica Brasileira**, the city's main equestrian center, and the headquarters of the Clube Regatas do Flamengo. Flamengo, along with Vasco da Gama, Fluminense, and Botafogo, is one of Brazil's top soccer teams and has won the National and South American titles on many occasions. All clubs have rowing divisions as the Lagoa is Brazil's main rowing center. Several international regattas have been held here.

Visitors can go boating, as *pedallos* and other craft are available for rent. It is also possible to rent bicycles.

The **Fundação Eva Klabin** is one of Rio's prolific cultural centers and museums. Its exhibits are part of the private collection of Eva Klabin, whose family made a fortune in paper in the mid-20th century.

The scenic **Parque da Catacumba** around Lagoa is interspersed with sculptures by artists Roberto Moriconi, Bruno Giorgi, and Caribé. Monkeys roam the park, which offers views over the Lagoa and toward Ipanema.

🏛 Fundação Eva Klabin
Av Epitácio Pessoa 2480. **Tel** (21) 3282 8558. **Open** 2:30–4pm Tue–Fri, hours vary according to exhibition.

🌳 Parque da Catacumba
Av Epitácio Pessoa 3000. **Tel** (21) 2521 5540. **Open** 8am–5pm daily.

🏛 Sociedade Hípica Brasileira
Av Borges de Medeiros 2448. **Tel** (21) 2156 0191. **Open** only for events. ♿ ♿

㉒ Jóquei Clube Brasileiro

Rua Jardim Botânico 1003, Gávea. **Map** 1 A2. **Tel** (21) 3534 9000. Ⓜ Botafogo. 🚌 **Open** from 6:30pm Mon, from 3:30pm Fri, from 7am Sat & Sun. ♿ ♿ 🌐 jcb.com.br

With a great view of the Lagoa and the Corcovado mountain, the Jockey Club has one of the most spectacular settings of any racecourse in the world. Races are held four days a week, all year round, so it is easy to catch the action. The club will allow even non-members and visitors into the members' stand to enjoy the race.

The track first opened in 1926, with the main stand designed in a Louis XV style. In total, there are five stands; a paddock, a turf track, two sand tracks, and an equestrian village. The biggest race of the year – and one of South America's most important – is the Grande Prêmio Brasil do Turfe, that was first run in 1933. It traditionally takes place every August.

㉓ Jardim Botânico

Rua Jardim Botânico 920 & 1008, Gávea. **Map** 1 A1. **Tel** (21) 3874 1808. 🚌 **Open** 8am–5pm daily (Mon: from noon). **Closed** Jan 1 & Dec 25. ♿ ♿ ♿ restricted. 🌐 jbrj.gov.br

Rio's fascinating Jardim Botânico was founded in 1808 by the Prince Regent, Dom João VI. Originally meant to acclimatize plants and spices coming from the Orient and the East Indies, it later became the Royal Garden and opened to the public in 1822. Among its many illustrious visitors were Charles Darwin in 1832 and Albert Einstein in 1925.

Today, Jardim Botânico includes an area of natural rainforest, and is home to many species of plants, as well as innumerable types of birds and animals. However, the

A track lined with palm trees in Jardim Botânico

garden's signature are the 200 imperial palms that line its main avenues.

Jardim Botânico has other attractions within its grounds. These include Rio's original gunpowder factory dating from 1808, the old gates of the Fine Arts Academy, and the Empress's Mansion, which became the headquarters of the National School of Tropical Botany in 2001.

㉔ Museu do Índio

Rua das Palmeiras 55, Botafogo.
Tel (21) 3214 8702. Ⓜ Botafogo.
Open 9am–5:30pm Tue–Fri, 1–5pm Sat, Sun & public hols. 🎨 🌐
Ⓦ **museudoindio.org.br**

Founded in 1953, the Museum of the Indian is run by the National Indian Foundation (Funai) with the aim of giving an insight into the lives of Brazil's Indian and indigenous groups. Housed in a 19th-century mansion, this dynamic institution has more than 14,000 indigenous artifacts, 50,000 photographs, and over 200 films. With 16,000 books and magazines, it also has one of the most complete libraries covering topics related to indigenous peoples.

There are several permanent exhibits in the gardens, including a Guaraní house and farm field, a Xingu kitchen and house, and Kuarup ritual tree trunks. There is also a well-stocked store that sells genuine indigenous artifacts.

㉕ Museu Villa-Lobos

Rua Sorocaba 200, Botafogo.
Tel (21) 2226 9818. Ⓜ Botafogo.
Open 9am–6pm Mon–Fri. 🌐
Ⓦ **museuvillalobos.org.br**

With over 1,000 compositions to his credit, Heitor Villa-Lobos (1897–1959) is considered one of the greatest composers in Latin America *(see p36)*. It is believed that it was through his work that Brazilian music first became popular abroad, eventually gaining universal appeal with the advent of *bossa nova*.

The Villa-Lobos Museum, which moved to a stately 19th-century mansion in Botafogo in 1986, helps organize the Villa-Lobos Festival that begins on the anniversary of his death, November 17, each year. His second wife, Arminda Neves d'Almeida, set up the museum in 1960, one year after his death. Its aim is to preserve the composer's personal collection of artifacts and keep his work alive. Exhibits include his books, music scores, photographs, and instruments.

Villa-Lobos's best-known work is his cycle of the nine *Bachianas Brasileiras*, which pays homage to both Bach and Brazilian folk music. Such was his versatility that he wrote a variety of music from *choros* (an upbeat waltz or polka), concertos, symphonies, and orchestral works, to chamber music, operas, and ballets, as well as guitar and solo piano pieces.

Stately building housing the Museu Casa de Rui Barbosa

㉖ Museu Casa de Rui Barbosa

Rua São Clemente 134, Botafogo.
Tel (21) 3289 4600. Ⓜ Botafogo.
Open 10am–5:30pm Tue–Fri, 2–6pm Sat & Sun. 🎨 free on Sun. 🌐
Ⓦ **casaruibarbosa.gov.br**

A renowned politician, diplomat, and jurist, Rui Barbosa de Oliveira (1849–1923) helped shape several important Brazilian policies, including those pertaining to direct elections and the abolition of slavery. He made his mark internationally during the 1907 Peace Conference at the Hague, where he argued that all countries should be treated equally. Barbosa contested twice for the Brazilian presidency – in 1910 and 1919 – but lost on both occasions.

Barbosa was also a great essayist and was one of the founders (and later president) of the Brazilian Academy of Letters. He was eventually elected as a judge to the International Court of Justice at the Hague.

The 1850 building that houses the Rui Barbosa Museum was the statesman's home from 1895 until his death in 1923. When it opened to the public in 1930, it was the first private residence in Brazil to be turned into a museum. The museum showcases a collection of Barbosa's personal possessions, such as furniture and art, and a library containing 200 of his own works.

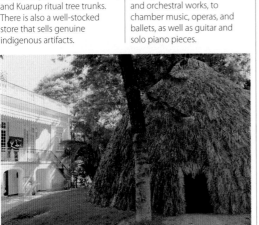

Indigenous roundhouse on the grounds of Museu do Índio

㉗ Morro do Corcovado & Cristo Redentor

The 2,316-ft (706-m) Corcovado mountain derives its name from *corcova* (hunchback), which describes the physical appearance of the mountain itself. On the summit, the iconic Cristo Redentor statue towers over Rio, and is Brazil's most recognizable landmark. It was officially inaugurated in 1931 to mark the centenary of Brazil's independence. The enormous statue sits in the center of the gorgeous tropical jungle of Parque Nacional da Tijuca.

Making the Head
Work on the statue began in Paris in 1926, with French sculptor Paul Landowski working on the head and hands. The head alone weighs 30 tons.

Wide Open Arms
The entire Rio City is embraced by Christ, and the statue's open arms are seen as a testament to the warmth of the Brazilians.

The Statue
Having been shipped from France to Brazil, the 98-ft (30-m) statue was faced in limestone and hauled up the mountain by rail to be assembled and attached to supporting pillars.

Famous Visitors
Pope John Paul II, Pope Pius XII, and Albert Einstein are some of the famous people to have visited Corcovado.

Morro o
Formiga

EST. DO CORCOVADO

Alto da
Boa Vista

Morro d.
Corcovac

Cris
Redent

0 km   2
0 miles   2

★ Museu Internacional de Arte Naïf
The museum has one of the largest collections of naive art in the world, featuring more than 6,000 works, dating from the 15th century to the present.

VISITORS' CHECKLIST

Practical Information
Morro do Corcovado. **P** at the base of Cristo Redentor.
i Corcovado, (21) 2558 1329.
Open 8:30am–6:30pm daily (entrance at Parque Nacional da Tijuca).
w corcovado.com.br

Transport
R Cosme Velhostation, Rua Cosme Velho 513, 8:30am–7pm daily. 180, 184, 583 & 584.

Parque Nacional Da Tijuca

The statue of Christ sits in this scenic national park, which contains the world's largest urban forest – Floresta da Tijuca. Dotted with natural springs, the park is home to more than 200 species of birds and several small mammals. It draws regular crowds of resident Cariocas, especially on the weekend (see p92).

Cog Train
Passing through the dense Atlantic rainforest, the train ride up the summit is a plus. The line was originally built in 1882 by Dom Pedro II; the current Swiss train dates from 1979.

Key
- Major road
- Other road
- Minor road
- Cog train route
- Tunnels
- Park boundary

KEY

① **Escalators** link the base to the train station and car park.

② **The pedestal**, on which the statue stands, is 26 ft (8 m) high.

③ **The chapel** at the base of the statue can accommodate 150 people.

④ **Largo do Boticário** is a lovely square surrounded by seven private houses. Colonial in appearance, the houses date from around 1920.

⑤ **Mirante Dona Marta** offers splendid views of Rio City.

★ Stunning Views
Corcovado is located right in the center of Rio and can be seen from most areas of the city. The views over and across Rio from the summit offer a sweeping aerial panorama.

For keys to symbols *see back flap*

㉘ Estádio do Maracanã

Rua Prof. Eurico Rabelo (gate 18), Maracanã. **Tel** (21) 8871 3950. Ⓜ Maracanã. **Open** 9am–10pm for tours. 🐾 💳 ♿

Rio's Maracanã Stadium is one of the most famous soccer grounds in the world. It is also the largest, having hosted crowds of up to 200,000 people.

The stadium, which was refurbished for the 2007 Pan-American Games, was built for the 1950 World Cup and inaugurated on June 16 the same year, with a game between Rio and São Paulo.

The first game played by the Brazilian team took place on June 24, 1950, with Brazil beating Mexico 4–0. A month later, a crowd of almost 200,000 tested the stadium's capacity to see Brazil play Uruguay in the final game. Brazil lost 2–1, and thus began its eternal rivalry with Uruguay.

It is not only soccer that has set stadium records. Big artists have attracted massive crowds to the Maracanã, including Frank Sinatra, Paul McCartney, Kiss, Madonna, the Rolling Stones, Sting, Tina Turner, and the second "Rock in Rio" Festival. Pope John Paul II's public appearances in 1980 and 1997 were also attended by thousands.

The Maracanã Stadium can be visited on the days of soccer matches and concerts (see p98), or as part of a daily guided tour that takes visitors behind the scenes and onto the pitch. In 2014, it hosted the World Cup final.

Rio Zoo's main gate, gifted to Dom Pedro I by an English aristocrat

㉙ Quinta da Boa Vista

Av Pedro II (between Rua Almirante Baltazar & Rua Dom Meinrdo, São Cristóvão). Ⓜ São Cristóvão. Museu Nacional: **Tel** (21) 2562 6900. **Open** 10am–4pm Tue–Sun. **Closed** Jan 1, Dec 25, Carnaval & Good Friday. 🐾 Jardim Zoológico: **Tel** (21) 2567 9504. **Open** 9am– 4:30pm Tue–Sun.

The Quinta da Boa Vista, the landscaped grounds of a former royal estate, includes the **Museu Nacional** and the **Jardim Zoológico** (Rio Zoo). Founded by Dom João VI in 1818, the Museu Nacional is the country's oldest scientific institution, which started out as the House of Birds before becoming the Royal Museum, the Imperial Museum, and, finally, the National Museum.

Its permanent exhibits cover a variety of fields from archaeology, biodiversity, and botany to ethnology, geology, and palaeontology. A part of the collection belonged to Emperor Pedro II, a botanist, and his wife,

the Empress Teresa Cristina, who was an archaeologist. The museum's gardens and the former royal palace are an attraction in their own right, and their lakes and grottos are a big draw on the weekends. They were landscaped by the French architect Auguste Glaziou in 1869.

The Jardim Zoológico is considered one of the best in the world and is Brazil's oldest zoo, having been founded in 1888. It is home to approximately 350 species and more than 2,100 animals, including one of the most complete collections of Brazilian mammals and butter-flies. Particular highlights are the Brazilian monkeys and birds. The zoo also boasts an excellent aviary and an aquarium that houses a variety of fascinating Brazilian river species.

The zoo's beautiful main entrance was a wedding gift, presented to Dom Pedro I and the Empress Leopoldina by an English aristocrat in the early 19th century.

㉚ Sambódromo & Cidade do Samba

Av Marquês de Sapucaí, Centro. **Map** 4 A4. **Tel** (21) 2563 9000. Ⓜ Praça XI. **Open** 9am–4pm daily. ♿ Cidade do Samba: Rua Rivadávia Correa 60, Gamboa. **Tel** (21) 2213 2503. **Open** 9am–5pm Wed–Mon; shows: 9am–11pm Thu. ♿ 🌐 cidadedosambarj.com.br

The Sambódromo, or Passarela do Samba, is where Rio's famous *samba* schools parade each February during Carnaval (see pp68–9).

Before Carnaval was as popular as it is today, the schools simply paraded on the streets and people stood on the sidewalk, and later, on specially built stands. As the crowds got bigger, the disruption caused by the building of the stands each year meant another solution had to be found.

The renowned Brazilian architect, Oscar Niemeyer (see p299), came up with a perman-ent solution. He built what is today the Sambódromo, which

Aerial view of the spectacular Estádio do Maracanã

The Sambódromo, venue of Rio's annual Carnaval

was inaugurated in time for the 1984 Carnaval. In order to complement the Sambódromo, a large complex, known as the **Cidade do Samba** (City of Samba), was established in 2005. This space is used by the main *samba* schools to build their floats and make their vibrant costumes.

Throughout the year, visitors are allowed in to watch the preparations and see how a *samba* school puts on its parade.

❸ Centro Cultural do Banco do Brasil

Rua Primeiro de Março 66, Centro. **Map** 5 E3. **Tel** (21) 3808 2020. Ⓜ Carioca. **Open** 9am–9pm Tue–Sun. ▨ ▣ ▥ bb.com.br/cultura

Located in what used to be the financial quarter of Rio de Janeiro's Centro district and housed in an impressive building dating from 1880, the Centro Cultural do Banco do Brasil (CCBB) was originally

the headquarters for the Trade Association and the Bank of Brazil. In 1989 the building was converted into a major cultural center consisting of three theaters, four exhibition rooms, a cinema, and a bookstore.

The gallery spaces offer a wide selection of changing exhibitions, ranging from paintings and sculpture to photography. There is one permanent exhibition on the evolution of Brazil's currency. The cinema screens art films and hosts experimental film festivals, while the theaters stage dance performances, lunchtime and evening concerts of both classical and modern music, as well as plays. Many of the cultural center's events are free of charge (*see also pp98–9*).

The building itself is worth a visit; it consists of imposing columns and a rotunda (the old trading floor stock exchange), a marbled lobby, and grand staircases.

Rio's Favelas

As much a part of the city's landscape as Corcovado and Sugar Loaf, Rio's *favelas* are famous, lately due to their prominence in Fernando Meirelles' 2002 film, *Cidade de Deus* (City of God). They are often erroneously referred to as slums, and while some are, the majority are simply Rio's main areas of poor housing. What started as one or two shacks on a hillside has slowly grown into cities in their own right. Estimates suggest that there are now as many as 800 *favelas* in Rio, and up to 20 percent of the city's population may now live in these areas. Some *favelas* have grown into giant communities, such as Rocinha in São Conrado, with over 150,000 residents. Others, such as Pavão, Cantagalo, Vidigal, and Chapéu Mangueira, are strategically located in hilly Zona Sul areas offering breathtaking views.

Favelas are complex and vibrant communities, deriving their name from the hardy *favela* plant. Many still have drug lords who run *boca de fumos*, where narcotics are openly sold and violence is not uncommon. However, the idea that these ghettos are dangerous warrens full of criminals is simply misplaced, as the majority of people who live here are law-abiding citizens working in low-paying jobs. That said, it is still advisable only to visit these areas as part of a guided tour. There are now several good tours on offer. The most traditional tour is organized by Marcelo Armstrong, who was brought up in an apartment block adjoining the Vila Canoas *favela*. He and his team have been escorting visitors around Vila Canoas and Rocinha since 1992. The tours offer valuable insights into the lives of thousands of Rio's less privileged citizens.

Rocinha, located in São Conrado, one of Rio's largest and most complex *favelas*

㉜ Barra

The fastest growing suburb of Rio, Barra da Tijuca houses the Riocentro, Latin America's largest convention and exhibition center, and the Sítio Roberto Burle Marx, one of the best collections of tropical plants around the world. Besides Barra Shopping Center, the largest shopping mall in South America, Barra boasts many other modern malls and supermarkets. There are also Rio City's most modern multiplex cinemas and an ever-growing number of restaurants, bars, clubs, and hotels. Barra is bordered by the city's longest beach, Praia da Barra da Tijuca.

Barra Shopping Center, the largest shopping mall in Latin America

Map of Barra da Tijuca

SERRA DO NOGUEIRA

SERRA DOS TRES RIOS

Projac-TV Globo ⑦

JACAREPAGUÁ

Rio Water Planet

Centro de Conveções Riocentro ⑥

Autódromo Internacional Nelson Piquet ⑤

ITANHANGÁ

Sítio Roberto Burle Marx (2km) ⑧

Lagoa de Jacarepaguá

Museu Seleção Brasileira ④

BARRA DA TIJUCA

Las Palmas

Barra Shopping Center ③ ②

RECREIO DOS BANDEIRANTES

Lagoa de Marapendi

Cidade das Artes

Downtown

Casa do Pontal ⑨

Lagoina

①

Praia da Barra da Tijuca

Praia dos Bandeirantes

Praia do Pontal

ATLANTIC OCEAN

Praia Prainha & Grumari ⑩

0 km   3

0 miles   3

① 🏖 Praia da Barra da Tijuca
Av Sernambetiba.

Stretching for over 11 miles (18 km), Praia da Barra da Tijuca is Rio's longest beach. The first 4 miles (6 km) are the most built-up, a modern-day Copacabana, with large condominiums.

There are different hot spots along the length of the beach, the most famous of which is Barraca do Pepê, a tremendously busy food outlet that has been a favorite with the surfing and hang-gliding crowd, with a kiosk that served organic food long before people had heard of it.

Crowds from all over Rio are drawn to this beach at weekends, but farther along it becomes less crowded and unspoilt. During the week, when schools are in session, it is even possible to find large isolated stretches.

② 🏬 Barra Shopping Center
Av das Américas 4666.
Tel (21) 4003 4131.

This massive and popular shopping center has an impressive range of shops. There are also eight movie theaters, a medical center, a bowling alley, and many coffee shops.

③ 🎭 Cidade das Artes
Trevo das Palmeiras. 🅿

This cultural center houses one of the largest concert halls in Latin America and is home to the Brazilian Symphony Orchestra.

With the main building suspended 33 ft (10 m) above the ground, the center has a 1,800-seater main hall, smaller halls, four movie theaters, and shops, bars, and restaurants.

④ 🏛 Museu Seleção Brasileira
Av Luís Carlos Prestes 130.
Tel (21) 3572 2006. 🅿

Soccer arrived in Brazil in 1894. Twenty years later, the Brazil squad played its first official

The long stretch of Praia da Barra da Tijuca

For keys to symbols *see back flap*

Fascinating collection of tropical plants at Sítio Roberto Burle Marx

VISITORS' CHECKLIST

Practical Information
Rio de Janeiro. 30,000.
Praça Pio X 119, (21)
2271 7000.
rio.rj.gov.br/riotur

Transport
Botafogo.
from Copacabana (No. 523).

match and won its first trophy, the Copa Roca. So began a legend. Trophies, photos, and more are on display at this shrine to the national team.

⑤ **Autódromo Internacional Nelson Piquet**
Av Embaixador Abelardo Bueno, Jacarepaguá. **Tel** (21) 3410 6850. **Open** race days only.

Named for Nelson Piquet, the only Brazilian to win a Grand Prix in Rio, this circuit opened in 1978 and held the Brazilian Formula One Grand Prix that year. Thereafter, the race returned to São Paulo before coming back to Rio from 1981 until 1990. A favorite with the drivers, it became one of the most glamorous motor-racing events. In 1991, Rio lost out to São Paulo and it has not held a Grand Prix since.

⑥ **Centro de Conveções Riocentro**
Av Salvador Allende 6555. **Tel** (21) 3055 9100.
riocentro.com.br

Latin America's largest exhibition and convention center, Riocentro received tremendous global attention when it hosted the 1992 United Nations Conference on Environment and Development. The event, better known as the Earth Summit, was unprecedented for its magnitude and the scope of its concerns.

The large complex has five pavilions, and includes a heli-port, lawns, gardens, a natural lake, and parking facilities.

⑦ **Projac-TV Globo**
Estrada dos Bandeirantes 6700, Jacarepaguá. **Tel** (21) 2540 2000.

Globo is one of the world's largest television networks and

produces most of its own prime-time programming, including its famous soap operas, called the *novelas*, three of which are screened daily. A complete entertainment factory, Projac includes four studios, two auditoriums, scenery and costume workshops, a restaurant, and the production offices.

⑧ **Sítio Roberto Burle Marx**
Estrada Burle Marx 2019. **Tel** (21) 2410 1412. **Open** 9:30am–1:30pm by appointment only.

This private garden belonged to Roberto Burle Marx *(see p299)*, one of the most important landscape architects of the 20th century. In 1949, Burle Marx bought a plantation and started to organize his private collection of amazing plants. He moved here in 1973 and stayed there until his death. In 1985, he donated the entire estate to the National Institute for Cultural Heritage (IPHAN).

With around 3,500 plant species, the garden is considered one of the most important collections of tropical and semitropical plants in the world. This horticultural paradise also displays the works of Burle Marx, from the designs for his landscape projects to his paintings and sculptures. The garden also has a small Benedictine chapel dating from the 17th century, dedicated to St. Anthony.

⑨ **Casa do Pontal**
Estrada do Pontal 3295. **Tel** (21) 2490 3278. **Open** 9am–5pm Tue–Sun.
museucasadopontal.com.br

Almost the entire collection in this charming museum is based

on the private collection by the Frenchman, Jacques Van de Beuque. Around 200 artists from every region of Brazil have had their works represented here.

The superb collection at the Casa do Pontal consists of more than 8,000 works of Brazilian folk art including sculptures, wood carvings, models, and mechanized sets. These are made from a variety of materials including clay, wood, cloth, sand, iron, aluminium, straw, wire, and even bread dough.

⑩ **Praia Prainha & Grumari**
Av Estado da Guanabara.

Prainha and Grumari are the city's most unspoilt beaches, and are deserted during the week as they are only accessible by car. Prainha, just 164 yards (150 m) long, is particularly popular with the surf crowd, while Grumari is larger and attracts couples and families. Some scenes from the 1984 Hollywood comedy *Blame It on Rio* were filmed along the road to Grumari.

The restaurant and bar, Point de Grumari, on the top of the hill to the west, offers spectacular views along the coast to the west.

A surfer at the picturesque and secluded Prainha beach

For hotels and restaurants in this region see pp370–71 and pp386–8

The lush setting of the Mayrink Chapel, Parque Nacional da Tijuca

❸ Parque Nacional da Tijuca

Tel (21) 2492 2253. 🚌 **Open** 8am–6pm daily. ♿ ℹ️ Estrada da Cascatinha 850, Terra Brasil, (21) 2492 2252.

Covering 15 sq miles (39 sq km), the Tijuca National Park encompasses the last remaining tracts of Atlantic rainforest that once surrounded Rio de Janeiro. It includes the Floresta da Tijuca (Tijuca Forest), Serra da Carioca (Carioca Mountains), and the monoliths of Pedra da Gávea and Pedra Bonita. The park's most famous landmark is the towering statue of Cristo Redentor atop Corcovado peak *(see pp86–7)*. Other well-known viewpoints are the Dona Marta, the Vista Chinesa (with a Chinese-style pavilion), and the Mesa do Imperador (Emperor's Table), all of which offer spectacular city views.

Sights within the Floresta da Tijuca include **Cascatinha do Taunay**, a waterfall near the main gate named after the French painter Nicolau Taunay

Cascatinha do Taunay, one of Parque Nacional da Tijuca's many waterfalls

(1755–1830); the 19th-century **Mayrink Chapel**, featuring the work of Candido Portinari (1903–62), one of the most important Brazilian painters; the lovely Os Esquilos restaurant; and the hundreds of species of plants, birds, and mammals that live here.

Many of the park's 150-odd trails, originally made by Brazil's indigenous people, exist even today. One of them, dating from the 19th century, takes walkers up from Largo do Bom Retiro, a picnic spot in the Floresta da Tijuca, to the 3,940-ft-(1,201-m-) high

Tiled map of park routes in Alto da Boa Vista

Tijuca Peak. It is easy to get lost in the dense foliage, so stick to the main trails and do not go without a guide if planning on trekking. Book in advance if a guide is required.

Another attraction near the Floresta da Tijuca is the **Museu do Açude**, a museum housed in the Neo-Colonial building that once served as the residence of the successful businessman, Raymundo Ottoni de Castro Maya (1894–1968). The museum is known for its French, Dutch, Spanish, and Portuguese tiles from the 17th and 18th centuries, and for Castro Maya's personal collection of Oriental art.

🏛 Museu do Açude

Estrada do Açude 764, Alto da Boa Vista. **Tel** (21) 2492 5443. **Open** 11am–5pm Wed–Mon. 🎟 free on Thu. 📷 ♿

❸ Baía de Guanabara

Without Baía de Guanabara, Rio de Janeiro would probably have been known by a different name. On January 1, 1502, the navigators Andre Gonçalves and Amerigo Vespucci became the first Europeans ever to sail into the bay. Assuming it was the mouth of a great river, they called it Rio de Janeiro or "River of January." Guanabara, meaning "Lagoon of the Sea," was the name given to the dominant bay by indigenous Brazilians and is rather more accurate.

The bay is flanked by Rio to its west and Niterói to its east, and encompasses countless islands. As well as the ferry services that begin at Praça XV, boats can be hired from the **Marina da Glória** in Flamengo Park, the center of all nautical activities in Rio. One of the more pleasant ways to enjoy the bay is by taking the special cruise that starts from the **Espaço Cultural da Marinha** (Navy Cultural Center) in Centro. Centro has a number of fine nautical exhibits, including an Imperial Barge built in Salvador in 1808, and also offers a cruise on the historic tugboat, *Laurindo Pitta*, which was built in England in 1910 and took part in World War I. The cruise lasts an hour and a half and passes several interesting sights along the way.

The Tom Jobim International Airport is located on the largest of the islands in the bay, **Ilha do Governador**, while the tiny **Ilha Fiscal** houses a palace built in 1889 at the request of Emperor Dom Pedro II in the style of a 14th-century French castle. The castle's highlights include its exceptional carved stonework and cast-iron work, and the turret's mosaic floor, which is made from different species of

Museu de Art Contemporârnea (MAC-Niterói), hovering like a flying saucer above Boa Viagem

hardwood. Also noteworthy are the wall paintings by 19th-century Dutch artist Frederico Steckel, and the tower clock and stained-glass windows, which were imported from England.

Ilha Paquetá, north of the bay, is an oasis of calm where no cars are allowed. Ferries and hydrofoils cruise up the bay to the island from the Estação das Barcas in front of the historic Praça XV. Crossing the bay is the Rio-Niterói Bridge (officially the Presidente Costa e Silva Bridge), which is one of the longest in the world at 9 miles (13 km). The project was financed by Britain, and construction began in 1968 in the presence of Queen Elizabeth II.

🏛 Espaço Cultural da Marinha
Av Alfred Agache, Centro. **Tel** (21) 2104 6025. **Open** noon–5pm Tue–Sun. 🎫 ♿

🏛 Ilha Fiscal
Baía de Guanabara. **Tel** (21) 2233 9165. **Open** only for tours at 1pm, 2:30pm & 4pm Thu–Sun. 📷 🚫

⚓ Marina da Glória
Av Infante Dom Henrique, Glória. **Tel** (21) 2255 2200. ♿

㉟ Niterói

🏔 475,000. 🚐 🚢
🌐 **niteroiturismo.com.br**

Cariocas like to joke that the best thing about Niterói is its view across the bay to Rio de Janeiro, and it is true that the city's popularity has shown a decline due to its proximity to Brazil's first city. Both cities, however, developed simultan-eously, and as the ferries got faster and more reliable, Niterói became a popular residential option for people working in downtown Rio.

The British preferred Niterói to Rio, and in 1872, founded the Rio Cricket and Athletic Club that is still active there today. Praia de São Francisco in Guanabara Bay is the city's answer to Copacabana beach, but for the most part is not ideal for swimming. Niterói's better beaches – **Camboinhas**, **Itaipu**, and **Itacoatiara** – lie on the Atlantic coast, and are very popular on weekends.

The two most popular sights in the city are the imposing **Fortaleza de Santa Cruz** and the **Museu de Art**

Contemporârnea (MAC-Niterói). The Fortaleza de Santa Cruz (Santa Cruz Fort) sits on a rocky outcrop just outside the city and guards the entrance to Guanabara Bay. Parts of the fort date from the 16th century, when the French built an improvised fortification to protect the city. The structure grew until it became the most important fortress in Brazil. It helped protect Niterói from two invasions, the first of which came from the Dutch in 1599, and the second from the French in 1710.

The stunning Museu de Art Contemporârnea (Contemporary Art Museum) appears to hover above the neighborhood of Boa Viagem. The illusion comes from its slender base pillar, which is only 30 ft (9 m) in diameter. Inaugurated in 1996, it was the brainchild of the acclaimed Brazilian architect, Oscar Niemeyer (see p299). Its exhibits are based on the 1,000 pieces of Brazilian art donated by the eminent art collector, João Sattamini. The most enchanting spectacle, however, is the view from inside the museum at dusk, when Rio's lights twinkle from across the bay.

🏛 Fortaleza de Santa Cruz
Estrada Gaspar Dutra, Jurujuba. **Open** 9am–5pm Tue–Sun. 📷 🚫

🏛 Museu de Arte Contemporânea
Mirante da Boa Viagem, Niterói. **Tel** (21) 2620 2400. **Open** 10am– 6pm Tue–Sun. 📷 🚫 book in advance. ♿

A panoramic view of the Marina da Glória, Baía de Guanabara

SHOPPING IN RIO

Resident Cariocas have turned shopping into something of an art form and use it as an alternative form of entertainment when they are bored with the beach. Visitors will be pleased to find out just how far their money goes in Rio's stores, especially when it comes to buying items that have been manufactured in Brazil. This includes top fashion clothing, beach and sportswear, leather goods, jewelry, and numerous other items. Until the 1980s, the best place to shop was along Visconde de Pirajá in Ipanema. Although the area is still considered to have

the hippest boutiques, Rio's residents have fallen in love with the experience of shopping in the larger malls, such as Rio Sul and Barra Shopping Center, the largest shopping and entertainment complex in Latin America. The historic districts of Centro and Copacabana (mainly the area along Avenida Nossa Senhora de Copacabana) cannot be overlooked, as it is here that most of Rio's quirky, special interest shops are found. The Hippie Fair is the best place to buy arts and crafts items, trinkets, curios, and souvenirs to take home as gifts.

Rio Sul, one of the two giant malls dominating Rio's shopping scene

Opening Hours

Most stores in Rio open from 9 or 10am in the morning until 6 or 7pm in the evening Monday to Friday, and between 9 or 10am until 1pm on Saturday. The big shopping malls, such as Barra Shopping and Rio Sul, stay open from 10am to 10pm Monday through Saturday and from 3 to 9pm on Sunday.

Most supermarkets are open from 8am to 10pm Monday to Saturday, with a limited selection remaining open on Sunday. There are also several 24-hour supermarkets scattered throughout the city.

Shopping Malls

Two giant malls have dominated Rio's shopping scene since the 1980s and offer just about anything people could want under one roof. The closest and most convenient for visitors staying in Copacabana and Ipanema is

the **Rio Sul** mall, which is located on the main artery linking the Sugar Loaf end of Copacabana to Botafogo and the city. Rio Sul has more than 400 stores, plus restaurants and cinemas. It also runs a free bus service that picks up shoppers from all the main hotels along the beachfront and drops them back with their purchases. Of course, there are always plenty of taxis at Rio Sul.

Barra Shopping Center (see p90), the largest shopping and entertainment complex in Latin America, can almost be treated as a tourist attraction in its own right. It has about 600 stores, as well as a good selection of bars and restaurants, and entertainment that includes a modern bowling alley, an 18-screen multiplex cinema, and a gaming area known as Hot Zone. Both Rio Sul and Barra Shopping Center have

branches of virtually all the top Brazilian retailers as well as some familiar international names. The two giant malls are not the only shows in town, and malls in every shape and size can be found all over Rio, including the popular **Fashion Mall** in São Conrado.

Jewelry

Brazil has huge deposits of precious and semi-precious gemstones, and, in some cases, holds more than 90 percent of the world's total supply. This has turned Brazil into one of the most important manufacturers of jewelry, both traditional and modern, and has made Rio de Janeiro into one of the jewel capitals of the world.

The two market leaders, **H. Stern** and **Amsterdam Sauer**, have stores in most of the city's major hotels, and at the airport. They also organize special jewelry tours at the Ipanema headquarters.

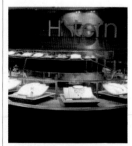

H. Stern, offering a wide range of traditional and modern jewelry

The famous Blue Man line of beachwear

Bikinis & Beachwear

The girls from Ipanema, Copacabana, and Barra have helped make the bikini a symbol of the city's lifestyle. Shops specializing in bikinis, swim, surf, and beachwear can be found all over Rio, especially in Copacabana, Ipanema, and all the big malls. Famous names in bikiniwear include **Blue Man**, **Bum-Bum**, and **Kitanga**.

What you wear to the beach is a fashion statement in Rio, so designs, shapes, and colors change with every season. Many stores offer a special line for visitors who find Brazilian fashions a bit daring.

Fashion Wear

Brazil features prominently in the international fashion scene, and Brazilians like to keep up with the latest trends. Walk around Ipanema or any of the large malls to get an idea of what is available. Items on display are usually of high quality and are also well priced.

Shoes

Brazil is one of the largest manufacturers of shoes and footwear in the world. Even the local supermarket is likely to stock fashionable flip-flops, and the two most famous brands are Havaianas and Grendha. The most popular stores, that sell well-made and reasonably priced leather shoes, are part of the **Mr. Cat** chain. Other stores worth checking include **Andarella** and Datelli.

Music

While no one music chain dominates in Rio, some music stores are better than others. **FNAC** megastore in Barra Shopping Center has a very good selection. **Biscoito Fino**, a music company that specializes in Brazilian music, especially *bossa nova*, has stands in Shopping da Gávea mall. Another top name is **Saraiva**, which has a large store in Rio Sul. Leading supermarkets, especially Lojas Americanas, sell cheap CDs.

Arts & Crafts Markets

The best and most famous arts and crafts market in Rio is the Hippie Fair, taking place every Sunday in and around Praça General Osório in Ipanema. The fair, which first began in 1968, runs from 8am to 6pm and is the perfect place to pick up souvenir paintings or Brazilian arts and craft works.

There are a number of specialized arts and crafts stores throughout the city, including those found in the Rio Sul and Barra Shopping Center malls. There is also a good selection in Copacabana, mostly along the historic Avenida Nossa Senhora de Copacabana, situated behind Copacabana Palace Hotel. In Ipanema, the H. Stern store has a good selection, as does **Brasil & Cia**.

Flip-flops

Ipanema's Hippie Fair, a great place for souvenir shopping

DIRECTORY

Shopping Malls

Barra Shopping Center
Av das Américas 4666, Barra da Tijuca.
Tel (21) 4003 4131.
W barrashopping.com.br

Fashion Mall
Estrada da Gávea 899, São Conrado.
Tel (21) 2111 4444.
W scfashionmall.com.br

Rio Sul
Rua Lauro Müller 116, Botafogo.
Tel (21) 3527 7257.
W riosul.com.br

Jewelry

Amsterdam Sauer
Rua Garcia d'Ávila 105, Ipanema. **Map** 2 A4.
Tel (21) 2512 1132.

H. Stern
Rua Garcia d'Ávila 113, Ipanema. **Map** 2 A4.
Tel (21) 2106 0000.

Bikinis & Beachwear

Blue Man
Rio Sul, Botafogo.
Tel (21) 2541 6896.

Bum-Bum
Rua Visconde Pirája 351, Ipanema. **Map** 2 B4.
Tel (21) 2287 9951.

Kitanga
Rua Santa Clara 70 loja 204, Copacabana.
Map 3 D2.
Tel (21) 2293 5053.
One of several branches.

Shoes

Andarella
Av Nossa Senhora de Copacabana 706, Copacabana. **Map** 3 D3.
Tel (21) 2236 2402.
W andarella.com.br
One of several branches.

Mr. Cat
Rua Visconde de Pirajá 414, Ipanema. **Map** 2 B4.
Tel (21) 2227 6521.
One of several branches.

Music

Biscoito Fino
Shopping da Gávea, Rua Marques de São Vicente 52.
Tel (21) 2540 7508.

FNAC
Barra Shopping Center.
Tel (21) 2109 2000.

Saraiva
Rio Sul, Botafogo.
Tel (21) 2543 7002.

Arts & Crafts Markets

Brasil & Cia
Rua Maria Quitéria 27, Ipanema. **Map** 2 A4.
Tel (21) 2267 4603.

ENTERTAINMENT IN RIO

As a major world city, Rio offers a wide variety of high-quality entertainment. However, these are targeted more toward local residents than casual tourists. The big local and international acts perform mainly for the Brazilians, and the same is true of what is presented at the theater, in the movie houses, clubs, and bars. Though some clubs offer a watered-down take on Brazilian culture, on the whole, visitors can enjoy a scintillating nightlife. The trendiest and most fashionable choices are found in Ipanema and Leblon, and around the Lagoa. Downtown Rio is also back in fashion, with Lapa being particularly popular when it comes to clubs and bars that play upbeat Brazilian music.

Information

For details of entertainment in Rio, check with the daily newspapers or their websites, most notably *O Globo* and *Jornal do Brasil*. For an update on on-going events, check *Veja Rio*, the special Rio supplement in Brazil's leading weekly news-magazine, *Veja*. It normally offers an accurate guide to the current scene. The concierge at any big hotel would also be of help.

Booking Tickets

Brazilians traditionally only buy their tickets at the very last moment. Even for the biggest events, tickets may go on sale only a few days ahead. In many cases, the tickets will be sold at the venue itself, or through an agency. Large ticket agencies, such as **Ticketmaster**, **Ticketronics**, and **Ingresso**, operate countrywide, and offer tickets to both events and particular venues.

Major Venues

Rio is an important venue and tour stop not only for the top names in Brazilian music, but also for all the leading inter-national acts. The major Brazilian acts tend to prefer to play in one of two big show houses in Rio, **HSBC Arena** and the **Citibank Hall** in Barra da Tijuca. Opened in 1967, Canecão has hosted many major concerts and a number of classic live Brazilian albums have been recorded here. Claro Hall, a purpose-built state-of-the-art facility, opened for business in 1994, with a show by Diana Ross.

Vivo Rio, located in the Modern Art Museum in Flamengo, puts on various shows. The **Cidade das Artes** in Barra is one of South America's largest concert halls and is home to the Brazilian Symphony Orchestra..

Smaller bands, or big names looking for a more intimate setting, also use the **Circo Voador** in Lapa and other smaller venues such as the **Teatro João Caetano** in Centro, the beautiful **Sala Baden Powell** in Copacabana, and even **Morro da Urca** on the halfway stage of Sugar Loaf *(see pp80–81)*.

The open-air venues of **Praça de Apoteose** and **Cidade do Rock** stage large acts. Even the Copacabana and Flamengo beaches sometimes hold free concerts.

Rio also hosts a number of festivals during the year that cover all genres. The largest and most famous festival is Rock in Rio, though this is not an annual event.

Over the years, Rio has offered a number of shows that primarily target the visitor who might want a quick, though somewhat over-simplified, version of the vast range of Brazilian culture. The glitziest show to outlast them all takes place daily at

Colorfully costumed *samba* performers in the floor show at Plataforma 1

Leblon's **Plataforma 1**. The kitschy variety show features *samba*, *bossa nova*, and other Brazilian sounds.

Samba, Bossa Nova & Gafieira

Most visitors to Rio will hope to catch a little live music and dance action when they are in town. While the big Brazilian acts will be found at Canecão and Claro Hall, there will also be a lot of artistes performing in smaller, more intimate venues, many of which are also bars and clubs.

Fans of *bossa nova* flock to **Vinícius** in Ipanema and **Bar do Tom** in Leblon. Celebrated for its outstanding music and a lively bar, the tiny **Bip Bip** in Copacabana is a well-frequented haven for MPB. **Arab** is a restaurant and bar in Lagoa that often hosts live music, including jazz, instrumental, and MBP.

Since the end of the 1990s, the reinvigorated nightlife in the city center has given a special boost to *samba* and *choro* (an upbeat waltz or polka). Lapa remains the main hub, with places such as **Carioca da Gema**, **Dama da Noite**, and **Rio Scenarium**. **Clube dos Democráticos** is a spacious club in Lapa particularly renowned for its *samba* and popular with a young crowd. Close by, in Praça Tiradentes, the **Centro Cultural Carioca** is known to host Brazilian music. Praça Mauá is also establishing itself on the nightlife scene. Head to Pedra do Sal, a small outdoor square where live *samba* and *choro* music are played on Friday, Saturday, and Monday evenings. Drinks and food are sold from street stalls around the square.

Even when the center of Rio was not in fashion, two clubs prospered there and still hold sway as the city's authentic ballrooms, or *gafieiras*. **Estudantina**, in Praça Tiradentes, dates from 1928, while the 1918 **Cordão da Bola Preta** in Lapa is the oldest carnival *bloco*. For those who

The Pé de Moleque group playing at the Carioca da Gema bar in Lapa

wish to learn the basics of dance there are a number of schools in Rio. The Centro Cultural Carioca offers beginner classes for individuals or groups for *samba*, *forró*, and *gafieira*.

Samba Schools

The number of shows and opportunities increase the closer it gets to Carnaval *(see pp68–9)*, with the "high season" for *samba* from December through February. However, those who are not visiting the city during this time can watch the *samba* schools in action.

The *samba* schools are also known to host programs featuring performances and other events at the **Cidade do Samba**, which opened in Centro in early 2006. Any good hotel will be able to organize a visit to the technical rehearsals or a guided tour of the Cidade do Samba.

People dancing to a live *gafieira* show in Rio Scenarium

Bars & Clubs

Rio enchants visitors with its unique range of bars and clubs. Bars go through every degree of sophistication, from periodically changing hot spots to those specializing in *cachaça* and *caipirinhas*, such as the popular **Academia da Cachaça** in Leblon and Barra. Enhancing the variety are several pub-like venues, the most famous of which is **Lord Jim** in Ipanema, while sophisticated bars in the top hotels offer a more formal elegance. Then there are the traditional *botequins*, or the corner bars, with plenty to eat and drink, well into the early hours. **Culinária Alemã** in Centro, **Lamas** in Flamengo, **Cervantes** in Copacabana, **Hipódromo** in Gavea, and **Bar Lagoa** on the Lagoa, have been drawing a steady clientele. Favored by visitors, **Garota de Ipanema** was where Tom Jobim and Vinícius de Moraes are said to have seen the girl who inspired them to write the song "A Garota de Ipanema." Trendy **Barril 1800**, an Ipanema landmark, attracts local celebs and tourists alike with its great atmosphere.

The line between bars, DJ bars, and clubs can get blurred in Rio, with a surfeit of bars offering dancing and music as the night goes on. The "in" venues change extremely quickly in terms of popularity and name. Therefore, it is always a good idea to ask a resident or the concierge at the hotel about the places that may be currently in vogue.

Gay & Lesbian

Rio has a very active gay and lesbian scene, much of which simply blends into the everyday life of the city. Among the most traditional gay and lesbian clubs are the upbeat **Le Boy** and **La Girl**, at the Ipanema end of Copacabana. **Dama de Ferro** is as popular.

A good starting point is Ipanema beach. The block running back from the beach also has a number of gay- and lesbian-friendly bars.

Eating Out

For many Cariocas, eating out *(see p382–3)* is an entertainment in its own right. Foreign visitors get the best value from dining at the *churrascaria rodizios*, the large barbecue houses with a fixed-price menu.

In Rio, trying traditional Brazilian cuisine normally means a *feijoada (see p384)*, a sumptuous feast usually served for lunch on Wednesday or Saturday.

Theater

Theater in Rio de Janeiro is of a high quality, but a majority of the productions will be in Portuguese. The main theaters, generally small and intimate, are found in Copacabana, Ipanema, and Leblon. In Centro, the **Centro Cultural Banco do Brasil** is a major venue. For listings, check *O Globo* and *Jornal do Brasil.*

Cinema

Brazil is one of the world's biggest cinema-going markets. However, the latest multiplex

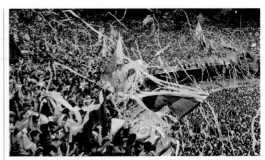
A soccer game in progress at the Estádio do Maracanã

operations all tend to be in Barra, such as the 18-screen **Cinemark**. Smaller and older theaters can be found in Copacabana and Ipanema.

International films quickly make their way into Brazil, and, unless they are aimed at children, will be left in their original language with subtitles added. At least one new Brazilian film is released each week, a few of which will go on to international acclaim.

Independent world cinema takes over the city each September and October, when the city's main film festival, Festival do Rio, holds public screenings.

Classical Music, Opera & Dance

Rio de Janeiro has a healthy and vibrant music, opera, and dance scene that is focused in the **Theatro Municipal** and the **Cidade das Artes** in Barra. Small concerts and recitals also use the **Sala Cecília Meireles** in Lapa.

Rio has its own music, opera, and dance companies, but also attracts the very best from the rest of Brazil and the world.

Helicopter Tours

One of the most popular tours with visitors to Rio, a helicopter ride takes people over the city and beaches, or around Sugar Loaf and Corcovado mountains.

Since 1991, **Helisight** has been offering eight different tours that vary from eight minutes to an hour. The most popular tours are those that circle Corcovado and the statue of Christ the Redeemer.

Helisight has modern heliports at Dona Marta, Morro da Urca, and the Lagoa. It also operates from Pier Maua when the cruise ships are in. Prices are much less than most people imagine.

Soccer

The mecca of soccer lovers, Rio is world-renowned for its abiding passion for the game. Matches take place all through the year, and are usually held on Wednesday evenings or Sunday afternoons. The city's four big clubs are Flamengo, Fluminense, Vasco da Gama, and Botafogo.

Almost synonymous with Brazil's legendary sport, the **Estádio do Maracanã** is widely acclaimed for hosting some of the best soccer matches.

Horse Racing

Unusual as it may seem to list it among the entertainment options, horse racing at the **Jóquei Club Brasileiro** on the Lagoa takes place four times a week. On Monday and Friday evenings, one can enjoy drinks or dinner in the members' stand, and watch the racing go on under the floodlights.

An aerial view of the Helisight heliport at Morro da Urca

DIRECTORY

Information

Jornal do Brasil
🆆 jbonline.terra.
com.br

O Globo
🆆 oglobo.globo.com

Booking Tickets

Ingresso
🆆 ingresso.com.br

Ticketmaster
🆆 ticketmaster.com.br

Ticketronics
🆆 ticketronics.com.br

Major Venues

Cidade das Artes
Trevo das Palmeiras, Barra.

Cidade do Rock
Av Salvador Allende, Barra
da Tijuca.

Circo Voador
Rua dos Arcos, Lapa.
Map 5 D5.
Tel (21) 2533 0354.

Citibank Hall
Av Ayrton Senna 3000,
Barra da Tijuca.

HSBC Arena
Av Embaixador Abelardo
Bueno 3401, Barra da
Tijuca.
Tel (21) 3035 5200.

Morro da Urca
Av Pasteur 520, Praia
Vermelha, Urca.
Tel (21) 2546 8400.

Plataforma 1
Rua Adalberto Ferreira 32,
Leblon.
Tel (21) 2274 4022.

Praça da Apoteose
Rua Marquês de Sapucaí,
Cidade Nova.
Map 4 A5.
Tel (21) 2563 9000.

Sala Baden Powell
Av Nossa Senhora de
Copacabana 360,
Copacabana.
Map 3 D3.
Tel (21) 2548 0421.

Teatro João Caetano
Praça Tiradentes, Centro.
Map 4 C4.
Tel (21) 2332 9257.

Vivo Rio
Av Infante Dom Henrique
85, Flamengo.
Tel (21) 2272 2901.

Samba, Bossa Nova & Gafieira

Arab
Av Borges de Medeiros,
Parque dos Patins, Kiosk 7.
Map 1 B2.
Tel (21) 2540 0742.

Bar do Tom
Rua Adalberto Ferreira 32,
Leblon. **Map** 1 A4.
Tel (21) 2274 4022.

Bip Bip
Rua Almirante Gonçalves
50, Copacabana.
Map 2 C4.
Tel (21) 2267 9696.

Carioca da Gema
Av Mem de Sá 79, Lapa.
Map 5 D5.
Tel (21) 2221 0043.

**Centro Cultural
Carioca**
Rua do Teatro 37, Praça
Tiradentes, Centro.
Map 4 C4.
Tel (21) 2252 6468.

**Clube dos
Democráticos**
Rua Riachuelo 91, Lapa.
Map 4 C5.
Tel (21) 2252 4611.

Cordão da Bola Preta
Rua da Relação 3, Lapa.
Map 4 C4.
Tel (21) 2240 8049.

Dama da Noite
Ave Gomes Freire 773,
Lapa. **Map** 4 C5.
Tel (21) 2509 4237.

Estudantina
Praça Tiradentes 79,
Centro.
Map 4 C4.
Tel (21) 2232 1149.

Rio Scenarium
Rua do Lavradio 20, Lapa.
Map 4 C4.
Tel (21) 3147 9000.

Vinícius
Rua Vinícius de Moraes
39, Ipanema.
Map 2 B4.
Tel (21) 2287 1497.

Samba Schools

Cidade do Samba
Rua Rivadávia Correa 60,
Gamboa.
Tel (21) 2213 2503.

Bars & Clubs

Academia da Cachaça
Rua Conde Bernadotte 26,
Leblon.
Tel (21) 2239 1542.
Av Armando Lombardi
800, Barra.
Tel (21) 2492 1159.

Bar Lagoa
Av Epitácio Pessoa 1674,
Lagoa. **Map** 2 A4.
Tel (21) 2523 1135.

Barril 1800
Av Vieira Souto 110,
Ipanema. **Map** 2 B5.
Tel (21) 2523 0085.

Cervantes
Av Prado Júnior 335,
Copacabana. **Map** 3 F1.
Tel (21) 2275 6147.

Culinária Alemã
Rua da Carioca 39, Centro.
Map 5 D4.
Tel (21) 2262 6900.

Garota de Ipanema
Rua Vinícius de Moraes
49, Ipanema. **Map** 2 A5.
Tel (21) 2523 3787.

Hipódromo
Praça Santos Dumont
108, Gávea.
Tel (21) 2274 9720.

Lamas
Rua Marquês de Abrantes
18, Flamengo.
Tel (21) 2556-0799.

Lord Jim
Rua Paul Redfern 63,
Ipanema. **Map** 1 C4.
Tel (21) 2259 3047.

Gay & Lesbian

Dama de Ferro
Rua Vinícius de Moraes
288, Ipanema. **Map** 2 B4.
Tel (21) 2247 2330.

La Girl
Rua Raul Pompéia 102,
Copacabana.
Map 2 C4.
Tel (21) 2247 8342.

Le Boy
Rua Raul Pompéia 102,
Copacabana.
Map 2 C4.
Tel (21) 2513 4993.

Theater

**Centro Cultural
Banco do Brasil**
Rua Primeiro de Março 66,
Centro. **Map** 5 E3.
Tel (21) 3808 2020.

Cinema

Cinemark
Av das Américas,
Barra da Tijuca.
Tel (21) 2494 5007.

Classical Music, Opera & Dance

Sala Cecília Meireles
Largo da Lapa 47.
Map 5 D5.
Tel (21) 2332 9176.

Theatro Municipal
Av Rio Branco.
Map 5 E4.
Tel (21) 2332 9195.

Helicopter tours

Helisight
Rua Conde de Bernadotte
26, sl. 119. **Map** 1 A4.
Tel (21) 2511 2141 (week-
days), (21) 2542 7895 (Sat,
Sun & public hols).

Soccer

Estádio do Maracanã
Rua Eurico Rabelo, São
Cristóvão.
Tel (21) 2334 1705.

Horse Racing

**Jóquei Clube
Brasileiro**
Rua Jardim Botânico
1003. **Map** 1 A2, A3,
B2, B3.
Tel (21) 3534 9000.

RIO DE JANEIRO CITY STREET FINDER

Map references given in this guide for entertainment venues and other attractions in Rio City refer to the Street Finder maps on the following pages. Map references are also provided for Rio City restaurants (see pp386–8) and hotels (see pp370–71). The first figure in the map reference indicates which Street Finder map to turn to, and the letter and number which follow refer to the grid reference on that map. The map below shows the different areas of Rio City – Leblon, Copacabana, Ipanema, and Centro – covered by the five Street Finder maps. Symbols used for sights and useful information are displayed in the key below. A list of important places of interest marked on the maps can be found on page 72.

Key

- ▦ Place of interest
- ▦ Other building
- 🚆 Train station
- ⛴ Ferry terminal
- Ⓜ Metro station
- Ⓜ Metro station under construction (opens 2016)
- 𝒊 Visitor information
- ✚ Hospital
- 🏛 Police station
- ✝ Church
- ═ Railroad
- ▬ Pedestrian street

Scale of Maps 1 & 2–3

0 meters		400
0 yards		400

Scale of Map 4–5

0 meters	200
0 yards	200

Streetwise in Rio

Though street crime is prevalent in Rio, a few precautions could help to prevent it from happening.

Contrary to general belief, it is probably best to avoid taking a stroll on the deserted streets of Centro on Sundays. Praça Mauá, just to the north of Centro, is best avoided after nightfall. Lapa, a popular nightspot in Rio, must be explored with great caution.

It is advisable not to wander unaccompanied around the darker corners of the Parque do Flamengo, or to walk between Cosmo Velho and Corcovado late at night. Robbery and assault in these areas are common.

Passengers taking a bus are easy targets for thieves, and need to be vigilant. Taxis are plentiful and inexpensive, so avoid walking along empty and unfamiliar streets.

Make sure the driver turns on the meter and ask for an estimate of the average fare to your destination.

Various instances of bag-snatching are common on the crowded beaches of Copacabana and Ipanema, especially during the weekends, so visitors must keep a keen eye on their belongings. Again, do not go down to the water after dark. Stay on the well-lit, busy sidewalks.

D   **E**   **F**   **5**

Baía de Guanabara

1

PIER MAUÁ

MORRO DA SÃO BENTO

PONTE ALM. ARNALDO LUZ

Ilha das Cobras

PRAÇA MAUÁ

Mosteiro de São Bento

R DOM GERARDO

2

R VISCONDE INHAÚMA

R BENEDITINOS

RUA ARCE

R MAYRINK

VEIGA

Espaço Cultural da Marinha

Niterói

Nossa Senhora da Candelária

Casa França-Brasil

AV RIO BRANCO

RUA PRIMEIRO DE MARÇO

useu Antônio go

PRAÇA PIO X

RUA DA ALFÂNDEGA

R MIGUEL COUTA

AIRES

RUA DE BUENOS

RUA DO ROSÁRIO

RUA DO OUVIDOR

RUA DO MERCADO

Estação de Barcas

ARGAS

guaiana **M**

CENTRO

RUA DO OUVIDOR

RUA URUGUAIANA

RUA GONÇALVES DIAS

RUA DA QUITANDA

RUA 7 DE SETEMBRO

RUA SÃO JOSÉ

PRAÇA XV DE NOVEMBRO

Paço Imperial

3

Confeitaria Colombo

RUA ASSEMBLÉIA

Palácio Tiradentes

Museu Naval e Oceanográfico

DE TEATRO

UA 7 DE SETEMBRO

R ERASMO BRAGA

Museu Histórico Nacional

UA DA CARIOCA

AV NILO PEÇANHA

AV PRES. ANTÔNIO CARLOS

AV GENERAL JUSTO

PRAÇA DO EXPEDICIONÁRIO

Igreja de São Francisco da Penitência

LARGO DA CARIOCA

M Carioca

AV ALM. BARROSO

N.S. do Bonsucesso

Catedral Presb.

AV RIO BRANCO

AV REP. DO CHILE

Museu Nacional de Belas Artes

R ARAÚJO PORTO ALEGRE

Santa Casa de Misericórdia

R DE SANTA LUZIA

AV MARECHAL CÂMARA

4

Theatro Municipal

R MÉXICO

GRAÇA

Palácio da Cultura

AV CHURCHILL

REPÚBLICA DO PARAGUAI

RUA SENADOR DANTAS

ARANHA

Santa Luzia

AV F. ROOSEVELT

Catedral etropolitana

Est. de Bondes

RUA EVARISTO DA VEIGA

RUA DE SANTA LUZIA

SANTA LUZIA

PRAÇA VERGÍLIO DE MELO FRANCO

RAÇAMONS RANCISCO PINTO

M Cinelândia

AV RIO BRANCO

PRES. WILSON

PRAÇA SENADOR SALGADO FILHO

Aeroporto Santos Dumont

R DOS

Teatro Mesbla

PRAÇA DO MONROE

TREVO DOS ESTUDANTES

Circo ador

ARCOS

R DO PASSEIO

AV INFANTE DOM HENRIQUE

AV J. NEVES DE FONTOURA

AV ALMIRANTE SILVIO DE NORONHA

Arcos da Lapa

Museu Instrumental

PRAÇA CARD. CÂMARA

PASSEIO PÚBLICO

RUA JARDEL JERCOLIS

Museu de Arte Moderna

5

LAPA

R TEIXEIRA DE FREITA

RUA DE LAPA

PRAÇA DEODORO

Santa Teresa

PRAÇA PARIS

PARQUE DO FLAMENGO

Enseada da Glória

D   **E**   **F**

RIO DE JANEIRO & ESPÍRITO SANTO

Beyond the capital cities of Rio and Vitória, the magnificent scenery dominating the areas continues unchecked by rapid modernization. Along the coast are giant boulder-strewn mountains, while farther inland are the steep, lushly forested ridges of the Mata Atlântica. Spectacular beaches, picturesque islands, and several resort towns are among the area's other attractions.

Stretching north and south of Rio City are long strands of beaches and half-moon coves lapped or pounded by a bottle-green Atlantic and visited by troops of sea turtles. Some surround the popular resort towns of Búzios, "discovered" by Brigitte Bardot in the 1960s, and Cabo Frio, while others lie close to the colonial port of Paraty, which once lay at the end of the mule route from the gold mines of Minas Gerais. Its cobbled streets are better preserved than others on the southeastern coast.

Inland, the steep ridges of the Mata Atlântica begin to rise vertiginously towards Minas Gerais and São Paulo, protecting a string of national and state parks, including Itatiaia and the Serra dos Órgãos, in their folds. This area, considered one of the world's biodiversity hot spots, has an astounding 950 species of birds and 40 percent of the plants here are unique, including the cattleya orchid, referred to as the "Queen of Flowers." The largest among the islands, Ilha Grande has no roads. Steep walking trails leave its only town Abraão, to cut through the forest to still more beaches deserted but for surfboards and fishing shacks.

The Espírito Santo coast is equally beautiful with its mountains, beaches, and small towns. One of them, Itaúnas, is backed by sand dunes large enough to swallow it. A stunning sight here is Pedra Azul, a granite monolith which changes from slate gray to fiery orange with the passage of the sun.

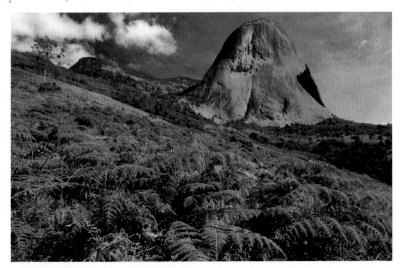

Pedra Azul, a spectacular granite monolith in Espírito Santo

◄ Colorful fishing boats lined up along the coast of Paraty, Rio de Janeiro state

Exploring Rio de Janeiro & Espírito Santo

Several towns pepper the coast of Rio de Janeiro state. Among these, Búzios draws the most visitors and has the best hotels and restaurants, while the colonial town of Paraty, nestled between the coastal mountains and an island-strewn sea, is emerging as a center for the arts. North of Rio is the imperial city of Petrópolis. Brazil's oldest national park, Itatiaia, lies just off the interstate between Rio and São Paulo. Ilha Grande, off the coast of Rio, and the resorts of northern Espírito Santo are relatively untouched. Vitória, the state's capital, dates to the 1550s. To its south is the beach town of Guarapari, while inland is the dramatic peak of Pedra Azul.

Statue of King Dom Pedro II, the founder of the magnificent city of Petrópolis

Lush Mata Atlântica in Parque Nacional do Itatiaia, Rio de Janeiro

Sights at a Glance

Towns & Cities

- ❶ Paraty pp110–12
- ❷ Angra dos Reis
- ❺ Petrópolis pp116–19
- ❻ Teresópolis
- ❾ Guarapari
- ❿ Vitória
- ⓬ Itaúnas

National Parks & Areas of Natural Beauty

- ❸ Ilha Grande
- ❹ Parque Nacional do Itatiaia
- ❼ Parque Nacional da Serra dos Órgãos
- ❽ Búzios pp120–21
- ⓫ Pedra Azul

Getting Around

The Rio and Espírito Santo coasts are served by the well signposted BR-101 interstate highway. Rio de Janeiro state has a good interstate bus service to all the beach towns. The Mata Atlântica, however, is best visited on a tour or with a hired car, as are the national parks of Itatiaia and Serra dos Órgãos. To visit northern and central Espírito Santo, visitors will need their own transport. Ilha Grande can be reached by passenger ferry twice a day.

Key

═══ Highway
━━━ Major road
⋯⋯⋯ Minor road
∼∼∼ Railroad
▬▬▬ State border
△ Peak

Colorful boats anchored on the Paraty shore

For keys to symbols *see back flap*

❶ Paraty

One of the most photographed colonial towns on the Brazilian coast, Paraty has been a UNESCO World Heritage Site since 1958. Though settled by the Portuguese in the 16th century, it was developed a century later as an important port from where gold was shipped to Europe. Extremely charming, the whitewashed churches and terra-cotta roofs offset the lush green of the rainforest-clad mountains, and the placid bay whose emerald waters lap at the town's quay. Paraty has an impressive literary tradition; the annual Festa Literária Internacional de Paraty (FLIP) is a big draw. It is also an ideal base for exploring the dazzling Brazilian coastline, and boasts lovely *pousadas* (exclusive hotels).

Statue of St. Benedict, Nossa Senhora do Rosário e São Benedito

Sturdy iron bars of the Casa de Cadeia, a former prison

🏛 Casa de Cadeia

Rua Travessa Santa Rita. **Tel** (24) 3371 1056. **Open** 9am–5pm daily. 🅿 📷 ✉

The 18th-century Casa de Cadeia served as the town's prison until 1890. Retaining its original iron prison bars, this building now serves as the public library, besides housing the Casa do Artesão (Artisan's House).

🏛 Santa Rita dos Pardos Libertos

Largo da Santa Rita. **Open** 9am–noon, 2–5pm Wed–Sun. 🅿 ✉

The façade of Paraty's oldest church now graces travel brochures of the city. It was built in 1722 by, and for, all those considered not white enough to attend the church of the ruling elite. These would have included the illegitimate offspring of the aristocracy, their children in turn, indigenous people, and freed slaves. In design the church is typically Jesuit, with three windows in the upper chancel and a curvilinear door. Except for the beautifully worked altarpiece in the sanctuary and fine woodwork on the doorways its interior is plain. Deconsecrated in the 20th century, the church now serves as the sparse Museu de Arte Sacra. Displayed religious artifacts include gold and silver remonstrances.

🔼 Nossa Senhora do Rosário e São Benedito

Rua Tenente Francisco Antônio. **Open** 9am–noon, 2–5pm Tue–Sun. 🅿 ✉

Slaves worshipped at Nossa Senhora do Rosário e São Benedito, which was built in 1725. The interior of this humble church is almost entirely free of embellishment, except for heavy gilt on the altarpiece. However, it retains a simple dignity and a sacred atmosphere. Its design resembles the Minas Gerais chapels of the same period. Every November, locals celebrate A Festa dos Santos (Feast of All Saints) here, where they remember some of the building's historical past. Mass is followed by a procession where churchgoers carry figures of a king and queen, recalling the Maracatú monarchs of Pernambuco, and icons of the various saints.

Paraty's whitewashed buildings reflected in the placid waters at the quay

For hotels and restaurants in this region see pp372–3 and p388

🏛 Matriz Nossa Senhora dos Remédios

Praça Monsenhor Helio Pires. **Open** 8am–noon Mon, Wed, Fri, Sat, 8am–noon, 2–5pm Sun. 🏛 ✉

Originally meant for the white elite, this stately church took 100 years to build, owing to financial constraints. When it was near completion in 1873, the architects discovered that Paraty's soil was too muddy to support the planned twin towers. It was left in its current squat state, slowly subsiding to the left. Today, it serves as a parish church.

🏛 Nossa Senhora das Dores

Rua Fresca. **Open** 9am–noon, 2–5pm Tue–Sun. ✉

The colonial aristocracy also attended the graceful chapel of Nossa Senhora das Dores. Built in 1800, it was renovated in 1901 and administered by the nuns of the convent of Our Lady of Sorrows. Just as the rest of Paraty's churches, it has an unembellished interior, although there is some fine carving on the balustrades in the upper chancel. A catacomb-like cemetery adjoins the chapel.

🏛 Forte Defensor Perpétuo

Morro do Forte. **Open** 9am–noon, 2–5pm Wed–Sun. 🏛 Centro de Artes e Tradições Populares: **Open** 10am–5pm Tue–Sun. ✉

Located on the northern headland, just outside town, this 19th-century fort looks more like an elongated squat town house. Rusted cannons and remnants of a wall sit in front of it. The Centro de Artes e Tradições Populares (Center for Popular Art) occupies its principal room, displaying local handicrafts and items related to the traditional way of life of the local people.

Cannons resting outside Forte Defensor Perpétuo

Paraty

① Casa de Cadeia
② Santa Rita dos Pardos Libertos
③ Nossa Senhora do Rosário e São Benedito
④ Matriz Nossa Senhora dos Remédios
⑤ Nossa Senhora das Dores
⑥ Forte Defensor Perpétuo

0 meters 150
0 yards 150

For keys to symbols *see back flap*

Beaches Around Paraty

Paraty, with its forest-swathed spurs of the coastal mountains, lies at the heart of a beautiful stretch of coastline. A short way offshore are a string of islands. Until only a few decades ago, this area was little-known even to Brazilian holiday makers. Much of the area, surrounded by a wealth of exotic flora and fauna, is protected by national and state parks. The islands can be reached by boat from Paraty town, or the nearby Paraty-Mirim.

Beaches & Islands Around Paraty

The small town of **Trindade**, 13 miles (21 km) south of Paraty, is popular with surfers from São Paulo. It offers a choice of simply appointed *pousadas* and some pretty beaches connected by footpaths. The scenic beach running south of Trindade, **Praia de Fora**, is backed by forest-covered hills. **Praia do Meio** is a long stretch of fine sand, washed by waves perfect for bodysurfing. **Laranjeiras**, a small distance downhill, is the hideaway for Rio's super-rich who flock to its private condo-miniums. Trails lead from here through the forest to a string of pristine beaches to the south. **Praia do Cepilho** is one of the best surfing spots along this stretch of coast.

Located 21 miles (34 km) from Paraty, **Ilha do Breu** is a tiny private island dominated by a single *pousada*. The owner breeds rare golden lion tamarins, which he lets run free on his island. He also maintains a small aviary, and has planted trees to attract Atlantic rainforest birds. **Poço das Andorinhas**, one of the many waterfalls in the region, is a popular spot for bathing.

Exploring Around Paraty

The bays and islands off Paraty are a favorite playground for Brazil's rich elite, who moor their expensive yachts in the Paraty Marina and fly in to the adjacent airport in their private jets for a weekend cruise.

Paraty's city beach, close to the historic center, is **Praia do Pontal** and it lies across the Rio Perequê-Açu. The water is not very clean, but the *barracas* (restaurants) are pleasant. A shallow and spacious beach, **Praia do Jabaquara**, is within walking distance of Paraty town. A glorious long beach, **Paraty-Mirim**, lies 17 miles (27 km) east of town, and can be reached by a bumpy dirt road. Just south, **Saco de Mamanguá** is lined with old fishing villages and plush holiday homes. A deep sleeve of water, it is good for snorkeling. **Ilha dos Meros**, 9 miles (14 km) northeast of Paraty, is another snorkeling spot, though marine life is limited to large shoals of sheepshead bream and the occasional turtle.

Secluded scenic Praia de Fora near Trindade

Mata Atlântica

The Atlantic coastal forest, or Mata Atlântica, is one of the best bird-watching sites in the world, with 950 resident species, almost 200 of which are endemic. It once covered the lowlands and coastal mountains from Rio Grande do Norte to Rio Grande do Sul. Today, less than 5 percent remains, concentrated mainly in Rio de Janeiro, Minas Gerais, São Paulo, and Paraná. Its proximity to the Atlantic blesses it with heavy rainfall. The vegetation is thick with epiphytic plants, and the forest is particularly rich in breathtaking orchid species. There are many rare mammals too, including the most endangered primate in the world, the woolly spider monkey, as well as several striking species of uniquely colored marmosets and tamarins.

Epiphytes are plants encrusting every available nook and cranny of the larger trees, drawing moisture directly from air.

Clearwater streams cut across the thick forest, which receives heavy rainfall, especially in the Southeast.

Vegetation at the water's edge tends to consist of fast-growing species that quickly replenish their numbers after floods.

BRAZIL

Locator Map
◼ Mata Atlântica

Biodiversity

Mata Atlântica is one of the world's most biodiverse regions, with some 20,000 plant species, 40 percent of which are endemic, and one of the highest numbers of threatened or endangered vertebrates in the world.

The seven-colored tanager is one of the local species listed as endangered or threatened by CITES.

The cattleya orchid, the world's most famous orchid genus, was discovered by Englishman William Cattley in 1818.

The woolly monkey, among South America's largest primates, can weigh more than 13 lb (6 kg).

The golden lion tamarin, one of the three lion tamarin species, lives on a few islands and in the Atlantic forest.

Ocelots, the third-largest of Brazil's eight indigenous big cats, are most abundant in southern São Paulo.

The Costa Verde

The Costa Verde (Green Coast) stretching south of Rio, past Paraty and Trindade (see pp110–12), deserves its name. Rainforests swathe the coastal mountains, which reach almost 9,143 ft (2,787 m) in the alpine meadows and the forests of Parque Nacional do Itatiaia. From here, they plunge down into steep ridges to meet an emerald ocean, tinged with turquoise at numerous long sandy beaches. Beyond are a scattering of breathtaking islands set in aquamarine and sitting in the deep, bottle-green Atlantic. The largest, Ilha Grande, is particularly lush, with trees covering its rocky mountains and sheltering its spectacular strands of fine white sand. The island is also the playground for the rich, who host extravagant parties in the summer.

❷ Angra dos Reis

Rio de Janeiro. 🏙 180,000. 🚢 from Rio. 🛈 Av Ayrton Senna 580, (24) 3367 7826. 🅆 angra-dos-reis.com

This unprepossessing port is today mainly a jumping-off point for the islands of Ilha Grande and Ilha da Gipóia. It was once a charming colonial town and vestiges of its once dignified past are hidden among the ever-expanding *favelas*. Angra dos Reis was once as pretty a town as Paraty. The main church, **Nossa Senhora da Conceição**, was built in 1626 in front of the docks, while the nearby **Nossa Senhora do Carmo** dates from 1593. The colonial naval complex lies some 2 miles (3 km) north of the town center towards the Praia do Bonfim.

Environs

Ilha da Gipóia, an hour's boat ride off the port of Angra dos Reis, is the second-largest island in the bay after Ilha Grande, and is known for its stunning white-sand beaches such as Jurubaíba, Praia do Dentista, and Norte. Most of the beaches here are bustling with bars floating offshore, which can be reached by the yachts and boats that ply the waters of the bay.

The forested **Serra do Mar** lies 25 miles (40 km) inland from Angra. On weekends and holidays, visitors can take a picturesque train journey there. Train tickets should be booked a day in advance from the tourist office.

Town church in Vila do Abraão, Ilha Grande, against a lush backdrop

❸ Ilha Grande

Rio de Janeiro. 🏙 6,000. 🚢 from Angra dos Reis. 🛈 Parque Estadual Peig, Av Beira Mar, Vila do Abraão, (24) 9922 9614. 🚤 Vila do Abraão. 🅆 ilhagrande.com.br

The most romantic and pretty of southeastern Brazil's many islands, Ilha Grande remains unspoilt by development and heavy tourism. The only settlement of any size is the two-street **Vila do Abraão**, the port town and main village on the island. Tour operators and hotels in Abraão offer a range of trips around the island, many of them on pretty, painted wooden fishing boats. The most popular trip is to the sheltered cove at **Palmas**, to the east of the village, from where a trail leads to **Lopes Mendes** to the east, one of Ilha Grande's longest beaches, washed by powerful surf. Other trips include snorkeling in the clear waters of the Saco do Céu or visits to the 18th-century **Igreja de Santana** at Freguesia de Santana.

Self-guided trails from Abraão lead throughout the island. Many of them are steep and rocky, but offer wonderful views out over the Atlantic. The most challenging is to the 3,248-ft- (990-m-) high peak of Pico do Papagaio.

Although most of the 75-sq-mile (193-sq-km) island now forms part of the Parque Estadual da Ilha Grande, Ilha Grande's pristine state owes more to its long isolation than to efforts at conservation. From the earliest colonial days the island was a notorious pirate lair. It then became a landing port for slaves destined for Rio and in the late 20th century an infamous prison for political prisoners. Ruins of the prison buildings remain, covered in thick vegetation.

Pristine beach alcove surrounded by lush green forest, Ilha Grande

Steep mountain ridges in Parque Nacional do Itatiaia, Brazil's oldest national park

❹ Parque Nacional do Itatiaia

Rio de Janeiro. 🚌 from Resende.
ℹ️ Centro Excursionista Brasileiro,
Av Almirante Barroso 2, 8th floor, Rio,
(21) 2252 9844. 🌐 ecoralph.com 📷
Ralph Salgueiro, (24) 3351 1823. 🏨
Hotel Donati, (24) 3352 1110.
🌐 hoteldonati.com.br

Brazil's oldest national park, Parque Nacional do Itatiaia, was founded in 1937. It was established to protect the high alpine meadows and the gradations of thick Atlantic rainforests that cover its steep mountain ridges. It is the only part of Rio de Janeiro state ever to see snow, albeit rarely.

The scenery here is magnificent. The highest regions of the park are capped with giant boulders, eroded into strange organic shapes by millions of years of rain and wind. They sit on expansive grassland coursed by babbling brooks, which become fast-flowing, clear-water rivers once they reach the warmer forested areas below. Here they tumble, roar, and fall over waterfalls and rapids.

The trees around them are busy with primates. Curious brown capuchin monkeys are a common sight on the numerous trails. Scarcer are the beautiful and shy black-faced titi monkeys, a threatened species.

Birdlife, too, is prolific in the park, which is home to 350 species, many of which are endangered. The park plays a crucial role in their conservation. Dusky-legged guans wander along the park's few paved roads, brilliant seven-colored and black and gold cotingas flit about with toucans, and the early morning air buzzes with the sound of dozens of different hummingbirds.

The park can be crowded on weekends when Brazilian families romp in the numerous waterfalls and wildlife makes itself scarce. But during the week the various trails are deserted and quiet. The ranger station provides rather poor walking maps but the trails are fairly clear. Hotel Donati, which is the best hotel in the park, can organize walking tours and, with advance notice, wildlife guides.

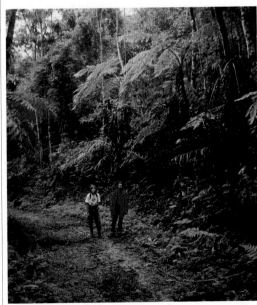

Trail through the verdant rainforests of Parque Nacional do Itatiaia

❺ Petrópolis

Located in the mountains near Rio, Petrópolis owes its creation to the Brazilian royal family. Dom Pedro I's dream of building a summer residence here was fulfilled by his son, Dom Pedro II, who was equally taken by the charms of the region. In 1843, before construction of the palace began, he decreed the creation of Petrópolis as the summer seat of his government. The city soon rose in importance, as trappings of royalty made their mark. Today, Petrópolis is popular for its royal attractions, as well as for its mountain scenery and the national park of Serra dos Órgãos (see p119).

🏛 Palácio Imperial
See pp118–19.

🏛 Palácio Rio Negro
Av Koeller 255, Centro. **Tel** (24) 2426 2423. **Open** 10am–5pm Tue–Sat.

Built in 1889 by Barão do Rio Negro, a wealthy coffee baron, the palace acted as the seat of the state government between 1894 and 1902, when Petrópolis was the capital of Rio de Janeiro state.

Between 1903 and 1960, the palace served as the summer residence of the presidents of the Republic. While Vargas converted a wine cellar into a Roman-style bathhouse, Kubitschek added built-in closets. All the original rooms are in excellent condition.

Exterior of French-Gothic Catedral de São Pedro de Alcântara

⛪ Catedral de São Pedro de Alcântara
Rua São Pedro de Alcântara 60, Centro. **Tel** (24) 2242 4300. **Open** 9am–6pm daily.

Though the cathedral's first stone was laid in 1884 by Dom Pedro II, much of its current structure dates from 1925. Built in French-Gothic style with a beautiful rose window, it has a striking interior decorated in Carrara marble. The walls here depict detailed scenes from the Crucifixion.

The Imperial Chapel, to the right of the main entrance, contains the mortal remains of King Dom Pedro II, Princess Regent Dona Teresa Cristina, their daughter Isabel, her husband Count d'Eu, and several other members of the royal family. Statues of the royal family are also featured inside the chapel. The 1848 baptismal font is the original.

🏛 Palácio de Cristal
Rua Alfredo Pachá, Centro. **Tel** (24) 2247 3721. **Open** 9am–6pm Tue–Sun.

The metal structure and glass enclosure of the Palácio de Cristal (Crystal Palace) were made in France in 1879 and shipped to Brazil. Inaugurated on February 2, 1884, the palace is a fine example of the architectural style that emerged during the French industrial revolution.

Although it was originally planned as a greenhouse for growing orchids, the Palácio de Cristal was later meant to be an exhibition hall for hosting regular displays of local products. However, it ended up as the imperial ballroom, and has been the sight of many spectacular

parties. Most momentous were the extravagant balls hosted by Princess Isabel and Count d'Eu, who is believed to have conceived the palace's basic design. It was during one such event in 1888 that Isabel signed an order liberating 103 slaves. On May 13 of the same year, Isabel went on to sign the Lei Aurea (Golden Law), the decree that, in theory, abolished slavery in Brazil.

Detail on the façade of Palácio Rio Negro

The metal-and-glass exhibition hall at the Palácio de Cristal

Although most of its former glory is lost, the palace today serves as an exhibition hall. It occasionally hosts art shows and cultural events.

Casa de Santos Dumont

Rua do Encanto 22, Centro. **Tel** (24) 2247 3158. **Open** 9:30am–5pm Tue–Sun.

In 1918, the great Brazilian aviator and inventor of the wristwatch, Alberto Santos Dumont (1873–1932), designed and built his summerhouse in the style of a French alpine chalet and named it "A Encantada," or enchanted. The three floors contain a workroom, a lounge-cum-dining room, a bedroom, and an office. The alcohol-heated shower in the bathroom was the first of its kind in Brazil. There is no kitchen because Dumont had all his meals sent in by the then Palace Hotel.

The fascinating personal collection of this delightful inventor includes everyday objects, such as furniture, photographs, and various artifacts, including beautiful vases and lamps.

Quitandinha

Av Joaquim Rolla 2. **Tel** (24) 2245 2020. **Open** 10am–5pm Tue–Sat, 10am–4pm Sun & public hols.

An imposing palace built in Norman style, Quitandinha is located southwest of the town center. Entrepreneur Joaquim Rolla built it in 1944 to be the largest casino complex in South America. For the exterior, Rolla copied the large casinos that were popular at the time along the Normandy coast, while the interior was by Dorothy Drape, a famous Hollywood set designer.

Quitandinha's glory ended in 1946, when President Dutra banned gambling. Remarkably well preserved, today it is mainly used for conventions and other events. Its interior still recalls the glamorous days of the 1940s when the guests were kings, queens, and Hollywood stars.

Casa de Rui Barbosa

Catedral de São Pedro de Alcântara ③

AVENIDA IPIRANGA

RUA 13 DE MAIO

Palácio de Princesa Isabel

PRAÇA PRINCESA ISABEL

R SÃO P EDRO DE ALCÂNTARA

RUA R DE LEÓN

RUA TAM ANDARÉ

AVENIDA TIRADENTES

Quitandinha AVENIDA KOELER

Palácio de Cultura

Palácio Rio Negro

Palácio Amarelo

PRAÇA VISCONDE DE MAUÁ

RUA DA IMPERATRIZ

Salão das Viaturas

RUA D PEDRO I

RUA D ANGELO

① Palácio Imperial

RUA M DETZI

PRAÇA DOM PEDRO II

RUA 16 DE MARÇO

| 0 meters | 500 |
| 0 yards | 500 |

Petrópolis

The Norman-style architecture of the Quitandinha palace complex

For keys to symbols *see back flap*

Petrópolis: Palácio Imperial

Built by Dom Pedro II between 1845 and 1864, the Neo-Classical Imperial Palace was used by the Emperor as his summer residence every year from 1848 until the end of the monarchy and declaration of independence in 1889. In that year, the palace was leased out as a college, and continued to function as such until President Vargas passed a decree in 1943 creating the Imperial Museum. Among the highlights of the museum, which faithfully reflect the daily life of the Brazilian royal family, are the Imperial Crown Jewels, as well as other artifacts, paintings, and furniture that belonged to the Emperor and his family.

★ Crown Jewels
The Imperial Crown of Dom Pedro II is the most valuable piece in the collection and was made for his coronation on July 18, 1841, when he was just 15 years old.

Sala do Primeiro Reinado
This room features the last painting of Dom Pedro I in Brazil prior to his abdication on April 7, 1831.

★ Cetro
The Imperial Scepter, depicting an open-mouthed dragon with outstretched wings, was made in 1822 for the coronation of Dom Pedro I.

Entrance

Ground floor

Museum Guide

The ground floor displays royal exhibits, and prominently features the Crown Jewels. The first floor houses the State Room, as well as the royal bedrooms. The museum is set in a pretty garden designed by Jean Baptiste Binot, a French landscape artist.

Elegant Neo-Classical façade of the Palácio Imperial

For hotels and restaurants in this region see pp372–3 and p388

Gabinete
The study features Brazil's first telephone, presented to Dom Pedro II in 1876 by Alexander Graham Bell.

First floor

★ Sala de Estado
The throne on show in the State Room came from the palace in São Cristovão.

Sala de Música
Besides a rare triangular spinet built by Mathias Bosten in 1788, the music room also has a beautiful harp.

Sala do Senado features the 1872 *Fala do Trono* (Speech from the Throne), a portrait of Dom Pedro II in full regalia.

Key

- The Dining Room
- The Music Room
- The Royal Costumes & Scepter
- The Imperial Throne
- Dom Pedro II's Study
- The Princesses' Room
- Imperial Brazilian Jewelry
- Dom Pedro I's Room
- Room of His Majesty
- Princesa Isabel's Room
- Lobby
- The Empress's Sewing Room
- The Empress's Piano Room
- Saleta
- Senate Room
- Other Exhibition Space
- Non-Exhibition Space

❻ Teresópolis

Rio de Janeiro. 140,000. from Rio de Janeiro City. Centro Turístico, (21) 2644 4095.

Set amid pretty countryside, Teresópolis is known for its artisan fair in Praça Higino da Silveira, which is lined with more than 700 stands at weekends. Just 3 miles (5 km) south of the town center, the **Orquidário Aranda** is one of Brazil's best orchid farms, with over 3,000 varieties on display.

❂ Orquidário Aranda
Rua João Daudt de Oliveira s/n.
Tel (21) 2742 0628. 9am–4:30pm Mon–Fri.

❼ Parque Nacional da Serra dos Órgãos

Rio de Janeiro. from Rio de Janeiro. (21) 2152 1100. **Open** 8am–5pm daily.

Created in 1939, this national park covers an area of approximately 46 sq miles (105 sq km) that stretches from Teresópolis across to Petrópolis. The park offers good climbing and treks, including a spectacular three-day guided trek of 26 miles (42 km) between the two towns. Among the park's most notable peaks are the 7,425-ft (2,263-m) Pedra do Sino, the highest in the mountain range, and the more famous Dedo de Deus (God's Finger), which stands 5,512 ft (1,680 m) high.

Of the many entrance points to the park, the most popular and best equipped is located 3 miles (5 km) south of Teresópolis.

Dedo de Deus (God's Finger), Parque Nacional da Serra dos Órgãos

Búzios

Rio de Janeiro. 🚌 from Cabo Frio.
ℹ️ Praça Santos Dumont, (22) 2623 2099. ✉️ 🌐 buziosturismo.com

Since Brigitte Bardot's visit to Búzios in 1964 with her then boyfriend, Brazilian actor Bob Zagury, this peninsula has developed from a quiet string of isolated fishing villages lost in semitropical *maquis*, into one of the country's most stylish low-key resorts. Private homes, designer boutiques, and little *pousadas* cling to its hills or watch over the numerous beaches. Beach buggies driven by vacationers buzz along the scruffy roads.

Statue of Brigitte Bardot on the Orla Bardot

Yachts bob in the bay in front of Búzios town, which is little more than a cluster of cobblestoned streets lined with smart boutiques and restaurants. During high season, the resort buzzes with cruiseship passengers and middle-class Brazilian tourists who shop by day on **Rua das Pedras**, the town's main thoroughfare, sip cocktails in the evening at one of the oceanfront *pousadas*, and then dance the night away in the Ibiza-style clubs and beachside bars.

Búzios's *raison d'être* is its beaches, which range from half-moon bays to long stretches of fine white sand. The best

One of the souvenir shops lining Rua das Pedras in Búzios

way to see them is to rent a beach buggy and explore, armed with one of the ubiquitous free maps of the peninsula available from every

---

Beaches of Costa do Sul

The southern coast, extending between Niterói and Búzios, is best known for its landscape, outstanding beaches, and upmarket resorts. Attractive beaches and sparkling waters make it ideal for a lazy stretch on the sand, or a dip in the clean waters. With its crashing waves and a steady breeze, this stretch is popular for windsurfing. It is easy to find accommodation here, both in busy resorts and isolated fishing villages.

SOUTHEAST BRAZIL
RIO DE JANEIRO & ESPÍRITO SANTO
Rio de Janeiro

Locator Map
🔲 Costa do Sul

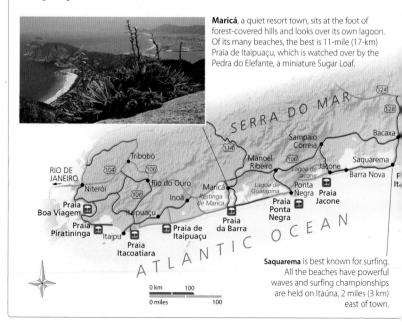

Maricá, a quiet resort town, sits at the foot of forest-covered hills and looks over its own lagoon. Of its many beaches, the best is 11-mile (17-km) Praia de Itaipuaçu, which is watched over by the Pedra do Elefante, a miniature Sugar Loaf.

Saquarema is best known for surfing. All the beaches have powerful waves and surfing championships are held on Itaúna, 2 miles (3 km) east of town.

other hotel reception. The peninsula is extremely well signposted, and since it is only 4 miles (6 km) long and 2 miles (4 km) wide, it is difficult to get lost here.

Many of the beaches, including the two sets of twin sheltered coves – at **Praia João Fernandes**, **Praia João Fernandinho**, **Praia Azeda**, and **Praia Azedinha** – are within half an hour's walk of town. Others are a beach buggy ride away. **Praia da Ferradura**, on the opposite side from Búzios, is one of the most beautiful beaches near town, and one of the least spoilt by hotel development. Fishermen still work from here at dawn and dusk. **Praia Brava**, at the peninsula's eastern extreme, is washed by

the fiercest waves and is a popular surf beach. **Olho de Boi**, which can be reached only via a rocky trail that runs from Brava's southern end, is surrounded by rocky hills on all sides, and is an unofficial nudist beach. **Ferradurinha**, at the peninsula's southern extreme, has clear, calm waters and natural swimming pools, good for a dip.

The small, isolated Praia Azeda, known for its tranquil waters

Cabo Frio is a triumph of concrete over natural beauty. The region's busiest resort, it overflows with locals at weekends. There is good surf on the numerous beaches and dune-boarding at Praia do Peró, 5 miles (8 km) north.

Praia da Tartaruga · Armação de Búzios
(106) (178) · Praia de Tucuns
(104) · Praia do Peró
São Pedro da Aldeia · Praia das Conchas
Iguaba Grande · Porto do Carro · Cabo Frio
(138) · Iguaba Pequena
Lagoa de Araruama
Araruama
Praia Seca · Figueira · (132) · Praia Grande · Arraial do Cabo
Ilha · Praia Massambaba · Praia do Cabo Frio · ILHA DO CABO FRIO
aia tur

Araruama, one of the largest lakes in Brazil, is ringed by myriad long white-sand beaches. A constant breeze makes for good windsurfing. It is also famous for its medicinal mud and high salinity.

VISITORS' CHECKLIST

Practical Information
Rio de Janeiro. Cabo Frio: Av Américo Vespúcio 200, (22) 2647 1689. Arraial do Cabo: Av do Liberdade 50, (24) 2622 1650. Araruama: Av Brasil 655 (22) 2665 5700. Saquarema: Secretaria de Turismo, Rua Coronel Madureira 77, (22) 2651 2123. Maricá: Av Ver Francisco Sabino da Costa 945, (21) 3731 5094.

Transport
from Rio.

Arraial do Cabo town itself is uninspiring but the confluence of currents around the cape provides the best diving in southeastern Brazil and a wealth of magnificent beaches.

For keys to symbols *see back flap*

Terceira Ponte Bridge connecting Vila Velha to Vitória

9 Guarapari

Espírito Santo. 🏔 2,000. 🚌 from Vitória. 🛈 Rua Paulo de Aguiar 68, Centro, (27) 3262 8759.

Espírito Santo's busiest beach resort is fringed by dozens of long, white beaches. People from Minas Gerais rush down on weekends to bask on the sandy beaches of Guarapari, said to have mildly radioactive healing properties. The best beach, **Praia do Morro**, lies to the north of the city and has a nature reserve. **Praia do Meio**, also to the north, has rock pools filled with clear water, and is good for snorkeling.

Guarapari offers light adventure activities, such as rappeling, rafting, and some of the best diving in the Southeast. The town also has a lively nightlife scene.

10 Vitória

Espírito Santo. 🏔 292,000. 🛬 🚌 from Rio. 🛈 Secretaria Municipal de Turismo, Rua Hélio Marconi 150, Bento Ferreira, (27) 3315 5540. 🎭 Carnaval (Feb/Mar).

The capital city of Espírito Santo is dominated by an expansive bay with sheltered crescent coves, and surrounded by a bottle-green open ocean. Vitória was originally made up of 36 distinct islands, but landfills have now reduced these to just a handful, connected by five bridges. **Praia do Camburí**, the main beach south of the city is a busy 4-mile (6-km) stretch, dotted with restaurants and hotels.

Across the river, **Vila Velha** (Old Town), the most interesting part of the city, is reached by the majestic bridge, **Terceira Ponte**. Although few colonial buildings remain, it is home to the architectural symbol of the city, **Convento da Nossa Senhora da Penha**. Sitting high on a lush palm-covered hill overlooking Vitória Bay, its thick fortified walls beautifully reflect both the sunrise and sunset. The monastery was founded in 1558 and preserves fine 16th-century wood carvings and one of Brazil's first paintings, *Nossa Senhora das Alegrias*, by an unknown early 16th-century Iberian artist. At the base of the hill is the simple Igreja Nossa Senhora do Rosário, the oldest church in the state, dating from 1551.

South of Vilha Velha, **Praia da Costa** is not as busy a beach as Camburí, but is a good place to go bodysurfing.

Manguezal de Vitória, situated northwest of Vitória, is the largest stretch of urban mangroves in South America. The mangroves are an important nursery for marine life and can be visited by boat alongside a number of the bay's wilder islands.

🏛 **Convento da Nossa Senhora da Penha**
Rua Vasco Coutinho, Prainha, Vila Velha, Vitória. **Tel** (27) 3329 0420. **Open** 5:30am–4:45pm Mon–Sat, 4:30am–4:45pm Sun.

🛶 **Manguezal de Vitória**
Santuário de Santo Antônio. 🚤 boat tours to Manguezal, Av Dario Lourenço de Souza, (27) 3345 6605.

Sunbathers on Praia do Morro in Guarapari

For hotels and restaurants in this region see pp372–3 and p388

⓫ Pedra Azul

Espírito Santo. 🚌 from Vitória.
ℹ️ Parque Estadual da Pedra Azul, (27)
3248 1156. **Open** 8am–5pm daily. 🚗
🚌 from 9am & 1:30pm daily (book in
advance). 🌐 **pedraazul.com.br**

Sitting in a tiny island of remnant Mata Atlântica forest, the 500-m- (1,640-ft-) high Pedra Azul (Blue Stone) rises in the middle of the Parque Estadual da Pedra Azul, forming a stunning centerpiece. Its natural color is an almost polished blue-grey, but shifts in hue and shade depending on the light: coal-black and brooding under a dark cloud, burning orange with the setting sun, or silvery white under a full moon.

The small visitors' center at the foot of the stone is a good place to collect a detailed map of the park. A ranger will also point out the trail leading up to the stone – a fairly easy but long walk punctuated by nine natural pools where visitors can take a refreshing dip. The trail is closed during and after heavy rains. Serious climbers are permitted to camp in the park for free.

The forest surrounding Pedra Azul is small but it is the nesting ground for a diverse variety of wildlife. Hummingbirds, tanagers, and tiny tufted-eared marmosets are a common sight.

Dramatic Pedra Azul, a granite monolith

⓬ Itaúnas

Espírito Santo. 🏠 2,500. 🚌 from
Vitória. 🎭 Festa de Forró (Jul).

This sleepy little fishing town lies tucked away in the far north of Espírito Santo on the border with Bahia. Long strands of beaches stretch to the north and south of the town. These have drifted into dunes so large that the first settlement here lies submerged, the remains of the original church tower occasionally appearing from the sand after a strong wind. The town lies next to the Rio Itaúnas which spreads into broad marshy meadows behind the sea. Ocelots, caimans, and capybaras live here, along with an impressive variety of rare waterbirds and small mammals.

The smattering of hotels in town offer dune buggy tours, during which you cross dozens of towering dunes and empty turtle-nesting beaches, eventually reaching the sandy cliffs on the state border with Bahia.

Itaúnas itself is surprisingly lively for a town so small. It is famous, particularly among students, for its exuberant *samba* and *axé* parties, which continue from December to March, and its exciting *forró* dance festival in July.

Sand dunes flanking the sleepy fishing town of Itaúnas along the Rio Itaúnas

MINAS GERAIS

The state of Minas Gerais is dotted with pretty colonial towns, set in a stunning landscape of rugged hills. Of these, Ouro Preto, Congonhas, and Diamantina are UNESCO World Heritage Sites. Beyond the towns is pastoral country broken by wilderness, much of which has been protected by a series of national and state parks, where several rare species of animals, birds, and plants can be seen.

Minas's old mining towns are laid out along the Estrada Real, once Brazil's first great wagon trail and now one of its major tourist routes. The most famous is Ouro Preto, named after the black gold that was discovered here in the late 17th century by an itinerant adventurer (*bandeirante*), who came through the vast interior in search of slaves. Gold brought a rush of speculators and new discoveries and by the mid-18th century ramshackle mining camps had grown into prosperous towns. Today, Ouro Preto, Tiradentes, Mariana, São João del Rei, Congonhas, and Diamantina preserve some of the finest ecclesiastical buildings and Baroque carvings in the Americas.

The state's spectacular parks are home to the maned wolf, as well as a plethora of endemic birds and plants. The Serra do Cipó and the Serra da Canastra lie on the tablelands of the Brazilian shield. Their *cerrado* forests are cut by several rivers that plunge dramatically over the edges of the *mesetas* (tabletop mountains), forming some of the world's highest waterfalls. The mountains of the Serra do Caparaó protect a swathe of the Mata Atlântica, dripping with orchids and the habitat of one of the few remaining populations of woolly spider monkey – the Americas' largest and rarest primate.

The state capital, Belo Horizonte, is a modern industrial city with a lively café life. President Juscelino Kubitschek's favorite architect, Oscar Niemeyer, adorned the city's Pampulha neighborhood with several structures before building the nation's capital, Brasília. Minas is also well known for its distinct cuisine and its rich literary and musical heritage.

A breathtaking view of mauve *ipê* flowers in full bloom outside Diamantina

◀ The cross at the top of the Igreja de São Francisco de Assis, Ouro Preto

Exploring Minas Gerais

Belo Horizonte, the capital of Minas Gerais, is the focus of life here. Most colonial mining towns, including Ouro Preto and Congonhas, lie immediately to its south. Mariana, another colonial city south of Belo Horizonte, is still a working mining center. Farther south, and a day's drive from the capital, is the hilly Serra da Canastra National Park. Northern Minas is much wilder, with large tracts of *cerrado* forest in the Serra do Cipó and around Diamantina. The extreme north is arid, dominated by the *sertão*, a region of scrub and grassland, whose distinct culture and language was mythologized in the most famous of all Brazilian novels, *Grande Sertão: Veredas*, by João Guimarães Rosa *(see p35)*.

Painting inside Igreja Nossa Senhora do Carmo, Diamantina

Sights at a Glance

Towns & Cities

National Parks & Areas of Natural Beauty

Historic Buildings

Ouro Preto, the architecturally stunning colonial city in Minas Gerais

Sunset in the *cerrado* landscape of Serra da Canastra

0 kilometers 100
0 miles 100

Matias Cardoso
Itacarambi
401 Monte Azul
Espinosa
Planalto
Januária
São João do Paraíso
do Brazil
122
Pardo
São Francisco
Janaúba
Taiobeiras
Pedra Azul
Jequitinhonha
135
251
Salinas
Medina
Almenara
Jacinto
Montes Claros
367
Jequitinhonha
Santa Fé Minas
Bocaiuva
Jequitinhonha
Araçuaí
Águas Formosas
365
Pirapora
Turmalina
Pavão
Várzea da Palma
135
Carbonita
Mucuri
Carlos Chagas
Pico de Itambé 6,670 ft (2,033 m)
Itamarandiba
Poté
Teófilo Otôni
Canoeiros
Corinto
🏛🏠 **1** DIAMANTINA
40
M I N A S   G E R A I S
Sêrro
Guanhães
Governador Valadares
Uberlândia
Curvelo
10
Virginópolis
Pompéu
381
116
Conselheiro Pena
Paraopeba
🎿📷 **2**
PARQUE NACIONAL SERRA DO CIPÓ
Ipatinga
Aimorés
Pará de Minas
🏛🏠 ✈ **3** BELO HORIZONTE
Caratinga
50
Divinópolis
🏠🏛
Manhuaçu
Formiga
OURO PRETO **4**
5 MARIANA
CONGONHAS **6** 🏠
🏠🏛
Viçosa
🏠🏛
SÃO JOÃO DEL REI **8** **7** TIRADENTES
Muriaé
381
Varginha
40
116
Agulhas Negras 9,143 ft (2,787 m)
Juiz de Fora
Além Paraíba
Itajubá

Key

- ▬ Highway
- ▬ Major road
- ▭ Minor road
- ▬ Railroad
- ▬ State border
- △ Peak

Getting Around

Belo Horizonte has two airports and is connected several times a day with all the Brazilian state capitals. There are few other airports in the state and transport beyond the capital is limited to buses, which are generally comfortable and frequent. Another option is to rent a car. Driving is possible during the day, even though many of the smaller roads are blighted with enormous potholes.

For keys to symbols *see back flap*

Old *fazenda* in the beautiful village of Biribiri near Diamantina

❶ Diamantina

🏚 48,000. 🚌 Largo Dom João 134, (38) 3531 1471. ℹ Praça Juscelino Kubitschek 25, (38) 3531 8060.
🌐 **diamantina.com.br**

Nestled in rugged hills and shrouded with *cerrado* forest, Diamantina is the prettiest and best preserved of all the colonial cities in the state, and also a UNESCO World Heritage Site. Diamonds were discovered here in 1728, when the city was a small settlement called Arraial do Tijuco. Within a few decades the mud huts and encampments transformed into one of the wealthiest towns in Brazil.

The city is tiny and most of its historic buildings and churches lie within easy walking distance of the main square, Praça Guerra. This is an obvious point of orientation as it is dominated by the twin towers of the largest building in the city – the Catedral Metropolitana de Santo Antônio, built in the 1930s. Just south of this in the adjacent Praça Juscelino Kubitschek is a small **Museu Casa do Diamante**, which houses a handful of the stones, together with iron collars once fitted onto slaves.

South again is the **Museu de Juscelino Kubitschek**, the modest former home of the Brazilian president, Juscelino Kubitschek (1902–76), who built Brasília *(see pp306–7)*. Two blocks west is the city's most beautiful landmark, the Casa da Gloria, consisting of two houses

on opposite sides connected by an enclosed, brilliant blue, second-story passageway. The building is not open to the public.

There are several churches in Diamantina. The oldest is the **Nossa Senhora do Rosário**, in the square of the same name, a short distance to the northeast of the Praça Guerra. It was built and used by the enslaved black community and the city's poor. Next to it is an original 18th-century fountain whose waterspouts are bas-reliefs of African heads.

A block south is the spectacular **Nossa Senhora do Carmo**. Built between 1760 and 1784, it was the town's richest church and attended by the elite white community. It is remarkable chiefly for the interior paintings by José Soares de Araujo, from Braga, Portugal. Araujo's works lie in many of the town's churches but those here are his finest. The ceiling paintings are very striking. Near the back of the church is a portrait of the Prophet Elijah ascending to heaven in a chariot of fire.

The **Casa de Chica da Silva**, a smart town house one block south of the Nossa Senhora do Carmo, is famous far more for its former owner than it is for its small collection of period furniture. During

the 18th century, Francisca (Chica) da Silva was a mulatta slave who became one of the few black people to become accepted by high colonial society through sheer force of personality.

Environs
A string of stunning natural locations lies within easy reach of Diamantina, the most impressive of which is **Biribiri**, located 7 miles (12 km) north of town. A historical village, Biribiri is home to many *fazendas* and is surrounded by waterfalls and mountains. Next to Biribiri is a winding blackwater river and the Parque Rio Preto, a good location for bird-watching.

🏛 **Casa de Chica da Silva**
Praça Lobo Mesquita 266. **Tel** (38) 3531 2491. **Open** noon–5pm Tue–Sat, 9am–1pm Sun.

🏛 **Museu Casa do Diamante**
Rua Direita 14. **Tel** (38) 3531 1382. **Open** noon–5:30pm Tue–Sat, 9am–noon Sun. 📷

🏛 **Museu de Juscelino Kubitschek**
Rua São Francisco 241. **Tel** (38) 3531 3607. **Open** 8am–5pm Tue–Sat, 8am–1pm Sun. 📷

⛪ **Nossa Senhora do Carmo**
Rua do Carmo. **Open** 8am–noon, 2–6pm Tue–Sun, 8am–noon Sun.

⛪ **Nossa Senhora do Rosário**
Largo do Rosário. **Open** 1–5pm Mon–Fri, 9am–noon, 2–5pm Sat & Sun.

Nave, Igreja de Nossa Senhora do Carmo

Magnificent waterfall at Parque Nacional Serra do Cipó

❷ Parque Nacional Serra do Cipó

🚌 from Belo Horizonte to Jaboticatubas, or Santana do Riacho. 🛈 Secretaria de Turismo, (31) 3718 7017. **Tel** (31) 3486 6771. **Open** 8am–5pm daily. 🅿️ 🅿️ Cipó Veraneio Hotel, Rodovia MG-10, Serra do Cipó, (31) 3718 7000.
🌐 **cipoveraneiohotel.com.br**

Just northeast of Belo Horizonte, the state capital, this 131-sq-mile (338-sq-km) national park lies in high rugged country in the Serra do Espinhaço mountains, which run through the middle of northern Minas Gerais. Cipó protects some pristine areas of *cerrado* as well as the watersheds of many of the tributaries of the São Francisco and the Doce rivers. Waterfalls, plants, rare animals, and birds are abundant, making this one of the most beautiful national parks in Minas Gerais.

It is particularly lovely in May and June when the skies are invariably blue, the rivers full, and many of the numerous wildflowers in bloom. This is also a good time to go on a guided tour, at dawn or dusk, to spot pumas, giant anteaters, ocelots, maned wolves, and howling monkeys on the quieter trails.

The park is a popular location for ecotourism – particularly rock climbing, with excellent facilities and accommodation options.

❸ Belo Horizonte

🏙️ 3,000,000. ✈️ 🚤 🚌 🚉
🛈 Aloturismo (Belotur's hotline), (31) 3277 9777. 🎭 Carnaval (Feb/Mar).
🌐 **pbh.gov.br**

The capital city of Minas Gerais was laid out in the 1890s and resembles a mini São Paulo. Clusters of seemingly endless skyscraper apartment blocks sit in a broad valley under lush hills. Belo Horizonte is known worldwide for its visionary architecture. Its architectural highlights lie in the suburb of Pampulha, often regarded as the blueprint for Brasília. The buildings are set in expansive gardens designed by Roberto Burle Marx (1909–94), gathered around a large, beautiful artificial lake. All were commissioned by the then mayor of Belo Horizonte, Juscelino Kubitschek, and designed by the renowned architect Oscar Niemeyer in the 1940s.

The most impressive of all the buildings is the **Igreja de São Francisco de Assis**, which was built in 1943 as a series of parabolic arches in concrete, and has a wonderful sense of light and space. On the outside walls are a series of *azulejos*, or Portuguese blue tiles, depicting scenes from the life of St. Francis and painted by Brazil's foremost Modernist artist, Candido Portinari (1903–62). Other important buildings in the Pampulha complex include the dance hall **Casa do**

Azulejos on the outside walls of São Francisco de Assis

Baile, with its sweeping curved walkway that functioned as a ballroom till 1946, and the twin sports stadia, which are a clear precursor to the gymnasium Niemeyer designed for Brasília.

In the inner city, the **Museu Mineiro** preserves some fine colonial-era religious art, including a number of paintings attributed to Mestre Athayde (1762–1830). Beyond this, Belo Horizonte's main attractions are the lively restaurant and nightlife scene around the inner-city neighborhoods of Lourdes and Savassi. These areas have many chic restaurants, which often have live music playing during the weekends (*see pp388–9*). The Lourdes and Savassi neighborhoods are easily explored on foot and make a pleasant walk.

Environs
The colonial towns of Sabará, Caeté, and Santa Luiza, to the east of Belo Horizonte, lie less than half an hour's drive away. All preserve fine Baroque churches and streets of 18th-century town houses.

🏛️ **Igreja de São Francisco de Assis**
Av Otacilio Negrão de Lima 3000, Pampulha. **Tel** (31) 3427 1644. **Open** 9am–5pm Tue–Sat, noon–5pm Sun. 🅿️ ♿ 🅿️

🏛️ **Museu Mineiro**
Av João Pinheiro 342. **Tel** (31) 3269 1168. **Open** 10am–5pm Tue–Fri, 10am–4pm Sat & Sun. 🅿️

Igreja de São Francisco de Assis in Pampulha, Belo Horizonte

❹ Street-by-Street: Ouro Preto

Ouro Preto, or "Black Gold," earned its name shortly after its founding in 1698 from tarnished gold nuggets mined in the surrounding areas. It still resembled a boom town when it was given city status in 1711. By the mid-18th century, however, the gold rush had turned Ouro Preto into a wealthy town with fine buildings. It nurtured a generation of some of Latin America's finest artists and craftsmen, including the ecclesiastical painter Mestre Athayde and the great sculptor Aleijadinho among others. Ouro Preto became the base of the Inconfidência rebellion led by Tiradentes against Portuguese colonists.

Casa dos Contos
Once the gold exchange, then a prison, the building is now a small museum dedicated to money and finance.

A cluster of colonial buildings in hilly Ouro Preto

★ Matriz de Nossa Senhora do Pilar
Exquisite artwork is showcased in this opulent Brazilian Baroque church, resplendent in gold. The carvings in the chancel are breathtaking.

RUA S. ROCHA LAGOA

RUA DIREITA

RUA COR ALVES

RUA B. MUSQUEF

RUA PARANÁ

RUA XAVIER DA V

RUA DO PILAR

Museu do Oratório

0 meters 100
0 yards 100

★ Matriz de Nossa Senhora da Conceição
Manuel Francisco Libsoa transformed this once-rustic church into one of the city's most magnificently decorated cathedrals.

Statue of Tiradentes
The leader of the Inconfidentes was the only rebel against the Portuguese colonizers to be executed. He is a cult figure in Brazil, mainly for the poor.

BERNARDO DE VASCONCELOS

RUA DO ALEIJADINHO

ROCHA LAGOA

RUA CLAUDIO MANOEL

DIREITA

Portrait of Aleijadinho
This likeness, which was painted long after the sculptor's death, is housed in the Museu Aleijadinho. The museum preserves a small collection of Aleijadinho's works.

Key
— Suggested route

RUA COSTA SENA

Museu da Inconfidência features relics related to the Inconfidentes, as well as drawings by Aleijadinho.

Igreja de Nossa Senhora do Carmo
The Rococo font (in the sacristy), door-case, the altars, and the statue of Santa Helena in this church are all attributed to Aleijadinho.

★ Igreja de São Francisco de Assis
One of Latin America's most important Rococo buildings, the church combines the finest work of Aleijadinho and Mestre Athayde.

Exploring Ouro Preto

One of the first gold towns in Minas Gerais and a former state capital, Ouro Preto is built on a series of hills. Steep, curving streets lined with 18th-century residences, many of which have now been converted into restaurants, bars, and shops, link the hills. Within the town, the streets lead to pretty little squares dominated by Baroque churches and stately town houses. These include the churches of São Francisco de Assis and Nossa Senhora do Pilar, whose interiors bear the stamp of some of Latin America's finest artists and craftsmen.

⬆ Igreja de São Francisco de Assis

Largo de Coimbra. **Tel** (31) 3551 4661. **Open** 8:30am–noon, 1:30–5pm Tue–Sun. 🖾

This understated, elegant little church was constructed between 1766 and 1802 and seems modest next to many of Latin America's grand Baroque churches. It is characterized by gentle curves, from the elegant S-shaped balustrades of its façade to the exquisitely unified, undulating lines of its interior. The quality of the church's beauty lies in the mastery of its art, created by two of Brazil's greatest artists, Aleijadinho *(see p135)* and his long-term partner Manuel da Costa Athayde (1762–1830). The tablet on the church's façade showing St. Francis receiving the stigmata

is believed to have been Aleijadinho's first great carving. It was followed by others, including the ornately carved door-case and the front of the sacristy at the rear of the church.

⬆ Matriz de Nossa Senhora do Pilar

Praça Mons Castilho Barbosa. **Tel** (31) 3551 4736. **Open** 9–10:45am, noon–4:45pm Tue–Sun. ⬆ 7am Mon–Fri, 7am & 7pm Sat & Sun, 7pm 1st Fri of the month. 🖾 🖾

Commissioned by two of the wealthiest ecclesiastical orders in Ouro Preto, this church was intended as a showpiece of their influence. Pomp and circumstance surrounded its inauguration in 1731, which witnessed grand processions of clergy in opulent vestments and horses in velvet mantles

mounted by knights in diamond-studded robes.

Nearly half a ton each of gold and silver were used to gild its interior, which is largely the work of 18th-century sculptor Francisco Xavier de Brito, an expatriate Portuguese. The gilt carving of Christ on the Cross on the door-case to the *capela-mor* (apsidal chapel) and the Resurrection scene on the tabernacle are regarded as de Brito's finest work.

Façade of Matriz de Nossa Senhora da Conceição

⬆ Matriz de Nossa Senhora da Conceição

Praça Antônio Dias. **Tel** (31) 3551 4661. **Open** 8:30am–noon Tue–Sat, noon–5pm Sun. 🖾

Built by Manuel Francisco Lisboa, this church was constructed between 1727 and 1770. It is most celebrated for its harmonious proportions – the unity of curves and straight lines on the façade and the sense of space generated by what is in reality a modest nave and chancel. Manuel Francisco only added the finishing touches to the heavily gilt interior, and the sculptors of the elaborate interior, with its eight splendid altars, remain largely unknown. Both Lisboa and his son Aleijadinho are buried in the church.

There is a small museum devoted to the life and times of Aleijadinho in the basement of the church, containing only very few of his pieces.

Ceiling painting by Athayde in Igreja de São Francisco de Assis

Praça Gomes Freire in Mariana, lined by fine 18th-century houses

❺ Mariana

🏔 47,000. 🚌 🛈 Praça Tancredo Neves, (31) 3557 1158.

The oldest colonial town in Minas Gerais, Mariana, which was also a significant mining town, was the capital of the state in the first half of the 18th century and far more important than its immediate neighbor, Ouro Preto.

The simple 18th-century **Basílica de São Pedro dos Clérigos** stands on top of the city's only hill. From here, there are spectacular views of Mariana's small colonial center.

The main focus of the old town is the **Praça Gomes Freire**, a lovely garden square surrounded by 18th-century town houses. A short distance west of Praça Gomes Freire are the twin churches of **São Francisco de Assis** and **Nossa Senhora do Carmo**. Both date

Unique window in Mariana

from the late 18th century and sit next to each other in front of the colonial building, the Casa de Camara.

The church of São Francisco de Assis is decorated with ceiling paintings by Manuel da Costa Athayde, who was buried in the church. Especially worth seeing are the evocative scenes of the death of St. Francis, showing the saint in serene contemplation in an Italian pastoral landscape, combined with the Brazilian landscape.

The Nossa Senhora do Carmo also has striking paintings by Athayde. Although damaged by fire in 1999, the church is still remarkable for its delicately balanced and very Portuguese exterior. Known for its gentle curves and round towers, it also has exquisite lozenge-shaped key windows.

The city's other famous church is the **Basílica de Nossa Senhora da Assunção**, which

dates from 1760 and is also referred to as the Basílica da Sé. Its exterior is modest, but the interior has some of the finest ceiling paintings by the 16th-century Portuguese artist, Manuel Rabello de Sousa. It also contains an exquisite 18th-century German organ and altarpieces by Francisco Xavier de Brito, and a portal and *lavebo* attributed to Aleijadinho. The organ was a gift to the diocese when Mariana was the foremost city in inland Brazil. Restored in 1984, it can be heard during regular weekend organ recitals.

Just around the corner to the south of the basilica is the most interesting of the civic buildings, the **Museu Arquidiocesano de Arte Sacra**. This preserves paintings by Athayde, *objets d'art* by Aleijadinho, and antique liturgical objects. Its façade is crowned with a medal by Aleijadinho.

🏛 **Basílica de Nossa Senhora da Assunção**
Rua Padre Gonçalves Lopes. **Tel** (31) 3557 1216. **Open** 6am–8pm Tue–Sun.

🏛 **Museu Arquidiocesano de Arte Sacra**
Rua Frei Durão. **Tel** (31) 3557 2581. **Open** 8:30am–noon, 1:30–5pm Tue–Fri, 8:30am–2pm Sat, Sun & public hols. 🛈

🏛 **Nossa Senhora do Carmo**
Praça Minas Gerais.
Open 9am–4pm daily.

🏛 **São Francisco de Assis**
Praça Minas Gerais.
Open 9am–5pm daily.

View of Mariana and the twin churches from Basílica de São Pedro dos Clérigos

❻ Basílica do Senhor Bom Jesus de Matosinhos, Congonhas

Completed in 1771, the Baroque church of Bom Jesus de Matosinhos was built by the diamond miner Feliciano Mendes, who, after recovering from the brink of death, vowed to build a church in homage to "Bom Jesus." At the entrance of the church, 12 soapstone statues of prophets from the Old Testament overlook a gently sloping garden, where six chapels containing life-size figures commemorate episodes from the Passion of Christ. The church is famous for preserving the most impressive ensemble of statues in Latin America, carved by Aleijadinho between 1780 and 1814.

Painted Ceiling
Painted by Bernardo Pires da Silva in 1776, the artwork on the ceiling is regarded as the finest Rococo church painting in Brazil.

Carved Altar
Designed by sculptor Aleijadinho, the altar was beautifully carved by his disciple, João Antunes de Carvalho.

KEY

① **The Crucifixion** is particularly grisly, depicting smiling soldiers hammering nails into a spread-eagled Christ, his face contorted in agony.

② Amos

③ Jonah

④ Obadiah

⑤ Baruch

⑥ Daniel

⑦ Hosea

⑧ Ezekiel

⑨ Jeremiah

⑩ Joel

⑪ Nahum

⑫ **Christ carrying the cross,** a sculpture portraying one of the stations in the Passion of Christ.

⑬ **The Flagellation of Christ and the Coronation with Thorns** depicts a prelude to the Crucifixion.

Isaiah
The sculpture of Isaiah has narrow shoulders and disproportionately short arms, and is thought to have been carved by Aleijadinho's students.

★ **The Prophet Habakukk**
Aleijadinho's sculptures are celebrated for having an air of theatricality and accentuated characteristics, both striking in his statue of Habakukk.

Façade of the church inspired by and modeled on the Santuário do Bom Jesus in Braga, Portugal, with the prophets at the entrance

VISITORS' CHECKLIST

Practical Information
Basílica do Senhor Bom Jesus de Matosinhos, Congonhas.
i FUMCULT, Praça Presidente Juscelino Kubitschek 135,
Tel (31) 3731 7394.
w cidadeshistoricas.art.br/ congonhas
Open 7am–6pm Mon–Fri, 8am–5pm Sat & Sun.
♦ 9am–1pm Sun.
▣ Jubileu do Senhor Bom Jesus do Matosinhos (Sep).

Transport
▭ Basílica from Av Júlia Kubitschek 1892.

★ **The Capture of Christ**
Jesus is captured by Herod's soldiers, led to him by his disciple, Judas Iscariot, in the Garden of Gethsemane.

Aleijadinho

Aleijadinho (1738–1815) meaning "Little Cripple," was nicknamed due to the disfigurement he suffered from leprosy. When he carved the statues at Bom Jesus de Matosinhos, he could no longer walk and had completely lost the use of his hands. His students carried him up the hill each day and strapped hammers and chisels to his arms. The figure watching the Crucifixion and hiding his hands is reputed to be a self-portrait by Aleijadinho. The statues are, without doubt, his masterpieces, and his final works of art.

Statue of Aleijadinho (standing, right) witnessing the Crucifixion

The Angel
The figure of an angel carrying a cup filled with Faith for Christ is in the chapel of the Mount of Olives.

★ **The Last Supper**
The figures are so life-like that when they were completed, some pilgrims are said to have greeted them as if they were real people.

Colonial Portuguese houses lining the cobbled streets of Tiradentes

❼ Tiradentes

🏠 6,000. 🚌 ℹ️ Largo dos Forros, Rua Resende Costa 71, (32) 3355 1212. 🎬 Festival de Cinema (Jan), Carnaval Mardi Gras (Feb/Mar).

Like Ouro Preto and Mariana, Tiradentes became rich on gold, producing some of the most lavish Baroque church interiors and façades in all of Brazil. The town takes its name from the nickname "Tiradentes" (Tooth-puller) of José da Silva Xavier (1746–92), an erstwhile resident who became a martyr of the Inconfidência Mineria, the first movement in Brazil towards independence from Portugal.

Tiradentes is a delightful colonial town. Its multicolored Portuguese cottages and miniature Baroque churches flank the cobbled roads on the steep, low São José hills around the Rio Santo Antônio. There is a craft shop, an arty little café, or a gourmet restaurant on every other corner. Pretty horse-drawn carriages gather in Largo das Forras, the town's main plaza, and a narrow gauge steam train, Maria Fumaça (see p424), with wooden Pullman coaches, puffs and heaves its way to and from neighboring São João del Rei on weekends and public holidays.

The center of Tiradentes is tiny and best seen on foot. Rua da Praia runs west from Largo das Forras following the course of the Rio das Mortes. Rua Direita runs parallel to it and a series of smaller streets cross the two. The most important of these is Rua da Câmara, whose steep cobbles rise to the town's most imposing church, the **Matriz de Santo Antônio**, built between 1710 and 1752. This is one of the finest Baroque churches in Brazil, with wonderful wood carvings and gilt interiors. Parts of the façade are attributed to the architect and sculptor Aleijadinho *(see p135)*.

There are various other small churches scattered throughout the town and these are all worth a visit. The best of these churches is **Igreja Nossa Senhora do Rosário dos Prestos**, on Rua Direita, which features some elegant statues and painted panels.

Also on Rua Direita is a cultural center, **Centro Cultural Yves Alves**, which hosts concerts, theatrical performances, films, and art exhibitions.

Gilt altar and interior of Matriz de Santo Antônio, Tiradentes

A highlight of Tiradentes is the magnificent blue soapstone public fountain dating from the 18th century, the **Chafariz de São José**, just across from Rua da Camara. It features an oratory with an image of São Jose de Botas and three faces representing love, good fortune, and health. The water comes from a spring in the São José hills overlooking the town, an area that offers excellent hiking.

🏛️ **Centro Cultural Yves Alves**
Rua Direita 168. **Tel** (32) 3355 1503.

🔆 **Matriz de Santo Antônio**
Rua da Camara. **Open** 9am–4:40pm daily. 🎨 📷 🎫 Dec–Mar: 8pm Fri & Sun, 8:30pm Sat (sound & light show), call (32) 3355 1238 to book.

Chafariz de São José, an 18th-century fountain in Tiradentes

❽ São João del Rei

🏠 79,000. 🚂 Maria Fumaça (only between São João del Rei & Tiradentes), Fri–Sun & public hols, (32) 3371 8485. 🚌 from Tiradentes. ℹ️ Rua Padre José Maria, Praça Frei Orlando, (32) 3372 7338. 🎬 Carnaval Mardi Gras (Feb), Semana de Inconfidência (Apr). 🌐 saojoaodelreisite.com.br

The largest of the historic towns of Minas Gerais, São João del Rei did not suffer from the decline of the gold boom in the 1800s. Today, it remains a bustling town, less than 19 miles (30 km) from Tiradentes, and boasts some beautiful churches, old mansions, and an attractive colonial center.

Façade, Igreja de São Francisco de Assis, São João del Rei

The principal reason for visiting São João is to see the **Igreja de São Francisco de Assis**, whose unusual curved façade, turtle-back roof and intricately carved medal overlook a square lined with towering palms. The square is in the shape of a lyre and at sundown the shadows of the palms form the instrument's strings. Together with the Santuário do Bom Jesus do Monte Sítio in Braga, Portugal, and the church of São Francisco in Ouro Preto (see p130–32), this church is one of the jewels in the crown of Baroque architecture.

The town has a handful of other interesting sights. The **Museu Regional de São João del Rei**, a colonial mansion, is full of antique furniture and sacred art and is one of the best in Minas Gerais. The **Museu Ferroviário**, at the Maria Fumaça railway station, is a tiny loco-motive museum housing an old,

Philadelphia-built, narrow gauge steam train. It sits alongside the Pullman carriages used by Emperor Dom Pedro II when he traveled to Minas Gerais from Rio by train in the 19th century.

⬆ Igreja de São Francisco de Assis
Praça Frei Orlando.
Open 8am–5:30pm Mon–Sat, 7am–4pm Sun. ✉

🏛 Museu Ferroviário
Estação Ferroviária, Av Hermílio Alves 366. **Tel** (32) 3371 8485. **Open** 8–11am, 1–4pm Wed–Sat, 9am–2pm Sun. 🐾

🏛 Museu Regional de São João del Rei
Rua Marechal Deodoro 12. **Tel** (32) 3371 7663. **Open** 12:30–5:30pm Tue–Sun. 🐾

❾ Parque Nacional Serra da Canastra

🚌 from Belo Horizonte. ℹ IBAMA, Av Mal Floriano Peixoto 465, São Roque de Minas, (37) 3433 1195. **Open** 8am–6pm daily. 🐾

The extensive Parque Nacional Serra da Canastra, tucked away in the far southwest of Minas Gerais, protects the head waters of one of South America's largest rivers – the Rio São Francisco. This great waterway flows 1,963 miles (3,160 km) through the rippling hills of Minas, and the bone-dry deserts of the northeastern interior. But in the Serra da Canastra it is little more than a large mountain stream cutting through rugged

Giant anteater in the Parque Nacional Serra da Canastra

terrain. Bare granite peaks rise to almost 4,920 ft (1,500 m). Sparse *cerrado* forest sprinkled with boulders gathers at their feet. Around the numerous waterfalls and along the wild rivers are stretches of lush, gallery forest. The most famed of the falls is the **Cachoeira d'Anta**. Here the river's ice-cold waters form a series of pools before plunging 186 m (610 ft) off an escarpment. The park's most famous trail, the **Trilha Casca d'Anta**, begins in front of the waterfall and offers a spectacular view out over the park to the denuded pasture land beyond.

There is plenty of wildlife in the Serra da Canastra, though it can be hard to see. Maned wolves and giant anteaters are relatively common here, as are the pig-sized giant armadillos. The park is especially rich in birdlife, and is one of the few places in the world where it is possible to see the endangered Brazilian Merganser duck.

Granite peaks looming over the *cerrado* and pasture land beyond, Parque Nacional Serra da Canastra

SÃO PAULO CITY

Bristling concrete towers extend interminably over São Paulo, an expansive, vibrant city located on a high plateau. The impressive number of immigrants settled in its many districts makes it one of the world's largest metropolises. Its immense cultural diversity has blessed it with the liveliest and most creative artistic, musical, and gastronomic scene in the country.

São Paulo was founded in 1554 by Manuel da Nóbrega and José de Anchieta, and established as a Jesuit missionary outpost. The 17th century saw the town become the headquarters for *bandeirantes*, or slave-trading pioneers. São Paulo became a major stopover point for explorers and pioneers, lured by the prospect of gold mines and slave trading in the interiors. The expansion of the sugar and coffee industries in the late 18th and 19th centuries attracted immigrants from the Middle East, Spanish America, the Russian republics, Central Asia, Europe – including Spain and Portugal – and Japan.

Internal migrants from every corner of the nation came to São Paulo in the mid-20th century. Among them was an impoverished metal-worker from Pernambuco, Luíz Inácio da Silva, who by

a wave of public support went on to become Brazil's president in 2002, and again in 2006. Regional festivals from all over the country are celebrated with great enthusiasm in the city's enormous *favelas* (shantytowns).

São Paulo's vastness and complex character can be intimidating to an outsider. The greatest pleasures of this magnificent city are to be found behind closed doors – in museums, galleries, concert halls, and in a wealth of restaurants and shops. A true haven for gourmets, São Paulo is known to serve the best food in South America. The city center offers a host of attractions, such as the 17th-century Igreja de São Francisco and the 20th-century Mosteiro São Bento. The city's finest museum, Museu de Arte de São Paulo (MASP), is one of the highlights of the famed Avenida Paulista.

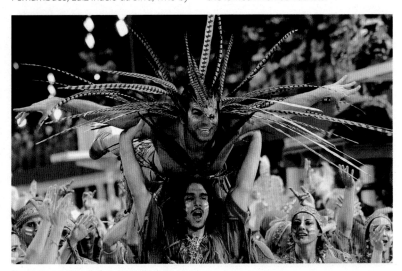

Carnaval dancers participate in the final night of the São Paulo parade

◀ View from the top of Banespa Tower, including the Palace of Justice and Metropolitan Cathedral of São Paulo

Exploring São Paulo City

Brazil's largest city covers an area of 6,332 sq miles (10,190 sq km). The conurbation of São Paulo, which includes the cities of São Bernardo de Campo, Guarulhos, and Sorocaba, is home to about 29 million people, making it the largest urban area in the world. There are three city centers – the old center preserves the few remaining historical buildings, including the Catedral Metropolitana. A short distance to the southwest is Avenida Paulista, home to the famous Museu de Arte Contemporânea (MAC). The commercial districts of Itaim and Brooklin lie south, on the banks of the Rio Tietê. The city's posh neighborhood, Jardins, is lined with South America's finest shops and restaurants. Another upscale area, Vila Mariana, is home to Parque do Ibirapuera, a green oasis among the relentless high-rises.

Sights at a Glance

Historic Buildings, Streets, Towns & Neighborhoods

❸ Pátio do Colégio
❺ Theatro Municipal
❼ Centro Cultural Banco do Brasil
❽ Edifício Itália
❾ Edifício Banespa
⓬ Estação da Luz
⓮ Sala São Paulo
⓰ Avenida Paulista
⓲ Liberdade

❹ Mosteiro São Bento
❻ Igreja da Consolação

Museums

❿ *Pinacoteca do Estado pp144–5*
⓫ Museu Arte Sacra
⓭ Estação Pinacoteca
⓯ *Museu de Arte de São Paulo (MASP) p147*
⓱ Museu do Futebol
⓴ Museu Paulista do Ipiranga
㉑ Museu de Arte Contemporânea (MAC)

Parks & Gardens

⓳ *Parque do Ibirapuera pp150–51*
㉒ Instituto Butantã
㉓ Jardim Botânico
㉔ Parque Burle Marx

Churches, Cathedrals & Monasteries

❶ Catedral Metropolitana
❷ Igreja de São Francisco de Assis

High-rise modern buildings dominating the skyline, central São Paulo

For hotels and restaurants in this region see pp373–4 and pp389–90

VISITORS' CHECKLIST

Practical Information

9,000,000 Praça Antônio Prado 9, (11) 3104 6898.

Festas Juninas (Jun), Bienal Internacional de São Paulo (Sep–Nov), Festa da Primavera (Sep).

cidadedesaopaulo.com

Transport

19 miles (30 km) NE of center.

9 miles (4 km) S of center.

Key

- Area of the main map
- Major road
- Minor road

Getting Around

São Paulo is well connected, with daily international flights to most major European, and North and South American cities. Most of these depart from Cumbica airport in Guarulhos, 19 miles (30 km) northeast of the city. Domestic flights leave from Congonhas Airport, just south of Ibirapuera Park in the main urban center. There are buses to every corner of Brazil and beyond to Bolivia, Argentina, Paraguay, and Uruguay. There is an extensive network of taxis and buses within the city. The metro and urban railway are clean, fast, and efficient. Cars can be rented at both the airports, although the city's numerous one-way systems and choking traffic make driving a little daunting.

For keys to symbols *see back flap*

❶ Catedral Metropolitana

Praça da Sé, Centro. **Map** 1 C3.
Tel (11) 3107 6832. Ⓜ Sé.
Open 8am–1pm, 3–5pm daily.
Closed last Sun of each month. 🚫
🕂 8:30am, 2pm, 6pm Mon, noon
Tue–Sat, 9am, 11am, 5pm Sun.

At the heart of old downtown São Paulo, the Catedral Metropolitana (also known as Catedral da Sé) watches over the large pebbled **Praça da Sé**, shaded by tropical fig and palm trees. Built between 1912 and 1954, the cathedral finally gained its full complement of 14 turrets in 2002.

Built by Maximiliano Hell, the exterior is a fusion of Neo-Gothic and Renaissance, with an overly narrow nave squeezed between two enormous 318-ft- (97-m-) high spires and a bulbous copper cupola. The cavernous interior, said to seat up to 8,000 people, looks starkly European. The only obvious local influences are visible in the capitals, delicately carved with distinctly Brazilian flora and fauna. The stained-glass windows were designed in Germany and Brazil.

The cathedral's façade has watched over the country's largest public protests, when crowds gathered in the square outside the cathedral in the late 1980s to demand the end of military rule.

Exterior of São Paulo Catedral Metropolitana, Praça da Sé

Carved altar in the interior of Igreja de São Francisco de Assis

❷ Igreja de São Francisco de Assis

Largo de São Francisco 133.
Map 1 A3. **Tel** (11) 3291 2400. Ⓜ Sé.
Open 7am–7pm Tue–Sat, 7am–noon, 5:30–7pm Sun. 🚫

Immediately to the west of Catedral Metropolitana is the Igreja de São Francisco de Assis, one of the city's oldest churches. Parts of the modest Baroque interior, featuring an intricately carved altar and ornaments, date from the mid-1600s. The church is often referred to as O Convento São Francisco after the exquisite Baroque convent that stood here until the 1930s, when it was demolished along with parts of the colonial center.

❸ Pátio do Colégio

Praça Pátio do Colégio 2. **Map** 2 D3.
Ⓜ Sé. **Open** 9am–4:30pm Tue–Sun.
🕂 noon Tue–Fri, 10am–noon Sun.
Museu Padre Anchieta: **Tel** (11) 3105 6899. 📷 🚫

Located within easy walking distance from the Praça da Sé, the Pátio do Colégio has an interesting history behind it. On January 25, 1554, the Jesuits inaugurated the Colégio de São Paulo de Piratinga on a small bluff overlooking an extensive forest. The original wattle-and-daub shack, built for them by their Guaraní cohorts, eventually became a school. That school became a church, and around the church arose the buildings that formed the core of the original city of São Paulo.

In 1760, the Jesuits were expelled from the city, but the college and chapel they founded remained and came to be known as the Pátio do Colégio. In 1886, the tower of the original church collapsed and the whole building was demolished.

Upon their return in 1954, the Jesuits immediately set about building an exact replica of their original church and college, which is what stands today as Pátio do Colégio.

Most of the buildings are occupied by the **Museu Padre Anchieta**, named after the Jesuit captain who led the first mission. The collection features a Modernist portrait of the priest, by the Italian artist Menghini, some of the priest's remains, a 17th-century font used to baptize indigenous people, as well as a collection of Guaraní artifacts from the colonial era. A model reproduction of São Paulo in the 16th century is also on display.

Visão de Anchieta by Menghini

❹ Mosteiro São Bento

Largo de São Bento. **Map** 1 C2.
Tel (11) 3328 8799. Ⓜ São Bento.
Open 7am–6pm Mon–Fri, 7am–noon Sat & Sun. 🕂 7am, 1pm & 6pm Mon–Fri, 6am, 7am Sat, 8:30am, 10am & 6:30pm (masses in Latin) Sun.
🆆 **mosteiro.org.br**

Brazil is the only South American country where the Benedictine order gained a foothold, arriving in São Paulo on this site in 1598. The current building, however, dates from the 1920s and was designed by Munich-based architect Richard Bernl.

The monastery has a beautifully painted Beuronese

interior. This style is named after techniques developed in the late 19th and early 20th centuries by Benedictines in the monastery of Beuron in southwest Germany. It is characterized by a compressed perspective and vivid colors. The finest representation of Beuronese art in Latin America is visible inside this beautiful Blessed Sacrament chapel. Scenes from the life of St. Benedict are depicted on the stained-glass windows and the ceiling. The church has a large organ, which is the centerpiece of a festival held in November and December every year. There is also a shop selling sweets and cakes made by the monks.

The 1920s interior of Mosteiro São Bento, with its painted ceiling

❺ Theatro Municipal

Praça Ramos de Azevedo.
Map 1 C2. **Tel** (11) 3397 0300.
Ⓜ Anhangabaú. ✉

Located near the Parque Anhangabaú, São Paulo's largest central park with some pretty fountains, the Theatro Municipal overlooks the Praça Ramos. The theater is one of the continent's most important venues, hosting a busy program of events. Opera and theater were very popular among the elite in turn-of-the-19th-century São Paulo and Rio de Janeiro. The theater was modeled on the Paris Opera

View of the exterior of Theatro Municipal

and the city waited in fevered anticipation for its inaugural night. It opened on September 12, 1911, with a production of *Hamlet*, starring the Italian baritone Titta Ruffo. Nijinski, Caruso, and Toscanini have all performed here.

❻ Igreja da Consolação

Rua da Consolação 585. **Map** 1 C3.
Tel (11) 3256 5356. Ⓜ Anhangabaú.
Open 7am–8pm. ✉

Designed by Maximiliano Hell, the architect of the Catedral Metropolitana, the Igreja da Consolação is a similar fusion of European styles. Some of the 19th-century master Benedito Calixto's *(see p34)* best religious paintings adorn the Blessed Sacrament chapel.

❼ Centro Cultural Banco do Brasil

Rua Álvares Penteado 112. **Map** 1 C3.
Tel (11) 3113 3649. Ⓜ São Bento/
Anhangabaú. **Open** 10am–9pm Tue–
Sat, 10am–8pm Sun. ✉ ⓦ **bb.com.
br/cultura**

This early 20th-century building with a lovely Art Deco glass ceiling was once the Bank of Brazil. It now houses the Centro Cultural Banco do Brasil. Inside, there are a series of spaces devoted to showing contemporary arts – from photography, installation works, and fine art to cinema and theater. The exhibition spaces are contained within the bank's original vaults, some of which retain their massive iron doors.

❽ Edifício Itália

Av Ipiranga 344. **Map** 1 B2 & B3.
Tel (11) 3257 3953. **Open** 8am–10pm
daily. Ⓜ República.

The Edifíco Itália, one of São Paulo's tallest buildings, was built in 1965 to honor the thousands of Italian immigrants to the city. The famous postcard shot of Oscar Niemeyer's Edifíco Copan with the vast environs of São Paulo behind was taken from the **Terraço Itália** restaurant *(see p389)* and viewing deck on the 45th floor of the building. People do not usually come for the food – most come for the unbeatable view of this incredible city, a view that is second only to that from the Edifício Banespa.

❾ Edifício Banespa

Rua João Bricola 24. **Map** 1 C3.
Tel (11) 3249 7466. Ⓜ São Bento.
Open 10am–5pm Mon–Fri.

The best panoramic view of São Paulo is from the observation deck on the 36th floor of the Edifício Banespa – a miniature version of New York's Empire State Building. Built in 1939, the building was inaugurated in 1947.

Every morning, a helicopter hovers through the thick smog to report on traffic conditions from here. Blocks of high-rise concrete towers crowd together as far as the eye can see, but the wonder of São Paulo is captured around late afternoon, when the lights start coming on in all the high-rises and the city takes on a different life.

⓾ Pinacoteca do Estado

The Pinacoteca is a significant repository of Brazilian art, with an archive of over 5,000 paintings and sculptures representing all major Brazilian artists and artistic movements. The galleries trace the evolution of Brazilian styles, which began as mock-European naturalism and gradually diversified into social realist, naive, and abstract forms. In the mid-1990s, the Pinacoteca was magnificently renovated by the noted architect Paulo Mendes de Rocha, who filled the original Neo-Classical building with carefully positioned partitions and capped it with a translucent roof. The magical sense of space and light perfectly complements the intensity of color and tone which characterizes Brazilian art.

★ Composição
This Brazilian Constructivist composition by Alfredo Volpi (1896–1988) fuses European style with tropical colors.

Serie Bahia Musa da Paz
Belonging to an infuential group of Paulista artists, José Pancetti (1902–58) rejected a European academic approach to art and strove to return to a more naive style.

Entrance

Octagonal Exhibition Hall

Façade
The Pinacoteca was tastefully refurbished in the 1990s, leaving only the shell of the original building.

The photography exhibition features Brazil's celebrated social documentary photographers.

Auditorium

First floor

Gallery Guide

The Pinacoteca's permanent collection is on the third floor, with galleries housing the Modernist collection, just above the main entrance. Brazilian 19th-century paintings and the more recent works flank this gallery, while sculptures by French artists, such as Aristide Maillol, occupy a prominent display. The second floor is devoted to temporary exhibitions and the first floor has the photography exhibition and also a bookshop and a café.

★ Tropical
Portraying a *caboclo* woman in a tropical setting, this painting by Anita Malfatti (1889–1964) is a fine example of Brazilian Modernism.

VISITORS' CHECKLIST

Practical Information
Praça da Luz 2, Jardim da Luz.
Map 1 C1.
Tel (11) 3324 1007.
Open 10am–5:30pm Tue–Sun.

w pinacoteca.org.br

Transport
M Luz.

Third floor

Formal portraits of Portuguese colonial dignitaries are the most European of the Brazilian paintings.

★ Caipira Picando Fumo
Almeida Júnior (1850–99) was one of the first to paint Brazil's rich tropical light and everyday Brazilians.

Génio do Repouso Eterno
This statue is regarded by many to be one of the most beautiful works of legendary French sculptor, Auguste Rodin (1840–1917).

Second floor

Pintura (1969)
Brazilian artist Tomie Ohtake (1913–2015), mother of the famous architect Ruy Ohtake, introduced Japanese elements into Brazilian art.

Second floor, with a temporary exhibition area

Key

- Brazilian Painting
- Landscapes (1850–1930)
- French Sculpture Yard
- Brazilian Contemporary Art
- Brazilian Constructivism
- Brazilian Sculpture
- Art by European Visitors
- Temporary Exhibition Gallery
- Photography Exhibition
- Non-Exhibition Space

Elegant façade of the Mosteiro da Luz, housing the Museu Arte Sacra

⑪ Museu Arte Sacra

Av Tiradentes 676. **Tel** (11) 3326 1373. M Tiradentes.
Open 10am–5:30pm Tue–Sun.

Often overlooked by visitors, this small museum boasts one of the finest collections of religious artifacts in the Americas. The exhibits are housed in a large wing of a distinguished colonial building, the early 19th-century Mosteiro da Luz. Restful and serene, the entire complex is a peaceful haven from the frenetic chaos of São Paulo.

The museum's priceless objects and artifacts include lavish monstrances (ceremonial vessels), ecclesiastical jewelry, and church altarpieces. Of particular note is the statuary, with pieces by many of the most important Brazilian Baroque masters such as Aleijadinho, Mestre Valentim, and Frei Agostinho da Piedade. One of the gems is the 18th-century Mary Magdalene by Francisco Xavier de Brito, which displays an effortless unity of motion and melancholy contemplation. Among the sculptures, mostly by anonymous Brazilian indigenous artists, two pieces stand out – a majestic African-Brazilian São Bento (with blue eyes) and an exquisitely detailed 18th-century Neapolitan nativity crib comprising around 2,000 pieces, which is the most important of its kind outside Naples. The collection also features works by

São Bento with baby, Museu Arte Sacra

18th-century masters such as Benedito Calixto and Mestre Athayde. Of special significance is the one that depicts Padre Anchieta taming a wild ocelot with the cross, a symbol of the Jesuit founder of São Paulo's mission to the indigenous Brazilians.

⑫ Estação da Luz

Praça da Luz 1. **Map** 1 C1. **Tel** (0800) 550 121. M Luz.

One of modern Brazil's prominent symbols of industrial progress, São Paulo's railway station was built in 1901. The design of the Estação da Luz is a homage to the English railroad, and imitates the Victorian eclectic style.

Just like all of São Paulo's railways, Estação da Luz was the creation of Brazil's first industrialist, the Visconde de Mauá. After a visit to London in the 1840s, Mauá was convinced that Brazil's future lay in rapid industrialization. He founded an ironworks, employing some 300 workers from England and Scotland. In 1854, Mauá opened his first railway, which was designed and run by the British. It linked Jundiaí, in the heart of São Paulo's coffee region, with Santos on the coast. Today, the Estação da Luz serves only the São Paulo city area. Romanesque red-brick arches and stately cast-iron pillars support a single vault that covers four tracks and platforms.

⑬ Estação Pinacoteca

Largo General Osório 66. **Map** 1 C1. **Tel** (11) 3335 4990. M Luz.
Open 10am–6pm Tue–Sun.
free admission on Sat.

Located in an attractive early 20th-century Neo-Classical building, the annex of the Pinacoteca do Estado (see pp144–5) is one of the city's best contemporary exhibition spaces. Some of Brazil's finest Modernist paintings, taken from the archive of the Fundação José e Paulina Nemirovsky, are displayed here.

An important milestone in Brazilian Modernism is Antropofagia by Tarsila do Amaral (1886–1973), the founder of the vital antropofagismo movement (see pp34–5). There are also key pieces by Candido Portinari, Anita Malfatti, and Lasar Segall. International art is represented by Marc Chagall, Pablo Picasso, and Georges Braque, among others.

⑭ Sala São Paulo

Praça Júlio Prestes 16. **Map** 1 B1. **Tel** (11) 3367 9500. M Luz.
Open 10am–6pm Mon–Fri. by appointment a day in advance, 1–4:30pm Mon–Fri, 2pm Sat.
W salasaopaulo.art.br

Known for the finest acoustics in Latin America, this concert hall was inaugurated in 1997. It is the city's premier classical music venue for symphonic and chamber music and the home of Brazil's top orchestra, the Orquestra Sinfônica do Estado de São Paulo (OSESP).

The orchestra's artistic director Arthur Nestrovski is a composer and classical guitarist specializing in Brazilian music.

The grand railway building, the Estação Júlio Prestes, in which the hall is housed, was designed in 1938 by Brazilian architect Cristiano Stockler. Largely inspired by New York, it contrasts strongly with the English Estação da Luz.

⑮ Museu de Arte de São Paulo (MASP)

One of Brazil's finest museums, MASP preserves a vast collection of European old masters and early Modernist paintings. Pietro Maria Bardi, a Brazilian of Italian origin, scouted around Europe between 1947 and 1953. He bought the now priceless works of Degas, van Gogh, Velázquez, Rembrandt, Turner, Titian, Bellini, and Raphael at absurdly low prices. By the 1960s, the works had become so important that Bardi persuaded the São Paulo authorities to build a gallery to house them.

The extensive collection is constantly rotating, as paintings are taken in and out of the archive. The works are loosely grouped by country.

VISITORS' CHECKLIST

Practical Information
Av Paulista 1578. **Map** 4 F2.
Tel (11) 3251 5644.
Open 11am–6pm Tue–Sun.
🖼 free admission on Tue. 🗂 🖼

Transport
Ⓜ Trianon–Masp.

The Schoolboy by van Gogh (1888), Northern European Collection

Resurrection of Christ (1501/1502) by Raphael, Italian collection

covering the 150 years of Venetian Renaissance and Baroque painting, from Bellini to Saraceni. A Titian and a Tintoretto are prominently featured, besides Bellini's beautiful *Madonna and Child*.

Italian Art

Of the museum's three dozen pre-19th-century Italian paintings, 17 date from the early Renaissance, prior to 1510. These include a series of iconogaphic religious works from Florence and Modena, a particularly haunting painting of a penitent St. Jerome in the desert by Andrea Mantegna, and *Resurrection of Christ* by Raphael. There are also 10 paintings of impeccable quality,

French Art and Parisian School

With more than 300 paintings, from the 18th to early 20th century, France dominates the museum. The collection has a wonderful chronological consistency. A few notable exceptions apart, including David, Millet, Seurat, and Braque, all the major artists are represented. Also showcased here are those who drew influence from late 19th- to early 20th-century Paris, such as Van Gogh, Chagall, and Picasso. Many of the works are among the artists' greatest masterpieces, especially those by Manet and Cézanne. Another gem is Toulouse-Lautrec's *Paul Viaud Dressed as an 18th-century Admiral* (1901).

Art from the Iberian Peninsula and Northern Europe

The rest of Europe is represented as a chronological mishmash of glorious paintings. Of particular note are very fine Spanish pieces by Velázquez, El Greco, and a magnificent series of etchings and portraits by Goya, the best of which is that of Cardinal Luís María de Borbón y Vallabriga (1800). Central Europe has some fine works by Bosch, Holbein, Memling, Rembrandt, Rubens, and Franz Hals. There are also a few paintings by Frans Post, depicting Dutch colonial Pernambuco. England is represented by a group of respectable works by Constable, Gainsborough, Joshua Reynolds, and Turner.

Brazilian Art

Though not as vast as Rio de Janeiro's Museu Nacional de Belas Artes *(see p78)*, or the Pinacoteca do Estado *(see pp144–5)*, MASP contains works by Almeida Júnior, Brecheret, Di Cavalcanti, Tomie Ohtake, and Candido Portinari, among others.

The room displaying works from MASP's French collection

Aerial view of the exclusive Avenida Paulista

⑯ Avenida Paulista

Map 4 E2, F2 & F3. **Ⓜ** Brigadeiro/Trianon-Masp/Consolação. 🏳️‍🌈 Gay Pride (Jun).

Modern São Paulo's first symbol of prosperity, Avenida Paulista and its crowded skyscrapers continue to attest to Brazil's status as South America's major economic power. Though often compared to New York's Fifth Avenue, it is actually a corporate valley, business-like and functional.

In the 19th century, when a Uruguayan named Joaquin Eugenio de Lima first set up house here, Paulista was a hill on the outskirts of a small colonial town surrounded by pastoral land and forest. Around this time, São Paulo was growing rich on trains and coffee. Others followed de Lima and began to build large houses here.

By the turn of the 19th century, the avenue had become São Paulo's most desirable address, and was lined with large, opulent mansions owned by extremely wealthy Brazilian moguls, or the coffee barons. Each mansion reflected the architectural predilections of the owner, be it Neo-Classical, Rhineland, or even mock-Tudor. Having suffered large-scale demolition after World War II, the avenue had lost its splendid character by the 1960s. Today, only one mansion remains, the French-style **Casa das Rosas**, which is now a cultural center managed and run by São Paulo state. Interesting art shows are occasionally held here, but the 1935 mansion itself is well worth visiting for its pretty rose garden and Art Nouveau stained-glass window.

There are a few other sights of interest along the street. The **Instituto Itaú Cultural**, near Brigadeiro metro station, hosts a range of concerts and exhibitions, all of which are free of charge. It also houses the largest currency museum in the country, the Itaú Numismática. The **Centro Cultural FIESP**, at Trianon-Masp, is a business headquarters with a small Centro Cultural that presents free live theater and hosts occasional art shows.

Immediately to its north and opposite MASP is the **Parque Trianon**, the only green respite from the concrete. It was named in homage to the gardens of the Palace of Versailles, to which it bears no resemblance. However, in the quiet of the early morning, small mammals, including agouti and marmosets, can be seen foraging here, and in the heat of the day, the trees provide welcome shade.

There are plenty of cinemas in and around Paulista, along the avenue itself, in the Shopping Paulista Mall, near Brigadeiro metro, and dotted along Rua da Consolação, near Paulista's northern end.

Together with the Praça da Sé (see p142), Paulista is one of the city's most important venues for protests and celebrations.

For a taste of Avenida Paulista as it once was, head a few blocks south, across the chic shopping streets of the Jardins and into Jardim Europa. Here, along Avenida Brasil and Avenida Groenlandia, the stately homes of the city's current rich can be seen.

🏛 **Casa das Rosas**
Av Paulista 37. **Tel** (11) 3285 6986. **Open** 10am–10pm Tue–Sat, 10am–6pm Sun & public hols.

🏛 **Centro Cultural FIESP**
Av Paulista 1313. **Tel** (11) 3146 7406.

🏛 **Instituto Itaú Cultural**
Av Paulista 149. **Tel** (11) 2168 1777. **Open** 9am–8pm Tue–Fri, 11am–8pm Sat & Sun. ✉

🌳 **Parque Trianon**
Rua Peixoto Gomide 949. **Open** 6am–6pm daily.

⑰ Museu do Futebol

Estádio do Pacaembu, Praça Charles Miller s/n. **Ⓜ** Paulista. **Open** 9am–5pm Tue–Sun (hours may change on match days). **W** museudofutebol.org.br

The Museum of Football is not to be missed by any fan of "the beautiful game." Explore the history of soccer in Brazil and its impact on both

Parque Trianon, with its lush greenery, on Avenida Paulista

For hotels and restaurants in this region see pp373–4 and pp389–90

local society and the global community. The focus here is as much on Brazilian people as it is on the sport itself, allowing visitors to get a sense of how habits and behaviors changed in this country throughout the 20th century.

The temporary exhibits at the museum are complemented by a 16-stage "fan path," which visitors may walk through. Each room along the route offers a mixture of some of the history and excitement of soccer.

⑱ Liberdade

Praça da Sé, via Av da Liberdade.
Ⓜ Praça de Sé/Liberdade.
🚌 Liberdade Rodoviária.

São Paulo is home to more ethnic Japanese people than any other city outside Japan. Liberdade, located just south of the city center, is the hub of the Japanese community. The neighborhood, small and easily manageable on foot, is best explored during the afternoon. Streets are lined with shops and restaurants selling everything, from woks and manga comics to sushi and sashimi. On Sundays, there is a lively market in the **Praça de Liberdade**, where stalls serve up steaming lacquer bowls of miso soup and yakisoba noodles.

Liberdade's main thoroughfare, Rua Galvão Bueno, runs south from this square, lined with the bulk of the shops and decorated with red Japanese arches, or *torii*. Many of Liberdade's most traditional Japanese restaurants are located on, and around, Rua Tomaz Gonzaga, which cuts across Galvão Bueno, south of the square.

At the corner of Galvão Bueno and Rua São Joaquim, an undistinguished block houses the **Museu da Imigração Japonesa** (Japanese Immigration Museum). The museum was opened in 1978 by the erstwhile prince, now Emperor Akihito of Japan. It has two floors of artifacts and displays devoted to telling the story of the Japanese immigrant

Shrine Gate at Oriental Quarter Japanese Town, Liberdade

community, their origins, and their lives in early 20th-century Brazil. These include a replica of the *Kasato-Maru* – the ship which brought the first immigrants in 1908 *(see p173)* and a complete early Japanese-Brazilian agricultural cottage. The building also features a lovely rooftop garden.

One of São Paulo's many Buddhist temples, built in 1995, the **Templo Busshinji** lies west of the Museu da Imigração Japonesa on the same street. Its traditional Japanese-style architecture comprising wood is topped with a pyramid-shaped roof. Visitors are welcome to attend the various ceremonies, the most impressive of which is the Cerimônia de Kannon, which takes place each month. The rituals, paying homage to the Buddha's compassionate nature, are accompanied by traditional Japanese instruments.

🏛 **Museu da Imigração Japonesa**
Rua São Joaquim 381. **Tel** (11) 3209 5465. **Open** 1:30–5:30pm Tue–Sun. 📷

🏯 **Templo Busshinji**
Rua São Joaquim 285. **Tel** (11) 3208 4515. **Open** 9am–5pm daily. 📷 by prior appointment. 📷

São Paulo Fashion Week

Established in 1996, São Paulo's fashion week is Latin America's most important fashion event. All of the top Brazilian names and faces, including Amir Slama and Havaianas, are showcased here, together with supermodels from around the world. The fashion fraternity can be seen in hip bars and boutiques in the wealthy corners of the city. Over 100,000 people visit the show itself, which takes place twice a year – usually in January and March or April – in Oscar Niemeyer's Bienal building in Parque do Ibirapuera *(see pp150–51)*. More column inches are devoted to the event than to any other activity in Brazil, except for soccer and political scandals. The event generates an estimated $45 million through the media alone, with more than 2,500 newspaper and magazine pages and almost 200 hours of television coverage.

A fashion show in full swing, with models displaying a collection

⑩ Parque do Ibirapuera

Parque do Ibirapuera is the largest green space in central São Paulo, and its native Brazilian woodlands and lakes are a welcome respite from the city's urban sprawl. Opened in 1954, it houses several museums and exhibition spaces, as well as a complex of buildings by the country's celebrated architect, Oscar Niemeyer (1907–2012). These stage major exhibitions such as the Terracotta Warrior exhibition from China and the Rodin retrospective.

Monumento às Bandeiras
Completed in 1950, this tribute to explorers or *bandeirantes*, who opened up Brazil's interior, is one of the more severe works by Brazil's foremost sculptor, Victor Brecheret.

★ **Hotel Unique**
Hotel Unique *(see p373)*, the intriguing, half-melon structure on stilts, is the most famous work of Brazil's leading contemporary architect, Ruy Ohtake, son of the artist Tomie Ohtake.

KEY

① **The Bosque da Leitura** or "reading wood" is the place to head for on Sundays. Visitors can borrow a book and read in the shade of the trees.

② **The small vivarium** houses a few species of native subtropical trees.

③ **The restored, state-of-the-art planetarium** is one of the most impressive in Latin America and is very popular with children. All shows are in Portuguese.

④ **A son et lumière** fountain show is held here on weekends.

⑤ **The Monumento do Pedro Álvares Cabral** honors the Portuguese explorer who first set foot on Brazilian soil in 1500.

⑥ **Museu Afro Brasil** is devoted to celebrating Afro-Brazilian culture. It hosts films, exhibitions, dance, music, and theater events.

⑦ **Auditório Ibirapuera**

⑧ **The Bienal Building**, also by Niemeyer, stages the city's flagship fashion, art, and other premier events – São Paulo fashion week and the Art Bienal, among others.

Pavilhão Japonês
This pavilion and its gardens were built in strict accordance with traditional Japanese design, using only Japanese materials. There is also an exhibition space and a Japanese tearoom.

The lush expanse of Lago do Ibirapuera (Ibirapuera Lake) in the park

VISITORS' CHECKLIST

Practical Information
Av Pedro Álvares Cabral.
Map 4 E5.
Open 5am–midnight daily.
Museu de Arte Moderna, Gate 3:
Tel (11) 5085 1300. **Open** 10am–
6pm Tue–Sun. free on Sun.
Museu Afro Brasil, Gate 10:
Open 10am–5pm Tue–Sun.
Bosque da Leitura, Gate 7: Av
República do Líbano 1551.
Open 9:30am–4pm Sun.

★ O Obelisco aos Heróis de 32
This giant Cleopatra's needle was built to honor the Paulistano rebels who died in 1932 when President Vargas crushed resistance to his Estado Novo regime *(see p59)*.

Oca do Ibirapuera
Designed by Oscar Niemeyer, this dome pays homage to the indigenous Brazilian roundhouse. It hosts major international art exhibitions and cultural events.

★ Museu de Arte Moderna (MAM)
The best of Brazilian contemporary art is showcased here. This work, *Cristo de Rapadura* by Caetano Dias, is a sculpture of Christ made from raw cane sugar. The idea is that it will gradually be consumed by visitors, thus symbolizing the lives of African slaves who died working in Brazil's sugar industry.

Façade of the imposing Museu Paulista do Ipiranga in the Parque de Independência, Ipiranga

⑳ Museu Paulista do Ipiranga

Parque da Independência s/n, Ipiranga. **Tel** (11) 2065 8000. 📧
Open 9am–5pm Tue–Sun. 📷 📵
🌐 mp.usp.br

In 1822, Dom Pedro I declared the famous "Grito de Ipiranga," or call for independence from Portugal (Independência ou Morte, or Independence or Death), on the banks of the Rio Ipiranga *(see p56)*. This large palace, built in 1890, was one of the earliest monuments of independent Brazil.

The Museu Paulista is housed in the palace at the top of extensive formal gardens in the Parque da Independência. The museum is devoted to the nation's history, containing a collection of exhibits which includes old maps, traditional colonial furniture, carriages, rare documents, old coins, clothing, and paintings. The artist Pedro Américo's monumental canvas *Independência ou Morte* (1888), depicting the young prince shouting his *grito* (cry), sits in the building's most handsome room, the Salão Nobre.

The mock French Renaissance gardens are dotted with sculptures and monuments. These include an enormous bronze sculpture to the nation's independence, *Monumento a Independência*, made by the Italian sculptor Ettore Ximenes in 1921. In the chapel at the base of the monument a

tomb contains the remains of Dom Pedro I and Empress Leopoldina. Also in the grounds is the **Casa do Grito**, a replica of the simple adobe house depicted by Pedro Américo in his painting.

㉑ Museu de Arte Contemporânea

Rua da Reitora 160, Cidade Universitária. **Tel** (11) 3091 3039. 📧
Open 10am–6pm Wed, Fri–Sun & public hols, 10am–8pm Tue & Thu. 🏛 by appointment. ♿ 📵
🌐 macvirtual.usp.br/mac

A treasure trove of modern and Post-Modern European and Brazilian art lies tucked away in the campus of São Paulo's most distinguished university. The collection at the Museu de Arte Contemporânea (MAC) is an amalgamation of donations given by wealthy individuals since the early 20th century and prizes from São Paulo's Art Biennials. The collection comprises

Estrada de Ferro Central do Brasil by Tarsila de Amaral at MAC

some 8,000 works of art. Prominent among these are important, little-seen European works by Amadeo Modigliani, Pablo Picasso, Max Ernst, and Henri Matisse, which sit alongside the cream of Brazil's artists. Brazilian Modernists, such as Anita Malfatti, Vitor Brecheret, and Candido Portanari, are well represented. MAC also holds three of the most celebrated works by Tarsila do Amaral – *A Negra*, *Estrada de Ferro Central do Brasil*, and *A Floresta*. Tarsila was the founder of *antropofagismo (see pp34–5)* – a movement that paved the way for many important artistic trends within postwar Brazil.

㉒ Instituto Butantã

Av Vital Brazil 1500, Cidade Universitária. **Tel** (11) 3726 7222. 📧 **Open** 9am–4:30pm Tue–Sun. 📷 📷 by appointment. 🌐 butantan.gov.br

The Instituto Butantã is a biomedical research center affiliated to the Cidade Universitária, the University of São Paulo. Founded in 1901 by Vital Brasil to conduct research into venomous animals, the institute is now one of the leading producers of anti-venoms and sera in the world. It is also one of the city's principal tourist attractions, as it is located in a pretty forested garden full of hummingbirds.

Pits alongside the center and an adjacent museum house many of South America's more exotic snakes and arachnids. Smaller but even deadlier creatures can be seen through microscopes in the institute's **Museu de Microbiologia**. This bright, modern space also includes excellent interactive displays which are particularly popular with children.

㉓ Jardim Botânico

Av Miguel Stéfano 3031. **Tel** (11) 5067 6000. **Open** 9am–5pm Tue–Sun.

Other than the Serra da Cantareira mountains on the city's western fringe, the Jardim Botânico is the largest area of green in São Paulo's metropolitan area. It combines formal gardens, laid out around a series of lakes with areas of forest large enough to support several resident troops of red howler monkeys. Their guttural calls can be heard here at dawn and dusk and sometimes the monkeys themselves can be seen in the trees. There is plenty of other wildlife too, including agoutis, pacas, and tufted-eared marmosets. The latter often loiter about in the trees around the lawns of the sculpture garden hoping to grab a fruity morsel.

The entrance to the park is through an avenue of magnificent royal palms, surrounded by tropical and subtropical trees. Most are labeled with their common and scientific names (the former in Portuguese only). The avenue leads to the **Jardim Lineu**, inspired by the gardens in Uppsala, Sweden, and, like them, are laid out in homage to 18th-century biologist Carl Linnaeus. Glass houses here contain a number of Atlantic rainforest plants and a botanical museum preserves a bank of Brazilian seeds from flowering plants and important fruit species.

Beyond the Jardim Lineu are areas of ponds and lawns popular with picnickers on the weekends. These are fringed

Pond with a tropical forest glade at the Jardim Botânico

with tropical forest cut by short trails and little running streams. Walkers should be wary of snakes.

㉔ Parque Burle Marx

Av Dona Helena Pereira de Morais 200. **Tel** (11) 3746 7631. **Open** 7am–7pm daily.

Roberto Burle Marx (1909–94) was South America's greatest landscape architect and one of the three core designers of Brasília *(see pp298–9)*. His designs were strongly influenced by Modernist ideas inspired by his studies in

Germany, and his early work with the architect Lucio Costa who had worked with Le Corbusier. Burle Marx was one of the first architects to combine sculptural and painting techniques with landscape design.

His gardens in the Parque Burle Marx have been compared to abstract paintings, utilizing simple shapes, and some curvilinear and rectilinear patterns to create blocks of color and texture, broken by paths and areas of woodland. Marx was a keen ecologist and promoted the use of Brazilian native species, and the park is surrounded by a small area of forest, comprising various Mata Atlântica species.

Although Marx contributed to Parque do Ibirapuera *(see pp150–51)*, this park is the only exclusive example of his work in his home city. The gardens were originally private, commissioned for the millionaire industrialist "Baby" Pignatari in the 1940s.

As well as landscaping, Burle Marx was allowed to experiment and place abstract structures in the gardens. These include mirrors of water and rectangular blocks reminiscent of the low Mixtec buildings in Mitla, Mexico. The constructions near the avenue of palms at the park's entrance are by Oscar Niemeyer.

Abstract rectangular structures, Parque Burle Marx

SHOPPING IN SÃO PAULO

Shopping in São Paulo is like shopping in a large North American city. It is largely mall- and boutique-based and geared toward high-end luxury goods. However, more interesting are markets and fairs that take place around town on weekends, selling traditional goods. Unlike many big cities in South America, São Paulo has no exclusive crafts markets or traditional artisan ware of note, but there are a few arts and crafts specialist shops. São Paulo is Latin America's fashion capital and the districts of Jardins, Pacaembu, and Vila Madalena are bursting with smart little fancy boutiques. Many others can be found in the city's numerous opulent malls, which are large, air-conditioned, and filled with restaurants, entertainment areas, and shops housing international brands and leading Brazilian designers. The city's other good buys, including CDs, books, coffee, and *cachaça* can also be bought from malls. High-quality household items can be found on Rua Gabriel Monteiro Silva in Jardins.

Designer shops lining Rua Oscar Freire

Shopping hours

Shops in São Paulo are open from 8am to 6pm. Street shops tend to open from 8 or 10am to 6pm. They are closed on Brazilian public holidays. Most shopping centers and malls are open from 10am to 10pm and on weekends (including Sunday) from 10am to 8pm. They often do not close on public holidays.

Fashion

The domestic fashion market in Brazil is flourishing, with almost all Brazilian labels coming from São Paulo. The market is strongest for women's clothing and the best place to begin a browse is in Jardins. Here, hundreds of tasteful little shops sell colorful, beautifully cut clothes. Many of the latest generation of young Paulistana designers, such as **Adriana Barra** and **Cris Barros**, have their showrooms in Jardins. These labels are particularly strong on dresses and evening wear. More established names can be found here too. **Amir Slama** opened his own store here and now stocks the world's sexiest and most fashionable bikinis.

Other designers, such as rising star **Santa Paciência**, celebrated for her elegant and original use of light, flowing fabrics, are based in Pacaembu, a short taxi drive away from central São Paulo.

Music & Film

Bossa nova, *samba*, *frevo*, *forró*, *axé*, *choro* – it is difficult to think of a country with as many homegrown musical genres as Brazil. São Paulo is the best place in the country either to begin an acquaintance with this diversity or to explore its variety.

Many of the larger stores give customers the chance to listen to CDs before buying. Such shops are to be found in many of the larger malls but the best in the city is probably **FNAC**, which also stocks an excellent selection of Brazilian DVDs. Its selections of Latin American art-house films are particularly strong.

Grandes Galerias, or the **Galeria do Rock**, has a large choice of rock CDs and DVDs. This arcade has around 100 different small shops selling every manner of CD and DVD. However, only a few stores offer the desirable option of listening before buying.

Beverages

The raw ingredient for the *caipirinha* cocktail, Brazilian *cachaça* or sugar-cane rum is sometimes difficult to find outside of Brazil. But in São Paulo, bottles are on sale in any corner shop at a reasonable price. The **Cachaçaria Paulista**, however, is a bar and shop for connoisseurs, selling more than 300 different *cachaças*, the best of which are said to be from Minas Gerais.

Very fine coffee beans and grounds can be bought here. **Santo Grão** in Jardins and boutiques in the various malls have shops selling gourmet and quality blends. Some of the very best are to be found in the shop of the Museu do Café in Santos (*see p172*).

Brazilian music CDs

Books & Magazines

Large bookshops can be found in the malls and are usually well-stocked with English-language novels. The greatest variety is to be found in FNAC, **Saraiva**, and **Livraria Cultura**. The bookshops attached to the **MASP** and **MAM** galleries are well worth a browse. Brazilian art books are of a very high international standard and much of the material, including reproductions of European art kept in Brazil, can only be found here. Particularly interesting are the gorgeous photographic books. Brazilian art and social photography is excellent and well represented in the gallery souvenir shops.

Overpriced international papers and magazines can also be bought at the larger bookshops. There are no English-language publications in Brazil. Portuguese readers will find newsstands or *bancas* dotted throughout the city, with a bewildering variety of glossy reading material to choose from.

Household knick-knacks on display at Jacaré do Brasil

Arts, Crafts & Design

Although arts and crafts are best bought regionally, particularly in centers such as Manaus, Palmas, or Caruaru, there are a few specialist shops in São Paulo. The **Casa das Culturas Indígenas** sells indigenous jewelry and household goods. **Jacaré do Brasil** stocks indigenous and regional items from household decoration to textiles.

Paulistanos adore decor. **Etel Interiores** has exquisite top-end home furnishings from furniture to small decorative items. The most interesting pieces are made from sustainable materials in Acre in the Brazilian Amazon. **Firma Casa** stocks the best of Brazil's furniture makers.

Shopping Malls

There are shopping malls throughout the city, many of which stock similar items and brands, making it difficult to choose between them. The best design names are to be found in South America's oldest mall, **Iguatemi**, which still looks as if it was built yesterday. **Shopping Ibirapuera** has the most shops and perhaps the greatest middle-brow choice.

São Paulo has only one department store, **Daslu**, but it is internationally famous and attracts élite and wealthy clients from around the continent. Many international and Brazilian big design names are sold here, together with Daslu's own brand.

DIRECTORY

Fashion

Adriana Barra
Alameda Franca 1243.
Map 4 F3.
Tel (11) 2925 2300.
W **adrianabarra.com.br**

Amir Slama
Rua Oscar Freire 977.
Map 4 D2.
Tel (11) 3061 0450.

Cris Barros
Rua Vitório Fasano 85.
Map 4 D3.
Tel (11) 3082 3621.

Santa Paciência
Rua Girassol 223, Vila Madalena.
Map 3 A1.
Tel (11) 3814 9188.

Music & Film

FNAC
Av Paulista 901.
Map 4 F3.
Tel (11) 2123 2000.

Galeria do Rock
Rua 24 de Maio 62 & Av São João 439. **Map** 1 B2.

Beverages

Cachaçaria Paulista
Rua Mourato Coelho 593, Pinheiro. **Map** 3 A3.
Tel (11) 3815 4756.

Santo Grão
Rua Oscar Freire 413.
Map 4 D3.
Tel (11) 3082 4892.

Books & Magazines

Livraria Cultura
Av Paulista 2073.
Map 4 E2.
Tel (11) 3170 4033.

MAM
Parque do Ibirapuera, Portão 3.
Map 4 E5.
Tel (11) 5085 1300.
W **mam.org.br**

MASP
Av Paulista 1578.
Map 4 F2.
Tel (11) 3251 5644.
W **masp.art.br**

Saraiva
Morumbi Shopping, Av Roque Petroni Jr. 1089, Morumbi.
Tel (11) 5181 7574.

Arts, Crafts & Design

Casa das Culturas Indígenas
Rua Augusta 1371, loja 107.
Map 4 E1.
Tel (11) 3283 4924.

Etel Interiores
Al Gabriel Monteiro da Silva, 1834.
Map 3 A4.
Tel (11) 3064 1266.
W **etelinteriores. com.br**

Firma Casa
Al Gabriel Monteiro da Silva 1487.
Map 3 B4.
Tel (11) 3068 0377.
W **firmacasa.com.br**

Jacaré do Brasil
Rua Melo Alves 555.
Map 4 D2.
Tel (11) 3081 6109.
W **jacaredobrasil. com.br**

Shopping Malls

Daslu
Av Juscelino Kubitschek 2041, Vila Olímpia.
Tel (11) 3841 4000.
W **daslu.com.br**

Iguatemi
Av Brig. Faria Lima 2232.
Map 3 A5.
Tel (11) 3816 6116.

Shopping Ibirapuera
Av Ibirapuera 3103.
Tel (11) 5095 2300.

ENTERTAINMENT IN SÃO PAULO

São Paulo has an incredible nightlife with a bewildering choice of activities on offer. Live music, in diverse styles, is performed every night by the most distinguished artists in the country. Brazil's finest orchestra, theater, and concert halls are also located in São Paulo. The city boasts myriad dance clubs offering *samba, forró,* and a dozen other traditional styles, alongside ubiquitous international club music, often with a Brazilian twist. A wide range of films can be viewed as well, with state-of-the-art multiplexes showing the latest blockbusters from Europe, Latin America, or Asia and art-house theaters offering popular national cinema. A progressive city, São Paulo has the largest Gay Pride parade in the world, which takes place in June. Children are welcome everywhere – even in bars and restaurants, and the largest theme park in South America, Playcenter, lies on the city's doorstep.

Guides & listings

The **Tourist Information Desk** at Guarulhos International Airport offers information in English about what's on in the city. The Friday edition of the *Folha de São Paulo* and *Estado do São Paulo* newspapers and *Veja* magazine's cultural insert, *Veijinha,* have comprehensive listings in Portuguese.

The central ticket-selling office in São Paulo is **Ticketmaster**, which sells tickets through the Saraiva and FNAC bookshops *(see p155).*

Live Music

A plethora of small venues in the *bairros* of Vila Madalena, Pinheiros, and Vila Olímpia play host to all manner of live acts. Almost all have a small restaurant area, a dance floor, and a sitting area. All have bars and serve beer and excellent cocktails. Musical performances may vary from week to week – from *samba* to Brazilian funk, *bossa nova,* or the latest post-*mangue* beat sounds from the state of Pernambuco. The best venues include **A Marcenaria** and the **Bourbon Street Music Club**, featuring jazz and Dixieland.

More popular performers, such as João Bosco or Otto, play in the **SESC**s – cultural centers with excellent concert halls. The best are in Vila Mariana and Pompéia. Legendary singers such as Milton Nascimento and Caetano Veloso play in numer-

Sergio Dias, Ceumar, and Rebecca Matta performing at SESC Pompéia

ous concert halls such as the **Via Funchal**. The most popular national and international groups, such as Ivete Sangalo and U2, play in the Pacaembu stadium.

Classical Music & Dance

Brazil's most reputable orchestra, the São Paulo State Symphony Orchestra, has its home in Latin America's best 1,500-seat concert hall, the **Sala São Paulo**. The acoustics here are almost perfect. The Sala São Paulo regularly advertises its upcoming programs on its website. The city's other key music venue for opera and classical concerts is the distinguished **Theatro Municipal**. The **Teatro Alfa** specializes in ballet.

Dance Bars & Clubs

Dance bars and clubs are concentrated in two areas of the city – Vila Madalena and Pinheiros, southwest of the center, and the contiguous *bairros* of Vila Olímpia, Itaim, and Moema in the south. The former is more lively, with live *forró* and *samba* bands playing to bars filled with university students. The **Bambú** and the **Canto da Ema** are always packed at weekends. Vila Olímpia, Itaim, and Moema are generally livelier

Popular Vila Madalena Club in São Paulo

neighborhoods and are home to the bulk of clubs which play host to big-name DJs, such as Marky and Patiffe, and play techno and trance music. The Consolação area is very popular for nightlife and has numerous trendy venues, including **Sonique**, **Volt**, and **Z Carniceria.**

Cinema & Theater

The city has some 250 cinema houses and hosts several important film festivals. Almost all the shopping malls have large multiplexes showing not only the latest films from Hollywood but also national releases. There are more than 20 art-house cinemas, including the **Cine SESC** and the **Reserva Cultural** off Avenida Paulista. Non-Portuguese films are subtitled rather than dubbed.

São Paulo has more than 100 theaters with shows almost exclusively in Portuguese. Most of the theaters are found in Bela Vista and Bixiga. The **Cultura Inglesa** features English-language films and TV shows.

Fans cheer during a championship match at the Estádio Morumbi

Children

São Paulo's urban environment makes outdoor attractions for children few and far between, although there are some popular amusement and theme parks scattered across the city. However, the biggest attraction, the largest theme park in Latin America, the **Playcenter**, is 50 miles (80 km) from São Paulo. The city also boasts the **Fundação Parque Zoológico de São Paulo** (São Paulo Zoo), set in a state preserve of coastal rainforest.

Soccer

Soccer is an obsession in São Paulo, as it is throughout the country, and the city has the most prestigious soccer teams in Brazil. There are three First Division teams based in São Paulo who play in the impressive Morumbi and Pacaembu stadiums. **Estádio Morumbi** is the home ground of São Paulo Futebol Clube. Matches are generally held on Wednesday and at the weekend. To watch a game check the schedules in ticket offices.

DIRECTORY

Guides & Listings

Ticketmaster
w ticketmaster.com.br

Tourist Information Desk
Guarulhos International Airport.
Tel (11) 6445 4029.

Live Music

A Marcenaria
Rua Fradique Coutinho 1378, Vila Madalena.
Map 3 A2.
Tel (11) 3032 9006.

Bourbon Street Music Club
Rua dos Chanés 127, Moema.
Tel (11) 5095 6100.

SESC
SESC Vila Mariana, Rua Pelotas 141.
Tel (11) 5080 3000.
w sescsp.org.br

Sonique
Rua Bela Cintra 416.
Map 4 F1.
Tel (11) 2628 8707.

Via Funchal
Rua Funchal 65, Vila Olímpia.
Tel (11) 3044 2727.

Classical Music & Dance

Sala São Paulo
Praça Julio Prestes 16.
Map 1 B1.
Tel (11) 3367 9500.

Teatro Alfa
Rua Bento Branco de Andrade Filho 722, Santo Amaro.
Tel (11) 5693 4000.

Theatro Municipal
Praça Ramos de Azevedo.
Map 1 C2 & C3.
Tel (11) 3397 0300.

Dance Bars & Clubs

Bambú
Rua Purpurina 272. **Map** 3 A1. Tel (11) 3031 2331.

Canto da Ema
Av Brig. Faria Lima 364, Pinheiros.
Tel (11) 3813 4708.

Sonique
Rua Bela Cintra 461. **Map** 4 F1. Tel (11) 2628 8707.

Volt
Rua Haddock Lobo 40.
Map 4 F1.
Tel (11) 2936 4041.

Z Carniceria
Rua Augusta 934. **Map** 4 F1. Tel (11) 2936 0934.

Cinema & Theater

Cine SESC
Rua Augusta 2075.
Map 4 E2.
Tel (11) 3087 0500.

Cultura Inglesa
Rua Deputado Lacerda Franco 333.
Tel (11) 3032 4888.

Reserva Cultural
Av Paulista 900, São Paulo.
Map 4 E2.
Tel (11) 3287 3529.

Children

Fundação Parque Zoológico de São Paulo
Av Miguel Stéfano 4241.
Tel (11) 5073 0811.

Playcenter
Rua José Gomes Falcão 20, Barra Funda.
Tel (11) 2244 7529.
w playcenter.com.br

Soccer

Estádio Morumbi
Praça Roberto Gomes Pedrosa 1, São Paulo.
Tel (11) 3749 8000.

SÃO PAULO STREET FINDER

Map references given in this guide for entertainment venues, shopping areas, and other attractions in São Paulo City refer to the Street Finder maps on the following pages. Map references are also provided for São Paulo City restaurants *(see pp389–90)* and hotels *(see p373–4)*. The first figure in the map reference indicates which Street Finder map to turn to, and the letter and number

that follow refer to the grid reference on that map. The map below shows the different areas of São Paulo City – Centro, Bela Vista, Jardins, and Jardim Paulista – covered by the five Street Finder maps. Symbols used for sights and useful information are displayed in the key below. A list of important places of interest marked on the maps can be found on page 140.

Aerial view of downtown São Paulo

0 meters 750
0 yards 750

Scale of Maps 1–2 & 3–4

0 meters 250
0 yards 250

Streetwise in São Paulo

São Paulo has one of the highest crime rates of any city in the world. However, most of the violence is restricted to the isolated areas dominated by the *favelas* (shantytowns), which lie on the periphery of the city far from the upmarket areas more frequented by visitors. Though you are unlikely to meet with serious trouble in São Paulo, it is important nonetheless to take all adequate precautions. Visitors are required to carry their identification documents at all times.

Visitors must exercise greater caution while traveling in certain parts of the city, including the district of Luz,

areas around the city's main train station, Praça da Sé, Praça da República, and Praça Roosevelt. Be careful in the city center late at night, as well as in the cheap accommodation area around Rua Santa Efigênia.

Cameras, credit cards, and cash should be kept out of sight, preferably in a money belt, with a few notes left in a pocket or handbag. It is wise to withdraw cash only during the day and use ATMs that are within the bank premises rather than in a crowded street.

The metro is safe for commuting during the day, but it is recommended to use taxis after dark. These can be booked through a hotel or rented at one of the many taxi stands.

Driving and navigation in São Paulo are difficult. Carjacking and red-light robberies are common after dark. As a result, the traffic law allows drivers to slow down at red lights and continue driving without stopping if there is little or no traffic on the roads.

Brigadeiro metro station entrance in Paulista Avenue, São Paulo

If held up or driven at gunpoint to an ATM machine, avoid any provocation that could prove fatal.

There have been many incidents of organized violence by the PCC (Primeiro Comando da Capital) against public servants and police. In the unlikely event of PCC activity, it is advisable to stay in your hotel.

Key

- ▢ Place of interest
- ▢ Other building
- 🚃 Train station
- Ⓜ Metro station
- 🚌 Bus station
- ℹ️ Visitor information
- ➕ Hospital
- 🚔 Police station
- ✝ Church

Crowded shopping street lined with a selection of stores, São Paulo

SÃO PAULO STATE

São Paulo is famous for its beaches, pristine island resorts, spectacular surf, and majestic rainforests. Divided into Litoral Norte and Litoral Sul, the state's coastline is one of the most incredible in the southern half of Brazil. São Paulo's agricultural hinterland is the reason it is Brazil's economic powerhouse. It is also home to a diverse range of immigrant communities.

The colony of Brazil was officially established in São Vicente (present-day Santos) in 1532 by Martim Afonso de Souza. The handful of sailors that remained formally named the beach São Vicente, and, as pioneers, had to fend for themselves in a new land, coping with assaults launched by the local Tamoio Indians. Settlements followed shortly after in nearby Santos and in São Sebastião, opposite the island of Ilhabela, now a beautiful resort. All towns in the region preserve interesting sights and legacies dating from their early colonial days.

Most visitors, however, come to the São Paulo coast not for history but for sand, surf, and rainforest. Ilhabela, Brazil's largest tropical island, Ubatuba, whose 70 beaches stretch to the state's far north, and Guarujá, similar to Copacabana in Rio

City, with similar numbers of high-rise buildings facing the ocean, are the most popular destinations. All three have beaches that have consistently been rated among the nation's top ten by the country's tourist magazines. Puma and ocelot still hunt in the wild Atlantic mountain forests which lie only a short distance behind them.

The full majesty of the Atlantic coastal forest, the Mata Atlântica, unfolds around Estação Ecológico Juréia-Itatins, and Cananéia in the Litoral Sul. Lush ridges, waterfalls, and abundant plant life are its main attractions. The forest is also home to a wide array of animals, birds, and brilliantly colored butterflies. One of the loveliest spots is Ilha do Cardoso, a boat ride from Cananéia, where caimans can be seen basking in the sun on the beaches.

Stream flowing through the lush Mata Atlântica near Ubatuba

◀ Ilha Urubuqueçaba, Santos, as seen from Morro Voturuá

Exploring São Paulo State

The São Paulo coast is divided into the Litoral Norte, which stretches towards Rio in the northeast from the port city of Santos, and the Litoral Sul, which stretches from Santos towards Paraná state. The Litoral Norte is one of the most heavily visited coastlines in southeastern Brazil. Beaches on the Ilhabela, Brazil's largest tropical island, and the resort of Ubatuba, are magnificently backed by towering spurs swathed in tropical rainforest. The sands of the Litoral Sul are darker and siltier than those of the Litoral Norte. Around Cananéia and Juréia, and stretching into Paraná, are the largest tracts of lowland coastal forest outside the Amazon. The beautiful beaches of the Ilha do Cardoso are just a boat ride away from Cananéia.

Key

Area illustrated

Sights at a Glance

Towns & Cities

1. Ubatuba
2. São Sebastião
5. Guarujá
6. Santos
7. São Vicente
9. Iguape
10. Cananéia

State Parks & Areas of Natural Beauty

8. Estação Ecológica Juréia-Itatins

Islands

3. Ilhabela
11. Ilha do Cardoso

Beaches

4. Maresias

Key

▭▭▭ Highway

━━━ Major road

▭▭▭ Minor road

∿∿∿ Railroad

▭▭▭ State border

△ Peak

For hotels and restaurants in this region see p374 and p391

The beautiful Praia das Toninhas in Ubatuba

Getting Around

There are two large airports – international and domestic – in São Paulo City. Regular bus services ply between São Paulo City and the major towns on the coast, but reaching the best of the beaches requires a car. The main routes to the coast are the Anchieta and Imigrantes highways between São Paulo City and Santos. From Santos, the route north follows the Rio–Santos (SP-055), which passes through all the major beach towns and heads into Rio de Janeiro state. The Litoral Sul can be reached by SP-055, which reaches only as far as the northern part of Juréia State Park. Towns farther to the south can be reached off highway BR-116.

Verdant Mata Atlântica (Atlantic rainforest) in São Paulo

For keys to symbols *see back flap*

Picinguaba beach in Ubatuba with Serra do Mar mountains in the distance

① Ubatuba

🏠 65,000. ✈️ 🚌 ℹ️ Av Iperoigi 214, (12) 3833 9123.

Lying at the northern extreme of São Paulo state and sitting at the feet of the Serra do Mar mountain range, Ubatuba is a little beach resort with a small colonial center lined with terraced houses. Glorious beaches surround the resort.

The most popular beaches, especially those south of the town center such as **Praia Grande**, have an excellent infrastructure, including play areas for children. Buses running along the coastal road pass other nearby beaches, such as **Enseada**, **Picinguaba**, and **Flamengo**. Even in high season it is easy to find a quiet stretch of sand or lonely cove tucked away along the coast to the south of Ubatuba.

The **Aquário de Ubatuba** in the center of the town contains some of the largest tanks and most diverse range of tropical marine life in all of Brazil. The office of the **Projeto Tamar**, a Brazil-wide organization that monitors and preserves turtle nesting beaches, is also located in town. Visitors are permitted to witness turtle hatchings under supervision.

The Serra do Mar rises in a vertiginous green wall only a short distance north of Ubatuba and an easy drive away from the town. Carpeted in thick primary forest, the Serra is home to many endangered endemic species. Birdlife, too, is prolific in this picturesque mountainous area.

🐟 Aquário de Ubatuba
Rua Guaraní 859. **Tel** (12) 3834 1382. **Open** 10am–8pm Sun–Tue & Thu, 10am–10pm Fri & Sat. 🐢

🐢 Projeto Tamar
Rua A. Atanázio 273. **Tel** (12) 3832 6202. **Open** 10am–6pm Mon, Tue, Thu & Sun, 10am–8pm Fri & Sat.

Environs
The twin beaches of **Domingas Dias** and **Lázaro**, whose white sands curve gently on either side of a forest-clad promontory, are located 11 miles (18 km) south of Ubatuba. The **Peninsula da Ponta da Fortaleza** lies just south of Domingas Dias and is fringed with many quiet beaches, including **Praia Vermelha do Sul**. Surfers head north of Ubatuba to **Praia Vermelha do Norte** for the best waves on the Litoral Norte.

② São Sebastião

🏠 58,000. 🚌 ℹ️ Av Doutor Altino Arantes 174, (12) 3892 2620. 🎉 Festas do 20 de Janeiro (Jan). 🌐 saosebastiao.com.br

São Sebastião was founded in the early 17th century, when Brazil's coastline was cloaked in a forest larger than the Amazon. North of Guanabara Bay was Tamoio indigenous country, and São Sebastião became the northernmost Portuguese outpost for the indigenous slave trade. As it grew, the city became one of the country's first sugar-growing centers and the thirst for slave labor became unquenchable. The city was also among the first to receive Africans in the slave trade.

Although most people who come to São Sebastião do so merely to pass through on their way to Ilhabela, the town has a colonial center of historical importance which merits at least a couple of hours' leisurely stroll before departing.

São Sebastião's colonial streets lie in the few blocks between the shoreline and the Praça Major João Fernandes at the heart of the city, easily recognizable by the imposing 17th-century church, the **Igreja Matriz**, which watches over it. This is largely a 19th-century reconstruction devoid of much of its original church art. However, the refurbished **Museu de Arte Sacra**, housed in the 17th-century chapel of São Gonçalo, a block to the south of the church, preserves a number of beautiful, delicate images of Christ. Dating from the 16th century, these images were found within cavities in the wall of the Igreja Matriz during its restoration in 2003.

There are also a few streets lined with Portuguese houses and a number of civic buildings, the most impressive of which is the **Casa Esperança** on the waterfront. Built from stone

Façade of Igreja Matriz, São Sebastião

and wattle and daub congealed with whale oil, the exterior is whitewashed with lime made from thousands of crushed shells. The Casa contains some faded but original 17th-century ceiling paintings and statuary.

Casa Esperança
Av Altino Arantes 144.
Open 9am–5pm Mon–Fri, 7–10am Sat & Sun.

Igreja Matriz
Praça Major João Fernandes.
Tel (12) 3892 1110. **Open** 9am–noon, 1–7pm daily.

Museu de Arte Sacra
Rua Sebastião Silvestré Neves 90.
Tel (12) 3892 4286. **Open** 9am–noon, 2–6pm Tue–Sat.

❸ Ilhabela

28,000. from São Sebastião to Perequê. Praça Vereador José Leite dos Passos 14, Barra Velha, (12) 3895 7220. Festa do Camarão (Aug).
W ilhabela.com.br

One of Brazil's largest islands, Ilhabela rises steeply out of the Atlantic, a short distance offshore from São Sebastião. With a coastline sculpted by dozens of bays and beaches, it is covered in rainforest, much of it cut by fast-flowing mountain streams. Visitors from São Paulo throng here during weekends, but during the week (outside of holiday season) the island is all but deserted. Much of the forest is protected as part of the **Parque Estadual de Ilhabela** and there is plenty of wildlife, including ocelots and several species of primates. The presence of biting flies, or *borrachudos*, on the island make insect repellent essential.

Ilhabela has just two roads. One is paved and runs the entire length of the western, leeward coast. Most of the numerous *pousadas* and guesthouses lie here, as do the villages of **Perequê** (where the ferry arrives), **Borrifos**, **São Pedro**, and **Vila Ilhabela**. The latter has a few colonial remains. Rusting 18th-century

Waterfront at Vila Ilhabela with 18th-century cannon

cannons adorn its waterfront and there is a little avenue of Portuguese buildings, including a 16th-century church, the Matriz de Nossa Senhora d'Ajuda.

The island's other road is a dirt track, usable only by four-wheel drives, which cuts across the interior from Perequê into the park and to the windward beaches. The most spectacular of these is the **Baía de Castelhanos**, a perfect half-moon of sand backed by rainforest-covered slopes. The island's longest beach, and the best for surfing, is **Bonete**, which is 9 miles (15 km) south from Borrifos village, along a rough forest trail.

Ilhabela's forests are dripping with waterfalls, but many are either completely inaccessible or reachable only by trail. A short distance inland from Perequê beach, **Cachoeira da Toca** waterfalls plunge in a series of little cascades into swimming pools, replete with waterslides. **Cachoeira da Água Branca** is larger, with more swimming pools. It is an hour's walk along a trail which begins at the entrance to the state park, a short distance beyond the turn-off to Cachoeira da Toca.

Numerous shipwrecks off Ilhabela also make it a popular scuba-diving destination, despite the murky water.

Blue dacnis, Ilhabela

Cachoeira da Toca
Estrada Baía de Castelhanos.
Open 24 hrs daily.

❹ Maresias

3,000. Praça Pôr-do-Sol, in Boiçucanga, 4 miles (7 km) W of Maresias, (12) 3865 4335.

South of São Sebastião lie a number of beautiful beach resorts. Maresias, the liveliest of the lot, is busy with young, hip Paulistanos at weekends and holidays. **Praia de Maresias** is famous for its powerful surf, which has been the site for many international surfing competitions. **Toque Toque Grande** and **Toque Toque Pequeno**, 6 miles (9 km) south-east, are smaller, quieter beaches, sheltered by rainforest-covered spurs. There are plenty of *pousadas* and restaurants on, or just off, the São Sebastião road, which runs along the coast.

❺ Guarujá

310,000. Av Marechal Deodoro da Fonseca 723, (13) 3344 4600.
W portal.guaruja.sp.gov.br

Situated close to São Paulo and on the way to Santos, this beachtown is a popular weekend and day-trip destination for São Paulo residents. It is known as the "Pearl of the Atlantic" and has about 14 miles (23 km) of white beaches that stretch along the coast. The longest of these, Enseada Beach, is popular with surfers, and its shores are lined with hotels and kiosks. For those who don't only want to soak up the sun, other activities include artisan fishing and looking at the town's historical buildings. The town also has an aquarium.

A fishing village on the coastal outskirts of the city of Santos, São Paulo State ▶

Stained-glass skylight, depicting a representation of Brazil, the *Mãe Douro*, Bolsa e Museu do Café, Santos

❻ Santos

🏙 418,000. 🚌 ℹ Setur, Largo Marquês de Monte Alegre, (13) 3201 8000. 🌐 **santos.sp.gov.br**

When Santos was founded in 1535, it was one of Portugal's first New World settlements. Since the mid-16th century, when neighboring São Vicente was established, Santos had been a port. First it dealt with sugar, and then with African slaves. However, it grew rich on coffee, which was brought out of the mountains on Brazil's first trains, built by the British in the late 19th century.

Scottish tram

Unlike São Vicente, Santos has preserved vestiges of its historical legacy, and, under recent enlightened municipal governance, is reinventing and refurbishing itself. Once decrepit, the city center is undergoing a spruce-up and is now very attractive. Scottish trams in British racing green run through its streets, taking visitors on a whistle-stop tour of the various attractions. The city center is also small enough to stroll around and have a closer look at these sights on foot.

The jewel in the city's crown is the Art Nouveau **Bolsa e Museu do Café**. Its modest Victorian exterior hides an opulent marble-floored turn-of-the-19th-century stock exchange and museum, together with a café shop serving excellent coffee and desserts. The Bolsa was once open only to wealthy (and exclusively male) coffee barons who traded here. When it was built, coffee was the most important and coveted commodity in Brazil.

The auction room is crowned by a magnificent stained-glass skylight, with an arresting representation of Brazil, the *Mãe Douro*; crowned with a star, she rises from flames in a landscape thick with tropical animals and startled-looking indigenous people. The skylight and the beautiful Neo-Renaissance painting of Santos that adorns the walls of the stock exchange are by Brazil's most celebrated mid-19th-century artist, Benedito Calixto *(see p34)*.

A number of Calixto's paintings are displayed in the **Fundação Pinacoteca Benedito Calixto**, which is housed in one of the few remaining coffee baron mansions. The landscapes shown here give an idea of the city's once breathtaking natural beauty.

Santos has a handful of interesting churches, but the only one open to the public is the **Santuário Santo Antônio do Valongo**. The church's mock-Baroque interior dates from the 1930s. The fine original 17th-century altarpiece remains preserved in the Franciscan chapel to the left of the main entrance; the statue of Christ is particularly striking. Next door to the church is the British-built terminus of the now defunct Santos–São Paulo railway. Built between 1860 and 1867, the station is vaguely reminiscent of London's Victoria.

The once-filthy city beaches are now much cleaner and are lively with bustling bazaars, and people playing volleyball and football, every evening and weekend.

A monument to the thousands of Japanese-Brazilians who

Pelé during Champions World Series 2003, New York

Football Legend Pelé

Regarded as the world's most famous sportsman, Pelé was born in Tres Corações, Minas Gerais. He started his career in Santos when, in 1956, the Santos Futebol Clube signed him. Soon, he was offered a place in the Brazilian national team, and went on to play in three of Brazil's five World Cup-winning teams. Since his retirement in 1977, Pelé has worked as a charity patron Goodwill Ambassador for UNICEF. In 1992, he became the UN Ambassador for Ecology and Environment. In 1995, he was appointed Minister of Sports, a post he resigned after becoming caught up in one of the rumored, or real, corruption scandals that blight Brazilian politics.

arrived in São Paulo state in the early 20th century sits here, together with the small but popular **Aquário de Santos**. In addition to a stunning range of tropical marine life, it displays three of the five species of sea turtles found in Brazil. The beaches lying farther out in the Baía de Santos (Bay of All Saints) bustle with activity at the weekends.

For all its history, it is for football that Santos is most famous outside Brazil. Pelé played here for almost all his professional life. The Santos Football Club has an excellent museum, the **Memorial das Conquistas**, devoted to the club's illustrious history.

🐠 Aquário de Santos
Av Bartolomeu de Gusmão, Ponta da Praia. **Tel** (13) 3236 9996. **Open** 9am–6pm Tue–Fri, 9am–8pm Sat & Sun. 🖼

🏛 Bolsa e Museu do Café
Rua 15 de Novembro 95. **Tel** (13) 3213 1750. **Open** 9am–5pm Tue–Sat, 10am–5pm Sun. 🖼 🖼

🏛 Fundação Pinacoteca Benedito Calixto
Av Bartolomeu de Gusmão 15. **Tel** (13) 3288 2260. **Open** 2–7pm Tue–Sun. 🖼

🏛 Memorial das Conquistas
Rua Princesa Isabel 77, Vila Belmiro. **Tel** (13) 3225 7989. **Open** 1–7pm Mon, 9am–7pm Tue–Sun. 🖼 🖼 prior booking required. 🖼

🏛 Santuário Santo Antônio do Valongo
Marquez de Monte Alegre 13. **Open** 8am–6pm Tue–Sun. 🖼

Proud display of trophies at the Memorial das Conquistas, Santos

Japanese Immigration

Brazil is home to the largest number of ethnic Japanese people outside Japan, and almost all their ancestors arrived at Santos. Immigration began in earnest after the Russo-Japanese War (1904–5). Although Japan emerged victorious, the penalty was high, leaving the poorer Japanese population with a bleak future. São Paulo seemed to offer hope, as the state was rich in coffee and workers were in short supply.

The first Japanese ship to land was the *Kasato Maru*, which brought 165 families to Santos on June 18, 1908. They left for the coffee plantations in the Mogiana region. By the beginning of World War II, almost 150,000 Japanese had arrived. After freeing themselves from their labor contracts, communities began to grow in metropolitan São Paulo *(see p149)* and other parts of Brazil.

Japanese Immigration Monument, Santos

🅰 São Vicente

🏙 418,000. 🚌 🌐 saovicente. sp.gov.br

The pleasant, laid-back port town of São Vicente is known more for its historical significance than the usual tourist attractions.

In 1532, Martim Afonso de Sousa established a small settlement on the eastern shores of South America. Thus Brazil was born, in the words of Afonso's brother, with "each man as lord of his own property, and private injuries redressed, and all the other benefits of a secure and sociable life." São Vicente is the scene of that noble beginning, though only a handful of relics belonging to that distinguished past can be found today.

First capital of the Captaincy of São Vicente, as São Paulo state was formerly known, São Vicente won the epithet of "Cellula Mater" (Mother Cell) for being Brazil's first organized town. The 18th-century Baroque parish church, the **Igreja Matriz de São Vicente Mártir**, is one of the very few historical buildings in the city to have survived the ravages of time. A tidal wave destroyed the first church, built close to this site by Martim Afonso shortly after his arrival. The second parish church was built inland on this present site. However, it fared no better, and was ransacked by pirates. The current building, standing on its ruins, is named in honor of the Spanish saint who is patron of the city.

Also in the city center are the remains of Martim Afonso's former home, and the first brick building in Brazil. These are housed inside the impressive late 19th-century **Casa Martim Afonso**, along with a few other interesting pieces of colonial bric-a-brac.

🏛 Casa Martim Afonso
Praça 22 de Janeiro 469, Centro. **Open** 10am–6pm Tue–Sun & public hols.

🏛 Igreja Matriz de São Vicente Mártir
Praça João Pessoa s/n, Centro. **Open** irregular timings.

Striking hills in the Estação Ecológica Juréia-Itatins

❽ Estação Ecológica Juréia-Itatins

🚌 to Iguape, then taxi. 🛈 Av São Pedro 189, Barra do Ribiera, Iguape, (13) 3849 1293. 🗺️ 🖼️

Brazil's coastal rainforest stretches in a series of rippling mountains and lowland forests cut by broad rivers, mangrove wetlands, and pristine beaches all the way through from Peruíbe in southern São Paulo state to Paranaguá in Paraná. The Estação Ecológica Juréia-Itatins sits at the northern end of this rainforest, protecting 316 sq miles (820 sq km) of Mata Atlântica.

Access to the ecological station is restricted to daytime visits only, and must be arranged through the park authorities in Iguape, just south of Juréia-Itatins. Only certain areas are open to the public, and most of these areas require prior permission before entering. Iguape is a good base for information on organized tours.

This is one of the most important breeding grounds for marine species in the southern Atlantic and the myriad forest types growing here protect one of the world's greatest diversities of vascular plant, vertebrate, and invertebrate species. There is a unique range of birds, butterflies, and mammals. Many larger animals, such as jaguars and tapirs, which have all but disappeared from coastal Brazil, live in healthy numbers here.

Juréia itself protects a wide variety of habitats; as a result the scenery is magnificent. Lush green forest swathes the high slopes of the Serra do Itatins in the eastern extremity of the park and continues all the way through to the lowland coastal areas, mixing with mangrove wetlands and perfuming the park's extensive beaches. These beautiful stretches of fine sand, many of which are cut by clear rivers or washed by waterfalls, are so deserted that caimans can occasionally be seen basking in the sun at dawn.

❾ Iguape

🏠 28,000. 🚌 🛈 Preifetura Rua 15 de Novembro 272, (13) 3841 3358. 🌐 **guiadeiguape.com.br**

This pretty little colonial town sits in a pocket of the Brazilian coastal rainforest, the Complexo Estuarino Lagunar de Iguape-Cananéia-Paranaguá, in the midst of breathtaking scenery. The verdant Serra do Mar mountains rise up behind the town which is surrounded by pristine mangrove wetlands and lowland subtropical forest on all sides including the wilds of the Estação Ecológico Juréia-Itatins to the north. The **Mirante do Morro do Espio** is a lookout point with a fabulous view of the port and surrounding area.

Iguape was founded in 1538 by the Portuguese. No buildings remain from that time but the city center preserves the largest collection of post-17th-century colonial architecture in the state. Most are civic buildings and town houses painted in thick primary colors and clustered around **Praça São Benedito**, a sleepy central square watched over by a towering 18th-century basilica.

There are also two small museums in the city center. The **Museu Histórico e Arqueológico** is housed in a 17th-century building which was once the first gold foundry in Brazil. It showcases a mixed bag of historical material, from pre-Columbian remains found in nearby middens to artifacts from the slaving era, and early

Rio Ribeira do Iguape estuary and Igreja do Rosário rising over Iguape town

For hotels and restaurants in this region see p374 and p391

photographs. The **Museu de Arte Sacra** in the 18th-century Igreja do Rosário houses some 100 ecclesiastical objects, most of which date from the 18th and 19th centuries.

🏛 Museu de Arte Sacra
Igreja do Rosário, Rua Papa XXIII s/n. **Open** 9–11:30am, 1–5:30pm Mon–Sat. 🖼

🏛 Museu Histórico e Arqueológico
Rua das Neves 45. **Tel** (13) 3841 3358. **Open** 8am–noon, 1:30–5pm Tue–Sat, 8am–noon Sun. 🖼 ✉

Environs
Just across the Rio Ribeira do Iguape estuary, east of the town center, are extensive stretches of fine white-sand beaches which make up the island of **Ilha Comprida**. They are accessible by road, or a 5-mile (8-km) walk across the estuary and sand flats via the pedestrian bridge.
 Boqueirão Norte, located immediately across the town, and **Praia do Viareggio**, 6 miles (10 km) south, are popular in high season and lined with holiday homes. Farther south still and reachable by dune buggy or by car is the far quieter **Praia das Pedrinhas**.

⑩ Cananéia

🔺 14,000. 🚌 ℹ Av Beira Mar 287, (13) 3851 1931. 🌐 cananéia.net

Cananéia is the farthest south of São Paulo's small colonial seaside towns, and like the others it lies nestled at the feet of the Serra do Mar mountains overlooking stretches of mangrove and an open ocean dotted with forest-covered islands. Outside of the high season few visitors ever make it here and the town's crumbling colonial streets and fig-tree-filled central square often have a sleepy feel to them.
 The most compelling reason to come to Cananéia is to take a boat trip out to the beaches and islands, preferably with plenty of time to spare. Fishing boats and launches can be chartered from the docks in

Stuffed great white shark, Museu Municipal, Cananéia

Cananéia to **Ilha do Cardoso** that lies in the Lagomar bay. Car and passenger rafts take 10 minutes to ferry across the estuary in front of the town to the southern reaches of the **Ilha Comprida**, east of Iguape, and do so several times per day. The beaches here lie a short distance beyond the island's ferry port along a sandy road, which is lined with a handful of tumble-down *pousadas*.
 While in Cananéia, it is worth visiting the tiny town museum, **Museu Municipal**, which preserves bits of nautical miscellany. Pride of place among the exhibits goes to what is reputed to be the largest great white shark ever, weighing a hefty 7,716 lb (3,500 kg), now stuffed, painted, and hanging safely from the museum ceiling.

🏛 Museu Municipal
Rua Tristão Lobo 78. **Tel** (13) 3851 1753. **Open** 9am–6pm Tue–Sun. 🖼

⑪ Ilha do Cardoso

🚤 from Cananéia. ℹ Núcleo Perequê, Cananéia, (13) 3851 1163. 🌐 cananeia.net

Just a 2-hour boat ride south of Cananéia, Ilha do Cardoso, a rugged 58 sq-mile- (150 sq-km-) island, rises dramatically out of the Atlantic Ocean. The island is primarily an ecological preserve which also has beautiful deserted beaches and walking trails. Together with Juréia-Itatins and Superagüi (*see p343*) across the border in Paraná, it forms the core protected area of the Brazilian coastal rainforest. Wetlands, mangroves, extensive beaches, coastal dunes, and all of the numerous forest types associated with the Mata Atlântica are found here. Several species of turtle nest on the island, caimans live in the rivers and estuaries, and jaguars and pumas still hunt in the forests that cover the upper reaches. The island is also rich in birdlife.
 Pre-Columbian shell middens, or *sambaquis*, dot the park's beaches and six traditional *caiçara* fishing communities live within the park, preserving a semi-indigenous way of life which has so far largely resisted the pressures of urbanization. *Caiçara* tidal fish traps can be seen in the shallows of the various little rivers and bays, attesting to the strong indigenous heritage the communities preserve to this day. Many of the *caiçaras* act as guides and boatmen.

Virgin beach on Ilha do Cardoso, near Cananéia

NORTHEAST BRAZIL

Northeast Brazil at a Glance

Comprising the nine states of Bahia, Sergipe, Alagoas, Pernambuco, Paraíba, Rio Grande do Norte, Ceará, Piauí, and Maranhão, the Northeast is truly a tropical paradise. Most of the states have three distinct areas – the fertile coastal strips with idyllic sand beaches giving way to the intermediate hilly areas with lush Atlantic rainforests, also home to a variety of fauna, and finally the vast semi-arid interiors. The beaches here range from the fascinating Canoa Quebrada beach in Ceará, to Genipabu and its sand dunes in Rio Grande do Norte, Porto de Galinhas in Pernambuco, and the Fernando de Noronha archipelago, among many others. The legacy of the Northeast's colonial history can still be seen in numerous, impressive historic monuments in Salvador, Olinda, and São Luís.

São Luís *(see pp256–8)*, capital of Maranhão, was founded by the French. It is a town with a beautiful historic core, Centro Histórico, with cobbled streets and 3,500 pastel-colored colonial buildings, which have been renovated. A UNESCO World Heritage Site, it is one of Brazil's finest examples of Portuguese architecture.

São Luís

Parr

Santa Inês

Teresina

Imperatriz

PIAUÍ & MARANHÃO
(See pp248–59)

Floria

Balsas

Teresina
(see p252)

BAHIA
(See pp184–2

Barreiras

Lenço

Lençóis *(see p208)*, in Bahia, is the perfect starting point to explore the Chapada's caves and waterfalls, or to hike up the 3,937-ft (1,200-m) surrounding peaks. Miners flocked to this area during the gold and diamond rush.

0 km — 200
0 miles — 200

◀ Dazzling white sand surrounds a lagoon at Parque Nacional dos Lençóis Maranhenses, Maranhão

Fernando de Noronha

0 km   3
0 miles   3

Fernando de Noronha *(see pp228–9)*, part of Pernambuco, comprises 21 islands. The warm, clear waters here offer Brazil's best scuba diving and snorkeling experience.

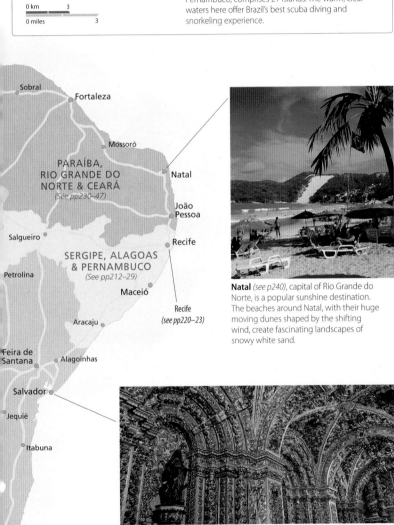

Sobral

Fortaleza

Mossoró

PARAÍBA, RIO GRANDE DO NORTE & CEARÁ
(See pp230–47)

Natal

João Pessoa

Salgueiro

SERGIPE, ALAGOAS & PERNAMBUCO
(See pp212–29)

Recife

Petrolina

Maceió

Recife
(see pp220–23)

Aracaju

Feira de Santana

Alagoinhas

Salvador

Jequié

Itabuna

Teixera de Freitas

Natal *(see p240)*, capital of Rio Grande do Norte, is a popular sunshine destination. The beaches around Natal, with their huge moving dunes shaped by the shifting wind, create fascinating landscapes of snowy white sand.

Salvador *(see pp188–99)*, capital of Bahia, has beautifully restored complexes of Baroque churches and palaces, built during the 18th-century sugar boom. Its historic center, a UNESCO World Heritage Site, offers a unique glimpse into Brazil's history and is the crown jewel of Portuguese architecture.

Afro-Brazilian Culture

A direct legacy of three centuries of slavery, the presence of African culture in the Northeast makes the region distinctly different from the rest of Brazil. Throughout the slavery period in colonial Brazil, there was little or no sanction on miscegenation. Over the years, masters, slaves, former slaves, and their descendants integrated into the new society of Brazil, creating an interesting blend of cultures and bloodlines with Portuguese, Dutch, West African, and Indian elements. This has uniquely resulted in what is now called Afro-Brazilian culture, visible in the people, clothing, food *(see pp182–3)*, religion, and music of the Northeast.

Colorful ribbons, bringing luck if tied around the wrist

Music

Africans brought along their fine command of percussion. Bahia's characteristic brand of Afro-Brazilian music grew in many forms, with axé becoming the signature sound of Salvador's Carnaval. In Pernambuco, as many as 13 distinct rhythms developed, including Recife's signature beat, frevó (see p221). During the 20th century, African music became part of the mainstream. Samba won acceptance in the 1930s.

Pop star Carlinhos Brown is one of the traditional singers who have become world-famous with their percussion-heavy rhythms. This noted advocate of Afro-Brazilian culture hails from Bahia.

Capoeira

A rhythmic, dance-like form of martial arts, capoeira was once practised only by slaves and former slaves. Over the years, it came to put less emphasis on fighting and more on the cooperative elements of dance and display, with rhythmic, graceful moves (see p203).

Traditional instruments used in *capoeira* mainly constitute *berimbau*, a single-stringed percussion instrument featuring a steel string and a hollowed-out gourd; *atabaque*, a large drum, and the *pandeiro*, which resembles a tambourine.

Capoeira was a way for the slaves to continue practicing martial arts, with kicks disguised as fluid body movements. Increasingly popular, today it is taught and performed all over the region, and indeed the world.

Religion

Of West African origin, most of Brazil's original slave population believed in a pantheon of deities, or orixás *(see p198). Each* orixá *was endowed with its own personality and unique powers, and was associated with a particular set of natural elements. The Portuguese, however, insisted that all new arrivals be forcibly converted to Catholicism. The struggle gave rise to Candomblé, a blending of Catholicism and the African beliefs (see p39).*

Festive celebrations, such as the Lavagem do Bonfim *(see p199)*, can be experienced in and around Salvador. The day is meant to honor Yemanjá, the Goddess of the Sea. The ceremonies blend Catholic-style processions with African beats and music.

Arts & Crafts

Many of the Bahian arts and crafts are strongly influenced by Afro-Brazilian traditions. The Mercado Modelo (see p196) in Salvador is a good place for souvenirs. Look for berimbaus and percussion instruments, sometimes painted in bright colors, as well as masks and pottery.

Wooden Masks are intricately carved and decorated with stones, shells, and beads. The northeastern masks are allegoric representations of the *orixás*.

Colorful figurines are produced by local artisans as part of the rich pottery tradition in the Northeast. Drawn from popular folklore, these figurines are sold throughout the region.

Dress

The most striking sartorial examples of African influence are the Baianas, the women in turbans and long white dresses, often seen on the streets of Salvador selling acarajé *(see p183). The ensemble is believed to be derived from the traditional dress of women in Nigeria. While their dresses are often similar, each Baiana wears a different set of jewelry to pay homage to her particular* orixá *(deity).*

Colorful beads and trinkets can be bought from the Baianas. Every color is known to denote a specific *orixá*; the blue is for Oshun, while red represents Yansã.

A young Baiana in traditional dress of layers of starched lace skirts, a shoulder cloth, high turban, and yellow and white beads and accessories.

The Flavors of Northeast Brazil

Northeast Brazil has two distinct regional cuisines, a reflection of both culture and climate. The narrow, densely populated coast, rich in fresh fruit and sugar cane and bordered by a generous sea, is home to an African-descended population who flavor their food with coconut milk and red *dendê* (palm) oil. The interior, or *sertão*, is arid semi-desert, largely given over to cattle tended by the cowboy descendents of Portuguese immigrants. The interior cuisine consists of sober, simple dishes, whose staples include sun-dried meat, manioc (cassava) root, rice, and black beans.

Spicy cayenne pepper

Distinctive *caju* fruit of the cashew tree, showing the nut

Cozinha Nordestina

When Brazilians refer to *cozinha nordestina* (northeastern food) they usually mean the dishes of the hot, dry hinterland. Fresh ingredients are few here, and refrigeration virtually nonexistent. Ingredients include the more resilient vegetables such as beans, corn and, especially, manioc. Meat – beef or, just

as often, goat – in the Northeast is usually either sun-dried *(carne de sol)* or air-dried and heavily salted *(carne seca)*. Both are served in small portions, often shredded, and mixed in with either beans, rice, or manioc. Manioc, indeed, is a centerpiece of northeastern cooking. Sliced into strips and fried, the sweeter version of this versatile root is known as *macaxeira*. Plain ground manioc flour *(farinha)* is often served as a side dish; locals put it in their morning coffee. Pan-fried with a little oil, the manioc flour becomes another common side dish, *farofa*. Finally, the lighter parts of the manioc root are made into tapioca, the base ingredient of desserts and breakfast

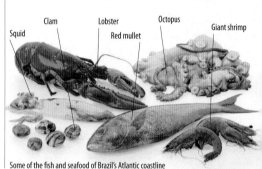

Clam — Lobster — Octopus — Giant shrimp
Squid — Red mullet

Some of the fish and seafood of Brazil's Atlantic coastline

Regional Dishes & Specialties

Dendê oil

Bahian cuisine is the most popular and sophisticated in all of the Northeast. The cooking is characterized by the use of coconut milk, hot peppers, and, importantly, *dendê* oil, which gives the dishes their deep orange color. This oil is extracted from a palm tree that was brought to Brazil by African slaves. Signature Bahian dishes include *moqueca*, *vatapá*, and *bobó de camarão*. All are variations on a tasty seafood stew. Traditionally, a *moqueca* is cooked in a large clay pot and served with white rice and a serving of *pirão*, a manioc paste. Both *bobó de camarão* and *camarão na moranga (see p385)* feature large, juicy prawns cooked in coconut milk. The *camarão na moranga* comes served in a hollowed-out pumpkin shell, its broth thickened with the addition of fresh, sweet pumpkin, locally called *jerimum*.

Bolinho de bacalhau is a Portuguese snack made from mashed potatoes and shredded salt cod.

Baiana woman in traditional all-white costume, selling *acarajé*

Acarajé

Acarajé is one of the most popular snacks, especially in Bahia. Cooked only by Baianas, it was originally served as an offering to Yansã, the Goddess of Tempests. Balls of mashed black-eyed beans are fried in *dendê* oil, then cut open and served with dried shrimp, *vatapá* (shrimp paste), *caruru* (okra stew), and hot sauce. *Abará* is another kind of *acarajé*, steamed and served on a banana leaf with the same toppings.

pancakes. Desserts in the Northeast are usually simple mixtures of sugar and tapioca or cornflour, often covered in condensed milk. Also popular are small and intensely sweet portions of dried and concentrated fruits, such as *caju* (cashew), *jaca* (jackfruit), *goiaba* (guava), and banana, usually consumed together with a small, very sweet cup of coffee.

Fish & Seafood

The long Atlantic coastline from Bahia to Maranhão yields a wealth of fish, shellfish, and crustaceans. Everywhere on the coast, the *guaiamu*, a small, blue-shelled crab with tasty meat, is usually steamed and served up as an appetizer. Larger, soft-shelled crabs are also popular, served steamed and eaten whole, including the shell. Another crustacean

is the *cavaquinha*, a small lobster known for its sweet and tender meat, but the full-size south Atlantic lobster is also found to the north, around Ceará. Large and succulent shrimp are another regular menu item. However, the tastiest northeastern shrimp, the *pitu*, is a freshwater variety. Spicy *pitu moqueca* is among the best featured on any menu.

Grated manioc root ready to be processed into tapioca

ON THE MENU

Baião de dois Made with rice, beans, cheese, and garlic, this dish is often served with sun- or air-dried meat.

Caldo de sururu A rich broth made from tiny clams with coconut milk, *dendê* oil, coriander, and spices.

Carne de sol Goat meat or beef is sun-dried to seal in moisture. It may be served grilled or sautéed.

Casquinha de siri A savory appetizer of shredded crab-meat flavored with coriander, coconut milk, and spices.

Tapioca Small pancakes made with tapioca, served stuffed with sweet or savory fillings.

Xinxim de galinha Chicken sautéed in *dendê* oil with ginger, dried shrimp, and cashew nuts. Served with white rice and manioc flour.

Moqueca is a rich fish dish made with coconut milk, *dendê* oil, cayenne pepper, and coriander (cilantro).

Ensopado is a seafood and coconut milk stew made without *dendê* oil, making it lighter in flavor.

Cocada is a sweet made with sugar and coconut. The darker variety is sweetened with dried sugar-cane juice.

BAHIA

The largest state in the Northeast, Bahia is known for its endless stretches of stunning beach along the Atlantic coast. The idyllic white-sand coast is dotted with laid-back resorts along its length. Beyond the gorgeous beaches and plains, where most of Bahia's population lives today, lies the *sertão*, an arid semi-desert partially covered in *caatinga*, a dry scrub forrest rich in plant and bird life.

When the Portuguese first arrived in Bahia in 1500, the entire 621-mile (1,000-km) coastline was covered in a swathe of lush green Atlantic rainforest. Today, only a few pockets of the rainforest remain along the coast in isolated patches. Inland from the coast, the Portuguese successfully established the cultivation of sugar cane, and later cotton and cocoa in the Recôncavo, a narrow, flat, well-watered plain, which they called the *agreste*.

Bahia played a key role in the history of Brazil. Salvador, its capital, was founded in 1549, and served for over two centuries as the administrative and political center of colonial Brazil. The legacy of that period is on display in Salvador's colonial core, Pelourinho, a jewel of colonial Baroque churches, cathedrals, and palaces.

Bahia was also the key point of entry for the thousands of slaves brought to Brazil from ports in Africa. The legacy of that transatlantic trade can be seen in Bahia's cultural diversity. The state has Brazil's highest percentage of Afro-Brazilian residents. Bahia's percussion-driven music, the fast fight-dance known as *capoeira*, and the spiritualist Yoruban Candomblé religion all have their roots in Africa.

In addition to these legacies, visitors to Bahia can experience one of Brazil's longest and most beautiful coastlines. Fine beach resorts such as Praia do Forte and Costa do Sauípe lie to the north of Salvador. To the capital's south, there are small villages such as Morro de São Paulo and Itacaré. Inland, Bahia provides unique hiking amid the mesas and valleys of the Chapada Diamantina.

A view of the Parque Nacional Marinho dos Abrolhos, comprising an archipelago of five islands

◀ The bright colors of Pelourinho's Old Town

Exploring Bahia

Living up to its official motto, *Sorria, você está na Bahia* (Smile, you're in Bahia), Bahia offers a diverse range of sights. The extensive coastline varies from fine Linha Verde resorts to sleepy villages with stunning unspoilt beaches such as Trancoso. Salvador and the historic towns of the Recôncavo provide fascinating glimpses into Brazil's history. The Chapada Diamantina is a highland region that resembles the mesas of Arizona and New Mexico in Southwest USA. Lençóis, founded during the area's 19th-century gold and diamond rush, boasts caverns, waterfalls, and some of Brazil's best hiking.

Sights at a Glance

Towns & Cities

- ❶ Salvador pp188–99
- ❸ Santo Amaro
- ❹ Cachoeira
- ❺ São Félix
- ❽ Itacaré
- ❾ Ilhéus
- ❿ Porto Seguro
- ⓫ Trancoso
- ⓭ Lençóis
- ⓯ Canudos

National Parks

- ⓬ Parque Nacional Marinho de Abrolhos
- ⓮ Parque Nacional de Chapada Diamantina pp208–9

Areas of Natural Beauty

- ❷ Ilha de Itaparica
- ❻ Morro de São Paulo
- ❼ Peninsula de Maraú

Beaches & Resorts

- ⓰ Linha Verde p211

0 kilometers 100
0 miles 100

A white-sand beach resort near Itacaré, with palm trees lining the shore

Key

- ▬ Highway
- ▬ Major road
- ▭ Minor road
- ▬ Railroad
- ▬ State border
- △ Peak

For hotels and restaurants in this region see pp374–5 and pp391–2

Key

Area illustrated

Fortaleza

São Francisco

Abáré

Curaçá

rolina
àzeiro

Macururé Glória

Paulo
Afonso

Recife

Formosa

Massaroca

Uauá **15** CANUDOS

Jeremoabo

Senhor do
Bonfim

Euclides
da Cunha

Campo Formoso

Cicero
Dantas

Queimadas
Tucano

Nova
Soure Cipó

Conceição
do Coité

Aracaju

Mangue Seco

Serrinha Inhambupe

Esplanada

Alagoinhas

Feira de
Santana

16 LINHA VERDE

Pojuca

Porto Sauípe

CACHOEIRA **4** **3** SANTO AMARO

SÃO FÉLIX **5** Camaçari

ILHA DE **2** **1** SALVADOR
ITAPARICA

Amargosa

6 MORRO DE SÃO
PAULO

Jequié

Camamu **7** PENINSULA
DE MARAÚ
Marau

Ipiaú

8 ITACARÉ

Itabuna **9** ILHÉUS
Ibicaraí

Buerarema

Itapetinga Una

Potiraguá Canavieiras

Itapebi Belmonte

Santa Cruz Cabrália

10 PORTO SEGURO

Guaratinga

11 TRANCOSO

Itamaraju

Monte Pascoal
1,758 ft (536 m)

Prado

Alcobaça

Caravelas

Helvécia

Mucuri

12
PARQUE NACIONAL
MARINHO DE ABROLHOS

A Baiana under Mario Cravo's towering
A Cruz Caída

Getting Around

Bahia is large, and the roads are mostly precarious. However, the Linha Verde (BA-099), which runs north along the coast from Salvador to the border with Sergipe, provides easy, quick access to the beach towns. South from Salvador, the BR-101 runs parallel to the coast, about 37 miles (60 km) inland. Access to beach towns on the southern coast is via secondary roads. The best way to get around is to fly to one of the major destinations, such as Salvador, Ilhéus, or Porto Seguro, and proceed by bus to explore the surrounding regions. The main destination inland, the Chapada Diamantina, is a drive from Salvador on the BR-324, BR-116, and BR-242 highways. Lençóis in the Chapada Diamantina can be reached by road and plane.

For keys to symbols *see back flap*

❶ Salvador

Founded by the Portuguese in 1549 on the protective shores of the Baía de Todos os Santos (Bay of All Saints), Salvador is Brazil's fourth-largest city, after São Paulo, Rio de Janeiro, and Belo Horizonte. Modern Salvador offers a fascinating blend of old and new. In the colonial heart, Pelourinho, the cobblestoned streets are lined with the restored 17th- and 18th-century palaces and Baroque churches. The city's recent growth has been eastwards along the beaches that face the Atlantic. The city's vibrant community of musicians draws from the region's African and Portuguese heritage, blending these into a unique Bahian sound.

Azulejos in the cloisters of Igreja e Convento de São Francisco

Imposing buildings in Pelourinho, the heart of Salvador

Sights at a Glance

Historic Buildings, Streets, Towns & Neighborhoods
① Pelourinho pp190–91
② Fundação Casa de Jorge Amado
⑦ Praça da Sé
⑧ Palácio Rio Branco
⑨ Elevador Lacerda
⑩ Mercado Modelo
⑮ Forte de Santo Antônio

Churches, Cathedrals & Monasteries
⑤ Catedral Basílica
⑥ Igreja e Convento de São Francisco pp194–5
⑯ Nosso Senhor do Bonfim

Museums
③ Museu Tempostal
④ Museu Afro-Brasileiro
⑪ Museu de Arte Sacra
⑫ Solar do Unhão
⑬ Museu de Arte da Bahia
⑭ Museu Rodin-Bahia

For hotels and restaurants in this region see pp374–5 and pp391–2

Getting Around

Most of the attractions in Salvador are concentrated in Cidade Alta (Upper City), linked to the Cidade Baixa (Lower City) by a funicular railway and the Carlos Lacerda elevator. The historic neighborhood of Pelourinho is located downtown, on top of a bluff overlooking the harbor. The main sights outside Pelourinho are within walking distance of the bustling waterfront. Bus services easily connect to every part of the city. Travelers coming from the south can take BR-101 around the Baía de Todos os Santos and connect to the BR-324. Those arriving from the north can follow the BR-009, called the Linha Verde.

VISITORS' CHECKLIST

Practical Information

2,900,000. Rua Francisco Muniz Barreto, Pelourinho, (71) 3321 2463. daily market at Mercado Modelo, Praça Cayru, (71) 3241 2893. Lavagem do Bonfim (Jan), Carnaval (Feb/Mar). **bahiatursa.ba.gov.br**

Transport

22 miles (35 km) from city center. Av Antônio Carlos Magalhães 4362, Pernambués, (71) 3450 3871. Av Oscar Pontes 1051, (71) 3254 1020.

| 0 meters | 200 |
| 0 yards | 200 |

Greater Salvador

Bonfim

São Caetano

Terminal da Estação Marítima

| 0 km | 1 |
| 0 miles | 1 |

Quintas

Barris

Rio Vermelho

Pituba

Barra

Ondina

Amaralina

ATLANTIC OCEAN

Key

- Area of the main map
- Highway
- Major road
- Minor road
- Railroad

For keys to symbols see back flap

① Street-by-Street: Pelourinho

The crown jewel of Salvador is the restored historic center, Pelourinho, which means whipping post. This originally described only the small triangular plaza in the heart of the city where slaves were publicly flogged. Located on a high bluff overlooking the commercial city below, Pelourinho was built by the Portuguese in the boom years of the 18th and 19th centuries as a residential and administrative center. Abandoned for a greater part of the 20th century, Pelourinho was designated a UNESCO World Heritage Site in 1985. Today, visitors can explore its magnificent colonial houses, Baroque churches, and museums.

④ ★ **Museu Afro-Brasileiro**
The large wood carvings of the Candomblé deities by renowned artist Carybé are the highlights of this museum of Afro-Brazilian culture.

⑤ **Catedral Basílica**
Built in 1657, the renovated cathedral has a cedar-wood altar, and two smaller side altars, both covered in thin layers of gold

⑦ **Praça da Sé** offers views across the Baía de Todos os Santos

Pastel-hued buildings along the slope of Pelourinho

LARGO DO CRUZEIRO DO SÃO FRANCISCO

RUA MONTE ALVERNE

Terreiro de Jesus, one of the most beautiful squares in Pelourinho, was laid out in 1549 by governor Tome de Souza.

Key

— Suggested route

⑥ ★ **Igreja e Convento de São Francisco**
A silver chandelier weighing 176 lb (80 kg) hangs over the ornate carvings of this richly embellished church

Locator Map
See Salvador map pp188–9

Igreja Nossa Senhora do Rosário dos Pretos
Built by slaves in the 18th century, the church remains the center of Afro-Brazilian traditions in Pelourinho.

② ★ **Fundação Casa de Jorge Amado**
The lovely café inside Foundation House, which is dedicated to the life of one of Brazil's most famous authors, is decorated with hundreds of book jackets from Amado's novels published around the world.

0 meters 100
0 yards 100

Museu Abelardo Rodrigues Solar do Ferrão
One of Brazil's largest private collections of sacred art is housed here.

Igreja da Ordem Terceira de São Francisco
The fine 18th-century sandstone façade of this church was rediscovered only in the 1930s. Craftsmen chipped away at plaster for nine years to reveal this marvelous building.

② Fundação Casa de Jorge Amado

Largo do Pelourinho s/n. **Tel** (71) 3321 0070. **Open** 10am–6pm Mon–Fri, 10am–4pm Sat. **W** jorgeamado.org.br

Although Brazilian author Jorge Amado (1912–2001) never lived in Pelourinho, many of his beloved novels were set in this neighborhood *(see p204)*. Opened in 1987, the Casa de Jorge Amado is a small museum housed in a pretty blue colonial building located at the top end of Largo do Pelourinho. It is one of the main monuments dedicated to Bahia's most famous author. Its four floors comprise the entire archive of his work and include a research center.

The collection on display consists mostly of covers of his books and personal belongings that tell the story of his life. A mural on the ground floor shows the languages into which his works have been translated – over 49 in total.

Covers of Amado's books exhibited at Fundação Casa de Jorge Amado

③ Museu Temostal

Rua Gregorio de Matos 33, Pelourinho. **Tel** (71) 3117 6383. **Open** noon–6pm Tue–Fri, noon–5pm Sat & Sun. 🖺

Housed in a beautiful colonial building in the heart of Pelourinho, this museum displays only a fraction of founder Antônio Marcelino's collection of 30,000 postcards and photographs. Most date from the 19th and 20th centuries. Antique postcards comprising the main display tell the history of Salvador as it

Antique postcard displayed at the Museu Temostal

has developed and grown. Some cards are enlarged to give visitors a better view of the photographic details. A smaller exhibit of *belle époque* postcards showcases some elaborate samples of postcard "art," some adorned with embroidery, others painted like aquarelles.

④ Museu Afro-Brasileiro

Praça XV de Novembro, Terreiro de Jesus s/n. **Tel** (71) 3283 5540. **Open** 9am–5pm Mon–Fri. 🖺

This small museum in the former Faculty of Medicine building houses a collection of photographs, artwork, and artifacts all related to the African diaspora in Brazil. The main exhibit displays objects and crafts from the original African cultures of regions such as Angola and Nigeria where Brazil-bound slaves were captured. The highlight of the collection is the 27 life-sized wood carvings of the *orixás* *(see p181)* by Bahian artist Carybé (1911–97), depicting their weapons and regalia, together with the animals or domain over which they are thought to rule. Yemanjá, Goddess of the Sea, is shown with a fish and seashells and the mirrors and trinkets offered to her by supplicants; the warrior Ogun is shown with his sword and armor.

Yansã, Candomblé Goddess of Tempests, at Museu Afro-Brasileiro

⑤ Catedral Basílica

Praça XV de Novembro, Terreiro de Jesus s/n. **Tel** (71) 3321 4573. **Open** 9am–5pm Mon–Sat, 1–5pm Sun. 🗓 11am–noon Sun; Baroque concert held every Sun at 11am. 🖺

Salvador's main cathedral, built between 1657 and 1672, is considered to be one of the richest examples of Portuguese Baroque architecture. The cathedral's façade is made of Portuguese *lioz*, a type of limestone. The interior walls and tall pillars are also covered with the pale-colored stone, giving the church a bright and spacious feel.

The vaulted ceiling of the main nave is made from wood. The decorations are carved in relief and stand out from the ceiling with an almost three-dimensional effect. The main altar and two smaller side altars are also carved out of wood and covered in gold leaf.

Dedicated to St. Francis, the altar contains a silver-plated statue of Nossa Senhora das Maravilhas (Our Lady of Miracles), which is said to have inspired Father Antônio Vieira, a 17th-century Jesuit priest who fought against the enslavement of indigenous people. His fiery, anti-slavery sermons did not sit well with the Inquisition, who subsequently ordered his arrest. The former Jesuit library now holds a small museum of religious art. The collection includes silver and gold religious artifacts such as chalices and candle-holders. The most modern piece in the cathedral is the powerful German organ with more than 500 pipes, 18 registers, and two keyboards.

Altar of Catedral Basílica, the main cathedral of Salvador

⑥ Igreja e Convento de São Francisco

See pp194–5.

⑦ Praça da Sé

Pelourinho's Praça da Sé blends the modern with the historic. The square is a transition point between the Terreiro de Jesus and the Praça Tomé de Sousa. Extensive renovations have added fountains and benches,

so people can linger and enjoy the *capoeira* presentations or other cultural events often held in the square.

There is a lookout point, the Belvedere, on the north side of the square which provides a beautiful view of the Lower City and the Baía de Todos os Santos (Bay of All Saints).

⑧ Palácio Rio Branco

Praça Tomé de Sousa s/n. **Tel** (71) 3116 6928. **Open** 10am–6pm Tue–Fri, 9am–1pm Sat & Sun.

The original Palácio Rio Branco has nothing in common with the building that currently goes by that name. The first palace was built on this site in 1549 to house Bahia's first governor, Tomé de Sousa. The Portuguese queen and later the prince regent resided in this palace temporarily in 1808, when the entire Portuguese court relocated to Rio de Janeiro in order to escape Napoleon's invasion of Portugal *(see p56)*. The building survived until 1900, when the whole structure was leveled and then rebuilt from scratch in Renaissance style.

A fire in 1912 forced another major overhaul by the Italian architect Júlio Conti, giving the building the eclectic look it still has today. Used as an official government building until 1979,

the Palácio Rio Branco was rededicated in 1986 as a cultural foundation, the Centro Memoria da Bahia. The former reception hall on the ground floor now tells the history of Bahia's 40 governors through paintings, historic documents, and their personal belongings.

The fine interior is a blend of Rococo plasterwork and frescoes. Of particular note are the big dome and the magnificent views from the belvedere in the wing looking onto the sea, as well as the iron and crystal stairway and a sculpture representing Tomé de Souza.

Art Deco Elevador Lacerda with market stalls below

⑨ Elevador Lacerda

Praça Tomé de Sousa s/n (Upper City); Praça Visconde Cairu (Lower City). **Open** 6am–11pm.

Built by merchant Antônio Francisco de Lacerda in 1873 from the original Jesuit-installed manual pulley, the famous Elevador Lacerda connects Salvador's Upper and Lower cities.

The Elevador Lacerda is a popular site in Salvador, used by more than 30,000 people daily. The elevator's current Art Deco look dates from a 1930s restoration. Four elevators make the 236-ft (72-m) trip up vertical shafts in just 30 seconds, where the view across the bay on a clear day is simply stunning.

Preparations for a cultural show outside Palácio Rio Branco

⑥ Igreja e Convento de São Francisco

The complex of the Church and Convent of St. Francis, which was constructed between 1708 and 1750, is one of Brazil's most impressive Baroque monuments. The convent's church stands out for its rich and opulent interior. The inner walls and the ceiling are largely covered in gold leaf. The main altar and the large side altars are magnificently carved out of wood and in typical Baroque style, ornately decorated with angels, birds, mermaids, fruits, and leaves. An enormous silver chandelier hangs above intricate wooden carvings, and hand-painted blue-and-white Portuguese tiles.

★ Franciscan Shield
Featuring the crossed forearms of Jesus and St. Francis, the shield represents the bond between the two.

São Pedro de Alcântara
The altar of São Pedro de Alcântara, carved by Brazilian artist Manuel Inácio da Costa, is a particularly fine example of Brazilian Baroque.

Façade
The church façade dominates the Largo de São Francisco with imposing twin bell towers.

KEY

① **Doors and windows** in bright tones adorn the outer walls of the church.

② **Detailing** of pure gold leaf decorates the church interior.

Oil Painting of St. Francis
The oil painting depicting an event in the life of St. Francis in the church entryway is one of the classic examples of Brazilian Baroque Illusionism.

★ **Main Altar**
A statue of Jesus on the cross with St. Francis by his side graces the main altar. The blue-and-white tiles behind the main altar tell the life story of the saint. The gold-and-white motif is offset by dark jacaranda wood hand railings.

VISITORS' CHECKLIST

Practical Information
Largo Cruzeiro de São Francisco, Praça Anchieta, Pelourinho.
Tel (71) 3322 6430.
Open 9am–5:30pm Mon–Sat, 10am–3pm Sun. 🅿 🅲 ♿
Igreja Terceira Ordem de São Francisco: Rua Inácio Accioli.
Open 8am–5pm daily. 🅿

Cloisters
These secluded interior arcades are where the monks of St. Francis would gather for prayer or quiet contemplation.

Black Saint, Saint Benedict
Two of the side altars are dedicated to black saints such as Santa Efigênia, an Ethiopian princess, and São Bento, the son of African slaves.

★ **Azulejos**
Brought over from Portugal in 1743, the decorative tiles are based on the etchings by Flemish painter Otto van Veen in his book of moral emblems.

Igreja Terceira Ordem de São Francisco

The ornately carved and detailed sandstone façade of the church of the Third Order of St. Francis next door is the only one of its kind in Brazil. The façade remained hidden for many years behind a layer of plaster, only to be uncovered accidentally when wiring was being installed in the 1930s. The church also has a museum and a room of Franciscan tombs.

Soapstone exterior of the church

Pretty lace hammocks displayed in the stalls outside the Mercado Modelo

⑩ Mercado Modelo

Praça Visconde de Cairu, Comércio, Cidade Baixa. **Tel** (71) 3241 2893. **Open** 9am–7pm Mon–Sat, 9am–2pm Sun.

The Mercado Modelo was built in 1861 as a customs building. The square behind the market, now used by *capoeiristas* (*see p203*), was where boats would dock to unload their merchandise for inspection. The building was transformed into an indoor craft market in 1971, and renovated after a major fire in 1984. Nowadays, the Mercado's two floors house 259 stalls that offer a variety of northeastern arts and crafts. Popular items include naive art paintings of Pelourinho, *berimbaus* (a stringed instrument), embroidered lace tablecloths, hammocks, colorful hats, spices, and sweets.

⑪ Museu de Arte Sacra

Rua do Sodré 276. Cidade Alta. **Tel** (71) 3283 5600. **Open** 11:30am–5:30pm Mon–Fri. 🖼

One of Brazil's best collections of religious art can be found in this museum, which is housed in a former Carmelite convent. The serene and beautiful structure was built between 1667 and 1697, and serves as the perfect backdrop for the varied exhibits, which include statues, icons, paintings, *oratorios* (portable altars), and numerous finely wrought silver crosses, candlesticks, chalices, censors, and other artifacts from the 16th to 19th centuries.

The Museu de Arte Sacra, housed in a 17th-century convent

⑫ Solar do Unhão

Av do Contorno s/n. **Tel** (71) 3117 6132. Museu de Arte Moderna: **Open** 1–7pm Tue–Fri, 2–7pm Sat & Sun. **Tel** (71) 3117 6132.

A renovated colonial sugar mill, the Solar do Unhão beautifully blends the old and the new. The original design is typical of the 17th century – a chapel, a big house with slave quarters on the lower floor, and a large mill where cane was transformed into sugar.

During the sugar boom of the 18th century, the owners added a courtyard fountain and a full-size church, Nossa Senhora da Coneição. After the sugar trade collapsed in the 19th century, the Solar was used variously as a factory, a warehouse, and naval barracks. Finally, in the 1940s it was designated a National Historic Monument and chosen as the site for the **Museu de Arte Moderna**. A series of renovations restored the buildings to their former glory, while upgrading the facilities to include eight exhibit rooms, a theater, and a library.

The complex also houses an excellent restaurant, besides displaying paintings, etchings, and sculptures by some of Brazil's best-known modern artists. In the evenings, it hosts a presentation of traditional Bahian dance and folklore, held in the former slave quarters.

Exterior of the Solar do Unhão, once a colonial sugar mill

⑬ Museu de Arte da Bahia

Av 7 de Setembro 2340, Vitória.
Tel (71) 3117 6903. **Open** 2–7pm Tue–Sun. 🖼️

The Museu de Arte da Bahia offers a glimpse of the opulent lifestyle of Salvador's colonial elite. The collection includes paintings, *azulejos*, furniture, silverware, glass, china, and crystal used by the local ruling families during the 18th, 19th, and early 20th centuries.

The south wing holds landscape paintings by such artists as José Joaquim da Rocha.

⑭ Museu Rodin-Bahia

Rua Graca 284. **Tel** (71) 3117 6910. **Open** 1–7pm Tue–Fri, 2–7pm Sat & Sun.

This small museum, in a 19th-century mansion near Barra, holds four original Rodin sculptures and 62 models made by Rodin prior to construction of the final pieces. Among them are *The Kiss* and *The Thinker*.

The Forte de Santo Antônio, topped by the lighthouse

⑮ Forte de Santo Antônio

Praça Almirante Tamandaré, Largo do Farol s/n, Barra. **Tel** (71) 3264 3296. **Open** 8:30am–7pm Tue–Sun. 🖼️

One of Salvador's best-known landmarks, the Forte Santo Antônio was erected in 1535. The fort was strengthened in the early 17th century, in response to Dutch attacks on the coast, and upgraded to its present star shape at the beginning of the 18th century. A lighthouse atop the fort was originally built in 1698, and is still used by boats navigating the entrance to the bay.

Inside the fort, the Museu Hidrográfico (Museum of Hydrography) shows historic navigation instruments and a variety of charts. There is also a notable collection of coins and China from a Portuguese galleon that foundered in 1668, off Rio Vermelho beach.

The fort also boasts a café with an outdoor terrace offering sweeping views of Salvador's skyline.

Carnaval in Salvador

Salvador's signature event, the Carnaval, is celebrated during February or March. The centerpiece is the *trio elétrico*, a giant flatbed truck carrying a massive array of speakers, topped by a rectangular stage. The tradition was started in the 1950s with Dodó and Osmar, two local musicians who took their music to the street on top of a 1929 Ford. Running out from behind the *trio elétrico* truck, a large roped-off area serves as a movable dance floor. Access to this area is restricted to those in an *abadá*, or uniform-style tank top. Revelers outside the roped-off area are called *pipoca*, or popcorn, as they pop up everywhere.

Blocos (neighborhood groups) parade along one of three routes – Pelourinho, mostly for smaller and more traditional groups; Campo Grande, which runs through the narrow streets of downtown Salvador; and Ondina, which goes through the beachside neighborhoods of Barra and Ondina. Performers at the

Carnaval include major Brazilian artists such as Daniela Mercury, Caetano Veloso, Gilberto Gil, Carlinhos Brown, and popular groups such as Olodum, Ara Ketu, and Chiclete com Banana. In addition to these name-brand performers, there are Afro-Brazilian *blocos* such as Ilê Aye, which only allows people of black heritage in their parade. The queen of the Carnaval is Ivete Sangalo, a noted exponent of *axé*, Bahia's unique rhythm that combines pop with *samba* and Afro-Brazilian beats.

The grand finale occurs in the wee hours of Ash Wednesday. All the various *blocos* make their way to Praça Castro Alves for the Encontro dos Trios, a last late-night jam that marks the closure of the Carnaval.

Costumed dancers at the Salvador Carnaval

Exquisite Portuguese *azulejo* (tile work) at Nosso Senhor do Bonfim

⑯ Nosso Senhor do Bonfim

Largo do Bonfim s/n. **Tel** (71) 3316 2196. **Open** 7am–6pm daily (Mon: from 9am; Fri & Sun: from 6am). ⊕ 7am, 8am, 5pm Tue–Sun.

Nosso Senhor do Bonfim (Our Lord of Good Success) stands atop a small hill on the Bonfim Peninsula, a strip of land jutting out into the Baía de Todos os Santos about 6 miles (10 km) north of Pelourinho. The church was built between 1746 and 1754 by Captain Rodrigues de Faria in fulfilment of a pledge he made in the midst of a fierce Atlantic storm. While the hilltop setting is picturesque, what sets the church apart is not its architecture but the role it plays in Bahia's Afro-Brazilian religion. The church is dedicated to God the Father, but it also honors Oxalá, the supreme deity in the Candomblé religion (*see p181*). On Fridays, worshippers dress in white and dedicate their prayers to Oxalá. On other days, in a small chapel just to the right of the main altar, one can visit the Sala dos Milagres (Chamber of Miracles). Believers come here to offer items made of wax, wood, or even gold. The item represents a miracle that has been bestowed upon them. The room is packed with replicas of hearts, lungs, livers, and breasts, as well as babies, houses, and even cars.

Outside, visitors are besieged with offers of *fitas*, little colored ribbons purchased as a good luck charm. The ribbon is meant to be tied around the wrist with three knots, and a wish is made for each knot. The ribbon is then worn until it falls off in order for the wishes to be granted.

The impressive 16th-century **Forte de São Felipe** is located

Salvador's Atlantic Coast

The tip of Porto da Barra is the beginning of a string of ocean beaches. The best beaches for swimming and sunbathing are close to the southern edge of the city. The best beach close to the city center is Porto do Barra. Farther out, Amaralina's *acarajé* (*see p183*) kiosks are popular on weekends. Itapoã is known for its calm waters and reefs that form natural pools at low tide.

Ondina's beautiful beach is lined with many of Salvador's biggest and best hotels that look out over the foamy waves.

Rio Vermelho is the starting point of a procession honoring Yemanjá (*see p45*).

Porto da Barra is the closest swimming beach to Salvador's historic center. The lighthouse here is a great place from which to watch a spectacular sunset over calm waters.

Historic Center

Porto da Barra · **BARRA**

AV. OCEÂNICA
AV. GARIBALDI

Praia do Farol da Barra

Ondina · Rio Vermelho
Praia de Ondina

Praia do Rio Vermelho

AV. MAGALHÃES JÚNIOR · AV. CARLOS JR

PARQUE DA CIDADE JOVENTINO SILVA

SANTA CRUZ · PIT

Amaralina · Pra

Praia de Amaralina · Pra Pi

close to the church, in the neighborhood of Boa Viagem. Just below the fort is the popular beach, **Praia de Boa Viagem**, which is usually bustling with locals and lined with busy stalls selling a variety of trinkets and snacks on weekends.

🏰 Forte de São Felipe

Rua Rita Durão s/n, Monte Serrat, Boa Viagem. **Tel** (71) 3313 7339. **Open** 8am–noon daily. 📷

Colorful ribbons on the railing outside Nosso Senhor do Bonfim

A group of colorfully dressed women during Lavagem do Bonfim

Lavagem do Bonfim

Salvador is home to some of the largest celebrations of the Candomblé religion. One event that occurs each year at the Nosso Senhor do Bonfim is the Lavagem do Bonfim (Washing Ceremony), which takes place on the third Thursday of January. A procession of thousands of devotees makes its way from Salvador city center to the church. Once the procession has reached the church, women in traditional white lace dresses wash the church steps with perfumed water in honor of Oxalá. The tradition is said to stem from the days when the slaves were not allowed inside the church and had to worship outside. The Catholic church does not entirely approve of the ceremony, and keeps its doors shut throughout the festival.

Amaralina, subject to large waves and strong winds, is an excellent beach for surfing and boardsailing. Baianas dressed in traditional garb sell *acarajé* at the numerous kiosks lining the shore.

VISITORS' CHECKLIST

Practical Information

Bahia. ℹ️ on the corner of Rua João de Deus & Laranjeiras, Pelourinho. **Tel** (71) 3321 2463. 🌐 **bahiatursa.ba.gov.br** 🎭 Festa de Yemanjá (Feb).

Transport

🚌 Barra from Praça da Sé.

0 km   1
0 miles   1

PARQUE METROPOLITANO DE PITUAÇU

PITUAÇU

AV PINTO DE AGUIAR

AV DORIVAL CAYMMI

Itapuã

Praia de Pituaçu

Praia de Piatã

Praia de Itapuã

BOCA DO RIO

AVENIDA OTAVIO MANGABEIRA

Praia de Jaguaribe

ATLANTIC OCEAN

ARMAÇÃO

Praia do Corsário

Praia Boca do Rio

AV M. NATO

Jardim de Alá

raia Jardim de Alá

Jardim de Alá, a seaside park with grassy slopes descending to the sea, has a coconut tree plantation.

Itapuã features turquoise waters and reefs teeming with marine life. Poet and lyricist Vinícius de Moraes (*see p35*) immortalized the place in a popular song.

Ilha de Itaparica, one of the tropical islands in the Baía de Todos os Santos

❷ Ilha de Itaparica

🏠 18,000. 🚢 from Salvador. 🛥
Zimbo Tropical, (71) 3638 1148.

The largest island in the Baía de Todos os Santos (Bay of All Saints), with summerhouses lining its shore, Itaparica is a popular weekend refuge for the residents of Salvador.

Located on the northern tip of the island, the main city is guarded by the Forte de São Lourenço, which was built by the Dutch in 1711. Among the island's main attractions are some historic buildings, including the 1622 Nossa Senhora da Piedade (Chapel of Our Lady of Piety) and the 1610 Igreja de São Lourenço.

The island is connected to the mainland by a bridge at its narrow southern tip. The **Praia da Penha**, 10 miles (6 km) south, is a lovely beach with views of Salvador. The region's biggest resort, **Club Med**, lies on the Praia da Conceição, 12 miles (19 km) south of town.

❸ Santo Amaro

🏠 60,000. 🚢 from Salvador.
🎭 Bembé do Mercado (May 13–18).

The laid-back town of Santo Amaro lies in the Recôncavo, the fertile zone at the top end of the Baía de Todos os Santos, which has formed the backbone of Salvador's colonial economy for almost 300 years. The region's high humidity, abundant rainfall, and rich soils were conducive to growing

tobacco and, more signicantly, sugar cane. Until the crash of the sugar economy in the 19th century, Santo Amaro remained the focus of Recôncavo's sugar industry. Dilapidated mansions of the erstwhile sugar barons can still be seen along the old streets. Nowadays, this unpretentious town is known for its paper industry. It is also famous as the hometown of Caetano Veloso and Maria Bethânia, two of Brazil's most popular singers.

Many of the slaves, who were brought from Africa to work on plantations, remained in the Recôncavo after slavery was abolished in 1888. The region still has a very high percentage of Afro-Brazilian residents, and Santo Amaro plays a key role in preserving their distinct traditions. Every year, the city commemorates the abolition of slavery with a five-day festival

Lush hillsides in the Recôncavo, covered with sugar cane

of the Bembé do Mercado. During this time, offerings are made to Yemanjá, Goddess of the Sea, to celebrate freedom of religion. In the main square in front of the town market, local groups put on capoeira performances. Theater performances of pieces, such as *Nego Fugido* (Runaway Slave), recount the story of slaves fleeing their masters to join *quilombos*, independent communities set up by runaway slaves.

In an effort to keep folkloric traditions alive, the Afro-Brazilian community also organizes presentations of the lesser-known *maculelê* sword dance, an African fight-dance, and *samba de roda* dances performed by women.

❹ Cachoeira

🏠 30,000. 🚌 🎗 Praça da Aclamação 4. 🎭 Festa da Boa Morte (Aug 13–15).

Historically more powerful than the other two main towns in the Recôncavo – Santo Amaro and São Félix – Cachoeira was also the most prominent. Its strategic location, between the Baía de Todos os Santos and the roads leading inland, made it an important crossroads between Salvador and the rest of the state.

The city once had a busy river port on the Paraguaçu. Boats sailed upstream from Salvador to load up with sugar and tobacco produced in the Recôncavo region. The town's

Cobblestoned streets lined with colorful houses in Cachoeira

privileged position as a commercial center is reflected in its imposing colonial architecture. However, with the creation of road access to Salvador, Cachoeira lost its key position and its port gradually faded away.

In the old city center, many of the city's churches and wealthy merchants' houses are still standing, although in a dilapidated condition. The city has, however, begun to renovate and preserve its historic center. As a cultural hub of the Recôncavo region Cachoeira celebrates the Festa da Boa Morte, one of the most important features of the Candomblé religion. Today, the city is as much celebrated for its robust wood-sculpting tradition as for its production of the best tobacco in Brazil.

Coronas cigar box, São Félix

❺ São Félix

🚃 from Cachoeira.

Regarded as the twin of Cachoeira, São Félix lies just across the Rio Paraguaçu, on a hillside overlooking the river. The railway bridge connecting the two towns was commissioned by Dom Pedro II, and built by British engineers in 1895. Cars, trains, and foot traffic all share the rickety railway bridge.

Several times a day, São Félix comes to a standstill as freight trains roll right through the town center.

Larger in size, though not as impressive as Cachoeira, São Félix used to earn a living in its own right as a producer of fine *charutos* (cigars). The heart of this industry was the Dannemann

cigar factory, founded in 1873 by German cigar-maker Gerhard Dannemann. Blessed by optimum conditions for growing and processing tobacco, the Dannemann factory quickly became one of the region's finest cigar producers. The region still produces Dannemann cigars, but the original factory has now been converted into a cultural center, known as the **Centro Cultural Dannemann**. A small exhibit of old machinery tells the story of the early factory days. On weekdays, it is possible to watch the factory workers rolling cigars.

🏛 **Centro Cultural Dannemann**
Av Salvador Pinto 29. **Tel** (75) 3438 3716.
Open 8am–noon & 1–5pm Tue–Sat.

Market scene in São Félix, with a vendor selling fruit

Festa da Boa Morte

Members of the Sisterhood of the Good Death in festive regalia

Celebrated from August 13 to 15, the Festa da Boa Morte (Festival of the Good Death) is one of the most important events of Candomblé (*see p39*), a blend of African spirituality and Catholicism. The ceremonies are held by members of the Sisterhood of the Good Death, a religious and self-help organization composed entirely of women of African descent. The festival honors both the *iyás* (female spirits of the dead) and the Assumption of the Virgin Mary. A Catholic mass is followed by a large procession through the historic streets of Cachoeira. The women come dressed in multilayered lace skirts and blouses, white turbans, and traditional accessories in honor of various *orixás* (deities). At the head of the procession, they carry a statue of the Virgin Mary. At the end, the women prepare an all-white meal of rice, fish, potatoes, onions, and other white-colored foods. *Samba de roda*, a dance based on the African circle dances, marks the end of the ceremonies. Women take turns dancing in the circle to the pounding rhythm of the drums. Onlookers may also be called on to dance.

The ruins of Fortaleza do Tapirando in Morro de São Paulo

❻ Morro de São Paulo

🏘 50,000. ✈ from Salvador. 🚢 from Salvador. 🛈 (75) 3652 1104. 🌐 **morrodesaopaulo.com.br**

Although within easy reach of Salvador, the coast immediately south of the state capital does not have many large, developed tourist areas, apart from Morro de São Paulo. Now a picturesque beach destination, Morro de São Paulo, on the northern tip of Ilha da Tinharé, once played a key role in the coastal defences of Bahia. In 1630, Governor General Diego Luiz de Oliveira ordered **Fortaleza do Tapirando** to be strategically built here where it could control the Itaparica channel, one of the main approaches to Salvador. The ruins of the fort have been designated a National Heritage Site. The view of the sunset from the fort's crumbling walls is spectacular, and dolphin sightings are quite common.

Still accessible only by boat or plane, Morro maintains much of its original charm. No cars are allowed in the village. Lined with *pousadas*, boutiques, and restaurants, the "streets" are made of sand, and wheelbarrows and bicycles are the primary means of transportation. In the evenings, the village square transforms into a craft market, the small stands often lit only by candlelight, making for a very cozy atmosphere. Morro's beaches are famous in Brazil for their parties. During high season, there are parties every night and the beaches are packed. Most nights start around midnight, when **Primeira** beach fills with locals and visitors, who dance *axé* and drink fruity cocktails. As you move away from the village, the beaches get wider and less developed. **Segunda** and **Terceira** beaches feature progressively more scattered *pousadas*. From **Quarta** beach onwards, the coast remains blissfully undeveloped, offering long stretches of white sand backed by waving groves of coconut palms.

Environs

Just south of Morro, **Ilha de Boipeba** offers a quiet, idyllic island getaway, with pristine, deserted beaches. Ponta de Castelhanos is especially known for diving. Travelers can get here via boat from Morro de São Paulo. Visitors coming from Salvador can drive to Valença, then take a boat (see www.ilhaboipeba.org.br).

❼ Peninsula de Maraú

🚢 from Itacaré or Camamu to Barra Grande. 🛈 Barra Grande, (75) 3258 9051. 🌐 **barragrande.net**

The main destination at the northern tip of the Peninsula de Maraú is **Barra Grande**, a delightful, remote fishing village. Beautiful beaches are scattered along the entire length of the peninsula, but it is difficult to get around without a car. Four-wheel drives ferry passengers from *pousadas* to various beaches around the peninsula. Alternatively, the 31-mile (50-km) walk across various palm-fringed beaches along the coastline is spectacular.

Most of the peninsula is covered in native Mata Atlântica rainforest, which has been relatively well preserved. The Baía de Camamu, one of Brazil's largest bays, separates the peninsula from the mainland. The long dirt road heading down the peninsula (often impassable after rains) leads to some of the best beaches facing the open ocean. **Praia Taipús de Fora**, 4 miles (7 km) south of Barra Grande, is considered one of Brazil's most beautiful beaches. At low tide, the coral reefs form a clear, natural pool, perfect for snorkeling and swimming.

There are also a handful of small fishing villages scattered along the coast. Local fishermen offer excursions to **Lagoa Azul** (Blue Lagoon), scenic view points, bay islands, and down the Rio Maraú.

Peninsula de Maraú, overlooking the Baía de Camamu

Capoeira

Bahia, the birthplace of *capoeira*, offers visitors plenty of opportunities to see this dazzling and mesmerizing mixture of dance, gymnastics, and martial arts. *Capoeira* was developed by African slaves within Brazil as a form of self-defense against their brutal slave masters. The music was added as a disguise. Many slaves successfully escaped and formed communities in the interior called *quilombos (see p219)*. Outlawed in 1890 and forced underground, the sport made a slow comeback over the next few decades as white Brazilians began to accept and celebrate the African aspects of Brazil's culture. *Capoeira* was fully rehabilitated in the 1930s, when President Vargas, calling it "the only true Brazilian sport," invited one of the most renowned *capoeiristas* of the day, Mestre Bimba, to perform in the presidential palace. Today, Mestre Bimba's school in Pelourinho is run by his son, Mestre Nenel.

Berimbau, a single-string instrument that produces a metallic droning sound, sets the *capoeira* beat.

African drums are the additional instruments used in *capoeira*.

The **roda**, or the circle in which *capoeria* is always performed, is created by participants who sit or stand and clap to the beat of a single-stringed *berimbau*. The people who form the *roda* will take turns, usually with no predefined order, to go inside the circle and participate.

Capoeira Moves

Capoeiristas *exhibit incredible muscle control, strength, and flexibility as they carry out acrobatic moves, while keeping their opponent at bay. The* capoeira *moves are carried out at lightning speed, but with a dance-like fluidity, where each move is a combination of skill, balance, and beauty.*

Escorpião, or the scorpion move, is a combination of back flips and cartwheels. Both participants try to create a beautiful performance.

Au malandro starts like a cartwheel, but only one hand goes down while the opposite leg kicks up in the air in a swift, fluid move.

The **esquiva** (escape), a low ducking move, is a very common one since *capoeiristas* primarily attack with kicks and sweeps.

The beautiful and unspoiled Prainha beach in Itacaré

❽ Itacaré

🏠 24,000. ✈ Ilhéus. 🚌 ℹ Rua João de Souza, Centro, (73) 3251 2329. 🌐 itacare.com

The small fishing town of Itacaré is part of Brazil's famous Discovery Coast. Portuguese explorer Pedro Álvares Cabral (*see p52*), who was the first European to officially "discover" Brazil, landed in Porto Seguro, close to Itacaré, in 1500.

Large areas of protected Atlantic rainforest, which were given World Heritage status by UNESCO in 1999, meet the sea along the coast of Itacaré. Relatively isolated, the town is favored by nature lovers. Itacaré is also known for its relaxed lifestyle and typical Afro-Brazilian culture.

The beaches have enormous waves, making it a popular surfing destination. Most are surrounded by lush forest and can only be accessed on foot. **Prainha**, Itacaré's main attraction, is considered to be one of Brazil's most beautiful beaches, and is accessible only by a trail through the rainforest from Ribeira beach, just south of town.

Environs

Known as the **Estrada Parque** (the Park Drive), the road that connects Itacaré to Ilhéus traverses a well-preserved strand of Atlantic rainforest. Care has been taken not to disrupt the ecosystem and to protect animals crossing the highway. In places, nets have been strung from tree to tree to provide safe passage for monkeys crossing the road. The 49-mile (80-km) drive follows the coastline and allows access to a string of beautiful, secluded beaches, many of which have little or no facilities.

❾ Ilhéus

🏠 220,000. ✈ 🚌 ℹ Setur, (73) 3634 6008. 🌐 brasilheus.com.br

When farmers began growing cocoa trees imported from the upper Amazon basin in the early 20th century, Ilhéus, the largest city on Bahia's southern coast, established itself as a major cocoa-growing region. A disaster of epic proportions struck in 1989, when a parasite infected most of the plantations and destroyed the entire crop. The industry has yet to recover, but several of the old plantations have been converted into museums.

Ilhéus is best known as the setting for several novels by Bahia's most beloved author, Jorge Amado. One of his best books, *Gabriela, Clove and Cinnamon*, takes place in the city's historic core at the height of the 1920s cocoa boom. Today, visitors can stroll along the promenades and see the famous Bar Vesúvio and Bataclã Cabaret that feature in his novel. The author's childhood home has been opened to visitors as the **Casa de Cultura Jorge Amado**.

Among the city's other sights is the 16th-century **Igreja de São Jorge**. There are several fine beaches to the north and south of town and **Cururupe**, near the village of Olivença, is a favorite.

🏛 **Casa de Cultura Jorge Amado**
Rua Jorge Amado 21. **Tel** (73) 3231 7531. **Open** 9am–noon, 2–6pm Mon–Fri, 9am–1pm Sat. 🗎

🏛 **Igreja de São Jorge**
Praça Rui Barbosa. **Open** irregular hrs.

Casa de Cultura Jorge Amado, childhood home of the famed author

Jorge Amado (1912–2001)

The son of a cocoa plantation owner, Jorge Amado was born near Ilhéus in 1912. In 1931, Amado moved to Rio to study law, but his heart was already given to literature. That very year, he published his first novel, *O País da Carnaval*. He based his 1958 novel, *Gabriela, Clove and Cinnamon*, on the warring cocoa barons of his native Ilhéus, but infused it with a sense of humor that won him acclaim in Brazil and around the world. *Dona Flor and her Two Husbands* (1966), *Tieta do Agreste* (1977), and *Gabriela, Clove and Cinnamon* were later turned into popular and successful films. Armado published 21 novels, which were translated into 49 languages. He died in 2001.

Life-like statue of Jorge Amado, Ilhéus

Main square and the Matriz Nossa Senhora da Pena, Porto Seguro

❿ Porto Seguro

🏔 140,000. ✈ 🚌 ℹ Av Portugal, Passarela do Alcool, Centro, (73) 3288 3708. 🅆 portosegurotur.com

Porto Seguro (Safe Port) is officially recognized as the site of the first Portuguese landing in 1500, where Pedro Cabral and his fleet arrived and said mass on Brazilian soil. The city's small historic center (Cidade Histórica) has several stately old buildings, including the **Matriz Nossa Senhora da Pena**, built in 1535. Its altar has an image of Saint Francis of Assisi, the first religious statue to be brought to Brazil in 1503. On the same square, the former jail built in 1772 is home to the **Museu de Porto Seguro**, which holds a collection describing the early colonization of the region.

Today, Porto Seguro is best known for its buzzing nightlife, beach parties, music festivals, and the notorious "Passarela do Alcool" (alcohol boardwalk), the nickname for the city's main street where vendors set up kiosks selling fresh fruit cocktails with a heavy alcoholic kick. Visitors looking for a more tranquil holiday experience usually head farther south to the lovely neighboring villages of Arraial d'Ajuda and Trancoso.

South of town are a few beaches that mainly attract backpackers. Less developed, but serene, these beaches can be accessed from Porto Seguro airport, which receives daily flights from all over Brazil. Road access can often be challenging, as distances are long and the coastal highways are in a state of disrepair.

🏛 Museu de Porto Seguro
Praça Pero Campos Tourinho s/n.
Tel (73) 3288 5182.
Open 9am–5pm daily.

⓫ Trancoso

🚏 Porto Seguro, then bus. 🚌
🅆 trancosobahia.com.br

Though just a short drive from Porto Seguro, Trancoso has a sense of tranquility that sets it apart from the nearby party town. Set on a high bluff overlooking the ocean, the town center, or *quadrado*, is a long, grassy space, anchored by a small church and framed by houses, many of which have turned their gardens into tasteful little cafés. Trancoso offers sophisticated services focusing on high-end travelers – upscale B&Bs, fine dining, and music. The beaches are backed by red sandstone cliffs, and remain largely secluded and unspoiled.

⓬ Parque Nacional Marinho de Abrolhos

🏨 ℹ Ibama, Praia do Kitongo, Caravelas, (73) 3297 1111.
🅆 abrolhos.net

Remote and uninhabited, the archipelago of Abrolhos, discovered by Amerigo Vespucci in 1503, offers excellent opportunities for viewing wildlife. The five islands are located off the coast of southern Bahia. In 1983, the islands, together with 351 sq miles (909 sq km) of surrounding ocean, were declared a National Marine Park, the first such park in Brazil. Known for its rare formations of south Atlantic coral, the park teems with sea turtles, squid, and a rich assortment of fish. A variety of bird species come to feed and lay eggs on the islands, which are otherwise dry and covered with grasslands. The best time for spotting humpback whales is between July and November, when the archipelago becomes a calving ground for them.

Only one of the five islands, Siriba, can actually be visited. Guided tours to the marine park should only be made with an operator accredited by Brazil's environmental agency, IBAMA. Visitors can also book a day or overnight excursion to the islands and surrounding coral reefs from the town of **Caravelas** on the mainland. For snorkeling and diving enthusiasts, underwater visibility is best between January and March.

Birds nesting on Siriba island, Parque Nacional Marinho de Abrolhos

Vacationers and locals relaxing at Praia do Forte, Bahia ▶

A view of the old diamond-mining town of Lençóis

⓫ Lençóis

🏚 9,000. ✈ 16 miles (25 km) E of town. 🚌 🛈 Sectur, (75) 3334 1380. 🎭 Festa de Senhor dos Passos (Jan), Festa de São João (Jun). 🌐 **guialencois.com**

Located in the foothills of the Chapada Diamantina mountains in central Bahia, the town of Lençóis sprang up almost overnight, as diamond fever struck in these interior highlands in the late 19th century. The name of the town, meaning "sheets," derives from the camp that grew up here during the diamond strike. The miners, too poor to afford tents, made do with sheets draped over branches.

Unlike many other mining boomtowns, however, Lençóis has a colonial air, with small Baroque churches, and tiny houses and shops painted in pastel colors. The town's distinguished main square, Praça Horácio de Matos, consists of 19th-century houses, characterized by high, arched windows. Another town landmark, Praça Otaviano Alves, lined with gracious colonial homes, is farther south of the main square.

Lençóis has reinvented itself as the base camp for ecotourists venturing out to explore the caves, waterfalls, and isolated mountaintops of the surrounding highlands. The town's pretty colonial homes now house trekking equipment stores, Internet cafés, and tasteful photo galleries.

⓮ Parque Nacional de Chapada Diamantina

Towering red rock formations, interspersed with lush vegetation, characterize this 587-sq-mile (1,520-sq-km) park in the hinterland of Salvador, established in 1985. Numerous small rivers crisscross the highlands, cascading over waterfalls, carving through canyons, and tumbling down waterslides. Countless trails lead to caves and caverns. These undefined paths are best navigated with a guide.

★ **Morro do Pai Inácio**
The striking mesa is the park's signature mountain formation. The 3,675-ft (1,120-m) plateau offers breathtaking views of the northern half of the park.

Cachoeira da Fumaça, or the Waterfall of Smoke, wears a veil of mist as the water plunges down the 1,150-ft (340-m) precipice.

★ **Vale do Paty**
The multiday hike up this scenic valley offers extraordinary views of the highlands from Morro do Castelo. Other attractions include abandoned miners' settlements and waterfalls with natural swimming pools at Cachoeira dos Funis, as well as the sound of Barbado monkeys that inhabit this vast wilderness.

Rappeling in the Chapada Diamantina
The Chapada's main adventure sport is rappeling down a cliff face or into a cavern. Tour companies in Lençóis offer thrilling rappeling alongside amazing waterfalls.

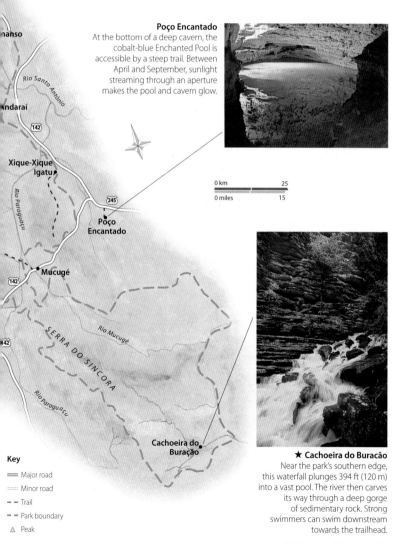

Poço Encantado
At the bottom of a deep cavern, the cobalt-blue Enchanted Pool is accessible by a steep trail. Between April and September, sunlight streaming through an aperture makes the pool and cavern glow.

0 km   25
0 miles   15

★ **Cachoeira do Buracão**
Near the park's southern edge, this waterfall plunges 394 ft (120 m) into a vast pool. The river then carves its way through a deep gorge of sedimentary rock. Strong swimmers can swim downstream towards the trailhead.

Key
▬▬ Major road
▭▭▭ Minor road
– – Trail
▬ ▬ Park boundary
△ Peak

For keys to symbols *see back flap*

Church and colorful houses in the small town of Canudos

⑮ Canudos

 59,000.

Traveling through the sleepy town of Canudos, it is hard to imagine that this was once the staging ground for a year-long rebellion in 1897. Led by Antônio Conselheiro, the war wound up costing the lives of more than 20,000 people and almost destroyed the future of the Brazilian Republic.

An eyewitness account at the end of the Canudos War was written by journalist Euclides da Cunha, who was on the scene to cover the events for a São Paulo newspaper. He went on to write a book based on his coverage of the war. Published in 1902, *Os Sertões* (*Rebellion in the Backlands*) is one of the most important works of Brazilian literature. In 1997, the University of Bahia turned the

site of the 19th-century Canudos War into a state park, **Parque Estadual de Canudos**. To access the park, visitors should get permission from the Memorial de Canudos.

The original settlement of Canudos now lies at the bottom of the Lagoa Cocorobó, which flooded the area in 1970. However, many of the original battlefields escaped the deluge and have been made into an open-air museum which is part of the park, just on the outskirts of the town. The principal museum sites include Morro do Conselheiro (Counsellor Hill), Vale da Morte (Valley of Death), the Estrada Sagrada (Holy Road), and the Vale da Degola (Valley of Beheadings). The dry *sertão* landscape is quite striking – vegetation consists of *caatinga* bushes, cacti, bromeliads, *umbu* trees, and *favelas*, a small

thorn-covered shrub very common in the dry interior in Bahia. After the April rains, the landscape briefly turns lush and animals such as deer, hyacinth macaws, and armadillos can be spotted frequently.

In the Canudos region during the war, Republican soldiers were camped in the hills that were covered by *favela* trees. Upon their return to Rio, the soldiers never received the land which they had been promised. They ended up squatting on the hills, naming their new-found community *favela* after the trees in the *sertão*. Hence the name *favela* (see p89), now used to refer to the urban ghettos traces, its origins to the Canudos War.

🏛 **Parque Estadual de Canudos**
Tel (75) 3494 2000. 📷 🎫 tours arranged by Memorial de Canudos.

Statue of Antônio Conselheiro

Antônio Conselheiro

Part Robin Hood, part religious fanatic, Antônio Conselheiro, the leader of Brazil's 1897 Canudos War, was born Antônio Vicente Mendes Maciel in 1830 in Ceará. Conselheiro traveled the dry *sertão* for decades, first as a salesman and legal *conselheiro* (counselor), then as a preacher and reformer, raging against the plight of the peasants. In 1893, Conselheiro, outraged at the newly imposed taxes on an already starving population, settled in the tiny upland town of Canudos and began creating what was, in effect, an independent state. Conselheiro began implementing an early form of socialism, heavily tinged with religious values. The poor of the region flocked to Conselheiro and Canudos quickly grew to a community of more than 8,000 people. With the prestige of the new Republican government at stake, the army sent three large forces against Canudos. All were destroyed. Finally, in November of 1897, the army mounted a full-scale invasion. Conselheiro died during the battle and all the residents of Canudos were slaughtered.

16 Linha Verde

The Linha Verde (Green Line) is the 152-mile (252-km) stretch of coast that runs north from Salvador all the way to Mangue Seco on the Sergipe border. It is often referred to as the Estrada do Côco, or Coconut Highway, because of the thick stands of palm trees that line the beaches. This part of the coast offers several popular holiday destinations and well-developed resorts. The most favored destinations are Praia do Forte and Costa do Sauípe. Farther north, the beaches are pristine and beautiful.

Praia Sítio do Conde, a popular beach, is visited by locals on weekends. Small reefs form natural pools at low tide.

Barra do Itariri
In a lovely setting with green palm trees, white sand dunes, and mangroves, Barra do Itariri is an ideal beach destination.

Sapiranga Reserve
This eco-preserve protects some of the last remaining Atlantic rainforest in Brazil.

0 km   15
0 miles   15

Costa do Sauípe
The custom-built village at Costa do Sauípe offers high-end recreation including spas, sailing, and golf.

Key
— Main Road
--- Minor Road

Projeto Tamar
As part of a conservation plan, four turtle species are reared at Praia do Forte.

Praia do Forte
Natural pools at the north end of Praia do Forte provide snorkeling and swimming areas.

Map labels: Mangue Seco, Praia do Coquiro, Praia Costa Azul, Praia Barra do Itapicuru, Barro do Itapicuru, Praia de Poças, Sítio do Conde, Praia Sítio do Conde, Conde, Barra do Itariri, Praia Baixio, Cardeal da Silva, Baixio, Subaúma, Praia Massarandupió, Porto do Sauípe, Costa do Sauípe, Itanagra, Imbassaí, Açu da Torre, Praia do Forte, Itacimirim, Guarajuba, Pajuca, Praia da Barra do Jacúpe, Mata da São João, Arembepe, Praia do Arembepe, Dias d'Ávila, Camaçari, Lauro de Freitas, SALVADOR, ESTRADA DO COCO, SERGIPE, BAHIA

SERGIPE, ALAGOAS & PERNAMBUCO

Long stretches of white beach bathed by a warm, blue-green ocean comprise the magnificent coastline of Sergipe, Alagoas, and Pernambuco. In contrast, much of the interior of this region is dry *sertão*, where the landscape is barren and harsh. Despite, or perhaps because of their material poverty, these northeastern states are culturally rich in music and folklore.

The states of Sergipe, Alagoas, and Pernambuco in the Northeast were among the first parts of Brazil to be colonized by Portugal, and for centuries afterward they were the richest region of colonial Brazil. The wealth of the region came from sugar. With slave labor, sugar cane could be cultivated in abundance, and sugar sold in the burgeoning markets of Europe. In 1654, the Portuguese reclaimed Pernambuco after a brief Dutch takeover, but opted to keep the new city, Recife, as the capital instead of Olinda.

Sugar still dominates the economy, but the beaches make this region one of Brazil's hottest tourist destinations. These states have also developed a rich culture and a penchant for lively festivals. Popular musical styles such as *forró* and *frevo* began or culminated in the Northeast.

All three states have pretty, historic towns, stunning coastlines, and picture-perfect beaches. Reefs of stone and coral provide natural habitats for fish, sea turtles, sharks, and other tropical marine life. The island archipelago of Fernando de Noronha, a municipality of Pernambuco, is one of Brazil's prime marine habitats and a preferred destination of scuba divers. The Rio São Francisco, the longest river in Brazil, passes through the beautiful scenery of Sergipe and Alagoas in the last leg of its journey before finally meeting the Atlantic Ocean.

Dois Irmãos (Mount of the Two Brothers), Parque Nacional Marinho de Fernando de Noronha

◄ View from Igreja de São Salvador do Mundo over the rooftops of Olinda

Exploring Sergipe, Alagoas & Pernambuco

Year-round warm weather makes this region a popular sunshine destination. The island archipelago of Fernando de Noronha in Pernambuco is Brazil's top scuba-diving destination, and it also offers a fascinating ecosystem rich in marine life. Recife and Olinda provide a captivating impression of 17th- and 18th-century Brazil, a legacy of Dutch and Portuguese colonization. São Cristóvão and Penedo, located on the border between the two states, are both charming Baroque colonial towns. Penedo has the added advantage of offering a spectacular view of the Rio São Francisco.

Rio São Francisco, the largest river in Northeast Brazil

Stunning blue sky and pastel-colored colonial houses in the picturesque town of Olinda

Sights at a Glance

Towns & Cities

❶ Aracaju
❷ São Cristóvão
❸ Penedo
❻ Marechal Deodoro
❼ Maceió
❾ *Recife pp220–23*
❿ *Olinda pp224–6*
⓬ Caruaru

Beaches, Islands & Areas of Natural Beauty

❹ Rio São Francisco
❺ Cânion Xingó
❽ Porto de Galinhas
⓫ Ilha de Itamaracá
⓭ *Fernando de Noronha pp228–9*

Getting Around

Recife, Aracaju, Maceió, and Fernando de Noronha have good flight connections to the rest of Brazil. However, only Recife has an international airport. Cities on the coast are easily accessible by bus or car. Bus connections are fast and convenient throughout the region. Highway BR-101 connects Aracaju, Maceió, and Recife, while smaller coastal destinations are only a short drive east on secondary roads off the main highway. However, roads in the interior require a bit more patience as they are often in poor condition, making night driving hazardous. Gas stations and services become scarce in the sparsely populated interior; drivers should be prepared with a full tank of gas, snacks, and plenty of water.

FERNANDO DE NORONHA 🔟

Fortaleza
Mossoró
Natal
Campina Grande
João Pessoa
Caruaru
Recife

0 km 200
0 miles 100

Key

▬▬ Highway
▬ Major road
▭▭▭ Minor road
◦▭◦ Railroad
▭▭▭ State border

Sailboats near Fernando de Noronha with Morro do Pico at a distance

For keys to symbols *see back flap*

The wide boulevards of Sergipe's capital, Aracaju

❶ Aracaju

Sergipe. 🏛 570,000. ✈ 🛈 Centro de Turismo, (79) 3179 7553. 🎭 Festa de São João (Jan), Forró Caju Music Festival (Jun), Festa de Yemanjá (Dec). 🌐 **aracaju.se.gov.br**

Sergipe's original capital was São Cristóvão, located inland from the Atlantic Ocean. A burgeoning trade in sugar, however, made a sizable port necessary, and in 1855, the capital transferred to Aracaju, situated at the mouth of the Rio Sergipe. By 1901, the sleepy fishing village soon transformed into a stately capital, with a horse-drawn streetcar and a movie theater.

Today, Aracaju is a small city with a commercial downtown area along the south riverbank. Sea-life enthusiasts should visit **Oceanário**, which has models of various marine habitats. The main highlights here include the sea turtles and the shark tank. Another of the city's top attractions is the **Museu da Gente Sergipana**, a state-of-the-art museum exploring the history, culture, and traditions of the Sergipe region with interactive exhibits.

🏛 Museu da Gente Sergipana
Av Ivo do Prado 398. **Tel** (79) 3218 1551. **Open** Tue–Sun. 🗫

🐟 Oceanário
Av Santos Dumont. **Tel** (79) 3243 3214. **Open** 9am–9pm daily. 🗫

Environs
Aracaju's lively beach neighborhoods lie 6 to 12 miles (10 to 20 km) south of the city center. The most popular suburban beach is **Atalaia**, with its sports and recreation facilities, stages for cultural events, and good seafood joints. The other favorite is **Praia Atalaia Nova**, on the Ilha de Santa Luzia, an island just off the coast, accessible by boat from the ferry station in the city center.

❷ São Cristóvão

Sergipe. 🏛 73,000. 🚌 from Aracaju. 🛈 Centro de Turismo, (79) 3214 8848. 🎭 Festival de Arte de São Cristóvão (Oct). 🌐 **turismo.se.gov.br**

A designated National Historic Heritage Site, São Cristóvão was founded in 1590, and is considered one of the oldest cities in Brazil. It served as the capital of Sergipe in the 17th and 18th centuries, but when the capital shifted to Aracaju it soon dwindled to the sleepy interior town it is today.

The town's charming historic center is a panoply of colonial squares and buildings, and is also a hub of commerce. The most beautifully preserved square, **Praça de São Francisco**, is easily identified by the large Franciscan cross at its center. Flanking the square are the Santa Casa Hospital, the former Governor's Palace, and the Convento de São Francisco, which now houses the **Museu de Arte Sacra** (Museum of Sacred Art). The museum has a fine collection of silver chalices and crosses, and a few beautifully sculpted statues of saints. The ceiling of the convent chapel was painted by the Bahian artist, José Teófilo de Jesus (1758–1847). In October, the annual Festival de Arte de São Cristóvão hosts popular art and music.

🏛 Museu de Arte Sacra
Praça de São Francisco. **Tel** (79) 3261 1385. **Open** 10am–4pm Tue–Sun. 🗫

Franciscan cross in front of Convento de São Francisco in São Cristóvão

Streets and historic buildings by the Penedo waterfront

❸ Penedo

Alagoas. 🏔 60,000. 🚌 from Maceió.
🛈 Teatro 7 de Setembro, Centro
Historico, (82) 3551 2727. 🎭 Bom
Jesus dos Navegantes (2nd Sun in
Jan). 🌐 **canalpenedo.com.br**

The oldest settlement in
Alagoas, Penedo was founded
in 1565 by Duarte Coelho
Pereira on a strategic bluff
overlooking the Rio São
Francisco, about 19 miles
(30 km) upstream of the delta.
Invading Dutch forces
conquered the town in 1637,
and after eight years, the
Portuguese managed to regain
control. Today, Penedo's historic
center has been designated a
National Historic Monument.
Particularly noteworthy is the
complex housing the **Convento
de São Francisco** and **Igreja de
Santa Maria dos Anjos**, built
over a period of 100 years.
  The **Igreja Nossa Senhora da
Corrente** (Church of Our Lady
of Chains), built in 1765 by the
Lemos de Gonzaga family, was
used as a refuge for runaway
slaves, who the family often
provided with forged certificates of freedom. It has a fine
Rococo-style main altar.

🏛 **Convento de São Francisco &
Igreja de Santa Maria dos Anjos**
Rua 7 de Setembro 218. **Open**
8–11:30am, 2–5pm Tue–Fri,
8am–11pm Sat & Sun.

🏛 **Igreja Nossa Senhora da
Corrente**
Praça 12 de Abril. **Open** 8am–4pm
Tue–Sun. 🎟

Environs
The **Rio São Francisco Delta** is
easily accessed from the town of
Piaçabuçu, 9 miles (15 km) east
of Penedo. The delta, situated on
the Sergipe side of the river, is
rich in lagoons and mangrove
forests, and is home to turtles
and migrating seabirds. The
riverbank in Alagoas features
low-rolling sand dunes.

❹ Rio São Francisco

Sergipe, Alagoas, Pernambuco &
Minas Gerais.

The largest and most important
river in the region, the Rio São
Francisco has long served as
the main transport and
irrigation lifeline for the people
in the small towns of the arid
northeastern interior to the
bigger cities along the coast.
Considered a symbol of
national unity, Brazilians revere
the São Francisco, and it is the
subject of many myths and
fables. Nicknamed Velho Chico
(Old Chico), the 1,963-mile
(3,160-km) river meanders
through five states. Originating
in the Serra da Canastra
mountains in Minas Gerais,
it flows north through Bahia,
and crosses briefly into
Pernambuco before continuing
east, toward the Atlantic,
marking the border between
Sergipe and Alagoas in its final
run to the sea.

Lampião & Maria Bonita

In the 1920s and 1930s, bandit leader Lampião and his
wife Maria Bonita led a band of 40 outlaws, nicknamed
cangaceiros (*cangaço* means badlands), on a 15-year
spree of robberies, hold-ups, rapes, and
shoot-outs across the Northeast. As
their raids continued, Lampião and
Maria Bonita became notorious figures
throughout Brazil.
  The duo even introduced their own
style of clothing, with the round leather
cangaceiro hat, the front brim turned
upward and decorated with stars or
coins. The police and militia searched
for them endlessly but were unable to
capture them. Finally, in 1938, Lampião,
Maria Bonita, and nine *cangaceiros* were
ambushed and killed by the police in
Sergipe. Their story has inspired
numerous songs, plays, and different
versions on film and TV.

Lampião and Maria Bonita
clay statues

❺ Cânion Xingó

Sergipe. 🚌 from Aracaju.
ℹ️ Reservatório de Xingó, (79) 9972
1320. 🚤 trips to the dam at 11:30am
Tue–Sun, call (79) 3346 1184 for
further departure details. 🏞️

Standing on the Rio São
Francisco, the Xingó Dam in
Sergipe is one of the largest in
Brazil. When it was completed
in 1994, the dam blocked off the
São Francisco canyon at a point
about 155 miles (250 km) from
the ocean, causing the river to
rise and create the Xingó
Reservoir. This artificial lake is
now a popular destination.

Catamarans and schooners
depart from the dam and travel
upstream, crossing the reservoir
and re-entering the main part
of the river. Several rock
passageways that previously lay
at the top of the canyon are now
open to exploration by boat.

Situated 2 miles (3 km) from
the dam, the **Museu de
Arqueológia de Xingó** displays
numerous archaeological
objects from nearby sites that
were flooded when the dam
was created. Artifacts from
the earliest sites, dating from
around 5000 BC, include
arrows, rock paintings, primitive
stone mortars, and fish-
cleaning tools. Later sites reveal
a variety of items including
bone jewelry, decorative
ceramics, and clay containers.

🏛️ Museu de Arqueológia
de Xingó

2 miles (3 km) from Xingó dam at
Rodoviaria Canindé-Piranhas. **Open**
9am–4pm Wed–Sun. 🏞️ ♿ ♿

Igreja de Santa Maria Madalena in Marechal
Deodoro's historic center

❻ Marechal Deodoro

Alagoas. 🅰️ 30,000. 🚌 from Maceió.
ℹ️ (82) 8856 9091 🌐 turismo.
maceio.com.br

The capital of Alagoas until 1839,
Marechal Deodoro was founded
in 1611 as Vila Madalena. The city
was renamed in honor of its
native son, Marshall Manuel
Deodoro da Fonseca (1827–92),
elected as Brazil's first president
in 1891. Fonseca's childhood
home is now a small museum,
displaying much of the original
furniture and family memorabilia.

The city's small, 18th-century
colonial center features the
Rococo **Igreja de Santa Maria
Madalena**. Adjoining the
church, the **Convento do São
Francisco** houses a museum.

Just a 15-minute bus ride
from the city is the **Praia do
Francês**, with powdery sand
and deep-blue water. It has
enormous waves for surfing at
one end, while the other end

is protected by a large reef.
The authorities are working
toward removing the
restaurants that have been
built right on the sand.

🏠 Convento do São Francisco
Praça Pedro Paulinho. **Tel** (82) 3551
2279. **Open** 8–11:30am, 2–5pm Mon–
Fri, 8–11am Sat & Sun.

🏠 Igreja de Santa Maria Madalena
Praça João 23. **Tel** (82) 3263 1623.
Open 9am–5pm Mon–Sun.

❼ Maceió

Alagoas. 🅰️ 930,000. ✈️ 🚌 (82) 221
4615. ℹ️ Rua Boa Vista 453, Centro,
(82) 3315 5700. 🎭 Maceió Fest (Nov).

The capital of Alagoas, Maceió is
known for its many beautiful
urban beaches. The best known,
from north to south, are **Jatiúca**,
Ponta Verde, **Sete Coqueiros**,
and **Pajuçara**. Protected by
reefs, the beaches have little or
no surf, warm water, and a
Caribbean turquoise-green
color. The shores are lined with
thick groves of coconut palms,
especially dense at Ponta Verde.

About 1 mile (2 km) offshore
from Pajuçara, a series of large
coral reefs are partially exposed
at low tide, forming sizable
natural pools that can be
explored with a mask and
snorkel. Small single-sail rafts
known as *jangadas* depart daily
at low tide from Ponta Verde
and take about 20 minutes to
reach the pools.

In addition to the beaches,
Maceió has a small historic
core. The neighborhoods of
Jaraguá and Centro, just inland
from the port, have a large
number of well-preserved
historic buildings which convey
some of the atmosphere of the
city's 19th-century sugar boom.
One of the loveliest mansions
on the waterfront has been
beautifully restored and now
houses the **Museu Théo
Brandão**. Named after a local
writer who wrote about
Alagoan folk art and
anthropology, the small
museum has a good collection
of native art. It also has some
wonderfully creative displays

View of Praia de Francês, one of the popular beaches of Marechal Deodoro

For hotels and restaurants in this region see pp375–6 and pp392–3

Jangadas, small sailboats, on the beach at Ponta Verde in Maceió

that use local crafts to depict the region's religious festivals, typical foods, the sugar-cane industry, and folklore.

The southern end of the city borders the **Lagoa Mundaú**, one of the many lagoons that have given Alagoas its name. The lagoon encompasses several mangrove islands teeming with crustaceans and other marine life. Boats make excursions into the lagoon's channels.

The **Pontal da Barra** neighborhood on the lagoon's shore is a small fishing village. There are several rustic restaurants overlooking the water, which serve the catch of the day. Dishes with *sururu* (a small type of clam) and crab are especially popular. In Pontal da Barra, visitors will find highly skilled *rendeiras*, or lace-makers, working on a variety of laces. The one most typical of the

neighborhood is known as *filé*, a loose weave that is often brightly colored.

🏛 Museu Théo Brandão

Av da Paz 1490, Centro. **Tel** (82) 3214 1713. **Open** 9am–5pm Tue–Fri, 2–5pm Sat. 🌐 📷

Environs

Praia do Gunga is a pretty, palm-fringed beach located 9 miles (15 km) south of Maceió. Access to the beach is gained via a private road cutting across one of the region's largest coconut plantations. Permission to enter must be obtained at the gate, but beaches in Brazil are public property and access cannot be denied. One side of the beach faces the lagoon, while the other side looks toward the ocean, offering the option of fresh- or salt-water swimming, as well as kayaking.

❽ Porto de Galinhas

Pernambuco. 🏔 10,000. ✈ Recife Guararapes International Airport, 38 miles (60 km) N of town, then bus. 🛈 (81) 3552 1728.

Porto de Galinhas is one of the most popular tourist destinations in Northeast Brazil, and deservedly so. There are no high-rises dwarfing the beach here, just low-scale *pousadas* and bungalows. The star attraction of the area, in additions to the beach, are the natural tide pools that form in the reefs just a short distance offshore. Colorful *jangada* rafts take swimmers and snorkelers out to swim in the clear shallow waters that teems with tropical fish.

Porto de Galinhas also offers a lively atmosphere with excellent restaurants and shopping, and, better still, it does not take much effort to get away from the bustle. The main mode of transportation is the dune buggy, which allows for easy transit along the dirt and sand roads that lead to local beaches. A short distance south along the beach leads to **Ponta de Maracaípe**, a beautiful spot with a large white sandbar, where the Rio Maracaípe runs into the ocean. The mangroves in the estuary are home to several species of seahorse that live amid the roots of the tree.

Quilombos

Portrait of Zumbi

In the African Yorubá language, *quilombo* means dwelling place. In Brazil, the term was used to describe a community of runaway slaves. Brazil's most famous *quilombo*, Quilombo dos Palmares in Alagoas, grew to the size of a small city, with 30,000 residents. In the late 1600s, Zumbi, the *quilombo*'s second leader, successfully defended it from repeated Portuguese attacks. However, the Portuguese were relentless, and finally, in 1694, Palmares fell. Zumbi was beheaded and the community destroyed. A number of such places escaped Palmares' fate and survive even today. There are now 1,000 *quilombos* registered in Brazil. Zumbi's legacy is remembered every year on November 20, when Zumbi dos Palmares Day, or Black Awareness Day, is celebrated.

Clear-water rock pools offshore from Porto de Galinhas

❾ Recife

The Portuguese, who had built Olinda on a hillside, ignored the swampy islands below. The site of present-day Recife was only a fishing village when the Dutch took over Pernambuco in 1630. Count Maurice of Nassau commanded the draining and dyking of the flat islands at the mouth of the Rio Capibaribe. The islands of Santo Antônio, Boa Vista, and Recife Antigo (Old Recife) were connected to each other and the mainland with an ingenious system of bridges. Boa Viagem, south of Recife, has a popular beach, many hotels, and excellent nightlife.

Exploring Recife Antigo

In the heart of downtown Old Recife is the **Marco Zero** and the surrounding square, which marks the official point where the city was founded. The site of the original pier, it controlled all arrivals and departures taking place in the bay. This bustling district of the city makes for a pleasant walk during the day. It is possible to take a boat from the square across to the **Parque das Esculturas**, which features an imposing collection of tall, exotic sculptures made by one of Brazil's leading ceramic artists Francisco Brennand *(see p223)*.

The most interesting street in the historic quarter is **Rua do Bom Jesus**. During the brief period of Dutch rule the street was known as Rua dos Judeus (Street of the Jews). The Jewish community thrived under Dutch rule, but once the Catholic Portuguese re-established their control, most fled, converted, or went underground. A large number of the buildings on this street have been restored to their original 17th-century condition. Every Sunday, the street comes alive, as an art and crafts fair, live music, and outdoor festivities take place.

🏛 Paço da Alfândega

Rua da Alfândega 35. **Tel** (81) 3194 2100. **Open** 10am–10pm Mon–Sat, noon–8pm Sun & public hols. ♿
🌐 pacoalfandega.com.br

Just on the edge of the historical quarter, the Paço da Alfândega brings together the old and the new elements

of the city. Overlooking the Rio Capibaribe, the former customs building dates back to 1826, when Recife was one of Brazil's major ports. The renovated building houses restaurants, an art gallery, and a shopping and entertainment center.

Recife City Center

① Paço da Alfândega
② Kahal Zur Israel Synagogue
③ Paço do Frevo
④ Torre de Malakoff
⑤ Museu Cais do Sertão
⑥ Forte do Brum
⑦ Forte das Cinco Pontas
⑧ Praça da Republic
⑨ Igreja São Francisco & Capela Dourada
⑩ Catedral de São Pedro dos Clérigos
⑪ Casa da Cultura
⑫ Instituto Ricardo Brennand
⑬ Oficina de Cerâmica Francisco Brennard

🏛 Kahal Zur Israel Synagogue

Rua do Bom Jesus 197. **Tel** (81) 3224 2128. **Open** 9am–5pm Tue–Fri, 2–5:30pm Sun. 🈂

Built in 1637, during the city's brief period of Dutch rule, this synagogue recounts the history of the Jewish community in Recife. It was the first synagogue anywhere in the Americas. Many of the Jews who immigrated to Dutch-

The well-preserved old buildings on Rua do Bom Jesus

For hotels and restaurants in this region see pp375–6 and pp392–3

controlled Recife, had originally come from Portugal, fleeing the Inquisition. At the height of Dutch rule, about half of Recife's white population was Jewish. Unfortunately, the period of religious tolerance was short-lived, and when the Dutch surrendered to the Portuguese in 1654 the Jews were given three months to liquidate their assets and leave. Many members of the Recife community set sail to New Amsterdam and helped found New York.

The synagogue was dismantled, and its role as a temple and meeting place of the Jewish community was completely forgotten.

The building was eventually torn down at the beginning of the 20th century.

Archaeologists have confirmed the exact location of the original synagogue after digging up part of a *mikveh* (ritual bath). The current synagogue has been rebuilt from the ground up, based on these findings, historical data, and other sources. The museum presents an excellent documentary and display on the history of the Jews in Recife.

🏛 Paço do Frevo

Praça do Arsenal da Marinha s/n. **Tel** (81) 3355 9500. **Open** 9am–6pm Tue–Fri (to 9pm Thu), noon–7pm Sat & Sun. 🅿 🅲 w **pacodofrevo. org.br**

Come to this culture center to learn and experience all about Recife's unique musical rhythm. It includes a Documentation Center, Music School, School of Dance, and various temporary and permanent exhibitions.

🏛 Torre de Malakoff

Praça do Arsenal da Marinha, Rua do Bom Jesus. **Tel** (81) 3184 3180. **Open** 10am–6pm Tue–Fri, 3–7pm Sun.

A relative newcomer to the Rua do Bom Jesus, the Malakoff Tower was built in 1845 as South America's first astronomical observatory, and is still functional today. Visitors can climb to the top terrace for a splendid view of the city courtesy of the LX 200 telescopes.

🏛 Museu Cais do Sertão

Av Alfredo Lisboa. **Tel** (81) 3089 2974. **Open** daily. 🅿

This modern, well-designed, interactive museum explores the history and culture of the Sertão region and pays tribute to the Recife carnival, giving a taste of the lifestyle here. In one section, kids over seven may even play with musical instruments.

🏛 Forte do Brum

Praça Comunidade Luso-Brasileira. **Tel** (81) 3224 4620. **Open** 9am–4pm Tue–Fri, 2–5pm Sat & Sun.

One of the few constructions to pre-date the Dutch, Forte Brum is located at the far end of Avenida Militar. Built by the Portuguese in 1629, it was taken over by the Dutch in 1630, and strengthened and expanded. Today it is a military museum.

🏛 Forte das Cinco Pontas

Praça das Cinco Pontas. **Tel** (81) 3355 3107. **Open** 9am–5pm Tue–Sat. 🅿 🅲

Somewhat deceptively, the Forte das Cinco Pontas (Five-Pointed Fort) actually only has four points. The original Dutch fort, built in 1630 to protect the new Dutch-Brazilian capital of Mauritsstad, had five. When the Dutch withdrew in 1654, the Portuguese leveled the unique shape and put up a more traditional four-pointer. Wonderfully restored, the fort now houses the city museum and contains an impressive collection of maps, paintings, and artifacts that tell the history of Dutch rule.

Frevo

Recife's signature beat is *frevo*. Fast, upbeat, almost polka-like, the rhythm is particularly popular during Carnaval *(see p45)*. This distinct musical genre is reputed to have derived its name from the verb *ferver* (to boil), which refers to the frenetic beat of the brass bands. One of the accessories of a *frevo* dancer is the brightly colored hand-held parasol that is used in the choreography. First recorded in the 1930s, the rhythm made its way into the repertoire of mainstream Brazilian musicians by the 1950s and 1960s.

A dancer performing *frevo* with a colorful parasol

Exploring Modern Recife

Though modern Recife stretches onto the mainland, its center comprises the islands of Santo Antônio, Boa Vista, and Recife Antigua. Skyscrapers exist alongside a handful of old colonial buildings and crowded markets, lending the city a striking character. The area north of the center is as appealing, with leafy suburbs and a few museums and parks. The squares, dotted with impressive churches, retain much of their old-world charm.

The courtyard of Igreja São Francisco, with a graceful, colonnaded arcade

🏛 Praça da República

Palácio do Campo das Princesas:
Tel (81) 3425 2124. **Open** 9am–5pm Mon–Fri, 10am–noon, 2–4pm Sun.
Teatro Princesa Isabel: **Tel** (81) 3355 3323. **Open** check for performance timings. Palácio da Justiça: **Tel** (81) 3419 3222.

Modern Recife's main civic square, Praça da República, is located at the tip of Santo Antônio island. Some of the city's finest public buildings can be found here.

The **Palácio do Campo das Princesas** (Governors' Palace) building was built in the 1840s. Over the years, renovations and additions have somewhat altered the original Neo-Classical design and made the building more eclectic. The lovely interior garden was designed by Brazil's premier landscape artist, Roberto Burle Marx. Unfortunately, the only view available to the public is the one through the wrought-iron fence posts.

The **Teatro Princesa Isabel**, a renovated pink theater, hosts many of Recife's prime cultural productions. The building is an elegant example of classic imperial architecture, marked by its symmetric forms and French and Italian decorative styles.

The **Palácio da Justiça,** with its dome-shaped cupola, was constructed in 1930 to mark the presidency of Getúlio Vargas *(see pp60–61)*.

🏛 Igreja São Francisco & Capela Dourada

Rua do Imperador, Santo Antônio. **Tel** (81) 3224 0530. **Open** 8–11:30am, 2–5pm Mon–Fri, 8–11am Sat. 🖼

One of the major attractions in Recife, Igreja São Francisco served as the convent of the Third Franciscan Order. It was built in 1606, when the island of Santo Antônio only had 200 inhabitants. The initial convent was small and rather plain. During the Dutch occupation of Recife (1630–54) it was used as army barracks. Renovations began after the return of the Franciscans. The courtyard was added with a surrounding arcade of delicate and ornate Tuscan columns. Blue-and-white Portuguese tiles (*azulejos*) were used to decorate the main altar and the walls of the small, charming cloister.

However, the *pièce de résistance* is the **Capela Dourada** (Golden Chapel), added in 1695, in an annex of the main church. All of the wood in the chapel is jacaranda and cedar and is covered in gold leaf or paint. The intricately carved altars, arches, and beams showcase some outstanding Portuguese Baroque art. Each altar consists of various arches, adding a depth of field to the statues on display. One of the walls in the church is adorned with a painting that depicts the Crucifixion of a group of Franciscan saints.

🏛 Catedral de São Pedro dos Clérigos

Rua São Pedro s/n, Santo Antônio. **Tel** (81) 3224 2954. **Open** 8am–noon, 2–4pm Mon–Fri.

Dating back to 1728, Catedral de São Pedro dos Clérigos is one of the most impressive churches in Pernambuco. Its striking façade is dominated by a statue of St. Peter, which was added in 1980. While from the outside the walls of the church look perfectly square and straight, on the inside the church nave is octagonal. The best features of the church are its stunning wood carving and the illusionistic ceiling. The main altar, balconies, and most of the remaining interior elements were renovated in the 19th century in the Rococo style. The only original pieces that remain are the two gold-painted wooden pulpits.

The square in front of the church, **Pátio de São Pedro**, is one of Recife's most popular public squares. The beautifully restored area hosts a number of cultural events. The most important, Terça Negra (Black Tuesday), takes place every Tuesday night. It is widely known for showcasing typical regional Afro-Brazilian musical styles, such as *afoxé*, *maculelê*, and *coco*. The area also has many fine restaurants.

Eye-catching ceramic figures and souvenirs on sale, Casa da Cultura

Casa da Cultura

Rua Floriano Peixoto s/n, São José.
Tel (81) 3184 3151. Open 9am–7pm Mon–Fri, 9am–6pm Sat, 9am–2pm Sun.

Used as a jail until 1973, the former penitentiary now houses the Casa da Cultura, the city's largest arts and craft market. Each of the old jail cells holds a shop showcasing some of the finest leather, lace, and ceramic crafts of this region. Built in 1850, the jail was modeled after US prisons in New Jersey and Pennsylvania. The four wings are in a cross shape, allowing a view of all four corridors from one vantage position in the center of the cross. The center brings out the monthly *Agenda Cultural*, an excellent listing of cultural events.

Instituto Ricardo Brennand

Av Antônio Brennand, Várzea. Tel (81) 2121 0352. Open 1–5pm Tue–Sun.

Founded by the cousin of ceramic artist Francisco Brennand, the Instituto Ricardo Brennand includes a small castle, the Castelo São João, which houses a large collection of European art, an impressive collection of medieval armory and weapons, and an extensive archive of paintings and documents from the years of the Dutch conquest of Brazil.

Also worth seeing is the Pinacoteca gallery that features a large collection of 17th-century paintings and drawings by landscape artists Frans Post and Albert Eckhout, both of whom were hired by Dutch count Maurice of Nassau to portray Brazil's fauna and flora, as well as scenes from everyday life. Over the years, Brennand has amassed the world's largest collection of Post's work. The exhibit also includes many antique maps and documents that recount the brief, but eventful, history of the Dutch in Brazil.

Oficina de Cerâmica Francisco Brennand

Access via Av Caxangá, Várzea.
Tel (81) 3271 2466. Open 8am–5pm Mon–Thu, 8am–4pm Fri.

Acclaimed as the most unusual cultural attraction in Recife, the Oficina de Cerâmica Francisco Brennand is the famed artist's personal gallery. Brennand

Ceramic tiles by Francisco Brennand

(b.1927) is best known for his large collection of phallic-shaped ceramic sculptures, nearly all of which are striking, potent, and larger than life. His collection is creatively displayed inside a ceramic-covered brick factory and its surrounding gardens, beautifully landscaped by Burle Marx, a renowned landscape architect of the 20th century.

In addition to Brennand's superb ceramic art, the collection also showcases thousands of playfully designed ceramic tiles, as well as some of his paintings and drawings. The bold mix of stylized imagery, embellishment, and erotic motifs, visible in all his works, led one critic to define Brennand's art as "tropical sensual Baroque."

Gardens in Oficina de Cerâmica Francisco Brennand, adorned with ceramic sculptures

⑩ Olinda

One of the best-preserved colonial cities in Brazil, Olinda was founded in 1535 by the Portuguese. Much of it was burned down during the Dutch occupation in 1631, and later beautifully restored to its former glory. Magnificent colonial buildings, gardens, Baroque churches, and numerous small chapels mark Olinda, which was designated a UNESCO World Heritage Site in 1982. Although much of this historic city lies on a steep hillside, it is only a short walk up, and the views of the Atlantic Ocean are splendid. Its narrow cobblestone streets are perfect for exploring on foot. The highlight of the walk suggested here is the Praça da Sé, which features historic churches and sweeping views of Recife *(see pp220–23)*, only 6 miles (10 km) to the south.

The view of Olinda from Alto da Sé, with the sea in the background

② Convento de São Francisco
Brazil's oldest Franciscan convent was built in 1585. When the Dutch invaded Olinda in 1630 the convent was abandoned, and rebuilt in the 18th century. The cloister walls, decorated with Portuguese tiles, depict the life of St. Francis.

① Praça do Carmo, the prominent city square, faces the splendid Igreja Nossa Senhora do Carmo, resting on a small hill above.

ATLANTIC

AVENIDA MARCOS FREIRE

RUA DO SOL

TRAVESSA DO FORTINO

RUA DO SÃO FRANCISCO

AVENID

RUA DO BONFI

TRAVESA J. ALFREDO

RUA DA PALHA

③ Igreja da Sé which was built in 1535, is the oldest parish church in Northeast Brazil. The church has undergone many renovations over the centuries. The last, in 1984, restored the building almost to its original 16th-century state.

R DO BISPO COUNTINHO

LADEIRA DA SÉ

RUA DAS BE

R DO BISPO COUNTINHO

Key

••• Walk route

Tips for Walkers

Starting point: Secretaria de Turismo, Praça do Carmo.
Walking time: 2–3 hours. Flat, non-slippery footwear is best.
Best days: Tue–Sat. Museums are only open in the morning.
Places to eat: Oficina do Sabor, Rua do Amparo 335; Olinda Sorvetes e Sucos, Rua São Bento 358.

④ Alto da Sé
The Alto da Sé is one of the highest points in Olinda and offers a magnificent view of Recife in the distance. In the evenings, locals gather here to browse the crafts market, and eat tapioca and pancakes made from manioc.

⑤ Mercado Ribeira
Originally the building where slaves were bought and sold, this 18th-century structure is now one of Olinda's busiest crafts markets. Especially popular are naive art ceramics, carnival masks, and *frevo* umbrellas (see p221).

⑥ Igreja e Mosteiro São Bento
Founded in 1582, this church holds a magnificient gold altar. It took more than a year and 30 professionals to fully restore the altar in 2001. Gregorian chanters add a special touch to the Sunday morning mass.

⑦ Museu de Arte Contemporânea is
a fine 18th-century building and a former jail. This building now houses an interesting collection of artwork by contemporary Pernambucan artists.

⑧ Museu do Mamulengo displays a large collection of puppets from all over the Northeast. Unique to Olinda's Carnaval, the giant puppets, carried by revelers along the parade route, are true works of art.

⑨ Rua do Amparo
More than a dozen artists have set up their studios in the historic buildings along Rua do Amparo. The street also boasts several excellent restaurants, cafés, and B&Bs.

0 meters 300
0 yards 300

For key to symbols *see back flap*

Exploring Olinda

A calm, colonial city, Olinda grew to be the capital of the rich sugar-growing region of Pernambuco. Reconstruction started in earnest only after Dutch forces were expelled in 1654. The city has maintained its 17th-century architectural fabric intact. Olinda is also home to a vibrant community of artists, musicians, and liberal professionals. The scenic city, though, is most renowned for its lively Carnaval.

The exterior of Igreja e Mosteiro de São Bento in Olinda

⛪ Convento de São Francisco

Rua de São Francisco 280. **Tel** (81) 3429 0517. **Open** 8am–noon & 2–5pm Mon–Fri, 9am–noon & 2–4:30pm Sat. 🖼

The Convento de São Francisco was the first convent built by the Franciscan order in Brazil. The complex includes a 1585 church, Nossa Senhora das Neves (Our Lady of the Snow), and the adjacent chapels of St. Anne and St. Roque, built in 1754 and 1811, respectively. The highlight of the convent is the beautiful arcade surrounding the cloister. The tiled walls tell the story of St. Francis of Assisi. The sacristy's beautiful Baroque furniture, carved from dark jacaranda wood, is as impressive.

⛪ Igreja e Mosteiro de São Bento

Rua São Bento. **Tel** (81) 3316 3290. **Open** 8am–noon & 2–6:30pm daily. ✞ 6:30am Mon–Sat, 10am & 6pm Sun (with Gregorian chants).

Built in 1582, this monastery was destroyed by the Dutch along with most of the city, and rebuilt in the late 18th century. It is acclaimed for its Baroque altar in the chapel and intricate wood carving, which features the image of São Bento (St. Benedict) himself. In 2001, the original wood altar was repainted with gold leaf. The sacristy's three large paintings, by 18th-century artist José Eloy da Conceição, portray scenes from the life of the saint.

🏛 Museu de Arte Contemporânea

Rua 13 de Maio 149, Carmo. **Tel** (81) 3184 3153. **Open** 9am–1pm Tue–Sun.

Housed in a fine 18th-century building that originally served as an *ajube*, or jail working in conjunction with the Catholic church, the Museum of Contemporary Art displays both permanent and temporary exhibits. During the Inquisition, religious prisoners were brought here to pray and confess their sins. Today, the place holds some interest for those looking for serious modern art. Works by local contemporary artists are regularly displayed in front of the stairs.

🏛 Museu do Mamulengo

Rua do Sao Bento 344. **Tel** (81) 3493 2753. **Open** 10am–5pm Tue–Sat.

One of the region's unique gifts to the cultural scene in Brazil, *mamulengo*, or puppetry, is showcased in this fascinating museum. Nearly 1,000 puppets are featured here, with a portion of the collection dating from the 1800s. Having performed before political figures, royalty, and luminaries through the ages, these puppets are today used as popular entertainment. During folk festivals, the puppets can be seen enacting comedies, skits, and Pernambucan folk legends. For those interested in the puppets' historical background, there is a curator who can explain it by asking the puppets themselves.

Revelers filling a street in Olinda, with larger-than-life papier-mâché puppets

The Olinda Carnaval

Every year during Carnaval, the cobblestoned streets of Olinda become the stage for a week-long street party. The meeting place is the square, known as *quarto cantos* (four corners), on the corner of Rua do Amparo and Rua Prudente de Moraes. Here, *blocos* (neighborhood groups) begin their parades through the streets, playing music, singing, and dancing as they go. The *blocos* often have themes or names such as "Virgins," "Elephant," or "Midnight Man." Dominating the festivities are enormous papier-mâché puppets that *bloco* members proudly carry along the parade route. The music varies from *frevo*, an upbeat, almost frenetic beat unique to Pernambuco, to *maracatu*, a much more African beat.

⓫ Ilha de Itamaracá

Pernambuco. 🚗 16,000.
🚌 from Recife.

The island of Itamaracá played an important strategic role during the Dutch interregnum in Brazil. In 1631, the Dutch built the **Forte Orange** here, to protect their new domain from invading forces. The Portuguese destroyed the Dutch-built adobe when they took over in 1654. However, the location was so unique that the Portuguese created a new fort in stone on the site. During past renovations, artifacts dating back to the Dutch period were found. Just across from the fort is a small island, Coroa do Avião, which has natural reef pools. Boat tours to the island leave from the beach in front of the fort.

Itamaracá is also home to the **Projeto Peixe Boi**, a manatee research and rehabilitation center. Manatees live along the Brazilian coast from Alagoas to Amapá, but are threatened by loss of habitat, as well as by speedboats and their often-lethal outboard propellers. Scientists estimate that there are only around 400 animals in the wild along this coast. The center works to rehabilitate injured manatees, and to study those that cannot be released. A natural history exhibit on the manatee is offered along with a host of interactive learning activities for children. Visitors are only allowed to observe those animals that cannot be released into the wild.

Pottery on display at a craft shop in Caruaru

The eastern part of Itamaracá, with its lovely ocean beaches, is also a popular weekend destination.

🏛 Forte Orange
Estrada do Forte. **Open** 9am–5pm Mon–Sat, 8am–5pm Sun. 🖼

🐟 Projeto Peixe Boi
Estrada do Forte Orange. **Tel** (81) 3544 1056. **Open** 10am–4pm Tue–Sun.
🖼 ♿

⓬ Caruaru

Pernambuco. 🚗 300,000. 🚌 from Recife. 🎭 Festa do Forró (Jun–Jul).
🌐 caruaru.pe.gov.br

Located 100 miles (160 km) on the mainland southwest of Itamaracá, Caruaru is a market town whose fame rests on its marvelous ceramic *figurinhas* (figurines). Artist Vitalino Pereira dos Santos (1909–63) made many of these brightly painted sculptures, and his hometown, Alto de Moura, a community of potters located 4 miles (6 km)

west of Caruaru, still specializes in producing figurines. **Casa Museu Mestre Vitalino** in Alto do Moura is dedicated to this great artist, and displays his tools and some personal possessions.

Caruaru's open market is the largest in the Northeast, and is a very popular tourist attraction. Besides figurines, leather bags, straw baskets, and ceramic pots are also sold at some of the best prices in Brazil. Apart from a bustling market scene, Caruaru, known as the capital of *forró (see p240)*, hosts Brazil's largest month-long *forró* festival. The **Museu do Barro** pays tribute to Luis Gonzaga, the father of *forró* music.

Figurine, Casa Museu Mestre Vitalino

Environs
Situated 17 miles (30 km) northwest of Caruaru, **Nova Jerusalém** is an intriguing re-creation of Jerusalem. In the week before Easter, thousands of people flock to watch an epic performance of the Paixão de Cristo (Passion of Christ). Local tour operators offer all-inclusive packages to the town and its annual play.

🏛 Casa Museu Mestre Vitalino
Rua Mestre Vitalino 281. **Tel** (81) 3725 0805. **Open** 8am–5:30pm Mon–Sat, 8am–noon Sun.

🏛 Museu do Barro
Praça José de Vasconcelos. **Tel** (81) 3721 2545. **Open** 8am–5pm Tue–Sat, 9am–1pm Sun.

Rehabilitated manatees at the Projeto Peixe Boi, Ilha de Itamaracá

⑬ Fernando de Noronha

Discovered in 1503 by Amerigo Vespucci, the 21-island archipelago of Fernando de Noronha was fought over for the next two centuries by the French, Dutch, and Portuguese, who built forts on strategic lookout points. The island, located 220 miles (354 km) off the coast, was used in a variety of ways, including as a political prison during World War II. In 1988, the Parque Nacional Marinho de Fernando de Noronha was created in order to protect the fragile marine and island ecology of the archipelago. Today, a combination of crystal-clear water, fascinating wildlife, diverse marine life which includes multicolored fish, turtles, sharks, and whales, and stunning beaches make Fernando de Noronha one of the most beautiful destinations in Brazil. One of the best ways to explore the island is to rent a buggy.

Key

--- Park boundary

Surfing on Praia do Boldró
Fernando de Noronha offers some of Brazil's best surfing, but only between December and March.

★ Baía do Sancho
The most beautiful and isolated beach on Noronha, Baía do Sancho is also a snorkelers' paradise with its clear, turquoise waters and myriad tropical fish.

Praia do Boldró

Praia Cacimba do Padre

Praia da Baía do Sancho

Praia da Baía do Porcos

BAÍA DOS GOLFINHOS

MORRO BRANCO

FERNAN

MORRO DA QUIXABINHA

Praia do Leão

ILHA MORRO DO LEÃO

Ponta Capim Açu

★ Spinner Dolphins
Hundreds of dolphins gather at sunrise to leap and spin at Dolphin Cove in the Baía dos Golfinhos.

KEY

① **Praia do Meio** is located close to the ruins of Forte Nossa Senhora Conceição.

② **Baía do Sueste** is the site for the Projeto Tamar (see p211), and it is possible to swim with the turtles.

★ Turtle Hatchlings
Ilha Morro do Leão is a prime hatchery for green sea turtles. Between December and May, around sunset, scores of tiny turtle hatchlings break out of their shells and make a dash for the sea.

Morro do Pico
The sharp basalt finger of Morro do Pico, a testament to the island's volcanic heritage, stands 1,053 ft (321 m) above sea level.

VISITORS' CHECKLIST

Practical Information
Pernambuco. 🗠 2,500.
ℹ️ Divisão de Turismo, Palácio São Miguel, Vila dos Remédios (81) 3619 1352, or Projecto Tamar, Alameda do Boldró (81) 3619 1171. 🗠 environmental tax assessed on all visitors to the island; to be paid on arrival at the airport. License required for scuba diving in national parks.
🔲 noronha.pe.gov.br

Transport
✈️ from Recife or Natal

ILHA DO RATA

ILHA DO MEIO

ILHA RASA

Ponta de Santo Antônio
Praia de Santo Antônio
Forte dos Remédios
Buraco da Raquel
Praia do Meio
Vila dos Remédios
Vila do Trinta

MORRO DO FRANCES

PICO

DE NORONHA

MORRO DO SÃO VISTA

Praia da Atalaia

E

★ **Praia da Atalaia**
A shelf of volcanic rock extends out into the surf line. At low tide, tropical fish take refuge in the natural pools.

Diving & Marine Life

Protected as a marine national park, Fernando de Noronha offers the best scuba diving in Brazil. Greatly suited for diving, its water temperature is a constant 28° C (82° F), and the depth of underwater visibility is almost 98 ft (30 m). Underwater there is an astounding variety of marine life – rays of all types, green sea turtles, and the even rarer hawksbill turtle, monkfish, lemon sharks and reef sharks, clownfish hiding in anemones, surgeon fish, and parrotfish are just some varieties. As a result of the island's volcanic heritage there are also numerous swim-throughs.

| 0 km | 1 |
| 0 miles | 1 |

A school of surgeon fish in the coral reefs of Fernando de Noronha

Key

— Major road

⋯ Minor road

- - Trail

–⋯ Park boundary

PARAÍBA, RIO GRANDE DO NORTE & CEARÁ

Pristine beaches, lively beach towns, and massive shifting sand dunes are the main attractions of these three states. Natal, the capital of Rio Grande do Norte, and João Pessoa are pleasant, historic cities with good urban beaches. However, this part of Northeast Brazil is best experienced along its coast, and in its quiet, relaxed fishing villages and beautiful, isolated beaches.

In 1532, Paraíba, Rio Grande do Norte, and Ceará were among the first states in the Northeast to be colonized by the Portuguese. These states never grew as rich or settled as their more southerly neighbors because sugar cane did not thrive here. However, the three states have taken advantage of the constant sunshine and beautiful beaches and have developed tourism as the mainstay of the economy.

Ceará is famous for its beaches, with their warm, turquoise waters, set against a backdrop of red sandstone cliffs. The most popular include Morro Branco and the lively beach town of Canoa Quebrada, both located to the southeast of Fortaleza, and the isolated beach of Jericoacoara, north

and west of Fortaleza. Parque Nacional de Ubajara lies in western Ceará and comprises caves, eco trails, and magnificent waterfalls.

Rio Grande do Norte lies in the extreme northeast corner of Brazil. The real growth industry here is tourism. Natal, the capital city, has become one the Northeast's main points of entry for tourists from Western Europe. Nearly all come here for the sunshine and beaches.

Wedged in between Pernambuco and Rio Grande do Norte, Paraíba boasts some of Brazil's least spoilt beaches. Agriculture plays an important role in the state economy. The capital, João Pessoa, is a pleasant city with a small historic center. The city of Campina Grande is famous for its June festival, the Festas Juninas.

View of the Rio Branco and João Pessoa, Paraíba

◀ Traditional wickerwork for sale at Mercado Central, Fortaleza

Exploring Paraíba, Rio Grande do Norte & Ceará

Most visitors to the states of Paraíba, Rio Grande do Norte, and Ceará focus on the natural beauty of the beaches and the coastline. The most popular gateway destinations are Natal in Rio Grande and Fortaleza in Ceará, which offer easy access to most of the region's attractions. Paraíba's capital, João Pessoa, with its colonial buildings, parks, and beaches, is a pleasant place to visit. In the interior of Paraíba, the monster rock formations in Cariri offer an almost other-worldly experience. Dinosaur fossils, discovered in Souza, have made the place archaeologically important. The harsh, arid interior landscape of these states has a unique, stark beauty.

Sights at a Glance

Towns & Cities
- ❶ *João Pessoa pp234–5*
- ❷ Campina Grande
- ❹ Souza
- ❺ Natal
- ❼ Genipabu
- ❿ Mossoró
- ⓬ *Fortaleza pp246–7*

National Parks
- ⓮ Parque Nacional de Ubajara

Areas of Natural Beauty
- ❸ Cariri
- ❽ Maracajaú
- ❾ Costa Branca
- ⓫ Canoa Quebrada
- ⓭ Jericoacoara

Beaches & Resort
- ❻ *Rota do Sol Beaches p241*

Downtown João Pessoa from across the lagoon

For hotels and restaurants in this region see pp376–7 and p393

Key

≡ Highway
— Major road
∷ Minor road
⊶ Railroad
▬ State border

Colorful old buildings in the historic center of Fortaleza

Getting Around

All major cities and some smaller destinations, such as Campina Grande in Paraíba, can be reached by domestic flights. There are regular buses between all towns and cities. However, roads in this part of Brazil are in poor condition and are very badly maintained. The BR-101 connects João Pessoa to Natal. From Natal, travelers continuing north to Fortaleza take the BR-304, which veers west and cuts inland across Rio Grande do Norte to Ceará. The stretch of the BR-230 towards Souza is in rough shape. Ensure that the vehicle, preferably a 4WD, is in good condition. Be sure to carry extra gas, water, and supplies.

❶ João Pessoa

Founded in 1585 as Nossa Senhora das Neves, the city derives its present name from a former governor of Paraíba. Brazil's third-oldest city, João Pessoa maintains an air of old-world charm, with a host of well-restored colonial churches, convents, and monasteries. Local visitors, however, flock here mainly for the easy atmosphere of its great white sandy beaches along the coastline. The dense tropical forest that once covered the coastal strip of Paraíba now thrives only in patches, one of which lies within João Pessoa, forming one of the largest areas of natural wilderness in any city in the world.

Rococo-style painting on Igreja de São Francisco's ceiling

Majestic colonial buildings, Centro Histórico

Exploring João Pessoa

One of the oldest and less developed cities in Brazil, João Pessoa has a small historic core, which remains little changed despite the modernization drive. It is located a bit inland, on a small hill overlooking the Rio Sanhauá and Rio Paraíba. Modern João Pessoa, with fast emerging skyscrapers, gravitates towards the beaches. Due to a state law restricting the height of buildings within 490 ft (150 m) of the shoreline to four stories or less, the waterfront is free of the curtain wall of concrete high-rises that afflict some other Brazilian beachfronts.

🏛 Catedral Basílica de Nossa Senhora das Neves

Rua General Osório, Centro. **Tel** (83) 3221 2503. **Open** 2–5pm Mon–Fri, 5–7pm Sat. 🕙 5pm Mon–Fri, 7:30pm Sat, 6am, 9am, 7:30pm Sun. 🚫

After four major renovations little remains of the original cathedral built in 1586. The interior maintains a striking harmony, unlike many of the elaborate Rococo-style churches in Brazil.

🏛 Igreja de São Francisco

Praça São Francisco, Centro Histórico. **Tel** (83) 3218 4505. **Open** 9am–5pm Mon–Fri, 9am–2pm Sat & Sun. 🚫 📷

One of the most spectacular churches in the city sits majestically atop a hill that bears the same name. The most striking feature of this impressive 18th-century church is the tower topped with an oriental dome. The altar contains an 18th-century statue of St. Benedict, one of the few black saints. The beautiful Rococo-style painting on

Façade of Igreja de São Francisco, João Pessoa's celebrated church

the ceiling of the church depicts various images of St. Francis. Even older than the church by a few decades is a stone cross across the courtyard. The church is part of the larger Centro Cultural de Sao Francisco complex, which also includes the Convento de Santo Antônio, chapels, and a museum of popular and sacred art, the result of grand-scale reforms carried out in 1718 and 1788.

🏛 Mosteiro de São Bento

Rua General Osório, Centro Histórico. **Tel** (83) 3241 1093. **Open** 8:30am–4pm Mon–Fri. 🕙 7am.

Built in the 17th century, this working monastery is a shining example of simplicity. Its unembellished, well-restored interior features a curved wooden ceiling.

🏖 Praia de Tambaú

4 miles (7 km) E of city center.

João Pessoa's most popular urban beach is Praia de Tambaú, a 4-mile- (7-km-) long stretch of sand lined with restaurants, cafés, and interesting food and craft stalls. In the evenings, locals stroll the seawall, enjoying the cool breeze.

🏖 Praia do Cabo Branco

S of Praia do Tambaú.

Better suited for swimming than Tambaú, Cabo Branco is a residential beach area looking out over the easternmost point in the Americas, **Ponta do Seixas** (Seixas Point). The point juts out into the ocean, and is topped by a small lighthouse, with a monument marking the spot.

🏖 Ilha de Picãozinho

N of Praia de Tambaú. 🗺

Actually a large coral reef, Ilha de Picãozinho is a popular spot. At low tide, boats depart from Praia do Tambaú, and take visitors over to swim and snorkel in the natural tide pools. Fish and starfish can be easily observed in the crystal-clear water. Check the tide table for specific times daily before taking a dip. For a few days every month, the tide is too high for the reef to be visited.

🏖 Ilha de Areia Vermelha

12 miles (20 km) N of town. 🗺

Another low-tide attraction is Ilha de Areia Vermelha (Island of Red Sand). For approximately 25 days every month, low tide exposes a beautiful beach of striking red-orange sand, a short distance off the coast of João Pessoa. With a choice of floating bars, it makes a perfect spot for swimming, snorkeling, or sunbathing. The temporary island is accessible from Praia da Camboinhas, 8 miles (13 km)

north of Tambaú. Trips to this island can be arranged by travel agencies.

🚩 Praia Tambaba

19 miles (30 km) S of town.

Tambaba is a beautiful, secluded nude beach with lush vegetation, small reefs, and tide pools. Two coves make up this splendid beach. Clothing is optional on one of the coves. The other cove, which is exclusively a nudist beach, is closed off by a

VISITORS' CHECKLIST

Practical Information
Paraíba. 🏠 723,000. ℹ Sectur, Parque Solonde Lucena 216, (83) 3218 9852.

Transport
✈ 7 miles (11 km) W of city center. 🚌 Rodoviária at Rua Francisco Londres, Varadouro.

gate and allows men only if accompanied by women.

Low tide at the expansive Ilha de Areia Vermelha

João Pessoa City Center

① Catedral Basílica de Nossa Senhora das Neves
② Igreja de São Francisco
③ Mosteiro de São Bento
④ Praia de Tambaú
⑤ Praia do Cabo Branco
⑥ Ilha de Picãozinho
⑦ Ilha de Areia Vermelha
⑧ Praia Tambaba

❷ Campina Grande

Paraíba. 🏘 400,000. ✈ 🚌 from João Pessoa. 🛈 Rua 13 de Maio 329, (83) 3310 6100. 🎭 Micarande (late Apr), Festas Juninas (Jun).

Ideal for experiencing the unique *sertão* culture, Campina Grande is a large market town with some degree of industrial growth.

The autumn harvest festival, Festas Juninas, although celebrated everywhere in the Northeast, is biggest in Campina Grande. The vast, purpose-built fairground, **Parque do Povo**, includes several smaller theme parks such as the Sítio São João, a reproduction of a traditional ranch where visitors can observe the rural *nordeste* lifestyle, and the Arraial Hilton Motta, a replica of a small interior town.

The **Museu de Arte Assis Chateaubriand** has a striking collection of modern works, with a focus on the work of artists from the Northeast.

🏛 **Museu de Arte Assis Chateaubriand**
Av Floriano Peixoto 718. **Open** 9am–noon, 2–10pm Mon–Fri.

Parque do Povo
Tel (83) 3310 6100. **Open** only during Festas Juninas. 🅿 ♿

The Lajedo do Pai Mateus rock formation, Cariri

❸ Cariri

Paraíba. 🚌 from Campina Grande. 🛥 Cariri Ecotours, (84) 9660 1818.
🌐 **caririecotours.com.br**

Situated in the Cariri Paraíbano, a large plateau in the Serra da Borborema, Cariri is the point at which the *sertão* proper begins. Tours in this area of aboriginal rock carvings and huge rock formations can be organized by Cariri Ecotours, based in Ponta Negra, Natal.

One of the formations, the **Lajedo do Pai Mateus**, sits on the private grounds of a *fazenda*. A vast slab of bare granite, it is littered with boulders bigger than houses, as if a giant had scattered his collection of pebbles – hence the local epithet, "Devil's Marbles." The most remarkable of these granite monsters is the Pedra do Capacete (Helmet Stone), a 20-ft- (6-m-) high boulder that is open in the front and hollow underneath, resembling a huge war helmet.

From the plateau, there are breathtaking views of the Borborema valley. The diverse landscape consists of small trees, bushes, cacti, and bromeliads. Sightings of emu birds, an ostrich-like avian, are common in this area.

❹ Souza

Paraíba. 🏘 60,000. 🚌 from Campina Grande. 🛥 Cariri Ecotours, (84) 9660 1818. 🌐 **caririecotours.com.br**

Brazil's most important prehistoric site, Souza is located deep in the Paraíba interior, almost on the border with Ceará. It was a large shallow lake where hundreds of dinosaur species roamed, 130 million years ago. Today, the dry riverbed of the Rio de Peixe, also known as the **Vale dos Dinossauros**, contains one of the world's best collections of dinosaur tracks. The largest and best track forms a perfect 164-ft- (50-m-) long trail across the meandering riverbed.

Scattered throughout the valley are numerous other tracks, most of which have not yet been catalogued or protected. Some, indeed, have yet to be discovered. Manary Ecotours can combine trips in this area with visits to Cariri.

A night scene of Campina Grande, lit up during the Festas Juninas

Festas Juninas

One of the most popular folklore traditions of the Northeast, the Festas Juninas began as a peasant celebration of the corn harvest and the June solstice, the longest night of the year in the Southern Hemisphere. June also coincided with the feasts of St. Anthony, St. John, and St. Peter. Over the years, the pagan rituals and Catholic events were melded together. The atmosphere is burlesque, as partygoers dress up in peasant outfits and perform square dances to the sounds of *forró (see p240)*. Bonfires are lit and fireworks sent aloft to safeguard the harvest and ward off evil spirits, as well as to bring light to the long night.

The Sertão

The *sertão* is a geographic region that encompasses almost half the territory of the Northeast. Aridity is its single most important characteristic. Rainfall is sparse, and the vegetation is primarily *caatinga*, which consists of small trees and bushes. Agriculture is difficult in the *sertão*, which makes it one of Brazil's poorest regions.

Traditionally, *sertanejos* have made a living herding goats or cattle. One of the country's original cowboy regions, the *sertão* has also seen the largest outflow of people in Brazil. Hard climatic conditions forced *en masse* migrations either to the coast, or to the big cities such as São Paulo and Rio de Janeiro. Not just the dislocated northeasterners, or *nordestinos,* but all Brazilians have an affinity for the *sertão* way of life: *forró* music is loved throughout the country, and Brazil's popular culture abounds with *sertanejo* stories and images.

After a sudden rain, the dry land will turn green and lush for a short period.

Palma cactus is often the only food available to livestock. The tough, chewy leaves are ground into a paste and used as cattle feed.

Caatinga, the vegetation growing in this arid landscape, consists of cacti, bromeliads, and scrubby trees and bushes. These plant species are suitable to the challenging conditions of the *sertão*.

Goats are the most important livestock in the *sertão*. More adaptable than other animals, the goat thrives in the dry and hot conditions. It is an important source of meat, milk, and leather.

Rio São Francisco is one of the main water sources in the *sertão*. Large irrigation projects are using the water to make agriculture possible. Many areas in Pernambuco grow fruits and vegetables.

Nordestino markets are where homesick communities of migrants from the Northeast meet, listen to *forró*, and eat some of their favorite foods. São Paulo and Rio de Janeiro have the largest *sertanejo* immigrant communities.

Luiz Gonzaga (1912–89), Brazil's most famous "Son of the *Sertão*," was a *forró* musician. Most of his songs celebrated or lamented the life of those living in the *sertão*.

A palm-lined beach in Fortaleza ▶

View of the small chapel in the central courtyard of the Forte dos Reis Magos

🟤 Natal

Rio Grande do Norte. 🚩 800,000. ✈️
🚌 ℹ️ Centro de Turismo, (84) 3211
6149. 🎭 Carnatal (Dec).

Natal is a pleasant, modern, and
safe city, increasingly sought out
as a sunshine destination for
winter-weary Europeans. Natal
has several attractions, including
beautiful beaches, dune buggy
rides, unusual sand art, and an
incredible nightlife. The city and
its most famous landmark, **Forte
dos Reis Magos**, date back to
December 25, 1598, when the
Portuguese established a fort
and settlement at the mouth
of the Rio Potengi. In honor of
the season, the city was named
Natal, the Portuguese word for
Christmas. The fort was named
after the three wise kings of
the east who had traveled to
Bethlehem bearing gifts. The
Dutch occupied the fort in 1633,
upgrading it into its current

five-pointed formation before
turning it back over to the
Portuguese in 1654. Access
to the fort is via a narrow
pedestrian walkway. At high
tide, the fort is cut off from
land by the waves. Visitors
have the full run of the fort,
from the garrisons and the
mess hall to the high
ramparts, which offer terrific
views of the city skyline.

Natal was never a large
trading center, and there
are few historic buildings.
The city's 19th-century
penitentiary has been
converted into the **Centro
de Turismo**, a showcase
for regional arts and crafts.
Each of the dozens of prison
cells along four corridors has
been transformed into a shop
selling leatherwork, lace,
hammocks, and figurines from
northeastern folk festivals.
A restaurant and a cafeteria

Sand art in
bottle

offer some regional dishes.
On Thursday evenings, the
courtyard of the old prison
becomes an outdoor dance
hall, as the center plays host
to *forró com o turista*, an
evening of *forró* dancing,
with live music and
instructors on hand to
help shy and left-footed
foreigners with the
dance steps.

Most visitors to Natal
stay in **Ponta Negra**, a
waterfront neighborhood
in a modern part of the city
featuring a lovely long
beach with good waves
for surfing. At the far end
of the beach the Morro
do Careca, a towering 390-ft
(120-m) sand dune, is now off-
limits to climbers because of
the danger of erosion.

On the coast between the old
downtown and the modern
parts of Natal there stands the
Parque das Dunas, a 12-sq-mile
(6-sq-km) reserve of coastal
dunes. The park has several
trails, but can only be visited
with a guide.

🏛️ **Centro de Turismo**
Rua Aderbal de Figueiredo 980.
Tel (84) 3211 6149. **Open** 9am–7pm
daily. ♿

🏰 **Forte dos Reis Magos**
Praia do Forte. **Tel** (84) 3211 3820.
Open 8am–4:30pm daily. 📷

🌳 **Parque das Dunas**
Av Alexandrino de Alencar s/n.
Tel (84) 3201 3985. **Open** 8am–6pm
Tue–Sun. 📷 📷

Couples dancing to the lively music
of *forró*

Forró

According to local legend, the
musical style known as *forró* is said
to have been inspired by visiting
foreigners. In the early days of
World War II, the Americans
created a massive air base near the
city. Locals invited the American
airmen to their parties, and to
make sure they felt welcome they
put up signs proclaiming that
simplified dances with a two-step
rhythm, were "for all." The label
stuck to the musical style, though
in common speech "for all"
became *forró*.

6 Rota do Sol Beaches

Head south from Natal on the Rota do Sol (Route of the Sun), for beaches and more beaches, stretching from the edge of the city to the far southern border of the state. Variety is the key feature of this golden stretch of coast. There are beaches with small reefs and little surf, and others with strong and steady waves, much loved by avid surfers. There are deserted beaches surrounded by tall dunes, accessible only by dune buggy or 4WD, far from the hustle and bustle of even the smallest fishing village. Other beaches, particularly Pipa, are full to bursting with energetic young Brazilians.

Mãe Luiza lighthouse north of Ponta Negra

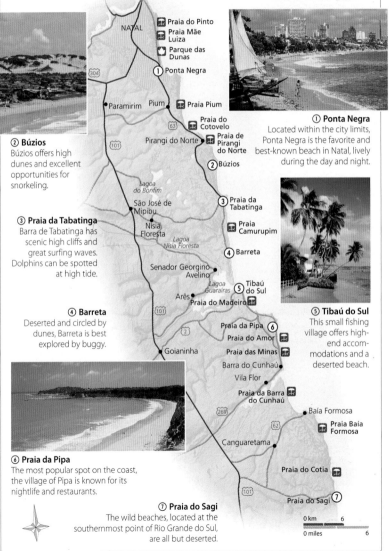

① Ponta Negra
Located within the city limits, Ponta Negra is the favorite and best-known beach in Natal, lively during the day and night.

② Búzios
Búzios offers high dunes and excellent opportunities for snorkeling.

③ Praia da Tabatinga
Barra de Tabatinga has scenic high cliffs and great surfing waves. Dolphins can be spotted at high tide.

④ Barreta
Deserted and circled by dunes, Barreta is best explored by buggy.

⑤ Tibaú do Sul
This small fishing village offers high-end accommodations and a deserted beach.

⑥ Praia da Pipa
The most popular spot on the coast, the village of Pipa is known for its nightlife and restaurants.

⑦ Praia do Sagi
The wild beaches, located at the southernmost point of Rio Grande do Sul, are all but deserted.

Map labels:
NATAL
Praia do Pinto
Praia Mãe Luiza
Parque das Dunas
① Ponta Negra
Paramirim
Pium
Praia Pium
Praia do Cotovelo
Pirangi do Norte
Praia de Pirangi do Norte
② Búzios
Lagoa do Bonfim
São José de Mipibu
Nísia Floresta
Lagoa Nísia Floresta
③ Praia da Tabatinga
Praia Camurupim
④ Barreta
Senador Georgino Avelino
Lagoa Guaraíras
⑤ Tibaú do Sul
Arês
Praia do Madeiro
Goianinha
Praia da Pipa ⑥
Praia do Amor
Praia das Minas
Barra do Cunhaú
Vila Flor
Praia da Barra do Cunhaú
Baía Formosa
Praia Baía Formosa
Canguaretama
Praia do Cotia
Praia do Sagi ⑦

0 km   6
0 miles   6

For keys to symbols *see back flap*

Snorkeling in the coral reefs, Maracajaú

❼ Genipabu

Rio Grande do Norte. ⌖ 5,000. ✈ Natal Airport. 🚌 ℹ Associação dos Bugueiros do Rio Grande do Norte, (84) 3225 2077.

The main reason to visit Genipabu is to experience the magnificent dunes. This small town is located north of Natal, close to the edge of an impressive landscape of shifting sands that pile up into high dunes and plunge down to the edge of the Atlantic Ocean. Though it is possible to ride a camel through the dunes or sandboard down them, the best way to enjoy these enormous ridges of sand is behind the roll bar of a dune buggy with an experienced driver at the wheel. The **Parque Dunas de Genipabu** is the perfect place to start. This area of 164-ft (50-m) tall shifting dunes is off-limits to all but licensed buggy drivers who know their way around every hump and dip. Passengers have the option of requesting a ride *"com ou sem emoção"* (with or without the thrills and heart palpitations). Well worth requesting, the thrill-ride is an amazing roller coaster of maneuvers up and down along the slippery front faces of the dunes, descending at almost 90-degree angles before zooming straight up another dune on the far side.

The best time of day to visit the Parque das Dunas is in the afternoon, to enjoy the lovely golden sunset over the dunes after the ride.

❽ Maracajaú

Rio Grande do Norte. 🚌 **Open** at low tide only.

Maracajaú's coral reefs offer one of the best spots for snorkeling along the whole of Brazil's north coast. The reefs lie approximately 4 miles (7 km) offshore. At low tide, the receding ocean leaves the reefs from just 3 to 9 ft (1 to 3 m) underwater, and forms natural pools, called *parrachos*, which combine the beauty of the tranquil water with a spectacular array of marine life. They are shallow enough for snorkelers and swimmers to observe dozens of species of colorful, tropical fish trapped inside the reefs. The water is crystal clear and warm round the year, making it a popular destination for scuba divers and swimmers alike. Tour operators offer scuba-diving trips, but the water is so shallow, it is hardly worth the effort or expense.

The best way to reach Maracajaú is by a dune buggy, departing from Natal (or Genipabu) and traveling north along the white, sandy beaches. Check the tide tables to time the journey in order to arrive in Maracajaú at, or a few hours before, low tide. The large **Manoa Water Park**, replete with slides and swimming pools, en route to the coral reefs in Maracajaú, is an enjoyable stop for children.

Tourists enjoying a buggy ride on the white sand dunes in Genipabu

For hotels and restaurants in this region see pp376–7 and p393

Sailboats, known as *jangadas*, on Tibaú beach, one of the beach-villages along Costa Branca

❾ Costa Branca

Rio Grande do Norte. 🚌 ℹ️
Catavento Turismo, (85) 3433 6999.

The Costa Branca lies in the extreme northwest of Rio Grande do Norte. Starting at **Porto do Mangue**, it stretches across the villages of **Areia Branca** and **Grossos** and ends at **Tibaú**. The name "Costa Branca" refers to both the white dunes and the salt works found along this coast. The region has not yet been discovered by mass tourism, and its beaches, mangroves, dunes, and lagoons are blissfully devoid of crowds. **Praia do Rosado**, just west of Porto do Mangue, is famous for its pinkish sand dunes. The red soil underneath the shifting dunes mixes with the white sand of the beach giving the dunes an unusual and distinctly soft, pink hue.

The largest village on this coast, Areia Branca has around 20,000 residents and offers the best tourist facilities for those wanting to spend a few days exploring the region. Tibaú is the last village in Rio Grande do Norte, right on the border with Ceará. Its beach is mostly used by residents of the inland city of Mossoró. Local artisans use sand from the colored dunes to make artistic and pretty designs inside small glass bottles.

Sand design in glass bottle

❿ Mossoró

Rio Grande do Norte. 🚹 225,000.
✈️ 🚌 ℹ️ Rua Ruy Barbosa 282
(84) 3315 4814. 🎭 Batalha do Mossoró (Jun).

Located 34 miles (55 km) inland from the coast, Mossoró is, in many ways, the archetypal *sertão* town of the northeastern interior. The main places of interest in Mossoró are connected to a glorious moment in history in 1924, when the townspeople fought off an attack by the legendary bandit leader Lampião and his gang of outlaws. The event is still commemorated every June 13 with great ceremony.

Mossoró is an ideal jumping-off point for visiting the **Lajedo de Soledade**, an archaeological site. Its limestone rocks were formed more than 90 million years ago. Tours begin at the visitors' center, at the Museu de Soledade. From here, visitors can depart on a guided walk featuring 10,000-year-old rock paintings, and impressive fossils containing the remains of extinct animals, including saber-toothed tigers.

🏛️ Lajedo de Soledade
Tel (84) 3333 1017. **Open** 7am–noon & 1–5pm Tue–Sun. 🈲 📷

Repentistas

Repentista is a popular form of entertainment in the interior of the Northeast. Its singers engage in a two-man musical duel, making their rhymes up on the spot, trying to score points off their opponent. Singers sometimes accompany themselves with a tambourine or the melodious *viola nordestina*, developed from the Portuguese seven-string guitar. The singing duelists take turns singing out a stanza, trying to win the favor of the audience by making fun of their opponent, preferably with a clever bit of rhyme. The adversary's manhood, sexual prowess, and ancestry are common topics, but politics and day-to-day events also play into the mix. In big cities with significant *nordestino* populations, such as São Paulo and Rio de Janeiro, *repentistas* make money on the downtown streets by creating impromptu songs to entertain homesick migrants.

Repentistas performing

⓫ Canoa Quebrada

Ceará. 🔼 65,300. 🚌 from Fortaleza.
ℹ️ Secretaría de Turismo, (88) 3446
2451. **W** canoaviagens.com.br

In just over four decades, Canoa Quebrada has transformed from a sleepy fishing village to a popular hippy hangout in the 1970s, and now a mainstream beach resort. According to a legend, the name Canoa Quebrada, meaning "Broken Canoe," originated with a Portuguese skipper who wrecked his ship close to shore and donated the useless craft to local fishermen. Never having seen such a craft before, locals named it a broken canoe.

The beaches of Canoa Quebrada, featuring red cliffs, fine sand, and offshore reefs, attract many visitors today. The village itself is a bustling place, known for its cafés and restaurants, and for the bars and clubs lining the main cobblestone street. It is also famous for its lacework. Even at the busiest times, however, it is not difficult to get away from the crowds and find a spot on one of the more deserted beaches or high sand dunes surrounding Canoa Quebrada. Buggy tours are a popular way to get out of town. The tour to Ponta Grossa, 18 miles (30 km) southeast, travels along miles of empty beaches framed by high red sandstone cliffs. Other activities include kite-surfing, riding, and sailing on a *jangada* (sailboat).

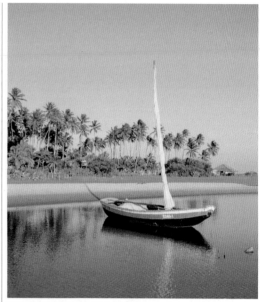

Beach along the fishing village of Jericoacoara

About 6 miles (10 km) northwest is the small town of **Aracati**. It is one of the few historic towns in this part of Northeast Brazil. An important center for the 18th-century cattle industry, Aracati has several buildings dating back to this time. Most noteworthy is the Mercado Central (Central Market), dating back to the 1700s, still used as the town's daily open-air market on Rua Pompeu.

⓬ Fortaleza

See pp246–7.

⓭ Jericoacoara

Ceará. 🔼 2,000. 🚌 from Fortaleza.
W jericoacoara.com

The isolated village of Jericoacoara is a beach lover's paradise. Although no longer the sleepy fishing community it once was, it preserves much of its original charm. The village consists of five streets made of sand, and houses and apartments are simple, even rustic. In 2002, the entire region was declared a national park, putting a complete halt to the construction of new buildings.

Red sandstone cliffs in and around the beaches of Canoa Quebrada

For hotels and restaurants in this region see pp376–7 and p393

The spectacular Ubajara Cave in Parque Nacional de Ubajara

Surrounded by dunes and lagoons, Jeri (as locals call it) is a place for those who like water, waves, and wind. From June to January, the winds pick up and kitesurfers, windsurfers, and sailors from around the world flock to Jeri.

Dune buggies are used to explore the surrounding beaches and dunes and visit the various lagoons. The most beautiful are **Lagoa Azul** and **Lagoa do Paraíso**, located about 12 miles (20 km) east of the village. Jeri's postcard view is that of **Pedra Furada**, a basalt outcrop, on the edge of the sea with a 13-ft (4-m) hole in the middle. It sits on the beach at Praia Malhada, about 2 miles (3 km) east, a 15-minute walk from the village. The red rock glows in the late afternoon light and from June to September, the aperture lines up perfectly with the tropical setting sun. Another beautiful spot is **Duna do Pôr do Sol** (Sunset Dune).

⑭ Parque Nacional de Ubajara

Ceará. 🚌 from Fortaleza. ℹ️
Secretaría de Turismo, (88) 3634 2365; Park Headquarters, (88) 3634 1388. **Open** 8am–5pm Tue–Sun. 🅿️ 🅲

Located almost exactly halfway between Fortaleza and Teresina, the Parque Nacional de Ubajara is the smallest national park in Brazil. Situated close to the small town of Ubajara, the park

features the **Ubajara Cave**. The entrance to the cave can be reached either by cable car (9am–3pm Fri–Sun) or via a steep, marked trail through the forest. The 3,937-ft- (1,200-m-) long cave is filled with stalactites and stalagmites, the work of several patient centuries of erosion and calcium deposition.

Fifteen chambers totaling 3,674 ft (1,120 m) have been mapped, of which 1,182 ft (360 m) are open to visitors. Eight galleries are lit up to display some of the amazing formations that have taken shape inside the cave. The main formations seen

inside are Pedra do Sino (Bell Stone), Salas da Rosa (Rose Rooms), Sala do Cavalo (Horse Room), and Sala dos Retratos (Portrait Room). The cave is also home to 14 different types of bat.

The elevation gain is just over 1,640 ft (500 m), and the trail leading up to the cave, though rather strenuous, offers some spectacular views of the Serra da Ipiapaba and several waterfalls and beautiful natural pools. The hike takes about two hours, one-way. There are also many local guides available here to show visitors around the park's eco trails, caves, and waterfalls.

Buggies

Dune buggies are found everywhere on Brazil's northeastern coast. Essentially a Volkswagen Beetle chassis with a fiberglass body and soft, fat tires, the Brazilian dune buggy is the perfect vehicle for exploring the endless beaches and towering sand dunes that characterize Northeast Brazil.

Popular places to buggy here are Genipabu (*see p242*), just north of Natal, and Cumbuco and Canoa Quebrada, respectively north and south of Fortaleza. They all feature towering mountains of sand, and dune-buggy drivers are trained to make the most of them.

High-speed runs up, down, and along the sheer, steep face of sand dunes are among the most hair-raising maneuvers one can expect from such a tour.

Multiday buggy expeditions include tours from Natal to Fortaleza – nearly 311 miles (500 km) of untouched sand.

Dune buggy in Canoa Quebrada

⑫ Fortaleza

With pretty urban beaches, a pleasant year-round climate, and a constant cooling breeze coming off the ocean, Fortaleza has an appealing resort-like atmosphere. Founded in the early 1500s, Fortaleza remained a small town until after Brazilian independence in 1822, then rapidly developed into one of Brazil's largest ports, exporting vast amounts of cotton to England in particular. There is a small historic section with a 17th-century fort near the old port, now renovated as a nightlife area called Praia de Iracema, but beyond that Fortaleza has a modern feel, with apartment high-rises, beach boulevards, and outdoor cafés.

Brightly painted colonial buildings lining the streets

🎭 Teatro José de Alencar

Praça José de Alencar s/n. **Tel** (85) 3101 2583. **Open** 9am–10pm Mon–Fri; 2–5pm Sat, Sun & hols. 🎦 🎟 ♿

Named after one of Brazil's famous novelists, the Teatro José de Alencar was built in 1908. The theater's high-Victorian cast-iron structure was imported straight from Glasgow. Additional elements, such as the stained-glass windows and interior furnishings, were done in the Art Nouveau style.

Ironwork, Teatro José de Alencar

🏛 Centro de Turismo

Rua Senador Pompeu 350. **Tel** (85) 3101 5508. **Open** 8am–6pm Mon–Fri, 8am–4pm Sat, 8am–noon Sun. ♿

This formerly grim Victorian prison has been transformed into a bustling market, with a different shop in each of the old jail cells. The market specializes in local handicrafts, including fine lace, leather, and figurines. The market is a good place to stock up on top-quality cashew nuts.

🏛 Museu do Ceará

Rua São Paulo 51. **Tel** (85) 3101 2609. **Open** 9am–5pm Tue–Sat. 🎦 🎟

The museum possesses a vast archive of things relating to the history of Ceará – coins, medals, paintings, furniture, indigenous artifacts, folk art, and more. Its most prized exhibit is the dagger belonging to notorious outlaw Lampião (see p217).

🏛 Centro Cultural Dragão do Mar

Rua Dragão do Mar 81, Iracema. **Tel** (85) 3488 8600. **Open** 8:30am–9:30pm Tue–Fri, 2:30–9:30pm Sat & Sun. 🎦 for movies & plays.
🌐 dragaodomar.org.br

Fortaleza's cultural center is a striking white building with a circular design. It houses the Museum of Contemporary Art, a history and anthropology museum, a planetarium, and a cinema and theater venue.

🏪 Mercado Central

Rua Maestro Alberto Nepomuceno 199. **Tel** (85) 3454 8586. **Open** 8am–6pm Mon–Fri, 8am–4pm Sat, 8am–2pm Sun. ♿

Fortaleza's central market is the cheapest place in town for fine leatherwork, lace, or textiles. The market is also an excellent place to sample local ice cream made from regional fruits.

Fortaleza

① Teatro José de Alencar
② Centro de Turismo
③ Museu do Ceará
④ Centro Cultural Dragão do Mar
⑤ Mercado Central
⑥ Praia de Iracema
⑦ Praia de Meireles
⑧ Praia do Futuro
⑨ Praia de Cumbuco

The Story of Iracema

Written by José de Alencar in 1865, the story of Iracema tells of the love that a Tabajara princess bore for Martim, a white Portuguese settler. Iracema uses magic to make Martim fall in love with her, and is ostracized by her community. Away from her people, she loses her magical powers and her lover. A statue of Iracema on Meireles beach is located where, according to legend, she stood awaiting the return of her beloved.

Statue of Iracema waiting for her lover

VISITORS' CHECKLIST

Practical Information
Ceará. 🚊 2,400,000. ℹ️ Casa do Turista, Av Beira Mar at Rua Frei Mansueto, (85) 3105 2670. 🛍️ daily craft market at Meireles beach. 🎭 Fortal (Jul), Regata de Jangadas (Jul), Semana do Folclore (Aug).
ⓦ **fortaleza.ce.gov.br/turismo**

Transport
✈️ 4 miles (6 km) S of town.
🚌 (85) 3235 0688.

🏖️ Praia de Iracema

Just east of the city center lies the Praia de Iracema. Though called a beach, it is actually the very urban former port, now renovated and transformed into the city's most popular nightlife and restaurant area. The centerpiece of the area is a long ocean pier called Ponte dos Ingleses (Englishman's Pier), first built in 1920, and modeled on the piers of Brighton. Many restaurants occupy other original turn-of-the-19th-century buildings in the area. Locally famous nightlife spots include Piratas (open Mondays), and Lupus Bier, known for its Wednesday evening folklore and variety show.

🏖️ Praia de Meireles

The city's prettiest urban beach is lined with thick groves of coconut palms and waterside cafés, although the water is not considered good for swimming. Meireles is a great place for strolling, shopping, sunbathing, or people-watching while

Visitors at a waterside café, Praia de Meireles

sipping on fresh cashew juice. Home to what has become the city's prime residential and hotel neighborhood in Fortaleza, Meireles' pedestrian boulevard, running beside the beach, becomes a night market every evening.

🏖️ Praia do Futuro

Praia do Futuro is one of the best beaches in the city for swimming, and a bustling nightlife destination in its own right. The 7-mile-(11-km-) long beach southeast of the center is lined with restaurants and beach shacks that serve local cuisine. There are several discos on the beach that are popular on weekends. On Thursday nights, Fortalezans head to Barraca Chico do Caranguejo to feast on fresh crab and listen to popular live *forró* (see p240) music.

🏖️ Praia de Cumbuco

21 miles (33 km) W of town.
Cumbuco is the city's favorite beach playground. The Lagoa da Banana offers a wide variety of watersports, including jet-skiing, boating, banana boating, and kayaking, and has become a major kitesurfing destination. Lagoa do Parnamirim, just south of Cumbuco, is surrounded by tall dunes, making it perfect for "ski-bunda" (bum-skiing), where skiers slide on wooden boards down a dune into the lagoon. Other activities on offer include horseback riding and sailing on *jangadas*, or single-sail rafts.

0 meters 500
0 yards 500

MUCURIPE

Atlantic Ocean

⑧ Praia do Futuro

RUA J
RUA B
RUA A
R. BRIZMAR
AV VICENTE DE CASTRO
RAV LEITE BARBOSA
R. ADOLPHO DUCKE
AV JOSÉ SABÓIA
AVENIDA ZEZÉ DIOGO
AV DIOGUINHO
RUA ISMAEL PORDEUS
AV JANGADEIRO
AV ABOLIÇÃO
RUA ANA BILHAR
ARJOTA
DOM LUIZ
AV DES COLOMBO SOUSA
AV SANTANA JR
R. VALDÉR RIO MOTA
AV DOLOR BARREIRA
RUA DO MORO
AV TRAIANO MEDEIROS
AV CÉSAR B CALIS
RUA HERMINIA BONAVIDES

For keys to symbols see back flap

PIAUÍ & MARANHÃO

Although part of the Northeast, Piauí and Maranhão are different from the rest of the region culturally and geographically. Both states have violent histories. Piauí was the site of many skirmishes between the indigenous population and cattle herders, and Maranhão was forcibly settled in 1612 by the French. Today, the area is abundant in natural and cultural riches.

Unlike its southern neighbors, Piauí was settled by ranchers on horseback pushing northwards from the sugar plantations of Bahia in the late 1700s.

Largely visited in transit, Piauí is sparsely populated and possibly the poorest state in Brazil. The economy here is greatly dependent on agriculture and livestock. The only significant industry revolves around the *carnaúba* palm, which yields a wax that is an important ingredient of shellac. However, Piauí boasts a few fascinating natural attractions. The state capital, Teresina, located more than 186 miles (300 km) inland, is the only capital in Northeast Brazil which is not on the ocean, and has some interesting sights.

For many years after they first came to Brazil, the Portuguese showed little interest in the area that now forms Maranhão. Taking advantage of the Portuguese neglect of the Maranhão coast, the French, in 1612, landed a sizable force and founded São Luís, named in honor of King Louis XIII. Portuguese forces laid siege for four years to drive the new French colony out.

Maranhão's golden age came in the 19th century, with a rich agricultural export economy based on cotton and sugar. Ports such as São Luís and Alcântara grew wealthy. When slavery was abolished in 1888, Maranhão's sugar and cotton industries collapsed, causing an economic slump that lasted for most of the 20th century.

Maranhão is today an exciting destination, both in terms of natural and cultural treasures. The state's main festival, Bumba-meu-boi, celebrates the indigenous, Portuguese, and African cultures.

Mesmerizing sand dunes of Lençóis Maranhenses in Maranhão

◄ Beautifully decorated ceiling of the Igreja da Sé, São Luis

Exploring Piauí & Maranhão

Most of Piauí's attractions are a long way from the coast. The Serra da Capivara is one of the largest archaeological sites in the world, containing more than 30,000 prehistoric rock paintings. The only important destination on Piauí's tiny 41-mile (66-km) coastline is the town of Parnaíba. It sits at the edge of the Delta do Parnaíba, one of the largest deep-water river deltas in the world, and now an ecotourism destination. Most of the delta itself lies in Maranhão. Its capital, São Luís, rivals Salvador for its collection of restored colonial homes and heritage buildings. Outside of São Luís, the biggest draw is a spectacular region of stark beauty in the form of coastal sand dunes known as Lençóis Maranhenses.

Sights at a Glance

Towns & Cities

1 Teresina
5 *São Luís pp256–8*
6 Alcântara

National Parks & Areas of Natural Beauty

2 Parque Nacional de Sete Cidades
3 *Parque Nacional de Serra da Capivara pp252–3*
4 *Delta do Parnaíba & Parque Nacional dos Lençóis Maranhenses pp254–5*
7 Reentrâncias Maranhenses

Key

— Major road
⋯ Minor road
⋯ Railroad
▬▬ State border

Carútapera
Turiaçu
Belém ➤
Camiranga 316
Cururupu
Santa Helena
ALCÂNTA
REENTRÂNCIAS MARANHENSES 7 Pinheiro
6
São Bento 5
Viana
Arari It
M
Santa Inês Pirapemas
Belém ➤
Santa Luzia *Lago Açu* 135
316
Coroatá
Lago da Pedra Bacabal
222 Arame
Pedreiras
Açailândia Presidente Dutra
M A R A N H Ã O 226
Imperatriz Amarante do Maranhão Barra do Corda 135
Montes Altos Grajaú Colinas
230 6
Alpercatas
Porto Franco Pastos Bor
Goiânia 10 Santo Antônio 230
BeneditoLeite Uruç
Carolina 230 Riachão Balsas 324 Bertolin
Eliseu
Brejo da Porta
Alto Parnaíba Santa Filomena Cristino Castro
135 Reder
Gilbués Cu
Corrente
Brasília ↓

Pedra do Elefante at the Parque Nacional de Sete Cidades

For hotels and restaurants in this region see p377 and pp393–4

Pristine Caburé beach at Lençóis Maranhenses

DELTA DO PARNAÍBA & PARQUE NACIONAL DOS LENÇÓIS MARANHENSES

Araiosos Parnaíba

Luzilândia Cocal
Fortaleza

Piracuruca

Batalha PARQUE NACIONAL
DE SETE CIDADES

Miguel Piripiri
Alves Pedroll
José de
Freitas Campo Maior

TERESINA Castelo
do Piaui

São Miguel
do Tapuio

Palmeirais

Valença Fortaleza
do Piaui

Floriano Fronteiras
enha
Oeiras Picos

São José Jaicós
do Peixe Recife

Costa
Simplício
Mendes Paulistana

São João
do Piaui

PARQUE NACIONAL DE SERRA DA CAPIVARA

ão Raimundo
Nonato

Brasília

0 kilometers 100

0 miles 100

Getting Around

The São Luís airport in Maranhão has international flights, and Piauí's capital city Teresina can be reached by flights en route to São Luís. There are buses linking almost every town in this region, but roads are in very poor condition. It is also possible to rent a car. The inland attractions of Piauí are far from Teresina, and from each other, so travel well equipped with plenty of gas, water, and supplies.

Most of Maranhão's highlights are on the coast. The Lençóis Maranhenses are best accessed from Barreirinhas, located just on the edge of the Lençóis Maranhenses National Park. From São Luís, it is a 45-minute flight in a single-engine plane, or a four-hour drive. Once there, most excursions are by boat or in a 4WD, as there are no paved roads in the region.

Colonial-style houses and Ponte José Sarney, São Luís

For keys to symbols *see back flap*

Church exterior, Nossa Senhora do Amparo

❶ Teresina

Piauí. ✈ 815,000. ✈ 🚌
ℹ️ Piemtur, (86) 3215 9426 or 3215 7476. 🌐 turismoteresina.com

Founded in 1852, Teresina was named in honor of the Empress Teresa Cristina, wife of Brazilian Emperor Dom Pedro II. Teresina has the dubious honor of being one of Brazil's hottest cities, although Rio Parnaíba and Rio Poty, as well as several large, tree-shaded squares scattered throughout Teresina, moderate the worst of the city's scorching heat.

Most historic buildings date back only to the end of the 19th century. One of the oldest buildings is the cathedral, **Nossa Senhora do Amparo**. Construction was started in 1851 but completed only in 1952. More modern, but also interesting, is the Palácio Karnak, Piauí's new state legislature. Built in 1926, the palace's façade was modeled on an ancient Egyptian temple. The former state legislature is now home to the **Museu do Piauí**. Its small collection provides a good overview of regional history, including both pre-historic artifacts and folk art.

🏛 **Museu do Piauí**
Praça Marechal Deodoro da Fonseca, Centro. **Tel** (86) 3221 6027.
Open 8am–5pm Tue–Fri, 8am–noon Sat & Sun.

🏛 **Nossa Senhora do Amparo**
Praça Marechal Deodoro da Fonseca s/n, Centro. **Open** daily.

Environs
Easily reached by bus, the **Parque Ambiental Encontro dos Rios** is located just north of Teresina, where the Poty and Parnaíba rivers join up. This pleasant park offers walking trails, fishing spots, gardens, two lookouts, a floating restaurant, a store with regionally made crafts and a statue of Crispim, the Bowl Head.

❸ Parque Nacional de Serra da Capivara

Piauí's most compelling park is the Serra da Capivara, located in the far south of the state. The park's impressive canyons, plateaux, and rock formations also form one of Brazil's most important prehistoric sites, one that was designated a UNESCO World Heritage Site in 1991. Over 30,000 rock paintings have been discovered within the park. The paintings portray aspects of prehistoric life such as the hunt, dances, and other rituals.

Andorinhas
Every evening, thousands of swifts (andorinhas) perform amazing aerial acrobatics before retiring to a nearby cave to spend the night.

Rock Painting
Scientists estimate that many of these rock paintings were created between 6,000 and 12,000 years ago. The oldest drawings may date as far back as 29,000 years.

Key

━━ Major road
═══ Other road
── Minor road
– – Trail
━━ Park boundary

Trails leading up to rock formations at Parque Nacional de Sete Cidades

heat, and erosion, the rocks resemble animals, people, mythological beings, and even man-made structures. Among the shapes are **Mapa do Brasil**, a backward-facing map of Brazil, and **Biblioteca** (Library), both in Quarta Cidade (Fourth City). Segundo Cidade, the second of the seven "cities", has a 147-ft- (45-m-) tall look-out with views out over five of the cities of stone. There are also more than 2,000 prehistoric rock paintings,

some 6,000 years old. The most impressive painting, **Pedra de Inscrição** (Inscribed Rock), said to be marked with cryptic Indian runes, can be seen at Quinta Cidade (Fifth City). Other formations include **Pedra do Elefante** (Elephant Rock) at Sexta Cidade (Sixth City), and lookout points such as the **Arco de Triunfo** (Triumphal Arch), a 59-ft- (18-m-) tall arch-shaped rock, lying between Quarta Cidade and Quinta Cidade.

❷ Parque Nacional de Sete Cidades

Maranhão. 🚌 from Teresina.
🛈 Ibama Office, Centro de Visitantes, (86) 3343 1342. **Open** 8am–5pm daily.
🎫 🛏 Parque Hotel Sete Cidades, (86) 3276 2222.

The name Sete Cidades (Seven Cities) refers to seven distinct and unusual rock formations, spread out in the park along 7 miles (12 km) of trails. Only the first six are accessible to the public. Sculpted by rain, wind,

Crispim, the Bowl Head

A popular Piauí legend tells the story of Crispim, a fisherman who lived by the banks of the Rio Parnaíba. He came home one day frustrated after not having caught any fish. Outraged with the meager lunch of beef-bone soup, Crispim took up a large bone and beat his mother. As she lay dying, she cursed him, condemning him to live in the river as a bowl-headed monster. The curse would be lifted when he devoured seven virgins named Maria. Locals still tell of spotting Crispim in the river, looking for virgins to eat.

Rio Parnaíba, reputedly haunted by Crispim

---

0 km   10
0 miles   6

Caldeirão dos Rodrigues, a walk through Baixão da Pedra Furada, leads to archaeological sites with rock paintings.

Desfiladeiro da Capivara is a 2-mile- (4-km-) long trail, leading to many rock-painting sites.

São João do Piauí

Grande

deirão dos odrigues

Baixão da Pedra Furada

Baixão do Sítio Meio

Coronel José Dias

São Raimundo Nonato

Baixão do Sítio Meio is the site where a pottery shard nearly 9,000 years old was found. It is the oldest in the Americas.

VISITORS' CHECKLIST

Practical Information
Coronel José Dias, Piauí.
🛈 Museu de Homem Americano, Bairro Campestre, São Raimundo Nonato, (89) 3582 1612. **Open** 9am–5pm Tue–Sun. Best time to visit is Mar–Jun. 🎫 valid for three days. 📷 tour groups up to a maximum of 10 people. 🛏 Hotel Serra da Capivara, Santa Luiza, (89) 3582 1389.

Transport
🚌 from Teresina to São Raimundo Nonato, then taxi.

Baixão da Pedra Furada
The trail leading to the large unusual-shaped rock, known as Pedra Furada (Pierced Rock), leads to 10 different archaeological sites.

For keys to symbols see back flap

Ⓐ Delta do Parnaíba & Parque Nacional dos Lençóis Maranhenses

The Delta do Parnaíba stretches roughly from the Piauí border some 56 miles (90 km) farther up the coast in Maranhão, where the Rio Parnaíba runs into the sea. Shaped like a hand, the river breaks into five fingers, meandering through some 83 islands. Small villages thrive on sea salt, cashews, and crabs. Tourism is still in its infancy. Straddling Piauí and Maranhão, the Parque Nacional Lençóis Maranhenses offers over 600 sq miles (1,555 sq km) of spectacular white sand dunes created by strong coastal winds. From May to August, rain collects in the basins between dunes, forming countless crystal-clear freshwater lagoons. In June, when the water levels are at their highest, the Lençóis dunes look like an array of white stripes, interspersed with sparkling ribbons of blue, turquoise, and green.

★ Queimada dos Britos
Deep inside the park is an oasis, surrounded by sand dunes. It can be visited by 4WD from Sucuruju.

★ Scarlet Ibis
Born gray, these birds obtain their distinct red color from eating tiny crustaceans found in tide flats in the estuary of the Rio Preguiças.

Lagoa de Santo Amaro
This beautiful clear-water lake near the tiny village of Santa Amaro do Maranhão sits isolated amid sand dunes.

Atlantic Ocean

Lagoa Travosa

Lagoa de Santo Amaro

Queimada dos Britos

Santo Amaro do Maranhão

Provoado de Sucuruju

Primeira Cruz

Alegre

Key

▬▬▬ Major road

▭▭▭ Minor road

– – Trail

▬▬▬ Park boundary

KEY

① **Baixa Grande** oasis can be reached by hiking across the dunes.

② **Barreirinhas** is a small town, and the main access point to the park.

★ Lençóis
On foot, visitors can only access a small portion of the park. To appreciate the size and scale of the dunes, it is worth taking a sightseeing flight from São Luís. The views of the large dunes and lagoons are breathtaking.

The Versatile Buriti Palm Tree

The delta area's dense vegetation is dominated by the multipurpose buriti palm tree. The fruit can be eaten or used for wine, the trunk is used for house poles, while the fronds make thatch roofs and baskets. Buriti fiber is crucial for the strong but limber pouch used to squeeze the poison from manioc root. The twigs make good placemats, the seeds can be fashioned into jewelry, and the bark can be spun into twine.

Buriti palm tree with its hanging fruit

Caburé
Sitting on a sandpit a short distance from the Atlantic Ocean, this tiny settlement is a good starting point for reaching the northeastern part of the Lençóis Maranhenses by ferry.

0 km 5

0 miles 5

Caburé

Atins

Mandacaru

Praia Pequenos Lençóis

Baía Tutóia

Delta do Parnaíba

Tutóia

34

Paulino Neves

Preguiças

2

São Luís 225

Pequenos Lençóis
This small desert of dunes rises out of Rio Preguiças. Ropes assist in hiking to the Boi hill.

Delta do Parnaíba
Formed where the Rio Parnaíba meets the Atlantic Ocean, the Parnaíba delta, comprising 83 islands with immense beaches, is one of the richest habitats for birdlife in the Northeast.

❺ Street-by-Street: São Luís

One of Brazil's finest examples of Portuguese colonial architecture, São Luís was, ironically, founded by the French in 1612, and later taken over by Dutch invaders. In 1644, the city was finally settled under Portuguese rule, serving as the export point for sugar and cotton. Expensive houses and buildings covered with brightly colored Portuguese tiles were built in the city's urban center. By the late 1800s, with slavery at an end, São Luís went into a decline. At the end of the 1970s, the state government began to invest in preserving the city's historic center, and in 1997, the historical core of São Luís was designated a UNESCO World Heritage Site.

A row of colorful houses along one of the streets in São Luís

★ Palácio dos Leões
Built in 1766 on the site of the original French Fort St. Louis, the Palácio dos Leões is now home to the Maranhão state government.

Beco Catarina Mina
This picturesque 18th-century alley connects the lower-lying streets of the historic center with Avenida Dom Pedro II.

Museu de Arte Visuais is covered in elaborate Portuguese tiles.

Casa do Maranhão
The former 19th-century customs building now houses a fine collection of Bumba-meu-boi folklore. Guides walk visitors through the colorful exhibits.

Igreja da Sé
The cathedral little resembles the original 1699 structure. Extensive renovations were carried out in 1922, including the addition of a Neo-Classical façade, giving the cathedral its imposing look.

VISITORS' CHECKLIST

Practical Information
Maranhão. **i** Central de Serviços Turisticos.
w cultura.ma.gov.br/en
Casa das Tulhas: Rua da Estrela 401. **Tel** (98) 3231 7431
Open 8am–6pm daily.
Palácio dos Leões: Av Dom Pedro II. **Open** 2–5:30pm Wed–Fri, 3–5:30pm Sat & Sun

Praça Benedito Lete is framed by historic, beautifully tiled houses. The statue in the center of the square is of former senator and state governor, Benedito Leite.

★ **Casa das Tulhas**
Regional delicacies, such as cashew nuts and dried shrimp, are on sale in the food stalls of this 19th-century market building.

Rua de Estrela is one of the liveliest streets in the historic center of São Luís.

RUA 28 DE JULHO

RUA DE ESTRELA

TRAV. M. ALMEIDA

RUA 14 DE JULHO

TRAV. BOAVENTURA

RUA DA ESTRELA

BECO DA PRENSA

★ **Centro de Cultura Popular**
This center exhibits costumes, artifacts, and photographs of the Festa do Divino, one of Maranhão's most popular religious festivals.

0 meters 100
0 yards 100

Key

— Suggested route

José Sarney Bridge connecting the historic district to São Francisco, São Luís

Exploring São Luís

The rich and diverse historical center of São Luís makes it ideal for touring on foot. This is the oldest part of the city, known interchangeably as the Praia Grande, the Reviver, and the **Centro Histórico**. All the city's museums and beautifully preserved historic sites are located here.

The **Casa do Maranhão** is one of the city's most interesting museums, offering two floors of colorful exhibits that elaborately explain the Festa do Bumba-meu-boi.

Cazumba figure, Casa do Maranhão

The **Centro de Cultura Popular** (also known as the Casa da Festa) is dedicated to showcasing the traditions and customs of the Festa do Divino Espírito Santo. The highlights of the museum are the poster-size photographs of the actual celebrations, including some compelling black-and-white images of the elderly women who once served as festival queens.

The building that once housed the city slave market is now home to the **Cafua das Mercês**, also known as the Museu do Negro. This small museum contains numerous artifacts from the slave era, including musical instruments and tribal artwork, and sinister tools of the slave trade, such as shackles and instruments of torture. One of the more poignant monuments is the Pelourinho, or the whipping post, on display in the museum's central courtyard.

The **José Sarney** Bridge leads from the Centro Histórico into the newer parts of the city. Across the bridge lies São Francisco, the city's small central business district. Just beyond São Francisco, there is a large freshwater lake, the Lagoa de Jansen, circled by a boardwalk with a number of bars and restaurants. Much calmer than the Centro Histórico, it is a very popular place to stroll in the evenings. São Luís is blessed with a string of excellent beaches, all of which can be easily accessed by bus from the Terminal de Integração in the city center. Farther south, beyond the Lagoa de Jansen, the popular beaches are Ponta d'Areia, São

Marcos, Praia do Calhau, **Calhau**, and Olho d'Agua. Calhau, located 6 miles (10 km) from São Luís, is considered by many to be one of the nicest beaches around the city. Many busy kiosks and restaurants line the beachside boulevard. The quiet far end of the beach, where the water is calm and restaurants fewer, is known as Caolho.

Ⅲ Cafua das Mercês
Jacinto Maia 54. **Open** 9am–6pm Mon–Fri.

Ⅲ Casa do Maranhão
Rua do Trapiche s/n. **Tel** (98) 3218 9954. **Open** 9am–6pm Tue–Sat, 9am–1pm Sun.

Ⅲ Centro de Cultura Popular
Rua do Giz 221. **Tel** (98) 3218 9926. **Open** 9am–6pm Tue–Sat, 9am–1pm Sun.

❻ Alcântara

Maranhão. ⬛ 21,000. ⬛ from São Luís. 🅸 Casa Municipal de Turismo, (98) 3231 4696. 🎭 Festa do Divino Espírito Santo (May).

Just across from São Luís, Alcântara lies on the other side of the Baía de São Marcos. The city was founded by the Portuguese in the 1640s, and used as a temporary capital and base during the campaign to drive the Dutch away from São Luís. Alcântara reached its zenith in the 19th century as the

Bumba-meu-boi

A unique folklore event endemic to Northeast Brazil, the Festa do Bumba-meu-boi revolves around a legendary folktale about the life, death, and resurrection of a magical Brazilian bull. Over the centuries, the celebration has grown into a huge carnivalesque festival, with different neighborhood groups competing to put on the best re-enactment of the story. In São Luís alone, more than 100 groups take to the streets. A papier-mâché bull is created each year and displayed in raucous parades, where participants take on the roles of medicine men, Indians, peasants, and cowboys. The largest celebrations take place in the second half of June. The music is upbeat and lively, with different groups using different rhythms and instruments.

A colorful celebration of the Bumba-meu-boi festival

Pillory, restored mansions, and ruin of a church in Alcântara

regional center for the surrounding sugar and cotton plantations. It was the place where wealthy slave-owning aristocrats built their splendid city mansions. When slavery was abolished in 1888, the local economy crashed, the white upper class departed, and many of the fine mansions stood abandoned.

Appreciation of Alcântara's heritage value began as early as the 1950s, but restoration has been slow and quite a few of its churches and mansions remain as ruins, giving the city its own charm. These ruins are now the town's main tourist attractions. Day-trippers from São Luís come here to stroll the quiet cobblestoned streets, peer among the ruins, and admire the often brightly tiled mansions of this former colonial capital.

The Brazilian Heritage Institute, Iphan, has restored several of the old mansions as museums. The best is the **Casa Histórica do Iphan**, featuring period furniture and glassware. Informative wall plaques and well-trained guides make getting around easy in the museum.

Another attraction to Alcântara is the Festa do Divino Espírito Santo, a vibrant religious festival held in May every year.

🏛 **Casa Histórica do Iphan**
Praça de Matriz s/n. **Open** 9am–5pm Tue–Sun. 🅿

❼ Reentrâncias Maranhenses

Maranhão. 🚌 from São Luís to Cururupu. 🚤 from Cururupu.
ℹ Sematur, Praça Joao Lisboa 328, São Luís, (98) 3232 2098. 🅿
Maramazon, (98) 3235 3994.
🅦 maramazon.com

One of the world's largest wetlands, the Reentrâncias Maranhenses is also one of Maranhão's more off-the-beaten-track natural attractions. The small town of **Cururupu** to the north of São Luís offers the best access to the Reentrâncias Maranhenses, with boats departing regularly.

Spread over an area of 10,350 sq miles (26,800 sq km), the Reentrâncias Maranhenses forms an important habitat for shorebirds such as scarlet ibis, spoonbills, whimbrels, egrets, willets, ruddy turnstones, and black-bellied plovers, as well as

Scarlet ibis, one of the shorebirds found in Reentrâncias Maranhenses

an array of marine life, including sea turtles and manatees. Many species of fish and crustaceans are also found in the Reentrâncias. The region is geographically diverse and consists of a complex riverine system of extensive bays, coves, and rugged coastline covered mainly by mangrove forest. Many low-lying islands are also found here.

In order to protect the flora and fauna of this region, the Reentrâncias Maranhenses was designated an Area de Proteção Ambiental (Area of Environmental Protection) and was also made a Ramsar site (a wetland site listed under the Convention on Wetlands of International Importance) in 1993.

One of the more popular destinations here is the **Ilha dos Lençóis**, to the northeast of Cururupu. The island's geography somewhat resembles the Lençóis Maranhenses (see pp254–5), with its endless landscapes of dunes and lagoons.

A small community of 300 people live here and still practice subsistence fishing. Some of them are descendants of the Filhos da Lua (Sons of the Moon), an albino community that settled here in the beginning of the 20th century. The isolation and flooding was harsh on the residents and not many survived. Some of the fishermen work as local tour guides for a small fee.

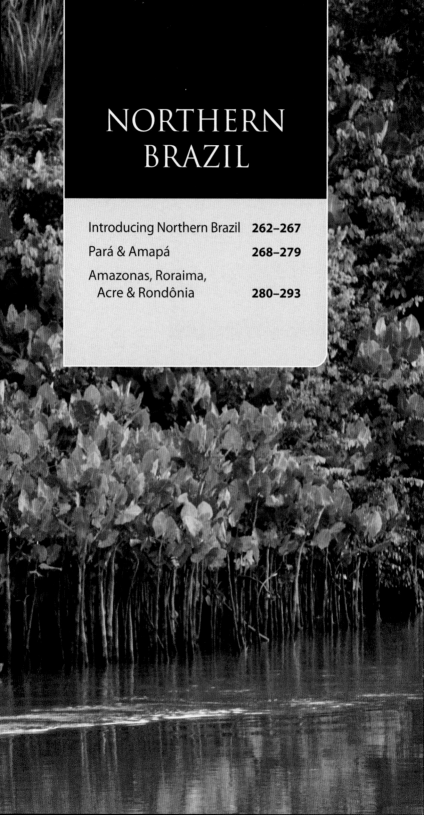

NORTHERN BRAZIL

Introducing Northern Brazil

The six states of Pará, Amapá, Amazonas, Roraima, Acre, and Rondônia cover almost half of Brazil. Northern Brazil was relatively quiet until the rubber boom in the late 19th century. With expansive savannas to the north, and a rich diversity of flora and fauna in the east, today the region's economy is sustained by traditional forest products. Belém, Manaus, Santarém, Rio Branco, and Porto Velho, cities created by the rubber industry, are growing fast, connecting Amazônia to the outside world.

Boa Vista's Monte Roraima *(see p292)*, with its massive uplifted plateau, inspired Sir Arthur Conan Doyle's book *The Lost World*.

Rio Branco *(see p292)* was founded during the rubber boom. Today, it is better known for its sustainable rubber-tapping forest reserves.

Boa

Amazon

AMAZONAS, RORAIMA, ACRE & RONDÔNIA *(See pp281–93)*

Tabatinga

Humaitá

Cruzeiro do Sul

Porto Velho

Rio Branco

Ji-Paraná

Madeira-Mamoré Museu Ferroviário *(see p293)*, in Porto Velho, houses several impressive locomotive steam engines, antique carriages, and other railway paraphernalia.

0 km	200
0 miles	200

◄ *Ribeirinhos* ("river people") boating down the Picanco River, Amazonian Estuary

The river scenery of Santarém *(see p278)*, known for its serene beauty, is the primary reason for visiting this popular Amazon port town.

Ilha de Marajó *(see p274)* is the world's largest inland river island. Its eastern half is savanna dotted with small woodland copses.

The old port of Belém
(see pp272–3) possesses more character than any other sector of the city. Attractive fishing boats bob up and down in the harbor, with the large old white fort on one side and the colorful Ver o Peso market on the other.

Macapá

Salinópolis

Óbidos

Amazon

Belém

Santarém

us

PARÁ & AMAPÁ
(See pp268–79)

Marabá

São Martinho

The Amazon river
(see pp288–91), known as Rio Solimões in its upper reaches, was first identified by Vicente Yáñez Pinzón. Its lower reaches are called Rio Negro.

Teatro Amazonas *(see pp286–7)*, in Manaus, exudes the opulence of its rubber-boom architects. It took the finest of materials and the most skilled of craftsmen to re-create an Italian Renaissance-style edifice, with a steel structure from Scotland and marble imported from Italy.

The Amazon Ecosystem

Brazil has over 1.3 million sq miles (3.5 million sq km) of rainforest, the largest in the world. This massive river system contains a fifth of the world's fresh running water at any moment. The Amazon is home to an incredible variety of plant, bird, fish and insect species. From the air, its magnificent canopy hides a variety of ecosystems, many with dramatic seasonal changes. Between December and April, visitors explore the flooded forest swamps and creeks that offer access to the fascinating flora and fauna.

Ecological Concern

An estimated 208,495 sq miles (540,000 sq km) of the rainforest is reported to have been destroyed by indiscriminate felling. Stringent measures being taken to save this ecological treasure include expansion of protected areas and sustainable use of forest resources.

Rubber trees (*Hevea brasiliensis*) growing on riverbanks are the source of valuable latex, which is later transformed into rubber.

The ceiba tree (*Ceiba pentandra*), with elegant buttress roots that surround the trunk's base, is the biggest tree in the Amazon, with an average height of 120 ft (37 m).

Walking palms appear to migrate across the forest floor due to their characteristic stilt roots loosely attached to the ground.

Flowering Bromeliads are epiphytes that gather water and nutrients from raindrops on leaves as well as from dew.

Amazon river winding through dense rainforest

Buriti Palm

The upper canopy, about 131 ft (40 m) above the ground, is active with reptiles, mammals, tropical birds, and other wildlife.

The guamo tree, found all across the Amazon, grows very fast to an average height of 30 ft (10 m).

Pau-d'arco-amarelo bears bright yellow flowers from August to November, while shedding all its leaves.

The black water owes its color to its source in low-lying forests where rotting vegetation is absorbed into the river system.

Fauna

One of the world's most diverse ecosystems, the Amazon harbors an infinite variety of animal life. There are plenty of remote areas that provide habitats for jaguars, tapirs, and wild pigs. However, spotting these elusive creatures is difficult. Monkeys, sloths, and alligators are more commonly sighted.

The emerald tree boa is not venomous, but feeds on rodents and small animals of the forest.

Hoatzins, one of the most primitive of birds, live in flocks and build their nests in low canopy trees.

The three-toed sloth inhabits the forest canopy, moving incredibly slowly in search of its vegetarian diet of fruits, leaves, and sprouting plants.

Tapirs, the largest of all Amazon mammals, can weigh up to 661 lb (300 kg). These vegetarians take refuge in water to escape danger.

Freshwater river dolphins, both gray and pink, live in the main rivers and lakes of the Amazon basin.

Piranhas are known for their razor-sharp teeth. Only a few species pose a threat to larger animals.

The People of Amazônia

Approximately 345,000 indigenous people, distributed among 215 groups, live in Brazil. Each group has its own unique dialect, mythology, arts, and culture. A majority of them are semi-nomadic, and live by hunting, gathering, fishing, and migratory farming. These indigenous people live in close harmony with the rhythms of the rainforest, and conservation and sustainability are an integral part of their life. The degree of exposure to western society varies greatly. Some people, such as the nomadic Maku, are incredibly isolated, while others, such as the literate Ticuna (see p30), are heavily reliant on modern Brazilian society.

Man peering through a *cokar* (headgear) of blue macaw feathers

Yanomami people

The Yanomami live in the rainforests of southern Venezuela and Northern Brazil. One of the most recently contacted tribes in Amazônia, they number around 20,000 today. Considered fierce warriors, the tribe consists of four subdivisions, each with its distinct language.

The patterns painted on a Yanomami adult have an aesthetic, as well as magical and religious significance.

During Rehao, a yearly ceremony of paying obeisance to the dead, the Yanomami decorate their arms and shoulders with colorful feathers.

Hammocks, slung under palm leaf roofs along the inside perimeter of the circular hut, are commonly used by old and young alike.

Tukano People

The name Tukano is used for a number of ethnolinguistic subgroups living in northwestern Brazil along the Rio Uapés. The individual groups live in communal houses, which are spaced out along the river at a distance of several hours by canoe. The Tukano grow bitter manioc and cultivate sweet potato, peanut, and plantain.

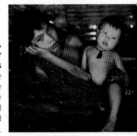

Tukano handicrafts are sold in local markets, or used as trade items favored by non-indigenous people in the area.

The traditional flute, played by male initiates, is characterized by a piercing echo. The flute is believed to be the earthly manifestation of spirits which dominate the magical and religious world of the Tukano.

The maloca, a hut made from wood and palm leaves, provides shelter to the whole village.

Impact of Globalization

The need for national development, fueled by globalization, is prompting the government of Brazil to enforce economic policies that are inimical to the tribal way of life. Pipelines to expand fuel production, and highway projects for transporting goods for global enterprises, are opening up indigenous lands to loggers, miners, ranchers, and colonists. The positive impact of globalization may involve easier access to the modern world, including medicines, education, and tools.

Women gaining access to modern tools

Kayapó People

Around 7,000 Kayapós live in the Amazon River Basin in an area the size of Austria, with villages along the Rio Xingú. Circles are one of the tribe's main symbols, representing the course of the sun and moon. Body paint, which is worn at all times, is equally symbolic. The Kayapó also wear ear plugs and lip discs, according to which their social status can be determined, particularly their right to speak and be heard.

A large lip disc is worn by older Kayapó men. Its size increases with the age and importance of the person within the community. Children and women usually wear ear discs.

Ritual communal dancing constitutes a crucial part of the Kayapó celebration of important events in the year. This is the time when Kayapó men and women show off their interesting headdresses – usually made from macaw and parrot feathers – and other ritual adornments.

Beautiful Bead Bracelets, created by Kayapó women, bear geometric designs with symbolic meanings. These are similar to the brightly colored patterns painted on their bodies with vegetable dyes.

Ashaninka People

Originally from Peru, the Ashaninka fled to parts of Brazil to escape the rubber boom from 1839 to 1913. Still possessing a fairly traditional material culture, the Ashaninka wear long *cushmas* that the women weave from cotton grown in small forest gardens. They make a living from hunting, fishing, and small-scale gardening. Rice, coffee, and chocolate supplement their way of life with bought-in goods including metal tools and soaps.

Small dugout canoes or balsawood rafts are regularly used by the riverine Ashaninka for traveling on the rivers along with their families.

Red face paint is traditionally applied by most of the Ashaninka people. The strong color comes from seeds of the garden-grown annatto bush.

Ashaninka women weave cotton cloth on primitive back-strap looms, almost every day, to make the men's pretty robes.

PARÁ & AMAPÁ

The states of Pará and Amapá in the eastern Amazon are the gateway to the world's largest river basin. In many ways, they are different from one another. Pará covers an enormous area, and has benefited from the natural wealth of the Amazon rainforest. Much smaller than Pará, Amapá is relatively poor. Both states rely on the mineral extraction industry.

It is the Amazon river itself that brings most visitors to this part of Brazil. Pará stretches west as far as the straits of Óbidos, where the river suddenly becomes narrow. This happens due to a geological meeting of the Guyana Shield from the north and the Brazilian Shield from the south. North of the Amazon, Amapá occupies an isolated region, stretching from the Amazon delta all the way to the borders of French Guyana and Suriname.

Pará has many places of cultural and ecological interest. The capital city, Belém, has been a vital Atlantic port since the colonial era, and still boasts many extravagant period buildings. Santarém, another sizable city, is a busy and attractive river port replete with fascinating beaches. The massive island, Ilha de Marajó, which has vast areas of mangrove swamps, some splendid beaches, and a scattering of resorts, is located in the heart of the Amazon river delta.

Pará is also known for large modern iron ore mines, such as Grande Carajás and the older gold mine of Serra Pelada, once infamous for the vast scale of human labor used for extraction. In southern Pará, the rainforest transforms into *caatinga*, a scrubby savanna landscape.

Once exploited for its natural resources, Amapá is now making concerted efforts towards sustainable development. More than half of the state is under environmental protection. Macapá, the state capital of Amapá, lies on the equator. The English, Dutch, and French clamored for a base in this part of Amazon, before the Portuguese settled at Macapá in 1738.

Fishing boats moored at the old harbor near Ver o Peso market, Belém

◀ Aerial view over the city of Belém, with the Basílica de Nossa Senhora do Nazaré in the foreground

Exploring Pará & Amapá

Even with their widespread rainforest canopy, which can only be seen clearly from the air, it is ocean and river travel that have long been the hallmark of Pará and Amapá states. Their highlights include the tasteful, restored historic buildings of Belém in Pará, along with the Amazon river itself, as well as splendid riverine beaches such as Alter do Chão, close to Santarém, and those found on the Ilha de Marajó. Macapá, the capital of Amapá, with its refreshing sea breeze, was founded around the Forte de São José. It lies on the equator in a strategic position on the north side of the Amazon river estuary. More than half of the state is under environmental protection.

Corner tower, Fortaleza de São José de Macapá, Macapá

Sights at a Glance

Towns & Cities

1. *Belém pp272–3*
2. Salinópolis
4. Macapá
5. Santarém
6. Óbidos
7. Monte Alegre

Areas of Natural Beauty

3. Ilha de Marajó

0 km   100

0 miles   100

Ferries moored on the shore of Rio Tapajós, Santarém, Pará

For hotels and restaurants in this region see p378 and p394

Mountains of fresh fruit at Ver o Peso market, Belém

Getting Around

Rivers are the transport arteries of Pará, where virtually every village has some form of riverboat service. There are regular riverboat services connecting Belém, Macapá, and Santarém. While there are very few bus routes in Pará, most access is by road in Amapá. However, the roads are mainly unsurfaced, and bus travel during the rainy season can be treacherous in both states. Air services are widespread. Belém and Macapá can be reached from most cities in Brazil by air, and there are daily flights from Belém to most larger towns in the Amazon.

Key

— Major road

===== Minor road

····· Railroad

▓▓▓▓ International border

░░░░ State border

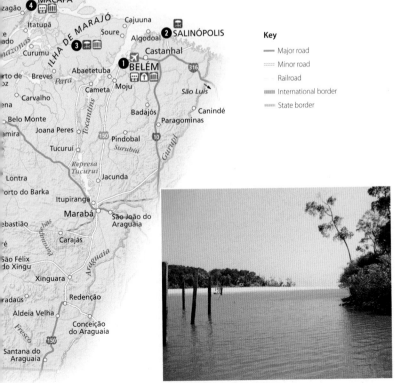

A creek near Araruna beach, Ilha de Marajó

For keys to symbols see back flap

❶ Belém

The attractive city of Belém was founded by the Portuguese in 1616 to guard the mouth of the Amazon river against other European powers. As the Amazon region's resources, mainly spices, were exploited, the city soon became a major trading port. It was ravaged during the 1835 Cabanagem Rebellion, when poor settlers attacked the wealthy local elite. By the end of the 19th century, Belém had more than recovered its economic position, largely due to the rubber boom. It is still the most important port in Northern Brazil, and a fascinating place in which to explore the wealth of colonial and republican architecture.

Cannon on display at the 17th-century Forte do Castelo

Ships docked on the waterfront at the Ver o Peso market

🏛 Estacáo das Docas

Blvd Castilho França, Campina.
Tel (91) 3212 5525.
Open noon–midnight daily.
W estacaodasdocas.com.br

Three former warehouses overlooking the river have been converted into a stylish, air-conditioned shopping, dining, and entertainment space. Visitors enjoy the lively atmosphere until late at night.

🏛 Ver o Peso

Av Castilhos França. **Open** 6am–2pm daily.

Incredibly hectic early in the morning, Ver o Peso, or "See the Weight," was originally a colonial customs point (Posto Fiscal), where goods were assessed for taxation purposes. These days, its most obvious feature is the iron-built fish market, the Mercado de Ferro, which was designed and made in England and assembled here in the late 19th century. The variety of seafood inside is staggering. Outside, the main market expands into stalls that sell everything from jungle fruits

and *farinha* (manioc, or cassava-root, flour) to medicinal herbs and aromatic oils. The market extends along the promenade where there are further stalls and kiosks selling craft goods and local food specialties.

🏛 Forte do Presépio

Praça Frei Caetano Brandão 117, Cidade Velha. **Tel** (91) 4009 8828.
Open 10am–6pm Tue–Fri, 9am–1pm Sat & Sun 📷

Sitting at the confluence of Rio Guamá and the Baía do Guajará,

this fort was first built of wood and mud plaster by the Portuguese colonists in 1616. It was rebuilt six years later, and again in 1878. It now houses the Museu do Encontro, a small historical museum presenting the city's history and the early conquest of the Amazon.

🏛 Palácio Antônio Lemos

Praça Dom Pedro II. **Tel** (91) 3114 1028. **Open** 10am–6pm Tue–Fri, 9am–1pm Sat & Sun. 📷

This splendid palace housed the municipal authorities between 1868 and 1883. It still has offices for the Prefeitura, but much of the building is open to the public, with some furnished period rooms upstairs. The palace is home to the Museu de Arte de Belém, which houses a fine collection of Brazilian 20th-century paintings.

🏛 Teatro da Paz

Praça da República. **Tel** (91) 4009 8750. **Open** 9am–5pm Tue–Fri, 9am–noon Sat, 10–11am Sun. 📷 on the hour.

This grand Neo-Classical opera house was built in 1878, along

Transamazônica

Until the middle of the 20th century, riverboat or mule trail were the only viable forms of travel across Amazônia and Northern Brazil. With the ambitious construction of Highway BR-230 during the late 1960s, the Atlantic port of Belém was effectively connected all the way to the Peruvian border. Known as the Transamazônica, this road is in a poor state of repair along much of its length. In 2005, a river bridge to Peru was opened in the remote jungle state of Acre, completing the Brazilian end of the Transamazônica.

Unpaved section of the Transamazônica

For hotels and restaurants in this region see p378 and p394

Elegant interior of the Neo-Classical Teatro da Paz

the very Parisian Avenida Presidente Vargas. Inspired by La Scala in Milan, the furnishings are still largely original. Legendary Russian ballerina Anna Pavlova was one of the great artists to have performed here.

🏛 Basílica de Nossa Senhora de Nazaré

Praça Justo Chermont. **Tel** (91) 4009 8400. **Open** 7am–8pm Mon–Sat, 7am–noon & 3–9pm Sun. Museu Círio de Nazaré: **Open** 9am–6pm Tue–Fri.

The basilica's spectacular interior makes it one of the most stunning churches in Brazil. Partially modeled on St. Peter's in Rome, it stands

on 16 major arches, each ornately covered in stone mosaics and supporting a breathtaking red cedar roof. It was completed in 1909, to house the miraculous Virgin image of Nossa Senhora de Nazaré, which is traced back to early Christian Nazareth.

Linked to the icon, the Círio de Nazaré, or the Festival of Candles, attracts over a million visitors to the city every October. In one of the main symbolic acts, hundreds of local people work together, dragging an enormous rope from the mud and water of the port, through the streets of the city to the Basílica de Nossa Senhora de Nazaré. For those who participate, their sins are purged, and their hopes and wishes for

the year are granted. The basilica also houses the **Museu Círio de Nazaré**, which is devoted to the cult of the Círio and exhibits over 500 pieces relating to the religious festival.

Nave of the Basílica de Nossa Senhora de Nazaré

Belém City Center

① Estação das Docas
② Ver o Peso
③ Forte do Presépio
④ Palácio Antônio Lemos
⑤ Teatro da Paz
⑥ Basílica de Nossa Senhora de Nazaré

0 meters   400
0 yards   400

❷ Salinópolis

Pará. 🏔 40,000. ✈ Belém Val de Caes Airport, 110 miles (180 km) SE of town, then bus. 🚌 Av Miguel Santa Brigada. 🛈 Paratur (91) 3423 2203.

The town of Salinópolis, locally known as Salinas, is just about as far east as the Amazon river delta reaches. Very much the traditional summer resort for city folk, Salinas has plenty of beaches fringed with beach huts and second homes. The busiest beach is the central **Praia do Maçarico**, which has several bars and restaurants. More pleasant still, there is the **Praia do Atalaia**, not far from the center of town, backed by sand dunes and well provided with *barracas* (tents) for food and drink. A continuation of this beach, the **Praia do Farol Velho**, is thickly lined with beach houses, and is most popular during July, when it can often get rather crowded.

Environs
About 19 miles (30 km) west of Salinópolis is the relatively sleepy fishing settlement and beach resort of **Algodoal**. The resort lies on the western edge of Ilha de Maiandeua, just a 40-minute boat ride away. There are no motorized vehicles in the

A secluded beach near Souré, Ilha de Marajó

village or on Maiandeua island, adding to the remote and idyllic feel. Electricity only reached the island in 2004, so facilities are improving.

The main beach for the village is the **Praia da Vila do Algodoal**. More popular, however, is the palm-fringed **Praia da Princesa do Farol**, a superb stretch of sand secluded from the main beach by a short walk at low tide or a canoe ride. There are trails on the island, offering the opportunity to spot wildlife and explore the area around an inland freshwater lake. It is advisable to carry adequate cash to visit the island, since there are no banks or ATMs.

❸ Ilha de Marajó

Pará. 🏔 250,000. ⛴ from Belém to Porto Camará. 🛈 Trapiche Municipal, Rua 1, Souré, (91) 3741 1326.

The world's largest river island, Ilha de Marajó covers over 18,533 sq miles (48,000 sq km), mostly dedicated to cattle ranches, or *fazendas*. The island is famous for having the biggest and finest buffaloes in Brazil. Their meat, leather, and dairy products are widely available to purchase. Ilha de Marajó was also the ancient home to the indigenous culture of the Marajoaras, notable for their exquisite ceramic burial and ceremonial urns.

The unofficial capital of the island is **Souré**, which has the most shops, restaurants, and other facilities, but the ferry port is **Porto Camará**, some 16 miles (27 km) south of Souré. Located between Porto Camará and Souré, the best and most secluded beach is at the small town of **Joanes**, some 3 miles (5 km) off the main road. There are good beaches at the other town on the island, **Salvaterra**, where there are also several hotels and *pousadas*. The Praia Grande beach in Salvaterra is well served with beach chairs, snack *barracas*, and refreshment stands.

During the peak rainy season (February–May) many of the roads are inaccessible for long periods; this includes the road to Joanes and Salvaterra at times. Boats for moving around the island can be found easily at Souré, Salvaterra, and Porto Camará.

Pottery on Ilha De Marajó

Marajó pottery displayed in Museu Goeldi, Belém

In 1948, anthropologists Betty Meggers and Clifford Evans discovered a large, painted anthropomorphic vessel on Ilha de Marajó. The ancient inhabitants, the Marajoaras, left behind not only burial mounds, some almost 3,000 years old, but also some very fine ceramics, leading archaeologists to believe that between the 5th and 13th centuries, there were sophisticated societies living along the banks of the Amazon river. Excavations reveal that the dead were buried in line according to their social ranking, with larger urns indicating higher status. Most of these ceramics, representing abstract feminine figures, demonstrate the matrilineal nature of this early Amazonian society. As well as funerary ceramics, there were also bowls, vases, spindle whorls, and stools. The larger urns generally took three main forms: humanoid, cyclindrical, and round; and around 15 different finishing techniques are known to have been utilized. Some excellent examples of the urns can be found in the Museu Goeldi in Belém.

❹ Macapá

Amapá. 🏔 395,000. ✈ 🚌 from Belém. 🚌 Bairro São Lázaro, (96) 3251 2009. ℹ Setur, Rua Independência 29, Centro, (96) 3212 5335. 🎭 O Marabaixo (May).

Split in two by the equator, Macapá is hot and humid all year round. The city occupies its position as Amapá's capital sitting on the northern bank of the Amazon river, very close to the giant river's mouth. It is rather isolated, with mostly air and boat transportation, rather than road connections.

The history of the city is rich and varied. Several European countries, including England and France, attempted to take it over from the Portuguese, but the Portuguese established their hold here by completing the grand **Fortaleza de São José de Macapá** in 1782, after almost 20 years of construction by black and Indian slave labor. The bricks used were brought over from Portugal as ballast on the ships.

Just to the north of the fort there is an attractive pier, the Trapiche Eliezer Levy, which dates back to the 1930s. The pier stretches far out into the water and it is an enjoyable stroll to the end of it, especially on a breezy evening. The charming Trapiche Restaurante, also located at the end of the pier, has a breathtaking view overlooking the river.

A replica of a typical indigenous home, Museu SACACA, Macapá

These days, Macapá is the capital of a progressive state. Following the election of the environmentalist João Capiberibe as state governor in 1995, successive governors have kept the spirit of environmentalism alive. One present project is to connect all the state's protected areas with wildlife or biodiversity corridors. The **Museu SACACA**, or the Museum of Sustainable Development, just a short distance south of the town center, offers fascinating guided tours of replica *ribeirinho* (river-dweller) houses.

The **Mercado dos Produtos da Floresta** offers a wide range of local art and craft goods, ranging from *balata* (ceramics) dusted with manganese ore to indigenous crafts, leather

Wooden artifact, Museu SACACA

goods, carved wooden statues, and all-natural medicines.

The Marco Zero monument, a large obelisk-cum-sundial, 4 miles (6 km) southwest of the city center, marks the equatorial line on Avenida Equatorial. A sports stadium and *sambódromo* also form part of the same complex.

🏰 **Fortaleza de São José de Macapá**
Av Candido Mendes. **Tel** (96) 3212 5118. **Open** 9am–6pm Tue–Sun. 📷

🏬 **Mercado dos Produtos da Floresta**
Rua São José 1500. **Tel** (96) 9 9961 0913. **Open** 8am–6pm Mon–Fri.

🏛 **Museu SACACA**
Av Feliciano Coelho, 1509. **Tel** (96) 3212 5361. **Open** 9am–6pm Tue–Sun. 📷

Buildings inside the Fortaleza de São José de Macapá

Wooden house on stilts on the Amazon River, with the rainforest behind ▶

⑤ Santarém

Pará. 📷 295,000. ✈ ✈
🚢 from Docas do Pará (W of center).
ℹ Santarém Tour, (93) 3522 4847.
w **santaremtur.com.br**

Amazônia's fourth-largest city, Santarém sits at the mouth of the Rio Tapajós, surrounded by brilliant white sandy beaches. Modern Santarém began in 1661 as a Jesuit mission, following 30 years of military action in the area to subdue the fierce, indigenous Tapuiçu Indians.

In 1867, there was an influx of ex-Confederates from the USA, a handful of whose descendants still survive. However, it was the rubber boom and Santarem's strategic position as a pit stop en route along the Amazon river that turned the town into a buzzing commercial center.

In the late 19th century, Henry Wickam, an English settler in Santarém, smuggled rubber tree seeds out to establish rubber plantations in Asia. Within 40 years, and just in time for World War I, Asian rubber plantations greatly outproduced the Brazilian Amazon.

The local economy is today based on rubber, logging, soya, brazil nuts, and tourism. Colorful boats and frantic movement of produce at the port and along the attractive riverfront are typical today.

Ferries moored on the shore of the Amazon river at Santarém

An ancient center for the production of fine ceramics, the town showcases its distinct Santarém Phase Pottery in a striking museum, the **Museu de Santarém**. The exhibits prominently feature burial urns, reputed to be among the oldest in South America. Also known as Centro Cultural João Foua, the museum has a striking interior, painted by João Foua, an artist from Pará.

Burial urn, Museu de Santarém

Another attraction is the **Museu de Arte Sacra de Santarém**, which has a decent collection of religious art.

Environs

Located 20 miles (33 km) west of Santarém, the river-beach town of **Alter do Chão** has fine sandy beaches set against a calm bay on the Rio Tapajós. Canoes ferry visitors across the bay in order to climb the low-lying hills that offer breathtaking views. Closer to the main beach is another prominently shaped hill that resembles a church altar. **Fordlândia**, 62 miles (100 km) south of town, was Henry Ford's first rubber plantation, founded

Belterra, a rubber plantation set up by John Ford in the 1930s

The Rubber Story in Brazil

In the mid-1700s, Charles-Marie de la Condamine was presented with latex syringes from the *Hevea brasiliensis* tree by the Omagua people living in Amazônia. He returned to France with samples, and rubber became known to the world. Soon it was being used for everything from insulation to tyres, and *Hevea brasiliensis* had become the oil of its day. In Amazônia, where the rubber tree grew in abundance, foreign banks and companies began to set up plantations. The rubber boom ushered Manaus and Belém into the *belle époque* era, with electric lights, lavish opera houses, and mansions for the rubber barons. Brazil emerged as the world's largest producer of natural rubber. The euphoria lasted until 1910, when the British colonies in Asia – Malaya, Ceylon, and Singapore – outproduced the Brazilian rubber. Unprepared for competition, Brazil was elbowed out of the rubber market by 1914. The indigenous Brazilians, who had been rounded up and forcibly settled to work on the plantations, returned to relative freedom. Today, much of Brazil's rubber is imported from Asia.

in the 1920s to produce rubber for the Ford Motor Company. In the 1930s, he also established **Belterra**, 12 miles (20 km) south. Both ventures failed, and Ford had to sell them to the Brazilian government in 1945. These towns are accessible by boat from Alter do Chão.

🏛 Museu de Arte Sacra de Santarém
Rua Siqueira Campos 439, Centro. **Tel** (93) 3523 0658. **Open** 8–11:30am Tue–Sat.

🏛 Museu de Santarém
Rua do Imperador, Praça de Santarém. **Open** 8am–5pm Mon–Fri. 🖼 donation expected.

❻ Óbidos

Pará. 🔼 47,000. 🚢 from Santarém. 🛈 Rua Rui Barbosa, Centro, (93) 3547 3244.

The real gateway to the deeper Amazon, Óbidos marks the narrowest section of the Amazon river valley. It was created 40 million years ago, when a massive inland lake burst through to the Atlantic at this point, where the Guyanan Shield meets the Brazilian Shield.

The pretty waterfront has some beautifully tiled buildings and the 17th-century Forte Pauxias. There is also a free museum featuring, among other exhibits, luxury items from the rubber-boom days. The museum opens on request.

A surfer catching the "Pororoca" tidal wave

Pororoca Wave

Revered by surfers, the Pororoca is a legendary wave, over 16 ft (5 m) tall, that regularly rolls up the Amazon river. The name Pororoca comes from a local Tupi Indian phrase which means "great destructive noise." Predicted to happen twice daily during full moons between January and April every year, the wave comes in from the Atlantic causing some devastation along the riverbanks. Following a low tide in the rainy season, the force of the mighty river against the turning tide creates the large and powerful wave that rolls, literally unstoppable, up the Amazon. The surfing record so far is 27 minutes in time and 7 miles (12 km) in distance, while the tidal waves are known to travel over 12 miles (20 km) per hour at times.

❼ Monte Alegre

Pará. 🔼 23,500. 🚢 🛈 Rua do Jaquara 320.

Located impressively on top of a small hill beside the Amazon river, the town of Monte Alegre was one of the first places on the river to be colonized by Europeans. A band of English and Irish sailors were the earliest to settle here in the 1570s, soon to be expelled by the Portuguese. Over the last 200 years, Monte Alegre has benefited from ranching and the rubber industry. It is best known for the rock paintings of **Serra Paytuna** and **Serra Ererê**, located 19 miles (30 km) out of town. Estimated to be 10,000 years old, the paintings feature abstract patterns, mostly geometric in form, and some stylized representations of human and animal figures. It is obligatory to hire a guide and a vehicle to visit them. Monte Alegre is also renowned for scenic waterfalls and its wealth of birdlife, for which a local guide and a canoe will be required.

Boats moored along the waterfront in Óbidos, with rows of houses in the background

AMAZONAS, RORAIMA, ACRE & RONDÔNIA

The states of Amazonas, Roraima, Acre, and Rondônia form the heartland of the vast Amazon rainforest region, which is drained by the world's largest network of freshwater lakes and rivers. Despite hundreds of years of European presence and the ravages of 20th century deforestation, the region is still home to some of the world's most isolated indigenous peoples.

Amazonas is larger than the other three states put together. Manaus, its capital, is the most popular place from which to explore the jungle. The city sits at the confluence of two of the world's largest rivers – the Solimões (as the Amazon river is called in this section) and the Rio Negro. The vast Rio Madeira lies downstream of Manaus.

Roraima, which literally juts up into Venezuela and Guyana, is best known for its superb plateau-topped mountains, lakes, and substantial rainforest. A host of indigenous groups live here, tenaciously holding on to their land and culture. Roraima also boasts open savannas that have been transformed into cattle ranches. The state capital, Boa Vista, is a well-planned city on the banks of the Rio Branco.

Acre and Rondônia, in the very southwest corner of the Brazilian Amazon, possess some fantastic protected areas of biodiversity, home to many indigenous communities. Acre, the rubber-tapping center of the Amazon, is known for its lush beauty. Environmental destruction has been met with equally forceful conservation movements here. The state capital, Rio Branco, was where activist Chico Mendes fought to defend the forest in the late 1980s.

Rondônia, an area which has developed beyond recognition, still retains some of Brazil's best flora and fauna. It also offers fascinating gems in terms of heritage, such as the Madeira-Mamoré railway museum in the state capital, Porto Velho.

Village huts surrounded by tall palm tree plantations in Acre

◀ A wooden canopy walkway through Brazilian nut trees, Rio Branco, Acre

Exploring Amazonas, Roraima, Acre & Rondônia

This region offers the ultimate rainforest experience. Most people travel here to explore the dense forests, picturesque river islands, and tranquil waterways. The sights include Manaus, the legendary capital city of Amazonas, which offers much architectural and cultural interest. Also located in Amazonas is the Mamirauá Reserve, Brazil's first sustainable development reserve. The secluded and beautiful mountains of Roraima are worth a visit, as is Acre, with its natural beauty, history, and *seringueiro* (rubber-tapping) culture. Porto Velho, the capital of Rondônia, overlooking the Amazon's longest tributary, the mighty Rio Madeira, is a lively place to visit. Riverboat excursions on the Rio Madeira are a good way to idle away a few hours and spot a few pink dolphins.

Spectacled caimans can be found near Manaus

Boats anchored on the Rio Madeira outside Porto Velho

Sights at a Glance

Towns & Cities

1. *Manaus pp284–7*
2. Parintins
3. Boa Vista
4. Rio Branco
5. Porto Velho

Getting Around

Joining an organized tour with one of the companies in Manaus, Boa Vista, Porto Velho, or Rio Branco is the best way to see the Amazon jungle. Most companies offer accommodation in tourist lodges and travel by a combination of road and riverboat or canoe. For those who want to travel independently, it is possible to move around the jungle on local riverboats. Road travel is also possible from all cities. Manaus, for instance, is only 6 hours by bus from Novo Airão, on the Rio Negro, where it is possible to bathe in jungle rivers and swim with pink dolphins.

0 km 200
0 miles 200

For hotels and restaurants in this region see pp378–9 and pp394–5

The Rio Branco snaking through Roraima

Key

—— Major road

==== Minor road

▦▦▦ International border

—— State border

△ Peak

Visitors exploring the forest near Manaus

For keys to symbols see back flap

❶ Manaus

Manaus is a legendary city, located at the heart of the Amazon forest on the banks of the Rio Negro, close to where this massive river blends with the even larger Amazon river, or Rio Solimões as it is known along this section of its course. Manaus is a busy city bringing together the hectic pace of a modern port with the hot, laid-back feel of a jungle town. The brief period of economic boom between 1888 and 1912, due to the export of rubber, catapulted Manaus into wealthy city status. The only signs that remain of this time are the fancy European buildings of the port and the even more splendid Teatro Amazonas.

🏛 Mercado Municipal Adolfo Lisboa

Rua dos Bares 46. **Open** 8am–5pm Mon–Sat, 6am–noon Sun.

The municipal market was built in 1902, very close to the port, and is an amazing building. Looking up to its elegant ceiling and Art Nouveau ironwork structure, it is not difficult to see that Gustave Eiffel himself had a hand in its design, which is said to be inspired by the Les Halles market in Paris.

🏛 Alfândega

Rua Marquês de Santa Cruz. **Tel** (92) 3622 3025. **Open** 8am–4pm Mon–Fri, 8am–noon Sat.

Constructed in 1906 at the height of the rubber boom, the Alfândega (Customs House), like many of the well-engineered features of Manaus from this period, was entirely pre-fabricated in England. The stone used for the building was

brought from Scotland. The tower used to be a lighthouse. Much of this refined building's glory can be seen from the Praça Adalberto Valle opposite.

🏛 Teatro Amazonas

See pp286–7.

🏛 Palacete Provincial

Praça da Policia, Centro. **Tel** (92) 3631 6047. **Open** 9am–5pm Tue–Wed, 9am–7pm Thu–Sat, 4–8pm Sun.

Built in 1874 originally to house the police headquarters, the Palacete Provincial is now a cultural center, which is home to several interesting small museums and collections, including the Museum of Image and Sound, the Military Police Museum, and the Numismatic Museum. The Palacete's highlight is the art gallery, which features modern and contemporary art by regional painters, photo-

graphers, and installation artists. The exuberant paintings of local flora and fauna by Manaus painter Rita Loureiro are especially noteworthy.

🏛 Homem do Norte

Centro Cultural dos Povos da Amazônia, Praça Francisco Pereira da Silva. **Tel** (92) 2125 5300. **Open** 8am–noon, 1–5pm Tue–Fri, 4–9pm Sun.

An anthropology and ethnology museum, the fascinating Museu do Homem do Norte (Museum of Northern Man) has exhibits on the way of life of the people of Northern Brazil. It is particularly dedicated to the *caboclos* (copper-colored) mixed descendants of the indigenous people and Portuguese who live along the riverbanks. Cultural, social, and economic aspects of life in Northern Brazil are detailed with photographs, documents, artifacts, and everyday objects, such as historic cooking utensils, costumes, and an interesting collection of indigenous weapons, including the infamous *furador de olhos* (eye piercer). There are also exhibitions on *guaraná* and rubber production.

🏛 Palácio Rio Negro

Av 7 de Setembro 1546. **Tel** (92) 3232 4450. **Open** 10am–4pm Tue–Fri, 5–8pm Sun.

A remarkably well-preserved colonial-period mansion, the almost garish Palácio Rio Negro

The Rio Negro with the Porto Flutante (Floating Port) and the Catedral Metropolitana in the background

was built in 1913 during the rubber boom. It was originally home to an eccentric German rubber baron, Waldermar Scholz. In later years, it housed the local government. These days, much of it has been opened to the public as a cultural center. The palace hosts art exhibitions and events, as well as film screenings.

🏛 Museu do Índio

Rua Duque de Caxias 296. **Tel** (92) 3635 1922. **Open** 8:30–11:30am & 3–4:30pm Mon–Sat (Sat: am only). 📷

An excellent ethnographic museum, the Museu do Índio was established by Salesian nuns and is based on their work as missionaries in the Rio Negro area. There are many feather-work exhibits and some weapons and tools, as well as household and sacred objects on display, along with musical instruments and artworks. The Tukano people *(see p266)* are particularly well represented here. Explanations of the displays are in Portuguese, English, and German. The museum has a good craft shop, with a wide range of handicrafts on sale.

Traditional indigenous longhouse at the Museu do Índio

VISITORS' CHECKLIST

Practical Information
Amazonas. 🗺 1,800,000. ℹ AmazonasTur, Manaus Airport, (92) 3182 9850. 🎭 Manaus Opera Festival (Apr/May), Festival Folclórico do Amazonas (Jun). 🌐 **manausonline.com**

Transport
✈ 🚌 Rua Recife 2784, (92) 642 5805. ⚓ Porto Flutuante.

🐆 Zoológico do CIGS

Estrada Ponta Negra 750. **Tel** (92) 2125 6402. **Open** 9am–5pm Tue–Sun. 📷

One of the few places around Manaus where you might see a jaguar at close quarters, the Zoológico do CIGS is a great place to take children. Located 8 miles (13 km) from Manaus toward Ponta Negra in the army jungle training center, this small zoo is home to over 300 animals including many caimans, monkeys, exotic birds, and an unforgettable large pit full of anacondas.

Manaus City Center

① Mercado Municipal Adolfo Lisboa
② Alfândega
③ Teatro Amazonas
④ Palacete Provincial
⑤ Homem do Norte
⑥ Palácio Rio Negro
⑦ Museu do Índio
⑧ Zoológico do CIGS

0 meters 200
0 yards 200

For keys to symbols *see back flap*

Manaus: Teatro Amazonas

Built at the end of the 19th century during the *belle époque*, when fortunes were made from the extraction of rubber in Manaus, the Teatro Amazonas remains one of the jewels of the Amazon region. This grand state-of-the-art, Renaissance-style opera house was designed by Gabinete Português de Engenharia de Lisbon (Portuguese Engineering Academy of Lisbon). Inaugurated on December 31, 1896, it was two more years before construction was completed and the prominent landmark with a glistening dome appeared above the port.

The Teatro façade, restored to pink at the close of the 20th century

★ The Painted Curtain
The main stage curtain was created by Manaus-based artist Crispim do Amaral (1845–1911) to depict the Meeting of the Waters *(see p289)*, and also a local river goddess, Iara. The curtain is pulled up into the specially designed cupola at the start of each performance.

The Wooden Floor
The opera-house floor, laid with thousands of pieces of Amazon timber, is a masterpiece of craftsmanship. The light and dark patterns represent the meeting of the Negro and Amazon rivers *(see p289)*.

KEY

① **The roof** is made of red tiles that were imported from Alsace in France.

② **The columns** are made from Italian Carrara marble.

③ **Outside balconies** are built in finely cut Portuguese stone.

Events
Regular musical events and operas include those of the Companhia de Dança and the resident Orquestra Filarmônica do Amazonas.

★ The Cupola
The impressive cupola was created using 36,000 colorful ceramic tiles, imported from Alsace on the Franco-German border.

VISITORS' CHECKLIST

Practical Information
Praça São Sebastião, Manaus.
Tel (92) 3232 1768.
Open 9am–5pm Mon–Sat.
Shows: opera, theater & dance performances through the year.

★ The Four Painted Pillars
A key feature of the main auditorium is a ceiling rosette whose four pillars were painted in Paris and reassembled in Manaus. The pillars create the impression of gazing up from underneath the Eiffel Tower.

Lobby
The lobby is furnished with *Murano* chandeliers made with Venetian glass and French bronzework.

Main Auditorium
Designed in the shape of a harp, the theater can seat almost 700 people. Like the main columns and the three curving balconies, the seats are made from English cast iron. The polished wooden armchairs are made from local jacaranda. The lower columns bear the names of many classical composers.

Amazon Excursions from Manaus

Manaus is well located as a base from which to explore the rainforest. The main destinations include the Rio Negro, Lago Mamori, Rio Juma, Lago Manaquiri, Presidente Figueiredo, and, farther west, the splendid reserve at Mamirauá. Operators run tours, offering everything from basic accommodation to four- or five-star luxury lodges and boats. It is good to have at least half a day out of Manaus in order to have a reasonable chance of seeing a wide range of tropical birds and mammal wildlife such as agoutis, monkeys, deer, or wild boar.

The Rio Urubuí and Cachoeira Iracema near Presidente Figueireido

Presidente Figueiredo

62 miles (100 km) N of Manaus. 🚌 🛈 Centro Turístico, (92) 3324 1308.

Presidente Figueiredo is a small town linked to Manaus by a relatively good road. There are more than 100 waterfalls dotted around the town, as well as some caves. Tours in and around the area can be booked from Manaus or directly with local guides through the tourist information office located at the bus stop. One of the best waterfalls is the **Pedra Furada**, where the water gushes out of a hole in the rocks. The waterfalls **Cachoeira Iracema**, **Pedra da Lua Branca**, and **Natal** are on the **Rio Urubuí** and only accessible by boat. The **Caverna Araras** is on a trail bordering the Rio Urubuí. Another attractive cave is **Caverna Maruaga**, which has shallow river running over its floor. Permission to visit the caves has to be obtained from the tourist information office in Manaus.

�⃠ Rio Negro & Ilhas de Anavilhanas

60 miles (90 km) NW of Manaus. 🚌 🛈 Amazonastur, Av Ajuricaba s/n, Novo Airão, (92) 3365 1391.

One of the least visited regions of South America, the Rio Negro area possesses distinctive flora created by its acidic waters and soil type. There is a lower density of wildlife here than any other area along the Rio Negro. There are few towns and even fewer tourist facilities along the river, which stretches right up to the Colombian and Venezuelan borders.

Ilhas de Anavilhanas is a biological reserve and the largest group of freshwater islands in the world. Tours to visit these islands are offered from Manaus or from Novo Airão. There are over 250

Sights at a Glance

① Presidente Figueiredo
② Rio Negro & Ilhas de Anavilhanas
③ Novo Airão
④ Encontro das Aguas
⑤ Lago Manaquiri
⑥ Lago Mamori
⑦ Instituto de Desenvolvimento Sustentável Mamirauá

0 kilometers   60
0 miles   60

Key

━━━ Main road
═══ Other road

The Rio Negro winding through the rainforest

uninhabited islands stretching for more than 187 miles (300 km). Depending on the season and time of day, it is possible to see caimans, sloths, snakes, frogs, and a wide range of bird species. Sprawled across an area of 1,350 sq miles (3,500 sq km) of protected rainforest on the left bank of the Rio Negro, the Estação Ecológica de Anavilhanas (Ecological Station of Anavilhanas) is part of the Anavilhanas islands. Created in 1998 and named after the Archipelago dos Anavilhanas, it boasts several species in great danger of extinction, including jaguars and night monkeys.

A day-and-a-half's journey from Ilhas de Anavilhanas, Barcelos, the only town of any size along the river, is an interesting place to start a jungle expedition. Another two days upriver is the town of São Gabriel Da Cachoeira, a beautiful place deep in the Amazon with stunning jungle scenery and wildlife.

Toco toucan in Amazonas

Visitor feeding fish to pink dolphins at El Delfin in Novo Airão

Novo Airão

71 miles (115 km) W of Manaus. 🚌 from Manaus. 🚢 from Manaus. Ibama: Rua Ministro João Gonçalves de Souza s/n, Manaus. **Tel** (92) 3878 7100. Parque Nacional Jaú: **Tel** (92) 3365 1345.

The small town of Novo Airão is located on the western side of the Rio Negro, opposite the Archipelago dos Anavilhanas. Pleasant, yet laid-back, with only a handful of attractions, the town draws tourists mainly for the pink dolphins that come to a platform behind the **El Delfin** restaurant at Novo Airão's small port. The restaurant owner has been feeding dolphins from the restaurant for several years. Along with its standard fare, the restaurant also sells raw fish to offer the dolphins from the wooden platform, giving visitors the opportunity of coming into close contact with these friendly creatures.

The area neighboring Novo Airão is home to a number of interesting sights, such as **Airão Velho**, the overgrown ruins of the old town center, with prehistoric spiral and figure-like petroglyphs. The beautiful and peaceful **Igarapé do Mato Grosso**, a forested section of a tributary river nearby, makes a great place for a walk or a swim in fresh water. The **Parque Nacional Jaú** is a two-day trip from Novo Airão, and is a wonderful opportunity to visit virgin Amazon rainforest. A permit is required from the **Ibama** office in Manaus.

🌿 Encontro das Aguas

🚢 from Manaus.

One of the main tours offered from Manaus, the Encontro das Aguas (Meeting of the Waters) is where the Rio Solimões joins the Rio Negro. The relatively creamy and alkaline light brown or "white" water of the Solimões (Amazon) river takes several miles to absorb the dark, acid water coming in from the Rio Negro. The Solimões is light because it starts mainly in the Andes and brings plenty of silt with it. The Rio Negro wells up primarily in the swamplands and smaller hills of the northeastern Amazon and contains much more decomposed plant life than it does soil or silt.

Small boats go out from Manaus allowing tourists to take photographs and see the clear line between light brown and black running down the middle of the river. It is a two-hour return trip from Manaus, and the best time to visit is between 7 and 10am.

Meeting of the Rio Solimões and Rio Negro at Encontro das Aguas

For hotels and restaurants in this region see pp378–9 and pp394–5

Limpid blue sky mirrored in the clear waters of Lago Mamori

🏞 Lago Manaquiri
40 miles (64 km) SW of Manaus.
🌐 visitamazonastour.com/site2/en

A 5-hour boat ride from Manaus, the backwater lake of Manaquiri is best entered first via the Rio Solimões, then upstream to a tributary that leads to the lake. Its waters rise and fall with the seasons. Relatively isolated, the Lago Manaquiri is usually a good spot for seeing waterbirds, including the great egret (*Casmerodius albus*) and fish eagles. It is not unusual to see caimans and large Amazonian alligators on the sandy shore.

The lake provides sustenance to the small fishing town of Manaquiri. Local economy depends more on fishing than on tourism. In 1995 and 2005, however, both were hit by the worst drought in over 40 years, when the lagoons evaporated, and thousands of dead fish lay on the bed of the dried-up lake. The changed climatic conditions continue to deplete fish in

the area. Nonetheless, fishing remains the main activity, and there are many tour operators based in Manaus, offering budget fishing packages.

It is always best to book your trip through a travel company registered with the Brazilian Tourism Bureau (Embratur) (*see p409*). Some of the tour agencies provide typical Amazon riverboats, which may come fully equipped with kitchen, dining area, canopied sundeck, bathroom, and shower. Fishing is best in the dry season, which usually lasts from August to December or January.

🏞 Lago Mamori
60 miles (96 km) SE of Manaus.
Gero's Tours: Rua 10 de Julho 679, Manaus. **Tel** (92) 9983 6273.
🌐 amazongero.com Nature Safaris: Rua Flavio Espiritu 1, Manaus. **Tel** (92) 3656 3357. 🌐 naturesafaris.com.br

Easily accessible by road and boat from Manaus, the elongated and breathtaking Lago Mamori is located in a lush

rainforest setting. Much of it is surrounded by narrow creeks, hidden among forests full of sloths, monkeys, and colorful, noisy tropical birds. The river and lake offer the opportunity to see both pink and gray river dolphins, as well as to go piranha fishing. Nearby, the Lago Arara is great for fishing, and home to a pink dolphin feeding ground. The local people, known as *caboclos*, have been here for generations and live in scattered riverside communities, occasionally coming together for celebrations. They earn their living by making *farinha* (manioc flour), rearing cattle, and fishing. Visits to the *caboclo* homes can be organized by **Gero's Tours**. Run independently by English-speaking Gero Mesquita, it can book hotels, arrange transport, and meticulously plan tours.

Farther upstream and deeper into the forest from here, the Rio Juma region offers better access to wildlife, but requires expedition-type preparation and several days.

Nature Safaris, a tour company based in Manaus, can arrange expeditions in Amazônia, offering short package tours, as well as longer safaris. It is possible to stay either in a floating lodge, or one of the many jungle lodges along the Rio Juma. Most of them offer jungle hikes, piranha fishing, and caiman spotting at night.

Caimans luxuriating on the sandy riverbank of Manaquiri, with a great egret in the foreground

For hotels and restaurants in this region see pp378–9 and pp394–5

Cormorants and great egrets in the Mamirauá Reserve

1 Instituto de Desenvolvimento Sustentável Mamirauá

280 miles (450 km) W of Manaus.
W uakarilodge.com.br Programa de Ecoturismo: **Tel** (97) 3343 4160.

Located at the confluence of two rivers, the Rio Solimões and Rio Japurá, the Mamirauá Sustainable Development Reserve covers an area of 5703 sq miles (14,770 sq km). Since 1990, when it was declared an ecological station, the Mamirauá Reserve has been one of Brazil's most prized ecotourism spots.

Splendid and luxuriant, its *várzea* (seasonally flooded) vegetation offers plenty of opportunity for spotting abundant wildlife, including endemic species such as the white uakari monkey and black-headed squirrel monkey. The annual flood transforms the life of the whole region. During the high-water season, fish invade the flooded forest and disperse seeds as they move about. More than 300 species of fish have already been catalogued in the reserve. Mamirauá is also home to pink river dolphin, great egret, and the rare scarlet macaw. The Neotropic cormorant, whose diet consists mainly of fish, can be spotted swimming and feeding in large, noisy flocks.

In the dry season, which lasts from September to December, one can walk on trails, or paddle almost silently through them on canoes. The preserve's eco-tourism program features a range of activities, which includes guided nature

expeditions in the lakes and trails in the forest.

The preserve also offers comfortable and ecologically sound accommodation at the floating Uakari Lodge *(see p378)* close to forest trails, pretty jungle lakes, and *caboclo* communities. Book through a Manaus tour company, or directly with the **Programa de Ecoturismo** in Tefé, 16 miles (25 km) south.

2 Parintins

Amazonas. 105,000.
from Manaus. Festa do Boi Bumbá (Jun); Festa das Pastorinhas (Dec–Jan).

A large jungle town, Parintins was originally the refuge of a community of indigenous riverine people, known as *caboclos*, who were escaping Portuguese slave traders. Today, Parintins is best known for its popular Festa do Boi Bumbá. The festival is celebrated in June, when the town gets so packed that visitors often stay on boats.

Though there is little else to see, besides the well-preserved colonial architecture, Parintins is known for its rich indigenous culture, and the local handicrafts make unique souvenirs. The flea markets sell everything from trinkets, lace, and bead-work to masks and mahogany carvings. During the dry season, boat trips can be taken to nearby lakes and river beaches.

Festa do Boi Bumbá

The vibrant festival, Festa do Boi Bumbá, is centered around a ritualistic dance recounting the death and rebirth of a legendary *boi* (ox). Originating on the 18th-century Northeast plantations, the festival arrived in Parintins almost 100 years ago with the Cid brothers from Maranhão. They brought with them the Bumba-meu-boi *(see p47)* musical influence, steeped in the vibrant rhythms of the Northeast. The last few decades saw the festival gaining in prominence. Every June, at least 35,000 people crowd into Bumbódromo, a purpose-built stadium in the town center, to join in the revelries. The fantastic procession incorporates dazzlingly dressed participants, including mythological beasts. The rivalry between the two competing camps, the red Garantido and the blue Caprichoso groups, is expressed in traditional songs. Over the years, this competitive spirit, which goes right down to who wears the most outlandish costume, has brought forth some radical and electrifying spectacles.

Garantido in bright red headgear, gearing up for the contest

Tranquil waters of the Rio Branco, flowing past Roraima's capital Boa Vista

❸ Boa Vista

Roraima. 285,000. ✈ 🚌 💬
ℹ Centro Turismo, (95) 2121 2561.
🌐 turismo.rr.gov.br 📷 Roraima
Adventures, (95) 3624 9611.
🌐 roraima-brasil.com.br

Created in 1991, Roraima is one of Brazil's newest states, and Boa Vista is its capital city. While the savannas surrounding it are an important cattle-ranching territory, the gold rush of the 1980s still drives development in the region.

The Praça Cívica forms the heart of the town's arch-shaped street layout. The modern Palácio Municipal is here beside the Monumento ao Garimpeiro, a local monument honoring the gold miners who have brought significant wealth to this state.

There are good swimming beaches on the Rio Branco, only 15 minutes by bus from Boa Vista. The sandy beaches right in the town center, opposite the Orla Taumanam, offer excellent swimming when the river is low.

Environs
Boa Vista is blessed with lush tropical rainforest, endless stretches of savanna plains, and pretty river beaches, which make the surrounding region well worth exploring. Though ecotourism is still in its initial stages, organized tours are fairly developed.

A significant staging port en route south to Manaus or north to Guyana and Venezuela, Boa Vista is easily connected by bus to the Venezuelan town of **Santa Elena de Uairén**, located 147 miles (237 km) north. The route from Boa Vista to Santa Elena is dotted with some interesting sights. The ecological island preserve of **Ilha do Maracá**, 62 miles (100 km) north of Boa Vista, is known for its species preservation and biodiversity. Fringed with groves of cashew trees, the enchanting **Lago Caracaranã** is located 112 miles (180 km) north.

Santa Elena de Uairén offers the best access to the **Parque Nacional de Monte Roraima**. The park is ideal for trekking through a variety of eco-niches with changing vegetation to climb **Monte Roraima**, a point where Brazil, Guyana, and Venezuela meet. At 8,970 ft (2,734 m) above sea level, good camping equipment and preparation is essential.

Several Boa Vista-based companies offer excellent week-long packages. International visitors require a Venezuelan tourist card, which can be obtained at the Venezuelan consulate in Boa Vista.

❹ Rio Branco

Acre. 335,000. ✈ 🚌 💬 ℹ Av
Getúlio Vargas 91, (68) 3901 3019.

Another relatively new state, Acre was annexed from Bolivia in the early 20th century by a pioneering army of Brazilian rubber-tappers. It was founded in 1904, under the name of a rubber company, Seringal Empressa, by Newtel Maia from Ceará.

The Parque de Maternidade has magically transformed a small town water canal into a long, green city walk. In the town center, just a couple of blocks north from the Rio Acre, which cuts the town in half, stands the **Palácio Rio Branco**. Though restored, the building maintains its original Neo-Classical façade with four columns at the entrance. It was built in the 1930s as headquarters for the state government, and retains a good collection of period furniture from the 1940s and 1950s.

Rio Branco city on the banks of Rio Acre

A main feature of the palace, the largest painting in Brazil, depicts a scene in homage to the revolutionary heroes who liberated Acre from Bolivia. The palace also contains several large rooms dedicated to the prehistory and history of the region. The main focus is on the 20th-century history of Acre, and there is a superb room dedicated to indigenous culture, displaying some stupendous feather headdresses. Artifacts relating to local history and tribes are also displayed in the palace.

A few blocks north, the **Museu da Borrachá** (Rubber Museum) focuses on the fascinating local ethnic culture, rubber-tappers, and *ayahuasca* churches, known for their ceremonial use of hallucinogenic herbs.

Rio Branco is transforming the city's south bank of the Rio Acre, which was the focal point during the rubber boom and until the new north-based commercial center emerged in the mid-20th century. The municipality is restoring many of the buildings, which once served the river port as hotels, bars, and a splendid movie theater, as well as merchants' stores, making for a lively atmosphere. The promenade, La Gameleira, makes a perfect location for a riverside walk.

The **Parque Ambiental Chico Mendes** (Chico Mendes Environmental Park) is located in the former rubber plantation at Itucumã near Vila Acre, 6 miles (10 km) south of Rio Branco. It contains virgin forest areas, some replica *malocas* (indigenous longhouses) and rubber-tapper dwellings, as well as a zoo and the Chico Mendes memorial.

🏛 Museu da Borrachá
Av Ceará 1441. **Tel** (68) 3223 1202.
Open 8am–5pm Mon–Fri.

🏛 Palácio Rio Branco
Praça E. Gaspar Dutra s/n. **Tel** (68) 3223 9241. **Open** 8am–6pm Tue–Fri, 4–9pm Sat & Sun. 🎫 📷 📹

🏞 Parque Ambiental Chico Mendes
Rodovia AC-40 Km 7, Vila Acre.
Tel (68) 3221 1933. **Open** 7am–5pm Tue–Sun.

Visitors walking through the ruined Forte Príncipe da Beira, Guajará-Mirim

⑤ Porto Velho

Rondônia. 🗺 425,000. 🚌 🚗 🚢
🛈 Departamento do Turismo, (69) 3901 3186.

A very fast growing jungle city, Rondônia's capital, Porto Velho, has grown out of a few streets beside the giant Rio Madeira in the last 100 years. River trips to the nearby beach of Santo Antônio are popular for freshly cooked fish at a waterside restaurant.

The star attraction, however, is the **Madeira-Mamoré Museu Ferroviário**, where several steam locomotives, some under cover, still defiantly symbolize a rusting industrial vision in the middle of the Amazon jungle. In the main museum shed, there are interesting exhibits from the turn of the 19th century, when the railway was being built. Unfortunately, its inauguration

in 1912 was just in time to witness the collapse of Brazil's rubber industry.

Environs
Guajará-Mirim is on the Bolivian border. From here, it is possible to visit the lonely jungle fort, the **Forte Príncipe da Beira**, built by the Portuguese in 1773.

The **Reserva Biologica do Guaporé** near Costa Marques town, which is located 12 miles (20 km) east of Principe de Beira town, is known for its diverse bird species. The Ibama in Porto Velho arranges trips for researchers.

🏛 Madeira-Mamoré Museu Ferroviário
Praça Madeira-Mamoré. **Open** 8am–noon, 2–6pm Mon–Fri. 🎫 ♿
Tel (69) 3901 3651.

🏞 Reserva Biologica do Guaporé
Av Cabixi com Limoeiro 1942.
Tel (69) 3651 2315.

Environmentalist Chico Mendes

Chico Mendes (1944–88)

A rubber-tapper union leader and environmental activist, Chico Mendes helped establish the National Council of Rubber Tappers. His design for extractive rainforest preserves won him recognition by the UN in 1987, with a Global 500 award. He received another award from the Better World Society, before his assassination by hired men employed by the ranchers on December 22, 1988. His untimely death brought international attention, for the first time, both to the plight of the rainforest and the positive solution offered simply by harvesting the rainforest's fruits and sustainable products. Many leading Brazilian human rights activists, environmental campaigners, and church organizations came together to establish the Chico Mendes Committee, which successfully dedicated itself to seeing his murderers brought to justice.

CENTRAL WEST BRAZIL

Introducing Central West Brazil

The Federal District of Brasília and four other states make up Brazil's Central West. Goiás and Tocantins in the east of the region and Mato Grosso and Mato Grosso do Sul in the west, are areas where the expansive wilderness of craggy *cerrado*-covered plateaus, vast wetlands, rainforests, and deserts are beginning to give way to industrialization. The slow pace of life in colonial mining towns such as Cidade de Goiás and Pirenópolis is being eclipsed by the urban attractions of cities such as Campo Grande and Brasília. However, the Central West remains one of the best regions in which to savor Brazil's traditional rural way of life as well as spot amazing wildlife.

Cristalino Jungle Lodge *(see p323)* is situated on the banks of the Rio Cristalino, in Alta Floresta. This region is rich in the Amazon flora and fauna, and has a number of splendid birding trails. Guided hiking tours are also on offer.

Bonito *(see p327)*, a small, quiet town located at the southern edge of the Pantanal, offers visitors light adventure activities such as snorkeling in clear-water rivers, visiting caves, and hiking along short wildlife trails.

◀ Cattle roaming the Pantanal

Ilha do Bananal *(see p315)*, one of the world's largest river islands, contains rivers that extend up to 155 miles (250 km), and is home to several indigenous peoples. A bird-watcher's paradise, the island's wild interior is not easily accessible.

Paraíso do Norte

Gurupi

BRASÍLIA, GOIÁS & TOCANTINS
(See pp302–17)

Uruaçu

Pirenópolis
Brasília

Goiânia

Rio Verde

Brasília *(see pp306–9)*, the country's capital, is renowned for its Modernist buildings, many of which were designed by the noted architect Oscar Niemeyer.

0 km   150

0 miles   150

Três oas

Pirenópolis *(see pp312–13)*, a picturesque former mining town with colonial buildings and impressive restaurants, is a popular weekend retreat. It is also a base for exploring the *cerrado* and the region's numerous waterfalls.

Creation of a Capital

President Juscelino Kubitschek and his team of designers, planners, and architects, led by Oscar Niemeyer, envisaged Brasília not only as a city, but also as a monument to the national motto – Order and Progress. In creating this, they turned to European Modernism, following the doctrine of Charles-Edouard Jeanneret (1887–1965), or "Le Corbusier," for their inspiration. The concept stated that modern cities should be zoned functionally with separate areas for housing (in high-rise blocks), recreation, and administration, broken by green belts and roads.

Juscelino Kubitschek was the president of Brazil between 1956 and 1961. He was responsible for the creation of Brasília as the new, modern capital of the country.

The Missão Cruls was commissioned by President Floriano Peixoto in 1892 and led by the Belgian scientist Luiz Cruls. It sought to find a possible site for a new capital in the Brazilian interior to make a more regionally neutral federal capital where resources could be equally divided.

Superquadra 309, a residential neighborhood, was built in one of the "wings" of Brasília.

The *candangos* were workers from the Northeast brought to Brasília in vast numbers to build the city. Homes for their descendants were not included in the grand plan and today Brasília is ringed with the slum cities of their children.

Brasília

Located at the heart of the country, Brazil's capital city is today on UNESCO's list of World Heritage Sites, and is famous for its innovative urban planning and daring architecture.

1892 Luiz Cruls sent to explore the area

Dom Bosco (1815–88)

1934 Possibility of a new capital formally discussed

1946 Land demarcated for a capital

1960 Brasília inaugurated, Eisenhower visits

1961–64 Work on remaining buildings continued

1880	1900	1920	1940	1960

1883 Dom Bosco predicts a new civilization arising between the 15th and 20th parallels of latitude

Catedral Metropolitana

1922 Foundation stone for a future city laid

1956 Juscelino Kubitschek elected as president; Project Brasília begins

Lúcio Costa and Roberto Burle Marx, the urban planner and the landscape designer behind Brasília, intended that every element, from the layout of the residential and administrative districts to the symmetry of the buildings, should be in harmony with the city's overall design.

Ministerial buildings were built to flank Praça dos Três Poderes and Eixo Monumental (see pp306–7).

Oscar Niemeyer

Born in Rio de Janeiro in 1907, Niemeyer went on to become one of the most important names in modern architecture. His first job was with Le Corbusier and Lúcio Costa on Rio's Ministry of Education in 1936. After this he went on to design a series of landmark buildings such as the Contemporary Museum of Art in Niterói (see p93). Niemeyer's socialist beliefs led to his exile under the coup of 1964. He returned to Rio in the 1980s and continued to work. He died in 2012.

Oscar Niemeyer at his office in Rio de Janeiro

Original pen and ink drawings submitted by Lúcio Costa in 1956 in the competition for a new capital city show Brasília's distinctive shape, which has been variously interpreted as an airplane, a bird in flight, and a bow and arrow.

Eixo Rodoviária Sul is one of the main roads in the "wings" connecting Brasília from one end to the other.

American President Dwight D. Eisenhower, on an official visit to Brazil, inaugurated the new capital city of Brasília with great fanfare on February 23, 1960. He also visited Rio de Janeiro and São Paulo.

The inauguration of Brasília by President Juscelino Kubitschek and President Eisenhower was attended by thousands of people. The new capital saw the installation of the three powers of the republic – parliament, judiciary, and presidency.

Flora & Fauna in the Cerrado

The Brazilian *cerrado* (meaning inaccessible in Portuguese) is a biome unique to South America and is the tropical world's largest woodland savanna. The *cerrado* landscape is made up of scattered woods and vast swathes of grassland along riverbanks and in small valleys. One of the richest ecosystems in the world, the *cerrado* is home to almost every species of large mammal found in South America, together with an enormously prolific birdlife. The *cerrado* landscape is home to some 10,000 plant species, of which 4,400 are endemic to the region.

BRAZIL

Key
- The *cerrado*
- The Pantanal

Hyacinth macaws are an endangered species due to overcollection for the caged-bird trade. They are also hunted by the Kayapó people *(see p266)*, who use their bright blue feathers in their headdresses.

The *cerrado*, a sprawling 1.2-million-sq-mile (3-million-sq-km) mix of forest and savanna, covers 75 percent of Brazil.

Capybaras, abundant in the *cerrado*, are semi-aquatic, herbivorous rodents. They live in herds and spend most of their time feeding on river-banks, where they are easily spotted during mornings and evenings.

The marsh deer is generally a solitary animal, or lives in herds of fewer than six. It has webbed feet which help it walk on flooded land.

The rhea is a large, flightless bird native to South America. Because rheas will eat almost any crop plant, farmers sometimes kill the birds. This, along with egg gathering and habitat loss, has led to a significant drop in their numbers. The species is listed among the wildlife of "special concern."

The maned wolf is the only large canid in the world that does not form packs. The animal, now endangered, was hunted by poachers for its body parts, notably the eyes, which were believed to be good-luck charms.

Buriti Palms often grow over subterranean water. They are an important source of food for many large parrots and primates.

Savanna formations in the *cerrado* are not homogenous. Hilly areas have denser, more varied flora than the grasslands.

Conservation of the Cerrado

Central Brazil's ancient *cerrado* forests are rapidly being cleared for soya plantations and cattle ranches. Since the late 1990s, steps have been taken to identify conservation-priority areas and better manage protected areas. Recently, private reserves, established under the Private Natural Heritage Reserve system, have become an important component of biodiversity protection in the *cerrado*. There have also been more intensive faunal and floral surveys of the region.

Tractors paving the way for a new farm in the *cerrado*

Ipê Tree is a large canopy tree. Its vibrant trumpet-shaped flowers bloom in spectacular yellow, pink, and mauve throughout the *cerrado*.

Flora in the Cerrado

The cerrado *is characterized by its vast expanses of grassland, scattered forests, and palm groves. The landscape varies between the "open* cerrado*," predominantly grassland, without trees and shrubs, and "closed* cerrado*," the more forested areas.*

Flora & Fauna of Pantanal

Although the world's largest wetland forms part of the southern extreme of the cerrado, *the Pantanal (see pp324–5) comprises habitats most associated with the Amazon. Many* cerrado *species live here, as well as marsh deer, capybara, caimans, waterbirds, and monkeys.*

The white-necked heron *is a common sight in the Pantanal, especially along riverbanks, where it feeds. This graceful bird builds its nest on a platform on trees close to the river.*

Caiman *numbers in the Pantanal have increased after a ban on hunting them for their skin and teeth (considered charms against witchcraft) took effect.*

Guira cuckoos are slightly scruffy-looking birds that nest, roost, and feed in groups, eating insects, frogs, and eggs off the ground.

BRASÍLIA, GOIÁS & TOCANTINS

The capital of Brazil since 1960, Brasília is the region's only metropolis. Its striking city plan and futuristic architecture make it vastly different from any other city in the country. Goiás and Tocantins make up Brazil's heartland. Northern Goiás and Tocantins are mainly wilderness areas of mountains and dry savanna, while in the south lie the colonial towns of Pirenópolis and Goiás Velho.

Until the mid-20th century, only *bandeirante* slavers and gold hunters had ventured into the wilderness of central Brazil, a land of *cerrado* (savanna) woodland, *mesetas* (tabletop mountains), and giant winding rivers, peopled by indigenous groups such as the Xavante. Some gold prospectors stayed on, building a handful of colonial towns near their mines. Cidade Goiás and Pirenópolis in central Goiás are very well preserved, so much so that the former is now a UNESCO World Heritage Site. Pirenópolis is famous for its festivals, the liveliest of which, the Festa do Divino Espírito Santo, re-enacts the battles between the Christians and the Moors. The city is also a center for ecotourism,

and a favorite watering hole for nearby Brasília's middle class. The Utopian, but impersonal, capital city sits on an exposed plain under an expansive sky. Its brave new domes, churches, and steel-reinforced monoliths, now ringed with *favelas*, should not be missed.

Northern Goiás and Tocantins remain frontier lands, where fields of soya are fast encroaching upon the foothills of the *mesetas* in Chapada dos Veadeiros National Park, the dune-filled expanses of the Jalapão *cerrado*, and indigenous lands on the world's largest river island, Ilha do Bananal. The scenery here is spectacular, and adventure activities, such as canyoning and rappeling, are well developed.

The Palácio do Itamaraty (Palace of Arches), one of the most impressive modern buildings in Brasília

◄ Tribute to Northeast Brazil's migrant workers, Bruno Giorgio's sculpture *Os Candangos*, in Brasília, the city they helped build

Exploring Brasília, Goiás & Tocantins

Cidade de Goiás and Pirenópolis in Goiás remain pleasant
colonial towns, while the spectacular Chapada dos Veadeiros
National Park in northern Goiás showcases the unique flora and
fauna of high-altitude *cerrado*. Brasília, the capital city of Brazil
from 1960 onward, was built from the dust and scrub of the
central western *cerrado*, and is a Modernist marvel. In Tocantins
state, the Ilha do Bananal, one of the largest islands in Brazil, is
also the point at which three ecosystems converge – rainforest,
cerrado, and wetland. The dune deserts of Jalapão in Tocantins
are fringed by dry *sertão*, vast horizons of soya farms, waterfalls,
crystalline rivers, and forests inhabited by the Xavante and
Xingú indigenous groups.

Rio Preto waterfall at Chapada dos Veadeiros

0 km   100
0 miles   100

Sights at a Glance

Towns & Cities

❶ Brasília *pp306–9*
❷ Pirenópolis *pp312–13*
❸ Cidade de Goiás
❺ Palmas

**National Parks & Areas of
Natural Beauty**

❹ Parque Nacional Chapada
   dos Veadeiros *pp316–17*
❻ Jalapão
❼ Ilha do Bananal
❽ Parque Nacional das Emas

For hotels and restaurants in this region see p379 and p395

Ministry buildings, Catedral Metropolitana, and Museu Nacional, in Brasília

Getting Around

Travel inevitably begins in Brasília. There is an international airport, and flights connecting with most larger Brazilian cities, including frequent flights to Goiânia in Goiás and Palmas in Tocantins. Roads radiate out from these cities to other towns and states cutting through the harvest land and the stunning scenery. Pirenópolis, a weekend getaway from Goiânia, is reached from Brasília via a filigree of small roads and regular buses. There are daily buses to Cidade de Goiás from Goiânia via the BR-070. The Chapada dos Veadeiros, which, together with Pirenópolis, boasts the best ecotourism infrastructure, is reached from the little towns of São Jorge or Alto Paraíso in northern Goiás. These are connected to Brasília via the GO-118. Apart from the main north–south artery, the BR-153, transportation in Tocantins is difficult. Ilha do Bananal in the west and Jalapão in the east are remote and best visited on tours.

Key

— Major road

===== Minor road

━━━ State border

Sweeping sand dunes in Jalapão

For keys to symbols see back flap

● Brasília

Brasília is the embodiment in concrete of President Juscelino Kubitschek's promise of "fifty years of economic and social development in five," and of the national motto – Order and Progress. The city was built by vast teams of *candangos*, workers from the Northeast, who carved it from the *cerrado* at breakneck speed. They were led by urban planner Lúcio Costa, architect Oscar Niemeyer, and landscape engineer Roberto Burle Marx *(see p299)*. The capital of Brazil shifted from Rio de Janeiro to Brasília on April 21, 1960. Brasília was added to UNESCO's list of World Heritage Sites in 1987 as an example of daring urban planning and modern architecture. Today, Brasília is a stately, organized city, albeit a little quiet.

View of the Eixo Monumental from atop the TV Tower at dusk

Memorial dos Povos Indígenas is fashioned like a *maloca*, a traditional longhouse. It is a tribute to Brazil's indigenous peoples.

TV Tower is the best place to get a bird's-eye view of the city. The observation deck is on top of the 426-ft- (75-m-) high building.

Quartel General do Exército

VIA N-1 OESTE

VIA S-1 OESTE

0 meters   250
0 yards   250

PARQUE SARA KUBITSCHEK

VIA S-1 OESTE

VIA S-2

VIA W3 NO

VIA W3 SUL

Eixo Monumental

The Eixo Monumental, Brasília's main thoroughfare, forms the centerpiece of the city. Kubitschek stands at one end of the Eixo, waving from his towering Modernist column to the seat of government, the Congresso Nacional and Palácio do Planalto, which sit around the Praça dos Três Poderes. Many of Brazil's most famous architects and sculptors were involved in its construction.

Memorial Juscelino Kubitschek
Built in honor of the president responsible for the construction of Brasília, this monument contains his mausoleum, with photographs of, and documents about, the construction of the city.

Quartel General do Exército
This fusion of curves, straight lines, and jagged waves echoes the Congress complex and is the headquarters of the Brazilian army – at times the key player in affairs of state.

For hotels and restaurants in this region see p379 and p395

Esplanada dos Ministérios
Tall ministry buildings, 19 in all, are lined up in disciplined rows along Esplanada dos Ministérios.

Congresso Nacional e Anexos
Oscar Niemeyer's most famous and celebrated group of Modernist buildings at the heart of Brasília is also Brazil's seat of government.

Os Candangos
Artist Bruno Giorgio's *Os Candangos* was built in homage to the thousands of migrant workers from Northeast Brazil who went by this nickname and who helped build Brasília.

Teatro Nacional, a set of four theaters, is the most important in the city.

Esplanada dos Ministérios

Palácio do Planalto, or the President's Office, is one of Niemeyer's best examples of Modernist architecture.

ESPLANADA DOS MINISTÉRIOS

Museu Nacional Honestino Guimarães,
a perfect white dome, is another of Niemeyer's buildings.

Palácio de Justiça,
the building of the Ministry of Justice, has a beautiful internal garden.

Catedral Metropolitana Nossa Senhora Aparecida
Niemeyer's iconic cathedral with its curved columns and stained-glass interior is flanked by haunting sculptures of the four apostles.

Supremo Tribunal Federal
The highest court in the country, the Supremo Tribunal Federal is the seat of Brazil's judicial power.

Exploring Brasília

The capital of Brazil, Brasília, is shaped like an airplane in homage to what was then the incipient jet age. While to its north and south lie the residential wings, the Eixo Monumental *(see pp306–7)* forms the body of the jet, with the city's major attractions.

Praça dos Três Poderes

Eixo Monumental.
Congresso Nacional e Anexos:
Tel (61) 3216 1771. **Open** 9:30am–5pm daily. 🦽 Palácio do Planalto:
Tel (61) 3411 2042. **Open** 9:30am–2:30pm Sun. Palácio Itamaraty:
Tel (61) 3411 6155. **Open** 2–4:30pm Mon–Fri, 10–11:30am, 1–3:30pm Sat, Sun & public hols. Palácio da Justiça:
Tel (61) 2025 3216. **Open** 9–11am, 3–5pm Mon–Fri.

This vast square is flanked by buildings that form the locus of the Brazilian government. The axis of the federal state, the **Congresso Nacional e Anexos** is a harmonious fusion of lines and curves, creating the most monumental and timeless architecture in the city. On the other side of the square are the seats of two other branches of power – the **Palácio do Planalto**, the executive office of the presidency, and opposite it, the **Supremo Tribunal Federal**, the Supreme Court headquarters, which is closed to the public.

Immediately below this group of buildings are the **Palácio Itamaraty** and the **Palácio da Justiça**, two of Brasília's few buildings that are more aesthetic than monumental.

Palácio da Justiça with lily pond in the foreground

The interior of Santuário Dom Bosco, bathed in blue light

The latter's Modernist columns seem to rise gently from the lily pond lying at its feet to form smooth arches. Inside is a vast hall decorated with fine sculpture and paintings. The highlight is 19th-century artist Pedro Américo's *O Grito de Ipiranga*, depicting the moment when Dom Pedro I proclaimed Brazilian Independence *(see p56)*.

🏛 Catedral Militar de Nossa Senhora da Paz

Canteiro Central do Eixo Monumental Oeste. **Tel** (61) 3323 3858.
Open 7am–10pm daily.

This brilliant white triangular church, with its jagged windows and vast gable, echoes the French Notre Dame du Haut, designed by Niemeyer's mentor, Le Corbusier. It was completed in 1991, and was built to house the papal altar used by John Paul II on his visit to Brasília in 1980.

Quartel General do Exército

Setor Militar Urbano.
At the northeastern end of the Eixo Monumental, this vast complex of imposing buildings is set in a sea of lawns and watched over by a towering obelisk. It was built during the military dictatorship and was intended to show the presence of military power in the government, which was notably absent from the Praça dos Três Poderes. The intimidating stature of the buildings conveys Niemeyer's objective of constructing something grand for the generals. He was determined that the monumentalism of these generals should not be eclipsed by that of President Juscelino Kubitschek *(see p62)*.

🏛 Santuário Dom Bosco

Av W3 Sul, Quadra 702. **Tel** (61) 3223 6542. **Open** 7am–7pm daily. ✉
The city's finest church honors the 19th-century Italian visionary saint and founder of the Salesian order. His proclamation that a new civilization would arise in the third millennium between the 15th and 16th parallels of latitudes, inspired Kubitschek to build Brasília on the edge of an artificial lake. The stunning interior features an almost seemless panoply of glass, which ranges from light to dark blue and indigo, as it ascends. In the late afternoon, shafts of light penetrate the building, illuminating the marble statue of the Virgin and the vast cross whose vertical was carved from a single piece of tropical cedar. The church was blessed by John Paul II on his 1980 visit.

Templo da Boa Vontade

Setor Garagem Sul 915. **Tel** (61) 3114 1070. **Open** 24 hrs daily.
Many religions, some orthodox, some decidedly alternative, thrive in and around Brasília. This marble pyramid with open sides was built to reflect the ecumenical attitude towards spirituality which characterizes the city. The building's geometry is based on multiples of seven in accordance with sacred numerology. The sides rise to 69 ft (21 m), the cavernous nave spans 92 ft (28 m), and spiral steps wind around the interior. The central portion of the temple is illuminated by light, filtering through an enormous and priceless rock crystal found at Cristalino in Goiás.

Catedral Metropolitana Nossa Senhora Aparecida

Designed by Oscar Niemeyer to resemble a crown of thorns, this cathedral features 16 soaring curved pillars spread like an open hand. Between them, a filigree of glass windows is united by a fluid series of colors. The main altar and the altarpiece was given by Pope Paul VI in 1967, who also blessed the metal cross sitting atop the building. The statues of the evangelists outside the cathedral are by the Mineiro sculptor Alfredo Ceschiatti, who also sculpted the archangels suspended from the ceiling inside.

VISITORS' CHECKLIST

Practical Information
Esplanada dos Ministérios.
Tel (61) 3224 4073.
Open 8am–6pm Tue–Sun.
Closed during masses: 12:15pm, 6:15pm Tue–Fri, 5pm Sat, 8:30am, 10:30am, 6pm Sun
W catedral.org.br

The Catedral Metropolitana, etched against a cloudy Brasília sky

Subterranean Entrance
The remarkable entrance was intended to recall the catacombs where Christ was interred, with visitors emerging out of darkness into the cathedral's light.

São Mateus
Designed by sculptor Alfredo Ceschiatti (1918–89), this 10-ft- (3-m-) high bronze figure of St. Matthew is one of the four sculptures that stand in front of the cathedral.

Curved Concrete Pillars, all 16 of them, are held together at their apex by a high-tensile steel ring.

Stunning Interior
Archangels hover over the central altar, while the light marble and ample daylight infuse the entire building with a transcendent glow. The glass panels in the interior reflect sunlight from the rippling water outside.

The breathtaking *cachoeira* (waterfall) that crashes into the Cânion do Rio Preto in the Parque Nacional Chapada dos Veadeiros, Goiás ▶

❷ Pirenópolis

The picturesque town of Pirenópolis is gathered around the Rio das Almas, surrounded by verdant *cerrado* woodlands, and tucked away at the feet of low ragged hills. Pirenópolis skillfully balances the old and the new, the traditional and the contemporary. Crowned by Portuguese Baroque churches, the cobbled streets clatter to the sound of cowboys on horseback. The streets are lined with chic little restaurants, housed in rustic 18th-century bungalows, or designed in low-key 20th-century Art Deco style. The entire historical center can be walked around in less than two hours. There are only a few streets – the principal ones being Rua Direita, Rua da Aurora, Rua do Bonfim, and Rua do Rosário, which has the bulk of the restaurants. At weekends, a bustling crowd from Brasília fills up the streets.

Display of costumes from the Festa do Divino, Museu das Cavalhadas

Souvenir shops selling traditional handicrafts on Rua Rui Barbosa

⌂ Igreja Nosso Senhor do Bonfim

Praça do Bonfim. **Open** check with tourist office before visiting.

This simple but elegant little church on Rua do Bonfim was built between 1750 and 1754. One of the best-preserved churches in Goiás, this modest Baroque building is architecturally similar to Matriz de Nossa Senhora do Rosário and has a plain white façade. The

The well-maintained Igreja Nosso Senhor do Bonfim

image of Nosso Senhor do Bonfim, in the main altarpiece, was brought here from Salvador by a convoy of 250 slaves.

⌂ Igreja Matriz de Nossa Senhora do Rosário

Praça da Matriz. **Open** check with tourist office before visiting.

This parish church, founded in 1728, is the largest and the oldest ecclesiastical building in Goiás. Until 2002, when the entire attractive colonial edifice was gutted in a fierce fire, it also had one of the finest Baroque interiors in the state. The church boasted an altarpiece decorated with motifs taken from the flora of the surrounding *cerrado*, and an impressive ceiling painted by the Brazilian artist, Inácio Pereira Leal, in 1864. The church was restored and opened anew in 2006, but a shortage of funds has left it with a plain interior.

Museu da Família Pompeu

▥ Museu das Cavalhadas

Rua Direita 39. **Tel** (62) 3331 1166. **Open** 10am–5pm daily.

This small museum contains an incredible display of Carnaval masks, ornate metal armor costumes, photographs, and folklore relating to the hugely popular Festa do Divino Espírito Santo. The festival was originally Portuguese but the court costumes and the animal masks are uniquely Brazilian, originating from Afro-Brazilian and indigenous custom. The collection occupies the ground floor of a home belonging to a family which has for generations played a central role in performances at the festival.

▥ Museu da Família Pompeu

Rua Nova 33. **Tel** (62) 3331 1299. **Open** 1–5pm Tue–Fri, 1–3pm Sat.

Set up in a corridor inside a large 18th-century house, this tiny museum displays regional historical items, including an odd collection of colonial bric-a-brac, furniture, Dickensian shelves of old documents, municipal newsletters, an old printing press, and silver jewelry. The museum preserves the most comprehensive and well-maintained records of the early years of the colonial town of Pirenópolis, including pictures and documents from its gold-mining days. The Pompeu family does not reside here. There is a proposal to turn this treasure-house into a public municipal museum.

Festa do Divino Espírito Santo

Also known as Cavalhadas, the festival is based on Iberian lore dating from the Crusades and Catholic Whitsuntide celebrations. The festival begins 15 days before Pentecost Sunday, with a gathering of riders, known as the Folia do Divino, at the Matriz. They then proceed out of Pirenópolis into the surrounding countryside. Masked dancers, parades of horsemen dressed as Crusaders, Moors, or Cavalhadas, and many cultural and musical events follow. The festival culminates on Pentecost Sunday in the stadium, the Cavalhadodrómo.

Cavalhadas parade costume

VISITORS' CHECKLIST

Practical Information
Goiás. 🖼 23,000.
ℹ️ Central de Atendimento ão Turista, (62) 3331 2633.
📷 Festa do Divino Espírito Santo (May/Jun).
🌐 **pirenopolis.com.br**

Transport
✈️ 🚌 Rodoviária, Rua Neco Mendonça, (62) 3331 1080.

🎭 Teatro de Pirenópolis
Praça da Matriz s/n. **Tel** (62) 3331 2029 (box office). **Open** box office open all day on show days.

This delightful, restored miniature 19th-century theater is one of the town's hidden treasures and commemorates the centenary of its foundation. The Teatro de Pirenópolis is best visited during one of the regular plays, performances, and shows. One of the most interesting small acts in the past has featured the popular Mato Grosso do Sul-born guitarist Almir Sater. The Goiás singer-songwriter, Maria Eugenia, and the Tocantins *forró* singer, Dorivã, regularly play here. Just around the corner, on the Rua do Direita, is the little

Art Deco **Cine Pireneus Art Cinema**, which has an impressive eclectic program.

The Art Deco façade of Cine Pireneus Art Cinema

🦋 Santuário de Vida Silvestre Fazenda Vagafogo
4 miles (6 km) NW of Pirenópolis. **Tel** (62) 3335 8515. **Open** 9am–5pm daily. 🎫

A beautifully preserved patch of forest lined with streams and exquisite trails, Santuário Vagafogo makes for a good excursion. This stunning nature preserve of *cerrado* and gallery forests (forests along a river or stream) is home to a number of bird and animal species such as brown capuchins and armadillos. On weekends and on holidays, a small restaurant at the visitors' center serves fantastic fare. Visitors can hire a motorbike taxi from pick-up points in town – an inexpensive way to get to the sanctuary – or hire a cab.

Pirenópolis

① Igreja Nosso Senhor do Bonfim
② Igreja Matriz de Nossa Senhora do Rosário
③ Museu das Cavalhadas
④ Museu da Família Pompeu
⑤ Teatro de Pirenópolis
⑥ Santuário de Vida Silvestre Fazenda Vagafogo

A cobbled street lined with town houses in Cidade de Goiás

❸ Cidade de Goiás

Goiás. 🅜 29,000. ✈ 🚌 ℹ
Secretaría de Turismo, (62) 3371
7714. 🎭 Semana Santa (Apr),
Festival Internacional de Cinema
Ambiental (Jun). 🆆 **cidades
historicas.art.br/goias**

Like most colonial towns in
Brazil's interior, Cidade de Goiás
grew rich on gold. Until the
middle of the 20th century, it
was the capital of what was
once the largest Brazilian state
apart from Amazonas. Also
known as Goiás Velho, or just
Goiás, Cidade de Goiás is a
magical little city nestled at the
foot of the rugged Serra
Dourado hills. Winding cobbled
streets lined with 18th-century
town houses lead to hills
capped with churches, leafy
squares and little markets. Life
here seems to trot along as it
has done for centuries.

While historic, Goiás is far
from being lost in a bygone age.
The city's busy social calendar is
a testament to its successful
fusion of the old with the new.
There is something happening
almost every weekend through
the year in Goiás, from
thoroughly traditional hooded
parades in Semana Santa (Holy
Week) to some of the best
world-cinema festivals and
classical music concerts in Brazil.

Many buildings and museums
testify to the city's illustrious
past, and Goiás is small enough
to see them all leisurely on foot.
The best place to begin a tour is
at **Praça Brasil Caiado**, the large
square which graces the town's
southern end. There are a
number of museums and

monuments here. These include
the **Museu das Bandeiras**, the
former seat of government,
which preserves a forbidding
dungeon and a set of rooms
with period furniture, a
magnificent Baroque public
fountain, Chafariz de Cauda, and
the Quartel do Vinte, an
18th-century barracks, which
now houses the tourist office.

Immediately north of Praça
Brasil Caiado and capped with
an attractive, though modest,
Baroque church is another
square, **Praça do Coreto**. The
most interesting of all the city's
museums, **Museu de Arte Sacra**
in the Igreja de Boa Morte, is
located here, preserving a series
of hauntingly lifelike religious
effigies by José Joaquim da
Veiga Valle (1806–74), a self-
taught sculptor. Opposite this
museum is the **Palácio Conde
dos Arcos**, complete with
18th-century furniture and
still used by the governor on
city visits.

🏛 **Museu de Arte Sacra**
Praça do Coreto. **Tel** (62) 3371 1207.
Open 9am–5pm Tue–Sat, 9am–1pm
Sun. 🎟

🏛 **Museu das Bandeiras**
Praça Brasil Caiado. **Tel** (62) 3371 1087.
Open 9am–5pm Tue–Sat, 9am–2pm
Sun. 🎟

🏛 **Palácio Conde dos Arcos**
Praça Dr. Tasso de Camargo. **Tel** (62)
3371 1200. **Open** 8am–5pm Tue–Sat,
8am–noon Sun. 🎟

❹ Chapada dos Veadeiros

See pp316–17.

❺ Palmas

Tocantins. 🅜 265,000. ✈ 🚌 (63)
3228 5600. ℹ CATUR (Centro de
Atendimento ao Turista), (63) 2111
0213. 🎭 Carnaval (Feb/Mar).

Built in 1989, Brazil's newest
state capital sits at the base
of a range of forested low
hills. It is a pleasant, but
sprawling, modern city. Most
visitors come to Palmas as
it is a good jumping-off point
for the numerous attractions
that lie within the interior
of Tocantins state, most
notably Jalapão and the Ilha
do Bananal.

Aside from the vast Palmas
lake formed by the dam on the
Rio Tocantins, Palmas' most
interesting area is its vast,
grassy main square, Praça
Giróssois, which is lined by
grandiose public buildings and
various monuments to its
founder, José Wilson Siqueira
Campos, and his legacy.

The sparkling Rio Tocantins in Palmas
at sunset

❻ Jalapão

Tocantins. 🎫 Korubo, (11) 9 8222
5028, 🆆 **jalapao.com**; or Bananal
Ecotour (63) 3028 4200.

A journey through Brazil's
interior would be incomplete
without a visit to Jalapão.
Located deep within eastern
Tocantins, this breathtaking area
is one of South America's great
wilderness destinations. Jalapão,
stretching across 13,130 sq miles
(34,000 sq km), is made up of
a state park, three private
protected areas, and an
ecological station, Estação

Ecológica. The best time to visit is the dry season between June and September.

Beyond the inaccessible reaches of southern Piauí, the arid *cerrado* forests and incipient *caatinga* thornlands are more pristine here than anywhere else. Many fast-flowing rivers cut through spectacular canyons and thunder over myriad waterfalls throughout Jalapão. A number of rivers are born in limpid glassy springs that bubble forth from the sands of Jalapão. Others wind their way through groves of buriti palms called *veredas*. These are visited by Spix's macaws and Brazilian Merganser ducks, two of the extremely rare birds lost to the rest of the continent but still found in Jalapão.

Towering over Jalapão's seemingly interminable plains and striding out to the endless horizons are stands of monolithic tabletop mountains, winding yellow sand dunes, and craggy rock pinnacles. The air is so clear that even when these are far in the distance, they appear close enough to touch. Trails running across the mountain summits range from moderate to difficult, depending on the experience of the hiker.

The views from the top of the mountains and dunes are mesmerizing. But for the whistling breeze, it is so silent that the infrequent pick-ups running across the very few dirt roads can be heard clearly even when they are quite a long distance away.

Dark waters of the Rio Javaés, one of Ilha do Bananal's rivers

❼ Ilha do Bananal

Tocantins. ⚐ 3,500. ⚑ Bananal Ecotour Quadra 103-S, Loja 28, Palmas, (63) 3028 4200.

The Rio Araguaia runs from southern Goiás across Tocantins state to join the Rio Tocantins before draining into the Amazon. In the middle of this river sits the Ilha do Bananal, an island so vast that it has its own rivers running through it and contends with Ilha de Marajó (see p274) for the title of the world's largest river island. Access to the island's wild interior is not easy. Visits here are only possible with a licensed tour operator.

Three ecosystems converge on the island – rainforest, wetland, and *cerrado*. Bananal's southern extremes are mostly Terras Indígenas (indigenous territories), where tourists are not welcome. Its center and north are impenetrable without a guide. Indigenous communities, including the Javaés and the Karajás, inhabit the island, some of whom produce carved wooden animals and pottery figurines. The southern part of the island also comprises seasonally flooded forests, lakes, and swamps filled with wildlife. This is a wonderful area for bird-watching, particularly waterbirds. There are also black caimans, which grow to an immense size in the dark, fish-filled waters.

❽ Parque Nacional das Emas

Goiás. 🛈 Rua do Bonfim, Centro Historico, (62) 3331 2633. ⚑ Drena, Rua Aurora 21, Centro Histórico Pirenópolis, (62) 3331 3336. ⚐ Fazenda Santa Amélia, (64) 3634 1380.

Tucked far away in the southwest corner of Goiás and surrounded by a sea of soya, Emas National Park is a 500-sq-mile (1,300-sq-km) island of grassland and sparse *cerrado*, dotted with millions of termite hills and cut by blackwater rivers. The park is considered the best preserved *cerrado* in the country. In 2001, it was designated a UNESCO World Heritage Site.

Populations of larger mammals, particularly the armadillo, maned wolf, and puma, are so healthy here that the park is a favorite location for film crews from the BBC Natural History Unit. It is also an important destination for bird-watchers, with the greatest concentration of blue-and-yellow macaws outside Amazônia.

Although there is no compulsion to go on a guided tour, it is a good idea to organize a trip through a tour operator in Pirenópolis, or through the tourist office in the nearby town of Chapadão do Céu, east of the park. Facilities at the park are minimal. Accommodation is limited to very rustic, simply appointed **Fazenda Santa Amélia** in Chapadão do Céu.

A breathtaking view of Tocantins landscape from a dune, Jalapão

❹ Parque Nacional Chapada dos Veadeiros

Named for the marsh deer that inhabit the area, this national park sits on the edge of the *cerrado*, one of the largest areas of wild country in the interior of Brazil. Most easily accessed from the small town of Alto Paraíso, the park is set in a stunning landscape. The surrounding area is just as magical; sprawling forest is broken up by rushing waterfalls and meadows, and dotted with stands of buriti palms. This remarkably isolated destination offers spectacular walks and pretty trails for nature lovers as well as exciting outdoor adventure activities, such as rappeling and canyoning.

Buriti palm groves, widely scattered in the Chapada

★ Cânion Rio Preto
The narrow gorges of the Rio Preto, which runs through the middle of the park, cut into the sandstone cliffs. The most stunning precipice has waterfalls gushing down the cliffs.

Rio Ronc

Colinas

Morro da Chapéu
3,300 ft (1,000 m)

SERRA DE SANTANA

Rio Preto

SERRA RIO PR

239

Cachoeira
Cariocas   Cânion I
Cachoeira do   Cânion II
Rio Preto
Salto do Rio Preto

Rio São Miguel

São Jorge
VALE DA LUA

Giant Anteater
One of the larger mammals in the Chapada, the giant anteater is a common sight.

| 0 km | | 10 |
| 0 miles | | 6 |

Vale da Lua The light in this shallow canyon is particularly beautiful at sunset. The rocks have been sculpted into strange Daliesque shapes by the Rio São Miguel.

Chuveirinho Flower
The *cerrado* has thousands of endemic plants and one of the highest numbers of species found in a single area. One such indigenous plant is this unusual meadow flower.

VISITORS' CHECKLIST

Practical Information
Goías. 🚹 Av Ari Valadão, Alto Paraíso, (62) 3446 1159; São Jorge, (62) 3455 1090. 🏠 in Alto Paraíso. **Open** 8am–5pm Tue–Sun. Best time to visit is April–October. 📷 🎟 visits are permitted only with a guide, available at the park entry station. Only 450 visitors may enter the park at any one time and for day trips only.

Transport
🚌 from Brasília to Alto Paraíso, then bus.

Key

━━ Highway

═══ Minor road

– – Trail

▬ ▬ Park boundary

△ Peak

Rio São Domingos

Palmas

Morro do Mresto
3,775 ft (1,150 m)

SERRA DE SANTANA

Rio Santana

Rio Montes Claros

SERRA POUSO ALTO

Morro Capão Grosso
5,050 ft (1,540 m)

118

114

ro Peito de Moça
0 ft (1,525 m)

eto

• Cachoeira
Aqua Fria

• Cachoeira
Rio Cristal

SERRA DAS COBRAS

Rio das Cobras

Rio do Caufos

Morro da Baleia
4,900 ft (1,495 m)

ℹ

• Alto Paraíso
de Goiás

239

239

aBuracão
(1,675 m)

• Fazenda
São Bento

Brasília

Rio Alméçegas

Adventure Sports
The Chapada is one of the most popular places in Brazil for outdoor adventure sports such as abseiling and canyoning.

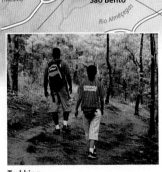

Trekking
The Chapada is home to several forest trails, which are perfect for avid hikers and nature lovers.

★ Cachoeira Almeçegas
A picturesque many-tiered waterfall drops over 260 ft (80 m) into deep pools, which are good for swimming. Access is along a rather tortuous trail.

For keys to symbols *see back flap*

MATO GROSSO & MATO GROSSO DO SUL

Once a destination for explorers and gold hunters, today Mato Grosso and Mato Grosso do Sul attract avid nature lovers. The world's largest wetland and a vital ecosystem, the Pantanal straddles both states. Blessed with crystalline rivers and spectacular national parks, and dotted with ranches and farms, this vast region is still home to a large population of indigenous groups.

Explorations of Mato Grosso were limited to nature expeditions and Jesuit missionaries until the discovery of gold in the 18th century. The gold rush led to clashes between Europeans and indigenous groups. Many of these groups, such as the Bororo and Kayapó, still live in this state.

The building of Brasília as the new capital of Brazil brought waves of migrant workers to the Central West in the mid-20th century. In 1979, the state was split into Mato Grosso and Mato Grosso do Sul, divided by the star attraction of the region, the wetlands of the Pantanal.

Very few places in the world can boast such enormous numbers of large birds as the Pantanal. While wildlife can be difficult to see in the closed forests of the Amazon, it is visible in abundance here. In July and August, storks, ibis, herons, and huge, colorful parrots swarm the Pantanal, and can even be seen while driving along dirt roads. The wetlands are home to a diverse range of wildlife, including the anaconda, the elusive jaguar, and giant otter.

Outside the Pantanal, large tracts of farmland are broken by low mountains and giant, sluggish rivers. Amazon forests cling on in places such as Alta Floresta, Chapada dos Guimarães, and Bonito despite the expansion of the soya industry. The entire region offers prime opportunities for bird-watching, angling, and snorkeling.

Capybara, the largest rodent in the world, frequently spotted in water ponds of the Pantanal

◄ Snorkelers in the Lagoa Misteriosa, Mato Grosso do Sul

Exploring Mato Grosso & Mato Grosso do Sul

Both Mato Grosso and Mato Grosso do Sul are regions of enormous plains with a handful of mountain ranges. The main attraction of this region is the Pantanal, the world's largest wetland. This harbors an important ecosystem with varied fauna such as caimans, jaguars, and a profuse variety of birds. Cuiabá, Corumbá, and Campo Grande are good springboards for ecotourists who wish to travel into or through the Pantanal. Alta Floresta, in the extreme north of Mato Grosso, is considered one of the best places for spotting rare birds and mammals. Bonito, in Mato Grosso do Sul, is an area of plunging waterfalls, caves, and crystal-clear rivers – ideal for walks through mountains and forests, and rafting and snorkeling. Flowing from central Mato Grosso, the Rio Xingú has indigenous peoples from nine distinct ethnic groups living along its banks.

Sights at a Glance

Towns & Cities

❶ Cuiabá
❻ Corumbá
❼ Miranda
❽ Campo Grande
❾ Bonito

National Parks & Areas of Natural Beauty

❷ Chapada dos Guimarães
❸ Xingú
❹ Alta Floresta
❺ Pantanal pp324–5

Jabiru storks, also known as *tuiuiú*, gather to feed in the Pantanal

For hotels and restaurants in this region see pp379–80 and p395

Clear water of the Rio Sucuri at Bonito

↑ *Santarém*

Peixoto de Azevedo

Xingu

Ipitinga

Villa Rica

S. José do Xingu

Tapirapé

de Azevedo

anissaná Missu

XINGÚ ③

Suiá Missu

322

Porto Alegre do Norte

Arraias

Culuene

Querência

Jatobá   Gaúcha do Norte   Garapu

Planalto do Mato Grosso

Canarana

Rio das Mortes

Manso

Mariembero

Araguaia

158

zargão   Paranatinga   Areões   Cocalinho

Nova Xavantino

PADA DOS MARÃES   General Carneiro   *Goiânia*

70

Poxoréu   Barra do Garças

Guiratinga

ndonópolis

364

163   *Correntes*

são   Pedro Gomes   *Goiânia*

im

Paraíso   Cassilândia

Camapuã   *MATO GROSSO DO SUL*   Inocência

hedo   *Coxim*   Aparecida do Tabuado

✈ CAMPO GRANDE ⑧   Água Clara

Sidrolândia   **262**

Três Lagoas

267   *São Paulo*

aju   Rio Brilhante   Bataguaçu

Dourados   *São Paulo*

Ivinheima

a Porã   *Paraná*

Naviraí

mambaí   **163**

Iguatemi

Getting Around

Distances are huge in these states and there are few paved roads. However, the capital cities – Campo Grande in Mato Grosso do Sul and Cuiabá in Mato Grosso have airports with good connections to the rest of Brazil. Alta Floresta also has an airport. Corumbá, Bonito, and Miranda in Mato Grosso do Sul are connected to Campo Grande by fast, comfortable buses. Tour operators are based in the capital cities and in Corumbá and Bonito. Most can organize bookings through their websites. Tours to the Pantanal are also organized, and usually enter the Pantanal by road and spend a couple of days exploring in canoes, motorboats, or on horseback from a land base. Rented 4WD are also a possibility, though visitors would be limited to only a few tracks along the fringes that is suitable for such vehicles.

| 0 km | | 100 |
| 0 miles | | 100 |

Key

═══ Highway

─── Major road

┄┄┄ Minor road

~~~ Railroad

▮▮▮ International border

▬▬▬ State border

For keys to symbols *see back flap*

The spectacular vista of the Chapada dos Guimarães plateau, Mato Grosso

❶ Cuiabá

Mato Grosso. 485,000. Sedtur, (65) 3613 9300. Festa de São Benedito (Jul).

Mato Grosso's capital and the warmest city in Brazil sits on a low, languid plain at the foot of the Chapada dos Guimarães hills. Situated on the banks of the Rio Cuiabá, a tributary of the Rio Paraguai, the city has some leafy squares and is known as the Cidade Verde or the Green City. Cuiabá is also a good starting point for excursions into the Pantanal, a vast wetland area (see pp324–5).

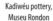

Kadiwéu pottery, Museu Rondon

Like Cidade de Goiás (see p314) and Ouro Preto (see pp130–31), Cuiabá was originally a flourishing gold-mining town, full of handsome buildings and fine churches. Almost all were demolished in a spate of hasty modernization in the late 1960s. The town has lost most of the splendid works of José Joaquim da Veiga Valle (1806–74), one of the country's great geniuses of the Baroque. Fortunately, some of his exquisite craftsmanship can still be seen in the well-preserved, vast, rectangular interiors of the new concrete Catedral do Bom Jesus, which has an unusual square, Moorish façade.

The most interesting of the city's sights is the small university-run **Museu do Índio Marechal Rondon**, in which some exquisite and priceless pieces of indigenous art are kept. These include exhibits of the Xavante, Bororo, and Karajá peoples. The museum houses some beautiful Bororo and Rikbaktsa headdresses and superb pieces of Kadiwéu ceramics from Mato Grosso do Sul.

🏛 Museu do Índio Marechal Rondon

Av Fernando Correia da Costa. **Tel** (65) 3615 8489. **Open** 8–11:30am, 1:30–5:30pm Tue–Fri; 1–5pm Sat, Sun & hols.

❷ Chapada dos Guimarães

Mato Grosso. 13,500. from Cuiabá. Eco Turismo, Av Cipriano Curvo 655, Centro, (65) 3301 1393. Festival de Inverno (Jul). 🌐 **chapadadosguimaraes.com.br**

The town of Chapada dos Guimarães is set on a plateau of the same name. Said to be about 500 million years old, the majestic honey-colored tablelands and escarpments of the plateau are among the oldest rock formations in the world. As the continent's geodesic center, the tablelands of the Chapada dos Guimarães are reputedly imbued with energizing powers strong enough to reduce the speed of a car and said to be attractive to UFOs. While the residents of the Chapada claim that this effect has been documented, skeptics believe otherwise.

The little town has numerous shops and cafés, and a daily fair selling local arts and crafts. There are also several spiritual centers devoted to the New Age movement, which is growing in Brazil. Nature lovers come here to admire the scenery. The edge of the Chapada offers sweeping vistas out over the patchy, remnant

Véu de Noiva, the highest waterfall in Chapada dos Guimarães

cerrado forests of the Mato Grosso plains. There are several waterfalls in the area, the most famous and tallest of which is the **Véu de Noiva**, or the Bridal Veil Falls.

Although the Chapada has seen far more aggressive agricultural development than its counterparts in Goiás and Tocantins, many upland bird species that are not found either in the Pantanal or the Amazonian forests can be seen here. The high *cerrado* forests, savannas, and pasturelands of the Chapada hold a special attraction for birdwatchers, who come here in droves to catalog the variety of birds, and perhaps to catch a lucky glimpse of mammals, such as maned wolves, ocelots, and blacktailed marmosets.

Red-capped cardinal, Alta Floresta

❸ Xingú

Mato Grosso. 🚌 🛈 Fundação Nacional do Índio (Funai), Rua 8, Qd. 15, (65) 3644 1245, Cuiabá.
🌐 **funai.gov.br**

By the end of the 19th century all of the great Amazon tributaries had been explored and colonized, and their indigenous peoples enslaved or completely wiped out. The remote region of Xingú, in the extreme northeast of Mato Grosso, was the only indigenous settlement to survive the onslaught and be established as a preserve.

Home to one of the largest areas of tribal lands in the country, it sits as a huge island of forest in a vast ocean of soya plantations. These tracts of land are concentrated around the beautiful clear-water Rio Xingú. Known to be sophisticated, the indigenous peoples flourishing in the Xingú specialize in furniture-making and basketweaving, among other things.

Tourism is extremely limited here and visits to indigenous villages can only be undertaken with prior permission from Fundação Nacional do Índio (Funai).

❹ Alta Floresta

Mato Grosso. 🏔 43,000.
🛩 to Cuiabá, then bus.
🛈 Anaconda Pantanal Operators, (65) 3028 5990. 🏕 Cristalino Jungle Lodge, (66) 3512 7100.
🌐 **cristalinolodge.com.br**

Situated in the extreme north of Mato Grosso, Alta Floresta sits on the edge of the pristine southern Amazon rainforest, and is a rapidly growing frontier town. This remote town is also a thriving agricultural settlement. Its surrounding areas are considered some of the best in the Brazilian Amazon for spotting rare birds and mammals. One of the highlights of Alta Floresta is the fourstar hotel, Floresta Amazônica, which serves as a base for the **Cristalino Jungle Lodge** *(see p379)*.

The Cristalino Jungle Lodge sits in the Cristalino Forest Reserve deep in the forest, north of Alta Floresta. The lodge is situated on the banks of the Rio Cristalino, which is the blackwater tributary of the Rio Tapajós, whose blue waters flow into the Amazon at Santarém *(see p278)*. The lodge is most famous for the profuse birdlife surrounding it, as well as an enormous variety of butterflies and other insects, reptiles, and mammals. All the

A view out over the forests of the Rio Cristalino preserve

large Neotropical rainforest mammals, including the endangered white-nosed bearded saki monkey, brown titi monkey, giant river otter, and three-toed sloth, as well as jaguar, puma, and tapir are present and can often be spotted here. Facilities for jungle walks and viewing wildlife are excellent and include Englishspeaking, specialist guides, a 164-ft- (50-m-) high canopy tower, and a very good library of decent field guides.

Other more challenging outdoor adventure activities, such as camping in the forest, trekking, survival techniques, rappeling, canyoning, and canoeing, can also be arranged through the Cristalino Jungle Lodge.

Cristalino Jungle Lodge, in the Rio Cristalino Forest Reserve, Alta Floresta

● Pantanal

The world's largest wetland, the Pantanal provides a habitat for the greatest concentration of animals in the Western Hemisphere. Innumerable waterbirds gather toward the end of the dry season. There are plenty of reptiles and large mammals, including caimans, tapirs, giant anteaters, and all of Brazil's eight feline species. The secret to the vast numbers of animals lies in the diversity of vegetation and the geography of the Pantanal, a gently sloping bowl which floods when nutrient-rich tributaries drain from the ancient sedimentary rocks of the Brazilian Shield and get trapped. Aquatic plants breed profusely and these provide ample food for fish and birds, who, in turn, feed the rest of the food chain.

Green Kingfisher
The green kingfisher is one of five types of kingfisher to inhabit the Pantanal. It is seen on the banks of small, undisturbed rivers and makes its nest in a tunnel.

Anhinga
The anhinga is a relative of the cormorant and is a common sight in the Pantanal. As it has no wax in its feathers, it must dry its wings in the sun after diving for fish.

Brahmin Cattle
The most common animals in the Pantanal are Brahmin cattle who are herded by local cowboys, or *pantaneiros*.

0 km   50
0 miles   50

Barra do Bugres

Sepotuba
Paraguai

174

Santa Bárbara ●

Barbado

Porto Esperidião
Jauru

Cáceres

Bento Gome...

Aguapei

San Matías

Corixa Grande

Paraguai

PN do Pantana Matogrossense

② Amo...

Palagu...

Paraguai

Corumbá
Urucur...

Piraputangas

① Puga ●

206...

Carandaza...

Bodo...

São Simão ●

Porto Murtinho

267

San Lázaro

KEY

① **The Estrada Parque** dirt road cuts through the southern Pantanal and leads to the wildlife-rich region of Nhecolândia. Like the Transpantaneira, it is lined with *fazendas* (farms).

② **The Parque Nacional do Pantanal Matogrossense** formally protects a small percentage of the Pantanal UNESCO World Heritage Site.

Key

▬ Major road
▬ Minor road
— Railroad
▬ ▬ International border

★ Estrada Transpantaneira

The dirt road of Estrada Transpantaneira is lined with *fazendas,* many of which have accommodation for tourists. Wildlife viewing is excellent and the road is navigable in a normal car.

VISITORS' CHECKLIST

Practical Information

Mato Grosso & Mato Grosso do Sul. ℹ️ Av Afonso Pena 3297, Campo Grande.
Tel (67) 3314 3588.
🚌 organized tours available in Campo Grande & Cuiabá. The dry season (Apr–May & Sep–Oct) is the best time to visit. Bird-watching ideal in Jul–Sep. Fishing best in Apr, but requires a permit from Ibama, (67) 3317 2966.

Transport

✈️ Campo Grande & Corumbá.
🚌 Caceres & Cuiabá.

★ Fazendas

Originally built as cattle ranches, many *fazendas* have been converted into ranch-style hotels. The *fazendas* are connected by excellent bird-watching walkways throughout the Pantanal.

Igapó Forest

Among the most diverse of the Pantanal's eco-systems, the *igapó* is a seasonally flooded forest on blackwater rivers. It is a wonderful place for wildlife-viewing by canoe.

River Excursions

Fazendas near Miranda *(see p326)* offer boat trips on the various Pantanal rivers. Binoculars are essential for bird and caiman spotting.

For keys to symbols *see back flap*

Boats moored on the Rio Paraguai, Corumbá

❻ Corumbá

Mato Grosso do Sul. 🚹 95,000.
✈️ 🚍 🚆 🚢 along Rio Paraguai.
ℹ️ Secretaría de Turismo, (67) 3231
2886. 🎭 Festa de Nossa Senhora de
Candelária (Feb).

Corumbá , on the banks of the
Rio Paraguai, is a small town
surrounded by the Pantanal
region's unspoilt beauty. Boat
rides along the river as well
as wetland excursions form
Corumbá's major attractions.
Sportfishing, one of the main
highlights, is provided at the
nature lodges, floating hotels,
and charming *fazendas* in
this area.

Corumbá was first explored
by Portuguese and Spanish
adventurers in search of gold. By
the 18th century, the growing
strategic importance of the Rio
Paraguai led to the construction
of forts. The **Forte Junqueira**,
built during the Paraguayan War
(see p57), is the only fort still
standing intact.

Another place worth a visit is
the **Casa do Artesão**, a former
prison housing an interesting
museum of indigenous and
local *objets d'art*. The **Museu do
Pantanal** also has a small
collection of indigenous art.

🏛 **Casa do Artesão**
Rua Dom Corrêa 405. **Open** 8am–
noon Mon–Sat.

🏯 **Forte Junqueira**
Rua Cáceres 425. **Tel** (67) 3231 5828.
Open 8am–5pm daily.

🏛 **Museu do Pantanal**
Praça da República. **Tel** (67) 3231
5757. **Open** 7:30am–5pm.

❼ Miranda

Mato Grosso do Sul. 🚹 23,000.
🚍 🚆 ℹ️ Setur, (67) 3242 3051.
🎭 Festa do Homem Pantaneiro (Oct).

The tiny town of Miranda, in the
heart of the Pantanal, hosts the
region's liveliest festival, the
Festa do Homem Pantaneiro.
This grand celebration of the
ranching and cowboy way of
life features lasso contests (in
the mornings for women, at
night for men), and rodeos. Live
sertanejo bands and dancing
carry on all night.

Miranda is an ideal base for
visiting the southern Pantanal's
various *fazenda* ranches *(see
pp379–80)*, many of which lie
on the outskirts of town. The
Fazenda San Francisco is one
of the best locations in inland
Brazil for big cats, especially
ocelot and jaguar. The **Fazenda
Baía Grande** preserves a diverse
range of Pantanal habitats,
including a large caiman-filled
lake and extensive forest. The

Fazenda Meia Lua lies just on
the edge of town and is an
ideal soft adventure option.

Environs
Known for their distinctive
painted terra-cotta ceramics,
the Terena indigenous villages
surround Miranda. Tour operators in Miranda can arrange
trips to a Terena village, as well
as to the **Rio Salobrinho**, a
beautiful clear-water river lined
with gallery forest. Expect to
find rare bird species, including
kingfishers and black-crowned
night herons.

❽ Campo Grande

Mato Grosso do Sul. 🚹 665,000. ✈️
✈️ 🚍 🚆 ℹ️ Centro Informação
Turística e Cultural, (67) 3314 3142.

Mato Grosso do Sul's capital,
Campo Grande is also known as
Cidade Morena because of its
red earth. It is a prosperous,
modern city devoted far more
to agro-business than tourism.
Yet most visitors to the southern
Pantanal arrive here because
the tourist infrastructure is
excellent. Commerce,
education, and tourism are
fast-growing industries here.
The city itself has few major
attractions, though there are
many good restaurants, hotels,
and bars, particularly along and
around Rua Barão do Rio
Branco. For those who do not
want to rough it out with a
Pantanal camping tour, travel
agencies sell packages to
comfortable farm hotels.

Rodeo at the Festa de Homem Pantaneiro

For hotels and restaurants in this region see pp379–80 and p395

Rio Sucuri flowing near Bonito, reflecting the lush greenery around

❾ Bonito

Mato Grosso do Sul. 🏔 17,000. 🚌 ℹ Comtur. 🚗 Taika Tour, R. Coronel Pilad Rebuá 2111, (67) 3255 1354; Ygarapé Tours, Pilad Rebuá 1853, (67) 3255 1733.

A one-street town, Bonito is lined with *pousadas*, restaurants, shops, and tour operators whose lifeline is tourism. It lies just beyond the Pantanal's southern extremities, in the Serra do Bodoquena, a low, *cerrado*-covered range of rugged hills busy with primates and birds, including the black-collared hawk. There are numerous sights around Bonito, all protected by regulations. Only Bonito-based tour agencies can organize trips and arrange permits.

Black-collared hawk

🐾 Aquário Natural Baía Bonita

4 miles (7 km) SE of Bonito. **Tel** (67) 255 1193. **Open** 7:30am–3:30pm daily. 🌐 🆆 aquarionatural.com.br

One of the natural springs in the area, the Baía Bonita features a pristine aquarium, which contains 30 different varieties of fish. Facilities within the complex include a warm swimming pool and relaxation cabin. Snorkeling trips to the Rio Sucuri and Rio da Prata are offered by tour companies. Wetsuits and snorkels are also provided.

🐾 Rio Sucuri

12 miles (20 km) SW of Bonito.

This glassy river is broken by waterfalls and large pools filled with 3-ft- (1-m-) long *piraputanga* (ray-finned fish, typical of the Rio Paraguai basin) and silver dourado fish. Many pools are set in woodland cut with wildlife trails. The gentle flow of the Rio Sucuri and the excellent facilities draws a plethora of snorkelers and rafters, from morning to afternoon, mainly in the high season. Particularly popular are the flotation points where visitors begin a pleasant 1-mile (1.6-km) float downstream. Tour agencies provide meals and equipment.

🐾 Gruta do Lago Azul

12 miles (20 km) W of Bonito. **Open** 7am–2pm daily. 🌐

The Serra do Bodoquena is dotted with caves, the most spectacular of which is the Gruta do Lago Azul. The main highlight is a radiant underground lake that shines as blue as a sapphire in the morning light. From the cave's spectacular mouth, a narrow path leads deep down through striking stalactite formations. At the bottom lies the lake, illuminated by ambient light that streams through the cave's opening.

🐾 Estância Mimosa

15 miles (24 km) NW of Bonito. **Tel** (67) 8403 5213. **Open** 8am–3pm daily. 🌐 🆆 www.estanciamimosa. com.br

Some of the best hiking opportunities are offered in the Estância Mimosa trail, which features rivers, natural pools, and as many as eight waterfalls. There are various bathing spots located in and around these natural features. The trail goes past the gorgeous riverside forest of the Rio Mimoso, with caves and a rich array of wildlife. The fauna includes a variety of birds and mammals, while various kinds of fern, orchid, and bromeliad are part of the lush vegetation found in this area. An optional horseback excursion is also available.

Lake and stalactites at the Abismo Anhumas cavern

🐾 Abismo Anhumas

16 miles (25 km) W of Bonito. **Open** 7:30am–noon daily. 🌐

A pothole that descends a vertical 240-ft (73-m) deep, the Abismo Anhumas is a cavern filled with a large, clear, blue lake featuring vast stalagmites, stalactites, and many other cave deposits. It is possible to snorkel in the lake. The entrance to the cave is by rappel. The growing number of adventure activities include cave diving and canopy tours using rope bridges and zip lines. A group of 16 people are permitted in the cave on any given day. Book with Bonito tour agencies in advance as training is required.

SOUTHERN BRAZIL

Introducing Southern Brazil

The states of Paraná, Santa Catarina, and Rio Grande do Sul form Southern Brazil – the only Brazilian region that lies entirely outside the tropics. Often dismissed as somehow not being truly Brazilian, this region is distinctive due to more than its temperate climate. Although there are vital indigenous, African, and Portuguese elements to the population, the region is largely associated with descendants of European immigrants. The landscape features tremendous contrasts – the pampas grasslands, mountains, and the highland plateau. The distinctive cultures that have emerged there, as along the equally varied coast, are a reflection of Brazil's diversity.

BRAZIL

SOUTHERN BRAZIL

Foz do Iguaçu *(see pp344–7)* is one of South America's most impressive natural features. These spectacular waterfalls are shared by Brazil and Argentina, with each side offering unique perspectives. From Brazil, visitors enjoy a complete panorama, while the trails in Argentina allow visitors to see the falls close-up.

Cascavel

Foz do Iguaçu

Chapecó

Ijuí

Pa
Fu

0 km   150
0 miles   150

Santa Maria

Uruguaiana

Rosário
do Sul

RIO GRAN
DO SUL
(See pp352–6

Bagé

P

São Miguel das Missões *(see p363)* is Rio Grande do Sul's best-preserved Jesuit ruin. This haunting place offers ample evidence of the sophistication of native Guaraní Baroque architecture that emerged in this remote region in the mid-17th century.

◄ Foz do Iguaçu (Iguaçu Falls), Paraná

Curitiba *(see p340)*, the capital of Paraná, is a pretty, well-planned town. Built during the city's cattle and coffee boom, today Curitiba has well-preserved historic buildings, less pollution and traffic than other Brazilian cities, plenty of green spaces, a great music scene, and several interesting sights.

ndrina

Iaringá

Ponta Grossa

Curitiba

Paranaguá

TA CATARINA & PARANÁ
(See pp336–51)

Joinville

Itajai

Florianópolis

Lajes

Florianópolis *(see pp350–51)*, the vibrant capital city of Santa Catarina on Ilha de Santa Catarina, is surrounded by quiet fishing communities and excellent beaches. The sheltered north shore has the most developed beaches, while the east coast lures surfers attracted by giant Atlantic rollers.

Caxias do Sul

Novo Hamburgo

rto
gre

Grande

Porto Alegre *(see pp356–7)*, the capital of Rio Grande do Sul, has a host of Neo-Classical buildings dating from the 19th and early 20th centuries. The Palácio Municipal is one such expression of civic pride, built in 1898, when Porto Alegre was developing into a significant city.

Multicultural Southern Brazil

More than anywhere else in the country, Southern Brazil has been shaped culturally and economically by immigrants. Unlike tropical Brazil to the north, this part was considered unsuitable for plantation agriculture, and instead immigrants were recruited for land colonization schemes. The legacy of its physical isolation from "mainstream" Brazilian society is reflected in the languages and cultures of the immigrants. The architectural heritage is highly valued, festivals showcase traditional music and dance, while handicrafts and local products are sold in villages and on farms.

An illustration of European immigrants aboard a ship bound for Brazil

Azoreans

In the 18th century, Azoreans settled along the coast of Southern Brazil, bringing with them fishing, farming, and lace-making skills. Villages were created, in particular on the island of Santa Catarina, whose white-and-blue buildings resemble those of the Portuguese mid-Atlantic islands.

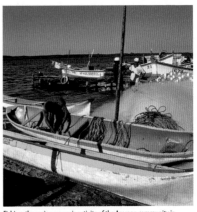
Fishing, the main economic activity of the Azorean community in Santa Catarina

Azorean lace-making is one of the important traditions that have been maintained by women in villages on the island of Santa Catarina.

Germans

Germans were the first non-Portuguese immigrants to settle in Southern Brazil, in the 1850s. They were drawn to the highlands of Rio Grande do Sul and the river valleys of north-eastern Santa Catarina. Their dialects and traditions continue in many rural areas, while German architectural styles are apparent in cities such as Blumenau and Nova Hamburgo.

Old-world architecture still dominates in the areas of Southern Brazil settled by German immigrants. Many buildings are exact replicas of ones found in towns in southern Germany. In the countryside, distinctive half-timbered farm-houses, built by pioneer immigrants, remain a common sight.

German-Brazilian celebration of Oktoberfest

Italians

The first Italian immigrants settled in Rio Grande do Sul in 1875, with tens of thousands arriving there, and in Santa Catarina and Paraná, over the next 50 years. The vast majority came from the northern Italian provinces of Veneto and Trento, introducing rich culinary traditions and the ability to cultivate lucrative grape vines on the steepest of hillsides.

Vineyards in the Serra Gaúcha *(see p359)* have become as much a part of the landscape as they are in Italy. These endless stretches of lush greenery form the center stage for the region's wine production, known both in and outside Brazil.

Slavs

Paraná is the state most closely associated with Slavic immigrants from Central and Eastern Europe, with Poles settling in and around Curitiba from 1869, Ukrainians in the south-center of the state from 1895, and Russians around Ponta Grossa in the early 1960s. The Ukrainians have been especially successful in maintaining their ethnic identity.

São Josafat, a typical Byzantine-style church in Prudentópolis, is easily recognizable by its onion dome features. The Ukrainian Catholic church is pivotal in maintaining Ukrainian identity in Brazil.

A log cabin, housed in the Museu da Imigração Polonesa in Curitiba, is one of the structures that were built by Polish immigrants in the 19th and 20th centuries.

Other Communities

At the beginning of the 20th century, Jews from Eastern Europe founded agricultural communities in Rio Grande do Sul. They later moved to Porto Alegre, establishing Brazil's third-largest Jewish community. In the 1920s and 1930s, many Japanese immigrants relocated to Paraná from São Paulo, setting up coffee and soya farms. Immigrants from other ethnic backgrounds were too few to leave legacies. Some exceptions are the Austrians who settled in central Santa Catarina in the 1930s, and the Dutch who came to Paraná after World War II.

Praça Ministro Andreas Thaler, in Treze Tílias, is named for the then Austrian Minister of Agriculture, who founded the city in 1933 for Austrian immigrants.

Castrolanda, a Dutch settlement thriving on dairy and agricultural products, mainly soya, continues to celebrate its past in the traditional folk dances of the Netherlands.

The Gaúcho Life

The *gaúcho* culture developed in colonial times in what is now northeastern Argentina, Uruguay, and Southern Brazil. In Rio Grande do Sul, the natives of the state – whether urban or rural, and regardless of their ethnic origin – are called *gaúchos*. Traditionally, *gaúchos* were semi-nomadic people who lived by hunting wild cattle. With the introduction of fencing and border agreements, they were reduced to being ranch hands. Nonetheless, their legacy continues to be strongly visible in the distinct *gaúcho* culture of today. In the interior of the state, in the grasslands of both the pampas and *serra*, the heirs of the traditional *gaúcho* employ their skills as tough horsemen on cattle *estancias* (ranches).

Old *estancia* Sobrado, a traditional ranch, Rio Grande do Sul

Clothing

Traditional gaúcho *attire remains commonplace among the rural population of the pampas and highlands of Southern Brazil. On special occasions, city dwellers also don* gaúcho *clothing, an outward sign of the distinctiveness of Rio Grande do Sul society.*

Gaúcho Dress is worn with immense pride. "Gaúcho pants" (*bombachas*), a linen shirt, kerchief, poncho, rimmed felt-hat, and pleated boots with fancy spurs are essential components of traditional *gaúcho* clothing.

A Silver Knife, delicately carved, is an important *gaúcho* tool, handy weapon, and eating implement.

Parade celebrating *gaúcho* culture in Argentina

Centro de Tradições Gaúchas

The worldwide Brazilian-*gaúcho* organization, Centro de Tradições Gaúchas, (Center for Gaúcho Traditions) was founded by eight Porto Alegre students in 1948, to preserve and promote *gaúcho* traditions. Today, it has more than 4,500 affiliate clubs that stage rodeos, *gaúcho* dances, parades, barbecues, and other social events. A *centro* can now be found wherever *gaúchos* live, both within Rio Grande do Sul and as far afield as Bolivia, Japan, and Portugal. The *centros* are perhaps the most convenient way for an outsider to observe *gaúcho* traditions, which are emerging as a part of popular culture even in non-*gaúcho* areas. Local tourist offices and hotels will be able to provide information on upcoming events.

Way of Life

The *gaúcho* way of life was originally a nomadic one, with the horsemen wandering the pampas, hunting wild cattle for their hides. Working as cattle hands today, *gaúchos* still cling to many of the traditions.

Rodeos, often lasting several days, test the skills of cattlemen, serve as social events for local townsfolk, and help break the isolation of rural inhabitants.

Cattle drives by *gaúchos* on horseback are common sights en route to Rio Grande do Sul's extensive grassland regions.

Dance & Music

Dance performances are integral to social gatherings. The music originates from a mixing of Portuguese, Spanish, Basque, African, German, and Italian cultures, with lyrics typically about local tales. Polkas and marches form the basis of traditional gaúcho *dance.*

A colorful kerchief is part of a *gaúcho's* typical dress.

Bombachas, or loose-fitting trousers belted with a *tirador* (sash), are traditionally worn by the *gaúchos*.

Accordion music first came to Southern Brazil with Portuguese colonists, but was transformed by exposure to other influences. The accordion and acoustic guitar are the most common folk instruments.

Food & Drink

Meat, especially beef, is central to the traditional gaúcho *diet. While the* gaúcho *grill is legendary, rice, usually cooked with* charque *(jerked beef), is also a staple. Pumpkin and other varieties of squash are often incorporated into stews.*

Chimarrão, a sugarless *chá mate* tea, is the characteristic and most popular drink of Rio Grande do Sul. The caffeinated herbal tea is sipped through a *bomba* (a silver straw) from a *cuia* (gourd). The same *cuia* is generally used by a group of *chimarrão* drinkers.

Churrasco, barbecued beef popular throughout Brazil, is cooked on metal or wood skewers rested on a support or stuck into the ground, and roasted over a charcoal or firewood flame.

SANTA CATARINA & PARANÁ

Brazil's southern states are a delight for nature lovers, with Paraná's spectacular Iguaçu Falls surrounded by lush rainforest and lovely beaches fringing the coast of tiny Santa Catarina. The region's long history of immigration from Europe has created a unique, multi-layered cultural identity.

During the 17th and 18th centuries, military garrisons were established all along the coast of Southern Brazil to guard against possible Spanish encroachment, and immigrants from the Portuguese mid-Atlantic islands of the Azores were brought in to establish farming and fishing settlements. Over time, these settlements grew into important towns, and Curitiba – on the trade route between Rio Grande do Sul and Minas Gerais – transformed into one of Brazil's most dynamic cities.

From 1840 to the mid-1900s, the interiors of Paraná and Santa Catarina were opened to immigration, with waves of European and other settlers staking out small farms. The newcomers settled along ethnic lines, with the Polish concentrated around Curitiba, Ukrainians in southern Paraná, Germans in Santa Catarina's Itajaí Valley, and Italians in the southern part of the state. The physical and cultural isolation of ethnic groups has resulted in distinct identities being maintained in rural areas to this day. The towns of Paranaguá, Antonina, and Morretes in Paraná, and Laguna, Florianópolis, and São Francisco do Sul in Santa Catarina also retain visible characteristics of their European origins.

The main destinations for visitors to Paraná are the Iguaçu Falls and the surrounding rainforest. The state's coast has escaped the excesses of development despite the natural beauty of Ilha do Mel, Guaraqueçaba, and Superaguï Island. Visitors to Santa Catarina make straight for the beaches of Florianópolis. The mountainous interior around São Joaquim and Lages is worth visiting for its spectacular scenery.

Turquoise waves hitting Florianópolis beach, Santa Catarina

◀ Catedral Metropolitana de Florianópolis, on the Ilha de Santa Catarina

Exploring Santa Catarina & Paraná

Although the uncontested highlights of this region are
Paraná's magnificent Iguaçu Falls and Santa Catarina's island
resort of Florianópolis, these two states have much more
to offer. Santa Catarina's 310-mile (500-km) coast features
sheltered coves and long expanses of beach, while in Paraná,
the Atlantic forest preserves of the Parque Nacional Ilha de
Superagüi encompass dense virgin forest. Ilha do Mel, at
the mouth of Paranaguá Bay, is a popular beach resort,
and just across the bay on the mainland is the scenic
port of Paranaguá. Inland, both states have a robust
agricultural industry. Vast soya farms dominate large
parts of Paraná, while small family holdings are
characteristic of Santa Catarina. Descendants of
European immigrants continue their traditions in
these states, such as the Austrians in Treze Tílias.

Sights at a Glance

Towns & Cities

❶ Curitiba
❸ Paranaguá
❼ *Florianópolis & Ilha de Santa
    Catarina pp350–51*

**National Parks, Islands & Areas
of Natural Beauty**

❷ *Serra da Graciosa p341*
❹ *Ilha do Mel*
❺ *Ilha de Superagüi*
❻ *Foz do Iguaçu pp344–7*

Façade of the Mercado Público in Florianópolis, Santa Catarina

For hotels and restaurants in this region see pp380–81 and p396

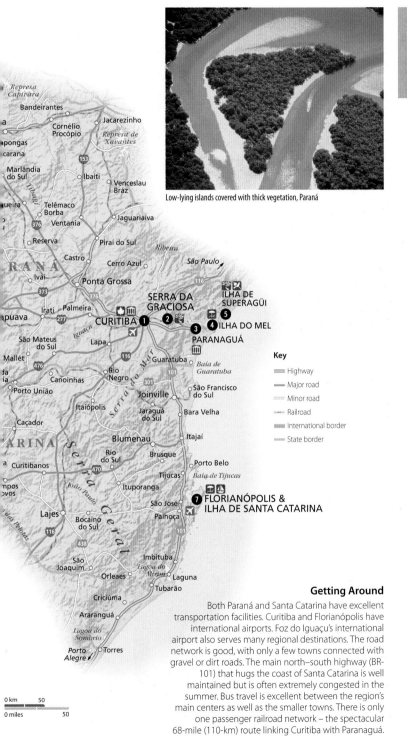

Low-lying islands covered with thick vegetation, Paraná

Key

═══ Highway

──── Major road

╌╌╌ Minor road

⤫⤫⤫ Railroad

▪▪▪ International border

▪▪▪ State border

Getting Around

Both Paraná and Santa Catarina have excellent transportation facilities. Curitiba and Florianópolis have international airports. Foz do Iguaçu's international airport also serves many regional destinations. The road network is good, with only a few towns connected with gravel or dirt roads. The main north–south highway (BR-101) that hugs the coast of Santa Catarina is well maintained but is often extremely congested in the summer. Bus travel is excellent between the region's main centers as well as the smaller towns. There is only one passenger railroad network – the spectacular 68-mile (110-km) route linking Curitiba with Paranaguá.

For keys to symbols *see back flap*

Colorful shops and restaurants around Praça Garibaldi

❶ Curitiba

Paraná. 🏛 1,730,000. ✈
🚉 from Paranaguá. ℹ️ Rua da Glória 362, (41) 3352 8000.
🌐 **viaje.curitiba.pr.gov.br**

Founded in 1693 as a gold-mining encampment, Curitiba developed to become the largest city in Southern Brazil. It emerged from being a minor administrative, commercial, and agro-processing center to grow into one of Brazil's most dynamic cities. Since the early 1990s, Curitiba has rivalled São Paulo as a location for corporate investment, in large measure attracted by the city's quality of life and public services, which are an example to the rest of the country.

The Largo da Ordem marks the heart of Curitiba's oldest quarter and features many well-preserved historic buildings. Dating from 1737, the Igreja da Ordem is the city's oldest church and the finest example of Portuguese ecclesiastical architecture in the state. The plain, whitewashed structure is decorated inside with typically Portuguese blue-and-white tiles and Baroque altars. Alongside the church is the **Museu de Arte Sacra** with its small but well-presented collection of relics gathered from churches in Curitiba. On the same side of the square is the **Igreja do Rosário**, originally serving Curitiba's slave population. First built in 1737, the church was completely reconstructed in the 1930s but retains its original Portuguese colonial style.

Across the square is the early 18th-century Casa Romário Martins, Curitiba's oldest surviving house and now a cultural center featuring exhibitions on the history of the city.

Up the hill from here, virtually adjoining the Largo da Ordem, are Garibaldi and João Cândido squares. The squares are surrounded by brightly painted late 19th- and early 20th-century houses, now used as art galleries, antique shops, and restaurants. The grandest building, however, is the Palácio São Francisco, built in 1929 and later serving as the state governor's official residence. Renovated and extended, the building now houses the **Museu Paranaense**,

its displays concentrating on Paraná's archaeology, anthropology, and history.

The city's commercial center extends along Rua XV de Novembro. Rua das Flores is the pedestrianized section lined with early 20th-century pastel-colored shops. This area's one truly distinctive building is the magnificent former city hall at Praça José Borges, just across from the flower market. Built in 1916, the French-style Art Nouveau structure was later used as the Museu Paranaense until the opening of the new site.

To celebrate the contributions of European immigrants to the city's development, parks have been built in their honor. The best example of these is the **Bosque Papa João Paulo II Memorial Polonês**, where log cabins built in the 1880s by Polish immigrants have been re-erected. The buildings – including a farmhouse, chapel, and barns, are set amid a small araucaria preserve, pine trees that originally dominated the landscape. Bordering the Bosque Papa João Paulo II and representing modern Curitiba is the **Museu Oscar Niemeyer**. Popularly referred to as "The Eye" after the construction's central feature, the building is considered one of Oscar Niemeyer's greatest architectural achievements.

Detail outside Museu Paranaense

🏛 **Bosque Papa João Paulo II Memorial Polonês**
Av Mateus Leme/ Rua Euclides Bandeira 1200 (Portal Polonês). **Tel** (41) 3313 7194. **Open** 9am–6pm Tue–Sun. ♿

🏛 **Museu de Arte Sacra**
Largo da Ordem s/n. **Tel** (41) 3321 3265. **Open** 9am–noon, 1–6pm Tue–Sun. ♿ 📷

🏛 **Museu Oscar Niemeyer**
Rua Marechal Hermes 999 (Centro Cívico). **Tel** (41) 3350 4400. **Open** 10am–6pm Tue–Sun. 📷 ♿

🏛 **Museu Paranaense**
Rua Kellers 289. **Tel** (41) 3304 3300. **Open** 9am–5pm Tue–Fri, 10am–4pm Sat & Sun. 📷 ♿

Façade of Igreja do Rosário on Largo do Ordem

For hotels and restaurants in this region see pp380–81 and p396

❷ Serra da Graciosa

The mountain range that separates Paraná state's coast from its interior is known as the Serra do Mar. Its southern extension, Serra da Graciosa, is one of the largest remaining areas of Mata Atlântica (Atlantic forest) in Southern Brazil. The Serra is rich in flora and fauna, ranging from lowland subtropical to cloud forest varieties. The road and railroad linking Morretes and Curitiba are amazing feats of 19th-century engineering, zigzagging through some of the most spectacular terrain in the country. The area is often shrouded with mist or fog, the result of cool air from the highlands colliding with the warm air of the subtropical coast. The forest thrives on such precipitation.

VISITORS' CHECKLIST

Practical Information
Paraná. 🛈 Largo Dr. José Pereira 43, Morretes, (41) 3352 8000.
🚉 in Morretes. Parque Estadual de Morumbi: **Tel** (41) 3462 3598.
Open 24 hours daily.
Litorina: **Tel** (41) 3888 3488; advance booking required.
🌐 serraverdeexpress.com.br

Transport
🚌 🚐 from Curitiba.

Parque Estadual de Marumbi
Usually shrouded with mist, trails with stunning vistas crisscross this vast expanse of Mata Atlântica.

The Estrada Graciosa
Completed in 1873, the Estrada Graciosa winds its way through the forbidding terrain of the Serra do Mar.

Serra do Mar, with its forest-covered mountain range, separates Paraná's coastal plain and highland plateau.

Morretes makes an excellent base to explore the surrounding region.

The Litorina
The remarkable Curitiba–Paranaguá railroad line passes through 13 tunnels and across 30 bridges. For much of the route, the line clings to a seemingly sheer mountainside from which, on clear days, there are wonderful views across untouched forest toward the coast.

Key
▬▬ Major road
═══ Minor road
— Railroad

0 km   10
0 miles   10

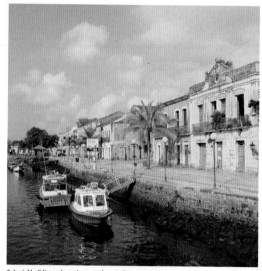
Colonial buildings along the waterfront in Paranaguá

❸ Paranaguá

Paraná. 🗻 142,000. 🚌 from Curitiba.
🚌 ℹ️ Rua Padre Albino 45, (41) 3420
2940. 🌐 **paranagua.pr.gov.br**

Founded in 1585, Paranaguá is
the oldest city in Paraná and is
one of Brazil's most important
ports today. Paranaguá's historic
center is small enough to
explore on foot. The oldest
buildings are located in the
compact historic core on the
shore of Paranaguá Bay. Most of
these dilapidated, but distin-
guished-looking, 19th-century
merchants' houses now serve as
shops or inexpensive hotels.
Also along the shore is the
former Colégio dos Jesuítas, an
imposing building that now
houses the **Museu de
Arqueologia e Etnologia**,
whose rich collection relates to
the region's indigenous inhabitants and popular culture.

Two churches in the historic
center are worth seeking out.
The **Igreja de Nossa Senhora
do Rosário**, built between
1575 and 1578, has suffered
considerable changes over
the centuries but the main
structure retains a Portuguese
colonial appearance. Built in
1784 for slaves, the **Igreja de
São Benedito** is an excellent
example of popular colonial
architecture. The simple,

whitewashed building has
undergone renovation and
contains a small collection
of sacred art.

🏛 Museu de Arqueologia
e Etnologia
Rua 15 de Novembro 575.
Tel (41) 3423 2511. **Open** 9am–noon,
1–6pm Tue–Fri, noon–6pm Sat, Sun &
public hols. 🛍

❹ Ilha do Mel

Paraná. 🗻 1,200. 🚢 from Paranaguá.
🌐 **ilhadomelonline.com.br**

The most beautiful of
Paraná's islands, Ilha do Mel
offers a combination of almost
entirely undeveloped beaches,
isolated coves, and sandy
trails. The island guards the
entrance to Paranaguá Bay and
there are well-preserved ruins
of the mid-18th-century fort,
**Fortaleza de Nossa Senhora
dos Prazeres**, that was
constructed to ward off English,
French, and Spanish attacks.
The **Farol das Conchas**
(Conchas Lighthouse),
imported from Glasgow and
placed on the island's most
easterly point in 1872, is the
best place for a stunning
panoramic view of the island,
bay, and mountains.

Tourist development is
low-key. Visitor numbers are
controlled, and there are no
roads or motor vehicles on the
island. Building work is also
strictly regulated. *Pousadas*
are all small and very simple,
but most are all the more
charming for this. The Ilha do
Mel attracts predominantly
young visitors and in the

Farol das Conchas lighthouse on the eastern tip of Ilha do Mel

A flock of migratory birds in the Parque Nacional de Superagüi, Ilha de Superagüi

summer it transforms into a party island, with beachside bars open through the night. In spite of this, there can be few more peaceful spots on the southern Brazilian coast than on this island. The beaches, some with waves suitable for skilled surfers, others with warm, calm water ideal for swimming, are never overcrowded. Some of the best beaches, such as **Praia Grande** and **Praia de Fora**, are located on the eastern part of the island.

❺ Ilha de Superagüi

Paraná. 🚌 from Paranaguá. 🛥 Pousada Superagui, (41) 3482 7149. 🌐 pousadasuperagui.com.br

Just a few dozen people who make a living from fishing and tourism inhabit the island of Superagüi. The island is part of the **Parque Nacional de Superagüi**, the largest stretch of intact Atlantic rainforest, or Mata Atlântica (see p113). The park is home to jaguars and parrots, and is known for its mangroves and salt marshes, where an amazing variety of orchids grow. The park is also part of the Atlantic forest reserves that were given UNESCO World Heritage listing in 1999. The island is reached by boat, most easily from Paranaguá, although arrangements can also be made

from Ilha do Mel. Most of the low-lying island is covered with shrub forest and mangrove. Very basic accommodation is available at **Barra de Superagüi**, a village located on the southeast of the island. The only other part of the island that is accessible to visitors is **Praia Deserta**, a glorious 24-mile-(38-km-) long expanse of white

sand. The island attracts various migrating birds, but the flocks of rare, red-faced parrot (*Amazona brasiliensis*) are endemic. Visitors can observe them during the early hours of the evening.

🏞 **Parque Nacional de Superagüi**
Barra de Superagüi. **Open** 24 hrs. 🏠 arranged at Pousada Superagüi.

Barreado, a regional specialty of Paraná

Barreado

In Paraná's coastal towns, *barreado* is listed on the menu of most restaurants. Now available throughout the year, *barreado*, considered a poor man's meal, used to be eaten during Carnaval. *Barreado* is a dish that can provide food for several days and requires little attention while cooking. The dish is made of beef, bacon, tomatoes, onion, cumin, and other spices. Traditionally these ingredients are placed in layers in a large clay urn, covered, and then sealed with a paste of ash and *farinha* (manioc flour), before being cooked in a wood-fired oven for up to 15 hours. Today, pressure cookers are sometimes used, and gas or electric ovens are substituted for wood-fired ones. *Barreado* is served with *farinha*, which is spread on a plate; the meat and gravy is placed on top, and the dish is eaten with banana and orange slices.

❻ Foz do Iguaçu

Iguaçu Falls rate as one of South America's great natural sights. The falls are formed by a succession of 275 interlinking cataracts up to 246 ft (75 m) in height cascading over a 1.8-mile- (3-km-) wide precipice. The falls owe their origins to several successive volcanic layers of rock built up over 110 million years. Shared between Brazil and Argentina, the falls are completely surrounded by nature preserves. The two preserves of Brazil's Parque Nacional do Iguaçu and Argentina's Parque Nacional Iguazú contain one of the largest surviving tracts of Atlantic forest in South America.

★ **Garganta do Diabo**
At the Garganta do Diabo (Devil's Throat), the river falls into the depths below with immense power, producing a thick cloud of misty spray.

Walkway
The walkway snaking along one tier of the falls is where visitors can peer into the depths of the magnificent, multiple cascading cataracts.

KEY

① **Estrada Velha de Guarapuava**

② **Porto Canoas Restaurant,** with its outdoor deck, has a wonderful view of the upper falls.

③ **Estación Cataratas** is the starting point of most of the trails. The station also has a rest area and a food court.

④ **The railroad track** runs through vast expanses of lush forest where wildlife and bird sightings are common.

⑤ **Pasarelas de la Isla San Martín**

0 meters   50
0 yards   50

★ **Hotel das Cataratas**
This majestic 1958 hotel *(see p381)* is the only one that lies in the Brazilian national park.

Tren Ecológico
Access to the trails leading to the falls in the Argentinian park is by a miniature train which runs on natural gas. The train stops at three stations along the way.

Isla San Martín Surroundings
Walkways lead up to views of seven cascading waterfalls, including the powerful Salto San Martín.

Powerboat Trips
The falls can be experienced from close up in hired powerboats that skim the rapids to the very foot of the falls.

★ Wildlife
The forests around Foz do Iguaçu host many rare wildlife species, including jaguar, ocelot, and harpy eagle.

The Argentina Falls

Although the Brazilian side is the best place for panoramic views of the falls, it is easier to get closer to both the main cataracts as well as a series of smaller ones from the network of trails on the Argentinian side. The Argentinian forest preserve is larger than the Brazilian one, with good walkable trails, requiring more time to explore. There is also a greater likelihood of being able to spot wildlife on the Argentinian side.

The Sheraton Internacional Iguazú, close to the falls

Exploring Iguaçu

The spectacular falls are located near the Brazilian city of Foz do Iguaçu and the sleepy Argentinian town of Puerto Iguazú. Thanks to excellent roads and tourist facilities, the huge numbers of visitors do little to detract from this majestic sight. Both sides are flanked by lush national parks, abundant with wildlife, and offering sweeping views of the falls, as well as options to go closer to the cascades by boat. The region of Iguaçu, meaning "Great Waters" in Tupi-Guaraní *(see p51)*, was declared a UNESCO World Heritage Site in 1986.

The ground-dwelling red-winged tinamou at Parque das Aves

Key

- ▬▬ Major road
- ══ Minor road
- ▪▬▪ International border
- ---- Park boundary

Medianeira

São Miguel do Iguaçu

BRAZIL

(277)

Santa Terezinha do Itaipu

Iguaçu

Foz do Iguaçu

PARAGUAY

Parque Nacional do Iguaçu

Parque das Aves

Puerto Iguazú

Parque Nacional Iguazú

Macuco Safari

Deseado

Tropical das Cataratas

ARGENTINA

0 km   15
0 miles   10

Foz do Iguaçu

400 miles (639 km) W of Curitiba. ✈ 🚌 🛈 Av das Cataratas, (45) 2105 8128. Itaipu Binacional: Av Tancredo Neves 6731. **Tel** (45) 3520 6999. **Open** 8am–4pm daily. 🅿 📷 mandatory. ♿ 🌐 **itaipu.gov.br**

Foz do Iguaçu, also referred to just as Foz, was a sleepy little border town until the 1970s, when construction work began on the nearby **Itaipu Binacional**, the world's largest hydroelectricity plant. Today, Foz is a base from which to visit the city's main attraction, the

spectacular waterfalls located to the east. Foz also boasts a wide range of accommodations, as well as reasonably good bars and restaurants.

🐦 Parque das Aves

Rodovia das Cataratas Km 17. **Tel** (45) 3529 8282. **Open** 8:30am–5:30pm daily. 🅿 ♿ 🌐 **parquedaves. com.br**

Located close to the main entrance to the **Parque Nacional do Iguaçu**, the Parque das Aves serves as an excellent introduction to Brazilian birdlife. The

park has large aviaries housing some 180 species of birds from different Brazilian ecosystems and include macaws, parrots, toucans, red-winged tinamous, and flamingos. Apart from a butterfly habitat and a reptile exhibit, the park also has a successful breeding program that concentrates on Brazilian endangered species.

🦋 Parque Nacional do Iguaçu

Tel (45) 3521 4400. **Open** 9am–5pm daily. 🅿 📷 ♿ 🌐 **cataratasdoiguacu.com.br**

Created in 1939, Brazil's first national park is today one of the most visited sights in the country. Public and tour buses leave visitors at the visitors' center near the park's entrance where they transfer onto electric-powered, open-topped buses for the falls, located 6 miles (10 km) into the park. The bus stops at the Estação Macuco Safari, where visitors can (for an additional charge) transfer onto a smaller electric-powered vehicle that takes them along a forest trail to the Rio Iguaçu. There, inflatable powerboats carry visitors across rapids toward the Garganta do Diabo (Devil's Throat) and to virtually the foot of the falls.

Along the way are various rest points from where there are spectacular panoramic views of the main series of falls. At the trail's lowest point there is a secure walkway that leads to a platform where one can peer into the stunning Garganta do Diabo, a deep gorge into which the fierce, cascading waters of the falls plummet.

Jungle Explorer trucks transporting visitors to the falls

Exploring the Argentinian Side

The Argentinian side of Iguaçu has a larger share of the waterfalls, and offers an intimate experience with a greater variety of perspectives. The quiet little town of Puerto Iguazú is a good place to make a base.

🗺 Parque Nacional Iguazú
Tel (54) 3757 491469.
Open 8am–6pm daily. 🎣 ⛵ ♿
🌐 iguazuargentina.com

Whereas the Brazilian park's great attractions are the spectacular panoramic views of the falls, the Argentinian park has an extensive network of forest and waterside trails, which offer visitors close-up views of the smaller falls. As well as the Passeio Garganta do Diablo, there are trails to the Passeio Inferiores and the Passeio Superiores.

From the park's excellent visitors' center, a miniature railroad takes visitors to the Estación Central where the Passeio Inferiores and Passeio Superiores circuits begin. From the Passeio Superiores, visitors can look down onto and across dozens of cataracts. This circuit has concrete catwalks going behind the falls, which used to lead to the Garganta do Diablo until the floods swept them away.

A rainbow arcs above the Rio Iguazú, Parque Nacional Iguazú, Argentina

The Passeio Inferiores is a short circuit offering even more spectacular views of the falls from below. This circuit takes a little over an hour and involves climbing up and down stairs. Especially remarkable are the parts of the trail across catwalks allowing amazing views over cascading water. At the lowest point, boats make the short crossing to the **Isla San Martín**, an island located in the heart of the falls. Walking on the island also requires a high level of fitness, as it involves clambering up steep slopes and across some jagged rock formations. The Passeio Garganta do Diablo catwalk begins at a quiet point upstream, passing several small islands before reaching its final, majestic destination.

Puerto Iguazú
6 miles (10 km) S of Foz do Iguaçu. 🚖
🚌 ℹ️ Av Victoria Aguirre 66, (37) 5742 0722. 🌐 iguazuturismo.gov.ar

Traveling between Foz and the Argentinian park by public transport involves changing buses in the Argentinian town of Puerto Iguazú. Although Puerto Iguazú boasts few sights, its quiet, tree-lined streets make for attractive wandering, with wooden, rather than concrete, buildings predominating.

A short walk along Puerto Iguazú's main artery, Avenida Victoria Aguirre, leads to the Hito Tres Fronteras (Triple Borders Landmark). From here there are superb views of the Rio Iguaçu and Rio Paraná rivers and across the rivers to Brazil and Paraguay.

Wildlife in the Iguaçu Region

The extent of native flora and fauna that the parks offer is varied. Over 2,000 species of flora have been identified, including ferns, bromeliads, orchids, and many large species of trees that serve as support for an equally large variety of climbing plants. In turn, this serves as a habitat for a similarly varied range of wildlife, lured by fruit, nesting spots, and dens. Although there are 450 varieties of bird amid this forested area, by far the most likely place to spot many of these is the Parque das Aves. With a practiced eye, birds can also be spotted within the forests and clearings of the national parks; the best time for bird-watching is early in the morning and at dusk when toucans, parrots, and hummingbirds abound. Some 80 kinds of mammals, with five varieties of feline, including jaguars and pumas, also rove the forest. Early morning and evening are the best time to see animals, with monkeys sometimes seen drinking from pools in the Argentinian park, or swinging overhead through the forest's canopy. The most commonly sighted mammal is the coati. One of the great joys of Iguaçu during the warm summer months is the immense quantity and variety of colorful butterflies that flutter about.

Capucin monkey, Parque Nacional Iguazú

Coati, one of the most commonly spotted mammals in the park

The bright colors of the historic downtown area of Curitiba, Paraná ▶

❼ Florianópolis & Ilha de Santa Catarina

Santa Catarina's capital, Florianópolis, is one of South America's hippest destinations. A gateway to the Ilha de Santa Catarina, the sprawling urban center of Florianópolis is also the transport hub for the rest of the island. The industrial zone occupies the mainland, while the colonial center sits across the bay on the island. The island's north shore has pretty beaches and warm, tranquil waters that are popular with families. The Atlantic rollers of the east coast have made the island one of the world's great surfing centers. In the daytime, Praia Mole and Praia Joaquina are crowded, while the bars of the town of Centro da Lagoa bustle until early morning.

Colorful fishing boats moored in the village of Riberão da Ilha

Canasvieras
During the summer (Dec–Feb), the warm water and safe swimming of the resort of Canasvieras especially attract families from São Paulo and Argentina.

Ingleses do Rio Vermelho

Praia dos Ingleses

Cachoeira do Bom Jesus

Praia Grande/Moçambique

Ponta das Canas

São João do Rio Vermelho

Praia de Canasvieras

Praia da Barra da Lagoa

Canasvieras

Vargem Grande

(403)

(406)

Praia de Jurerê

Rio Ratones

(402)

Praia de Daniela

(401)

Costa Lag

Forte de São José

Santo Antônio de Lisboa

Praia do Forte

Sambaqui

Cacupé

BAÍA NORTE

★ Santo Antônio de Lisboa
This charming little village, with the church as its focal point, is the best preserved of the island's 18th-century Azorean settlements. Fishing provides the community's basic livelihood.

KEY

① **Centro da Lagoa,** an important fishing center, is primarily known for its lively nightlife, stylish bars, and restaurants.

② **Campeche** is renowned for some of the finest beaches on the island.

③ **Ribeirão da Ilha** is mainly visited for its excellent seafood restaurants, the prime attraction being oysters, farmed just offshore.

FLORIANÓPO

Biguaçu (101)

(407)

Angelina

★ Florianópolis
The attractions of Florianópolis include Mercado Público, which features upbeat bars, as well as some 150 stands with fruits, vegetables, seafood, and handicrafts.

For hotels and restaurants in this region see pp380–81 and p396

Barra da Lagoa
This pleasant fishing village and beach sits at the mouth of the Rio Barra. Lined with a choice of accommodations and restaurants, it is particularly lively in the summer season (Dec–Feb). The clear river water is perfect for swimming.

★ Praia Mole
Surfers and hang-gliding enthusiasts favor the laid-back Praia Mole to showcase their talents. A number of pleasant beach bars and eateries line the relaxed beach.

Praia Joaquina
Brazil's famous surfing center is backed by huge dunes. The cold water and the rough sea make it fit only for the strongest of swimmers.

Key

— Major road

--- Minor road

0 km   5
0 miles   3

RIO GRANDE DO SUL

The vast rolling pampas, rugged landscape, and fertile valleys of the Serra Gaúcha range are the dominant physical features of Rio Grande do Sul. A distinctive regional identity emerged with the semi-nomadic *gaúcho*, whose culture is still most apparent here. Although arable farming is important, the area is dominated by large, sprawling cattle *estancias* or ranches.

In 1494, even before Brazil was officially "discovered," the Treaty of Tordesillas divided South America between Portugal and Spain. An imaginary line was drawn through the continent with land to its west awarded to Spain and that to its east to Portugal. Although Brazil was Portuguese, the area that is now Rio Grande do Sul was Spanish. Neither power, however, controlled this frontier region.

Even after Brazil's independence in 1822, only a few military garrisons and small coastal settlements existed here until the mid-1800s. Apart from its obvious strategic significance, the economic potential of this sparsely populated province was gradually being recognized. Until the mid-19th century, indigenous Guaraní people and *gaúchos* inhabited the pampas, largely the preserve of wild cattle.

The forested highlands had an even smaller population. European immigrants settled here on small farms in the mid-18th century. These agricultural, wine-producing colonies grew rapidly and soon transformed the Serra's landscape and economy. By the early 19th century, Rio Grande do Sul had become synonymous with beef. The *charque* (dried beef) industry developed around the southern town of Pelotas. The introduction of railroads and refrigeration gave a further boost to the industry.

Beautiful mountain resorts and extraordinary hiking can be found around the canyons of Parque Nacional dos Aparados da Serra. Both *gaúcho* and European influences have instilled a distinct cultural identity in this state, offering a unique Brazilian experience.

Pastoral scene of cows grazing in Rio Grande do Sul

◄ A tourist steam train readying for departure in Caxias do Sul

Exploring Rio Grande Do Sul

The pampas that characterize the interior of southern and western Rio Grande do Sul are the state's economic heartlands. Porto Alegre, the state's capital, is a bustling city which is culturally rich and ethnically diverse. The windswept coast is for the most part unrelentingly bleak, and is fringed by lagoons and sandbars, making it one of the world's longest beaches. The araucaria pine forests, immense canyons, and terraced vineyards of Bento Gonçalves and Flores da Cunha in the northeast make perfect backdrops for charming country hotels, wineries, and mountain resorts. In the far west, the ruins of São Miguel das Missões are a haunting reminder of the Jesuit legacy in Brazil.

Key
Area illustrated

Sights at a Glance

Towns & Cities

1 *Porto Alegre pp356–7*
2 Nova Petrópolis
3 Gramado
4 Canela
6 Bento Gonçalves
7 Caxias do Sul
8 Flores da Cunha
9 Antônio Prado

National Parks & Beach Resorts

10 Parque Nacional dos Aparados da Serra
11 Torres

Churches

12 *São Miguel das Missões p363*

Tour

5 *Vale dos Vinhedos p359*

Forested hill, Parque Nacional dos Aparados da Serra

For hotels and restaurants in this region see p381 and p397

Freshwater fishing bird on the coast of Rio Grande do Sul

Key

═══ Highway
─── Major road
═══ Minor road
──── Railroad
═══ State border

Getting Around

Porto Alegre, the state's capital, has an airport which serves the capital cities of neighboring countries and major Brazilian cities. Excellent roads and good bus services connect all parts of Rio Grande do Sul with Porto Alegre. Well-surfaced highways even connect most of the smallest towns and villages. It is essential to have a hire car, or to make advance arrangements to be met by a guide in the nearest town, if an *estancia* (ranch) stay has been organized. The Serra range is about two hours from Porto Alegre, and the most direct route is the congested BR-116 highway.

For keys to symbols *see back flap*

● Porto Alegre

Founded in 1755 on the right bank of the Rio Guaíba, Porto Alegre served as a Portuguese military garrison that guarded against Spanish encroachment into southern Brazil. Today, it is Rio Grande do Sul's capital and an important trading port. The city has some impressive public buildings and a lively street life. Most sights are located in the Cidade Baixa (Lower Town) and Cidade Alta (Upper Town) areas of downtown, while the best restaurants, bars, and hotels are mainly concentrated in the suburbs.

🏛 Mercado Público

Praça XV de Novembro.
Open 6am–6pm Mon–Sat. ♿

Dating back to 1869, the Neo-Classical-influenced Mercado Público has a vast collection of stalls selling household goods, fruit, vegetables, herbs, wine, meat, and fish. Characteristic of the region are the herb stalls selling *chá mate* (herbal tea) as well as *bombas* and *cuias* (silver straws and drinking gourds). Also of interest are the stalls devoted to African-Brazilian religious rituals, a reminder of the importance of those traditions in a part of the country associated primarily with European culture.

Façade of the Mercado Público, an excellent market for regional items

🏛 Praça da Matriz

Catedral Metropolitana: **Tel** (51) 3225 4980. **Open** 9:30am–6:15pm Mon–Fri, 9am–4:30pm Sat. ♿ Museu Júlio de Castilhos: **Tel** (51) 3221 3959. **Open** 10am–6pm Tue–Sat. Palácio Piratini: **Tel** (51) 3210 4100. **Open** 9:30–11am, 2–5pm Mon–Fri. 📷 ♿ Teatro São Pedro: **Tel** (51) 3227 5100. **Open** noon–6pm Tue–Fri, 4–6pm Sat & Sun. 📷

Designed by the renowned Italian architect Giovanni Giovenale, the 1772 **Catedral Metropolitana** features graceful classical columns, geometrically perfect designs, and a large hemispherical dome. The present structure dates from 1921. There are a number of fine 19th- and early 20th-century buildings around Praça da Matriz.

Just off the square is the **Museu Júlio de Castilhos**, with an interesting collection of artifacts relating to the region's history. The imposing **Palácio Piratini**, just west of the cathedral, serves as the governor's residence. It was built in 1909 in a fascinating mix of Neo-Classical, Baroque, and Rococo styles. To the square's north, the grand Neo-Classical **Teatro São Pedro** is the city's

Porto Alegre City Center

① Mercado Público
② Catedral Metropolitana
③ Museu Júlio de Castilhos
④ Palácio Piratini
⑤ Teatro São Pedro
⑥ Museu de Arte do Rio Grande do Sul
⑦ Santander Cultural
⑧ Memorial do Rio Grande do Sul
⑨ Casa de Cultura Mário Quintana
⑩ Usina do Gasômetro

Ornate foyer of the Neo-Classical Teatro São Pedro

prestigious concert and theater hall. Built in 1858, it is a popular venue for lunch and tea.

🏛 Museu de Arte do Rio Grande do Sul

Praça da Alfândega. **Tel** (51) 3227 2311. **Open** 10am–7pm Tue–Sun.
🚻 🏛 💻 **w** margs.rs.gov.br

Late 20th-century works by local artists are prominently displayed in this museum. More absorbing, however, is the small section devoted to 19th-century art. The museum also hosts a number of interesting traveling exhibitions.

🏛 Santander Cultural

Rua 7 de Setembro 1028. **Tel** (51) 3287 5500. **Open** 10am–7pm Mon–Fri, 11am–7pm Sat & Sun. 🚻

This vibrant arts complex has an impressive repertoire featuring art, music, and cinema. The Neo-Classical building originally served as a bank between 1927 and 1932. Despite extensive renovations, it retains many of its original features including stained-glass windows.

Works on display at the Museu de Arte do Rio Grande do Sul

🏛 Memorial do Rio Grande do Sul

Praça da Alfândega. **Tel** (51) 3224 7210. **Open** 10am–6pm Tue–Sat, 1–5pm Sun. 🚻
w memorial.rs.gov.br

The memorial features exhibits relating to the state's social and political history. It also houses the state archives and an oral history center.

🏛 Casa de Cultura Mário Quintana

Rua dos Andrades 736. **Tel** (51) 3221 7147. **Open** 2–9pm Mon, 9am–9pm Tue–Fri, noon–9pm Sat & Sun. 🚻
w ccmq.rs.gov.br

This Neo-Classical building was designed as a hotel in 1923 by German architect Theo Wiederspahn. For many years, it was also the home of Mário Quintana, one of the state's foremost poets. Today, it hosts exhibitions relating to modern art and literature.

🏛 Usina do Gasômetro

Av Presidente João Goulart 551. **Tel** (51) 3289 8112. **Open** 9am–9pm Tue–Sun.

Built in 1928 as a thermo-electrical power station, the Usina opened in 1991 as a cultural center hosting theater and art exhibitions. It also houses a wine museum and an art-house cinema. The west-facing terrace offers spectacular views of the sunset over the river. There are daily boat trips from the adjacent pier.

The picturesque Parque Aldeia do Imigrante, Nova Petrópolis

❼ Nova Petrópolis

66 miles (106 km) N of Porto Alegre.
🏠 18,700. 🚌 ℹ️ Av XV de Novembro, (54) 3281 1398. 🎭 Festa do Folklore (Aug), Frühlingsfest (Oct).
w novapetropolis.rs.gov.br

German immigrants arriving in the 1820s were the first to settle in the rolling hills north of Porto Alegre. The town of Nova Petrópolis, founded in 1858, remained relatively isolated until the mid-20th century and retains a strong German character even today.

Stretching along Avenida 15 de Novembro, the town's commercial center features a number of German-style buildings. Midway along the avenue is the interesting **Parque Aldeia do Imigrante**, which pays tribute to the region's early settlers. Set within an araucaria forest, the park houses a collection of beautifully reconstructed, half-timbered buildings dating between 1870 and 1910. The Lutheran church, houses, school, smithy, and cemetery help re-create the atmosphere of a 19th-century German hamlet. The park also hosts festivals and concerts and features a large bandstand and beer hall.

The hamlets and farmsteads surrounding Nova Petrópolis also have a distinctly German flavor. Here, German is still the dominant language and old-world traditions, such as music and dance, thrive.

🏛 **Parque Aldeia do Imigrante**
Av 15 de Novembro 1966. **Tel** (54) 3281 1254. **Open** 8am–5:30pm daily.
📷 🚻

Swiss-style chalet, a common sight in Gramado

❸ Gramado

🏔 32,000. 🚌 from Porto Alegre.
ℹ️ Av Borges de Medeiros 1647, (54)
3286 1475. 🎬 Festival de Gramado
(Aug), Natal Luz (Nov 3–Jan 15).
🌐 **gramadosite.com**

Brazil's best-known mountain
resort, Gramado does all it can
to mimic a central European
village. Although there are
no Alpine peaks, the hilly
landscape, reaching just 2,706 ft
(825 m) around Gramado, is
quite dramatic and the views
are fantastic. The flower-filled
Parque Knorr and the **Lago
Negro**, an artificial lake
bordered by pine trees
imported from Germany's Black
Forest, allow for pleasant strolls.

"Swiss chalet" is the dominant
architectural style and, with the
profusion of geranium-filled
window boxes, chocolate shops,
and restaurants specializing in
cheese fondues, one is
encouraged to believe that
Gramado has connections with
Switzerland. This is entirely an
affectation as only a very tiny
minority of the population is of
Swiss origin and, beneath its
veneer, Gramado has more in
common with an American
shopping mall.

Gramado survives almost
entirely on tourism. During
the first two weeks in August,
the city hosts the Festival de
Gramado, one of Brazil's most
prestigious film festivals,
which also attracts an international crowd.

Environs

Just 4 miles (6 km) north from
Gramado's main avenue is the
Vale do Quilombo. Approached
by a steep dirt road, much of
the valley's original dense Mata
Atlântica (Atlantic rainforest)
remains and the climate is
warmer and more humid.
The **Ecoparque Sperry** supports
an abundance of fauna
including coati, toucans, and
howler and capuchin monkeys.
Forest trails pass magnificent
waterfalls that enhance the
valley's scenic splendor.

The valley floor is cultivated
and picturesque. Half-timbered
farm buildings, which were built
by German immigrants in the
19th century, are to be seen
alongside the road.

🌳 Ecoparque Sperry
Vale do Quilombo. **Tel** (54) 9629
8765. **Open** 9am–5pm Tue–Sun.
🅿️ 🚻 ♿

❹ Canela

🏔 38,000. 🚌 from Porto Alegre.
ℹ️ Central de Informações, Lago da
Fama 227, (54) 3282 2200.
🌐 **canelaturismo.com.br**

Chilly winters, refreshing
summers, and unspoilt nature
attract visitors to Canela, once a
stop-off point for cattle being
herded across Rio Grande do
Sul's grasslands. The town is
dominated by the Igreja Matriz
Nossa Senhora de Lourdes, an
imposing stone church built in

1953 in English Neo-Gothic
style, with other buildings in
an eclectic mix of local and
European styles. Thanks to the
presence of students attracted
to highly regarded tourism
colleges, the town has a vibrant
feel to it.

Environs

Most of the forests of the Serra
were devastated in the 19th
century in the quest for
araucaria pine. Today, some
of this forested area is being
preserved. Approximately
5 miles (8 km) north of Canela is
the **Parque do Caracol**, a forest
reserve with a 429-ft (131-m)
waterfall. A highlight here is the
927-step stairway leading to the
base of the cascade from where
visitors can best appreciate its
force and the surrounding
forests. A farther 3 miles (5 km)
north along the road from
Caracol is the **Parque da
Ferradura**, a forest reserve
notable for the dramatic views
of the horseshoe-shaped Rio Caí
and of the Arroio Caçador
canyon and waterfall.

The area is a popular
destination for adventure
tourism, with rafting along the
fast-flowing Rio Paranhana.
Rappeling down its gorge
allows for close-up views of
the terrain.

🌳 Parque da Ferradura
Estrada do Caracol. **Tel** (54) 9962 5927.
Open 9am–5:30pm daily. ♿

🌳 Parque do Caracol
Estrada do Caracol. **Tel** (54) 3278 3035.
Open 8:45am–5:45pm daily. ♿

Majestic waterfall, Parque do Caracol,
near Canela

For hotels and restaurants in this region see p381 and p397

❺ Tour of Vale dos Vinhedos

Some of the best wine in Brazil is produced in Vale dos Vinhedos. The majority of inhabitants here are descendants of immigrants from Veneto, Italy, and life in the Vale dos Vinhedos follows a pattern very similar to that in the corner of northeast Italy. In an area of virtual monoculture, grape is central to the year's activity, while the Catholic chapels are cornerstones for the maintenance of Italian traditions.

Picturesque vineyard in the Vale dos Vinhedos

⑥ Casa Valduga
Comfortable guest rooms and excellent food is offered by this pioneer of the production of high-quality Brazilian wines and agritourism.

⑦ Capela das Neves
Built in 1907, this is the earliest surviving chapel in Vale dos Vinhedos.

⑤ Vinícola Pizzato
Still small-scale producers, the Pizzato family offers tastings and sell an extensive range of wines.

Veranópolis [470]

Monte Belo do Sul

Santa Teresa

Bento Gonçalves

[470]

[444]

0 km   1

0 miles   1

Caxias do Sul
Porto Alegre ↓

④ Famiglia Tasca
These typical stone and wood farm buildings are among the oldest wineries in the valley.

② Memorial do Vinho
This small, fascinating exhibition charts the development of the local wine production from 1875 to present.

① Capela das Graças
Honoring Our Lady of Grace, this *capela* is one of the many Catholic chapels that are central to the valley's Italian immigrants.

Key

━━ Tour route

══ Other road

Tips for Drivers

Starting point: Bento Gonçalves (*see p360*).

Length: Allow a full day to visit several wineries and a stop for lunch.

Driving conditions: The main road is paved while the side roads have good-quality gravel surfaces.

③ Vinícola Miolo
The largest vineyard in the valley, Vinícola Miolo produces some of Brazil's best wine. The visitors' center tells the story of Miolo's development and allows tastings.

Vinhos Salton, one of the many wineries in Bento Gonçalves

⑥ Bento Gonçalves

🏔 100,000. 🚌 ℹ️ Rua Mal Deodoro 70, (54) 3454 3169. 🌐 **turismobento. com.br**

Examine a bottle of Brazilian wine and, in all likelihood, the label will indicate Bento Gonçalves as its place of origin. Bento, as the city is usually called, is one of the largest producers of wine in Brazil, with virtually every patch of land outside the city growing vines. The city's economy relies solely on grapes and wine production, as a result of which Bento's vintners dominate the Brazilian market.

Wine produced in Bento Gonçalves

Bento was one of the earliest Italian communities established in the Serra Gaúcha in 1875. However, the rapid growth of the city's urban center in recent decades has left few traces of Italian influence during the early years of immigration. The **Museu do Imigrante** has a rich collection of artifacts relating to Bento's pioneer settlers, with rooms focusing on the arrival of the immigrants and the central role of the Catholic church in the community and farming, in particular viticulture.

Wine is still produced in town by large commercial operations. The **Cooperativa Vinícola Aurora** is the best known, and Aurora is the most prominent wine producer in Brazil, with a membership of some 1,300 families, most of whom farm in the valley.

Visitors to the cooperative are shown the entire production process from the crushing of grapes to bottling. Tours culminate with tastings. There are also numerous *cantinas* (wine cellars) dotting the town center which also offer free tours and tastings.

Smaller producers also produce fine wines. These are located just a short distance from downtown Bento, and indeed vines extend right up to the city limits and through the beautiful Vale dos Vinhedos, the Valley of Vineyards (see p359).

Cooperativa Vinícola Aurora
Rua Olavo Bilac 500, Cidade Alta.
Tel (54) 3455 2000.
Open 8:15am–5:15pm Mon–Sat, 8:30–11:30am Sun. 🔲 🚻

🏛 **Museu do Imigrante**
Rua Erny Hugo Dreher 127, (Planalto).
Tel (54) 3451 1773. **Open** 8–11:15am, 1:30–5:15pm Tue–Fri, 1–5pm Sat, 9am–noon Sun. 📷

Environs
Garibaldi, a small town just 12 miles (20 km) south of Bento Gonçalves, is known for its surprisingly good champagne-style sparkling wines. Part of the attraction of getting to this little town is the ride on the steam engine known as Maria Fumaça, or "Smoking Mary," a name commonly given to tourist steam trains (see p424).

Passing through the landscape's patchwork of vineyards, the 15-mile (23-km) route is covered in an hour and a half. The high point of the journey is the stop at an observatory overlooking the Rio das Antas at the point where the route curves in a horseshoe shape.

⑦ Caxias do Sul

🏔 395,000. ✈️ 🚌 ℹ️ Praça Dante Alighieri, (54) 3202 2255.

Founded in 1875, Caxias do Sul – or simply Caxias, as it is usually called – along with Bento Gonçalves, was one of the earliest Italian *colonias* to be established in the Serra. Like its neighboring settlements, commercial activity at first revolved entirely around wine production, but over the next century other agro-processing industries, as well as textiles and metalworking, developed. Today, Caxias is Rio Grande do Sul's second-largest city after Porto Alegre.

Although tower blocks and other concrete buildings have overtaken much of Caxias, some

Maria Fumaça, plying between Bento Gonçalves and Garibaldi

Artifacts displayed in Museu Casa de Pedra in Caxias do Sul

visible traces of the city's heritage survive. The **Museu Municipal**, built in 1880 as a private residence, documents the history of Caxias, starting with the arrival of the first immigrants from Veneto. The museum's permanent collection includes objects, documents, and photographs charting the development of the city.

The **Museu Casa de Pedra**, housed in a carefully preserved stone farmhouse built in 1878, sheds light on the lives of the pioneer settlers with interesting displays of tools, furniture, and photographs.

Museu Casa de Pedra
Rua Matteo Gianella 531, Bairro Santa Catarina. **Tel** (54) 3221 2423.
Open 9am–5pm Tue–Sun.

Museu Municipal
Rua Visconde de Pelotas, 586.
Tel (54) 3221 2423. **Open** 9am–5pm Tue–Sun.

❽ Flores da Cunha

27,000. from Caxias do Sul.
floresdacunha.com.br

The fact that Flores da Cunha boasts one of the highest concentrations of wineries in Rio Grande do Sul will come as little surprise to visitors. Just about every available patch of land in the municipality is given to grape vines and *cantinas*, ranging from small artisan wine producers to huge cooperatives.

The town of Flores da Cunha itself is unremarkable, but the surrounding villages and hamlets could easily be mistaken for simple northern Italian farming communities, even maintaining the Venetian dialect of their immigrant forbears, making it the most Italian of Brazilian towns.

Environs
Located in a fertile and picturesque valley, **Otávio Rocha**, 8 miles (13 km) southwest of Flores da Cunha, is especially striking, with vines extending down to the main streets. The village has become a popular place to eat and there is a good choice of restaurants specializing in simple, but tasty, northern Italian country fare.

Another 4 miles (7 km) west of Otávio Rocha is **Nova Pádua**, another wine-producing *município*, whose inhabitants are descended from Venetian immigrants. The village's focal point is the church, characteristically Italian in style with a bell tower set slightly to the side of the main structure. A short distance farther west, there are breathtaking views below onto the fast-flowing Rio das Antas and a landscape of the Antas Valley, a mix of vineyards and primary forest.

❾ Antônio Prado

14,000. Rua Luiza Bocchese 68, (54) 3293 1500. **antonioprado. com.br**

The last of the major settlements, Antônio Prado was established in the Italian colonial zone in 1886. Located in the zone's northern extreme and, until fairly recently, with poor links to other centers, Antônio Prado failed to make the transition from farming community to industrial town.

The lack of development is one of the reasons why the town was declared a National Heritage Site in 1989. Its particular attraction is its concentration of wooden, stone-base buildings erected by Italian immigrants.

Clustered around the town's central square, **Praça Garibaldi**, and the roads that extend immediately off it, some 48 historic buildings are protected and perfectly maintained. Most of the brightly painted clapboard structures with their unchanged interiors have been turned into shops or small government offices.

One of these buildings is now the town hall on Praça Garibaldi. Also located on Praça Garibaldi, the **Museu de Antônio Prado** offers a useful historical overview of the development of the town.

Museu de Antônio Prado
Rua Francisco Marcantônio 77.
Tel (54) 3293 1277. **Open** 8:30–11:45am Tue–Fri, 1:30–5pm Sat & Sun.

Colorful stone-base wooden houses in Antônio Prado

Araucaria pine trees above the Cânion do Itaimbezinho, Aparados da Serra

❿ Parque Nacional dos Aparados da Serra

🚌 from Canela to Cambará do Sul, then taxi. ℹ️ Rua Pres Getúlio Vargas 978, (54) 3251 1262. **Open** 9am–6pm Wed–Sun. ♿

The highland plateau of Southern Brazil emerged from the accumulation of layer upon layer of ocean sediment, with the resulting rock formations lifted up to form the Brazilian Shield. Some 150 million years ago, lava poured onto the shield to create a thick layer of basalt rock. Cracks emerged at the edge of the plateau, taking the form of narrow, but deep, canyons. It is around one of the largest of these canyons – **Canion do Itaimbezinho** – that the Parque Nacional dos Aparados da Serra, one of Brazil's first national parks, was created in 1959.

Canion do Itaimbezinho is a 2,360-ft- (720-m-) deep, 4-mile- (6-km-) long canyon featuring several ecosystems merging into one another with transition zones between them. The plateau around Itaimbezinho is mainly given over to cattle pasture, while dense Mata Atlântica (see p113) covers Itaimbezinho's lower reaches. The abundant flora ranges from lichens and mosses to orchids and other flowering plants and giant araucaria pines. Trails around the edge of the canyon are well marked, varying in length between 1 mile (2 km) and 4 miles (6 km), with

observatories offering views of the canyon. The longest trail, Trilha do Rio do Boi, can be challenging for unseasoned hikers. It is closed in the rainy season due to the danger of flooding.

The best season to visit the park is in winter (May to August), when visibility stretches to the base of the canyon and toward the coast. September is the worst time to come here, with low cloud and heavy rainfall. During the rest of the year, fog often obscures views, though it can lift very quickly.

⓫ Torres

🏙️ 34,000. 🚌 from Porto Alegre. ℹ️ Rua José A. Picoral 171, Centro, (51) 3626 3226. 🌐 **torres.rs.gov.br**

The main highlight of the long coastline of Rio Grande do Sul is Torres, located near the

border with the neighboring state of Santa Catarina. Torres is named for a series of huge basalt rocks, or "towers," that jut into the ocean and break the otherwise seemingly unending beach. The towers are located in the **Parque da Guarita**, on the southern perimeter of town. Between the sea-cliff towers are sandy coves offering protection from fierce Atlantic rollers. Stairs lead to caves on the cliffs facing the open sea, which were formed over the course of millions of years by the force of the ocean. From a hill at the southern edge of the park, visitors can enjoy tremendous views of the beautifully rugged coastline or trek through the dunes of 2-mile- (4-km-) long Praia de Itapeva. The water at Itapeva is tranquil and favorable for swimming.

Waves lapping against the cliffs, Parque da Guarita

The Rise and Collapse of Jesuit Missions

Santa Cecilia, wood sculpture

For much of the 17th and 18th centuries, the Guaraní Indians of what is now northwestern Rio Grande do Sul, as well as parts of Argentina and Paraguay, were controlled by the Jesuits. The first *redução* (community) was established in 1610; 30 others followed, including Brazil's São Miguel, which was founded in 1632. Over time, Guaraní-influenced Baroque music, architecture, painting, and sculpture began to flourish. The Spanish and Portuguese authorities became increasingly concerned about the power of the Jesuits, while Rome was worried that the order was too independent of papal authority. In 1756, Spanish and Portuguese forces expelled the Jesuits. The missions were razed to the ground or abandoned to nature.

⓬ São Miguel das Missões

Surviving through centuries of neglect, the São Miguel Mission presents a fine example of the Guaraní-Baroque style, a blend of Iberian and indigenous architectural elements. These influences are visible in architectural details, particularly in the carved stonework and in the wooden sculptures housed in the museum. The mission was designated a UNESCO World Heritage Site in 1984. Although the area around São Miguel has been given over to farmland, the mission retains an air of isolation.

VISITORS' CHECKLIST

Practical Information
São Miguel. 🛈 (55) 3381 1294.
🚏 🎭 Semana Farroupilha (Sep).
🆆 rotamissoes.com.br
Museu das Missões: Rua São Nicolau s/n. **Open** 9am–noon, 2–6pm daily (winter); 9am–noon, 2–8pm daily (summer). 🚻 💻
🏠 Sound & Light Show: 7pm (winter), 9pm (summer) daily. 📷

Transport
🚌 from Porto Alegre to Santo, then bus.

The Bell
The mission's bell was not only rung as a call to prayers, but also to warn of attacks by roving gangs hunting for slaves.

Inner Corridors
A network of corridors gives a sense of the extent of the original mission site, which at its height housed 4,000 people.

The façade is a replica of Il Gesù, the Jesuits' mother church in Rome. Only one of the two original towers remains intact.

Brick and stonework, made from local materials, was mainly used in the mission's construction.

Entrance

Museu das Missões
Designed in 1937 by Lúcio Costa, this early Modernist building was inspired by Jesuit-Baroque architecture. The museum houses statues and other relics excavated locally.

Ruins of Jesuit Buildings
Little remains of the workshops, school rooms, cloisters, and living quarters of the Jesuit mission. However, it is still possible to make out their distinct areas in the ruins.

TRAVELERS' NEEDS

WHERE TO STAY

Given the size and diversity of Brazil, it is no surprise that the country offers an excellent selection of accommodations to suit every taste and pocket. Large cities have a wide range of business hotels that comprise everything from budget brands and deluxe international properties such as Grand Hyatt, Sofitel, and Belmond (the latter formerly known as Orient-Express), to privately owned, cutting-edge boutique hotels such as the Fasano and Unique in São Paulo.

In tourist areas, the options include large, fancy, all-inclusive, internationally known resort properties, as well as Brazilian-owned chain and individual hotels. There are also small, privately owned establishments, or *pousadas*, that may only have two or three rooms and are either very simple and basic or very sophisticated and, depending on size, border on being boutique hotels. There has also been a growth in good-quality hostels.

Booking

Brazil is one of the most active Internet countries in the world, and the majority of hotels, *pousadas*, and lodges have their own websites through which it is possible to make reservations and look at facilities in more detail. Many larger properties also appear on international booking engines and travel sites such as **Expedia** and **Last Minute**. In places where there is an English-speaking staff, it is also possible to make telephone and email reservations.

In the age of the Internet, it is important for the traveler to check how financially protected they are if they do book directly and the property they choose goes out of business. Under European regulations, any company based in the EU that sells a "package" (a combination of flight, hotels, car rental, among other things) must be bonded through an approved body that will protect the client's financial security; this will probably not be the case if the traveler books direct.

During the high season, and especially during Carnaval and the Christmas-to-New Year period, many hotels and *pousadas* in Brazil will expect guests to stay for a minimum number of nights. This will need to be taken into consideration, since one- or two-night stays may be difficult to find if you want to move around. Book in advance during high season, as good rooms are not easy to come by last minute. Weekends can also get quite crowded. In all cases, prices will be higher in the high season or at the weekend in leisure locations.

Prices & Payments

Just as travelers want financial security, so do hotel and *pousada* owners. A deposit will certainly be required, whereas many smaller properties may require payment in advance to cover the entire duration of the stay, especially in high season or for weekend specials.

It is also normal for hotels in Brazil to ask the client to send a photocopy of the credit card used to make the reservation. The reason for this is due to the increasing number of travelers who change their travel plans and then try to deny they ever made the reservation. A copy of the credit card – if not reported stolen – does tend to prove that the person did make the reservation. Credit cards are accepted as payment at most properties, especially in bigger cities.

Only the larger hotels in bigger cities will handle traveler's checks. Checks drawn on Brazilian banks are generally acceptable, as is cash. Many places accept payment in US dollars, but they will set

A swanky new Serhs Natal Grand Hotel on Via Costeira, Natal

◀ Street cafés in the World Heritage Site of Paraty, Rio de Janeiro

Plush lobby of Hotel Bourbon Curitiba, one of Curitiba's premium hotels

the exchange rate, which will often be high.

When booking, it is important to check what taxes are included in the price. These may include a 10 percent service tax, a 5 per-cent sales tax, and, in some areas of Brazil, a nightly tourist tax.

Prices throughout Brazil vary greatly, and it is rare that any traveler should ever need to pay the rack rate as advertised by the hotels. Like airlines, hotels often make special offers available even through their own websites. Some hotels – normally smaller, privately owned properties – still think they can charge different prices for Brazilian travelers and foreign visitors, so it is worth checking the rates on the Portuguese-language version of the website. Prices also vary due to exchange rates.

In Brazil, the price often reflects not only the quality of accommodation, but also the location. A traveler on a budget needs to decide if the priority is a beachfront location or a better-quality hotel a couple of blocks back from the beach. There will also be notably different rates for rooms at the front of a beachfront property and those at the side or behind.

Tipping

It is customary and much appreciated for guests to leave a tip for the staff who have served them well during their stay. This could be the chamber-maid, the bellboy, or bar staff. Many of the people who serve visitors will be earning the minimum wage of around US$300 per month, so any tips can make a real difference.

Children

Many Brazilian families travel with their nanny in tow and are quite happy taking their children with them wherever they go. Children are always welcome at most hotels, with only a very few smaller, normally romantic *pousadas* having any restrictions, which will be clearly stated on their websites or at the time of booking. The vast majority of hotels and *pousadas* in Brazil are child-friendly. Larger properties will have high chairs and possibly cots, and many resorts also have special child-friendly areas, playrooms, and even separate kitchens for mothers needing to prepare food for babies and smaller children. Many large hotels can also organize babysitters.

Advise the hotel of the age of your children and any special requirements you may need for them in advance. If the hotel does not have it already, it may be willing to obtain it by the time you arrive.

Disabled Travelers

The situation for disabled travelers in Brazil has greatly improved in recent years, but not all accommodation options, especially the smaller properties with narrow lifts or those in the remoter areas of the country, can offer wheel-chair access or the facilities that disabled travelers may require. Brazilians by nature, however, will do everything they can to assist, so do not hesitate to ask.

Children's playroom, a feature in many Brazilian hotels

The lush gardens of Pousada do Sol, Morro de São Paulo

Chain Hotels

Brazil's hotel chains include a number of long-established Brazilian groups, such as **Othon** and **Tropical**. There are also several hundreds of modern hotels throughout the country that operate under different international brands, such as the **Accor** and **Marriott** groups.

Brazilian hoteliers have not been left behind, with the introduction of **Blue Tree, Bristol**, the **Atlântica Hotels** group (which operates as Radisson, Clarion, Quality, Comfort Suites, Four Points, Sleep Inn, and Go Inn), **Transamérica**, and in Rio de Janeiro, **Windsor Hoteis**.

The majority of chain hotels, which vary greatly in terms of price, infrastructure and quality, tend to be targeted at Brazilian and South American business travelers unless they are in obvious tourist destinations. Only the properties in the tourist areas are likely to consider adding a Brazilian or tropical flavor to the surroundings or decorations.

Apart-Hotels

Though not strictly for budget travelers, apart-hotels, in most of the main Brazilian cities, offer good value for money. These come with one, two, or more bedrooms, a living area, and a kitchen. Some will have restaurants and cafés, as well as swimming pools and gyms.

One of the main chains with properties throughout Brazil is Accor's Parthenon group, while in São Paulo, Transamérica Flats is a very prominent brand.

Apart-hotels are the most convenient self-catering option in Brazil. Most houses and apartments are rented individually, and it may be easier to organize the rental through a local agency.

Pousadas

Outside of the main city and town centers, the majority of accommodations on offer are smaller, privately owned properties. *Pousadas* vary dramatically in terms of cost, quality, and facilities offered. Some will be very basic but certainly clean, while others can be considered world-class boutique hotels set in lovely locations. *Pousadas* are usually charming, offer good value, and give a real flavor of Brazil.

It is a good idea to visit the website of an individual *pousada* to see the pictures of the property and what it has to offer. Most good tour operators know the best *pousadas* in each category and area. **Roteiros de Charme**, a network of outstanding *pousadas*, is also very useful, as is the **Hidden Pousadas** website.

If staying in Rio de Janeiro, check out **Cama a Café**, an organization that looks after many bed-and-breakfast options across the city, the majority in Santa Teresa. These offer the chance to stay in a room in a local resident's house.

Resorts

World-class resorts, many all-inclusive, can be found across Brazil. One of the largest is the Costa do Sauípe, just north of Salvador, and close by in Praia do Forte, Tivoli Ecoresort, Iberostar Praia do Forte, and Iberostar Bahia. Among the best are Transamérica on Ilha de Comandatuba in Bahia, Ponta dos Ganchos in Santa Catarina, Nannai in Porto de Galinhas, and Sofitel Jequitimar in Guarujá, to name but a few.

The Marriott Resort in Costa do Sauípe, Bahia

Budget Options

In the main areas visited by tourists, there are many *pousadas* that can be considered budget accommodation. There is also a good and growing network of modern and comfortable hostels in Brazil for those on a really tight budget. New independent hostels can be found right across Brazil, from the tourist areas of Rio de Janeiro, to the business heart of São Paulo. The website of the **Federação Brasileira de Albergues da Juventude** has a full list of hostels in Brazil that are approved by the organization.

Motels

Motels in Brazil have nothing in common with the ones to be found in North America or in Europe. In Brazil, these tend to be "love hotels," renting rooms out to couples by the hour. Guests are not normally encouraged to spend more than one night at these establishments.

Camping

Brazil offers a massive number of places where it is possible to camp. However, campers should make sure they have not wandered on to private property or into a restricted area. Security, too, is an issue, and not just from miscreants, but also from Brazilian wildlife.

Camping in the Serra dos Órgãos National Park

If you are not an experienced camper, you should stick to official campsites, the majority of which are run and organized by the **Camping Clube do Brasil**. If using one of the national parks, check first with the park authorities where camping is permitted. Having your own tent, or hiring one, is useful in ecotourist regions, such as the Amazon and the Pantanal.

Lodges

The majority of wildlife lodges that will help visitors to see and enjoy some of the remoter parts of Brazil are located in the Amazon *(see p378)* and the Pantanal *(see pp379–80)*. While there are some outstanding exceptions, the facilities and home comforts of many of these lodges may be quite basic, since visitors are more keen on exploring the surrounding countryside, flora, and fauna.

It is recommended for travelers to consider traveling light, leaving the bulk of their belongings back in the main hotel, an airport locker, or at the city office of the lodge prior to making the transfer.

Recommended Hotels

The many different hotels, resorts, *pousadas*, and lodges in this book have been carefully selected for their facilities, good location, and value. A wide variety of accommodations is covered, from lodges in remote rainforest locations, to stylish boutique hotels in Brazil's towns and cities.

Entries labeled as DK Choice highlight establishments that are exceptional or notable in some way – for their stunning location, outstanding rooms, superb restaurant, excellent service, or a combination of these.

DIRECTORY

Booking

Expedia
W expedia.com

Last Minute
W lastminute.com

Chain Hotels

Accor
Tel (0800) 703 7000.
W accor.com.br

Atlântica Hotels
Tel (0800) 55 5855.
W atlanticahotels.com.br

Blue Tree
Tel (0300) 150 5000.
W bluetree.com.br

Bristol
Tel (0800) 645 1816.
W bristolhoteis.com.br

Marriott
W marriott.co.uk

Othon
Tel (0800) 725 0505.
W othon.com.br

Transamérica
Tel (0800) 012 4400.
W transamericagroup.com.br

Tropical
Tel (0800) 70 12670.
W tropicalhotel.com.br

Windsor Hoteis
Tel (11) 3259 5323.
W windsorhoteis.com

Pousadas

Cama a Café
Tel (21) 2225 4366.
W camacafe.com.br

Hidden Pousadas
Tel (21) 98122 2000.
W hiddenpousadasbrazil.com

Roteiros de Charme
Tel (21) 2287 1592.
W roteirosdecharme.com.br

Budget Options

Federação Brasileira de Albergues da Juventude
W hihostelbrazil.com.br

Camping

Camping Clube do Brasil
W campingclube. com.br

Where to Stay

Rio de Janeiro City

AIRPORT: Linx $$
Business
Av Vinte de Janeiro s/n, 21941 900
Tel (21) 2468 3400
W linxinternationalairportgaleao.
com
This is the best choice if you
need suitable accommodation
near the international airport for
connecting flights.

BARRA DA TIJUCA:
Royal Tulip São Conrado $$
Resort
Rua Aquarela do Brasil 75, 22610 170
Tel (21) 3323 2200
W royaltulipriodejaneiro.com
Resort property that hosted the
England soccer team during the
2014 World Cup. Great views.
Pool area is one of the best in Rio.

BARRA DA TIJUCA:
Windsor Barra $$$
Business
Av Lucio Costa 2630, 22620 172
Tel (21) 2195 5000
W windsorhoteis.com.br
Large modern beachfront
property that is popular for
conferences due to its extensive
event facilities. Good beach and
sea views from most rooms.

CENTRO: Manga $
Hostel   **Map** 5 D5
Rua do Lavradio 186, 20230 070
Tel (21) 3852 5742
W mangahostelrio.com
Popular hostel that is situated
close to Rio's party central in
Lapa. Well located for sightseeing
and the metro for the beach,
Ipanema, and Copacabana.
Dormitories only.

The façade and entrance of the Porto Bay
Rio Internacional, Copacabana

CENTRO: Novotel Santos
Dumont $$
Business   **Map** 5 F4
Rua Marechal Câmara 300, 20020 080
Tel (21) 3506 8500
W novotel.com
Modern, well-equipped, no-frills
Novotel that is well positioned if
you are working downtown or
taking domestic flights from
Santos Dumont airfield.

CENTRO: Vila Galé Rio de
Janeiro $$
Historical   **Map** 5 D5
Rua Riachuelo 124, 20230 014
Tel (21) 2460 4500
W vilagale.com/en/rio-de-janeiro
Located close to Lapa and
downtown Rio, this renovated
Colonial-era mansion has a
pleasant mix of new and old. The
rooms are tasteful and elegant.
Good base for sightseeing.

CENTRO: Windsor Asturias $$
Business   **Map** 5 E5
Rua Senador Dantas 14, 20031 000
Tel (21) 2195 1500
W windsorhoteis.com.br
This good, standard business
hotel, housed in a 1930s building,
is centrally located and close to
the metro station. There are lovely
views from the rooftop terrace.

COPACABANA & LEME:
Rio Lancaster $$
Business   **Map** 3 F2
Av Atlântica 1470, 22021 000
Tel (21) 2169 8300
W hotelriolancaster.com.br
The front rooms of this Art Deco
building on Copacabana beach-
front have balconies and beautiful
views. The breakfast buffet
includes a wide variety of fruit.

COPACABANA & LEME:
Sofitel Rio $$
Luxury   **Map** 3 D5
Av Atlântica 4240, 22070 002
Tel (21) 2525 1232
W sofitel.com
Located at the Ipanema end of
Copacabana beach. Stunning
views back along the beach from
the large pool area. All rooms
have a balcony. Good facilities.

COPACABANA & LEME:
Windsor Excelsior $$
Business   **Map** 3 E2
Av Atlântica 1800, 22021 001
Tel (21) 2195 5800
W windsorhoteis.com.br
This is a solid choice for a beach-
front business hotel near the
metro station. Rooftop pool. Same
block as the Copacabana Palace.

COPACABANA & LEME:
Windsor Leme $$
Boutique   **Map** 3 D4
Av Atlântica 656, 22010 000
Tel (21) 2195 5400
W windsorhoteis.com.br
This is a luxury, stylish, top-of-the-
line hotel on the beachfront, with
chic rooms. The rooftop pool area
has a glorious view over Copaca-
bana beach. Superb breakfast.

DK Choice

COPACABANA & LEME:
Copacabana Palace $$$
Historic   **Map** 3 E2
Av Atlântica 1702, 220121 001
Tel (21) 2548 7070
W copacabanapalace.com.br
Famous in Rio and around the
world, with a guest list of
celebrities to match, this top-end
luxury grand beachfront hotel
from Belmond, first opened in
1923. It features Rio's best and
most glamorous hotel pool.

COPACABANA & LEME:
JW Marriott $$$
Luxury   **Map** 3 D3
Av Atlântica 2600, 22041 001
Tel (21) 2545 6500
W marriott.com
This boutique hotel is one of Rio's
best choices for a Copacabana
beachfront property. The rooftop
terrace offers amazing views of
Sugar Loaf Mountain.

COPACABANA & LEME:
Porto Bay Rio Internacional $$$
Business   **Map** 3 F2
Av Atlântica 1500, 22021 000
Tel (21) 2546 8000
W portobay.com
Beachfront hotel with a great roof
terrace that has sweeping views
of Copacabana. The corner rooms
have floor-to-ceiling windows.

COPACABANA & LEME: Rio
Othon Palace $$$
Business   **Map** 3 D3
Av Atlântica 3264, 22070 000
Tel (21) 2196 1500
W othon.com.br
Towering, landmark hotel on the
beachfront. The rooms and
facilities are a bit dated, but many
have spectacular views.

The opulent lobby at the Windsor Atlântica

COPACABANA & LEME: Windsor Atlântica $$$
Luxury   Map 3 F1
Av Atlântica 1020, 22010 000
Tel (21) 2195 7800
W windsorhoteis.com.br
Flagship property from the
Windsor Group. Wonderful views
and excellent facilities. Many
people, including taxi drivers, still
know this hotel as Le Méridien.

FLAMENGO & BOTAFOGO: Discovery $
Hostel
Benjamin Constant 26, 20241 150
Tel (21) 3449 0672
W discoveryhostel.com
Terrific little hostel located in
Glória and just a few steps from
the metro station. As well as
dorms, it offers private rooms
and a studio apartment.

FLAMENGO & BOTAFOGO: El Misti $
Hostel
Praia de Botafogo 462, Casa 9, 22250
040
Tel (21) 2226 0991
W elmistibota.com
Close to Botafogo metro station,
beach, and Sugar Loaf Mountain,
this excellent hostel has shared
dorms and private rooms.

DK Choice
FLAMENGO & BOTAFOGO: Oztel $
Hostel
Rua Pinheiro Guimarães 91,
20081 311
Tel (21) 3042 1853
W oztel.com.br
Located at the Lagoa end of
Botafogo, this trendy hostel
borders on being a hotel, with
suites as well as dorms, a
lounge, TV room, and popular
bar. Good for public transport.

IPANEMA & LEBLON: Rio Hostel Ipanema $
Hostel   Map 2 C5
Rua Canning 18, Casa 1, 22081 040
Tel (21) 2287 2928
W riohostelipanema.com
Conveniently located hostel that
is in walking distance of both
Copacabana and Ipanema
beaches. Dorms and suites. The
pleasant rooftop terrace has
hammocks to relax in.

IPANEMA & LEBLON: Arpoador Inn $$
Business   Map 2 C5
Rua Francisco Otaviano 177,
22080 040
Tel (21) 2523 0060
W arpoadorinn.com.br
A little gem that sits at the
Copacabana end of Ipanema, in
Arpoador. Simple but slightly
dated rooms. There isn't a pool,
but it's just a short path between
the hotel and sand. Book a high-
up oceanfront room.

IPANEMA & LEBLON: Ipanema Plaza $$
Business   Map 2 B5
Rua Farme de Amoedo 34,
22420 020
Tel (21) 3687 2000
W ipanemaplaza.com.br
This popular hotel is located one
block back from the beach in the
heart of Ipanema. Close to many
restaurants and bars. Great views
from the rooftop terrace.

IPANEMA & LEBLON: Mar Ipanema $$
Business   Map 1 C4
Rua Visconde de Pirajá 539, 22410 003
Tel (21) 3875 9191
W maripanema.com.br
Located on the main shopping
street and just two blocks from
the beach. The elegant rooms
are tastefully decorated. Friendly
and helpful staff.

IPANEMA & LEBLON: Praia Ipanema $$
Business   Map 1 C5
Av Vieira Souto 706, 22410 060
Tel (21) 2141 4949
W praiaipanema.com
Pleasant hotel with small
rooftop pool, bar, and restaurant.
All the rooms are light and airy
and have tiled floors and a
balcony. Fantastic location on
Ipanema beachfront.

IPANEMA & LEBLON: Sol Ipanema $$
Business   Map 2 A5
Av Vieira Souto 320, 22420 004
Tel (21) 2525 2020
W solipanema.com.br
Excellent beachfront location in
the very heart of Ipanema close
to restaurants, bars, and stores.
Small rooftop pool. Book a
seafront room for the view.

IPANEMA & LEBLON: Caesar Park $$$
Luxury   Map 2 A5
Av Vieira Souto 460, 22420 000
Tel (21) 2525 2525
W sofitel.com
Under Sofitel management, the
stylish Caesar Park has been a
popular choice for business and
leisure travelers for decades.
Small pool and rooftop terrace.
One of Ipanema's very best.

IPANEMA & LEBLON: Fasano $$$
Luxury   Map 2 B5
Av Vieira Souto 80, 22420 000
Tel (21) 3202 4000
W fasano.com.br
Chic, stylish, world-class luxury
boutique hotel, with lovely sea
views from all the rooms.
Gorgeous rooftop pool deck. Great
restaurant and fashionable bar.

IPANEMA & LEBLON: Sheraton Rio $$$
Resort
Av Niemeyer 121, 22450 220
Tel (21) 2529 1122
W sheraton-rio.com.br
Rio's largest resort property
is located almost on its own
beach just a short hop along
the coast from Leblon. A great
choice for families.

SANTA TERESA: Santa Teresa $$$
Luxury
Av Alm Alexandrino 660, 20241 260
Tel (21) 3380 0200
W santateresahotel.com
This boutique hotel is tucked
away in bohemian Santa Teresa.
Far from the beach and
Copacabana, but an oasis of
calm. Spacious and stylish room.

For more information on types of hotels see pages 368–9

Rio de Janeiro State & Espírito Santo

Rio de Janeiro State

ANGRA DOS REIS: Vila Galé Eco Resort $$$
Resort
Estrada Vereador Benedito Adelino 8413, Fazenda Tanguá, 23909 901
Tel (24) 3379 2800
W vilagale.pt
This well-structured, comfortable resort property is located on its own beach and is excellent for families. One of the closest major resorts to Rio.

The sun deck at Vila d'Este, Búzios, offering beautiful views of sea and sky

BÚZIOS: Abracadabra $$$
Pousada
Alto do Humaitá 13, 28950 000
Tel (22) 2623 1217
W abracadabrapousada.com.br
Just 5 minutes from the center of the action in Rua das Pedras, this small, well-appointed *pousada* has lovely views over Búzios.

BÚZIOS: Casas Brancas Boutique Hotel & Spa $$$
Boutique
Rua Alto do Humaitá 10, 28950 000
Tel (21) 2623 1458
W casasbrancas.com.br
Charming hotel that is slightly larger than the *pousadas* but has the extra facilities you might expect from a hotel. The rooms have been individually decorated and some have a balcony.

DK Choice

BÚZIOS: Insolito Boutique Hotel $$$
Boutique
Rua E1, Lotes 3 and 4, Praia da Ferradura, 28950 000
Tel (22) 2623 2172
W insolitos.com.br
Beautiful location on the edge of Praia da Ferradura, one of the region's very best beaches. This French-owned hotel is stylish, cool and fashionable, as well as comfortable and relaxing. It has individually styled suites, a wellness center, lovely pool areas, and a good restaurant.

BÚZIOS: Vila d'Este $$$
Pousada
Alto do Humaitá 11, 28950 000
Tel (22) 2623 1546
W viladeste.eco.br
A cross between a *pousada* and boutique hotel, within walking distance of town, this spot has a good restaurant and a pool deck. Great views and sunsets.

ILHA GRANDE: Ancoradouro $$
Pousada
Rua da Praia 121 A1, Abraão, 23960 000
Tel (24) 3361 5153
W pousadancoradouro.com.br
Cute *pousada*, typical of those to be found in and around the main town of Ilha Grande, offers spacious and clean rooms.

ILHA GRANDE: Naturalia $$
Pousada
Rua da Praia 149, 23960 000
Tel (24) 3361 9583
W pousadanaturalia.net
A short walk from where the boats dock and from the center of town, this comfortable *pousada* is well positioned for exploring the island.

DK Choice

ILHA GRANDE: Estrela da Ilha $$$
Boutique
Praia Pequena, Freguesia de Santana Lagoa Azul, 23900 970
Tel (24) 9 9831 0020
W estreladailha.com
Tucked away on its own beach, away from the main action and surrounded by rainforest, this is a special, relaxing little lodge from which to explore the beauty of Ilha Grande. Comfortable and stylish, yet also rustic with an eco-friendly infrastructure. All rooms have a private balcony with a hammock. Excellent food. Hotel will transfer you from mainland.

PARATY: Sandi $$
Pousada
Largo do Rosário 1, 23970 000
Tel (24) 3371 2100; (11) 2503 0195
W pousadadosandi.com.br
Set in Paraty's historic center, the Sandi is full of character, which captures the spirit of the town. Comfortable rooms.

PARATY: Casa Turquesa $$$
Pousada
Rua Doutor Pereira 50, 23970 000
Tel (24) 3371 1037
W casaturquesa.com.br
Stylish and romantic *pousada*. Understated class in the historic center, and a perfect base from which to explore the town.

PARATY: Literária $$$
Pousada
Rua Ten Francisco Antônio 362, 23970 000
Tel (24) 3371 1460
W pousadaliteraria.com.br
This *pousada* has a literary theme, reflecting the fact that the town holds South America's leading literary festival. The rooms are spacious and have tasteful decor.

PETRÓPOLIS: Grande Hotel $$
Historic
Rua do Imperador 545, 25620 130
Tel (24) 2244 6500
W grandehotelpetropolis.com.br
Perfect location for sightseeing. This place balances the modern with the historic.

PETRÓPOLIS: Solar do Império $$
Historic
Av Koeller 376, 25685 060
Tel (24) 2103 3000
W solardoimperio.com.br
Small classic hotel that is set in two large houses that date from 1875 and 1983. Well positioned for sightseeing.

Espírito Santo

VITORIA: Golden Tulip Porto Vitoria $
Business
Av Nossa Senhora dos Navegantes 635, 29050 335
Tel (27) 3533 1300
W goldentulipportovitoria.com
This modern, well-appointed hotel with good facilities enjoys a central location. Good value.

VITORIA: Ilha do Boi $$
Business
Rua Bráulio Macedo 417, 29052 640
Tel (27) 3345 0111
w hotelilhadoboi.com.br
Part of Brazil's national hotel and catering school. Lovely setting with great views on Ilha do Boi, one of Vitoria's nicest neighborhoods. Lovely pool area.

Minas Gerais

BELO HORIZONTE: Holiday Inn Belo Horizonte $$
Business
Rua Professor Moraes 600, 30150 370
Tel (31) 3064 6555
w ihg.com
This convenient and modern Holiday Inn offers all you would expect from the chain.

BELO HORIZONTE: Ouro Minas Palace $$
Business
Av Cristiano Machado 4001, 31160 342
Tel (31) 3429 4001
w ourominas.com.br
Considered by many to be the top business hotel in Belo, this is a fashionable place for events and conferences.

OURO PRETO: Grande Hotel Ouro Preto $
Pousada
Rua Senador Rocha Lagoa 164, 35400 000
Tel (31) 3551 1488
w grandehotelouropreto.com.br
Historic, small hotel designed by Oscar Niemeyer in 1938, with gardens created by Burle Marx. The panoramic restaurant offers views over Ouro Preto, as do many of the rooms.

The pool at Belo Horizonte's top business hotel, Ouro Minas Palace

OURO PRETO: Mondego $$
Pousada
Largo de Coimbra 38, 35400 000
Tel (31) 3551 7700
w mondego.com.br
This comfortable *pousada*, set in a colonial building, is located close to the main square. Perfect base for exploring Ouro Preto. Pleasant bar and restaurant.

DK Choice

OURO PRETO: Solar do Rosário $$
Pousada
Rua Getúlio Vagas 270, 35400 000
Tel (31) 3551 5200
w hotelsolardorosario.com.br
This small hotel has traditional charm, yet with the modern touches that today's travelers demand. Lovely gardens and pool and an excellent restaurant. Handy for the historic center and sightseeing around Ouro Preto on foot.

PARQUE NACIONAL DA SERRA DO CIPÓ: Cipó Veraneio $$
Pousada
Rodovia MG-010, Km 94, 38830 000
w cipoveraneiohotel.com.br
Pleasant hotel with a lovely garden and pool on the edge of the River Cipo. Simple rooms.

TIRADENTES: Pequena Tiradentes $$
Historical
Av Governador Israel Pinheiro 670, 36325 000
Tel (32) 3355 1262
w pequenatiradentes.com.br
Small hotel inspired by the history and architecture of old Tiradentes. The rooms look like typical houses, and the corridors are like streets, with plants and streetlights. A fun spot for families.

TIRADENTES: Solar da Ponte $$
Pousada
Praça das Mercês 1, 36325 000
Tel (32) 3355 1255
w solardaponte.com.br
Old-style hospitality and modern comforts are found at this well-maintained *pousada* in the heart of Tiradentes, set up in 1974 by a British artist and his Minas wife.

TIRADENTES: Três Portas $$
Pousada
Rua Direita 280A, 36325 000
Tel (32) 3355 1444
w pousadatresportas.com.br
Delightful and rustic *pousada* ideally located close to the city's main square. The rooms are cozy and comfortable.

São Paulo City

AIRPORT (GUARULHOS): Pullman São Paulo $
Business
Rodovia Hélio Smidt s/n, 07190 100
Tel (11) 2124 5800
w pullmanhotels.com
Close to the airport, this is a good option if you have flight connections to make. The shuttle takes 10 minutes to reach the terminals.

JARDINS & AVENIDA PAULISTA: Viva Hostel Design $
Hostel
Rua Girassol 1262, 05433 002
Tel (11) 3812 9142
w vivahostel.com.br
This colorful, popular, well-located hostel has clean, modern, spacious rooms or small dorms.

JARDINS & AVENIDA PAULISTA: Porto Bay L'Hotel $$
Business **Map** 4 F3
Alameda Campinas 266, Jardim Paulista, 01426 000
Tel (11) 2183 0500
w portobay.com
A popular, small, friendly hotel that is well-located for Avenida Paulista. It offers European-style elegance and service.

JARDINS & AVENIDA PAULISTA: Emiliano $$$
Luxury **Map** 4 D3
Rua Oscar Freire 384, 01426 000
Tel (11) 3069 4369
w emiliano.com.br
Stylish boutique hotel that is considered one of the city's best. It is well located for both business and leisure.

DK Choice

JARDINS & AVENIDA PAULISTA: Fasano $$$
Luxury **Map** 4 D3
Rua Vittorio Fasano 88, 01414 020
Tel (11) 3896 4000
w fasano.com.br
Exclusive style, charm, and five-star comfort. Fasano São Paulo boasts the Fasano Italian restaurant and the bar Baretto, both considered among the best in their class. Pool and spa.

JARDINS & AVENIDA PAULISTA: Unique $$$
Luxury **Map** 4 E5
Av Brigadeiro Luís Antônio 4700, 01402 002
Tel (11) 3055 4710
w hotelunique.com.br
This trendy boutique hotel has a beautiful pool area and superb restaurant. Stunning city views.

For more information on types of hotels *see pages 368–9*

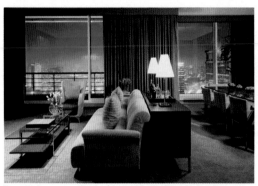

The upstairs lounge area with views of the city at the Grand Hyatt, São Paulo City

MORUMBI & BROOKLIN:
Grand Hyatt $$
Luxury
Av das Nações Unidas 13301,
04578 000
Tel (11) 2838 1234
w saopaulo.grand.hyatt.com.br
Top of the line and elegant, the
Grand Hyatt Hotel has stylish and
spacious rooms. Great facilities
include a highly rated spa and a
gourmet center.

MORUMBI & BROOKLIN:
Hilton Morumbi $$$
Business
Av das Nações Unidas 12901,
04578 000
Tel (11) 2845 0000
w hiltonmorumbi.com.br
Large Hilton that is in demand
for conferences and events. It's
handy for the business district of
Brooklyn and Morumbi. Rooms
have mountain or sea views.

São Paulo State

GUARUJÁ: Casa Grande Hotel
Resort & Spa $$$
Resort
Av Miguel Stefano 1100, 11440 530
Tel (13) 3389 4000
w casagrandehotel.com.br
Comfortable, colonial-style resort
directly on one of the beaches
closest to São Paulo. There are
five restaurants and four bars.
Wonderful for children.

GUARUJÁ: Sofitel Jequitimar
Guarujá $$$
Resort
Av Marjori da Silva Prado 1100,
11444 000
Tel (13) 2104 2000
w accorhotels.com
In a lovely spot, this exceptional
Sofitel is also a well-regarded spa,
resort, and convention center.
Outstanding restaurant.

DK Choice

ILHABELA: DPNY Beach
Hotel $$$
Boutique
Av José Pacheco do Nascimento
7668, 11630 000
Tel (12) 3894 3000
w dpnybeach.com.br
One of Brazil's trendiest and
most fashionable beach
properties, DPNY is weekend
party central for some of São
Paulo's most demanding jet-
setters looking to relax in style.
Three charming restaurants,
great beach and pool setting,
and popular spa. Day passport
offered if you are not staying at
the hotel or are arriving by boat.

ILHABELA: Maison Joly $$$
Pousada
Rua Antônio Lisboa Alves 278,
11630 000
Tel (12) 3896 2364
w maisonjoly.com.br
Charming *pousada* situated
close to the historic center of
the island's main town. It offers
amazing ocean views from
public areas and rooms.

MARESIAS: Maresias Beach $$
Pousada
Rua Francisco Loup 1109,
11620 000
Tel (12) 3891 7500
w maresiasbeachhotel.com.br
Great beach location, pool, and
grounds make up for the average
standard of the rooms at this
pousada. Good for families.

SANTOS: Mendes Plaza $$
Business
Av Floriano Peixoto 42, 11060 300
Tel (13) 3208 6400
w mendeshoteis.com.br
This friendly hotel is conveniently
located for the beach and some
of the city's shopping malls.

UBATUBA: Picinguaba $$
Pousada
Rua G 130, Vila Picinguaba, 11680 000
Tel (11) 2495 1586
w picinguaba.com
A charming *pousada* in an excep-
tional coastal setting. It is an oasis
of understated style and comfort
and within easy reach of Paraty.

Bahia

COSTA DA SAUIPE: Costa do
Sauipe Golf & Spa $$$
Resort
Rodovia BA 099, Km 76, s/n,
48282 970
Tel (71) 2104 7020
w costadosauipe.com.br
Massive resort with several
properties that used to be
managed by the Costa da Sauípe
chain. Accommodations range
from luxury to simple *pousadas*.

ILHEUS: Transamérica Ilha de
Comandatuba $$$
Resort
Estrada P/Canavieiras, Km 77, Una,
45690 000
Tel (73) 3686 1122
w transamerica.com.br
Since opening in 1989, this place
has been regarded as one of
Brazil's best and most consistent
resort properties. Located one
hour from Ilheus on the Ilha de
Comandatuba. Great for families.
Excellent golf course.

ITACARÉ: Itacaré Eco Resort $$$
Resort
Rodovia Ilhéus, Km 65, Condomínio
Vila São José, 45530 000
Tel (73) 3251 3133
w ier.com.br
This eco-resort is located in an
old coffee plantation. You can
stay in the main hotel or chalets
in the rainforest. Lovely beach.

ITACARÉ: Txai $$$
Boutique
BA-001, Itacaré, 45530 000
Tel (73) 2101 5000
w txairesorts.com.br
One of Brazil's most fashionable
and in-demand boutique hotels
offers bungalow accommodations.
Understated luxury and wonderful
setting. Good spa and restaurant.

LENÇOIS: Canto das Aguas $$
Pousada
Av Senhor dos Passos 01, 46960 000
Tel (75) 3334 1154
w lencois.com.br
The best hotel in Lençóis from
which to explore the town and
national park offers lovely grounds
and views and a superb restaurant.

**MORRO DE SÃO PAULO:
Vila dos Orixas** $$
Boutique
Praia do Encanto s/n, 45428 000
Tel (75) 3652 2055
W hotelviladosorixas.com
Intimate haven on a quiet beach.
This is one of the most stylish
options on Morro de São Paulo.
Pretty rooms and bungalows.

**PRAIA DO FORTE: Iberostar
Bahia & Praia do Forte** $$$
Resort
*Rodovia BA 099, Km 56, Praia do
Forte, 48280 000*
Tel (71) 3676 4300
W iberostar.com.br
Two neighboring resort
properties have over 1,000 rooms
between them and the necessary
infrastructure to handle that
number of guests. Great choice
for families. Closed Jun 7–Jul 1.

**PRAIA DO FORTE: Tivoli
Ecoresort** $$$
Resort
Av do Farol, 48280 000
Tel (71) 3676 4000
W tivolihotels.com
Family-friendly eco-resort in a
pleasant setting. The spacious
rooms all have a balcony with sea
views. Lovely restaurants.

SALVADOR: F Design Hostel $
Hostel
*Travessa Prudente de Moraes 65,
41950 030*
Tel (71) 3035 9700
W fdesignsalvador.com.br
Top-end design hostel, with clean,
wacky rooms. The facilities include
a small pool, restaurant, and bar.
Private rooms and small dorms.

SALVADOR: Casa Amarelindo $$
Historical
Rua das Portas do Carmo 6, 40026 290
Tel (71) 3266 8550
W casadoamarelindo.com
Attractive and popular *pousada*
in a 19th-century house in the
historic Pelourinho area. There is
a pool, a restaurant, two bars, and
a roof terrace with lovely views.

DK Choice

**SALVADOR: Convento do
Carmo** $$
Historic
Rua do Carmo 1, 40301 330
Tel (71) 3327 8400
W pestana.com
Small hotel set in an old convent
building dating from 1586 that
is located in the historic heart of
the city. It is elegant and refined
and has a lovely pool area and
courtyard. Good service.

**SALVADOR: Sheraton da
Bahia** $$
Business
Av 7 de Setembro 1537, 40080 001
Tel (71) 3021 6700
W sheratondabahia.com
Located close to Castro Alves
square and theater, this property
has been fully refurbished and
offers minimalist rooms with
warm decor. Good breakfast.

**SALVADOR: Solar dos
Deuses – Suítes de Charme** $$
Boutique
*Largo do Cruzeiro do São Francisco
12, 40020 280*
Tel (71) 3322 1911
W solardosdeuses.com.br
Enchanting hotel located in the
historic heart of Salvador in a
17th-century building. There are
just six individually themed suites
based on the Candomblé gods.
Closed in June.

SALVADOR: Zank by Toque $$
Boutique
Rua Almirante Barroso 161, 41950 350
Tel (71) 3083 4000
W zankhotel.com.br
This stylish and good-value
hotel is located out of the city
center in Rio Vermelho, close
to Farol da Barra. Sea views
from all rooms.

SALVADOR: Villa Bahia $$$
Historical
*Largo do Cruzeiro do São Francisco
16, 40020 280*
Tel (71) 3322 4271
W lavillabahia.com
Set in the Pelourinho area in
two magnificent colonial
mansions, the rooms here have
been renovated but preserve
their original character. Two
garden courtyards and a
panoramic terrace.

TRANCOSO: Etnia Pousada $$
Pousada
Trancoso, 45818 000
Tel (73) 3668 1137
W etniabrasil.com.br
This stylish and fashionable
pousada offers eight themed
bungalows tucked away in the
greenery. Closed in June.

**TRANCOSO:
Uxua Casa Hotel** $$$
Boutique
Trancoso
Tel (73) 3668 2277
W uxua.com
Located in a tropical garden off
the main square, this has become
one of the places to see and be
seen in Trancoso. The ten rustic-
style houses include four
fishermen's cottages.

**TRANCOSO: Villas de
Trancoso** $$$
Pousada
Trancoso, 45818 000
Tel (73) 3668 1151
W villasdetrancoso.com
Luxury beachfront boutique hotel
in a lovely setting, great for a
romantic hideaway or for families.
This is one of the best for a special
Brazilian and Bahian experience.

Sergipe, Alagoas &
Pernambuco

Sergipe

ARACAJU: Radisson Aracaju $$
Business
*Rua Dr. Bezerra De Menezes, Atalia
40, 49035 240*
Tel (79) 3711 3300
W atlanticahotels.com.br
Modern, comfortable Radisson
off Atalaia beach. Close to
beachfront, bars, and restaurants.

Alagoas

MACEIÓ: Jatiúca $$
Resort
*Dr. Mario Nunes Vieira 220,
Mangabeiras, 57035 553*
Tel (82) 2122 2000
W hoteljatiuca.com.br
This urban resort property is well
located in front of Jatiúca Beach
and is good for families.

MACEIÓ: Radisson Maceió $$$
Business
*Av Doutor Antônio Gouveia 925,
57030 17*
Tel (82) 3202 4900
W atlanticahotels.com.br
Great location, close to the town's
best urban beach and other
attractions. Good-sized rooms.

Tasty breakfast options at Solar dos
Deuses – Suites de Charme, Salvador

For more information on types of hotels *see pages 368–9*

Pernambuco

FERNANDO DE NORONHA:
Vale $$
Pousada
Rua Pescador Sérgio Lino 18, 53990 000
Tel (81) 3619 1293
W pousadadovale.com
Comfortable *pousada* located in
Jardim Elizabeth and one of the
nicest on the island. A short walk
to the sea, bars, and restaurants.

DK Choice

FERNANDO DE NORONHA:
Maravilha $$$
Pousada
BR-363 s/n, Vila do Vai quem
Sabe, 53990 000
Tel (81) 3325 5302
W pousadamaravilha.com.br
One of the more luxurious
pousadas on the island. The
rooms have spectacular sea
views, and there is a gorgeous
pool area and a spa. Choose
between romantic bungalows
or more family-friendly rooms.
Tours of the island, by land and
sea, are organized, plus diving
and fishing. Lovely restaurant.

FERNANDO DE NORONHA:
Solar dos Ventos $$$
Pousada
Rod BR-363, Vila Do Sueste, 53990 000
Tel (81) 3619 1347
W pousadasolardosventos.com.br
This place has a stunning setting
and is a perfect base for explor-
ing the island. Rooms are set in
bungalows and have their own
verandas with astonishing views.
Close to the beach. No pool.

DK Choice

OLINDA: Amparo $$
Pousada
Rua do Amparo 199, 53020 190
Tel (81) 3439 1749
W pousadadoamparo.com.br
The best known of the *pousadas*
located in the historic center of
Olinda. Charming and quirky,
with a great colonial atmosphere,
Amparo is a good base for visit-
ing and exploring both Olinda
and Recife. Good restaurant.

OLINDA: Quatro Cantos $$
Pousada
Rua Prudente de Moraes Carmo 441,
53020 140
Tel (81) 3429 0220
W pousada4cantos.com.br
A popular and charming *pousada*
in the heart of Olinda. It is set
on the carnival route in an old
family home.

A king-size bed in one of the bungalows at
Solar dos Ventos, Fernando de Noronha

OLINDA: Sete Colinas $$
Historical
Rua São Francisco 307, 53120 080
Tel (81) 3493 7766
W hotel7colinas.com.br
Small hotel, with larger grounds
and more facilities than the
pousadas. There are beautiful
gardens with tropical vegetation
and a pool. Simple and tranquil.
Good choice for families.

PORTO DE GALINHAS:
Armação $$
Resort
Lot. Merepe II, Quadra G1, Lote 1A,
55590 000
Tel (81) 2126 2160
W hotelarmacao.com.br
This unpretentious, good-value
property is on one of the best
stretches of beach in Brazil. It
offers simple, tasteful rooms and
a beachfront pool area. Easy
access to village.

PORTO DE GALINHAS:
Tabajuba $$
Pousada
Lot. Merepe II, Quadra I, Lotes 5/6,
55590 000
Tel (81) 3552 1651
W tabajuba.com
A gorgeous, beachfront *pousada*,
this charming and intimate place
is within walking distance of the
village. Good restaurants. No
children under 12 allowed.

PORTO DE GALINHAS:
Nannai Beach $$$
Resort
Praia de Muro Alto, 55590 000
Tel (81) 3552 0101
W nannai.com.br
Stylishly decorated resort property
with Polynesian influences. The
bungalows have their own dip
pools. Good spa.

RECIFE: Atlante Plaza $$
Business
Av Boa Viagem 5426, Boa Viagem,
51030 000
Tel (81) 3302 3333
W atlanteplaza.com.br
One of the most popular high-rise
beach properties on Boa Viagem,
this has comfortable, large rooms
and lovely views. Rooftop pool.

RECIFE: Beach Class Suites $$
Business
Av Boa Viagem 1906, Boa Viagem,
51111 000
Tel (81) 2121 2626
W beachclasssuites.com
Another excellent beachfront
option centrally located on Boa
Viagem. All rooms have sea
views. Good amenities.

RECIFE: Courtyard Recife
Boa Viagem $$
Business
Av Eng Domingos Ferreira 4661,
51021 040
Tel (81) 3256 7700
W marriott.com
Modern hotel in the Marriott
chain. It has well-equipped
rooms and is near the beach.

Paraíba, Rio Grande do Norte & Ceará

Paraíba

JOÃO PESSOA: Verdegreen $$
Business
Av João Maurício, Manaíra 255,
58038 000
Tel (83) 3044 0000
W verdegreen.com.br
Not a great deal of accommo-
dation options in João Pessoa, but
this beachfront hotel will tick most
boxes. Clean, modern rooms.

Rio Grande do Norte

NATAL: Manary Praia Hotel $$
Boutique
Rua Francisco Gurgel 9067, 59090 050
Tel (84) 3204 2900
W manary.com.br
Gorgeous and charming hotel on
Ponte Negra that has consistently
delivered high standards and
comfort. Wonderful restaurant.

NATAL: Serhs Natal Grand $$
Resort
Av Senador Dinarte Medeiros Mariz
6045, 59090 002
Tel (84) 4005 2000
W serhsnatalgrandhotel.com
Large, sophisticated beachfront
resort has good restaurants, a
lovely beach, and sea views.

PRAIA DE PIPA: Sombra e Água Fresca $$
Resort
Rua Praia do Amor 1000, 59178 000
Tel (84) 3246 2376
W sombraeaguafresca.com.br
This property is divided into a resort, hotel, and spa and is 165 yards (150 m) from Praia do Amor. The decor has an Asian vibe. Popular with couples.

PRAIA DE PIPA: Toca da Coruja $$$
Pousada
Av Baia dos Golfinhos, 59190 000
Tel (84) 3246 2226
W tocadacoruja.com.br
Wonderful garden setting close to the centre of Pipa. This place has a perfect mix of rustic charm and understated luxury. Excellent restaurant. There is a free transfer to the beach, where the hotel has its own bar/restaurant.

TIBAU DO SUL: Ponta do Madeiro $$
Pousada
Av Antônio Florêncio 2695, 59178 000
Tel (84) 3246 4220
W pontadomadeiro.com.br
Breathtaking ocean views from this *pousada*'s clifftop location. Take the staircase (over 200 steps) down to the beach, where the hotel has its own beach bar and facilities. Transfers to Pipa.

Ceará

CANOA QUEBRADA: Azul Marinho $
Pousada
Rua Leandro Bezerra s/n, 62800 000
Tel (88) 3421 7003
W azul-marinho.com
This charming clifftop *pousada* is one of the town's best, with great ocean and beach views. Closed in May.

CANOA QUEBRADA: Long Beach $$
Boutique
Rua Quatro Ventos, 62800 000
Tel (88) 3421 7404
W longbeachcanoa.com
Gorgeous, unpretentious hotel with rustic charm. The pool area has sea views. It is a short walk to the beach and 15 minutes to the town center. Good for families.

FORTALEZA: Ibis Fortaleza $
Business
Rua Doutor Atualpa Barbosa Lima 660, 60060 370
Tel (85) 3052 2450
W ibis.com
A short walk from the main beach area of Iracema, this modern hotel has a small pool and sun deck.

FORTALEZA: Gran Marquise $$
Business
Av Beira Mar 3980, Meirelles, 60165 121
Tel (85) 4006 5000
W granmarquise.com.br
Standard beachfront hotel in a location that is good for business or leisure trips. Good facilities. Try to book an oceanfront room.

FORTALEZA: Luzeiros $$
Boutique
Av Beira Mar 2600, 60165 121
Tel (85) 4006 8585
W luzeirosfortaleza.com.br
Impressive hotel on the beachfront at Meireles Beach. Close to many amenities and attractions. Most rooms have verandas.

JERICOACOARA: Recanto do Barão $
Pousada
Rua do Forró 433, 62598 000
Tel (85) 9989 2469
W recantodobarao.com
A typical example of the charming *pousadas* that make up the bulk of the accommodation options at Jericoacoara.

DK Choice

JERICOACOARA: My Blue Hotel $$
Boutique
Rua Ismael s/n, 62598 000
Tel (88) 3669 2203
W mybluehotel.net
Attractive beachfront property with two pool areas that has set the standard for other hotels in Jericoacoara. The colorful rooms and suites are stylish and sophisticated and have sea, pool, or garden views. Some also have a terrace. There is a spa, a gym, a restaurant, and a wine bar directly on the beach with panoramic views.

Piauí & Maranhão

Piauí

BARREIRINHAS: Encantes do Nordeste $$
Pousada
Rua Boa Vista s/n, 65590 000
Tel (98) 3349 0288
W encantesdonordeste.com.br
Simple *pousada* located by a river outside of the town. Good base from which to visit the Lençóis park and dunes. Organized tours and activities.

TERESINA: Metropolitan $$
Business
Av Frei Serafim 1696, 64001 020
Tel (86) 3216 8000
W metropolitanhotel.com.br
Teresina does not have many hotels, but the Metropolitan has consistently been the best on offer. Centrally located.

Maranhão

SÃO LUIS: Pestana São Luis $
Business
Av Avicênia 1, Praia do Calhau, 65071 370
Tel (98) 2106 0505
W pestana.com
Well located for both business and leisure, this hotel is a short walk to Calhau Beach and a short cab ride to the historic center. Excellent pool area.

SÃO LUIS: Luzeiros $$
Business
Rua João Pereira Damasceno 02, 60077 630
Tel (98) 3311 4949
W luzeirossaoluis.com.br
Modern design hotel on the beachfront at Ponta do Farol. Lovely setting. There are sea views from all the large, airy rooms.

The beautifully kept, tranquil gardens at Toca da Coruja, Praia de Pipa

For more information on types of hotels *see pages 368–9*

Pará & Amapá

Pará

BELEM: Crowne Plaza $$
Business
Av Nazaré 375, 66040 145
Tel (91) 3202 2000
W crownebelem.com.br
Consistently one of Belém's best, this hotel is close to tourist attractions, restaurants, bars, and the financial district. Great for business or sightseeing, too.

BELEM: Radisson Maiorana Belem $$
Business
Av Comandante Bras do Aguir 321, 66035 395
Tel (91) 3205 1399
W atlanticahotels.com.br
This Radisson property delivers the standards expected of the brand. Centrally situated, with comfortable and functional rooms for business travelers.

ILHA DE MARAJO: Fazenda Sanjo $$
Fazenda
Margens do Igarapé São Sebastião, 68870 000
Tel (91) 3228 1385
W sanjo.tur.br
There are limited accommodation options on the island, but this lodge is the best base for exploring, since it is located in the heart of the island. Offers one-, two-, and three-night stays.

SANTAREM: Barrudada Tropical Hotel $
Business
Av Mendonça Furtado 4120, 68050 040
Tel (93) 3222 2200
W barrudadatropicalhotel.com.br
You don't go to Santarem for the hotels. Barrudada is probably the best one available.

The comfort of Amazon Ecopark, perfectly located for Manaus

Amapá

MACAPÁ: Ekinox $
Pousada
Rua Jovino Dinoá 1693, 68900 075
Tel (96) 3223 0086
W ekinoxpousada.yahoostore.com
This friendly, well-located little *pousada* is ideal if you want to avoid staying in the mediocre hotels on offer in Macapá.

MACAPÁ: Ibis Macapá Hotel $
Business
Rua Tiradentes Centro 303, 68900 098
Tel (96) 2101 9050
W accorhotels.com
Comfortable, modern, and well-located, this Ibis hotel is simple but does the job.

Amazonas, Roraima, Acre & Rondõnia

Amazonas

MANAUS: Holiday Inn Manaus $
Business
Av General Rodrigo Otávio 3775, 69077 000
Tel (92) 3182 0100
W holidayinn.com
Modern and comfortable Holiday Inn hotel. Although basic, it offers exactly what many travelers require as a base.

MANAUS: Caesar Business $$
Business
Av Darcy Vargas 654, Bairro do Chapada, 69050 020
Tel (92) 3306 4700
W accorhotels.com
Good-quality, attractive business hotel run by Accor. It is close to the huge Amazonas Shopping Center and convention center and about a 20-minute taxi ride to the downtown waterfront.

DK Choice

MANAUS: Tropical $$
Historical/Resort
Av Coronel Teixeira 1320, Praia da Ponta Negra, 69037 000
Tel (92) 2123 5000
W tropicalmanaus.com.br
Almost an attraction in its own right, this place is in a secluded riverside location and has been the first choice for visitors for decades. Large, colonial-style eco-resort that may have seen better days, with faded elegance, but still an excellent choice for Amazon light, before heading in to the rainforest proper. On-site zoo and other attractions.

MANAUS: Amazon Ecopark $$$
Rainforest Lodge
Tel (92) 9146 0594; (21) 3005 5536
W amazonecopark.com.br
Pleasant, comfortable lodge in a lovely river setting that is one of the closest to Manaus. Rooms and bungalows are available. Meals are included in the price.

MANAUS: Amazon Jungle Palace $$$
Rainforest Lodge
Tel (92) 3211 3955
W amazonjunglepalace.com.br
Unusual option since this is a modern floating lodge – an easy, comfortable, slightly sanitized way to be introduced to the rainforest. There are panoramic river views from all the rooms.

MANAUS: Anavilhanas $$$
Rainforest Lodge
Tel (92) 3622 8996
W anavilhanaslodge.com
This family-friendly lodge is one of the region's best. Transfer is 3 hours by road or by seaplane. There is a viewing platform to see across the rainforest. Stay in beautiful wooden bungalows or chalets.

MANAUS: Dolphin Lodge $$$
Rainforest Lodge
Tel (92) 3663 0392
W dolphinlodge.tur.br
This rustic lodge is popular with international tour operators. Located 78 miles (126 km) southeast of Manaus. Transfer is by van and boats, which is an adventure in itself. Rooms are wooden buildings with thatched roofs.

DK Choice

MANAUS: Juma Lodge $$$
Rainforest Lodge
Tel (92) 3232 2707
W jumalodge.com
A popular lodge for travelers looking to immerse and integrate themselves in the full Amazon experience. Lovely rooms on stilts. Tasty food is on offer in the restaurant, and there are lots of organized activities. Three hours from Manaus by boat, or 30 minutes by hydroplane, but the transfer is part of the adventure.

MANAUS: Uakari Lodge $$$
Rainforest Lodge
Tel (97) 3343 4160
W uakarilodge.com.br
Well-regarded floating lodge that can handle just 24 guests at any one time. Special packages are also offered. Set in pristine jungle surroundings.

Windows galore at Cristalino Jungle Lodge, one of the best ecolodges in the world

Roraima

BOA VISTA: Aipana Plaza $
Business
Praça Centro Cívico 974, 69301 380
Tel (95) 3212 0800
W aipanaplaza.com.br
If you need a place to stay in Boa Vista, you cannot go far wrong with the Aipana Plaza, in a good downtown central location.

Acre

RIO BRANCO (ACRE): Holiday inn Express Rio Branco $
Business
Rua Rio Grande do Sul 332, 69990 324
Tel (68) 3302 2300
W hiexpress.com
Rio Branco is another town not blessed with many hotels. This centrally located Holiday Inn Express, though, has a rooftop pool and fitness center.

Rondônia

PORTO VELHO: Oscar Hotel Executive $
Business
Av 7 de Setembro, 934, 78916 100
Tel (69) 2182 0600
W oscarhotelexecutive.com.br
This hotel is located in the city center and is close to restaurants and bars. There's a small rooftop pool and bar with city views.

Brasília, Goiás & Tocantins

Brasília

BRASÍLIA: Kubitschek Plaza $$
Business
HN Quadra 2, Bloco E, Asa Norte, 70702 904
Tel (61) 3319 3543
W kubitschek.com.br
Reliable, centrally situated hotel that is popular for events and small conferences. Front rooms have lovely views of the city.

BRASÍLIA: Meliá Brasíl 21 $$
Business
Setor Hoteleiro Sul, Quadra 6 Bloco D, 70316 000
Tel (61) 3218 4700
W solmelia.com
This towering hotel is close to the TV Tower and National Stadium. Offers a "Women Traveling Alone" program. Elegant rooms.

BRASÍLIA: Quality Hotel $$
Business
SMAS Trecho 3, Conjunto 2, Bloco A, 71215 300
Tel (61) 2196 6090
W atlanticahotels.com.br
This popular, modern, low-rise hotel is situated about 15 minutes from the center.

DK Choice

BRASÍLIA: Royal Tulip Brasília $$
Business
Setor Hoteleiro Norte, Trecho 01, Conjunto 1B, Bloco C, 70800 200
Tel (61) 3424 7000
W royaltulipbrasiliaalvorada.com
In a city full of fairly nondescript hotels, the stylish Royal Tulip is more of a resort property that sits on the edge of Lake Paranoá. Excellent large pool area. Front rooms have lake views. Ten-minute taxi ride to the city center. Close to the residence of the Brazilian president.

Goiás

CHAPADA DOS VEADEIRO: Casa Rosa $
Pousada
Rua Gumercindo Barbosa 233, 73770 000
Tel (62) 3446 1319
W pousadacasarosa.com.br
Simple *pousada* with a pleasant garden and pool, close to the entrance to the national park. Accommodation is in the main house and a number of chalets.

Mato Grosso & Mato Grosso do Sul

Mato Grosso

DK Choice

ALTA FLORESTA: Cristalino Jungle Lodge $$
Rainforest Lodge
Av Teles Pires 2001, 78580 000
Tel (66) 3521 1396
W cristalinolodge.com.br
This highly regarded place is considered one of the world's best ecolodges. Located within a private forest reserve, it has 16 stylish and comfortable guest quarters offering every convenience. There's a floating deck, a restaurant with views, and two 165-ft (50-m) observation towers to look over the canopy of trees. Full program of activities.

CUIABÁ: Deville Cuíabá $$
Business
Av Isaac Póvoas 1000, 78032 015
Tel (63) 3319 3000
W deville.com.br
Modern hotel situated in the city center, close to bars, restaurants, and nightlife. Good base for heading in and out of the Pantanal.

CUIABÁ: Gran Odara Hotel $$
Business
Av Miguel Sutil 8344, Ribeirão da Ponte, 78040 400
Tel (65) 3616 2014
W en.hotelgranodara.com.br/hotel
This comfortable, well-run hotel is ideal when having to stay overnight in Cuiabá before or after transfers to and from the Pantanal.

POCONÉ: Araras Lodge $$
Rainforest Lodge
Est Parque Transpantaneira Zona Rural, 78175 000
Tel (65) 3682 2800
W araraslodge.com.br
This ecolodge is particularly popular with birders but offers a full range of Pantanal activities for which it is well sited and equipped. The transfer from Cuiabá takes 2 hours and 30 minutes.

Mato Grosso do Sul

BONITO: Zagaia Eco-Resort $$
Resort
Rod Bonito–Três Morros, Km 0, 79290 000
Tel (0800) 979 4400
W zagaia.com.br
Close to Bontio, this family-friendly ecolodge is a good base from which to explore the surrounding area and the crystal-clear waters.

For more information on types of hotels *see pages 368–9*

The lush greenery of the grounds at Meia Lua, which also has a pool for guests

CAMPO GRANDE: Grand Park Hotel $$
Business
Av Afonso Pena 5282, 79040 010
Tel (67) 3044 4444
W grandparkhotel.com.br
Modern, centrally located hotel close to bars and restaurants and in front of the city's main shopping center. Good choice if staying overnight before or after a visit to a Pantanal lodge.

CAMPO GRANDE: Jandaia $$
Business
Rua Barão do Rio Branco 1271, 79002 174
Tel (67) 3316 7700
W jandaia.com.br
Slightly dated, this is still a good hotel option for overnight stays before or after visiting the Pantanal. It is also conveniently located for the airport.

MIRANDA: Meia Lua $
Rainforest Lodge
BR 262, Km 547, Zona Rural, 79380 000
Tel (67) 9686 9064
W pantanalranchmeialua.com
This ranch a few miles outside of Miranda makes a simple, unfussy base from which to explore parts of the Pantanal. Organized activities. Lovely grounds.

MIRANDA: Refúgio Ecológico Caiman $$$
Rainforest Lodge
Estância Caiman s/n, Zona Rural, 79380 000
Tel (67) 3242 1450
W caiman.com.br
One of the best-equipped Pantanal lodges, in the heart of the region, this comprises two comfortable *pousadas* and private villas and is still a working farm. Rates include guided tours and transfers.

Santa Catarina & Paraná

Santa Catarina

FLORIANÓPOLIS: Blue Tree Towers Florianópolis $$
Business
Rua Bocaiuva 2304, 88015 530
Tel (48) 3251 5555
W bluetree.com.br
Modern, centrally situated hotel close to restaurants, bars, and a shopping center. It is better for business than leisure, as it is away from the island's main beaches.

FLORIANÓPOLIS: Quinta do Bucanero $$
Resort
Estrada Geral do Rosa s/n, 88780 000
Tel (48) 3355 6056
W bucanero.com.br
Charming, romantic *pousada* in a glorious setting overlooking Praia do Rosa; it is an oasis of calm at the end of a dirt track. About 53 miles (85 km) south of Florianópolis. No children under 14.

FLORIANÓPOLIS: Vila Tamarindo $$
Business
Av Campeche 1836, 88063 300
Tel (48) 3237 3464
W tamarindo.com.br
Popular *pousada* on Praia do Campeche and a 10-minute stroll from the activities at Riozinho. Lovely setting and grounds.

FLORIANÓPOLIS: Costão do Santinho Resort & Spa $$$
Resort
Rodovia Vereador Onildo Lemos 2505, 88058 700
Tel (48) 3261 1000
W costao.com.br
Large resort that is popular for conventions and events. Lovely beach setting. Rooms can be pot luck; some are more modern than others. There is a golf course.

DK Choice

FLORIANÓPOLIS: Ponta dos Ganchos $$$
Resort
Rua Eupídeo Alves do Nascimento 104, 88190 000
Tel (48) 3262 5000
W pontadosganchos.com.br
This stylish, romantic boutique resort is one of the best in Brazil, and truly world-class. Stunning beachfront setting on a headland north of Florianópolis, with breathtaking views. Stay in deluxe bungalows. No children under 18. Book well in advance.

FLORIANÓPOLIS: Quinta das Videiras $$$
Boutique
Rua Afonso Luiz Borba 113, 88062 070
Tel (48) 3232 3005
W quintadasvideiras.com.br
This stylish hotel appears to be a colonial mansion but is in fact a new-build with historic touches. Located on Lagoa da Conceição, close to bars and restaurants.

Paraná

CURITIBA: Four Points by Sheraton $$
Business
Av Sete de Setembro 4211, 80250 210
Tel (41) 3340 4000
W starwoodhotels.com
Good standard Four Point hotel that is located in the Batel residential area, close to restaurants, bars, malls, and the historic center. There is a floor exclusively for women.

CURITIBA: Mercure Curitiba Golden $$
Business
Rua Desembargador Motta 2044, 80420 190
Tel (41) 3322 7666
W mercure.com
This well-located hotel in the Batel area offers all the facilities you expect from the Mercure group.

CURITIBA: Slaviero Conceptual Full Jazz Hotel $$
Business
Rua Silveira Peixoto 1297, 80240 120
Tel (41) 3312 7000
W slavierohoteis.com.br
With jazz as its theme, this Slaviero property makes a welcome change from the town's more standard business hotels. Large rooms with city views. Live jazz twice a week in the bar.

FOZ DO IGUAÇU: Che Largato $
Hostel
Av Juscelino Kubitschek 874, 85851 210
Tel (45) 3027 8300
W chelagarto.com
Centrally located in Foz and close to public transport, this popular hostel offers dorms or private rooms. Nice roof terrace and bar.

FOZ DO IGUAÇU: Nadai Confort $
Business
Av República Argentina 1332, 85852 090
Tel (45) 3521 5050
W nadaiconforthotel.com.br
Popular option in the center of Foz for visitors on a budget. It is pleasant and comfortable.

FOZ DO IGUAÇU: Bourbon Resort $$$
Resort
Rodovia das Cataratas, Km 2, 85853 000
Tel (45) 3521 3900
w bourbon.com.br
This large, self-contained resort is frequented by both Brazilian and foreign visitors. Located between the town and the falls and good for families.

DK Choice

FOZ DO IGUAÇU: Hotel das Cataratas Belmond $$$
Historical / Resort
Iguaçu National Park, 85863 000
Tel (45) 2102 7000
w hoteldascataratas.com
This grand hotel is the place to stay when visiting the falls, as it is the only property located in the park itself. Standards are everything you would expect from Belmond: lovely rooms, pool area, and so on. The park closes at night, so early in the morning and during the night, guests have the Brazilian side of the falls to themselves, which is worth paying a price for.

MORRETES: Santuário Nhundiaquara $$
Lodge
Est das Prainhas, Km 02, Porto de Cima, 83350 000
Tel (41) 9972 5543
w nhundiaquara.com.br
This is a good base when exploring Morretes and the Serra do Mar. Rustic charm at a reasonable price.

PARANAGUÁ: San Rafael $$
Business
Rua Julia da Costa 185, 83203 060
Tel (41) 3721 9000
w sanrafaelhotel.com.br
There is not a lot of choice if you need to stay in Paranaguá, but San Rafael is well located and comfortable, if unremarkable.

Rio Grande do Sul

BENTO GONÇALVES: Don Giovanni $$
Pousada
Linha Amadeu 28, Km 12, 95700 000
Tel (54) 3455 6293
w dongiovanni.com.br
This 20th-century Italian-style farmhouse surrounded by the Don Giovanni vineyards is 8 miles (12 km) outside of Bento Gonçalves. Mix of rustic charm and contemporary style.

BENTO GONÇALVES: Villa Valduga $$$
Pousada
Linha Leopoldina, Vale dos Vinhedos, 95700 000
Tel (54) 2105 3154
w villavalduga.com.br
Four charming, modern *pousadas* are offered at the Villa Valduga winery, close to Bento Gonçalves. Breakfast and a wine course and tasting are included. No children under 15.

CANELA: Cravo & Canela $$
Pousada
Rua Ten Manoel Correa 144, 95680 000
Tel (54) 3282 1120
w pousadacravoecanela.com.br
Delightful little *pousada* that is ideal for exploring Canela. The rooms and grounds are lovely, and it is close to the town center in a quiet residential road.

GRAMADO: Saint Andrews $$$
Boutique
Rua das Flores 171, 95670 000
Tel (54) 3295 7700
w saintandrews.com.br
Elegant, well-kept intimate hotel, with lovely mountain views. The restaurant is excellent and the service impeccable.

GRAMADO: St Hubertus $$$
Boutique
Rua da Carrieri 974, 95670 000
Tel (54) 3286 1273
w sthubertus.com
Welcoming, romantic hotel overlooking Lago Negro, 1 mile (2 km) from the city center. Lovely grounds. It is a good base for exploring Gramado and the surrounding countryside.

PORTO ALEGRE: Solar 63 $
Hostel
Rua Octávio Corrêa 63, 90050 120
Tel (51) 3092 0063
w solar63hostel.com.br
Clean and friendly hostel close to the historic center, bars, and restaurants. It has four small dorms and one double room.

PORTO ALEGRE: Laghetto Viverone Moinhos $$
Business
Rua Doutor Vale 579, 90560 010
Tel (51) 2102 7272
w hotellaghettomoinhos.com.br
The reception here is in a restored historic building at the front of the modern hotel. It is centrally located and close to restaurants and bars.

PORTO ALEGRE: Sheraton Porto Alegre $$
Business
Rua Olavo Barreto Viana 18, 90570 070
Tel (51) 2121 6000
w sheraton-poa.com.br
Smart hotel in a central location, and next to the elegant Moinhos Shopping Mall. It has spacious rooms and offers everything you would expect of a Sheraton.

SÃO MIGUEL DAS MISSÕES: Missões $
Pousada
Rua São Nicolau 601, 98865 000
Tel (55) 3381 1202
w pousadadasmissoes.com.br
Simple, well-located property with private rooms and dorms, near the Jesuit ruins. It is a good choice when visiting the missions. Lovely grounds and pool.

A choice of pools at the large Bourbon Resort, popular with foreign tourists and Brazilians

For more information on types of hotels *see pages 368–9*

WHERE TO EAT & DRINK

As a melting pot of races and influences, Brazil has a rich diversity of regional culinary styles *(see pp182–3 and pp384–5)*.

Although the term "haute cuisine" does not strictly apply to Brazilian fare, the art of eating well, or *arte do comer bem*, is known to all Brazilians. A light breakfast, a hearty lunch that can last from noon to 3pm, and a late afternoon snack are followed by an even later dinner that may go on beyond midnight. Saturday and Sunday lunches

are an elaborate, extended family affair, possibly a *feijoada* (meat and bean stew). Everywhere in Brazil it is easy to get well-cooked, filling meals. For light snacks, there are umpteen *lanchonetes*, or corner snack bars. For lunch, a *botequim*, or simple gastro pub, can be fun, while dining at a formal *rodízio* all-you-can-eat barbecue is a must. Famous for offering the widest varieties of cuisine, São Paulo is seen as the best place for an authentic culinary experience.

Restaurants & Bars

In Brazil, restaurants and bars come in every shape and size. From the corner *botecos* (pubs) and beach bars to elegant world-class restaurants, Brazil has it all. There is a good range to suit every budget. Even dining in top-notch restaurants, especially away from Rio de Janeiro and São Paulo, offers value for money in comparison to anywhere in Europe or North America.

Most Brazilian restaurants have a website, so check the photos to get a clearer idea of whether or not a place is to your taste.

Local Eating Habits

Visitors will recognize that many Brazilian eating habits have been influenced by European countries. People eat leisurely and throughout the day, although those who want to snatch a quick bite will not be disappointed. Several restaurants are open all through the day, so the lunch hour is spread over many hours.

Brazilians generally eat dinner late, many of them preferring to start at 10pm or later. At the weekend, numerous restaurants in the bigger cities, such as Rio de Janeiro and São Paulo, take orders well after midnight. It is not unusual to see Brazilians retreating to the bar if they have to wait for a table. Most restaurants take reservations, and this is often necessary at the more fashionable restaurants, especially those in the larger cities.

Due to the many different culinary styles, it is virtually impossible to say what a typical

Brazilian meal will be, although rice and beans will probably make an appearance at some point. Many of the dishes are specific to a region. Breakfast can be a meal in itself, and in most cases it will be a hearty spread of fruits, cold meats, cheeses, and breads. Often this is included in your hotel room rate, so make good use of it.

Dress Code

The easygoing Brazilian nature is also reflected in the dress code. In corner bars, one can walk in wearing casual attire. In Rio and other coastal areas, it is not unusual to see women in bikinis at beach bars. Dress codes, usually more relaxed and tropical in the north, tend to become more formal in the south.

A collar and tie for men may be the norm only in restaurants in the business quarter of cities, or in Brasília, where the politicians and civil servants prefer formal dressing.

Paying & Tipping

The majority of restaurants take credit cards. By far the most widely accepted credit cards are MasterCard and Visa. Amex and Diners Club cards are also useful. However, it is recommended to check first, especially at the more expensive restaurants, where you might not have the cash to cover the bill. If you do get stuck in a "no credit card" situation, do remember that you can probably get cash out of the local ATM machine on your credit card.

Technically, restaurants are not meant to add a 10 percent service charge to the bill; however, in many places, it will be expected as a tip for the staff. If the service charge has not been added, the waiter will normally let you know. It is ideal to leave 10 to 12 percent or, if the service charge has been included, simply round up the bill to the next suitable number. Given the average wage of the staff, tips, however small, are always welcome.

Inside the Box 32 bar in Florianópolis

Food Hygiene

As most of Brazil is hot and tropical, every Brazilian knows the importance of keeping food fresh and well refrigerated. Food poisoning, even among visitors, is rare.

The majority of restaurants use ice cubes made from filtered water. However, in small back-street bars, it is best to avoid ice.

Alcohol & Drinks

On the whole, Brazilians are not great alcohol drinkers. Beer, however, is extremely popular. It is the most popular alcoholic beverage, and the majority of Brazilian beer is a refreshingly cold light lager that comes in bottles (*cerveja*) or on tap (*chopp*). Also common, and much stronger, is a wide variety of drinks containing *cachaça*, a sugar-based spirit. The most notable and well known of these is the *caipirinha* with fresh lime.

Though Scotch is regarded as a status symbol, wine is rapidly growing in popularity, but it is still expensive and can add to the bill. Brazil already produces some excellent table wines, as do neighboring Argentina and Chile. Brazilians also like soft drinks, especially *guaraná*, which is as omnipresent as Coca-Cola. Most bars and restaurants will have bottled water *com* (with) and *sem* (without) gas.

Smoking

There are strict regulations about smoking in Brazil. Visitors should be aware that smoking inside enclosed public spaces, including bars and restaurants, is absolutely forbidden. It is also not permitted in the outside areas of restaurants that are partially covered.

Children

Brazil is a child-friendly country. Most restaurants, however sophisticated or simple, will welcome children. Staff will normally go out of their way to entertain them. If they don't have a suitable chair, they will almost certainly try to improvise something. Do not be shocked

Drinks kiosk on the beach in Morro de São Paulo

by young children eating out late with their parents. That is considered quite normal in Brazil.

Vegetarians

Vegetarian options are limited in Brazil. However, there are a few specialized restaurants offering vegetarian dishes, ranging from basic to highly innovative. *Por quilo* restaurants *(see below)* can be a good option, since they offer large salads and a range of vegetable-based dishes.

Churrascaria Rodízio/ Por Quilo

There are two styles of eating out in Brazil that can take visitors by surprise. The first is the *churrascaria rodízio*, or large barbecue houses, found throughout the country. Here, one fixed price covers the starter and main course. Go to a *churrascaria rodízio* when you are really hungry, as they will keep bringing you succulent pieces of grilled meat. Many offer a "traffic-light system" where each diner will have a card. Leave the green side up if you want more food; red, if not – then back to green for them to start again.

The *por quilo* type are self-service restaurants with a buffet of varying degrees of sophistication and a variety of dishes. What you pay for at the check-out, as far as the food is concerned, will be based on exactly what your plate weighs – hence the name *por quilo*, or "by-the-kilo."

Recommended Restaurants

The restaurants featured on the following pages have been carefully selected to give a cross-section of options in every region: you will find everything from the equivalent of Michelin-starred fine dining and traditional restaurants, to contemporary Brazilian, international cuisine, and bistro fare. The entries are divided into geographical areas corresponding to the chapters in this guide; the entries are then organized by town.

The fine-dining options include some of the best restaurants in Brazil, often in atmospheric and scenic locations. Given the size of Brazil, Brazilian cuisine varies dramatically from region to region. So a typical Bahian dish will be very different to that served in the rest of the Northeast or in the south. The barbecue house is probably the only constant. The international options serve mostly global favorites, while bistros generally offer a range of cuisine alongside Brazilian fare. All will reflect Brazilian influences and ingredients.

The DK Choice entries highlight exceptional establishments that offer more than just excellent food. The majority of these are popular with local residents and visitors, so be sure to inquire regarding reservations well in advance, or you may face a lengthy wait for a table.

Por kilo self-service buffet at the Mangai restaurant *(see p393)*

The Flavors of Brazil

Brazil offers a vast range of regional cuisines. Climate and geography influence ingredients, from the exotic tropical fruits and spices in Northern Brazil to Bahian seafood *(see p183)* and the heavy meat dishes of the southern states. Cultural heritage plays a part as well. In Amazônia, the diet is based on fruits and fish native to the forest and the rivers, with many dishes adapted from indigenous recipes. Farther south, settlement by Portuguese and, later, Italian and German immigrants put a distinctly European stamp on the cooking.

Brazilian Coffee

Freshly caught Bonito tuna on sale at a coastal fish market

Meat

Brazil is a nation that truly enjoys its meat and the wide variety of ways in which beef, chicken, and pork are prepared. The ability to devour large quantities of succulent Brazilian beef is considered a mark of manliness. The family barbecue (*churrasco*) is a Sunday tradition, but for visitors the best way to enjoy

Brazil's superb beef is at a *churrascaria rodízio* (barbecue house). Waiters bring large skewers of freshly barbecued beef and other meats, and slice off cuts directly onto the plate. You can state your preference for *mal passado* (rare), *ao ponto* (medium), or *bem passado* (well done), or you can just point to the part that looks good. Cuts include *filet mignon* (tenderloin), *fraldinha* (bottom sirloin), *picanha* (sirloin), *alcatra* (top sirloin), and *maminha* (sirloin tip). *Cupim* is the soft floppy hump on a cow's shoulders. This tender beef, mixed heavily with fat, is an acquired taste and may not necessarily be liked by all.

Fish & Seafood

Brazilians inherited a love of fish from their Portuguese

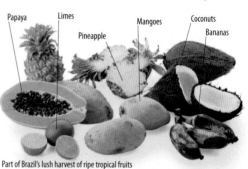
Papaya | Limes | Mangoes | Coconuts | Pineapple | Bananas
Part of Brazil's lush harvest of ripe tropical fruits

Brazilian Dishes & Specialties

Now considered Brazil's national dish, *feijoada* was not always the chic cuisine it is today. The rich black-bean stew traces its humble origins to the kitchens of the country's slave quarters. To make a meal with the leftovers from their masters' tables, the slaves improvised by combining the cast-off bits of meat into a hearty stew with black beans, flavored with garlic, onion, and bay leaves. Nowadays, a full *feijoada completa* spread is typically eaten for lunch on Wednesdays and Saturdays. In addition to the black beans, the stew contains several kinds of meat, including sausage, bacon, and sun-dried beef. Side dishes include rice, roasted cassava flour (*farofa*), sautéed kale, and slices of orange. A *batida de limão* (*cachaça* with ice shavings and lime) is served before the *feijoada*.

Black beans

Salgados, such as deep-fried pastries stuffed with cheese or meat, are popular Brazilian snacks.

Table laid out with all the elements that make up a *feijoada completa*

of Southern Brazil, one finds small, tart *jaboticaba*, and red *acerola* berries, often mixed in juices with other fruits. Farther north are vast orchards of cashew (*caju*) – not the nut, but the large fruit that grows above. In the Amazon, there are *taperaba*, *cupuaçu*, and the queen of Amazon berries, *açaí*. These are often puréed with *guaraná* berry powder or syrup and can be mixed with banana for a high-nutrition smoothie.

forebears. Cod, a Portuguese staple, is sold dried and heavily salted in grocery stores, while cod balls (*bolinhos de bacalhau*) or cod fillets are found on many menus. For fresher fare, Brazil's long coastline offers a bounty of excellent fish and seafood. The colder waters off Santa Catarina offer the country's best oysters. Ilhabela, off São Paulo's green coast, is known for its cold-water jumbo shrimp (*camarão*). Farther north are mollusks, squid, octopus, crab, lobster, shrimp, and, of course, fish. Some of Brazil's best fish come not from the ocean but from the fresh waters of the Pantanal

and the Amazon rainforest. The Pantanal's prize fish is the *dourado*, a fish with firm flesh that is delicious when grilled. Other popular and tasty fish include the *pacú* and *pintado*. In the Amazon, the astounding variety of freshwater fish includes the *tambaqui*, *aruanã*, and tucanaré. They are often served grilled, or in soups with local herbs. Another Amazon freshwater favorite is *caldo de piranha* (piranha broth).

The celebrated Brazilian *caipirinha*

Brazilian Fruits

Along with tropical staples, there are regional fruits, most of which have no English name. In Rio and parts

WHAT TO DRINK

Brazil's best-known drink is almost certainly the *caipirinha*, made with lime, sugar, ice, and *cachaça* (sugar-cane liquor). A better choice for quenching thirst, however, are the wide variety of tropical fruit juices. Brazil's most popular soft drink is the domestically produced *guaraná*. This fizzy drink is prepared with wild *guaraná* berries from Amazônia. Also enormously popular is *chopp*, or draft beer, served ice-cold after a hot day on the beach. *Chá mate*, herbal tea, is usually consumed hot in Southern Brazil, but in the rest of Brazil, it is served cold as iced tea. Although Brazil is very much a cold beverage country, the exception is the ubiquitous *cafézinho*, strong filter coffee. Most Brazilians drink it very sweet and at almost any time of the day.

Camarão na Moranga is a stew of large, juicy prawns cooked in coconut milk and served in a pumpkin.

Picanha steak is a sirloin steak and usually comes served with only a dusting of coarse salt.

Pudim de Leite, a traditional Portuguese dessert, is made from eggs, condensed milk, and caramelized sugar.

Where to Eat & Drink

Rio de Janerio City

BARRA DA TIJUCA: Fratelli $$
Italian
Av Sernambetiba 2916
Tel (21) 2494 6644
This popular eatery close to Barra beachfront opened in 1988 and serves rustic, traditional Italian, including pizza. Good wine list.

BARRA DA TIJUCA: Gero $$
Italian
Av Érico Veríssimo, 190
Tel (21) 3523 5700 **Closed** *Mon*
Gero is part of the exclusive Fasano family. This place serves sophisticated cuisine in a fashionable setting. Less expensive executive menu offered at lunch.

BARRA DA TIJUCA: Enotria por Joachim Koerper $$$
Mediterranean
Av Ayrton Senna 2150, Bloco G Piso ljs.104/105
Tel (21) 2431 9119 **Closed** *Mon dinner*
One of Barra and Rio's best restaurants. The chef Joachim Koerper has already earned a Michelin star from his work in Spain. Here, in CasaShopping, he delivers a menu of contemporary Mediterranean-inspired dishes. .

CENTRO: Albamar $$
Seafood **Map** 5 E3
Praça Marechal Âncora, 184
Tel (21) 2240 8378 **Closed** *Sun dinner*
Open since 1933 and set in the last surviving tower of the old Municipal Market, close to Praça XV. Ask for a window seat, and enjoy views over Guanabara Bay and dine on traditional seafood.

CENTRO: Atrium del Rey $$
International **Map** 5 E3
Praça XV de Novembro, 48
Tel (21) 2220 0193
Pleasant café in what was a palace for the Imperial family from 1808. This is a good choice if looking for a place for lunch during a tour of downtown.

CENTRO: Cais $$
Brazilian **Map** 5 E3
Rua Visconde de Itaboraí, 8
Tel (21) 2203 0178
Attractive and eclectic restaurant set in a warehouse dating from 1878. It is popular for lunch and dinner with those working downtown or going to the cultural corridor. The menu focuses on contemporary Brazilian dishes.

CENTRO: Confeitaria Colombo $$
International **Map** 5 D3
Rua Goncalves Dias, 32
Tel (21) 2505 1500 **Closed** *Sun*
A tourist attraction in its own right, this place has changed little since opening in 1894. It is a coffee shop, tearoom, and restaurant. Many famous people have visited, including King Albert of Belgium and Britain's Queen Elizabeth II.

DK Choice

CENTRO: Nova Capela $$
Brazilian **Map** 5 D5
Av Mem de Sá, 96
Tel (21) 2252 6228
Much loved in Rio's bohemian nightlife scene, this authentic and unpretentious institution dates back to 1903 and serves consistently good food until 3am or later. The signature dish is roast goat with broccoli rice, but other highlights include Brazilian cod balls. Expect large portions. Superb *chopp* on tap.

COPACABANA & LEME: Cervantes $
Botequim **Map** 3 F1
Av Prado Junior 335
Tel (21) 2275 6147 **Closed** *Mon*
A mix of small bar, *botequim*, and restaurant. Famous for sandwiches, late-night snacks, and "one for the road" as night turns to day. Always buzzing and fun.

COPACABANA & LEME: Don Camillo $$
Italian **Map** 3 D3
Av Atlântica, 3056
Tel (21) 2549 9958
Most of Copacabana's beachfront bars are not up to much when it comes to food. Don Camillo is one of the exceptions, serving excellent Italian cuisine. Choose to sit either on the outside terrace or inside in a more formal dining area.

COPACABANA & LEME: Cipriani $$$
Italian **Map** 3 E2
Av Atlântica, 1702 (Copacabana Palace)
Tel (21) 2548 7070 **Closed** *Sun dinner*
This is an outstanding restaurant offering top northern Italian cuisine. The setting, overlooking the pool of the Copacabana Palace, makes it even more special. Not surprisingly, it is popular with visiting celebrities.

Price Guide

Prices are based on a two-course meal and non-alcoholic drinks for one person, plus service charges.

$	up to $25
$$	$25 to $55
$$$$$	over $55

COPACABANA & LEME: Le Pré Catelan $$$
French **Map** 3 D5
Av Atlântica (Sofitel), 4240, Nível E
Tel (21) 2525 1160 **Closed** *lunch, Sun*
One of Rio's most sophisticated French restaurants and one of the best. On offer is a traditional menu of French favorites, with some sublime Brazilian touches and flavors, including dishes from the Amazon region.

FLAMENGO & BOTAFOGO: Fogo de Chão $$
Brazilian
Av Repórter Nestor Moreira, s/n
Tel (21) 2279 7117
One of Brazil's best-known *rodízio* all-you-can-eat barbecue houses serving tender, tasty meats. Beef is the specialty, but chicken, pork, and lamb are also available. Enjoy views over Sugar Loaf Mountain and Guanabara Bay as you eat.

FLAMENGO & BOTAFOGO: Irajá $$
Brazilian
Rua Conde de Irajá 109
Tel (21) 2246 1395
This restaurant has helped build Botafogo's growing reputation as a hub for interesting, inventive, and contemporary dishes in fun surroundings. Special tasting menu of 10 to 12 courses.

Stunning views across Guanabara Bay at Albamar

FLAMENGO & BOTAFOGO:
Majoríca $$
Steakhouse
Rua Senador Vergueiro, 11/15
Tel (21) 2205 6820
At this traditional and reliable barbecue house, you order from an extensive menu. It is a favorite with residents and visitors alike for some of the best meat dishes in town.

FLAMENGO & BOTAFOGO:
Miam Miam $$
French/Brazilian
Rua General Goes Monteiro, 34
Tel (21) 2244 0125 **Closed** *Sun & Mon*
Contemporary and creative comfort food and a relaxed retro vibe have made Miam Miam a popular option. Try the oxtail in crispy-crust pastry, or shrimp with spaghetti, peach palm, and garlic couscous. If you can't decide, go for the tasting menu.

FLAMENGO & BOTAFOGO:
Lasai $$$
Spanish/Brazilian
Rua Conde de Irajá 191
Tel (21) 3449 1834 **Closed** *Sun & Mon*
The chefs here have both worked at Spain's two-Michelin-starred Mugaritz. On offer are two daily-changing contemporary set menus of innovative and inventive dishes. A gourmand paradise.

FLAMENGO & BOTAFOGO:
Porcão $$$
Brazilian
Av Infante Dom Henrique s/n, Aterro do Flamengo
Tel (21) 3389 8989
The flagship branch of Rio's own *rodízio* all-you-can-eat barbecue chain is always excellent, with a choice of dishes that offers much more than just grilled meats. Plenty to satisfy vegetarians, too.

IPANEMA & LEBLON:
Capricciosa $$
Pizzeria **Map** 2 B5
Rua Vinícius de Moraes, 134
Tel (21) 2523 3394
This popular and family-friendly pizzeria is considered by many to offer the best pizza in Rio, but it isn't the cheapest.

IPANEMA & LEBLON:
Casa da Feijoada $$
Brazilian **Map** 2 B5
Rua Prudente de Moraes 10
Tel (21) 2523 4994
Feijoada is one of Brazil and Rio's most traditional dishes, but often only to be found on a Saturday. Casa das Feijoada solves this problem by serving this and other traditional Brazilian dishes every day of the week.

Modern meets rustic at the innovative, inventive Lasai

IPANEMA & LEBLON:
Satyricon $$
Seafood **Map** 2 B4
Rua Barão Da Torre, 192
Tel (21) 2521 0627
Smart, elegant, reliable seafood restaurant, of which there is a surprisingly limited choice in Rio. It made a name for itself after Madonna dropped in, quickly followed by Diana Ross and other celebrities.

IPANEMA & LEBLON:
Sawasdee $$
Asian **Map** 2 A4
Rua Barão da Torre, 446
Tel (21) 3322 2150
This Ipanema branch is the flagship of a well-dressed group that consistently serves some of the city's best and most interesting Asian cuisine, with a focus on Thai. The curries are excellent, or try the squid stuffed with pork and shrimp.

IPANEMA & LEBLON:
Le Vin Bistro $$
French **Map** 2 A4
Rua Barão da Torre, 490
Tel (21) 3502 1002
Comfortable and relaxing French bistro in the heart of Ipanema. Instantly recognizable dishes, such as duck confit with sautéed potatoes. Another branch can be found in Barra Shopping Center.

IPANEMA & LEBLON:
Antiquarius $$$
Portuguese **Map** 1 A5
Rua Arístides Espínola 19
Tel (21) 2294 1049
An elegant, old-school institution serving quality Portuguese fare, international favorites, and a highly regarded *feijoada*. For four decades, this has been one of Rio's better restaurants.

IPANEMA & LEBLON:
Esplanada Grill $$$
Steakhouse **Map** 1 C4
Rua Barão da Torre, 600
Tel (21) 2512 2970
Cozy steakhouse in the middle of Ipanema that delivers consistently high standards. There are more than 30 cuts of meat to choose from. This is a good alternative to the larger barbecue houses.

IPANEMA & LEBLON:
Fasano al Mare $$$
Italian **Map** 2 B5
Av Vieira Souto 80
Tel (21) 3202 4030
Italian, Mediterranean, and seafood are on offer at this elegant (and expensive) flagship restaurant of the Fasano chain. Designed by Philippe Starck, this hotel is also home to Baretto-Londra, one of Rio's top bars. It gets very busy at weekends, so book ahead.

LAGOA & JARDIM BOTÂNICO:
Bar Lagoa $
German/Botequim **Map** 2 A4
Av Epitacio Pessoa, 1674
Tel (21) 2523 1135 **Closed** *lunch Mon–Fri*
Art Deco bar overlooking the Lagoa that serves a menu of snacks and main meals with a German touch. Great draft beer. Built in 1934 as Bar Berlin, this has become a Rio institution.

LAGOA & JARDIM BOTÂNICO:
Lagoon $$
International **Map** 1 B3
Av Borges Medeiros 1424
Tel (21) 2529 5300
Lagoon is an entertainment complex, so it has several restaurants, including Giuseppe Grill Mar, Gula Gula, Quadrifoglio, Pax Delícia, and Sushi Lagoa.

For more information on types of restaurants *see page 383*

LAGOA & JARDIM BOTÂNICO:
Roberta Sudbrack $$
Brazilian
Av Lineu de Paula Machado, 916
Tel (21) 3874 0139   **Closed** *Sun*
Located in a house close to the
Botanical Gardens, Roberta
Sudbrack offers modern Brazilian
dishes with a twist. Exquisite food.

DK Choice

LAGOA & JARDIM BOTÂNICO:
Olympe $$$
French   **Map** 2 A2
Rua Custódio Serrão 62
Tel (21) 2539 4542   **Closed** *Sun*
Claude Troisgros may come
from France, but he is also Rio's
most famous and respected
chef, who has been perfecting
the art of combining Brazilian
ingredients and style with the
best he can bring from France.
Small, elegant Olympe is the
flagship of the Troisgros empire.

LAGOA & JARDIM BOTÂNICO:
Rubaiyat $$$
Steakhouse   **Map** 1 A2
Rua Jardim Botânico 971
Tel (21) 3204 9999   **Closed** *Sun
dinner*
In 2014, Rio finally got a branch of
São Paulo's upmarket steakhouse.
The views of Christ the Redeemer
and the Jockey Club are a bonus.
Ask for a table on the balcony.

DK Choice

SANTA TERESA: Aprazível$$$
Brazilian
Rua Aprazível 62
Tel (21) 2508 9174   **Closed** *Sun
dinner, Mon*
This is one of those places to
which locals take visitors for long
lunches. Hidden in Santa Teresa,
and with superb views, offering
tropical dining and interesting
dishes. Rustic, yet classy. Try the
grilled salt-water fish with
orange sauce, coconut rice,
cashew nuts, and baked plantain.

Rio de Janeiro State & Espírito Santo

Rio de Janeiro State

BÚZIOS: Estância Don Juan $$
Steakhouse
Rua das Pedras, 178
Tel (22) 2623 2169   **Closed** *Mon;
lunch Tue & Wed in low season*
Seafood rules in Búzios, but if you
want a good steak in relaxed
surroundings, head for Don Juan.

*A beautifully presented dish at Glouton,
Belo Horizonte*

BÚZIOS: Cigalon $$$
French
Av José Bento Ribeiro Dantas 199
Tel (22) 2623 1249
One of the prettiest restaurants in
Búzios with views across the bay,
Cigalon is located in the house
where Brigitte Bardot stayed in
1964. French-inspired dishes and
seafood take pride of place.

BÚZIOS: Satyricon $$$
Seafood
Av José Ribeiro Dantas 500
Tel (22) 2623 2691
Satyricon is considered one of
Rio's best seafood restaurants,
and the produce is as fresh as
can be. Consistently good.

DK Choice

BÚZIOS: Sollar $$$
Italian
*Avenida José Bento Ribeiro
Dantas, 994*
Tel (22) 2623 5392   **Closed** *Sun–
Wed*
Italian chef Danio Braga made
his name in Rio and now
spends his time between the
mountains and Búzios. He is
responsible for one of the
town's very best menus. Tasty
Italian dishes predominate,
along with seafood.

PARATY: Banana da Terra $$
Seafood
Rua Doutor Samuel Costa, 198
Tel (24) 3371 1725   **Closed** *lunch
Mon–Thu*
Located in the historic center
in a 17th-century house, this
charming, innovative Brazilian
restaurant is under the command
of Ana Bueno.

PARATY: Bartholomeu $$
French
Rua Doutor Samuel Costa, 176
Tel (24) 3371 5032
Delightful contemporary French
restaurant that captures the
historic spirit of Paraty in its
setting. It also offers the more
informal garden setting of Bartô
in the city square.

PARATY: Punto Divino $$
Italian
Rua Marechal Deodoro, 129
Tel (24) 3371 1348
Seafood and pizza – and even a
seafood pizza – take pride of place
on the menu in this romantic little
restaurant just off the main
square. There is often live music.

**PETRÓPOLIS: Imperatriz
Leopoldina – Solar do
Império** $$
Portuguese
Av Koeller, 376
Tel (24) 2103 3000
Elegant setting within Petrópolis's
centrally located hotel, which
itself is situated within two grand
19th-century houses. It is well
known for its tea served on Friday
and Saturday at 5pm.

PETRÓPOLIS: Majórica $$
Steakhouse
Rua do Imperador, 754
Tel (24) 2242 2498
High in the hills of Petrópolis, this
is the place to come if you need
a meat fix. The traditional, reliable
steakhouse offers a full menu,
including seafood and salads.

Espírito Santo

VITÓRIA: Lareira Portuguesa $$
Portuguese
Av Saturnino de Brito, 260
Tel (27) 3345 0331
This attractive, modern restaurant
is famous for its *bacalhau* (cod)
and *moquecas* (fish stews).

Minas Gerais

DK Choice

BELO HORIZONTE:
Glouton $$
Brazilian
Rua Bárbara Heliodora, 59
Tel (31) 3292 4237   **Closed** *Mon*
Come here for innovative, high-
quality, creative, contemporary
Brazilian and international fare
as part of an ever-changing
menu. Simple yet elegant
setting. There is also a small,
pretty garden area.

**BELO HORIZONTE:
Hermengarda** $$
Brazilian
Rua Outono, 314
Tel (31) 3225 3268   **Closed** *Mon*
Come here for excellent contemporary Brazilian cuisine with a strong infusion of Minas, set in a house that pays homage to the chef's grandmother.

BELO HORIZONTE: Trindade $$
Regional
Rua Alvarenga Peixoto 388
Tel (31) 2512 4479   **Closed** *Mon, lunch Tue–Sat*
Mineiro cooking is given a contemporary and creative touch in this modern and comfortable restaurant. Choose to sit either on the veranda or in the main room.

**BELO HORIZONTE:
Vecchio Sogno** $$
Italian
Rua Martim de Carvalho, 75
Tel (31) 3292 5251 **Closed** *Sat lunch & Sun dinner*
Classic Italian dining with local touches that keep the menu fresh. For over 20 years, this central restaurant has been considered one of Belo Horizonte's best and most consistent.

OURO PRETO: O Passo $
Italian
Rua São José 56
Tel (31) 3552 5089
Known for its pizza and live jazz, O Passo also offers a fuller menu of a surprisingly high standard. Try to get a table on the terrace, with views over the historic town.

**OURO PRETO: Senhora do
Rosário** $
Regional
Rua Getúlio Vargas 270
Tel (31) 3551 4200
In an elegant setting in one of Ouro Preto's most charming and well-structured *pousadas*, here you

will find a menu of local favorites and international dishes.

OURO PRETO: Bené da Flauta $$
Regional
Rua São Francisco de Assis, 32
Tel (31) 3551 1036
Located close to the church of São Francisco, this place serves traditional Mineiro fare in a beautiful colonial house. The upper floor has the best views.

OURO PRETO: Chafariz $$
Regional
Rua São José 167
Tel (31) 3551 2828   **Closed** *dinner, Mon*
Very popular for its large, well-priced buffet of Mineiro dishes – a great way to try many of the local specialties at one sitting.

**TIRADENTES: Estalagem do
Sabor** $$
Regional
Rua Ministro Gabriel Passos 280A
Tel (32) 3355 1144   **Closed** *dinner*
One of the oldest and most respected restaurants in Tiradentes serves typical Mineiro cuisine from the freshest local ingredients. Small and homely.

TIRADENTES: Kitanda Brasil $$
Brazilian
Rua Padroeiro Santo Antônio, 240
Tel (32) 3355 1560   **Closed** *Mon–Thu*
Superb, creative Brazilian dishes have resulted in this small restaurant being included on the list of Brazil's best. Excellent *caipirinhas*, and there's even a colorful hammock to sleep it off.

TIRADENTES: Theatro da Villa $$
French
Rua Padre Toledo 157
Tel (32) 3355 1275   **Closed** *Sun*
One for a special night out, this restaurant has a small but interesting menu. It is in the town's old theater, and musicians

often take to the small stage or garden at the weekend.

TIRADENTES: Tragaluz $$
Regional
Rua Direita, 52
Tel (32) 9968 4837   **Closed** *Tue*
Wonderful romantic setting in a small colonial town house. The menu features dishes that have a modern take on Mineiro cuisine, as well as international favorites.

São Paulo City

CENTRO: La Casserole $$
French   **Map** 1 B2
Largo do Arouche, 346
Tel (11) 3331 6283   **Closed** *Sun dinner, Mon*
This intimate, traditional French restaurant opened in 1954. The vibe is business at lunch and romantic in the evening.

CENTRO: Terraço Itália $$
Mediterranean   **Map** 1 B2
Av Ipiranga, 344
Tel (11) 2189 2929
Very few come to Terraço Itália for the food. The main attraction is the stunning views over the city center from the 42nd floor.

CENTRO: Famiglia Mancini $$$
Italian   **Map** 1 B3
Rua Avanhandava, 81
Tel (11) 3256 4320
In a city with many fine Italian restaurants, this traditional *cantina* is one of the favorites with the locals. Book ahead.

HIGIENÓPOLIS: Carlota $$
Brazilian
Rua Sergipe, 753
Tel (11) 3661 8670   **Closed** *Sun dinner*
Charming and inventive "multicultural" bistro. Owner Carla Pernambuco hosts cooking programs and writes cookbooks.

HIGIENÓPOLIS: Ici Bistro $$$
French
Rua Pará, 36
Tel (11) 3259 6896
Cozy and romantic French bistro of a high standard. The steak is a highlight. Good wine list.

**JARDINS & AV PAULISTA:
Amadeus** $$
Seafood   **Map** 4 E2
Rua Haddock Lobo, 807
Tel (11) 3061 2859
This elegant, traditional family restaurant serves high-quality modern and traditional seafood dishes. It's considered the place to go for seafood in São Paulo.

Airy and spacious dining room at the Bené da Flauta, Ouro Preto

For more information on types of restaurants *see page 383*

JARDINS & AV PAULISTA:
Tordesilhas $$
Brazilian **Map** 4 D2
Alameda Tietê, 489
Tel (11) 3107 7444 **Closed** *Sun dinner, Mon, lunch Tue–Fri*
One of the few restaurants in town to take traditional Brazilian cuisine seriously, this is the place to go for a true taste of Brazil's culinary arts. A good English-language menu helps visitors on this voyage of discovery.

DK Choice

JARDINS & AV PAULISTA:
D.O.M. $$$
Brazilian **Map** 4 D3
Rua Barão de Capanema 549
Tel (11) 3088 0761 **Closed** *Sat lunch, Sun*
Chef Alex Atala is globally recognized as one of the world's most creative. His flagship restaurant regularly features in the list of the world's top ten. A meal at D.O.M. is not something you are going to forget, but that also means making a reservation before you arrive in town. This may be one of the highlights of your visit to São Paulo.

JARDINS & AV PAULISTA:
Fasano $$$
Italian **Map** 4 D3
Rua Vittorio Fasano, 88
Tel (11) 3062 4000 **Closed** *Sun*
Sophisticated, classy Italian with prices to match, this is the highly regarded eponymous flagship of the Fasano group.

JARDINS & AV PAULISTA:
Figueira Rubaiyat $$$
Steakhouse **Map** 4 D3
Rua Haddock Lobo, 1738
Tel (11) 3087 1399
Diners come here for some of the best beef in town in an informal, chic setting. Fish and vegetarian dishes are also available.

JARDINS & AV PAULISTA:
Rodeio $$$
Steakhouse **Map** 4 D3
Rua Haddock Lobo, 1498
Tel (11) 3474 1333
One of the city's oldest and most charming barbecue houses opened in 1958 and helped make the Jardins fashionable. It is walking distance from some of the city's most exclusive boutiques.

LIBERDADE: Sushi Yassu $$
Asian **Map** 1 C4
Rua Américo de Campos, 46
Tel (11) 3288 2966 **Closed** *Mon*
São Paulo has one of the largest Japanese communities in the world, and they consider this the best traditional Japanese restaurant in town. Located in the heart of the Japanese quarter.

PINHEIROS: Arturito $$
Mediterraneanl
Rua Artur de Azevedo 542
Tel (11) 3063 4951
The food here is creative and tasty; the setting, modern and charming. Chef Paola Carosella hails from Argentina and is a judge on Brazilian TV's *MasterChef*.

PINHEIROS: Mani $$$
Brazilian **Map** 3 B3
Rua Joaquim Antunes, 210
Tel (11) 3085 4148 **Closed** *Mon*
Mani is regularly on the list of the world's best restaurants, and Helena Rizzo is its award-winning chef. Stylish and modern, yet homely – all of which is reflected in the menu. Try the tasting menu.

PINHEIROS: Vecchio Torino $$$
Italian
Rua Tavares Cabral, 119
Tel (11) 3816 0592 **Closed** *Sun dinner, Mon*
Hidden away in a fairly nondescript house in a side road, this place offers sophisticated, traditional Italian cuisine. The *gnocchi* is highly rated, and there is an impressive wine list.

VILA OLÍMPIA & ITAIM BIBI:
Attimo $$
Italian
Rua Diogo Jácome, 341
Tel (11) 5054 9999 **Closed** *Mon*
Modern, well-dressed, and cool, this restaurant has a creative and interesting menu that mixes Italian and Brazilian influences. Well-priced executive menu for lunch.

DK Choice

VILA OLÍMPIA & ITAIM BIBI:
Rascal $$
Buffet
Av Presidente Juscelino Kubitschek, 2041
Tel (11) 3152 6111
The flagship branch of Rascal has built a reputation for its high-quality, competitively priced all-you-can-eat buffet, to which other dishes may be added from the à la carte menu, including pizza. Well-priced wine list.

DK Choice

VILA OLÍMPIA & ITAIM BIBI:
Fogo de Chão $$$
Barbecue (Churrascaria)
Av dos Bandeirantes, 538
Tel (11) 5505 0791
When it comes to upmarket *rodízio* all-you-can-eat barbecue houses that really deliver, then Fogo de Chão is often found at the top of the list. It may appear pricey at first glance, but the variety and quality of the food on offer is worth the cost.

VILA OLÍMPIA & ITAIM BIBI:
Kinoshita $$$
Asian
Rua Jacques Félix, 405
Tel (11) 3849 6940 **Closed** *Sun*
Highly regarded authentic Japanese cuisine with a twist of fusion and Kappo cuisine. It is all delivered in a stylish, elegant, and tasteful atmosphere. In a city well renowned for its good Asian options, this is one of the best.

VILA OLÍMPIA & ITAIM BIBI:
Skye $$$
International **Map** 4 E5
Av Brigadeiro Luís Antônio, 4700
Tel (11) 3055 4702
This is the rooftop restaurant and bar that São Paulo's most stylish and fashionable boutique hotel deserves, with jaw-dropping views across São Paulo. It is the place to see and be seen, and the contemporary international menu does not disappoint.

One of the superb dishes created by Alex Atala at D.O.M., São Paulo City

Elegant, relaxed dining area at A Casa Vidal, Salvador

São Paulo State

GUARUJÁ: Casa Grande $$
International
Av Miguel Stéfano, 1001
Tel (13) 2102 4000
Casa Grande is a sprawling colonial resort on the beachfront with five restaurants and four bars of varying levels of sophistication. Good choice if visiting for the day or touring in the area.

GUARUJÁ: Il Faro $$
Italian
Av Miguel Stéfano, 4659
Tel (13) 3351 5559 **Closed** *Mon–Thu*
Opened in 1972, this popular beachfront eatery offers Italian- and Mediterranean-inspired dishes. Good selection of fresh seafood. Lovely views over the sea.

ILHABELA: Viana $$
Seafood
Praia do Viana
Tel (12) 3896 1089
Fresh and tasty seafood drive the menu here. Sit either in the main restaurant overlooking the beach or on the deck and tables on the sand. Dip in and out of the sea between courses.

DK Choice

SÃO SEBASTIÃO: Manacá $$$
International
Rua Manacá, 102
Tel (12) 3865 2546 **Closed** *Mon–Wed*
Tucked off the road and surrounded by luscious vegetation, this is one of those places you have to make the effort to visit, but it offers a special experience. It started out in 1988 to supply breakfast to surfers but is now known for its ambience and excellent fresh fish and seafood.

UBATUBA: Solar das Águas Cantantes $$
Seafood
Estrada do Saco da Ribeira 951
Tel (12) 3842 0178
Seafood and traditional *moquecas* (fish stews) are served in this *pousada's* restaurant, which sits on one of the prettiest beaches in Ubatuba. Family-friendly.

Bahia

ITACARE: Boca de Forno $$
Pizzeria
Beco Das Flores
Tel (73) 3251 3121
The eclectic and cool decor here, including chandeliers and colorful artworks, help this hip eatery stand out from the crowd. The pizzas, including the sweet ones, are well worth coming for.

LENÇOIS: Cozinha Aberta $
International
Av Rui Barbosa, 42, Centro
Tel (75) 3334 1321
Just off the main square, this charming restaurant serves a varied international menu of "slow food." This covers everything from Hungarian goulash to Thai curry.

LENÇOIS: Os Artistas da Massa $
Italian
Rua da Baderna, 49
Tel (75) 3334 1886 **Closed** *times vary; call in advance to check*
This is a simple Italian-owned restaurant that serves excellent well-priced pasta, as well as other Italian dishes.

MORRO DE SÃO PAULO: Pimenta Rosa $$
Seafood
Quarta Praia – Morro de São Paulo
Tel (75) 3652 1506
Located right on the fourth beach, this beach bar and restaurant has a good infrastructure, great views, and friendly staff. Try the Caipfruta, a version of a *caipirinha*.

SALVADOR: Solar Café $
International
Rua da Graça, 284
Tel (71) 3328 3444 **Closed** *Mon*
This small, unpretentious café/ restaurant is located in the Palacete das Artes, which also houses a cultural center and a museum of modern art. Guests can also enjoy great views over the bay of Todos os Santos from the terrace.

DK Choice

SALVADOR: A Casa Vidal $$
Spanish
Rua Afonso Celso, 294
Tel (71) 3565 8008 **Closed** *Mon*
This small, pretty, contemporary Spanish restaurant, with a large infusion of Bahian and other Brazilian influences, has quickly established itself high on the list of the best and most interesting places to eat in Salvador. Located in Barra, close to the historic Farol da Barra. Don't miss the variety of tapas to start, and then try the mixed seafood platter.

SALVADOR: Al Carmo $$
Italian
Rua do Carmo, 42
Tel (71) 3242 0283 **Closed** *Sun*
Located in a beautifully restored colonial building off the Pelourinho that, from the back terrace, overlooks the bay of Todos os Santos and the lower city, this simple Italian is a good choice when sightseeing.

SALVADOR: Fogo de Chão $$
Barbecue (Churrascaria)
Praça Colombo, 4, Rio Vermelho
Tel (71) 3555 9292
When you are looking for a change from seafood and Bahian cuisine, try this branch of São Paulo's excellent upmarket all-you-can-eat barbecue chain. Meat lovers will not be disappointed.

SALVADOR: Quattro Amici $$
Pizzeria
Rua Dom Marcos Teixeira, 35
Tel (71) 3264 5999
Popular and charming pizzeria hidden away in a historic house down a side street.

SALVADOR: Soho $$
Asian
Av Lafayete Coutinho (Av Contorno) 1010, Bahia Marina
Tel (71) 3322 4554
Popular and fashionable chain of upmarket Japanese restaurants. The stunning flagship branch in the marina offers glorious views over the bay of Todos os Santos.

SALVADOR: Yemanjá $$
Brazilian
Av Otávio Mangabeira, 4661
Tel (71) 3461 9010
Sited on the coast, and with beach views, this is the place to come for an introduction to and immersion into the local Bahian cuisine and customs – something of a gastronomic institution.

For more information on types of restaurants *see page 383*

TRANSCOSO: O Cacau $$$
Brazilian
Praça São João Batista, 96
Tel (73) 3668 1266   **Closed** *Mon*
The entrance to this attractive restaurant is off the main square, with a candlelit path leading up to the wide deck. Bahian cooking with an Oriental twist.

TRANSCOSO: Capim Santo $$$
Seafood
Rua do Beco, 55
Tel (73) 3668 1122   **Closed** *Sun*
There is a wonderful ambience here in the colorful grounds of the *pousada* of the same name. Creative modern Brazilian menu.

Atmospheric dining area at the Capim Santo, Transcosco, Bahia

Sergipe, Alagoas & Pernambuco

Sergipe

ARACAJU: Cariri $$
Brazilian
Rua Niceu Dantas, 775
Tel (79) 3243 1379
Lively restaurant serving large portions of meat and seafood regional dishes. The show house offers *forró* and other entertainment.

ARACAJU: Muratto $$
Mediterranean
Rua Doutor Bezerra de Menezes, 102
Tel (79) 3255 2376   **Closed** *Mon*
Choose between contemporary Mediterranean-inspired dishes and Japanese sushi at this elegant venue. Live music also features.

Alagoas

MACEIO: Wanchako $
Peruvian
Rua São Francisco de Assis, 93
Tel (82) 3377 6024   **Closed** *Sun*
This is one of Maceio's most popular eateries, serving Peruvian recipes with Brazilian ingredients.

MACEIO: Sur $$
Regional
Rua Professora Maria Esther da Costa Barros 306
Tel (82) 9808 9090 **Closed** *Mon & Tue*
This critically acclaimed restaurant serves exquisite contemporary dishes with an Alagoan influence.

Pernambuco

FERNANDO DE NORONHA: Cacimba Bistro $
International
Praça Pres Eurico Dutra 9, Vila dos Remedios
Tel (81) 3619 1200
Romantic bistro that is beautifully lit at night. Choose between the pretty veranda or the cozy indoor atmosphere.

FERNANDO DE NORONHA: Ecologikus $$
Seafood
Estrada Velha do Sueste
Tel (81) 3619 1807   **Closed** *Sun*
This simple, cozy mom-and-pop restaurant offers a nice selection of fresh seafood and other dishes. It's not the easiest place to find but is worth the effort.

OLINDA: Don Francesco $
Italian
Rua Prudente de Morais, 358
Tel (81) 3429 3852   **Closed** *Mon*
Tucked away in the cobbled streets of Olinda, this simple *trattoria* serves up tasty, unpretentious Italian cooking.

DK Choice

OLINDA: Oficina do Sabor $$
Brazilian
Rua do Amparo, 335
Tel (81) 3429 3331   **Closed** *Mon*
This "workshop of flavors" is the best known of Olinda's restaurants and perfectly captures the spirit and atmosphere of the area. It offers a creative menu of local Pernambucan and Brazilian dishes, many featuring fresh seafood. Try for a table on the veranda with views over Olinda.

PORTO DE GALINHAS: Domingos $
Brazilian/French
Rua Beijupirá 116, Galeria Paraoby
Tel (81) 3552 1464
Charming and romantic restaurant that, along with Beijupira, is the best in town. A varied menu of French and Brazilian influences offers something for every taste. Good wine list. Live piano music.

PORTO DE GALINHAS: Peixe na Telha $
Seafood
Av Beira Mar, 40-B
Tel (81) 3552 1323
Informal beachfront restaurant that works in tandem with its neighbor, the Encontro dos Mares bistro, serving northeastern specialties along with fresh seafood. Perfect spot for long lunches after a day on the beach. Try the "fish on a tile."

DK Choice

PORTO DE GALINHAS: Beijupirá $$
Seafood
Rua Beijupirá s/n, Praia dos Carneiros
Tel (81) 3676 1461
Colorful and atmospheric spot to test some inventive contemporary Brazilian dishes with a tropical feel. The restaurant is almost as famous as the town itself – a must-visit.

RECIFE: Chica Pitanga $
Buffet
Rua Petrolina, 19
Tel (81) 3465 2224
A pleasant "by the kilo" restaurant offering a good-quality buffet at reasonable prices, where you only pay for what you take. It is popular with locals and visitors, and well located for hotels on Boa Viagem.

RECIFE: Leite $$
Portuguese
Praça Joaquim Nabuco, 147
Tel (81) 3224 7977   **Closed** *Sat*
A piece of history, Leite has been operating since 1882 and is still going strong, one of the oldest in Brazil. The menu features regional and Portuguese influences served in an elegant, colonial setting.

RECIFE: Ponte Nova $$
French
Rua do Cupim, 172
Tel (81) 3327 7226   **Closed** *Mon*
The decor and menu here are inspired by French Art Nouveau, but with a distinctively contemporary Brazilian feel to both. The restaurant is as charming by candlelight as it is by the natural light of day for Sunday lunch.

Paraíba, Rio Grande do Norte & Ceará

Paraíba

JOÃO PESSOA: Mangai $
Brazilian
Av General Édson Ramalho, 696
Tel (83) 3226 1615
The very large buffet here – they work with more than 200 recipes – offers a great introduction to many northeastern specialties and delicacies. Look for branches in Natal and Brasília, too.

JOÃO PESSOA: Quintal Restô $$
Brazilian
Rua Eutiquiano Barreto, 863
Tel (83) 9179 3900   **Closed** *Sun–Tue*
Call to make a reservation, and wait to be charmed by the culinary skills on display in the city's best restaurant in terms of food. The menu changes almost daily.

Rio Grande do Norte

GENIPABU: Bar 21 $$
Brazilian
Praia de Genipabu
Tel (84) 3224 2484
The setting – on stilts above the sea at the bottom of a sand dune – is the main attraction of this thatched-roofed bar/restaurant. Stick to catch of the day and you won't go far wrong. Lunch only.

One of Camarões Potiguari's tasty prawn and shrip dishes, Natal

NATAL: Âncora Caipira $
Brazilian
Av Campos Sales 474
Tel (84) 3202 9364   **Closed** *Mon & Carnaval*
This is a firm favorite with the locals for its authentic northeastern cuisine. It is also famed for its sun-dried meat (*carne do sol*).

NATAL: Camarões Potiguari $$
Seafood
Rua Pedro Fonseca Filho, 8887
Tel (84) 3209 2425
If you like shrimp or prawns, you will be in heaven here, but there are many other dishes on offer. One of Natal's largest and most popular restaurants.

NATAL: Manary Gastronomia & Arte $$
Seafood
Rua Francisco Gurgel, 9067
Tel (84) 3204 2900
Glorious setting for lunch or dinner in Natal's best boutique hotel with sea views and sounds. This very special place is worth at least one visit while in Natal.

PRAIA DE PIPA: Dall'Italiano $
Italian
Rua do Céu
Tel (84) 9152 8651   **Closed** *Mon & Wed in low season*
Nicely decorated, cozy, informal pizzeria located just off the main street. The menu also includes seafood, pasta, and salads.

TIBAU DO SUL: Camamo $$
Brazilian
Av Governador Aluísio Alves 184
Tel (84) 3246 4195
Here you will be treated to a set menu of six courses at a table on the candlelit veranda of the chef's lovely house. Numbers are very limited each night, so make a reservation for this exclusive dining experience.

Ceará

CANOA QUEBRADA: L'Atelier do Brasil $
International
Rua Nascer do Sol, 360
Tel (88) 8817 9964   **Closed** *Wed*
Track down this cozy, romantic, atmospheric restaurant, one block off the bustle of "Broadway," and sample its menu of international favorites.

CANOA QUEBRADA: Pizza Nostra $
Pizzeria
Rua Dragão do Mar 2040, Broadway
Tel (88) 9680 5863   **Closed** *Mon*
Grills, seafood, and vegetarian options are also all on offer at this pizzeria in the center of the village. Balcony tables available.

FORTALEZA: L'O $
Brazilian
Av Pessoa Anta 217
Tel (85) 3265 2288
A mixture of Art Deco and more modern touches has resulted in one of the city's most sophisticated and striking dining spots, with a lovely garden bar in which to start or end the meal. Don't mis the rack of lamb or the smoked haddock risotto.

DK Choice

FORTALEZA: Coco Bambu $$
Seafood
Av Beira Mar, 3698
Tel (85) 3198 6000
Founded in Fortaleza in 2001 this is a reliable and fast growing chain of modern, informal seafood restaurants that won't disappoint. This branch is one of three in Fortaleza and is right on the seashore. The menu is very varied and includes a wide selection of salads and traditional dishes. Try the fish fillet with banana and white sauce, or with mango sauce. and nuts.

FORTALEZA: Colher de Pau $$
Brazilian
Rua Ana Bilhar, 1178
Tel (85) 3267 6680
Lovely outdoor restaurant offering all the color and flavor of the regional cuisine of both the coast and interior of Ceará. There is also often live music.

Piauí & Maranhão

Piauí

TERESINA: Coco Bambu $$
Seafood
Rua Professor Joca Vieira, 1227
Tel *86 3232 8100*
This popular branch of the reliable Coco Bambu seafood chain is one of the best in town and a favorite meeting point. Outdoor and indoor seating. Pasta, pizza, and steaks, too.

TERESINA: Favorita Comida Tipica $$
Brazilian
Rua Angélica, 1059
Tel (86) 3232 2020
Rustic yet comfortable, this spot is generally thought to serve the best regional fare in town. The Favorito group has five more restaurants in Teresina, including the pizzeria Favorito Forneira.

For more information on types of restaurants *see page 383*

Maranhão

LENCOIS MARANHENSES: Luzía $
Seafood
Canto do Atins
Tel (98) 9 8709 7661
The only restaurant and *pousada* within the Parque dos Lençóis Maranhenses, on the edge of the sand dunes, serves specialties of prawn, fresh fish, and goat.

SÃO LUIS: Antigamente $
Brazilian
Rua da Estrela, 220
Tel (98) 9 8876 7151
Located in the historic center of the old town, this pretty restaurant is good for snacks and a beer, as well as full meals. Large patio for musical entertainment.

DK Choice

SÃO LUIS: Cabana do Sol $
Brazilian
Rua João Rereiro Damasceno 24, Km 5, Ponta do Farol
Tel (98) 3304 4235
Sun-dried beef (*carne de sol*), goat, chicken, and other local dishes are the specialties at this popular, well-regarded restaurant. Ambience and bar all inspired by local culture. Another branch at Av Litorânea and one in Imperatriz.

SÃO LUIS: Senac $
Buffet
Rua de Nazaré, 242
Tel (98) 3198 1100
Part of the national hotel and catering school, this exceptional all-you-can-eat buffet is in a large house in the historic center. Good introduction to local and other Brazilian dishes.

Bright and lively dining area at Antigamente, São Luis

Key to Price Guide *see page 386*

Pará & Amapá

Pará

BELEM: Lá em Casa $
Brazilian
Estação das Docas – Av Boulevard Castilho França, Galpão 2
Tel (91) 3212 5588
Serving regional Amazon dishes, Lá em Casa is located inside the dock area in the beautiful mall, offering views over the river. There is an open-air terrace, too.

DK Choice

BELEM: Remanso do Bosque $$
Regional
Av Rômulo Maiorana, 2350
Tel (91) 3347 2829   **Closed** Mon
Innovative and creative use of local Amazon ingredients makes this the most interesting choice for foodies who want a gourmet experience – Amazonian chic, if you like. It has the same owners as the less sophisticated Remanso de Peixe, considered Belém's best for seafood.

Amapá

MACAPA: Estaleiro $
Seafood
Av 1 Maio
Tel (96) 3222 8375
Macapa is not overly blessed when it comes to restaurants, but Estaleiro is considered one of the best and most reliable. Nautically themed.

Amazonas, Roraima, Acre & Rondônia

Amazonas

MANAUS: Fiorentina $
Italian
Rua José Paranaguá, 44
Tel (92) 3215 2233
This is a pleasant, popular Italian restaurant in the center of Manaus that serves a good range of pasta, sushi, and other standard dishes. *Feijoada* is offered on Saturdays.

MANAUS: Canto da Peixada $
Seafood
Av Ayrão, 1677
Tel (92) 3234 3021
One of Manaus' best-known fish restaurants, this is the ideal place to try many of the local Amazon river fish that you will not find anywhere else in the world.

DK Choice

MANAUS: Banzeiro $$
Brazilian
Rua Libertador, 102
Tel (92) 3234 1621
This attractive, functional restaurant is credited with breathing new life into Amazonian cuisine. It is considered the best option at which to try out an Amazonian cuisine that uses a selection of exotic ingredients. If you have come all the way to Manaus and like to experiment, don't miss the experience.

MANAUS: Bufalo Churrascaria $$
Barbecue
Rua Pará 490
Tel (92) 9219 7243
Considered the best in town for meat, this is a popular *rodízio* all-you-can-eat barbecue house – plus sushi and an American bar.

MANAUS: Himawari $$
Asian
Rua 10 de Julho, 618
Tel (92) 3233 4229   **Closed** Mon
The best and most traditional Japanese restaurant in Manaus is conveniently located right next to the famous Opera House. Great sushi is served here.

Roraima

BOA VISTA: Tropical Peixada $
Seafood
Rua Ajuricaba, 1525
Tel (95) 3224 6040   **Closed** Wed & 3rd Sun of month
Popular street-corner restaurant with an airy outdoor seating area. Popular for lunch. The menu favors seafood and Amazon fish.

Acre

RIO BRANCO: Point do Pato $
Regional
Praca Jose Bisteni
Tel (68) 9972 8112   **Closed** Sun
Popular and trendy with locals, young and old alike, this spot specializes in regional dishes such as alligator steaks, as well as international favorites, including pasta and pizza. Live music.

Rondônia

PORTO VELHO: Caravela do Madeira $
Seafood
Rua José Camacho, 104
Tel (69) 3221 6641   **Closed** Mon
This rustic but comfortable restaurant, with views of the Madeira river and rainforest, specializes in river fish, including grilled piranha.

A large portion of tasty food that's ideal for sharing at Casa do João, Bonito

PORTO VELHO: Miyoshi $
Asian
Av Amazonas 1280, Nossa Senhora das Graças
Tel (69) 3224 4600
Amazon ingredients are used here to create traditional Chinese and Japanese dishes on a large menu. Modern and pleasant.

Brasília, Goiás & Tocantins

Brasília

BRASÍLIA: Corrients 348 $$
Steakhouse
Setor de Clubes Esportivos Sul Trecho 2, Lote40
Tel (61) 3345 1348   **Closed** *Mon*
This is a branch of the excellent Argentine steakhouse chain that has restaurants in São Paulo and Rio. Informal, relaxed atmosphere and views over Lagoa Paranoá.

BRASÍLIA: Dalí Camões $$$
Portuguese/Spanish
Setor Hoteleiro Sul, Qd 6, Bl B (Brasil 21)
Tel (61) 3039 8156   **Closed** *Sun*
Located in Hotel Brasil 21, this smart, elegant restaurant serves a nice selection of Portuguese and Catalan specialties. Don't miss the seafood selection platter.

BRASÍLIA: Fogo de Chão $$$
Barbecue (Churrascaria)
SHS Quadra 5, Bloco E, Asa Sul
Tel (61) 3322 4666
This is a branch of the excellent Fogo de Chão barbecue house, recognized as one of the best all-you-can-eat barbecues in Brazil. Centrally located, it is, not surprisingly, one of the city's most popular, and it seats 600.

BRASÍLIA: Gero $$$
Italian
SHIN, CA 4, Lote A, loja 22
Tel (61) 3577 5520
Located in Shopping Iguatemi, this is a branch of Fasano's fashionable and popular contemporary Italian eatery. Stylish, yet relaxed. One of the best in town.

DK Choice

BRASÍLIA: Taypá $$$
Peruvian
Setor de Habitações Individuais Sul, Quadra 17, Bl 9, Shopping Fashion Park
Tel (61) 3248 0403
Highly regarded by critics and considered one of the city's very best, this unpretentious Peruvian restaurant is away from the city center and has an innovative, ever-changing menu. Excellent ceviche, but it also has contemporary international dishes and a *pisco bar*.

BRASÍLIA: Trattoria da Rosario $$$
Italian
Shopping Fashion Park – SHIS Qi 17, Bl H s/n
Tel (61) 3248 1672   **Closed** *Mon*
One of the most consistent Italian restaurants in town – although not the cheapest – is this smart spot located in Fashion Park.

Goiás

CHAPADA DOS VEADEIROS: Massa da Mamma $
Italian
Rua São José Operário, 305
Tel (62) 3446 1362
As its name suggests, this is a simple Italian *cantina*. Its specialty is pasta, but it also offers pizza.

Tocantins

PALMAS: Adelaide Bistro $
Brazilian
Quadra 110 Sul, Alameda 21 lotes 73/75
Tel (63) 9214 0792
Although in a residential area, this is still the best place for a relaxing meal. Pretty veranda and pool area. Reliable food and service.

Mato Grosso & Mato Grosso do Sul

Mato Grosso

CUIABÁ: Getúlio $$
Regional
Av Presidente Getúlio Vargas, 1147
Tel (65) 3624 9992   **Closed** *Mon*
Reliable steaks and other grills, including fish, are served here. High-end yet casual, and always a lively buzz. There is a popular nightclub above the restaurant.

CUIABÁ: Mahalo Cozinha Criativa $$
Regional
Rua Pres Castello Branco 359
Tel (65) 3028 7700   **Closed** *some Sundays (call to check)*
This smart, charming, creative contemporary restaurant made a name for itself during the 2014 World Cup. The menu is international with regional touches.

Mato Grosso do Sul

BONITO: Casa do João $
Seafood
Rua Coronel Nelson Felício dos Santos 664A
Tel (67) 3255 1212
Not a lot of choice in Bonito, but Casa do João should satisfy most diners, offering a good variety of tasty dishes. Large portions, too.

CAMPO GRANDE: Cantina Romana $$
Italian
Rua da Paz 237
Tel (67) 3324 9777
This is a popular, reliable Italian *cantina* that has built a name and local following since opening in 1978. The owner also operates the busy Pizzeria Romana in Campo Grande.

CAMPO GRANDE: Fogo Caipira $$
Brazilian
Rua José Antônio Pereira 145
Tel (67) 3324 1641   **Closed** *Mon*
This restaurant is the best in town for regional Pantanal fare. It is very popular at weekends, so consider booking in advance.

For more information on types of restaurants *see page 383*

Santa Catarina & Paraná

Santa Catarina

FLORIANÓPOLIS: Arante $$
Seafood
Rua Abelardo Otácilio Gomes 254, Pântano do Sul
Tel (48) 3237 7022
This large beachside bar and restaurant is something of a local fixture. Crowded at the weekends and on summer evenings, it serves reliable seafood dishes. The walls are covered in notes left by visitors since the 1970s.

FLORIANÓPOLIS: Ostradamus $$
Seafood
Rod Baldicero Filomeno, 7640
Tel (48) 3337 5711   **Closed** *Mon*
Oysters are a specialty here and are freshly harvested from the neighboring oyster beds, 18 miles (30 km) from the center of Florianópolis. Other seafood options are available, too.

FLORIANÓPOLIS: Restinga Recanto $$
Seafood
Rodovia Rafael da Rocha Pires, 2759
Tel (48) 3235 2093   **Closed** *Sun dinner, Mon*
This popular, inviting rustic restaurant serves super-fresh Portuguese seafood. Panoramic beach and sea views from the terrace. Folk-dancing at the weekends.

FLORIANÓPOLIS: Villa Maggioni $$
Mediterranean
Rua Canto da Amizade 273, Canto da Lagoa
Tel (48) 3232 6859 **Closed** *Mon & Tue*
Intimate restaurant on the shores of Lagoa da Conceição. The international menu features Italian and Mediterranean influences.

Paraná

CURITIBA: Barolo Trattoria $$
Italian
Av Silva Jardim, 2487
Tel (41) 3243 3430
This excellent, charming Italian *trattoria* also has a few Brazilian influences to keep it interesting. Nice atmosphere. Good wine list.

CURITIBA: Batel Grill $$
Brazilian
Av Nossa Senhora Aparecida, 78
Tel (41) 3342 8101
This large, modern, popular *rodizio* all-you-can-eat barbecue house is considered the best of its type in Curitiba.

Notes written by diners adorn the walls of Arante, Florianópolis

CURITIBA: Famiglia Caliceti – Ristorante Bologna $$
Italian
Alameda Doutor Carlos de Carvalho, 1367
Tel (41) 3076 9477   **Closed** *Tue*
Pretty, well-decorated and traditional Italian restaurant; it has been something of an institution since opening in 1972, when the owners arrived from Bologna.

CURITIBA: Madalosso $$
Italian
Av Manoel Ribas, 5875
Tel 41 3372 2121
A very large restaurant – it sits 4,500 – Madalosso is an attraction in its own right, serving a good-quality, fixed-price Italian buffet though a number of salons. Located in the Italian quarter of the city, in Santa Felicidade.

DK Choice

CURITIBA: Madero Durski $$
International
Av Jaime Reis 254
Tel (41) 3225 7893   **Closed** *Sun*
Durski, which, unusually, offers an international menu with Ukrainian and Polish specialties, is one of the city's most talked and written about, and in a very good way. In 2015 it expanded to join forces with its neighboring Madero Steakhouse and now offers diners the best from both menus in a more relaxed, less formal setting.

CURITIBA: L'Épicerie $$$
French
Rua Fernando Simas, 340
Tel (41) 3079 1889   **Closed** *Sun & Mon*
Considered the city's best French restaurant, this is a charming, reliable, comfy bistro in one of Curitiba's best neighborhoods. It has a good wine list, too.

CURITIBA: Terra Madre $$$
Italian
Rua Desembargador Otávio do Amaral, 515
Tel (41) 3335 6070 **Closed** *Mon lunch*
Modern Italian and international fare is offered here, with Brazilian influences on a well-balanced menu. Also a wine bar and store.

FOZ DO IGUAÇU: Clube Maringá $
Seafood
Rua Dourado, 111
Tel (45) 3527 9683   **Closed** *Mon*
Part of the local fishing club, this is a good choice for lunch, with a great view across the river and on to Paraguay. The fixed-price buffet includes local fish and other international dishes.

FOZ DO IGUAÇU: La Mafia $
Italian
Alameda Watslaf Nieradka, 195
Tel (45) 3572 1015
This fun, quirky Mafia-themed Italian *trattoria* and wine bar is popular with visitors and serves tasty food at reasonable prices.

FOZ DO IGUAÇU: Bufalo Branco $$
Brazilian
Rua Engenheiro Rebouças, 530
Tel (45) 3523 9744
Probably the best barbecue house in town, Bufalo Branco is centrally located but offers free transfers from some of the out-of-town hotels. Casual and fun.

DK Choice

FOZ DO IGUAÇU: Itaipu $$$
Brazilian
Hotel das Cataratas, Iguaçu National Park
Tel (45) 2102 7000
Even if not staying at the Hotel Cataratas, you should head out for dinner either at the Itaipu, with its terrace overlooking the falls, or the more popular poolside Ipê Grill. Itaipu offers an interesting fusion of international and Brazilian, while Ipê serves an outstanding high-class buffet including barbecue. Dining here also allows you to see and visit the falls at night when the park is shut.

PARANAGUÁ: Danúbio Azul $$
Seafood
Rua XV de Novembro, 95
Tel (41) 3423 3255 **Closed** *Sun dinner*
On the water's edge, this restaurant, open since 1953, specializes in seafood and Paraná cuisine. Try for a table by the window. A buffet is served at lunch.

Rio Grande do Sul

DK Choice

BENTO GONÇALVES:
Casa di Paolo $$
Brazilian
RSC-470, Km 221.6
Tel (54) 3463 8505 **Closed** *Sun dinner*
One of the specialties in the south is mouthwatering, slow-barbecued chicken (*galeto*), and the Casa di Paolo chain, which also serves other dishes, is often voted best in class. You will find branches across the south including Porto Alegre, Caxias, and Gramado. Comfortable and informal eatery.

BENTO GONÇALVES: Maria
Valduga $$
Italian
Via Trento, 2355 – Vale dos Vinhedos
Tel (54) 2105 3122
Four charming, rustic dining areas make up Maria Valduga, which is located within the Valduga winery. A set Italian meal is served at lunch, and it will open for dinner for groups of 20 or more. The food is superb and beautifully presented.

GRAMADO: Belle du Valais $$$
Swiss
Av das Hortências, 1432
Tel (54) 3286 1744 **Closed** *lunch*
This popular, cozy, elegant spot is great for fondue and *raclette* during the colder winter months, and one of the best Swiss restaurants in Brazil through the year. Extensive wine cellar.

GRAMADO: La Caceria $$$
Brazilian
Av Borges de Medeiros 3166
Tel (54) 3295 7575
The charming top restaurant of the Casa da Montanha hotel has a small but interesting menu with a focus on game and other by-products of the hunt. The hotel also houses the cozy Bistrô da Varanda.

GRAMADO: Saint Andrews $$$
International
Rua Leopoldo Geyer – Cond V Bosque 171
Tel (54) 3295 7700
Saint Andrews is one of Gramado's most attractive and best boutique hotels. Its elegant Primrose restaurant offers high-quality fine dining (and a chance to see the hotel, which is part of Relais & Châteaux).

PORTO ALEGRE:
Al Dente $$
Italian
Rua Mata Bacelar, 210
Tel 51 3343 1841 **Closed** *Sun*
A small, cozy, intimate Italian restaurant. Classic, consistently well-prepared north Italian dishes are the main thrust here.

PORTO ALEGRE:
Chez Philippe $$
French
Av Independência, 1005
Tel (51) 3312 5333
Excellent, high-quality French cuisine with a strong Brazilian accent is served in a lovely, centrally located garden setting.

PORTO ALEGRE:
Koh Pee Pee $$
Asian
Rua Schiller, 83
Tel (51) 3333 5150 **Closed** *Sun*
Stylish, authentic Thai restaurant that has kept its standards high since opening in 1997. It is regarded as one of Porto Alegre's very best restaurants of any type.

PORTO ALEGRE: NB Steak $$
Barbecue (Churrascaria)
Av Nilo Peçanha, 2131
Tel (51) 3333 1413
This is part of a growing chain of smart, comfortable *rodízio* all-you-can-eat barbecue houses, with a more elegant presentation than many of its rivals.

PORTO ALEGRE: Puppi
Baggio $$
Italian
Rua Dinarte Ribeiro, 155
Tel (51) 3346 3630 **Closed** *Mon*
Some of the best and most reliable pasta dishes in town are served here, as well as pizza, in a rustic, chic setting in a lovely house. Well loved by the locals.

PORTO ALEGRE: Steinhaus $$
German
Rua Coronel Paulino Teixeira, 415
Tel (51) 3330 8661 **Closed** *Sun*
Generally named as the best traditional German restaurant in a town with many German influences, this has built a solid reputation since opening in 1979.

PORTO ALEGRE: Via Veneto
Galeteria $$
Brazilian
Rua José de Alencar, 501
Tel (51) 3233 1400 **Closed** *Sun dinner*
Barbecued chicken is the specialty at this excellent restaurant, but there is also a full buffet of other dishes and accompaniments.

DK Choice

PORTO ALEGRE: Floriano
Spiess Cozinha de autor $$$
International
Praça do Japão, 155
Tel (51) 3237 7601 **Closed** *Sun & Mon*
This is the city's most talked about and written about contemporary restaurant, yet still with a culinary foot in the best of the past. Serious gourmands should follow the creative tasting menu prepared by the owner and chef. Make sure you save room for dessert. Book ahead.

PORTO ALEGRE: Le Bateau
Ivre $$$
French
Rua Tito Lívio Zambecari 805
Tel (51) 3330 7351 **Closed** *Sun & Mon*
For over a decade, the French chef here has been serving some of the city's best Provençal cooking in comfy surroundings.

The warm decor at Koh Pee Pee, Porto Alegre

For more information on types of restaurants *see page 383*

SHOPPING IN BRAZIL

The most exciting aspect of shopping in Brazil is that it never fails to surprise visitors with its amazing variety. Major cities, such as Rio *(see pp94–5)* and São Paulo *(pp154–5)*, have expansive, world-class shopping centers that have everything from sophisticated boutiques to high-tech items. Craft centers, artisans' houses, and *ateliers* (workshops) showcase the unique, attractive products manufactured by the local people. Colorful street markets and *camelódromos* offer a truly exhilarating Brazilian shopping experience. The prices are, by and large, reasonable, and large items can be shipped home. In most state capitals and tourist areas the opening hours are extended for convenience.

Opening Hours

Business hours are normally 8am to 6pm on weekdays and 8am to 1pm on Saturdays. In large cities, tourist areas, and resorts, hours are more flexible. Stores in central areas stay open until 7 or 8pm on weekdays and 4pm on Saturdays. Shopping centers are open 10am to 10pm from Monday to Saturday. In resorts and tourist areas, even small stores are open daily until midnight in the high season.

How to Pay

Major credit cards are accepted in most stores in large cities and resorts, though there may be a minimum spend value (about R$50). International debit cards are commonly accepted even for small amounts. US dollars are sometimes accepted in tourist areas, but in small towns it is best to pay in cash using the *real (see p415)*.

Interior of an upmarket clothing store in Jardins, São Paulo

Shopping Centers & Hypermarkets

More convenient than street stores and offering much more than shopping alone, shopping centers have multiplied in the last few years. Fast-food chains and restaurants, department stores and boutiques, clothes repair, cobblers, and other services can all now be found within one complex. A combination of supermarket and department store, hypermarkets are often located on main roads and the outskirts of towns. Apart from the ubiquitous local chain, Extra, foreign names such as Wal-Mart and Carrefour also have a formidable presence in Brazil.

In resorts, smaller shopping centers sell souvenirs and fashionable items. Department stores such as C&A and Lojas Americanas have found their way into shopping centers, although they exist more prominently as street shops in the large city centers.

Markets & Camelódromos

Almost every medium-size city in Brazil has its own special market, some located in beautiful historical buildings. Lively and picturesque, these markets sell an array of fresh products from meat and fish

Ver o Peso, Belém's picturesque waterfront *mercado* (market)

to fruit and cheese. Authentic regional food, typical sweets, and crafts can also be found here. Ver o Peso market in Belém (*see p272*) and public markets in Olinda (Pernambuco), Manaus (Rua dos Bares), and Porto Alegre (Rio Grande do Sul) are good examples.

Everywhere in Brazil, street traders or *camelôs* sell goods on improvised stands, or at places called *camelódromos*. A wide range of items, from clothes to electronics of fairly decent quality, are sold at reasonably reduced prices.

It is possible for shoppers to bargain at open-air markets. Vendors will often start at double the price of products, but with a little skill and some charm on the part of the buyer, this can be reduced. Be on guard in crowded street markets, as pickpockets are not uncommon. Be discreet when taking out money to pay.

Traditional musical instruments and masks for sale in Bahia

Art & Crafts

Every region in Brazil has its own distinctive handicrafts. The use of specific raw materials makes every piece of work unique. The best way to buy these pieces is to go directly to the *ateliers*. Tourist information offices can provide the addresses. Craft centers, where artists can be seen at work, offer lower prices than the upmarket souvenir shops.

Typical Amazonian crafts include indigenous masks, jewelry, plume helmets, basketwork, and bows and arrows in Manaus, Belém, and Santarém. Attractive replicas of Marajoara pottery are sold

in Belém and the Ilha de Marajó. Delicate lacework is found in all northeastern states, while Pernambuco and Bahia are famed for their fine ceramics.

Woven items, hand-crafted furniture, and Arraiolo tapestry are popular in Minas Gerais. In the south, Santa Catarina's crystalware is exceptional. In the state of Rio Grande do Sul, it is worth looking for good-quality leather as well as woolen items in Gramado and Caxias do Sul.

Gems

Brazil has 60 percent of the world's gem reserves. It is the world's largest exporter of rough-cut gems and the sixth-largest exporter of worked gems. The variety and quantity of precious stones are spectacular. Amethyst, citrine, diamond, emerald, opal, and royal topaz are just a few of the gems that Brazil is famous for. Rough and worked pieces can be bought in the cities of Ouro Preto (Minas Gerais), Cuiabá (Mato Grosso), Salvador and Chapada Diamantina (Bahia), and Porto Alegre. Designed jewelry can also be found in these places, as well as in São Paulo and Rio de Janeiro.

Although gems are largely sold in open-air markets, it is best to buy them at stores offering origin warranty certificates, which gives the weight (in carats), quality, origin, and – in the case of ready-made jewelry – the characteristics of any precious metal used.

Salesman displaying gems, Howard Stern Jewelers, Ipanema

Food & Drink

Brazil is known for its rich variety of conserves, dried fruits, and cakes (*see pp384–5*). Another favorite is fruit – figs, citron ciders, pineapples, and oranges – crystallized in compôte. These delicacies can be bought at public markets, craft centers, and confectioners' shops, found everywhere in Brazil.

An immensely popular beverage, *cachaça* (sugar-cane liquor) is produced all over the country and locally distilled (*see p385*). The best *cachaça* comes from Minas Gerais, Rio de Janeiro, Bahia, Pernambuco, and Ceará. It can also be bought at craft centers, local bars, and in hypermarkets in the larger cities.

Excellent coffee and gourmet blends are easily available in all big cities in Brazil. Look out for the ABIC seal on the packets, as this certifies the coffee quality.

Cachaça emporium in Paraty, with a large array of different types for sale

ENTERTAINMENT IN BRAZIL

Entertainment in Brazil varies according to the region and the city, but one thing is certain – Brazilians love going to bars, cafés, or *botecos* (a kind of bar with snacks and an old-fashioned atmosphere) to meet with friends and drink cold beer. This usually happens before and after other activities such as watching movies, plays, and shows. Dancing is another popular activity with Brazilians. In a country known for the richness of its rhythms, there are venues catering to all kinds of music and dancing, from *forró*, *samba*, and *axé* to techno and hiphop. Outdoor activities, such as soccer and volleyball, are national pastimes. Water parks, beaches, and public gardens are also good places to enjoy the warm weather and outdoor activities.

Information & Booking

Most Brazilian shows, such as plays and operas, do not run for very long and tickets must be booked quickly. Rio and São Paulo have specific magazines with a good listing of events and entertainment *(see p99 & p157)*. In most other Brazilian cities, local newspapers are the best way to find out what's on. They usually come with special sections or supplements on Fridays or on weekends showing cinema, theater, and other entertainment listings.

Only the most active theaters and concert houses provide listings on the Internet. In some big cities, shows can also be booked via Ticketmaster using Visa, MasterCard, and American Express, for a small additional service fee. Hotel concierges can often be helpful and informative when it comes to finding out what shows are on and booking them as well.

Discount Tickets & Free Events

In general, students and seniors (over 60) get a 50 percent discount for most events. The conditions for students vary from state to state. Students must usually show their university identity card or proof of enrollment. There are many free events at museums and cultural centers, but as they become crowded quickly, arriving early is wise.

Almost every city has one or more cultural centers. Supported by the government or by private companies, they often offer cheap tickets or free access to a variety of events, such as plays, dance, and art exhibitions, performed by professional or amateur companies.

Performing Arts

Theater and dance shows are popular in bigger cities in Brazil, where the theaters feature regular shows. At some resorts, dance or musical performances take place during the high season, or during specific summer or winter festivals. Most plays run only for a season. There is a fair amount of traditional and experimental theater, many dance performances, and chamber and classical music recitals to attend. Some performances have become annual traditions, such as *The Passion of Christ* play staged during Passion Week at an open-air theater in Nova Jerusalém *(see p227)* in the state of Pernambuco. Another big performance takes place every January in São Vicente *(see p173)*, retelling the story of the foundation of the town.

Musical shows are as prolific in Brazil. They take place at venues ranging from bars and theaters to sophisticated cultural centers. During music festivals, concerts are held in open-air areas, such as squares, public parks, or beaches. The really big and famous acts, which can be costly, usually perform in the stadia and require advance booking of tickets.

Cinema

In larger cities, modern multiplex cinemas, most of which are located in shopping

A view of the private boxes in the Teatro Amazonas, Manaus *(see pp286–7)*

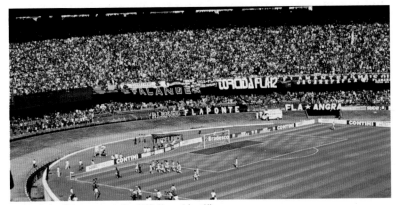

Inside Rio City's world-famous soccer stadium, Estádio Maracanã *(see p88)*

centers, mainly feature recent Hollywood and European as well as good Brazilian films. There are also a few good cineclubs, especially in Rio and São Paulo, that screen feature- and short-film festivals, often screening films with English subtitles. There are three main cinema chains operating in Brazil – United Cinemas International (UCI), Cinemark, and the Brazilian Playarte. They offer facilities for disabled people and sell tickets in advance via the Internet or at the box office.

Bars, Cafés & Botecos

Nightlife is always exciting in large cities, resorts, and tourist areas. Bars are open through the week, usually after 6pm until 1 or 2am (some continue until sunrise, especially those on the beaches); some are open 24 hours. Most cities offer a wide variety of bars to visit – dance bars, bars with live music, and in the bigger cities, gay and lesbian bars. *Botecos* – traditionally *carioca* bars known for their simplicity and good snacks – have now been adopted by many cities and have increased in popularity and sophistication.

Happy hour is an institution in many of the larger cities. It begins at 6pm and extends until 9 or 10pm, after which many people carry on at all-night bars. Bars and kiosks on and near the beaches are often crowded and buzzing with activity through the week, and especially on weekends. Cities without beaches generally make do with tables and chairs spread over the sidewalks with impromptu cafés sprouting up outside restaurants.

Soccer Matches

Soccer is a national passion – across Brazil there are 800 soccer clubs, 13,000 amateur teams, and 300 stadia, including Rio City's Estádio Maracanã *(see p88)*, which hosted the 2014 World Cup final. There are many championships through the year, with matches on Wednesdays, Thursdays, and weekends.

It is not always easy to get a ticket for these games, and very often there are immense queues to purchase tickets. Clubs and stadia do not sell tickets on the Internet. There are some websites that sell tickets online, provided this is done well in advance. Most travel agencies and hotel concierges are able to assist with the finding and buying of soccer tickets.

Gardens & Theme Parks

Public gardens and parks are always crowded on weekends. Many of them offer jogging tracks, roller-skating rinks, sports courts for playing soccer, volleyball, basketball, tennis, and other games.

Theme parks are becoming increasingly popular everywhere in Brazil. Nowadays, most of these parks include some form of outdoor activity, such as swimming pools, waterslides, water tobogganing, horse-riding, and roller coasters.

Live music in the popular Carioca da Gema, Lapa district, Rio de Janeiro

SPECIALIZED HOLIDAYS & OUTDOOR ACTIVITIES

The climate and great variety of landscapes – mountains, flatlands, waterfalls, and forests – make Brazil an outstanding outdoor destination. This ecological paradise offers great opportunities to observe its fascinating flora and fauna, or to indulge in adventure sports that allow close contact with the environment. Visitors can choose from a range of thrilling activities such as rappeling down cliffs, canyoning, or climbing peaks in spectacular settings. However, the infrastructure varies from region to region. It is best to get in touch with reputed tour operators licensed by Embratur, a government tourism agency. Other interesting activities may involve learning to dance to the beautiful rhythms of *forró* and *samba*, performing the legendary *capoeira*, or even joining a game of soccer.

Ecotourism

Brazil's rich and varied ecosystem has much to offer, and ecotourism is becoming a popular form of tourism. Visitors can capture on film the splendor of the Amazon rainforest near Manaus, or enjoy excursions into the forest organized by jungle lodges. Similar ecotours can also be undertaken from Belém or Santarém (Pará). **Amazon Mystery Tours** is based in Manaus; in Belém contact **Amazon Star**. **Pantanal Explorer** offers tours and expeditions into the vast wilderness of Pantanal, Nobres, and Chapada dos Guimarães from Cuiabá.

Serra da Capivara *(see pp252–3)* and Sete Cidades parks (Piauí) *(see p253)* offer amazing rock formations, while Chapada Diamantina in Bahia *(see pp208–9)* and Chapada dos Veadeiros *(see pp316–17)* in Goiás have good trekking trails, forested areas, and scenic waterfalls. National parks such as Serra dos Órgãos *(see p119)*, Parque Nacional do Itatiaia *(see p115)*, and Aparados da Serra *(see p362)*, and natural reserves such as Ilha do Cardoso *(see p175)* offer a broad range of biodiversity. Look for **Fazenda Palomas** or contact **Fellini Turismo** for special rural tours in Rio Grande do Sul.

Bird-Watching & Safaris

Home to almost a fifth of the world's bird population, Brazil offers a surfeit of bird-watching excursions. **Birding Brasil Turismo**, based in Manaus, provides good deals. **Iara Turismo** conducts special programs. **Estação Ecológica Santa Lúcia**, run by renowned naturalist Augusto Ruschi, organizes regular bird-watching. Ornithologist **Edson Endrigo** organizes tours to Parque Nacional Itatiaia *(see p115)* and Ubatuba. A typical safari can be experienced at Jalapão State Park *(see p314–15)*. The travel agency **Korubo Expedições** uses a truck with hatches for professional photo equipment.

Spectacular golden sand dunes in Jalapão

Off-Road Driving

Many beautiful sites in Brazil are accessible only by off-road vehicles. The Transpantaneira road (Pantanal) and the Estrada Park road are attractions in themselves, allowing passengers to leisurely observe the flora and fauna. The Transpantaneira extends 93 miles (149 km) from Poconé to Porto Jofre in Mato Grosso and has 126 wooden bridges to cross. Many inns and farms receive visitors along this road. Stretching 73 miles (117 km), the Estrada Park road links Corumbá to Buraco das Piranhas

The rare and striking scarlet ibises that inhabit the Ilha de Marajó *(see p274)*

(Piranha's Hole) in the state of Mato Grosso do Sul. Another enjoyable road experience is to cross Jalapão State Park, a wonderful contrast of golden dunes and gushing waterfalls. **Korubo Expedições** offers week-long packages leaving from Palmas. The Northeast region's off-road adventure *Rota das Dunas* (Dunes Route) runs from Fortaleza (Ceará) to São Luís (Maranhão), passing through Jericoacoara Beach and Delta do Parnaíba (a group of 80 islands) and Parque Nacional dos Lençóis Maranhenses *(see pp254–5)*. For bookings contact **Jeri Off-Road**.

Cycling & Biking

Cycling and mountain biking have been attracting increasing numbers of enthusiasts to Brazil. Many tour operators rent bikes, and provide necessary equipment, food, and accommodation. Trancoso (Bahia) is the starting point of the Discovery Route – a crossing that passes through wonderful beaches. Contact **Sampa Bikers** for details. Another popular mountain-biking destination in Bahia is the Chapada Diamantina. **Terra Chapada Expedições** organizes multiday tours through the park.

Mountain biking is an interesting way to discover the attractions of Florianópolis (Santa Catarina). There are 30 trails that traverse its 42 beaches,

Ecotourism by bicycle, Parque Nacional dos Lençóis Maranhenses

lakes, and stunning landscape. These and other options in the state can be found at **Caminhos do Sertão** and **Ecos da Serra**. Cycling tours near the Parque Nacional Aparados da Serra covering the cities of Gramado, Canela, and the Vale dos Vinhedos *(see p359)* are organized by **Casa da Montanha Adventures**. Accommodation can be found at the Parador Casa da Montanha, a kind of luxurious camping site.

Water Sports

Vast stretches of beach, and an abundance of rivers, lakes, and waterfalls make water sports widely available and accessible in Brazil. Fernando de Noronha (Pernambuco) and Itacaré (Bahia) are hot destinations for water sports such as snorkeling, surfing, and windsurfing. Búzios and Rio (Rio de Janeiro), and

Ubatuba and Guarujá (São Paulo) are easier, while Praia Joaquinas and other beaches in Florianópolis offer more challenging water-sports activities *(see pp350–51)*.

The country has many scuba-diving options. **PDIC Brasil** (Professional Diving Instructor's Corporation) is a good place to contact. Rio de Janeiro state, Cabo Frio, Angra dos Reis, Paraty, and Ilhabela in São Paulo are outstanding places for diving and exploring shipwrecks. Beaches in the Northeast are a snorkeler's paradise.

Among the sail sports, kitesurf reigns in Ceará's beaches and lakes near Jericoacoara. **Kite Club Preá** provides facilities, tours, and safaris for intermediate to advanced kiters in Preá, a small fishing village east of Jericoacoara.

Rafting and canoeing enthusiasts should head to Brotas and Socorro, in São Paulo; Três Rios, in Rio de Janeiro; Domingos Martins, in Espírito Santo; Jaguariaíva and Tibagi, in Paraná; Apiúna, in Santa Catarina; and Rio Cristlino, in the Amazon rainforest of Mato Grosso.

Cascading and canyoning can be challenging, but highly enjoyable, in the waterfalls of Chapada dos Veadeiros in Goiás, and in the Cipó mountains in Minas Gerais where visitors can get in touch with **ABETA (Brazilian Adventure Travel Trade Association)**.

For those who enjoy fishing, **Clube de Pesca Cananéia** helps organize expeditions. This club also makes arrangements for the obligatory fishing license.

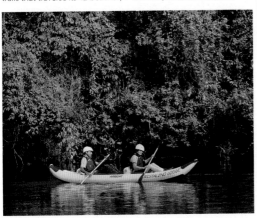
Canoeing on the Rio Cristalino near Cristalino Jungle Lodge *(see p323)*

Language & Culture

Almost 70 universities in the country offer Portuguese classes to foreign students. Many of these courses are now open to visitors. Some language schools also offer flexible Portuguese courses, which can stretch from one week to many months. These lessons may include lectures on Brazilian culture and guided tours of museums and galleries. Some of them prepare for the Portuguese Proficiency Certificate (CELPE-Bras), the Portuguese-language qualification granted by the **Ministério da Educação**. **Excellence Idiomas, Idiomas to Go**, and **Diálogo Language School** are some of the better private-school options.

Music & Dance

The sensuous dance forms of Brazil have evoked a lot of interest worldwide. With their natural hospitality Brazilians are easily motivated to teach dance steps at bars, dance houses, parties, and local performances. But you can also arrange to take professional dancing classes in the cities. In Rio de Janeiro, it is possible to learn with the famous dancer Carlinhos de Jesus at **Casa de Dança**. Diálogo Language School conducts

Couples dancing the *forró* on a festive occasion

workshops on dancing and singing to Brazilian rhythms, which may be tied in with Portuguese-language classes. These lessons are a good way to familiarize oneself with the most representative artists of Brazilian popular music. Also, keep your ears open for reggae beats on the streets throughout the Northeast.

Soccer

Soccer was introduced into Brazil by a Scottish railway engineer in the 1890s and grew to become the nation's favorite sport. It is possible to arrange day and residential soccer camps, as well as team and individual training sessions or family packages. The coaching

programs vary from a week to several months and may include friendly games and tournaments for players between 6 and 18 years of age. Good options are **Central de Intercambio** in São Paulo City and **Cruzeiro Esporte Clube** in Belo Horizonte (Minas Gerais).

Capoeira Classes

The amalgam of acrobatic movements, rhythm, music, and song make *capoeira (see p203)* a big draw. Almost every city has an academy. **Zebra & Pepi** take lessons on the Itacaré beaches. In Salvador, **Filhos de Bimba** is one of the best and most famous *capoeira* schools. With several branches outside Brazil, it strives to keep alive the regional spirit of *capoeira*.

Volunteer Programs

Volunteers can work in non-profit organizations contributing in the fields of education, child welfare, health, ecology, and the environment. This is a good way of getting to know local people, and at the same time making a social contribution. These programs are open to adults of any age, and may include homestay with a Brazilian family. The program duration commonly varies from two to ten months. To enroll contact **Diálogo Language School**, **World Study**, **AFS Intercultura Brasil**, or **Soul Brasileiro**. For all such programs, a basic knowledge of Portuguese is required.

A rigorous soccer training session, Ipanema beach, Rio de Janeiro City

DIRECTORY

Ecotourism

Amazon Mystery Tours
Rua 2, Casa 23 Parque Tropical.
Tel (92) 9 8430 7763.
W amazon-outdoor.com

Amazon Star
Rua Henrique Gurjão 236, Belem, Pará.
Tel (91) 3212 6244.
W amazonstar.com.br

Fazenda Palomas
BR-158 Santana do Livramento, Rio Grande do Sul.
Tel (55) 3505 6417.
W fazendapalomas.com

Fellini Turismo
Rua Gen Bento Martins, 24 Conj. 401, Porto Alegre, Rio Grande do Sul.
Tel (51) 3216 6300.

Pantanal Explorer
Av Governador Ponce de Arruda 670, Varzea Grande, Mato Grosso.
Tel (65) 3682 2800.
W pantanalexplorer.com.br

Bird-Watching & Safaris

Birding Brasil Turismo
Conjunto Acariquara 214, Manaus, Amazonas.
W birdingbraziltours.com

Edson Endrigo
Rua Antonio Aggio 1296/11, São Paulo.
Tel (11) 3742 8374.
W avesfoto.com.br

Estação Ecológica Santa Lúcia
Av José Ruschi 4, Museu Mello Leitão, Santa Teresa, Espírito Santo.
Tel (27) 3259 1182.

Iara Turismo
Av Gov José Maicher 815, Belém, Pará.
Tel (91) 4006 3850.
W iaraturismo.com.br

Korubo Expedições
Rua Traipu 260, São Paulo.
Tel (11) 4063 1502.
W jalapao.com

Off-Road Driving

Jeri Off-Road
Rua Principal 208.
Jericoacoara, Ceará.
Tel (88) 3669 2268.
W jeri.tur.br

Cycling & Biking

Caminhos do Sertão
Rua Caminho do Arvoredo 169, Rio Vermelho, Florianópolis, Santa Catarina.
Tel (48) 3234 9527.
W caminhosdosertao.com.br

Casa da Montanha Adventures
Av Borges Medeiros 3116, Gramado.
Tel (54) 3504 5302.
W paradorcasadamontanha.com.br

Ecos da Serra
Rua Presidente Lincoln 76.
Lages, Santa Catarina.
Tel (49) 9972 9672.
W ecosdaserra.com.br

Sampa Bikers
Rua Baluarte 672, São Paulo.
Tel (11) 5517 7733.
W sampabikers.com.br

Terra Chapada Expedições
Tel (75) 3334 1428.
W terrachapada.com.br

Water Sports

ABETA (Brazilian Adventure Travel Trade Association)
Rua Rio Grande do Norte 1560, Sala 401, Belo Horizonte, Minas Gerais.
Tel (31) 3261 5707.
W abeta.com.br

Clube de Pesca Cananéia
Rua João Maciel, Porto Cubatão, Cananéia, São Paulo.
Tel (13) 3851 6117.
W pescacananeia.com.br

Kite Club Preá
Preá Villa, Jericoacoara, Ceará.
Tel (88) 3669 2359.
W kiteclub prea.com

PDIC Brasil (Professional Diving Instructors Corporation)
Av Presidente Vargas 446, Grupo 1006, Rio de Janeiro.
Tel (21) 2263 8068.
W pdic.com.br

Language & Culture

Diálogo Language School
Rua João Ponde 240, Barra, Salvador, Bahia.
Tel (71) 3264 0053.
W dialogo-brazilstudy.com

Excellence Idiomas
Rua Barata Ribeiro 391, Copacabana.
Tel (21) 2225 7430.
W excellenceidiomas.com.br

Idiomas to Go
Al Jauaperi 1020, São Paulo.
Tel (11) 5052 4802.
W idiomastogo. com.br

Ministério da Educação
Esplanada dos Ministérios, Bloco L, Sala 227, Brasília.
Tel (0800) 616161.
W mec.gov.br/sesu

Music & Dance

Casa de Dança
Rua Álvaro Ramos 11, Botafogo, Rio de Janeiro.
Tel (21) 2541 6186.
W carlinhosdejesus.com.br

Soccer

Central de Intercambio
Av Paulista 726, Loja 7, São Paulo.
Tel (11) 3262 4012.

Cruzeiro Esporte Clube

Av Otacílio Negrão de Lima 7100, Bairro Bandeirante, Belo Horizonte.
W cruzeiro.com.br

Capoeira Classes

Filhos de Bimba
Rua Gregório de Mattos 51, Pelourinho, Salvador, Bahia.
Tel (71) 3322 5082.

Zebra & Pepi
Rua Pedro Longo 385, Pituba, Itacaré, Bahia.
Tel (73) 3251 2354.

Volunteer Programs

AFS Intercultura Brasil
Travessa do Ouvidor 50, Rio de Janeiro.
Tel (21) 3724 4464.
W afs.org.br

Soul Brasileiro
São Clemente 185 / 303 Rio de Janeiro.
Tel (21) 2538 9409.
W soulbrasileiro.com.br

World Study
Av do Contorno 4480, Sala 1509, Belo Horizonte, Minas Gerias.
Tel (31) 3224 4293.
W worldstudy.com.br

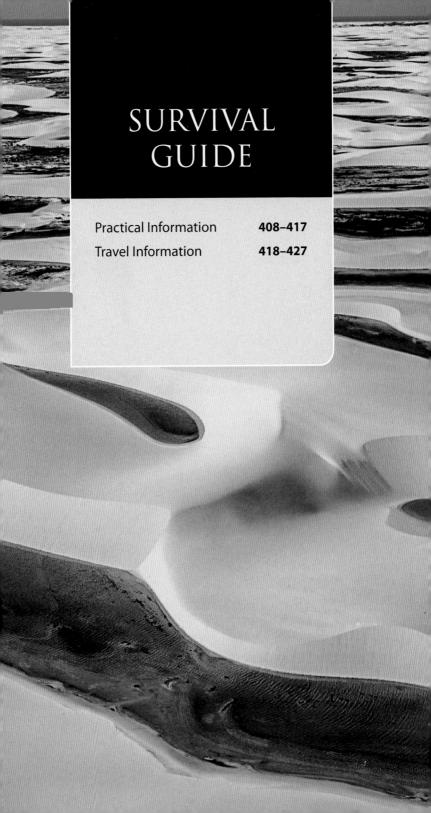

SURVIVAL
GUIDE

PRACTICAL INFORMATION

Tourism is one of the fastest growing industries in Brazil, and the country has been investing heavily in new airports, hotels, and other facilities designed to make it more attractive to visitors. Brazil offers a variety of travel experiences for all ages and tastes. Its sheer size makes air travel almost a necessity for those interested in exploring beyond just one region. All major tourist destinations are very well set up to receive international visitors. English and Spanish are generally spoken by those who work in the tourism industry. However, very few other Brazilians speak English. Fortunately, the friendliness and outgoing nature of the people more than makes up for these challenges and Brazilians overall are very helpful in assisting foreigners.

When to Go

High season in Brazil runs from Christmas to Carnaval (held in February or early March). Many musical and cultural events take place in these months. Although not as busy, a second peak season is during July and August when schools and universities have their winter break and many Europeans and North Americans visit on their summer holidays. The best times of year for lower prices and fewer travelers are the low seasons from March to May and September to November.

What to Take

Dress standards in Brazil seem largely a matter of personal taste. A sarong or sheet sleeping bag is invaluable for use as a towel, a bedsheet, or beach towel. Bring a first-aid kit, raincoat, sun hat, penknife, flashlight, wax earplugs, insect repellent, eye mask for sleeping on buses, and a chain for securing luggage to bus seats. For a jungle trip, a hammock is a good idea.

Visas & Passports

All travelers to Brazil must have a valid passport. Holders of European Union or New Zealand passports do not require a visa. Those with US, Canadian, or Australian passports need to apply for a visa at the Brazilian embassy or consulate in their country of residence. Always check the latest entry requirements with the Brazilian embassy in your country before leaving.

Upon arrival, visitors receive a 90-day entry stamp, which can be extended for another 90 days by the **Polícia Federal**, up to a maximum of 180 days per year. (Some nationalities are unable to extend beyond 90 days; check prior to traveling if this is relevant to you.) Visitors must also fill out an entry card to be kept with their passport at all times. It must be surrendered on leaving Brazil. Failure to produce this slip of paper may lead to a fine, and will certainly result in a hassle.

The 90 days are added on the day of renewal, so request the extension close to the expiry date. Keep in mind that an expired visa cannot be extended.

The Polícia Federal may ask to see an outbound ticket and proof of sufficient funds for the remainder of your stay. Those who outstay their visa term will be fined upon departure.

Map of Canoa Quebrada in one of its streets to assist tourists

Tourist Information

All international and domestic airports in Brazil have tourist information booths that offer maps, brochures, and general information. These are usually run by either the state or city's tourist office. The **Brazilian Ministry of Tourism**'s website is a useful source of information. Brazil's embassies or larger consulates have tourist sections, where visitors can get information brochures and advice. Popular destinations such as Rio and Salvador have helpful tourist offices.

Polícia Federal badge

Language

The language of Brazil is Portuguese, but it is quite different in style and pronunciation from the Portuguese spoken in Portugal. The language has quite a few similarities with Spanish. In major tourist areas, the staff will speak some English and/or Spanish. However, in general, English is not widely spoken and often Brazilians will only have a basic intermediate knowledge of the language.

A local travel agency with Internet facilities, Morro de São Paulo

◀ A small airplane flies over Parque Nacional dos Lençóis Maranhenses

Religion

Brazil is often called "the largest Catholic country on earth," although, to be accurate, one should probably call it the "largest and least devout" of Catholic nations. Many Brazilians consider themselves culturally Catholic, without being regular churchgoers. In recent years, the influence of the Church has greatly diminished. Traditional Afro-Brazilian religions are still followed, especially in the North and Northeast, with the religious ceremonies and practices gaining more acceptance over the years.

Time

Brazil has four time zones. Most of the country is three hours behind GMT (known as the Brasília Time Zone). Both Rio de Janeiro and São Paulo, as well as all of Southern and Northeast Brazil and Pará and Amapá states are three hours behind GMT. The island group of Fernando de Noronha is two hours behind GMT. The states of Mato Grosso, Mato Grosso do Sul, Amazônia, Rondônia, and Roraima are four hours behind GMT. The state of Acre, in the far western corner, is five hours behind GMT. During daylight saving hours it gets a little bit more complicated. The southern states set their clocks back an hour, but the states in the North and Northeast do not.

Electricity

There is no uniform voltage across Brazil. Some states are 110 volts, others 220 volts. Rio de Janeiro and São Paulo are both 110 volts. Brasília is 220 volts. Hotels will often have plugs for both voltages and are good at labeling the outlets. Adaptors for laptops and cell phone chargers can normally handle the full range of voltage, but it is always better to check the specifications of your equipment to be sure.

Local tour guide with a group of tourists in Cachoeira

Etiquette

Brazilians are very friendly and outgoing, even when meeting someone for the first time. When introduced, men will greet each other with a handshake and a friendly slap on the shoulder. Good friends usually embrace. When introduced to a woman, it is customary to greet her with a handshake and a kiss on the cheek (one kiss in São Paulo and the South, two kisses in Rio, the North, and Northeast). When introduced to a group of people, everybody has to kiss or shake hands with everybody else.

Women Travelers

A woman alone, especially at night, will attract some form of attention. It usually depends on where you are. Steer clear of the area around bus stations, since it is likely to be a red-light area at night. The transport terminals themselves, though, are usually policed and fairly safe at all hours.

Special needs

Travelers with mobility problems will find Brazil a very challenging country. Although it is relatively easy to find wheelchair-accessible hotels and restaurants, very few public places are accessible or wheelchair-friendly. Older buildings may still lack elevators or ramps, and streets and sidewalks are often uneven or broken.

Wheelchair parking sign

The metro system in Rio has electronic wheelchair elevators, but these are not always operational. For short distances, buses are not the best option for disabled travelers to get around. Taxis are better, and plentiful in most cities. For long distances, however, buses are generally comfortable, with special services offering fully reclining seats. Wheelchairs are available at all main airports.

Traveling with Children

Those traveling with small children will find Brazilians very child-friendly and accommodating. There are virtually no places that do not welcome children. Brazilians themselves think nothing of bringing their children to restaurants, theaters, cafés, concerts, or other events.

Public toilets

Public toilets are not that hard to find in Brazil, but vary greatly in cleanliness. Clean toilets can usually be found in hotel lobbies, shopping centers, and in public locations such as bus stations, parks, or beaches. A fee is sometimes charged. Note that toilet paper is sometimes dispensed from a central dispenser outside the stalls. It is a good idea to carry a roll of toilet paper.

Directory

Visas & Passports

Polícia Federal
Aeroporto Internacional Antônio Carlos Jobim, Terminal 1, Rio de Janeiro.
Tel (21) 3398 3198.
W dpf.gov.br

Tourist Information

Brazilian Ministry of Tourism
W braziltour.com

US State Department
W travel.state.gov

Health & Medical Matters

Brazil has a free national public health-care system. Even foreign tourists will receive medical attention in any of the public hospitals, should they require it. Unfortunately, the public health system is overloaded and inadequately funded, especially in the rural areas of Brazil. Queues can be long and tedious, and facilities are not always up to European or North American standards. However, Brazil's private hospitals and clinics, though not free, offer world-class medical facilities. A good travel insurance policy will give access to these private facilities in an emergency, but remember to read the fine print carefully. Overall, hygiene standards in Brazil are high. Normal care is required with food and drink, and with preventive vaccinations, particularly when visiting the most remote parts of the country.

prevent it. It is much more common in the summer months, from December to March. Symptoms include high fever, joint pain, and headaches (especially behind the eyes). The illness usually runs its course in a week or 10 days, but a check-up is recommended to avoid any complications.

Cholera occasionally occurs in remote areas, but is mostly preventable by taking proper hygiene precautions such as drinking filtered water and washing and peeling fruit and vegetables. The most important precaution is to wash hands frequently.

Pharmacies

For minor ailments, travelers can turn to Brazil's *farmácias*, or pharmacies. These can be found everywhere, are always well supplied, and are often open late. Every city will have at least one that is open 24 hours. Many medications that in other countries are available only by prescription can be bought over the counter in Brazil. Take care to remember the generic name of a medication taken regularly. A trained pharmacist is normally on hand to recommend the appropriate medication for common ailments such as diarrhea, allergies, rashes, or infections. It is possible to get injections and free medical advice in pharmacies all over Brazil.

A fire brigade ambulance parked outside a fire control office

Vaccinations

It is a good idea to consult a travel clinic or family doctor for an International Certificate of Vaccinations, an up-to-date list of the required vaccinations. The most commonly recommended are a DTP (diphtheria, tetanus, and polio) booster, as well as vaccinations for typhoid and hepatitis A.

A yellow fever vaccination is also required. This disease is endemic to many parts of South America, including Brazil. Officially, all visitors to Brazil are required to show proof of yellow fever vaccination. Although the requirement is not regularly enforced for visitors coming from North America or Europe, it is compulsory for those from other countries in South America. Entry can be denied upon failure to show proof of vaccination. Anti-malarial tablets may be advisable for those visiting some of the more remote parts of the Amazon.

Tropical diseases

Visitors to Brazil's major tourist destinations rarely have to worry about tropical diseases. The one tropical disease that can occur anywhere in the country, even in urban areas, is dengue fever. It is a viral infection that prevails throughout South America. The disease is transmitted by mosquitoes, and there is no vaccine to

A well-stocked pharmacy in São Paulo

Vacationers relaxing under umbrellas on the beach

Private Hospitals

Brazil does not offer the best medical facilities in its public hospitals. Foreign visitors, in particular, may find it difficult getting a bed, unless for an infectious disease. In most public hospitals, the level of health care will not match European or US standards.

Private hospitals, however, offer excellent facilities. Though good medical care may be rare to find in rural areas, in the larger cities you will never be far from a decent private hospital. In many big cities, local tourist offices and some good hotels can provide a list of doctors who can speak English, French, and German.

For medical emergencies in a remote area, an air ambulance service offers a pick-up within 24 hours of calling. However, it is advisable to contact the travel insurance company before requesting this service.

Though fairly affordable by international standards, private treatment in Brazil may turn out to be expensive. Many doctors and hospitals do not accept travel-health insurance, and insist on payment in cash.

Health precautions

A visit to Brazil, by and large, does not require special health precautions. Impure water and contaminated food are usually the reasons for most diseases. However, hygiene standards of food and drink are high, especially in major tourist areas. Water is usually filtered or bottled and ice cubes are made from filtered water. Even in the most remote parts, mineral water is easily available. As long as fruit, vegetables, and meat are handled properly, they can be eaten safely.

A local drink seller on a Rio de Janeiro beach

Sun protection

Visitors from the Northern Hemisphere should take extra care with Brazil's intense tropical sun, especially for the first few days in the country. Brazil basks in almost year-round sunshine, making adequate sun protection absolutely crucial. Avoid exposure between 11am and 3pm and apply sunscreen to all exposed parts of the body. Wear sunblock (minimum SPF 30) and limit tanning to only a few hours. Pharmacies and grocery stores sell a variety of national and international sunscreen brands. Those sold on the beach itself, or in street markets, are best avoided. The contents may either be fake, or have been kept in storage for a long time, which causes the active ingredients to deteriorate.

Safety for Travelers

Brazil is known to have a higher crime rate than anywhere in North America and Europe. However, in reality, the kind of violence that affects travelers is mostly limited to the bigger cities, and is usually restricted to crimes that target valuables such as cameras, credit cards, cell phones, or cash. Such assaults are rare in the countryside and smaller towns. While some parts of Brazil can truly be regarded as violent and dangerous, travelers can be assured of personal security by using common sense and observing some very basic precautions.

A Guarda Municipal policewoman patrolling on a bicycle, Rio City

Local showing the way to visitors, Salvador

Personal safety

The large cities, especially Rio de Janeiro, São Paulo, and Salvador, are generally considered more prone to violence than the rest of Brazil. Statistically, crime rates in these cities are significantly higher than in cities in Europe or the US. However, much of the violent crime is confined to poorer neighborhoods and *favelas* in parts of the city where travelers should not venture on their own without a tour guide. The crime that visitors are most likely to be susceptible to is theft or robbery. The most basic precaution is not to carry anything worth stealing and to avoid empty beaches and nearly empty streets after dark. Avoid ostentatious behavior such as walking around with expensive equipment; instead keep it in a plain bag.

When sightseeing, keep all belongings in a bag that can be placed in a money belt. Never carry large amounts of cash. Credit cards are widely accepted and can be used for purchases in most hotels and stores. Keep a few small bills handy in a pocket so that when making small purchases, the wallet doesn't have to be pulled out in a busy area. Public transport is safe in the daytime, but in the evenings taxis are a better option. If you get robbed, just hand over your valuables, as robbers are often armed with a gun or a knife. Streets and public places can be unsafe at times. A very common technique is to distract the victim by spraying something on their shoulder. An accomplice may then offer to clean the mess, while the thief will make off with your belongings. The best and safest way is to politely turn down any such offer.

It is always best to exercise caution when someone unknown offers a drink, or even cigarettes. Instances of drugging, or spiked drinks are not uncommon in Brazil.

Police

Brazil has several different types of police that travelers are likely to encounter. Known to be the most efficient by far, the **Polícia Federal** (*see p408*) are responsible for passport control at airports and border crossings. Dressed in plain clothes, they deal with visas and their extensions.

Dressed in gray uniforms and caps, the **Polícia Militar** are responsible for public safety and can be seen patrolling the streets, beaches, and highways. These policemen often carry out "blitzes" (traffic checks) along major streets or roads. These can appear a little intimidating as the Polícia Militar come out in full gear, carrying automatic weapons. If you are driving a car, slow down, turn on the interior light, and roll down the windows.

A few cities with a strong tourist presence, such as Rio and Salvador, also have **Polícia de Turismo**, or tourist police, who offer assistance in case

A brightly painted tourist police station in Olinda

of any difficulty. Unfortunately, many of them do not speak English. A special Delegacia do Turista (tourist department) is available for those who require further help or wish to report a crime.

The state-controlled **Polícia Civil** handle local laws and investigate more serious crimes. When there is no tourist police post in the vicinity, thefts are reported to these policemen. Rio City has an unarmed guard force, **Guarda Municipal** (Municipal Civil Guards), to complement state police patrolling of parks and beaches.

Reporting a crime

If you have been the victim of a crime, it can be reported at the nearest police station or tourist police office. This should be done within 24 hours of the crime. To obtain a report of the incident or theft for insurance purposes, insist that you receive a copy of the *boletim de ocorrência*. There may be nobody at the police station who speaks English, so it may be useful to request a hotel employee or tour guide to accompany you if you need to file a report. Missing credit cards should be reported to the relevant company

Polícia Militar booth in São Paulo, responsible for traffic checks

(see p414). If you have lost or damaged your passport, it is recommended that you contact your nearest consulate or embassy.

Identification

It is mandatory in Brazil to carry some form of photo identification. Often you will be asked to show some form of ID when entering an office building or government agency, or sometimes even a museum or library. To avoid carrying around a passport, keep a photocopy, and carry some other form of less valuable ID such as a student card, or a health card that has your picture, name, and date of birth.

Polícia Federal car

Guarda Municipal car

Directory

Police

Guarda Municipal
W rio.rj.gov.br/web/gmrio

Polícia Civil
Tel 197 or 147.

Polícia Militar
Tel 190.

Polícia de Turismo
RIO DE JANEIRO
Av Afrânio de Melo Franco 159, Leblon. **Map** 1 B4.
Tel (21) 2332 2924.
SALVADOR
Praça São Francisco 14, Pelourinho. **Tel** (71) 3322 1188.
SÃO PAULO
Av São Luíz 91, Centro. **Map** 1 B3.
Tel (11) 3214 0209.

Consulates

Australia
Av Presidente Wilson 231, Centro, Rio de Janeiro.
Map 5 E5. **Tel** (21) 3824 4624.
W dfat.gov.au

Canada
Av Atlântica 1130, 5th Floor, Copacabana, Rio de Janeiro.
Map 3 F1. **Tel** (21) 2453 3004.
Av Nações Unidas 12901, São Paulo. **Tel** (21) 2543 3004.
W brazil.gc.ca

Ireland
Alameda Joaquim Eugênio de Lima 447, São Paulo. **Map** Off 4
F3. **Tel** (11) 3147 7788.

New Zealand
SHIS QI 09, Conjunto 16, Casa 01, Brasília.
Tel (61) 3248 9900.

UK
Praia do Flamengo 284, Rio de Janeiro. **Tel** (21) 2555 9600.
Rua Ferreira de Araújo 741, Pinheiros, São Paulo.
Tel (11) 3094 2700.

USA
Av Presidente Wilson 147, Rio de Janeiro. **Map** 5 E5.
Tel (21) 3823 2000.
Rua Henri Dunant 500, São Paulo.
Tel (11) 3250 5000.

Banking & Local Currency

Brazil provides a range of accessible banking facilities and money exchange services. Except for the US dollar and euro, foreign currencies are rarely accepted outside of major tourist regions. Exchange rates for cash transactions are usually not very good, and the best rates can be obtained on credit card or *caixa automática* (automated teller machine) transactions. Credit cards, widely accepted in most establishments, can be used to withdraw local currency (*real*), giving a more favorable exchange rate, and are by far the most convenient. Traveler's checks are not widely accepted and can be difficult to cash.

Banking Hours

HSBC has a number of banks that are open from 9am to 5pm on all weekdays. Most other banks, including **Banco do Brasil**, are also open on weekdays, but only from 10am to 4pm. Hours for changing money or traveler's checks are even more limited, usually falling between 11am and 2pm. Automated teller machines (ATMs) have more flexible hours but are not always open 24 hours.

ATMs

The easiest way of getting cash in big cities is by using ATMs (*caixa automática*), which are widely found and accept foreign cards. Check with your bank prior to traveling to Brazil whether your ATM card can be used internationally for cash withdrawals and that you have the appropriate PIN (*numero de identificao*). In addition to ATM cards, most bank machines will

Automated teller machine (ATM) at a branch of Banco do Brasil

also give a cash advance on a credit card. Banco do Brasil, HSBC, Citibank, Bradesco, and Banco 24 Horas have reliable networks that work with international cards.

Bank machines are often updated and adjusted so other banks may join the network. For safety reasons, bank machines are not always open 24 hours. ATMs may close at 8 or 10pm,

or be programmed to dispense only a small amount of money. It is also good to plan ahead on weekends or statutory holidays when machines sometimes run out of cash. Keep in mind, too, that some small towns and islands do not have ATMs.

Credit Cards

Credit cards are widely accepted in Brazil. The most commonly used cards are **AmEx**, **MasterCard**, and **Visa**. **Diners Club** is less widely used. Credit cards can be used in almost all establishments. Street markets and kiosks, of course, only take cash. When you pay by credit card the cashier will usually ask "*débito ou credito*" (debit or credit). It is important to state "*credito*" as most international credit cards do not work as debit cards. Debit cards are also widely accepted. Credit cards with a PIN can also be used to make cash withdrawals from ATMs at banks. The service fee is higher for using a credit card instead of a regular ATM card.

Directory

Credit Cards

AmEx
Tel +1 336 393 1111.

Diners Club Citibank
Tel (0800) 4004 2484.

MasterCard
Tel (0800) 891 3294.

Visa
Tel (0800) 891 3680.

Banks

Banco do Brasil
Av Paulista 2163, São Paulo.
Map 4 E2. **Tel** (11) 4004 0001.

Rua Joana Angélica 124,
Ipanema, Rio de Janeiro.
Map 2 A4. **Tel** (21) 3554 9700.
W bb.com.br

HSBC
Av Paulista 949, São Paulo.
Map 4 E2. **Tel** (11) 4004 4722.

Av Nossa Senhora de
Copacabana 583, Rio de Janeiro.
Map 3 E2. **Tel** (21) 3816 8100.
W hsbc.com.br

Branch of Banco do Brasil with *caixa automática* (ATMs)

It is a good idea to instruct your bank that you will be using your card in Brazil, so as to avoid any transaction problems at a later stage.

Traveler's checks

Very few banks will cash traveler's checks, and at those that do, there is a high fee and a long wait. The Banco do Brasil, for example, charges a flat fee of US$20 per transaction. Some hotels and some tour operators will accept traveler's checks, but the exchange is always bad. American Express will cash AmEx traveler's checks for free, but they only have offices in a few major cities in Brazil. It is more convenient to use a credit card for major expenses incurred at hotels and on excursions.

Currency

The currency of Brazil is the *real* (R$, plural *reais*). All bank notes have a print of a Brazilian animal on them. The smallest R$2 note is blue, featuring a sea turtle. The purple R$5 and the red R$10 have pictures of a heron and a macaw respectively. The yellow R$20 notes feature the endangered *mico-leão dourado* (golden lion tamarin) monkey. The brown R$50 notes come with a picture of a jaguar. R$100 bills, featuring the endangered dusky grouper fish, are often impossible to break at small shops, so stock up on change at drugstores and grocery stores.

Banknotes

Brazilian reais bills come in denominations of 2, 5, 10, 20, 50, and 100. Brazilian bank notes are bright, with each denomination coming in a different color.

2 reais

5 reais

10 reais

20 reais

50 reais

100 reais

Coins

Coins come in the following denomination: 1, 5, 10, 25, 50 centavos and 1 real. 100 centavos make up 1 real.

5 centavos

10 centavos

25 centavos

50 centavos

1 real

Communications & Media

Brazil has an efficient and modern communication system. Telecommunication systems are reasonably advanced and cell phones are widely used, making it one of the world's biggest networks, with more than 270 million registered phones. Postal services, including registered post and express mail, are quite reliable. Most hotels subscribe to a digital or satellite television service with international channels. Although there are no foreign-language Brazilian newspapers, foreign magazines and some newspapers are available in all major cities, mostly in the main airports, business districts, and tourist centers.

Public telephones, available all over Brazil, particularly in urban areas

Local & International Phone Calls

Most telephone numbers in Brazil (fixed or cell) are now eight or nine digits. If you do come across a seven-digit number (or eight-digit cell), it is best to confirm if it is still correct. All cell phone numbers begin with a 9.

Local calls do not require a two-digit area code, whereas long-distance calls do. All long-distance calls (within Brazil and international) also require the use of a long-distance service provider (*prestadora*). The two-digit code of the *prestadora* needs to be dialed before the area code or country code for international calls; there are different services for fixed and cell lines. In listings, long-distance numbers often look like this – 0-XX-11-3455-3288. The two-digit *prestadora* number is inserted in place of the "XX" and is known as the *código de seleção de prestadora* (CSP). Customers have several options, depending on the region. **Embratel** (Brazil's

largest telecommunications company) phone cards work everywhere in Brazil, and its number is 21. If using Embratel to call São Paulo, the number would look like this: 0-21-11-3455-3288. This can be confusing because some *prestadora* codes are the same as some area codes – Embratel and Rio, for example.

Cell Phones

Cell phones are common all over Brazil, and are generally used in most public places, including in restaurants. Most tri-band GSM phones will work in Brazil. You can purchase a local SIM chip upon arrival and obtain a local number. Most local cell operators offer a very straightforward package for international visitors, including for data. Some phones need to be unlocked before they can be used in a foreign country. Check with your phone company before leaving home. If your service provider has a roaming agreement with Brazil, you can use your regular

A woman on her cell phone in the Ipanema neighborhood of Rio de Janeiro

number. However, inquire about roaming fees to avoid nasty surprises on your phone bill. Due to the size of Brazil, most cell phone packages are relevant to the city or state it is issued in, so you may still be charged roaming fees even when using a Brazilian cell number – for example, using a Rio cell number in São Paulo. Brazilians who regularly visit different cities in Brazil often have cell numbers for each one.

The main cell operators in Brazil are **Claro** (21), **Oi** (31), **Tim** (41), and **Vivo** (15). It is always cheapest to use the *código de seleção de prestadora* (CSP) of the network you are linked to when calling.

Public Telephones

As in many countries, public telephones (*orelhões*, or "big ears") are diminishing in Brazil. Pay phones do not take coins. You must purchase a phone card (*cartão telefonico*), available at newsstands, drugstores, and post offices. To make overseas collect calls from a pay phone, you have to contact the operator (dial 21) to complete the call for you. Local or long-distance collect calls within Brazil can be made by dialing 9090 before the number.

Dialing Codes

- A local call requires only the eight- or nine-digit number of the land line or cell without the area code. Some key area codes are: Belo Horizonte, 31; Brasília, 61; Curitiba, 41; Fortaleza, 85; Manaus, 92; Natal, 84; Porto Alegre, 51; Recife, 81; Rio de Janeiro, 21; Salvador, 71; São Paulo, 11.
- To make a long-distance call, dial 0 or +, then the *prestadora* code (CSP), followed by the area code, and phone number.
- To call abroad from Brazil, dial 00, then the *prestadora* code, followed by the country code, area code, and phone number.
- Contact Embratel at 0800 703 2100 or 0800 703 2111 to ask for collect calls or international calls.

The distinct blue and yellow colors of a post office in Rio de Janeiro

Internet

Internet service is widely available in Brazil and usually quite cheap. If traveling with a laptop, ask about the hotel's in-room Internet access rates, although at more and more business hotels it is free. Cyber cafés are a cheap option for accessing the Internet and are usually found in shopping centers, many of which already have free Wi-Fi zones and large bookstores. Some of the bigger Internet cafés include **FNAC Centro Cultural** and **Icone Espaço Cultural** in São Paulo, and **Livraria da Travessa** and **Cyber Copa Café** in Rio.

Postal Services

The Brazilian postal service is quite efficient. Post offices (*correios*) are open from 9am to 5pm Monday to Friday. Large shopping centers and airports will have branches with longer opening hours, including Saturdays. Regular delivery service within Brazil takes two to four days, and overseas six to 12 days. For guaranteed or registered delivery, the *correios* offer the excellent SEDEX (domestic Brazilian express mail) service, which functions like a courier service. For international mail, there is SEDEX Mundi and Express Mail Service (EMS). The *correios* has a good website, parts of which are in English, which allows you to check addresses, postal codes (known as CEP), locate post office branches, or track deliveries. In larger cities, there are also

several international couriers for express overseas delivery, such as **DHL**, **FedEx**, **Skynet**, and **World Courier**. Delivery from Brazil to the main cities and towns in the US or Europe normally takes 48 hours.

Addresses

Most addresses are fairly straightforward, giving the street name first, followed by the number. Landmark buildings or houses in small towns may be listed as s/n (*sem número*, or without number). Other abbreviations in addresses include lj or *loja* (shop) and sl or *sobreloja* (first floor or mezzanine). You should add the zip or postal code and the CEP, if you have it.

Newspapers & Magazines

Brazil does not have any English-language daily newspapers or magazines. The main Brazilian dailies are, like in the US, regional, the best known being *O Globo* (Rio de Janeiro) and the *Folha de São Paulo* (São Paulo). The Friday editions include a cultural and entertainment section with detailed information on concerts, plays, movies, and exhibitions. The bestselling weekly news magazines are *Época, Veja,* and *Isto É.* In Rio de Janeiro, São Paulo, and other large cities, the *Veja (see p156)* includes a separate magazine and listings related to cultural events.

Newspapers and magazines are most commonly sold at a newsstand (*banca de jornal*). Newsstands in Ipanema in Rio and Praça de Republica in São Paulo have a good range of international magazines, as do the better bookstores, especially in major shopping centers.

Television & Radio

Brazil is well served when it comes to both television and radio, although most of the local programming will be in Portuguese, but this can add to the flavor of a local football match or sporting event. The media giant in Brazil is Globo. It is responsible for the country's

most popular TV network, as well as a large number of national and regional radio networks, newspapers, magazines, and websites. At hotels and in many houses, visitors will have access to hundreds of digital or satellite channels that include international news services such as CNN and the BBC. On the Internet, you will be able to access radio stations from around the world.

Directory

Local & International Phone Calls

Embratel
ⓦ embratel.com.br

Cell Phones

Claro
ⓦ claro.com.br

Oi
ⓦ oi.com.br

Tim
ⓦ tim.com.br

Vivo
ⓦ vivo.com.br

Internet

Cyber Copa Café
Av Nossa Senhora de Copacabana 1077, Rio de Janeiro.
Map 2 C4. **Tel** (21) 2287 9403.

FNAC Centro Cultural
Praça do Omaguás 34, Pinheiros, São Paulo. **Tel** (11) 3579 2000.

Icone Espaço Cultural
Rua Augusta 1415, São Paulo.
Map 4 F1. **Tel** (11) 3288 9206.

Livraria da Travessa
Rua Visconde de Pirajá 276, Ipanema, Rio de Janeiro.
Map 2 4A **Tel** (21) 3205 9002

Postal Services

Correios
ⓦ correios.com.br

DHL
ⓦ dhl.com.br

FedEx
ⓦ fedex.com/br

Skynet
ⓦ skynetsao.com

World Courier
ⓦ worldcourier.com

TRAVEL INFORMATION

Most travelers arrive in Brazil by plane. There are regular scheduled flights from Europe and North and South America. Travelers from Asia or Africa will most likely have to connect elsewhere before continuing to Brazil. Several airlines offer stopovers to or from Brazil at no extra cost. Almost all direct flights land at São Paulo's international airport or in Rio de Janeiro. There are a few regular flights to Salvador, Recife, Brasilia, Belo Horizonte, and Fortaleza. However, most direct flights to these and other destinations in the Northeast, such as Natal, are European charter flights. Air travel within Brazil is efficient, and most remote locations are accessible by plane.

Arriving by Air

Most direct international flights land either in Rio de Janeiro or São Paulo, but there are also flights into other major cities, such as Brasília, Manaus, Belo Horizonte, Recife, and Salvador. Convenient connections are available for other domestic destinations. Travelers will clear customs at the airport where they first enter Brazil.

Modern, well-equipped Belém International Airport

International Airlines

Most major European and North and South American airlines operate regularly scheduled flights to Brazil. Delta, **American Airlines**, Continental Airlines, KLM, Lufthansa, Air France, British Airways, Alitalia, Iberia, Tap, and others offer nonstop flights to Rio de Janeiro and São Paulo. The largest Brazilian airline, **TAM**, has regular flights to Europe and the USA. There are also nonstop flights to Salvador de Bahia from Madrid with **Air Europa**, and from Miami with American Airlines. **Gol**, Brazil's second-largest airline, flies internationally to Latin American destinations only.

On Arrival

All tourists must fill out a *cartao de entrada/saida* (entry/exit card). Immigration officials will keep half and return the other to you. This card serves as proof of stay in Brazil and will be checked on departure. Loss of the card may result in a major hassle and possibly a fine *(see p408)*. Officials will also stamp your passport, and in case they are not granting you the usual 90-day stay in Brazil, the number of days will be written beneath the word *Prazo* on the stamp in your passport. For an extension of the 90-day entry stamp, contact the Polícia Federal *(see p408)*.

A Gol aircraft at the Deputado Luíz E. Magalhães International Airport, Salvador

Taxis waiting outside Congonhas Airport, São Paulo City

Customs Requirements & Duty Free

All international travelers are allowed to purchase up to US$500 at the Brazilian duty-free shop in the arrival hall. Purchases must be made prior to exiting the customs area. Visitors may bring items for their personal use, including electronics. Gadgets, such as cameras or laptops, may need to be registered upon arrival to ensure that they will be taken out of the country again. Gifts up to a value of US$500 can be brought in without additional duties; Brazilian duty-free purchases are not included in this amount.

Getting from Airports

In Rio City, taxis can be a rip-off. Either take a set-price yellow cab from Rio airport or, instead, go for the **Real Auto Bus**, which runs an efficient half-hourly bus service. São Paulo City offers excellent air-conditioned shuttles known as the "Airport Service." These run every 30 minutes, and depart from the arrivals terminal.

Taxis, too, are easily available at a fixed price. Salvador's international airport is linked to the city center by an hourly shuttle express bus service.

Travel Agencies & Packages

European residents have access to attractive package deals to Northeast Brazil. Packages typically include hotel and airfare to a popular destination such as Fortaleza, Natal, or Recife. Though affordable, these package tours do not offer a lot of flexibility. Independent travelers who wish to visit several destinations, must book their own airfare and hotels. Confirm hotel prices with travel operators, as Brazilian hotels often reserve their best prices for agencies.

A number of travel agencies, such as **Brazil Nuts**, offer customized tours or programs, including activities for seniors, youths, gay travelers, or for those interested in cultural activities. **Journey Latin America**, a UK-based travel

agency, offers tailor-made tours across Brazil. Based in Miami, **Brol** (BR Online Travel) is the first American online travel company to specialize in Brazil. It sells air passes for multiple flights around Brazil or South America.

Airport	Information	Distance to City Center	Average Taxi Fare	Average Journey Time
Internacional de Guarulhos	(11) 2445 2945	São Paulo City 17 miles (28 km)	US$50	40–120 minutes (in rush hour)
International Airport Tom Jobim	(21) 3398 5050	Rio de Janeiro City 12 miles (20 km)	US$40	40–90 minutes (in rush hour)
Deputado Luíz E. Magalhães	(71) 3204 1010	Salvador 17 miles (28 km)	US$55	40 minutes
Internacional dos Guararapes	(81) 3322 4188	Recife 11 miles (18 km)	US$30	20 minutes
Eduardo Gomes	(92) 3652 1210	Manaus 10 miles (16 km)	US$40	25 minutes
Internacional Salgado Filho	(51) 3358 2000	Porto Alegre 4 miles (6 km)	US$15	15 minutes

Domestic Air Travel

The sheer size of Brazil makes air travel the preferred mode of transportation. The country has an excellent network of airlines and most airports have been modernized. Air travel is an important means of transportation to reach remote areas in Amazônia and the interior of Brazil. All towns in the country have at least an airstrip, and all cities have an airport, usually some distance from the city, or located fairly centrally, as in the case with São Paulo City and Rio City.

Gol Linhas Aereas Inteligentes aircraft taxi at Congonhas Airport, São Paulo

Domestic Airlines

Domestic air travel within Brazil is a well-organized and efficient form of transportation. There are currently two major airlines that fly both international and domestic routes – TAM and Gol (see p421). Domestic bargain airlines include **Avianca Brazil**, **Azul**, **Gol**, and **Trip**. The nation's largest airline, **TAM Airlines** operates flights between São Paulo and Mato Grosso do Sul and has built up a wide and inexpensive network throughout the Amazon region.

Checking In

Check-in for domestic flights is normally 60 minutes prior to departure. A valid ID is required, and foreigners are required to show their passport upon check-in. Make sure to keep the luggage claim tags handy upon arrival, as airport staff will check for those when exiting the baggage claim area.

Airpass

Nonresidents of Brazil who arrive on an international flight are entitled to buy an airpass with TAM, making long-distance flights within Brazil quite affordable. The airline sells the pass for US$479, for which you are allowed four domestic flights within a 21-day period. Additional segments can be purchased. No direct return flights are allowed. For example, Rio–Manaus–Rio–Salvador is not allowed but Rio–Manaus–Salvador–Rio is. A travel agent can explain the detailed terms

and conditions, or else check the airline's website for more information.

High Season

High season for domestic air travel corresponds with the major holidays and vacation periods in Brazil. The peak season is in the Brazilian summer, from the week of Christmas until Carnaval in mid-February or early March. The month of July is also peak season when schools and universities are off on their winter break. Other popular periods are Easter, Corpus Christi, and Independence Day (September 7).

TAM offers significant discounts for those who take night flights or fly at off-peak hours. As unpleasant as departures and arrivals in the wee hours may be, the savings can be significant. It is also advisable to book well ahead of time when planning to take flights Friday evening or Monday morning between major cities.

Air Taxi

Many parts of Brazil, and particularly Amazônia, feature air taxi companies. Air taxis, known locally as teco-tecos, are not the most reliable form of transportation. Before taking one, be aware that the airstrips are often dangerous. These small planes routinely fly overloaded, and are very often in questionable condition. There are no checks made on the qualifications of pilots, so taking an air taxi is at the traveler's own risk.

Teco-teco (air taxi) in the Amazon region

An Avianca flight taking off at Curitiba Airport

Reservations & Cancellations

Flights tend to be booked in advance so book your tickets as far ahead as possible. The only exception to this is the Rio–São Paulo shuttle, where you can purchase tickets on the spot. Flights at the beginning and end of working days and on weekends are usually quite crowded.

Confirm onward flights a day or two in advance. This can be done over the phone, as most airlines have English-speaking staff.

If you have an airpass and you happen to change your flight, remember to cancel the original flight. If you don't do so, the computer will flag you as a no-show, and all your other airpass reservations will also be canceled. Similarly, if you miss a flight, reconfirm all onward flights on your airpass. If you don't, all your other flights will be canceled.

Domestic Airports

Along with domestic airports, such as **Aeroporto de Congonhas** in São Paulo, and **Aeroporto Santos Dumont** in Rio de Janeiro, there are small domestic airports all over Brazil, including Recife, Belo Horizonte, Cuiabá, Campo Grande, Curitiba, Fernando de Noronha, Florianópolis, and Fortaleza. Both Congonhas and Santos Dumont airports are close to the commercial areas. The shuttle service from Congonhas Airport to the city center takes 50 minutes.

DIRECTORY

Domestic Airlines

Avianca Brazil
Tel 4004 4040.
w avianca.com.br

Azul
w voeazul.com.br

Gol
Tel (0300) 115 2121.
w voegol.com.br

TAM Airlines
Tel (0800) 026 0728.
w tam.com.br

Trip
Tel (0800) 887 1118.
w voetrip.com.br

Domestic Airports

Aeroporto de Congonhas
Tel (11) 5090 9000.

Aeroporto Santos Dumont
Tel (21) 3814 7070.

Flight Duration Chart

1:15 = Duration in hours:minutes

Rio de Janeiro	São Paulo	Florianópolis	Brasília	Manaus	Belém	São Luís	Fortaleza	Recife	Salvador	Belo Horizonte
0:45	São Paulo									
2:30	1:00	Florianópolis								
1:30	1:35	2:17	Brasília							
3:00	2:55	6:00	2:45	Manaus						
3:35	5:25	4:40	2:20	1:00	Belém					
4:00	5:45	5:25	2:27	4:20	1:00	São Luís				
3:00	2:30	0:55	2:30	4:25	2:50	1:10	Fortaleza			
2:45	3:00	6:18	2:20	7:30	4:20	2:45	1:10	Recife		
1:50	0:45	5:10	1:55	7:30	7:45	4:35	1:40	1:10	Salvador	
0:50	1:00	3:00	1:10	7:00	5:00	4:45	4:00	3:55	1:35	Belo Horizonte

GETTING AROUND
Due to the size and distances across Brazil, the fastest and easiest way to travel around the country is by air. All big cities, smaller towns, and even more remote areas across the country have airports, or at least an airstrip of some sort. Domestic flights are available to and from just about any major city across Brazil.

Bus & Car Travel

Bus and car travel is a challenge in Brazil, both because of the distances, and because of the often poor quality of the roads. Brazil possesses a total of 932,000 miles (1.5 million km) of federal, state, and local roads but only 49,000 miles (79,000 km) are paved and in decent condition. Intercity bus travel is well organized and most routes offer efficient and comfortable express services. Though car rentals are widely available, given the distances and the high cost of gasoline, a car is not really advisable for longer trips, but it is a convenient way to explore attractions closer to the city.

Busy *rodoviária* (central bus terminal) in São Paulo

Buses

Brazil has an excellent network of long-distance buses which makes traveling around the country easy and economical. Intercity buses leave from a central station, called a *rodoviária*, usually built on the outskirts of the city. Buses are operated by numerous private companies, but prices are standardized, and very reasonable. Several categories of buses operate on longer routes. Regular buses (*ônibus comum*) sometimes do not have air-conditioning, so ask. *Comum com ar* are regular buses with air-conditioning. The *executivo* bus is more comfortable, its chairs wider and equipped with footrests. The best buses for overnight trips are known as *semi-leito* or *leito*. *Semi-leito* have seats that recline almost horizontally and have large footrests. *Leito* buses offer a fully horizontal bed-like seat. Both normally offer onboard refreshments, blankets, and pillows. Nearly all buses have onboard bathrooms. Buy your tickets from the *rodoviária* ahead of time, especially on holidays.

Car Rentals

All major cities and most smaller cities and towns offer car rental services, such as **Avis** and **Localiza**. Car rental offices, known as *locadoras*, can be found at every airport and in most towns. Foreigners need to show a valid driver's license from their home country, state, or province, their passport, and a major credit card. It is also a good idea to carry an International Driver's Permit (IDP). A wide variety of cars are available in Brazil, from small economy models with no air conditioning, to large air-conditioned 4WDs. Rental agreements can be with full or partial insurance, with unlimited driving or with a per-kilometer charge. In terms of price, a four-door mid-size sedan with air conditioning, unlimited driving, and full insurance will cost about R$150 (US$83) per day in a larger city. In smaller towns and remote areas, prices go up by 50 to 100 percent. It is a good idea to check with locals about the condition of the roads you plan on taking.

Gas Stations

Cars in Brazil run on either gasoline or alcohol, but many new models run on both. Service stations selling gasoline are more common, especially in remote areas. On long-distance road trips, service stations may be few and far between, so ensure that the car is in good condition. Always be well prepared with some cash, water, enough car fluids, a good spare tire with tools, and a flashlight.

Driving in Towns

Driving in Brazilian towns and cities can sometimes be a frustrating experience. Any time after about 9pm, especially in Rio and São Paulo, drivers begin to treat red lights as strictly optional. Be especially alert at intersections at night (even as a pedestrian). Often the driver running the red light won't even slow down, because of the risk of robberies at isolated intersections.

Posto de Gasolina (gas station) in Rio de Janeiro

On highways and secondary roads, drivers tend to be fearless overtaking other vehicles, even when they can't see what's around the bend.

Parking, especially in cities, can be a bit tricky due to security and space constraints. It is worth paying extra for a hotel with a lock-up garage facility. Do not leave valuables in the car. It is also worth paying a few *reais* to self-appointed "guards" who may approach you to watch over your car.

Parking sign

Rules of the Road

Officially, the rules of the road are much the same as in Continental Europe or the United States. Drive on the right side of the road; unlike the USA, right turns on red lights are not allowed. Roundabouts are common only in Brasília. The right of way is always with the car already in the roundabout, or to the left.

However, it is the application of these rules – or lack thereof – that sets Brazil apart. Most Brazilians are aggressive and impatient drivers. They tend to drive fast, overtake often, either on the right or left, and when they cannot, they hang impatiently on your back bumper. Do not expect the large bus driving next to you to stay in its lane. Drivers switch lanes constantly, for no apparent reason, normally without signaling.

However, the use of photo radar and regular alcohol checks have improved driving conditions. Seatbelt laws are also rigorously enforced. Note that in larger cities such as São Paulo, Rio, and Salvador, traffic is still very chaotic. In case of an emergency, it is best to call the Polícia Militar *(see pp412–13)* or **Highway Police**.

Road Network

Brazil's intercity road network is made up of state and federal highways. Federal highways are denoted by the initials BR followed by the number of the highway (BR-163). State roads are indicated by the state initials (RJ for Rio de Janeiro, PA for Pará, and so on) followed by the highway number (PA-150). Toll roads have become more common. Most are run by private companies. They are usually well maintained and offer roadside assistance.

Most other state and federal highways are undivided two-lane blacktops, with occasional passing lanes. Care is required when driving on these roads. Generally speaking, the roads in southern states such as Rio and São Paulo are much better than in northeastern or Amazônian states such as Bahia or Rondônia. Even in the South, roads in bad condition are not uncommon.

Traveling by night is best avoided. With very few exceptions, highways in Brazil are poorly lit, and completely lacking in reflective paint, reflective signage, and the roadside reflectors that show the edge of the road.

The best compilation of national road maps come bundled with the *Guia Quatro Rodas*, a publication brought out by a Brazilian motoring organization of the same name, available at newsstands, bookstores, and magazine stalls.

Directory

Car Rentals

Avis
Tel (11) 2155 2847 (São Paulo) or (0800) 725 2847.
W avis.com.br

Localiza
Tel (0800) 979 2000 (Reservations).
W localiza.com.br

Emergency

Highway Police
Tel 191 (Road Emergencies).

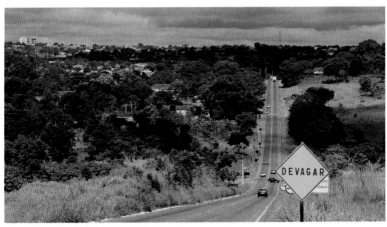

Road sign meaning "slow down" on a highway near Goiás

Train & Boat Travel in Brazil

Train travel is not a common mode of transportation in Brazil. While large parts of the country have never seen train tracks, in other areas, many routes have been deactivated in favor of roads. Today, the few remaining routes are of more interest to train aficionados, and are often of great scenic beauty. In some parts of Brazil, boat travel is still the only mode of transportation. With few roads connecting the major cities, particularly in the Amazon and along the northern coast, locals depend entirely on boats to get around. On the Rio Paraguay, on the western edge of the Pantanal, boats are used for multiday fishing charters.

The interior of a Maria Fumaça steam locomotive train

Trains waiting at the Luz railroad station in São Paulo

Train Travel

Although Brazil does not have a large train network, there are a few specific routes that can be useful for travelers and are good for a scenic ride. The Minas–Vitória train journey is an excellent day trip, and perfect for those traveling between the cities of Belo Horizonte, in the heartland of Minas Gerais, and Vitória on the Espírito Santo coast.

The quickest and most comfortable way to travel between São Luís and the interior of Pará, in Northern Brazil, is the São Luís Carajás railroad. In the state of Amapá, also in Northern Brazil, a passenger and cargo train runs from the port of Santana, 124 miles (200 km) inland, to the former mining town of Serra de Navio. Its passenger cars, though old and in need of maintenance, are still functional. Brazil offers a few charming, short historic routes. Steam locomotive trains, lovingly called Maria Fumaça, or "Smoking Mary," run on these routes. One of the journeys this unique steam engine makes is a regular 7-mile (12-km) run on weekends between São João del Rei and Tiradentes *(see p136)*, historic towns in Minas Gerais. An appealing short trip is offered along the route between the beautiful, historic mining town of Ouro Preto, one of Brazil's best-preserved colonial towns, and Mariana, also in Minas. Even though the towns are only 7 miles (12 km) apart, the route buzzes with history, as gold miners and gem hunters in the days of the gold rush used to travel through these hills. Contact the **Estação Ferroviária** for further details.

Another spectacular route is the Curitiba–Paranaguá train ride through the Atlantic rainforest of the Serra do Mar. The most unforgettable stretch is between Curitiba and Morretes *(see p341)*. For information, contact the **Curitiba Ticket Office**.

Boat Travel

In many parts of Brazil, boats are a vital form of transport. The network is extensive, and services are regular, although the facilities largely depend on the type of boat chosen for traveling.

In the Amazon, rivers are still the major highways, and old-style wooden riverboats are an important part of the transportation system. The most common and popular route runs between Manaus and Belém. The journey takes four days downstream and five days upstream. On this route, there are also several larger and more modern boats, which feature air-conditioned cabins and even enclosed air-conditioned hammock spaces. Continuing right up to Tefé, **AJATO** runs a speedboat service every Wednesday and Saturday, with airplane-style seating.

On most other routes, the boats are the older, smaller traditional type, with small wooden cabins, and two open

A picturesque view of one of the Maria Fumaça steam trains

Cruise ship Iberostar moored on the Manaus harbor

decks – upper and lower – where passengers sling their hammocks. Meals and water are provided.

Boats of the old style ply dozens of routes throughout the Amazon basin. The most common routes run between Manaus and Porto Velho, Manaus, Tabatinga, and São Gabriel de Cachoeira, near the borders of Peru and Columbia, respectively, and Manaus and Santarem, halfway to Belém. The Manaus–Santarem route also has a high-speed catamaran which makes the journey in a single day. Those more keen on tours than transportation can go for one of the comfortable boats for charter in Manaus, such as **Viverde**, that take passengers on a personal exploration of the Amazon River. For information on buying tickets in advance, contact **Amazonastur**, the state tourism agency.

The Rio Paraguay on the western edge of the Pantanal has a large fleet of boats, most of which are outfitted for multi-day sportfishing cruises. These boats depart from both Corumbá in Mato Grosso do Sul and Caceres in Mato Grosso.

On the Northeast coast, an absence of roads connecting the Maranhão and Piauí coast makes boat travel the only alternative to long detours inland. The most scenic option is to travel from Parnaíba in Piauí through the islands and inlets of the Delta da Parnaíba to Tutóia, one of the gateways to the Lençóis Maranhenses.

Cruise Travel

A very leisurely way to travel the Brazilian coast is on board a cruise ship. Several companies offer three- to five-day cruises, most typically between Santos, Rio de Janeiro as far as Salvador, or other northeastern cities. Another route starts in Recife and travels to Fernando de Noronha. There is now also a regular cruise ship, the **Iberostar Grand Amazon**, that departs from Manaus on three- and four-day cruises on the Amazon. The old-style **Amazon Clipper Cruises** can be excellent for a tour of the Rio Negro.

Directory

Train Travel

Curitiba Ticket Office
Tel (41) 3888 3488.
W serraverdeexpress.com.br

Estação Ferroviária
Praça Cesário Alvim 102, barra,
Ouro Preto. Tel (31) 3551 7705.
W tremdavale.org

Boat travel

AJATO
Rua Bares 3, Centro, Manaus
Tel (92) 3622 6047.

Amazonastur
Tel (92) 2123 3819.
W amazonastur.am.gov.br

Viverde
Rua das Guariúbas 47, Manaus
Tel (92) 3248 9988.
W viverde.com.br

Cruise travel

Amazon Clipper Cruises
Tel (92) 3656 1246.
W amazonclipper.com.br

Iberostar Grand Amazon
Tel (71) 3676 4300.
W iberostar.com.br

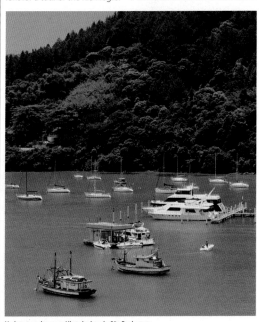

Yachts at anchor near Ubatuba beach, São Paulo state

Getting around Brazilian Towns

Public transportation in Brazil varies greatly from city to city and region to region. Large cities such as São Paulo and Rio de Janeiro have modern metro systems that offer quick access to many parts of the city and decent bus systems. However, in most cities and towns, the main mode of transportation is the bus and its variations, such as minivans and minibuses. Taxis are plentiful and quite affordable. In very small communities where there is little in the way of regular public transportation, people often use motorcycle taxis (moto-taxis). It is a cheap and fast one-person ride.

Moto-taxi stand, and drivers, in Camamu town, Bahia

Visitors exploring the town of Búzios on foot

On foot

Visitors to Brazil often seem preoccupied with street crime. What they should really worry about is traffic. Pedestrians get little or no respect. It is safest to assume that cars have the absolute right of way everywhere at all times. Even when the pedestrian has the right of way, such as when crossing with a green light, extreme care should be exercised at all times.

After dark, or when traffic is light, or when police are absent, cars tend to run red lights. Also, when making a right turn, cars rarely give preference to pedestrians trying to cross. Pedestrians should also be aware of bikes or motorcycles that may go down the wrong way on a one-way street. Always look both left and right.

Motorcyclists often weave in and out between the cars at high speeds. Be very careful when walking in between stationary or slow-moving traffic.

Taxis & Moto-taxis

Taxis are affordable and a quick mode of transportation. Prices generally run 50 to 70 percent lower than in Europe or North America. Most taxis work on the meter. When starting the ride, make sure that the meter is cleared and shows "tariff 1" except from 11pm to 6am, Sundays, and in December when "2" is permitted. Drivers sometimes "forget" to start the meter and end up charging a flat rate.

The only taxis allowed to charge a flat rate are radio taxis or cooperatives at airports, bus stations, or other specific locations. The price will be set before the passenger gets in. Rates are typically 30 to 40 percent higher than regular metered taxis, but you know what the final price will be. Although these prepaid taxis are not a bargain, they may be good value when taking a taxi from the international airports in Rio de Janeiro and São Paulo (see p419), where taxi drivers have developed the unfortunate habit of taking advantage of tourists who don't speak Portuguese and aren't familiar with Brazil.

In most cities, taxis can be hailed on the street or at numerous taxi stands. Renting a taxi for the day is an inexpensive alternative to renting a car. The price is negotiated with the driver. Taxis in small towns do not have meters, so it is best to agree upon a price in advance.

Another option in smaller towns is the moto-taxi, or motorcycle-taxi. The driver carries an extra helmet and the passenger just hops on the back and rides pillion after fixing a price.

Metro

The metro is the safest form of public transport in Rio and São Paulo. Both cities have metro systems that are very convenient for visitors, as they offer quick and reliable transportation to a number

Yellow Rio taxis, plentiful and relatively inexpensive

Passengers waiting to board the bus at a city bus stand in Paraná

of interesting sites. It is much easier and faster to take the metro to the stop closest to your destination and then take a taxi, rather than figure out a complicated and often slow bus system.

In Rio de Janeiro, the metro runs from 5am to midnight Monday through Saturday, and from 7am to 11pm on Sundays and holidays. During Carnaval, the metro runs nonstop for the five days of the festival. The metro has two main lines, both of which are clean and safe, even in the evenings. The main line from Gal Osório in Ipanema to Uruguai has 20 stops. The line splits at Central, with one line continuing west, while the secondary line goes north to São Cristóvão and beyond. The stops of most interest to visitors are downtown and along the southern beach neighborhoods, as well as the first few stops along the northern line to the Maracanã Stadium and Boã Vista Palace. Rio's metro now also offers a series of integrated metro-bus routes, which offer connections on air-conditioned buses to many of the city's attractions that are off the metro system, such as Santa Teresa, Sugar Loaf, and Ipanema. Passengers must request a special integrated ticket (integração) at the time of purchase.

São Paulo's metro system covers quite a large part of the city. It runs from 4:40am to midnight on all days of the week and is also clean, efficient, and safer than the buses.

For both systems, one-way (unitário), round-trip (duplo), or ten-ride (múltiplo) tickets are available. However, no discounts are offered for multiple-ride tickets. Transfers between lines are allowed. Free metro maps are available at most ticket booths of both metro systems.

Buses

Buses are plentiful in the big cities. Most buses list their destination in large letters on their front window, while another sign with smaller lettering lists key landmarks along the route. Buses in Rio and São Paulo run 24 hours a day, but with fewer circulating in the middle of the night. In Rio, most buses going from the south to the center will go to Copacabana. Keep in mind that buses are often crowded, and get stuck in terrible time-consuming traffic snarls. They are also often the sites of many of the city's robberies. To avoid pickpockets, try to sit at the front of the bus.

In São Paulo, a couple of the main bus transfer points are at Praça da Republica and the busy Terminal Bandeira, where it is also possible to catch different buses to far-off destinations within the city.

Tickets are sold on the bus by a ticket-seller who sits at a turnstile. Keep small change handy. Brazilian bus drivers can drive fast, so hold on at all times and be alert for sudden stops when standing. It is safer to take buses in the daytime. In the evenings, it is advisable to take taxis.

São Paulo metro arriving in the Barra Funda station

General Index

Acknowledgments

Dorling Kindersley would like to thank the many people whose help and assistance contributed to the preparation of this book.

Main Contributors
Shawn Blore, a Rio de Janeiro-based journalist, publishes travel and investigative articles in magazines and newspapers in Canada, the USA, the UK, and elsewhere.

Dilwyn Jenkins (1957–2014) began travelling in South America in 1976. Anthropologist, sustainable development expert, and travel writer, he made documentaries for television for 30 years.

Oliver Marshall has been visiting Brazil regularly since 1982. Specializing in travel and history, he has written extensively on Latin America.

Christopher Pickard has lived in Brazil for nearly 20 years and written widely about the country. He is vice-chairman of the Latin American Travel Association.

Alex Robinson is a travel writer and photographer with a client list that includes *Conde Nast Traveller*, *Wanderlust*, *Footprint*, BBC, and Channel 4.

Neiva Augusta Silva writes for Brazilian travel guides and magazines, as well as on adventure sports and rural tourism.

Fact Checkers
Alexandra de Vries, Fernanda Drummond, Stephen Wingrove

Proofreader
Susanne Hillen

Indexer
Hilary Bird

Design and Editorial
Publisher Douglas Amrine
Publishing Managers Jane Ewart, Scarlett O'Hara, Anna Streiffert
Senior Designer Paul Jackson
Senior Cartographic Editor Casper Morris
Editorial Assistance Alexandra Farrell, Fay Franklin
DTP Designer Natasha Lu
Picture Researcher Ellen Root
Production Controller Shane Higgins
XML Coordinator Bulent Yusuf

Additional Photography
Geoff Brightling, Geoff Dann, Barnabus Kindersley, Cyril Laubscher, Ian O'Leary, Jose Olimpio.

Additional Illustrations
Chapel Design and Marketing Ltd.

Additional Picture Research
Julia Harris-Voss, Phoebe Lowndes, Susie Peachey, Ellen Root, Lucy Sienkowska

Cartography Credits
Base mapping for São Paulo derived from Netmaps, and assistance from Ed Merrit.

Special Assistance
Dorling Kindersley would like to thank José Mayrink, Sônia Lúcia da Costa Conrado, Leonardo A. P. Silva, and Adriana Teixeira for their assistance.

Additional Editorial and Design
Rachel Fox, Rhiannon Furbear, Lydia Halliday, Kaberi Hazarika, Bharti Karakoyi, Priya Kukadia, Jude Ledger, Phoebe Lowndes, Alison McGill, Rada Radojicic, Alex Robinson, Sands Publishing Solutions, Beverly Smart.

Picture Credits
The publisher would like to thank the following for their kind permission to reproduce their photographs:

Key: a-above; b-below/bottom; c-center; f-far; l-left; r-right; t-top.

Alta Floresta: Cristalino Jungle Lodge; Belém: Basílica de Nossa Senhora de Nazaré, Teatro da Paz; Brasília: Catedral Metropolitana Nossa Senhora Aparecida, Santuário Dom Bosco; Caxias do Sul: Museu da Casa de Pedra; Congonhas: Basílica do Senhor Bom Jesus de Matosinhos; Curitiba: Hotel Burbon; Diamantina: Igreja Nossa Senhora do Carmo; Itamaracá Island: Projeto Peixe Boi; João Pessoa: Igreja de São Francisco; Manaus: Teatro Amazonas; Olinda: Convento de São Francisco, Mosteiro de São Bento; Ouro Preto: Casa dos Contos, Igreja de São Francisco de Assis, Matriz de Nossa Senhora da Conceição de Antônio Dias, Museu do Aleijadinho; Paraty: Casa de Cadeia, Igreja de Nossa Senhora do Rosário e São Benedito; Petrópolis: Museu das Cavalhadas, Palácio de Cristal; Piauí & Maranhão: Maranhão State Government Tourist Board, Sea and Air Maranhão; Porto Alegre: Museu de arte de Rio Grande do Sul, Teatro São Pedro; Recife: Casa da Cultura, Oficina Cerâmica Francisco Brennand, Kahal Zur Israel Synagogue; Rio de Janeiro: Barra Shopping, Blue Man, Confeitaria Colombo, H. Stern, Museu do Índio, Museu Nacional de Belas Artes, Nossa Senhora da Candelária, Rio Scenarium Bar; Salvador: Catedral Basílica, Fundação Casa de Jorge Amado, Igreja e Convento de São Francisco, Memorial das Conquistas do Santos, Museu Afro-Brasileiro, Museu Tempostal; Santos: Bolsa e Museu do Café; São Paulo City: Igreja São Francisco de Assis, Jacaré do Brasil, Mosteiro de São Bento de São Paulo, Museu de Arte Contemporânea, Museu de Arte de São Paulo, Museu de Arte Sacra de São Paulo, Museu de Arte Moderna de São Paulo, Vila Madalena; Tiradentes: Igreja Matriz de Santo Antônio.

Works of art have been reproduced with the kind permission of the following copyright holders:

Alfredo Volpi, *Composição* (1976) 144tr; José Pancetti, *Serie Bahia Musa da Paz* 144cl; Anita Malfatti, *Tropical* 145tc, Almeida Júnior, *Caipira Picando Fumo* 145cra; Tomie Ohtake, *Pintura* (1969) 145crb.

4Corners: Antonino Bartuccio 336; Giordano Cipriani 406–7; Guido Cozzi 328–9; Schapowalow/Chris Seba 348–9; SIME/Antonino Bartuccio 184, 206–7.
A Casa Vidal: 391tl.
Alamy Images: 1Apix 404t; age fotostock/P&R Fotos 280; AM Corporation 149tr; Arco Images GmbH 22tl, 24br, 325tl, /Therin-Weise 248, 258tc, 403tr; Aurora Photos/Matthew Wakem 394bl; Ricardo Beliel 30tr; BrazilPhotos /Ricardo Beliel 31tl, 43br, /Nando Neves 293cb, /Marco A. Rezende 37tr, /Ricardo Siqueira 107b; George Brewin 242b; Cristiano Burmester 253cr; Gary Calton 260–61; Cephas Picture Library 359cla, 359br; Gary Cook 181br, 287cr; David Crausby 62bc; David Davis Photo Productions 384cla, 89br; Danita Delimont 324tr; Nigel Dickinson 266cr; Didi 230; dpa picture alliance 44b; Redmond Durrell 265bc; Dynamic Graphics Group/Creatas 182cl; Chad Ehlers 81cla; Julio Etchart 41cb; Eye Ubiquitous 28cl; Robert Fried 108cl, 115br, 265cla, 347tr; Mike Goldwater 267crb, 267bl; Andrew Holt 60tr; ImageState 159br; IML Image Group Ltd 401br; James Davis Photography 306tr; Jacques Jangoux 113cla; Jon Arnold Images 265tl; Brian Kelly 262cla; David Laudien 37br; Alex Maddox 181cla; Mediacolor's 42–3c, 237bl, 420br; David Muscroft 81bl; Network Photographers 286cla; niceartphoto 106; David Parker 212; Beren Patterson 197bl; Natalie Pecht 30–31c; Pictorial Press Ltd 61tl, 81crb; Fabio Pili 350br, 351tl; Popperfoto 40br, 41bl, 41bc, 59bc, 61tr, 172bl; Ricardo Ribas 396tc; Richard Wareham Fotografie 345crb; Robert Harding World Imagery/Michael Runkel 15tr; Robert Harding World Imagery/Yadid Levy 20; Marcelo Rudini 352; Kevin Schafer 29bl; Sdbphoto Brasil 335cr; Andre Seale 179b, 199br, 228br, 301cb; David South 178bl; StockBrazil 121c, 208br, 209cl, 365tr; Sue Cunningham Photographic 30cl; Angel Terry 87cr; Travelstock44 31bl, 96b; Peter Treanor 25t, 68bl, 82tl; Genevieve Vallee 252c, 297tr, 301cra, 315tc; Mireille Vautier 8–9, 180br; Visual Arts Library (London) 56bc; Andrew Woodley 83tl; Worldwide Picture Library 137tr, 267cr, /Sue Cunningham 183c; Noel Yates 83tr.
Albamar: Mauro Motta 386br.
Amazon Ecopark: Fabio Colombini 378bl.
AWL Images: Christian Heeb 364–5; Alex Robinson 138, 268, 310–11, 318.
Bené da Flauta: 389bl.
Bourbon Resort: 381bl.
Bridgeman Images: Archives Charmet/Bibliothéque de L'Arsenal, Paris – *Cross-section of a model of a slave ship, late 18th century* (wood) by French School 54br; Archives Charmet/Bibliothéque National, Paris *The Dinner, a white couple being served and fanned by black slaves,* from Voyages Pictoresque et Historique au Brésil 1839 Jean Baptiste Debret 57bc; Giraudon/Museu de Arte, Sao Paulo *The Slave Hunter* (oil on canvas) Jean Baptiste Debret 54tl;

Giraudon/Private Collection *The Funeral of the Emperor of Brazil: The Carriage* from 'Le Petit Journal December 1891 Henri Meyer 58tc. Index/Museu Historico Nacional, Buenos Aires *The Surrender of Uruguaiana,* Candido Lopez 1865 57tr, 57bc; Index/Museu Historico Nacional, Rio de Janeiro *'Independence or Death', the Shout of Ipiranga on the 7th September 1822* Dome Pedro di Figueredo 56tl; Stapleton Collection *Botocudos family,* Rio Grande, from *Le Costume Ancien et Moderne, Volume II plate 37,* Jules Ferrario, published c. 1820s–30s 53tr.
Marcio Cabral: 208c.
Camarões Potiguar: 393bl.
Capim Santo: 392tr.
Casa do João: 395tl.
Sonia Conrado: 191crb.
Corbis: Alinari Archives 58bc; Theo Allofs 265crb, 319b; Archivo Iconografico, S.A. 54crb, 56crb; Ricardo Azoury 97tr, 120clb, 253br; Yann Arthus Bertrand 26bc, 26br, 41cra, 345br; Bettmann 36tr, 58cl, 59tc, 59c, 60br, 60–61c, 62c, 299crb; Tom Brakefield 265cr, 300cl, 316bl; Joao Luiz Bulcao 404bl; Pierre Colombel 51bc; Andrea Comas 180cl; Corbis Sygma 266cra, 266cl, 266br, /Bernard Bisson 38bl, /Collart Herver 63br, 266bl, /Le Segretain Pascal 25cl, /Manchete 86clb; /Whitemore Hank 267cla; Ecoscene/Joel Creed 345cra; EPA/Caetano Barreira 47br; Eye Ubiquitous/James Davis 195br, 344br, Paulo Fridman 63bl, 299cra, Gallo/Martin Harvey 300br; Farrell Grehan 299tc; Darrell Gulin 113br; Martin Harvey 28cb, 264bl; Collart Herve 226br; Eric and David Hosking 113clb; Wolfgang Kaehler 264clb, 287tl; Kipa/Rault Jean Franchois 37tl; Kuba 399br; Lawrence Manning 52tr; Stephanie Maze 399tr; Joe McDonald 265fcra; Wilson Melo 267cra; Diego Lezama Orezzoli 257tl; Fabio Polenghi 40tr; Jose Fuste Raga 71b; Reuters/Paulo Whitaker 420cla, /Sergio Moraes 279tr; Kevin Schafer 113bl, 300bl, 301br; Staffan Widstrand 26cl, 265ca; Paulo Whitaker 157tr, 267tr.
Cristalino Jungle Lodge: Katia Kuwabara 379tl.
D.O.M.: Cassio Vasconcelos 390bl.
Dorling Kindersley Ltd: Andy Crawford/Courtesy of the Football Museum, Preston 40clb.
Dreamstime.com: Dabldy 11crb; Alexandre Fagundes De Fagundes 10cl; Filipe Frazao 2–3, 159tr; Jakazvan 303b; Lazyllama 12bl, 13br; Giancarlo Liguori 11tl; Marchello74 70; Pixattitude 124, 302; Luca Roggero 176–7; Sjors737 43bl; Thiagogleite 13tl; Tupungato 14br, 421tl.
Getty Images: AFP/Mauricio Lima 35tr; Bloomberg 416bc; EACC 64–5; Lonely Planet Images/John Maier Jr 350tr; Rebeca Mello 170–71; SambaPhoto/Cassio Vasconcellos 294–5; SambaPhoto/Eduardo Barcellos 183tl; Stone/Will & Deni McIntyre 181bl; Time Life Pictures 62tl; Priscila Zambotto 164.
Glouton: 388tc.
The Granger Collection, New York: 35cl, 50, 52cla, 52bl, 52–9c, 53tl, 53cl, 55t, 57cb, 332tr.
Hyatt Hotels: 374tl.
Imagem Brasil: Gentil Barreira 27tl, 44cr, 254clb; Alex Uchôa 255bl; Flávio Veloso 38cl.
Imperial Palace: 118tr, 118cl, 118c, 119tl, 119ca, 119cb.
Koh Pee Pee Restaurant: 397br.
Lasai: 387tl.

Latin Photo: Biosfera 267tl, 267br; Carlos Ortiz Fragalá 334bl.
Marriott Resort & Spa: 368b.
Mary Evans Picture Library: 53bl, 60bl.
Masterfile: Mark Leibowitz 32tr; F Lukasseck 29crb; David Mendelsohn 21b, 23t; Brian Sytnyk 43tr; Jeremy Woodhouse 24tl, 29cr.
Meia Lua: 380tl.
Paul Mowatt: 290tl.
Octavio Campos Salles: 289bl.
Olhar Imagem: Aristides Alves 201bl, 208tl; Daniel Augusto Jr. 37c, 198cr; Ricardo Azoury 32clb, 69br, 74clb, 113crb, 181tr, 262cl, 262bl, 283tr; Flávio Bacellar 291br; Cynthia Brito 199tr; Maristela Colucci 228clb; Salomon Cytrynowicz 46tl, 231b; Adri Felden 357tr; Iolanda Huzak 332cr; Marcos Issa 210bl, 237cla, 337b; Zig Koch 27cr, 300–1c, 317cr; Stefan Kolumban 180–81c; Delfim Martins 29tc, 174b; Juca Martins 31tr, 31cr, 34bc, 38crb, 39tr, 42cl, 110cl, 115t, 123b, 148tl, 178cl, 199cl, 237cr, 237br, 272br, 290b, 292t, 325cra; Renata Mello 27br; Sonia Oddi 343t; Saulo Petean 39br; Rogério Reis 36bl, 180bl, 258br, 331cr; Zaida Siqueira 264cla; Monica Vendramini 279b; Luciana Whitaker 121bl, 293tr.
Ouro Minas Palace: 373bl.
PA Photos: Peter Robinson 41tl.
Photographers Direct: David Davis Photoproductions 43c; Chris Fairclough Worldwide 254br;Jahan Images 285c; Marcelo Krause Photography 121br.
Photolibrary: JTB Photo 334–5c, 385tl.
Popperfoto.com: 40ca, 40cl, 40bc, 41br.
Porto Bay Hotels & Resorts: 370bl.
Peter Price: 300cb.
Private Collection: 35br, 55b, 298cl.
Pulsar Imagens: Nelson Almeida 63tc; Ricardo Azoury 45tl, 68–9c, 213b, 256tr, 256br, 324clb; J. L. Bulção 185b; Armando Catunda 113c; Daniel Cymbalista 145bl, 423b; Adriano Gambarini 28crb, 245t; Artur Keunecke 29bc, 322br; Marcio Lourenço 28bl; Delfim Martins 33br, 46b, 122t, 122bl, 234cla, 241cla, 241cr, 251br, 301tc, 418b, 422cl; Juca Martins 30bl, 33cl, 200t, 289t, 427br; Manoel Novaes 28cr, 29cb; Rogério Reis 28bc, 47tl, 120tr; André Seale 28tr, 205br, 229br, 265br; Paula Simas 23br; Mauricio Simonetti 29tl, 29tr, 29cl, 66ca, 127tr, 137b, 240bl, 322t, 404tr; Luciana Whitaker 93bl; Palê Zuppani 325cr.

Reuters: Alexandra Beier 41fbr; Andrea Comas 37cb; Alex Grimm 40–41c; Lucas Jackson 36bc; Jose Patricio 30br; Claudio Pedroso 139b; Paulo Whitaker 36–7c, 149br.
Robert Harding Picture Library: Holger Leue 276–7; Sakis Papadopoulos 238–9.
Sofitel Hotels & Resort: Christian Knepper 188cl, 190clb, 191tc, 367bc, 399cl.
Solar dos Deuses: Alessandro Iglesias 375bl.
Solar dos Ventos: José Henrique Moura 376tc.
Lori Stilger: 300cla.
SuperStock: age footstock/Haroldo Palo Jr. 169clb.
Toca da Coruja: 377br.
Tyba Photographic Agency: J.R. Couto 80cl, 88bl, 90bl; Alberto Ferreira 298clb, 298bc, 298–9c, 299bl; Antonio Gusmão 36clb; Paulo Jares 36ca, 299tl; Marcello Lourenço 281b, 292br; Ciro Mariano 210tc; L.C. Marigo 291tl; Claus Meyer 135cr, 299cr, 335tr; OBrito News 298tr; Rogério Reis 68cb, 91tl, 98tr, 236clb, 243br, 249b; Ricardo Ribas 333br; David Santos Júnior 209tl; André Valentim 282cl; Flávio Vidigal 351cl.
Alex Sandro do Amaral Uchôa: 209br, 229cr, 244tr.
Viana Photography: Sergio Viana 252tl.
Vila d'Este: 372tr.
Visage Media Services: Hulton Archives/Evans 61cr, 61bl, 61br; Iconica/Wild Pics 351cr; Photographer's Choice/ Fernando Bueno 86cla; Time & Life Pictures/Leonard Mccombe 60cl.
Wikipedia: 53clb, 86tr, 298bl.
Windsor Hotels: 371tl.

Front Endpaper:
4Corners: SIME/Antonino Bartuccio Lbc, Rcra; **Alamy Images:** age fotostock/P&R Fotos Lcl; Arco Images GmbH/Therin-Weise Rtl; Didi Rtc; niceartphoto Rcrb; David Parker Rtr; Marcelo Rudini Lbl; **AWL Images:** Alex Robinson Ltl, Lc, Rbc; **Dreamstime.com:** Marchello74 Rfcb; Pixattitude Lbr, Rbr; **Getty Images:** Priscila Zambotto Rbl.

Jacket:
Front and spine – **Getty Images:** Jeremy Walker.

All other images © Dorling Kindersley
For further information see: www.dkimages.com

Phrase Book

The Portuguese spoken in Brazil differs in various ways from the Portuguese spoken in Portugal. In general, Brazilian pronunciation tends to omit far fewer sounds, especially the sounds at the end of words, and rarely runs two words together, both of which are common practice in Portugal. One feature of Brazilian Portuguese, particularly in the Rio de Janeiro area, is that an "r" sound can be spoken like an "h." So *carro* (car) may sound like "ka-hoo." Another difference lies in the ways of saying "you." The Portuguese form of placing the definite article in front of a person's name (o João, a Cristina), as a way of saying "you," does not exist in Brazil, where *você* and *vocês* are the most common words for "you." The Portuguese *tu* is not used much in Brazil. A huge number of other vocabulary differences exist, many at the level of everyday speech: train is *trem* in Brazil, *comboio* in Portugal; breakfast is *café da manhã* in Brazil, *pequeno almoço* in Portugal; bathroom is *banheiro* in Brazil, *casa de banho* in Portugal; goalkeeper is *goleiro* in Brazil, *guarda-redes* in Portugal; to drive is *dirigir* in Brazil, *conduzir* in Portugal. The sound indicated by "i" in the phrase book is like the "i" in English word "hi." "J" sounds like the "s" in the word "pleasure."

In an Emergency

Help!	**Socorro!**	sooko*rroo*
Stop!	**Pare!**	*pah*ree
Call a doctor!	**Chame um médico!**	shamih oong mehjikoo
Call an ambulance!	**Chame uma ambulância!**	shamih ooma amboolans-ya
Where is the hospital?	**Onde é o hospital?**	ohnd-yeh oo oshpital
Police!	**Polícia!**	poolees-ya
Fire!	**Fogo!**	fohgoo
I've been robbed	**Fui assaltado**	fwee asaltadoo

Communication Essentials

Yes	**Sim**	seeng
No	**Não**	nowng
Hello	**Olá**	ohla
How are you?	**Como vai?**	kohmoo vï
How is it going?	**Tudo bem? tudo bom?**	toodoo bayng/ toodo bong
Goodbye	**Tchau**	tshow
See you later	**Até logo**	ateh logoo
Excuse me	**Com licença**	kong lisaynsa
I'm sorry	**Desculpe**	dishkoolp
Thank you	**Obrigado (if a man is speaking)/ obrigada (if a woman is speaking)**	obriga*doo*/obri*ga*da
Good morning	**Bom dia**	bong jeea
Good afternoon	**Boa tarde**	boh-a tarj
Good evening/ night	**Boa noite**	boh-a noh-itsh
Pleased to meet you	**Muito prazer**	mweengtoo prazayr
I'm fine	**Estou bem/ tudo bem**	shtoh bayng/ toodoo bayng
Today	**Hoje**	ohJ
Yesterday	**Ontem**	ohntayng
Tomorrow	**Amanhã**	aman-yang
What?	**O que?**	oo kay
When?	**Quando?**	kwandoo
How?	**Como?**	kohmoo
Why?	**Por que?**	poorkay

Useful Phrases

On the left/right	**À esquerda/direita**	a-shkayrda/jirayta
I don't understand	**Não entendo**	nowng ayntayndoo
Please speak slowly	**Fale devagar por favor**	falee jivagar poor favohr
What's your name?	**Qual é seu nome?**	kwal eh say-oo nohm
My name is...	**Meu nome é...**	may-oo nohm eh
Go away!	**Vá embora!**	va aymbora
That's fine	**Está bem**	shtah bayng
Where is...?	**Onde está/fica...?**	ohnj shtah/feeka
When does the bus leave/arrive?	**A que horas sai/ chega o ônibus?**	a kih orash sï/ shayga oo ohniboosh
Is this the way to the...?	**Este é o caminho para...?**	aysht-yeh oo kameen-yoo pra

Useful Words

big	**grande**	granj
small	**pequeno**	pikaynoo
hot	**quente**	kayntsh
cold	**frio**	free-oo
bad	**mau**	mow
good	**bom**	bong
enough	**suficiente**	soofis-yayntsh
open	**aberto**	abehrtoo
closed	**fechado**	fishadoo
dangerous	**perigoso**	pirigohzoo
safe	**seguro**	sigooroo
full	**cheio**	shay-oo
empty	**vazio**	vazee-oo
straight on	**reto**	rehtoo
under	**debaixo**	dibïshoo
over	**em cima**	ayng seema
in front of	**em frente de**	ayng frayntsh ji
behind	**atrás de**	atraJ jih
first floor	**primeiro andar**	primayroo andar
ground floor	**térreo**	tehrryoo
lift	**elevador**	elevadohr
toilet	**banheiro**	ban-yayroo
men's	**dos homens**	dooz ohmaynsh
women's	**das mulheres**	dash mool-yehrish
quick	**rápido**	rapidoo
soon	**cedo**	saydoo
late	**tarde**	tarj
now	**agora**	agora
more	**mais**	mïsh
less	**menos**	maynoosh
a little	**um pouco**	oong pohkoo
a lot	**muito**	mweengtoo
too much	**demais**	dimïsh
entrance	**entrada**	ayntrada
exit	**saída**	sa-eeda
passport	**passaporte**	pasaportsh

Post Offices & Banks

bank	**banco**	bankoo
bureau de change	**(casa de) câmbio**	(kaza jih) kamb-yoo
exchange rate	**taxa de câmbio**	tasha jih kamb-yoo
post office	**correio**	koorray-oo
postcard	**cartão postal**	kartowng pooshtal
postbox	**caixa de correio**	kïsha jih koorray-oo
ATM	**caixa automática**	kïsha owtoomatshika
stamp	**selo**	sayloo
cash	**dinheiro**	jeen-yayroo
withdraw money	**tirar dinheiro**	tshirar jeen-yayroo

Shopping

How much is it?	**Quanto é?**	kwantweh
I would like...	**Eu quero...**	ay-oo kehroo
clothes	**roupa**	rohpa
This one	**Esta**	ehshta
That one	**Essa**	ehsa
market	**mercado**	merkadoo
supermarket	**Supermercado**	soopermerkadoo
Do you accept credit cards?	**Aceitam cartão de crédito?**	asaytowng kartowng jih krehditoo
expensive	**caro**	karoo
baker's	**padaria**	padaree-a
butcher's	**açougue**	asohgee
chemist's	**farmácia**	farmas-ya

Sightseeing

museum	**museu**	moozay-oo
art gallery	**galeria de arte**	galiree-a jih artsh
national park	**parque nacional**	parkee nas-yoonal
beach	**praia**	prï-a
park	**parque**	parkee
river	**rio**	ree-oo
church	**igreja**	igray-Ja
cathedral	**catedral**	katidrow
district	**bairro**	bïrroo
garden	**jardim**	Jardeeng
tourist office	**informações turísticas**	infoormasoyngsh tooreeshtsheekash
guide	**guia**	gee-a
guided tour	**excursão com guia**	shkoorsowng kong gee-a
ticket	**bilhete/ingresso**	bil-yaytsh/ingrehsoo
map	**mapa**	mapa

Transport

bus	**ônibus**	**oh**niboosh
boat	**barco**	**bar**koo
train	**trem**	trayng
airport	**aeroporto**	a-ayroo**pohr**too
airplane	**avião**	av-**yow**ng
flight	**vôo**	**voh**-oo
bus station	**rodoviária**	roodoh**vyar**-ya
bus stop	**ponto de ônibus**	**pohn**too j-**yohn**iboosh
train station	**estação de trem**	stas**ow**ng jih trayng
ticket	**passagem**	pasa**jayng**
taxi	**táxi**	**tax**ee
subway	**metrô**	metr**oh**

Health

I feel bad/ill	**Sinto-me mal/doente**	**seen**toomih mow/**dwaynt**sh
I need to rest	**Preciso descansar**	pris**eez**oo jishkans**ar**
diarrhoea	**diarréia**	j-yar**reh**-ya
pharmacy	**farmácia**	**far**mas-ya
headache	**dor de cabeça**	dohr jih kab**ay**sa
medicine	**remédio**	ri**mehd**-yoo
sanitary towels/ tampons	**absorventes/ tampões**	absoorv**ay**ntsh/ tamp**oy**ngsh
mosquito	**repelente de**	ripel**ay**ntsh dih
repellent	**mosquito**	moosh**kee**too
doctor	**médico**	**meh**jikoo
condom	**camisinha**	kamiz**een**-ya

Staying in a Hotel

hotel	**hotel**	oh**teh**-oo
boutique hotel	**pousada**	poh**zad**a
guesthouse	**pensão**	payns**ow**ng
hostel	**albergue**	ow**beh**rgee
Do you have a room?	**Tem um quarto?**	tayng oong **kwar**too
I have a reservation	**Tenho uma reserva**	**tayn**-yoo ooma ris**eh**rva
single/double (room)	**(quarto de) solteiro/casal**	(**kwar**too jih) soolt**ayr**oo/kaz**ow**
shower	**chuveiro**	shoov**ayr**oo
sheet	**lençol**	layns**oh**
bed	**cama**	**kam**a
pillow	**travesseiro**	travis**ayr**oo
towel	**toalha**	tw**al**-ya
toilet paper	**papel higiênico**	pap**eh**-oo iJ-**yeh**nikoo

Eating Out

I want to reserve…	**Quero reservar…**	**keh**roo rizirv**ar**
Do you have…?	**Tem…?**	tayng
The bill, please	**A conta, por favor**	a **kohn**ta, poor fav**ohr**
menu	**cardápio/menu**	kard**ap**-yoo/mayn**oo**
wine list	**lista de vinhos**	**leesh**ta de veen-**yoosh**
glass	**copo**	**ko**poo
bottle	**garrafa**	gar**ra**fa
fork	**garfo**	**gar**foo
knife	**faca**	**fa**ka
spoon	**colher**	kool-**yehr**
restaurant	**restaurante**	rishtow**ra**ntsh
breakfast	**café da manhã**	ka**feh** da man-**ya**ng
lunch	**almoço**	ow**mohs**oo
dinner/supper	**jantar**	**Jant**ar
(mineral) water	**água (mineral)**	**a**gwa (miner**ow**)
vegetarian	**vegetariano**	vigitar-**ya**noo
Is service included?	**O serviço está incluído?**	oo sirv**ees**oo shtah inklw**ee**doo

Menu Decoder

açúcar	as**oo**kar	sugar
alho	**al**-yoo	garlic
arroz	ar**rohsh**	rice
azeite	az**ay**tsh	olive oil
batatas fritas	batatsh **free**tash	chips
bebida	bib**ee**da	drink
bem passado	bayng pas**ad**oo	well done
bife	**bee**fee	steak
café	ka**feh**	coffee
carne	**kar**nee	beef
cerveja	sirv**ay**.la	beer
chá	sha	tea
churrasco	shoor**rash**koo	barbecue
feijão (preto)	fay.l**ow**ng (**pray**too)	(black) beans
feijoada	fayJw**ad**a	bean and meat stew

farofa	far**of**a	dish based on manioc/cassava meal
frango	**fra**ngoo	chicken
fruta	**froo**ta	fruit
grelhado	gril-**ya**doo	grilled
lanche	**lan**shee	snack
leite	**lay**tsh	milk
manteiga	mant**ay**ga	butter
muqueca de peixe	mook**eh**ka jih **pay**shee	fish stew with coconut milk
ovo cozido	**oh**voo kooz**eed**oo	hard-boiled egg
pão	powng	bread
pão de queijo	powng jih **kay**-Joo	cheese cookie
pastel de carne	pasht**eh**-oo jih **kar**nee	puff-pastry patty filled with mince
pastel de queijo	pasht**eh**-oo jih **kay**-Joo	puff-pastry patty filled with cheese
peixe	**pay**shee	fish
pimenta	pim**ay**nta	pepper
mal passado	mow pas**ad**oo	rare
ao ponto	ow **pohn**too	medium
quindim	keen**jeeng**	coconut and egg sweet
refrigerante	rifrig**ir**antsh	soft drink
sal	sow	salt
sorvete	sohrv**ay**tsh	ice cream
suco	s**oo**koo	fruit juice
vinho	**veen**-yoo	wine

Time

minute	**minuto**	min**oo**too
hour	**hora**	**or**a
half an hour	**meia hora**	**may**-a ora
next week	**na próxima semana**	na pr**os**ima sim**an**a
last month	**no mês passado**	noo maysh pas**ad**oo
Monday	**segunda-feira**	sig**oo**nda **fay**ra
Tuesday	**terça-feira**	**tayr**sa **fay**ra
Wednesday	**quarta-feira**	kw**ar**ta **fay**ra
Thursday	**quinta-feira**	**keen**ta **fay**ra
Friday	**sexta-feira**	s**ay**shta **fay**ra
Saturday	**sábado**	s**ab**adoo
Sunday	**domingo**	doom**een**goo
January	**janeiro**	Jan**ay**roo
February	**fevereiro**	fever**ay**roo
March	**março**	**mar**soo
April	**abril**	ab**ree**-oo
May	**maio**	m**i**-oo
June	**junho**	J**oon**-yoo
July	**julho**	J**ool**-yoo
August	**agosto**	ag**ohsh**too
September	**setembro**	sit**aym**broo
October	**outubro**	oht**oo**broo
November	**novembro**	noov**aym**broo
December	**dezembro**	diz**aym**broo

Numbers

1	**um/uma**	oong/**oo**ma
2	**dois/duas**	**doh**-ish/**doo**-ash
3	**três**	traysh
4	**quatro**	kw**at**roo
5	**cinco**	s**een**koo
6	**seis**	saysh
7	**sete**	seht
8	**oito**	**oh**-itoo
9	**nove**	n**o**vee
10	**dez**	dehsh
11	**onze**	**ohn**zee
12	**doze**	**doh**zee
13	**treze**	tr**ay**zee
14	**catorze**	kat**ohr**zee
15	**quinze**	k**een**zee
16	**dezesseis**	dize**saysh**
17	**dezessete**	dize**seh**tee
18	**dezoito**	diz**oh**-itoo
19	**dezenove**	dizen**o**vee
20	**vinte**	v**een**tee
21	**vinte e um**	v**een**tih-oong
30	**trinta**	tr**een**ta
40	**quarenta**	kwar**ay**nta
50	**cinqüenta**	sinkw**ay**nta
60	**sessenta**	ses**ay**nta
70	**setenta**	set**ay**nta
80	**oitenta**	oh-it**ay**nta
90	**noventa**	nohv**ay**nta
100	**cem, cento**	sayng/**sayn**too
1000	**mil**	m**ee**-oo

Rio de Janeiro Transit Map

Belford Roxo ↑

Pavuna [2]

Costa Barros

Barros Filho

Honório Gurgel

Rocha Miranda

Mercadão de Madureira

Cavalcante

Tomás Coelho

Pilares

Del Castilho

Jacarezinho

Nova América/ Del Castilho

Maria da Graça

← Santa Cruz, Campo Grande

Eng. Rubens Paiva

Acari/Fazenda Botafogo

Coelho Neto

Colégio

Irajá

Vicente de Carcalho

Tomas Coelho

Eng. da Rainha

Inhaúma

Triagem

Maracanã

São Cristóvão

↑ *Saracuruna, Vila Inhomirim*

Vigário Geral

Vigário

Lucas

Cordovil

Braz de Pina

Penha Circular

Penha

Olaria

Ramos

Bonsucesso

Manguinhos

Central

Cidade Nova

Praça Onze

Estácio

Afonsa Pena

São Francisco Xavier

Saens Peña [1]

Uruguai

Pres. Vargas

Uruguaiana

Carioca

Cinelândia

Glória

Catete

Largo do Machado

Flamengo

Botafogo [2]

Cardeal Arcoverde

Siqueira Campos

Cantagalo

General Osório [1] [4]

Gávea

[4] Jardim Oceânico — São Conrado — Antero de Quental — Jardim de Alah — Nossa Senhora da Paz

Getting Around

Rio's comfortable and efficient metro network is limited to two lines. The main line, Linha 1, which has 19 stops, runs from Ipanema Gal Osório, north through Central, out to the Saens Peña station. Linha 2 comes in from Pavuna to the city center and goes via the Maracanã to meet Linha 1 at Central. The commuter line Supervia connects downtown Rio to its suburbs, but is not commonly used by visitors.

Key

━━ Linha 1

━━ Linha 2

••• Linha 4 under construction

━━ Supervia

São Paulo T

Itapevi, Amador Bueno

[8] Osasco

Pres. Altino [9]

Imper Leopo

Ceasa

Jaguaré

Cidade Universitaria

Pinheiro

[4]

[17]

Vila Sônia

Capão Redondo [5]

V B

Campo Limpo